Routledge Handbook of International Family Law

Globalisation, and the vast migrations of capital and labour that have accompanied it in recent decades, has transformed family law in once unimaginable ways. Families have been torn apart and new families have been created. Borders have become more porous, allowing adoptees and mail order brides to join new families and women fleeing domestic violence to escape from old ones. People of different nationalities marry, have children, and divorce, not necessarily in that order. They file suits in their respective home states or third states, demanding support, custody, and property. Otherwise law-abiding parents risk jail in desperate efforts to abduct their own children from foreign ex-spouses.

The aim of this Handbook is to provide scholars, postgraduate students, judges, and practitioners with a broad but authoritative review of current research in the area of International Family Law. The contributors reflect on a range of jurisdictions and legal traditions and their approaches vary. Each chapter has a distinct subject matter and was written by an author who was invited because of his or her expertise on that subject. This volume provides a valuable contribution to emerging understandings of the subject.

Barbara Stark is Professor of Law and Hofstra Research Scholar at the Maurice A. Deane School of Law at Hofstra University, where she teaches Family Law, International Law, Human Rights, and International Family Law.

Jacqueline Heaton is Professor of Law at the University of South Africa. She specialises in Family Law, Law of Persons, and Child Law.

Routledge Handbook of International Family Law

Edited by Barbara Stark and Jacqueline Heaton

Routledge
Taylor & Francis Group
LONDON AND NEW YORK

First published 2019 by Routledge
2 Park Square, Milton Park, Abingdon, Oxon OX14 4RN

and by Routledge
605 Third Avenue, New York, NY 10017

First issued in paperback 2021

Routledge is an imprint of the Taylor & Francis Group, an informa business

Publisher's Note
The publisher has gone to great lengths to ensure the quality of this reprint but points out that some imperfections in the original copies may be apparent.

British Library Cataloguing-in-Publication Data
A catalogue record for this book is available from the British Library

Library of Congress Cataloging-in-Publication Data
Names: Stark, Barbara, 1952– editor. | Heaton, J., editor.
Title: Routledge handbook of international family law / edited by Barbara Stark and Jacqueline Heaton.
Description: Abingdon, Oxon [UK] ; New York, NY : Routledge, 2019.
Identifiers: LCCN 2018042265 | ISBN 9781472483829 (hbk) | ISBN 9781315613079 (ebk)
Subjects: LCSH: Domestic relations (International law)
Classification: LCC K670 .R69 2019 | DDC 346.01/5—dc23
LC record available at https://lccn.loc.gov/2018042265

ISBN 13: 978-1-03-209382-6 (pbk)
ISBN 13: 978-1-4724-8382-9 (hbk)

Typeset in Bembo
by Apex CoVantage, LLC

Contents

Contributors

Aziza Ahmed is Professor of Law at Northeastern University, where she teaches Property Law, Reproductive Rights, and International Health Law. She is also Affiliated Faculty at Northeastern University Bouvé College of Health Sciences. She has published widely in leading law journals, including the *Wisconsin Law Review* and the *University of Miami Law Review*, and she has an article forthcoming in the *Fordham Law Review*. She was a Law and Public Affairs Fellow and Visiting Scholar at Princeton University in 2017–2018.

Bill Atkin is Professor of Law at Victoria University of Wellington, New Zealand. He chaired the Ministerial Adoption Practices Review Committee, and was on the Working Group on Matrimonial Property and Family Protection, and the Ministerial Committee on Assisted Reproductive Technologies. He is on the Expert Advisory Group for the Law Commission's relationship property project. From 2007 to 2016, he was the General Editor of the International Society of Law's *International Survey of Family Law*. He has published extensively, especially in the field of Family Law, including in 2018 the third edition of his book *Relationship Property in New Zealand*.

Nicholas Bamforth is a Fellow in Law at The Queen's College, Oxford. He teaches Constitutional Law, Administrative Law, and Human Rights. He is the author or co-author of *Sexuality, Morals and Justice* (Cassell), *Patriarchal Religion, Sexuality and Gender* (with David A.J. Richards, Cambridge), and *Discrimination Law: Theory and Context* (with Maleiha Malik and Colm O'Cinneide, Thomson/Sweet & Maxwell), and the editor or co-editor of *Public Law in a Multi-layered Constitution* (with Peter Leyland, Hart), *Accountability in the Contemporary Constitution* (with Peter Leyland, Oxford), *Sexual Orientation and Rights* (Ashgate), and *Sex Rights: The Oxford Amnesty Lectures 2002* (Oxford).

Margaret F. Brinig is the Fritz Duda Family Chair in Law at Notre Dame School of Law, Indiana, USA. She sits on the executive council of the International Society of Family Law. An interdisciplinary scholar, she specialises in Family Law, Law and Economics, and Dispute Resolution. She has written or co-authored more than 100 articles and her books include *Family, Law, and Community: Supporting the Covenant* (University of Chicago Press, 2010), *The Economics of Family Law* (2 vol., ed. 2007), and *From Contract to Covenant: Beyond the Law and Economics of the Family* (Harvard University Press, 2000).

Edit Frenyo is S.J.D. candidate at Georgetown University Law Center, Washington D.C. Her research uses perspectives of law and the social sciences to explore contemporary transnational families. Her latest works analyse transnational parenting and the right to family life. Previously she has served as an Adjunct Professor at Georgetown Law and at McDaniel College, Budapest. In 2013 and 2014 she co-taught the Family Law course at Georgetown Law with Professor Judith C. Areen. In 2016 she taught "Children on the Move and the European Migrant Crisis – Status and Rights of Unaccompanied Minors in the European Union" at McDaniel College.

Nuria Gonzalez-Martin is Professor and Senior Researcher at the Institute for Legal Research, National Autonomous University of Mexico. In 2015 she was selected as a Weinstein JAMS International Fellow. From 2012 to 2016 she was Visiting Scholar and Visiting Fellow at Stanford Law School. She is the author of many publications on Family Law, Comparative Law, Private International Law, and Alternative Dispute Resolution. She is also external counsellor to Mexico's Foreign Affairs Ministry and a certified mediator. She is a member of several international scientific committees and participates in various Experts Groups of The Hague Conference on Private International Law and International Social Service to create a Global Network of International Family Mediation.

Maebh Harding is Associate Professor of Law at the Warwick School of Law, Coventry, United Kingdom. Her interests revolve around Family and Child Law, Conflicts of Law with a focus on cross-border family issues, and Legal History. Her books include *Conflict of Laws* (2013), *Family and Succession Law in England and Wales* (with Rebecca Probert, 2013), and the forthcoming *From Catholic Outlook to Modern State Regulation: Developing Legal Understandings of Marriage in Ireland* (Intersentia, 2019). From 2006 to 2008 she held the National University of Ireland E.J. Phelan Fellowship in International Law at University College Dublin.

Colin P.A. Jones is Professor at Doshisha Law School, Kyoto, Japan. He has also taught at Duke Law School, the University of Victoria, and Osaka University and he has been a Visiting Fellow at the National University of Singapore. His teaching areas include International Business Transactions, Japanese Law, and International Family Law. He has published widely, in English and in Japanese. His books include *The Japanese Legal System* (with Frank Ravitch, 2018) and *The Child Abduction Problem: How the Japanese Legal System Tears Parents and Children Apart* (in Japanese, Heibonsha shinsho, 2011).

Rashida Manjoo is Professor of Law at the University of Cape Town where she teaches and convenes the Human Rights Program. She was the UN Special Rapporteur on Violence Against Women between 2009 and 2015. She served as the Parliamentary commissioner on South Africa's Commission on Gender Equality, the Des Lee Distinguished Visiting Professor at Webster University, and the Eleanor Roosevelt Fellow with Harvard Law School's Human Rights Program. Among her numerous reports, journals and book publications are *Women's Charters and Declarations: Building Another World* (2013) and *The Legal Protection of Women from Violence: Normative Gaps in International Law* (2018).

Thandabantu Nhlapo is Emeritus Professor of Private Law and Former Deputy Vice-Chancellor of the University of Cape Town, South Africa. He was a full-time Commissioner of the South African Law Reform Commission and has served on the Executive Council of the International Society of Family Law. He has written widely on African Customary Law and has authored, co-authored, and edited several books, including *The Changing Family: Family Forms and Family Law* (ed. with John Eekelaar, Hart, 1998), and *African Customary Law in South Africa: Post-Apartheid and Living Law Perspectives* (ed. with Chuma Himonga, Oxford Southern Africa, 2014).

Rachel Rebouché is Professor of Law and Associate Dean of Research, Temple University Beasley School of Law, Philadelphia, USA. She is a co-investigator for a project on adolescent reproductive health at the Emory School of Public Health. She is an author of the casebook, *Family Law*, with Harris and Carbone, and a co-author of *Governance Feminism: An Introduction* with Halley, Kotiswaran, and Shamir. She is completing a book on reproductive justice for NYU Press and editing a collection of rewritten family law opinions for Cambridge University Press. She has published law review articles on a variety of reproductive rights topics.

Philipp M. Reuss is *Privatdozent* at the Institute of International Law – Comparative Law, Ludwig-Maximilians-Universität of Munich, Germany and is currently acting Professor at the University of Bonn, Germany, which will continue in the winter term 2018–2019. He is a member of the *Wissenschaftliche Vereingung für Familienrecht* (Scientific Association for Family Law) and has published in the field of Family and Child Law.

Geoffrey Shannon is the Adjunct Professor in Child and Family Law at the School of Law of the University of Limerick, Ireland. He is the current Chairman of the Adoption Authority of Ireland and the Special Rapporteur on Child Protection for the Irish government. In 2017, Mr Justice Peter Kelly, President of the Irish High Court presented him with the Dublin Solicitors Bar Association Award for outstanding contribution to legal scholarship for his entire work to date. He is also the recipient of several awards for his work in the field of national and international family law.

Barbara Stark is Professor of Law and Hofstra Research Fellow at the Maurice A. Deane School of Law, Hofstra University, New York, USA. She teaches Family Law, International Law, and International Human Rights. She is the author or co-author of three books, *International Family Law* (2005), *Global Issues in Family Law* (with Ann Estin, 2007), and *Family Law in the World Community* (with Marianne Blair et al., 2015). Her edited or co-edited books include *Human Rights and Children* (ed. 2017) and *Family Law in New York* (with Joanna Grossman, 2015.)

Elaine E. Sutherland is Professor of Child and Family Law, Stirling Law School, University of Stirling, Scotland, and Distinguished Professor of Law Emeritus, Lewis and Clark Law School, Portland, Oregon, USA. In 2012, she founded the United Nations Convention on the Rights of the Child Implementing Project. She is the sole author of more than 100 articles, book chapters and three books. Her recent edited or co-edited books include *The Future of Child and Family Law: International Predictions* (2012) and *Implementing Article 3 of the United Nations Convention on the Rights of the Child* (with Barnes Macfarlane, 2016).

Frederik Swennen is Dean and Full Tenured Professor of Family Law and Kinship Studies at the Faculty of Law of the University of Antwerp, Belgium. He chairs the Research Council Flanders, Scientific Research Network RETHINKIN_ (Rethinking family law and kinship studies in the Low Countries) and is co-promoter of the interdisciplinary University of Antwerp Centre of Research Excellence FAMCARE (Family Dynamics and Care). He teaches, and has broad research experience with publications and research projects in, International Family Law.

Geraldine Van Bueren QC is Professor of International Human Rights Law at Queen Mary University of London and Visiting Fellow at Kellogg College, Oxford in the United Kingdom.

She was appointed honorary Queen's Counsel in recognition of her scholastic contributions, and in 2003, she was awarded the Child Rights Lawyer Award. She is one of the drafters of the United Nations Convention on the Rights of the Child and other international laws. She has published widely on Child Law, International Law, Human Rights Law, and Constitutional Law.

Introduction

Barbara Stark and Jacqueline Heaton

Globalisation and the vast migrations of capital and labour that have accompanied it in recent decades have transformed families, and family law, in once unimaginable ways. Families have been torn apart and new families have been created. Borders have become more porous, allowing adoptees and mail order brides to join new families and women fleeing domestic violence to escape from old ones. People of different nationalities marry, have children, and divorce, not necessarily in that order. They file suits in their respective home states or third states, demanding support, custody, and property. Otherwise law-abiding parents risk jail in desperate efforts to abduct their own children from foreign ex-spouses. All these scenarios, and many more, give rise to cross-border issues and bring international family law (IFL) into play.

IFL has historically been regarded primarily as the province of "private international law", which refers to the rules regarding conflict of laws in disputes between private persons, such as spouses. Private international law draws on conflict of laws principles in general, as well as the conventions drafted by the Hague Conference on Private International Law, in particular. "Public international law", in contrast, refers to the rules and norms governing disputes among nation states. But public international law plays an increasingly important role in IFL. It includes human rights law, such as women's rights, children's rights, and lesbian/gay/bisexual/transgender/queer (LGBTQ) rights, which have transformed family law almost everywhere.

Comparisons of domestic family law rules play an integral role in the field of IFL. The ways in which different domestic systems address particular aspects of family law provide different perspectives on, and alternative solutions to, cross-border problems and also influence the ways in which domestic systems interpret and apply principles and rules of private and public international law. However, domestic social context must always be borne in mind when undertaking comparative family law investigations and evaluating their results.

Aims and rationale

The aim of this Handbook is to provide scholars, postgraduate students, judges, and practitioners with a broad but authoritative review of current research in the area of IFL. The contributors reflect on a range of jurisdictions and legal traditions and their approaches vary. Each chapter has a distinct subject matter and was written by an author who was invited because of his or her expertise on that subject. Since the authors are all subject experts, we were not prescriptive about the issues to be included by each author. Nor did we restrict the approach each author had to adopt in respect of the scope or meaning of "International Family Law". Rather, it is our hope that this volume will contribute to emerging understandings of the subject.

Not every chapter in the book has a comparative component, although several do. Some of the latter chapters include references to the national law in several jurisdictions (e.g. "Same-sex marriages and civil or registered partnerships"; "Divorce"; "Distribution of property on divorce"; "Child custody and cognate concepts: the challenges"), while others focus on a single jurisdiction (e.g., "Customary marriages" deals exclusively with South Africa and, as the title suggests, "Father's rights: Japan as a different paradigm" deals exclusively with Japan).

The restriction on length imposed by the publisher meant that it was difficult for the authors to discuss all the topics they might have wished to cover in their chapters, or to devote extensive attention to all the topics they selected for discussion.

Structure of the Handbook

The Handbook is divided into five parts. Part I addresses the requirements and consequences of marriage and marriage-like relationships. This includes restrictions on entry into marriage; alternatives to marriage, including German partnerships and French *pacte civil de solidarité* (PACS); relationships involving bisexual, transgendered, and questioning people; and state sanctions against such relationships. Finally, it addresses customary marriages, which may involve polygamy and payment of bridewealth.

In Chapter 1, Maebh Harding discusses the recognition of marital status across national boundaries. Harding focuses on the complications generated by different domestic rules regarding consanguinity and consent. Through rigorous scholarship, she shows how domestic conflict of laws rules – here, traditional principles of English conflicts law – treat the recognition of foreign marriages as clashes between different family values rather than the "multi-layered adjudications they truly are". Harding argues that by deciding these cases solely based on choice of law, that is, which domestic law should be applied, courts risk failing to take human rights and the needs of vulnerable parties into account. In cases of non-recognition of a marriage in the international context, similarly, she points out that blanket non-recognition may ill-serve a vulnerable spouse, whose immigration status or support may be adversely affected.

In "Same-sex marriages and civil or registered partnerships", Nicholas Bamforth undertakes an ambitious survey of law that is very much in flux. He begins with a nuanced comparative account that sets out the forms of legal recognition of same-sex relationships in four jurisdictions. The chapter then discusses same-sex relationships under international and regional human rights law. This leads to an analysis of non-discrimination norms in this context, including the challenges posed by claims of "religious freedom". The chapter concludes with a brief but sobering account of jurisdictions that legally sanction hostility towards same-sex couples.

In the final chapter in Part I, Thandabantu Nhlapo describes customary marriages in South Africa. In contradistinction to societies and legal systems that view marriage as one of many suitable forms of intimate relationship or reject it altogether because of its patriarchal and constricting history, marriage is considered desirable and an indispensable milestone in African societies and African customary law. In the first part of the chapter, Nhlapo explains the legal requirements for a customary marriage. They *inter alia* entail family involvement in negotiations relating to the marriage, property/bridewealth (*lobolo*) being given by the prospective husband or the head of his family to the head of the prospective wife's family in consideration of the marriage, and the handing over of the bride to the husband or his family. Another notable feature of customary marriage in South Africa the author deals with is that it permits polygamy, in this case specifically polygyny (i.e., a husband is allowed to take more than one wife). Nhlapo also discusses developments regarding the proprietary consequences of customary marriages and the dissolution of a customary marriage.

Part II of the Handbook explores divorce and its consequences. One of the central premises of the first chapter in this part is that divorce and the particular society in which it occurs are related. Departing from this basis, Barbara Stark considers substantive and procedural aspects relating to the availability and grounds of divorce, the effort that is required to obtain a divorce, and the procedure to be followed to obtain a divorce. Extrajudicial divorce, specifically a husband's power in terms of *Sharia* (Islamic religious law) unilaterally to divorce his wife by pronouncing a *talaq* without involving a judicial or administrative authority, and consensual divorce also receive attention. In the last part of the chapter, Stark provides an overview of the recognition of foreign divorces and explains that foreign divorces granted in respect of religious or same-sex marriages may present special difficulties, including "limping" marriages where the spouses' divorce is recognised by one jurisdiction but not by another.

The next two chapters in Part II consider the financial consequences of divorce. Geoffrey Shannon surveys post-divorce maintenance for spouses in Chapter 5. He assesses the rationales of such maintenance and, in view of the strengths and weaknesses of each rationale, concludes that neither a "clean break" nor the indefinite provision of post-divorce maintenance is ideal. The author also evaluates what he terms a "clean break with a cushion", that is rehabilitative maintenance where the spouses' matrimonial property is divided and a short-term maintenance order is made in favour of the economically dependent spouse. He draws on Irish law as an example of a jurisdiction that provides for indefinite post-divorce maintenance but permits a "clean break" if there are ample means. The author is critical of this approach, as it may lead to a two-tier system where wealthy parties can achieve finality and certainty through lump sum orders while other divorcing couples have to contend with the possibility of repeated court applications for variation of post-divorce maintenance.

In Chapter 6, Bill Atkin examines distribution of property on divorce. He indicates that in jurisdictions where the traditional view of marriage as a union between a man and a woman with the man as the head of the family applies, wives usually have limited or no property and/or control over property. Where the less traditional notion of marriage as a "partnership" or a relationship of "solidarity" applies, property is frequently divided equally on divorce. Although equal division may seem progressive, it does not always take into account children's needs and may result in inequality and inequity because it is misaligned with the reality that one spouse may be financially vulnerable due to the circumstances, such as unequal discharging of domestic and child-care responsibilities, that operated during the marriage. The author further notes that property is commonly divided according to either the rules-based or the discretionary approach. In jurisdictions where financial provision is determined by way of judicial discretion, division of assets and provision of maintenance are generally viewed holistically and the issue of how matrimonial property is defined does not have the same potentially far-reaching consequences it has in jurisdictions where property division is strictly separated from maintenance. Atkin further explores agreements relating to property and their enforcement upon divorce.

The last chapter in Part II was written by Nuria Gonzalez-Martin. In it, she sets out recent developments in international family mediation, focusing specifically on efforts to enhance cross-border recognition and enforcement of voluntary agreements in child-related family matters, the collaborative process in international family mediation, and principles that should apply in international family mediation processes. The author charts the investigations, conclusions, and recommendations of the Experts' Group on Cross-border Recognition and Enforcement of Voluntary Agreements in Family Matters involving Children established by the Permanent Bureau of The Hague Conference on Private International Law, and summarises the steps the broader community of experts in international family mediation has taken to promote and implement a collaborative process in international family mediation. Arguably the most important of these steps is the development of the Charter for International Family Mediation Processes. The author devotes considerable attention to the ten core principles in international family mediation that are at the heart of the Charter.

Part III of the Handbook focuses on children in families, including single parent families. In "Child custody and cognate concepts: the challenges", Elaine Sutherland traces the evolution and contemporary application of custody. She provides an outline of the international standards that form the backdrop to obtaining and exercising custody, and sets out the rules relating to the allocation of custody to married and unmarried parents in light of comparative examples. She also highlights the complicated position where a child is born as a result of assisted reproductive technology, including the possibility of a child having three or more parents. She then turns to the resolution of custody disputes. When courts are tasked with resolving custody disputes, they employ the best interests test, which sometimes involves using a checklist of factors and/or applying presumptions. The author pays particular attention to two issues that loom large in this context: the growing support for the continued involvement of both parents in the child's life, and the increased recognition of the dangers of exposing a child to domestic abuse.

In Chapter 9, Margaret Brinig discusses the duty to support children, found in all national laws as well as the United Nations Convention on the Rights of the Child. Brinig considers where the duty lies, and the responsibilities, if any, of the parents, other adults, and the state. This chapter proceeds to examine the scope of the duty, including the factors that determine the amount of support and its duration. It is followed by a survey of enforcement mechanisms, domestic and international, and the circumstances under which the duty ends.

In Chapter 10, Frederik Swennen examines personal relations and contact with children. Referring to international and regional instruments and examples, the author explores the various categories of persons who hold the right to have visitation and other forms of contact with a child. As far as the content of these relations is concerned, the author distinguishes between direct contact and indirect means of maintaining personal relations. He further indicates when and why personal relations and contact can be restricted and what types of restrictions can be imposed. He also reviews the enforcement of personal relations and contact, and points out that access to a speedy and effective enforcement procedure is required. In the final part of the chapter, the author addresses private international law aspects relating to cross-border exercising and enforcement of personal relations and contact. Lastly, he draws attention to the fact that the international and regional instruments that apply to cross-border exercising and enforcement of personal relations and contact strongly emphasise international co-operation.

In the chapter on adoption, Barbara Stark begins with a brief historical overview, showing how domestic adoption policies influenced intercountry adoption, which emerged after World War II. She describes the surge in intercountry adoption in the 1990s, and the unprecedented problems raised by the migration of babies and children over long distances. These included human rights issues as well as financial abuses. In response, the Hague Conference invited non-member states of origin to join with member states in drafting the Convention on Protection and Co-operation in Respect to Intercountry Adoption (the Adoption Convention). The chapter concludes with an analysis of the decline of intercountry adoption.

The four chapters in Part IV of the book concern human rights within and affecting the family. The opening chapter, "Children's rights in the family", was written by Geraldine Van

Bueren. It starts with a brief consideration of the recognition afforded to the family in human rights instruments and the evolution of human rights law to the point where states are not only obliged to protect children by not interfering with family life, but also have the duty to protect children's rights within the family. Then the author discusses one of the universally accepted fundamental principles relating to children's rights – the child's best interests. Next, the child's right to have recognition afforded to his or her evolving capacities receives attention. The author further considers the question of whether a child acquires rights within the family before birth. She also investigates areas where children's rights and those of their parents or the state frequently diverge. She specifically deals with the child's rights to health advice and treatment (especially contraception and abortion), religious choice, to know his or her birth parents, to have a relationship with his or her parents after their separation, and to privacy in the family; discrimination against non-marital children; adoption and the Islamic practice of *kafalah* where a child is placed in a family that is as closely related to the child's birth family as possible; intercountry adoption; early marriage; and physical punishment.

The topic of Chapter 13 is reproductive rights, with the spotlight falling specifically on abortion law reform. The analysis in the chapter centres on a 2016 decision by the First Chamber of the Supreme Court of Brazil, where it was held that persons who clandestinely performed abortions with the consent of pregnant women in violation of the near absolute prohibition on abortion imposed by Brazilian law could not be detained before their trial *inter alia* because punishing first trimester abortion violates women's human rights. Rachel Rebouché uses this case to reflect on three arguments that have been used internationally to support reproductive rights. The first argument is that universal values such as autonomy, physical and psychological integrity, and (substantive) gender equality, which underpin human rights, intersect with domestic laws and influence domestic interpretations of abortion laws. The second is that, separately from these values, a particular state's stance on abortion signals its affiliation with likeminded states. Transnational agreement about abortion in turn affords legitimacy to the states' shared values. The last argument is that public health data demonstrates the pitfalls of ignoring reproductive rights. The author concludes that, although issues such as abortion have been clothed in transnational importance, political considerations and differences in national context impose limits on a rights-based approach.

Chapter 14 explores domestic and international regulation and recognition of surrogacy. After providing an overview of the origins of and recent data on surrogacy practices, Philipp Reuss distinguishes between the different forms of surrogacy. Then he sets out the human rights framework that forms the background to the regulation of domestic surrogacy, and the recognition of cross-border surrogacy and the parent – child relationship that may have come into existence in the other state. He further sketches the human rights implications of surrogacy for intended parents, surrogate mothers, and children. Citing comparative examples, he also describes the approaches towards domestic surrogacy and the recognition of cross-border surrogacy. In conclusion Reuss makes the point that the lack of uniformity between the legal regimes relating to cross-border surrogacy results in uncertainty for all the parties. The author favours an international instrument that sets standards for surrogacy and regulates uniform prerequisites for the recognition of the parent – child relationship as a means to address the uncertainty.

Chapter 15, "Father's rights: Japan as a different paradigm", by Colin Jones describes the purportedly neutral dispute resolution procedures available to separated fathers in Japan. Jones depicts a family law system designed primarily to serve the interests of the state and society rather than family members. Until its revision following Japan's defeat in World War II, Japan's family registry system, the *koseki*, identified the head of household, who had the authority to manage the family property and decide whether family members could marry or adopt. Rights and duties among family members were left to the family to resolve. While family law is now technically governed by Part IV of the Japanese Civil Code, Jones notes, it was not until 2011 that the Code was amended to refer to post-divorce visitation and child support. These matters may be addressed by a court, but only at divorce and only after efforts to reach an agreement through a usually protracted process of judicial conciliation have failed. As Jones concludes, despite the changes in blackletter law, a status quo in which mothers remain responsible for children and fathers have no recognised "right" of access is remarkably persistent.

Part V concludes this volume with three chapters examining relationships between families, especially international families, and the state. It begins with Aziza Ahmed's thoughtful analysis of the role of family law in the state's regulation of the family. Drawing on work by Janet Halley and Kerry Rittich, Ahmed explains how the state relies on the family to assume responsibility for carework. She shows how this plays out in the context of Muslim Personal Law, which India relies on to manage its Muslim minority.

In Chapter 17, Rashida Manjoo examines normative developments regarding violence against women. She maps its emergence as a subject of international law, from its origins as soft law in international human rights law to its detailed articulation in regional human rights systems in Africa, the Americas, and Europe. Focusing on violence by current or former intimate partners, she concludes with a frank appraisal of what remains a grim and pervasive problem with far-reaching consequences. Noting dramatic breakthroughs in European and Inter-American jurisprudence, she points to the ongoing absence of a specific treaty, and the related lack of internationally binding definitions or effective monitoring of states, as obstacles to the elimination of violence against women.

In Chapter 18, Edit Frenyo examines emerging forms of transnational parenting among migratory families in an era of global capitalism. She vividly contrasts the very different experiences of migrating men and women, particularly from Central Eastern Europe to Western Europe. Noting the lack of data, she draws on anecdotal accounts to show the difficulties faced by migrating parents, especially mothers, who are criticised both for leaving young children and for being unable to provide for them unless they do.

Themes

Although each of the chapters in the Handbook has a unique subject matter, common themes emerge from many of the chapters.

A dominant theme is that social change is a vital factor in dictating legal developments, and globalisation has driven both dramatic social change, and an equally dramatic backlash. More specifically, the increased mobility and internationalisation of families have changed societal values, including views on marriage, and has resulted in, *inter alia*, a reduced focus on fault in the context of divorce, a growing acceptance of non-marital and same-sex families, and restrictions being imposed on a husband's right unilaterally to divorce his wife without the involvement of a court or another authority in terms of *Sharia* law, at least in some states. Several chapters show that advances in the field of medicine, particularly assisted reproduction techniques, have also resulted in social change and a concomitant need for legal development.

Another theme, especially in chapters dealing with support, adoption, immigration, and caregiving responsibilities, is the reduction in social services, or safety nets, as states have accepted austerity or structural adjustment programmes. Once-public programs have been privatised, and that means that responsibility for the very young, the very old, the sick, and the disabled has fallen on their families, many of which are already stretched thin.

Because the law and the legal developments required by social change are inseparably linked to the specific circumstances in each state, it comes as no surprise that there is a lack of uniformity in laws regulating international family law. Religious and cultural values play an important role in this regard.

International and regional instruments have been drafted in an attempt to address problems arising from the lack of uniformity in specific areas of family law, and harmonisation of rules has been attempted in some regions. Several chapters in this Handbook show that, despite these attempts, even greater international co-operation is required in cross-border cases, especially those involving children.

In the context of family law matters involving children, another prominent theme is the movement away from subsuming children's rights and interests under those of parents. For instance, children are no longer viewed solely as the object of a parental right to contact, but are rights holders, too; the child's best interests have been virtually universally accepted as the central concept in any matter concerning a child, despite the ongoing inability to agree on what, exactly, is in a "child's best interests", and the evolving capacities of the child are increasingly recognised.

Unsurprisingly, the misalignment of supposed gender equality with the lived realities of women also features as a common theme in the Handbook. It is especially marked in respect of maintenance for spouses after divorce, the division of property on divorce, and child care. Apart from financial inequality and the unequal distribution of domestic and child care responsibilities, domestic violence and oppressive limitations on the right to reproductive choice (especially the choice to terminate a pregnancy) are particular challenges.

Part I

Marriage and marriage-like relationships

1

Marriage

Maebh Harding

Introduction

Marriage is an ancient social institution, present in all cultures. However, understandings of what constitutes a marriage and its legal and social consequences differ from nation to nation. This diversity raises different legal issues in cross-border situations where a particular marriage is linked to more than one national legal system.[1] Efforts have been made to create a multilateral international agreement to recognise marriages across international borders,[2] but consensus has been difficult to obtain. While regional agreements do exist,[3] generally speaking, the rules determining whether or not a state will recognise a foreign marriage are determined by national or state conflict of law rules.

Marriage is both a private commitment between two spouses, creating obligations towards each other, and also a public commitment that is recognised by the state as creating a changed legal status. Many national legal systems treat married couples differently from unmarried couples, according benefits to the marital family in order to encourage the creation of stable, economically contributing family units. The state therefore has a national interest in determining who is married.

Parties to a particular marriage have a stake in ensuring that their horizontal commitment towards each other is upheld when borders are crossed. Some types of marriages are more universally accepted than others. A state's failure to recognise certain types of marriages or to recognise such relationships as imposing a lower level of legal obligation from that agreed to by the parties undermines the validity of such relationships and may leave the more vulnerable spouse without appropriate legal protection.

1 Referred to throughout this chapter as 'foreign marriages'.

2 For example, the Hague Convention on Celebration and Recognition of the Validity of Marriages 1978.

3 E.g. the Nordic Convention on Marriage Amendment Agreement 2006; American Law Institute, *Restatement of the Law Second: Conflict of Laws 2d* (1971) s 283 which, although not an agreement, has been widely adopted as a methodology in the USA; see S. Symeonides, *Choice of Law* (Oxford University Press, 2016) 555–556.

While the right to marry is recognised internationally as a universal human right,[4] within many international human rights instruments, priority is often given to national law to determine both what marriage is and its consequences. Article 12 of the European Convention on Human Rights limits the right to men and women of 'marriageable age' to marry according to the national laws governing the exercise of this right. However, the European Court of Human Rights has found that a state may not restrict the right to marry in such a way that the very essence of the right is impaired,[5] and has held Article 12 to be violated where national law creates an arbitrary or disproportionate infringement.[6] Similarly, Article 9 of the EU Charter guarantees the right to marry in accordance with the national law; however, national restrictions must be 'rational, reasonable and non-arbitrary'.[7] In the USA, marriage law is generally within the law-making competence of states rather than the federal government, although the US Supreme Court has long recognised the right to marry as a fundamental right protected by the US constitution.[8] Most recently, in *Oberfell v. Hodges*[9] all state prohibitions on same-sex marriage were found to be unconstitutional under the Due Process and Equal Protection clauses of the fourteenth amendment.

Moreover, other international human rights instruments protect against certain forms of harmful marriage practices. For example, Article 16 of the UN Convention on the Elimination of All Forms of Discrimination against Women (CEDAW) requires marriage law to treat both spouses equally and also establishes that child marriages should have no legal effect.[10] General Recommendation No. 21[11] makes it clear that polygamy is considered a violation of a woman's right to equality with men. Although not all human rights protections are directly incorporated into national law, courts should take them into account as at least persuasive authority when considering whether to recognise a foreign marriage.

Conflict of law rules determining whether a marriage should be recognised must therefore grapple with three different normative goals: maintaining the forum state's historical and social understanding of what marriage is and why it should be valued, ensuring that commitments to international human rights values are upheld, and dispensing justice for the individual spouses in question.

Traditionally, national systems have focussed on connecting a marriage to a single national legal system rather than considering the international context of these types of cases. Nonetheless, the application of such conflict of law rules often grants recognition to a broader range of relationships than the equivalent domestic law. The recognition of cross-border marriages can thus be a highly politicised issue. Where more lenient rules apply to foreign marriages than to purely domestic marriages this raises the risk of deliberate evasion of national law and requires

4 For example, Universal Declaration of Human Rights, Article 16; European Convention on Human Rights, Article 12; Charter of Fundamental Rights of the European Union, Article 9; International Covenant on Civil and Political Rights, Article 23.

5 *B and L v. UK*, Application No. 36536/02 (ECtHR, 13/09/2005), [34]; *Schalk and Kopf v. Austria*, Application No. 30141/04 (ECtHR, 24/06/2010) [49]; *F v. Switzerland*, Application No. 11329/85 (ECtHR, 18/12/1987) [32].

6 *O'Donoghue and others v. UK*, Application No. 34848/07(ECtHR, 14/12/201), [84].

7 EU Network of Independent Experts on Fundamental Rights, *Commentary of the Charter of Fundamental Rights of the European Union* (2006) 99.

8 *Loving v. Virginia*, 388 U. S. 1, (1967).

9 135 S.Ct, 2584 (2015).

10 Article 16.

11 UN Committee on the Elimination of Discrimination against Women (CEDAW), CEDAW General Recommendation No. 21: Equality in Marriage and Family Relations, 1994, available at: www.refworld.org/docid/48abd52c0.html (accessed 30 June 2017), [14].

states to consider the recognition of abusive relationships, such as forced marriages or child marriages. On the other hand, conflicts of law rules can be utilised as a positive force to modernise conservative family law.[12] There are many high-profile examples of the use of cross-border cases by campaigns to extend the right to marry within national law, from the furore over marriages to one's deceased wife's sister in England in the nineteenth century[13] to the much more recent extensions of equal marriage to same-sex couples in the Western world.[14]

This chapter will examine complications caused by differing rules of domestic legal systems relating to capacity to marry within a cross-border context; in particular, the class of relatives who are permitted to intermarry and the need for both spouses to consent to the union. Focussing on English common law principles of conflicts of law, the chapter will raise two critical questions: What factors should the courts consider when deciding whether or not to recognise a foreign marriage that differs from forum state ideals? Is blanket refusal of all legal recognition at a national level a proportionate way of showing state disapproval for marriages that offend national policy and international human rights protections?

Prohibited degrees of relationships

Most societies place some sort of prohibition on marriage between close blood relatives and/ or those connected by other sorts of kinship ties. However, the class of relatives prohibited from intermarriage in any particular legal system has varied substantially depending on culture and prohibitions have also evolved over time. For example, in Europe, the extensive rules of the Catholic Church in the sixth to eighth centuries prohibited marriage between those related by blood, marriage and 'spiritual kin' (for example, an individual and his or her godchild).[15] In the USA, earlier colonial laws prohibited many different forms of marriage between those related by marriage, whereas from the nineteenth century onwards, prohibitions on marriages between first cousins were increasingly introduced.[16] In Islamic law, marriage is also prohibited between those related by 'milk kinship' (for example two otherwise unrelated individuals who were breastfed by the same woman).[17]

The policy reasons underpinning these sorts of prohibitions have also varied widely. Goody argues that the extensive marriage prohibitions of the Catholic Church in early medieval Europe were designed to break the continuity of family property ownership.[18] Although originally based on the biblical text of Leviticus, the common underpinning for the prohibited degrees in common law countries is Archbishop Parker's table, itself composed to suit the personal needs of King Henry VIII to sire an heir in the sixteenth century.[19] Such prohibitions were later justified at the start of the nineteenth century as necessary to prevent jealousy and inappropriate sexual

12 Maebh Harding, 'Does Transnational Family Law Exist? Should Adult Relationships be Freed from National Protective Norms?' in P. Jurčys, P.F. Kjaer, and R. Yatsunami (eds) *Regulatory Hybridization in the Transnational Sphere* (Martinus Nijhoff, 2013) 263–281.

13 Discussed infra.

14 For example, *Obergefell v. Hodges*, 135 S.Ct, 2584 (2015), *Wilkinson v. Kitzinger* [2006] EWHC 2022.

15 M. Ottenheimer, *Forbidden Relatives* (University of Illinois Press, 1996) 63–68.

16 M. Ottenheimer, *Forbidden Relatives* (University of Illinois Press, 1996) 19–41.

17 A. Gil'adi, *Infants, Parents and Wet Nurses: Medieval Islamic Views on Breastfeeding and their Social Implications* (Brill, 1999) 71–114.

18 J. Goody, *The Development of the Family and Marriage in Europe* (Cambridge University Press, 1983) 48–82.

19 M. Harding, 'The Curious Incident of the Marriage Act No. 2 1537 and the Irish Statute Book' (2012) 32 *Legal Studies*, 78–83.

feelings within the family group.[20] Ottenheimer argues that prohibitions on marriages between first cousins in the USA, ostensibly based on genetic risk,[21] also encouraged the assimilation of ethnic communities at a time of large-wave immigration.[22]

Today, the tendency in the Western world is towards a reduced class of prohibited relatives,[23] viewing wider prohibitions as disproportionate infringements on the right to marry.[24] However, in the nineteenth century, clashes between the rules relating to prohibited degrees of different European systems generated case law in which fundamental common law principles of conflicts of law were challenged. The traditional approach of recognising foreign marriages if they were valid in the place of celebration unless contrary to public policy[25] gave way to a more complicated set of principles when it came to determining essential validity (i.e. whether or not either spouse lacked the capacity to marry rendering the marriage invalid). At this point, English law parted ways with the US *lex loci celebrationis* approach.[26] The distinction set out in *Brook v. Brook*[27] between rules regulating the formalities for marriage which are determined by the law of the place of the marriage[28] and rules determining the essential elements of marriage which are generally determined by the law of each spouse's pre-marital domicile[29] is still an important distinction in the English common law.

In nineteenth-century England, marriage to the sister of a deceased wife was prohibited under national law.[30] The evasion of national law by the upper and middle classes[31] and the subsequent legal challenges to these marriages generated polemic debate which subsequently led to domestic reform.

In *Brook v. Brook*[32] a man and his sister-in-law, British subjects domiciled in Britain, travelled to Denmark to evade English law and marry. The case was about the later administration of Brook's will. During the case, arguments were raised to the effect that the marriage should be recognised because many in England approved of the marriage between a widower and the sister of his deceased wife and such marriages were permitted in Protestant states in Europe and in most states in America.[33] The direct role of legal activist was rejected by Lord Campbell who noted that, '[c] hange of opinion on any great question, at home or abroad, may be a good reason for the legislature changing the law, but can be no reason for judges to vary their interpretation of the law'.[34]

Brook's marriage to his sister-in-law was not recognised by the English court and the three children of the marriage were rendered illegitimate. The case itself caused great controversy and inspired many attempts at immediate legislative reform.[35] Domestic English law was eventually changed by the Deceased Wife's Marriage Act 1907 and the Deceased Brother's Widow's Marriage Act 1921.[36]

20 S. Cretney, *Family Law in the 20th Century: A History* (Oxford University Press, 2003) 45.
21 M. Ottenheimer, *Forbidden Relatives* (University of Illinois Press, 1996) 42–60.
22 M. Ottenheimer, *Forbidden Relatives* (University of Illinois Press, 1996) 151–152.
23 See e.g. the English Marriage Act 1949, Schedule 1.
24 *B and L v. UK*, Application No. 36536/02 (ECtHR 13/09/2005).
25 *Herbert v. Herbert* (1819) 2 Hagg. Cons. Rep. 271.
26 S. Symeonides, *Choice of Law* (Oxford University Press, 2016) 554–556.
27 *Brook v. Brook* (1861) 9 HL Cases 193; 11 ER 703.
28 *Lex loci contractus.*
29 *Lex loci domicilii.*
30 The Marriage Act 1835, 5 & 6 Will 4, c54.
31 S. Cretney, *Family Law in the 20th Century: A History* (Oxford University Press, 2003) 44.
32 (1861) 9 HL Cases 193; 11 ER 703.
33 Ibid., [209].
34 Ibid., [209] – [210].
35 S. Cretney, *Family Law in the 20th Century: A History* (Oxford University Press, 2003) 46.
36 Ibid., 46–51.

The rule laid down in *Brook* itself was ambiguous. Both Lord Campbell and Lord Cranworth refused to recognise the marriage as an exception to the general rule in favour of recognising a marriage if that was valid in the place of celebration. Lord Campbell justified the non-recognition as falling into a public policy exception,[37] whereas Lord St Leonards imposed a higher threshold that foreign law should not be given force in England where it was considered opposed to 'God's Law'.[38]

Lord Cranworth justified the non-recognition because the marriage was prohibited by 'the laws of the country to which the parties contracting the marriage belong'[39] providing the basis for what would become known as 'the dual domicile rule' which requires both parties to the marriage to have capacity to marry under the laws of the country of their pre-marital domicile. In contrast, Lord Wensleydale emphasised that English law was applicable as the contemplated future matrimonial residence.[40] He emphatically rejected an international approach to the issue: 'What have we to do with the general consent of Christendom, on the subject of incest, in a question which relates to our own country alone?'[41]

It was not long before the English courts had to consider the converse situation to that in *Brook*; a case where foreign nationals had married in England to evade their own national law. In *Sottomayer v. De Barros No. 1*,[42] two Portuguese first cousins, aged 14 and 16, married in England in 1866 before returning to live in Portugal in 1873. Evidence accepted by the Court at first instance, suggested that the marriage was an ineffectual sham. The wife's father had been declared legally insane in Portugal and the marriage was entered into to free up his property from the consequences of bankruptcy.[43] Under Portuguese law at the time, marriage between first cousins was forbidden on the basis of consanguinity, unless a dispensation had been given. The wife had been assured by her parents that the English marriage would not be binding and it was accepted that the marriage had not been consummated.[44] The wife petitioned the English courts to have the marriage annulled and this was unopposed by her husband.[45] At the initial hearing, the Divorce Court accepted that both parties had been domiciled in Portugal at the time of the marriage.[46]

Although the marriage appeared to have little real connection to England, and neither spouse seemed particularly keen for it to continue, the Divorce Court dismissed the petition upholding the marriage as valid according to *lex loci celebrationis*. The prohibition on marriage between first cousins was considered to be a matter of Portuguese law, insufficient to invalidate the marriage on the basis of an English public policy exception or on the basis that the marriage was incestuous according to the general law of Christendom.[47]

The Court of Appeal gave more force to the principles of Portuguese law and held that marriage should be annulled. Cotton LJ set out strong support for a dual domicile approach to matters of capacity in English conflicts of law as follows:

> The law of a country where a marriage is solemnised must alone decide all questions relating to the validity of the ceremony by which the marriage is alleged to have been constituted;

37 *Brook v. Brook* (1861) 9 HL Cases. 193; 11 ER 703, [210].
38 Ibid., [231].
39 Ibid., [224].
40 Ibid., [240].
41 Ibid., [243].
42 (1877) 2 PD 81.
43 Ibid., 85.
44 Ibid.
45 Ibid.
46 Ibid., 85.
47 Ibid., 86.

> but, as in other contracts, so in that of marriage, personal capacity must depend on the law of domicile; and if the laws of any country prohibit its subjects within certain degrees of consanguinity from contracting marriage, and stamp a marriage between persons within the prohibited degrees as incestuous, this, in our opinion, imposes on the subjects of that country a personal incapacity, which continues to affect them so long as they are domiciled in the country where this law prevails, and renders invalid a marriage between persons both at the time of their marriage subjects of and domiciled in the country which imposes this restriction, wherever such marriage may have been solemnised.[48]

As the Court of Appeal lacked the ability to make a declaration of nullity, which is a decision that requires the determination of fact, the case was returned to the Divorce Court for rehearing. Under a new President, the court concluded that the wife's pre-marital domicile was Portugal but that the husband had been domiciled in England at the time of the marriage.[49] Within this differently constructed version of the facts, the rules of the pre-marital domiciles of both spouses were in conflict; Portuguese law forbidding the marriage, whereas English law allowed it. There is no reference in this second judgment to the parties returning to Portugal shortly after the marriage nor to the non-consensual appearance of the marriage.

The marriage was upheld and the English courts simply ignored the foreign incapacity. In his judgment, Sir James Hannen focussed on the nature of marriage as a public status 'to which each country is entitled to attach its own conditions'.[50] He held that injustice would be caused to a British domiciliary if the marriage was declared invalid on the basis of the wife's foreign incapacity. There was no reference to the injustice caused to the foreign wife, tricked into a sham marriage that was now binding or to the fact that the husband showed no great desire to remain married. Instead, Sir Hannen emphasised the equal legitimacy of English law to determine such a case, but did not entirely justify why it should be *preferred* in a case where the only remaining link to England at the time of the case was as the place of celebration of the marriage.

The decision of Sir James Hannen in *Sottomayer No. 2* to give effect to the English *lex fori* where one of the parties has an English domicile, has been criticised as giving an unfortunate national bias to English private international law.[51] Murphy argues that the rule is xenophobic in its prioritisation of the English capacity rules[52] and notes that there are no equivalent rules where the marriage was celebrated abroad in the country of the non-English domiciliary's domicile.[53] Clarkson in contrast, defends the rule on the basis it was an appropriate protection of English interests.[54]

The orthodox academic position put forward by the current editors of Dicey and Morris considers *Brook* and the Court of Appeal decision in *Sottomayer No. 1* to lay down a general principle in English law that capacity to marry is governed by the law of the parties' premarital domicile.[55] The application of this dual domicile rule was also supported by the English Law Commission[56]

48 *Sottomayer v. De Barros No. 1* (1877) 3 PD 1, 5.
49 *Sottomayer v. De Barros No. 2* (1879) 5 PD 94, 98.
50 Ibid., 101.
51 *Dicey, Morris & Collins on the Conflict of Laws* (15th edn, Sweet & Maxwell, 2016) [17–061].
52 J. Murphy, *International Dimensions in Family Law* (Manchester University Press, 2005) 63.
53 Ibid., 90.
54 C.M.V. Clarkson, 'Marriage in England: Favouring the *Lex Fori*' (1990) 10 *Legal Studies* 80–91, 85.
55 *Dicey, Morris & Collins on the Conflict of Laws* (15th edn, Sweet & Maxwell, 2016) [17–059].
56 Law Commission, *Private International Law: Choice of Law Rules in Marriage* (Working Paper No. 89, 1985) [3.37].

although the enactment of a statute to this effect was not recommended.[57] However, on closer inspection of individual judgments, *Brook v. Brook* marked the beginning of an ambiguous body of English case law that attempts to refer the question of essential validity to one closely connected national legal system. The subsequent case law is not wholly consistent on how this appropriate law is determined. Three tests have received some judicial support – the dual domicile test,[58] the intended marital home test[59] and a case by case determination of the national law with a real and substantial connection.[60]

In earlier case law, the different options for choice of law often pointed to the same national legal system – for example in *Brook* itself, England was both the law of premarital domicile and the law of the intended matrimonial home.[61] Such cases can be used to support the acceptance in English case law of both the dual domicile test and the intended matrimonial home test. In more recent cases judges continue to look at all three options of dual domicile, intended matrimonial home and the real and substantial connection test and seem relieved where all three tests refer to the same legal system.[62]

However, even where a marriage is found to be valid under the applicable national law, the English court retains a public policy discretion not to recognise the marriage. This overriding discretion has recently been made use of in forced marriage cases where the domestic machinery of English law has made it otherwise difficult to declare the marriage to be without any legal effect. The appropriateness of non-recognition on the basis of public policy alone, and the benefits of complete non-recognition of a forced marriage, are discussed in the next section.

Traditional academic commentators on English conflicts of law principles are relatively uncritical of referring a marriage's validity to the rules of a national legal system, merely disagreeing on which legal system is the most appropriately connected.[63] Shakargy[64] in contrast argues that choice of law rules for marriage focus too much on state ownership of marriage, which is anachronistic given the increasingly privatised nature of marriage law in Europe. She argues that party autonomy, identity and freedom of choice should be incorporated into choice of law rules. Briggs too argues that adults of sound mind should be able to choose the law to determine the effects of their marriage and that public policy could be the means to override any 'unpalatable consequences'.[65] While court recognition of the expressed choices of married couples would be welcome, it is clear that in many of the transnational marriage cases, at least one of the parties has not had the opportunity to exercise any choice.

57 Law Commission, *Private International Law: Choice of Law Rules in Marriage* (Law Com. No. 165, [1987) [2.11] – [2.13].

58 For example, *Re Paine* [1940] Ch 46.

59 For example, *Radwan v. Radwan* (No. 2) [1973] Fam 35.

60 The term is used in *Vervaeke v. Smith* [1983] 1 AC 145 and *City of Westminster v. IC (by his Friend the Official Solicitor) and KC and NN* [2008] EWCA Civ 198; See also R. Fentiman, 'The Validity of Marriage and the Proper Law' (1985) 44 *Cambridge Law Journal* 265–279 who argues that the decisions in many older cases can be justified on this basis.

61 See Lord Campbell and comments by J. Murphy, *International Dimensions in Family Law* (Manchester University Press, 2005) 59–60.

62 *City of Westminster v. IC (by his Friend the Official Solicitor) and KC and NN* [2008] EWCA Civ 198.

63 For example, A.J.E. Jaffey, 'The Essential Validity of Marriage' (1978) 41 *MLR* 38; T. Hartley, 'The Policy Basis of the English Conflict of Laws of Marriage', (1972) 35 *MLR* 571; R. Fentiman, 'The Validity of Marriage and the Proper Law' (1985) 44 *Cambridge Law Journal* 265.

64 S. Shakargy, 'Marriage by the State or Married to the State? On Choice of Law in Marriage and Divorce' (2013) 9 *JPIL* 499.

65 A. Briggs, *The Conflict of Laws* (3rd edn, Oxford University Press, 2013) 328–329.

It is argued in this chapter that in an increasingly internationalised world, simply focussing on connecting a marriage to one national system over another or referring to the forum's national public policy alone are inappropriate approaches to international cases that create transnational problems and engage international human rights issues. Instead the courts should adopt a more nuanced, reasoned, approach that considers the real connection of the marriage before the court to any national legal system, the human rights obligations on the state of the adjudicating court and the need to achieve justice for the parties.

Consent

In the Western world, marriage has historically been viewed as type of contract[66] formed by the exchange of consent.[67] Consent of both parties to marriage is required in Christian, Hindu, Jewish, Muslim and Sikh marriage customs. The necessity of free and full consent to marry is now expressly set out in several international human rights treaties.[68]

While all countries require consent for a marriage, there are regional differences in laws determining who has capacity to consent, the quality of consent required, the way in which consent must be expressed[69] and the need for parental consent. Countries therefore differ in the robustness of their safeguards to ensure that both parties have given 'free and full consent' to marry.

The issue of forced marriage, where one of the parties is married without consent, is now a matter of international scrutiny as a human rights abuse. The Council of Europe Convention on preventing and combating violence against women and domestic violence[70] contains provisions requiring forced marriage to be criminalised[71] and such marriages to be easily annulled.[72] The Statute of the International Criminal Court considers forced marriages to constitute enslavement.[73] The Protocol to Prevent, Suppress and Punish Trafficking in Persons, Especially Women and Children to the UN Convention against Transnational Organized Crime of December 2000[74] contains multiple prohibitions against promoting or engaging in forced or service marriages.[75]

In 2009, the Department for Children, Schools and Families estimated that there were between 5,000 and 8,000 cases of forced marriage in England in that year.[76] English domestic law allows

66 See, for example, R.J. Pothier, *Traité du Contrat de Mariage* (Vve Rouzeau-Montaut, Paris 1768); *Turner v. Meyers (falsely calling herself Turner)* (1808) 1 *Hagg Cons* 414, 161 ER 600; *Hyde v. Hyde and Woodmansee* (1866) 1 P&D LR 130, 133.

67 M.M. Sheehan, *Marriage, Family and Law in Medieval Europe* (University of Toronto Press, 1997) 98; J. McAreavey, *The Canon Law of Marriage and the Family* (Four Courts Press, 1997) [93].

68 For example, Universal Declaration of Human Rights, Article 16; International Covenant on Civil and Political Rights, Article 23(3); International Covenant on Economic, Social and Cultural Rights; Article 10(1): The UN Convention on Consent to Marriage, Minimum Age for Marriage and Registration of Marriage 1962.

69 For example, the need for specific vows to be exchanged and the availability of proxy marriage.

70 CETS No. 210.

71 Ibid., Article 37.

72 Ibid., Article 32.

73 Under Article 7(1)(c) of the Rome Statute of the International Court. See W. Schabas, *The International Criminal Court: A Commentary on the Rome Statute* (Oxford University Press, 2010) 161.

74 United Nations, Treaty Series, vol. 2237, 319;

75 See UN, *Model Law against Trafficking in Persons* (2009) 17.

76 Department for Children, Skills and Families, *Forced Marriage: Prevalence and Service Response* (Research Brief No. DCSF-RB128, July 2009).

for Forced Marriage Protection Orders to be made to prevent such marriages from occurring[77] and practical assistance is provided by a Forced Marriage Unit. Those who use coercion to cause a person to marry without free and full consent are now guilty of a specific criminal offence.[78]

There is often an international element to forced marriage cases in England. Forced marriage is most common among Pakistani, Bangladeshi and Indian communities[79] and English domiciliaries often travel to the Indian sub-continent to marry. In 2016, the Forced Marriage Unit handled 1,428 cases of which 43% related to a forced marriage in Pakistan and 8% to a forced marriage in Bangladesh. Only 11% of cases had no overseas element.[80] The criminal offence of forced marriage claims extra-territorial jurisdiction over the coercion and deception elements of the offence.[81]

The validity of an overseas forced marriage is determined by English conflicts of law principles. Consent is considered a matter relating to capacity and the dual domicile rule is commonly used.[82] Thus marriages will be invalidated where either party lacks capacity to consent to marriage under the law of their domicile or where their consent has been given under duress as defined by the law of their domicile. This rule leans towards non-recognition of the marriage which is appropriate in the context of forced marriages. However, the nullity machinery of English domestic law was not designed for international cases. As a result, conflicts of law cases involving forced marriages have led to judicial activism and provide powerful arguments for domestic reform.

Under domestic English law,[83] marriages where there is no adequate consent are classified as merely *voidable* not *void ab initio* as is the case in other common law legal systems. This means that an application to annul the marriage can only be brought by one of the parties to the marriage, not a third party, and applications become time-barred after 3 years.[84] These two changes in policy were recommended by the English Law Commission in 1971[85] on the basis that rendering such a marriage *voidable* would not cause hardship to the parties who would be able to decide for themselves if they wanted to remain married.[86] Three years was considered more than enough time to make this decision.[87] There was simply no consideration in the report of overseas cases. Courts are now precluded from shortcutting the domestic nullity procedure and simply making a declaration that a marriage is *void ab initio* by section 58 of the Family Law Act 1986. Another quirk of English domestic law is that financial relief is potentially available to an ex-spouse after a decree of nullity is made.[88]

Recent international forced marriage cases have highlighted practical problems with the way in which English domestic law deals with the consequences of a forced marriage. In *City of*

77 Forced Marriage (Civil Protection) Act 2007.
78 Anti-social Behaviour, Crime and Policing Act 2014, s 121.
79 Home Affairs Committee, *Domestic Violence, Forced Marriage and "Honour"-Based Violence* (Sixth Report of Session 2007–08, HC 263), [31].
80 Home Office, *Forced Marriage Unit Statistics 2016* (2017).
81 Anti-social Behaviour, Crime and Policing Act 2014, s 121(7) – (8).
82 *Apt v. Apt*[1948] P 83, [1947] 2 All ER 677.
83 Matrimonial Causes Act 1973, ss 12–13.
84 Ibid., s 13(2).
85 Law Commission, *Report on Nullity of Marriage* (Law Com. No. 33, 1970).
86 Ibid., [12].
87 Ibid., [85].
88 The Matrimonial Causes Act 1907, 7 Edw 7 c. 12, s 1(1) allowed applications for financial relief to be made during nullity proceedings by a petitioning wife. However, English law did not offer incidental relief for void marriages as opposed to voidable marriages until the Matrimonial Causes Act 1973.

Westminster v. IC (by his Friend the Official Solicitor) and KC and NN[89] the husband was a vulnerable adult who was married over the telephone in a Muslim ceremony to a Bangladeshi woman. The court held that the husband lacked the capacity to marry under English law and at the time of the marriage had been domiciled in England. The first instance judge held that the marriage had taken place in Bangladesh and that the marriage was valid under the law of Bangladesh. If the marriage had been deemed to take place in England it would have had no legal effect whatsoever.[90] As it was deemed to have taken place in Pakistan, its validity fell to be determined by English conflicts of law principles.

Thorpe LJ accepted that, under statute, the English court had only two options, it could only make a declaration of validity or grant a decree of nullity.[91] However, he held that in conflicts of law cases the statute did not apply and marriage could simply not be recognised under either the dual domicile rule[92] or on public policy grounds.[93]

In *Hudson v. Leigh*[94] Bodey J confirmed the jurisdiction of the English courts to make a declaration that a foreign marriage had no legal recognition in England and Wales and laid down guiding principles for marriages where there was no compliance with the necessary formalities of the *lex loci celebrationis*. In this case, the couple had married in a religious but non-binding ceremony in South Africa. The relationship had now broken down and the woman had applied for divorce or nullity from the English courts with a view to applying for financial relief. The man applied for a declaration that the ceremony in South Africa did not give rise to a marriage that could be recognised in England and Wales. Bodey J drew a distinction between the status of void and non-marriage in English domestic law and declared s 58 of the Family Law Act to be no impediment to a declaration that there never was a marriage, acknowledging that this would mean no right to apply for financial relief for either party.[95]

In *SH v. NB*[96] Moylan J struggled with the consequences in English law of a forced marriage carried out in Pakistan between a 27-year-old Pakistani man and a 16-year-old English girl. Five years after the marriage, the 'husband', who had become a British citizen, applied to the English courts for a divorce on the basis of his 'wife's' unreasonable behaviour. She sought a declaration that no marriage existed. Moylan J held that the marriage was not valid by either English or Pakistani law.[97] However, an application for nullity for lack of consent under the Matrimonial Causes Act 1973 was at this stage time-barred. Following the Court of Appeal's decision in *City of Westminster v. IC* Moylan J made a declaration that the marriage simply was not recognised as a valid marriage in English law.[98] He further justified this declaration on the basis that the marriage should not have greater status in English law than it did in Pakistani law.[99]

In *B v. I (Forced Marriage)*[100] an application for nullity had again been time-barred under English law and an application for a declaration of non-recognition was made under inherent jurisdiction. The marriage had taken place while on a family holiday in Bangladesh. The

89 [2008] EWCA Civ 198.
90 Ibid., [38].
91 Ibid., [26].
92 Ibid., [29].
93 Ibid., [31].
94 [2009] EWHC 1306 (Fam).
95 Ibid., [80] – [85].
96 [2009] EWHC 3274 (Fam).
97 Ibid., [90].
98 Ibid., [103].
99 Ibid., [104].
100 [2010] 1 FLR 1721.

plaintiff was 16 and believed that she had taken part in an engagement ceremony but had in fact been married. The court followed the distinction drawn in *Hudson v. Leigh* between declaring a marriage void and declaring it never to have existed and noted the approval of the Family Law Division in using the law as flexible tool in these circumstances.[101]

In *Re RS*[102] the 'husband' had intellectual disabilities and the local council had sought a Forced Marriage Protection Order to prevent any marriage taking place. However, a marriage in Pakistan took place before the Forced Marriage Protection Order could be granted. Proceedings were taken under inherent jurisdiction to consider the 'husband's' capacity to consent to marriage and whether the court should declare the marriage to be not recognised in England and Wales. It was concluded that the 'husband' lacked the capacity to consent to marriage under English law.[103] In this case the marriage could still have been annulled by bringing nullity proceedings as 3 years had not passed since the marriage. The court exercised its discretion not to recognise the marriage, which was formally valid, in Pakistan. However, Hayden J emphasised the need to consider the effects of the marriage on the incapacitated individual in question, as well as their rights to autonomy and to develop relationships with other human beings. In this case, Hayden J was persuaded by arguments that the marriage was under the permanent threat of criminal prosecution because the 'husband' lacked capacity to consent to sexual relations,[104] as well as the argument that it left the 'husband' subject to legal obligations of marriage that he was unlikely to be able to understand or discharge.[105]

This line of case law clearly permits the courts to make a declaration of non-recognition in cases of forced marriage where the possibility of a nullity petition has been time-barred. Even where the possibility of a nullity petition remains open, such as in *Re RS*, the court may still exercise its discretion not to recognise a marriage. What is unclear from this case law are the principles on which the court should exercise its discretion to make such a declaration. While all the forced marriages discussed were impugned by a lack of capacity, the decisions to grant a declaration were generally rooted in 'public policy'.

The use of vague public policy grounds to deny recognition of an overseas marriage has been criticised by Murphy, who argues that incompletely-articulated reasons for non-recognition, particularly when the tests of essential and formal validity are satisfied, leaves the court open to accusation of cultural imperialism and irrational justification.[106] Probert too raises questions about the 'dogged insistence' of the English courts as to the types of marriages that should be recognised or not recognised by English law, suggesting that a more considered approach is necessary.[107]

In relation to *City of Westminster* both Thorpe LJ and Wall LJ spelled out specific factors that justified the non-recognition of the marriage on the basis of public policy.[108] In *RS*, public policy concerns and the effect of the declaration on the vulnerable individual in question were carefully considered. However, what is missing from these cases is a discussion of whether denying the vulnerable individual in question the possibility of financial relief is an appropriate response to the issue of forced marriage in the circumstances.

101 Ibid., [17].
102 [2015] EWHC 3534 (Fam) [2017] 1 FLR 141.
103 Ibid., [30].
104 Ibid., [41].
105 Ibid., [51].
106 J. Murphy, 'Rationality and Cultural Pluralism in the Non Recognition of Foreign marriages' (2000) 49 *ICLQ* 643.
107 R. Probert, 'Hanging on the Telephone: *City of Westminster v JC*' (2008) 20 *CFLQ* 407.
108 Ibid., 401.

Probert argues that there is no need for the English courts to resort to public policy to categorise the resulting union as a non-marriage in overseas marriage cases.[109] However, where a marriage is simply not recognised in English law as opposed to being declared a nullity, there is no possibility of financial relief for either party and several cases relating to overseas marriages have been brought specifically on this point.

For example, in *Burns v. Burns*[110] the couple had married in California in a hot air balloon without a marriage licence. Under Californian law the marriage would have no legal effect whatsoever. However, the woman had sought a decree of nullity from the English courts under English domestic law and was specifically seeking financial relief.[111] Coleridge J held that both parties had intended to legally marry and had not properly understood the paperwork formalities.[112] Coleridge J accepted that Californian law as the *lex loci celebrationis* was determinative of the validity of the marriage, but not of the remedy.[113] The marriage was declared a nullity in English law, leaving it open to the wife to apply for financial relief.

For some vulnerable individuals, the continued legal existence of the forced marriages appears to be the matter of most concern. For example, in *P v. R*,[114] a case of overseas forced marriage where the wife applied in a timely fashion for a decree of nullity in English law, the court noted the importance of granting a decree of nullity as opposed to a divorce to remove any potential stigma from the vulnerable party that divorce or being considered married would bring.

The use of the concept of non-marriage in *B v. I* has been praised by Gaffney-Rhys[115] as facilitating B's wishes in the individual case, although she acknowledges that blanket use of such a declaration has the potential to be detrimental to women who are unable to petition for financial relief.[116]

The question of whether according vulnerable spouses some of the protective legal consequences of their impugned marriage is compatible with English public policy concerns about that particular type of marriage was discussed by the English Law Commission in relation to polygamous marriages in the 1970s. It was concluded that the failure at that time to allow 'wives' of polygamous marriages to make maintenance claims against their 'husbands' merely pushed the burden to maintain them on to the state and away from the potentially reprehensible 'husband'.[117]

The issue also arises in relation to child marriages that may be recognised under English conflicts of law principles if they satisfy the dual domicile test, although the court retains a public policy discretion to make a declaration of non-recognition.[118] Murphy notes that while it is difficult to imagine a scenario in which the English court would recognise a child marriage considering its international human rights obligations and domestic public policy, the individual circumstances of each case are important.[119]

109 R. Probert 'The Evolving Concept of 'Non-marriage' (2013) 25 *CFLQ* 331.
110 [2007] EWHC 2492 (Fam).
111 Matrimonial Causes Act 1973, s 14.
112 *Burns v. Burns* [2007] EWHC 2492 (Fam) [29] – [30].
113 Ibid., [45].
114 [2003] 1 FLR 661.
115 R. Gaffney-Rhys, '*Hudson v Leigh* – the Concept of Non-marriage' (2010) 22 *CFLQ* 351.
116 Ibid., 362.
117 Law Commission, *Family Law: Report on Polygamous Marriages* (Law Com. No. 42 1972) [28] – [29].
118 *Alhaji Mohamed v. Knott* [1969] 1 QB 1; See R. Deech, 'Immigrants and Family Law' [1973] *New Law Journal* 110, 111.
119 J. Murphy, *International Dimensions in Family Law* (Manchester University Press, 2005) 109.

Conclusion

The traditional principles of English conflicts of law determine the essential validity of marriage according to the law of a relevant national system or systems, subject to a public policy discretion to grant no recognition whatsoever. It is argued that the traditional principles of English conflicts of law approach international marital status cases as simple clashes between national family values rather the multi-layered adjudications they truly are. An emphasis on determining the appropriate national legal systems often means that the court fails to articulate its duties to uphold international human rights obligations or the need to ensure justice for vulnerable parties.

The chapter has also queried whether blanket non-recognition of a marriage is always an appropriate remedy in situations where a vulnerable individual has been coerced into marriage. Blanket non-recognition may prevent the vulnerable party from benefiting from the protections of marriage law such as immigration status, property rights and the possibility of financial relief which may, in individual cases, help to improve the situation of the coerced spouse.

Bibliography

Briggs, A., *The Conflict of Laws* (3rd edn, Oxford, Oxford University Press, 2013).

Clarkson, C.M.V. 'Marriage in England: Favouring the *Lex Fori*' (1990) 10 *Legal Studies* 80–91.

Cretney, S., *Family Law in the 20th Century: A History* (Oxford, Oxford University Press, 2003).

Deech, R., 'Immigrants and Family Law' (1973) 123 *New Law Journal* 110.

Department for Children, Skills and Families, *Forced Marriage: Prevalence and Service Response* (Research Brief No. DCSF-RB128, July 2009).

Dicey, Morris & Collins on the Conflict of Laws (15th edn, London, Sweet & Maxwell, 2016).

EU Network of Independent Experts on Fundamental Rights, *Commentary of the Charter of Fundamental Rights of the European Union* (2006).

Fentiman, R., 'The Validity of Marriage and the Proper Law' (1985) 44 *Cambridge Law Journal* 265–279.

Gaffney-Rhys, R., '*Hudson v Leigh* – the Concept of Non-marriage' (2010) 22 *Child and Family Law Quarterly* 351–363.

Gil'adi, A., *Infants, Parents and Wet Nurses: Medieval Islamic Views on Breastfeeding and their Social Implications* (Leiden, Brill, 1999).

Goody, J., *The Development of the Family and Marriage in Europe* (Cambridge, Cambridge University Press, 1983).

Harding, M., 'Does Transnational Family Law Exist? Should Adult Relationships be freed from National Protective Norms?' in P. Jurčys, P.F. Kjaer and R. Yatsunami (eds) *Regulatory Hybridization in the Transnational Sphere* (Leiden, Martinus Nijhoff, 2013).

Harding, M., 'The Curious Incident of the Marriage Act No. 2 1537 and the Irish Statute Book' (2012) 32 *Legal Studies* 78–108.

Hartley, T., 'The Policy Basis of the English Conflict of Laws of Marriage' (1972) 35 *Modern Law Review* 571–583.

Home Affairs Committee, *Domestic Violence, Forced Marriage and "Honour"-Based Violence* (Sixth Report of Session 2007–08, HC 263).

Jaffey, A.J.E., 'The Essential Validity of Marriage' (1978) 41 *Modern Law Review* 38–50.

Law Commission, *Family Law: Report on Polygamous Marriages* (Law Com. No. 42 1972).

Law Commission, *Report on Nullity of Marriage* (Law Com. No. 33, 1970).

Law Commission, *Private International Law: Choice of Law Rules in Marriage* (Working Paper No. 89, 1985).

Law Commission, *Private International Law: Choice of Law Rules in Marriage* (Law Com. No. 165, 1987).

McAreavey, J. *The Canon Law of Marriage and the Family* (Dublin, Four Courts Press, 1997).

Murphy, J., *International Dimensions in Family Law* (Manchester, Manchester University Press, 2005)

Murphy, J., 'Rationality and Cultural Pluralism in the Non Recognition of Foreign marriages' (2000) 49 *International and Comparative Law Quarterly* 643–659.

Ottenheimer, M., *Forbidden Relatives* (Illinois, University of Illinois Press, 1996).

Pothier, R-J., *Traité du Contrat de Mariage* (Paris, Vve Rouzeau-Montaut, 1768).

Probert, R., 'Hanging on the Telephone: *City of Westminster v JC*' (2008) 20 *Child and Family Law Quarterly* 395–407.

Probert, R., 'The Evolving Concept of 'Non-marriage' (2013) 25 *Child and Family Law Quarterly* 314–335.
Shakargy, S., 'Marriage by the State or Married to the State? On Choice of Law in Marriage and Divorce' (2013) 9 *Journal of Private International Law* 499–533.
Sheehan, M.M., *Marriage, Family and Law in Medieval Europe* (Toronto, University of Toronto Press, 1997).
Symeonides, S., *Choice of Law* (Oxford, Oxford University Press, 2016).

2

Same-sex marriages and civil or registered partnerships

Nicholas Bamforth

Many national legal systems in the global north and west now provide legal recognition to same-sex partnerships. The United Nations High Commissioner for Human Rights notes that "[a]s at April 2015, 34 States offered same-sex couples either marriage or civil unions, which bestow many of the same benefits and entitlements as marriage".[1] By contrast, there was a total absence of such protections around the world in 1978.[2] Recognition has come through legislative action, litigation, or a combination, and has taken different forms – including the opening up of marriage to same-sex couples, the creation of an additional institution of civil or registered partnership, or both.[3] International law does not yet require recognition, and the European Convention on Human Rights (ECHR) – as a regional system – has done so only in specific contexts. Since those in same-sex relationships often face social hostility, non-discrimination protections may also be needed to provide redress for unequal treatment, including the denial of services. Furthermore, homosexual acts remain unlawful in some parts of the world, and same-sex marriage is prohibited in many jurisdictions. As this more global perspective suggests, the degree and type of legal protection – if any – available to same-sex couples depends heavily on the jurisdiction in issue, although international requirements may potentially play some part – particularly in western Europe – and analogous constitutional arguments relating to dignity and equality are sometimes invoked at national level.

The first section below highlights, using examples from four jurisdictions, the varying forms of national-level legal recognition, and the differing methods by which it has been achieved. This analysis illustrates the central part played by national-level factors, including the political and

1 *Discrimination and violence against individuals based on their sexual orientation and gender identity: Report of the Office of the United Nations High Commissioner for Human Rights*, A/HRC/29/23, 4 May 2015, para 67. See also Dominic McGoldrick, 'The Development and Status of Sexual Orientation Discrimination under International Human Rights Law' (2016) 16 *HRLR* 613, 653.

2 Robert Wintemute, 'Conclusion', in Robert Wintemute and Mads Andenaes (eds), *Legal Recognition of Same-Sex Partnerships: A Study of National, European and International Law* (Hart Publishing, 2001), 759–760; John Eekelaar, 'Perceptions of Equality: The Road to Same-Sex Marriage in England and Wales' (2014) 28 *International Journal of Law, Policy and The Family* 1, 1–2.

3 Due to constraints of space, this chapter will not discuss unmarried same-sex couples.

social climate and constitutional structure (influenced in some jurisdictions by international legal obligations). In the second section, the implications of international human rights law, including regional systems such as the ECHR, are examined. The third section considers the extent to which the religious freedoms of those with belief-based objections to same-sex partnerships are sometimes balanced against the protection of such partnerships. The conclusion highlights examples of legally sanctioned hostility towards same-sex couples in some jurisdictions.

Forms of and routes to legal recognition in national law

Robert Wintemute notes that legal recognition has assumed a "huge variety of forms",[4] while John Eekelaar emphasises the diversity of "routes taken" to same-sex marriage.[5] The forms of recognition in national law can be broadly divided as follows:[6]

(a) '*equal marriage*': the same status and protections for same-sex and opposite-sex marriages, under the same legal scheme;
(b) '*alternative marriage*': the same status and level of protection, under different schemes;
(c) '*partnership*': civil or registered partnership for same-sex and opposite-sex couples, involving the same status and protections as marriage but as an alternative, with marriage available to both;
(d) '*LQBTQ partnership*': civil or registered partnership, involving the same status and protections as marriage but open only to same-sex couples, with marriage confined to opposite-sex couples;
(e) '*alternative partnership*': a registered arrangement open only to same-sex couples or also to opposite-sex couples, involving lesser protections than are available within marriage (which might or might not also be open to same-sex couples).

In considering the formal status(es) created and the route(s) leading to legal recognition, contrasts can be drawn between the United Kingdom, France, the United States and South Africa. In the first two jurisdictions, legislative development has been crucial; in the US, the Supreme Court has played a central role; and in South Africa, legislation followed judicial decision-making.[7] However, in none of the first three jurisdictions was one institution *exclusively* responsible. *Both* legislatures *and* courts played a part, with the real question being where the balance is drawn between the two: a matter that turns on national constitutional law and sometimes political circumstances. In most European jurisdictions, an additional factor – absent in the US and South Africa – is the need to comply with the 'trans-national' legal obligations associated with membership of the ECHR and of the European Union (EU). The arrangement chosen may also not depend *solely* on the treatment of same-sex couples. For example, Claude Martin and Irène Théry note in relation to the development of France's *Pacte Civil de Solidarité* (PACS) scheme that there was long-standing divergence between advocates of a new legal status open to *any* kind of 'pair' – couples, friends, siblings – and of something more akin to marriage and designed *specifically* "to achieve legal recognition of same-sex couples [and] open only to couples, heterosexual

4 Wintemute (n 2), 760. The same may be said for accommodations with conservative religious beliefs: Bruce MacDougall, Elsje Bonthuys, Kenneth McK Norrie and Marjolein van den Brink, 'Conscientious Objecting to Creating Same-Sex Unions: An International Analysis' (2012) 1 *Can J Hum Rights* 127.

5 Eekelaar (n 2), 2.

6 The options set out here are not incompatible with the existence of technical differences (concerning, for example, grounds of divorce).

7 In the Republic of Ireland and Australia, referenda have preceded legislative action.

or homosexual".[8] Key to this debate was the treatment of caring adult relationships *generally*, alongside the respective merits of expanding an existing status or creating a new one.

The UK is in transition. Civil partnership, granting the legal rights and responsibilities of marriage but using a separate institution of equivalent status, was created solely for same-sex couples under the Civil Partnerships Act 2004 (CPA) – 'LGBTQ partnership', point (*d*) in our scale.[9] Same-sex couples were included in the statutory definition of and provisions governing marriage via the Marriage (Same Sex Couples) Act 2013[10] – 'equal marriage',[11] point (*a*). However, it is currently unclear whether civil partnership will be abolished or opened to all: the latter constituting 'partnership', point (*c*), *alongside* 'equal marriage'. That the national legislature has played a key role in the UK is unsurprising in a jurisdiction in which Parliament retains legislative sovereignty. The judiciary has also played an important part, however: section 3(1) of the Human Rights Act 1998 requires legislation to be interpreted as far as possible in the light of ECHR rights, and where this is impossible section 4 permits a non-binding declaration of incompatibility to be issued. The 2013 Act requires Parliament to review the future of civil partnerships,[12] and proposals have been made for their reform.[13] Meanwhile, pressure for legislative resolution has increased following the Supreme Court's issuing of a declaration concerning the same-sex-only format in *R (Steinfeld and Keidan) v. Secretary of State for International Development*.[14]

On one view, civil partnership was, in the circumstances of 2004, "something very like 'gay marriage'",[15] even if it turned out to be a transitional stage on the path to full recognition. In *Bull v. Hall*, Baroness Hale observed that it was "not called marriage but in almost every other respect it is indistinguishable from the status",[16] and in *Wilkinson v. Kitzinger*, Family Division President Sir Mark Potter suggested that it accorded same-sex couples "the benefits of marriage in all but name".[17] Nonetheless, the pre-legislative Consultation Paper emphasised that it was *not* marriage,[18] and speaking for the government during the legislative process, Baroness Scotland stressed that "[c]ivil partnership is aimed at same-sex couples who cannot marry".[19] Meanwhile, Sir Mark Potter accepted in *Wilkinson* that its separateness entailed "preserving and supporting the concept

8 Claude Martin and Irène Théry, 'The PACS and Marriage and Cohabitation in France' (2001) 15 *International Journal of Law, Policy and The Family* 135, 147–8.

9 See Paul Mallender and Jane Rayson, *The Civil Partnership Act 2004: A Practical Guide* (Cambridge University Press, 2005).

10 Ss 1 and 11. The references to 'United Kingdom' are in fact to England, Wales and Scotland: a distinct situation prevails in Northern Ireland.

11 S 9 allows earlier civil partnerships to be converted into marriages.

12 S 15.

13 See *Hansard*, HC Deb, 2 February 2018, cols 1119–24 (Victoria Atkins MP, Parliamentary under-Secretary of State); *R (Steinfeld and Keidan) v. Secretary of State for International Development* [2018] UKSC 32, paras [7]–[10].

14 *Steinfeld* (n 13).

15 Mallender and Rayson (n 9), para 1.2.

16 [2013] UKSC 73, para [26]. See also Lord Mance, para [123]; *Secretary of State for Work and Pensions v. M* [2006] UKHL 11, para [99]. (Baroness Hale); *Ghaidan v. Godin-Mendoza* [2004] UKHL 30, para [82] (Lord Millett).

17 [2006] EWHC 2022 (Fam), para [88]. Note also the European Court of Human Rights' assessment: *Burden v. United Kingdom*, application no 13378/05, 29 April 2008 (Grand Chamber), paras [63]–[65].

18 Department of Trade and Industry, Women and Equality Unit, *Civil Partnership: A framework for the legal recognition of same-sex couples*, paras 1.3, 2.6–2.8 (2003); see also *Responses to Civil Partnership: A framework for the legal recognition of same-sex couples* (2003), para 3.4.

19 *Hansard*, HL Deb, 22 April 2004, col 388 and 10 May 2004, col GC31; see also HL Deb, 24 June 2004, cols 1361–2. For a balanced summary, see Mark Harper, Martin Downs, Katharine Landell and Gerald Wilson, *Civil Partnership – The New Law* (Jordan Publishing, 2005), para 4.4.

and institution of marriage as a union between persons of opposite sex or gender".[20] In addition, prior to the 2013 Act, the "differences" between same-sex marriage and civil partnership (for example, the names and registration formalities)[21] were emphasised. From this alternative viewpoint, civil partnerships – whether or not a transitional step for same-sex couples – might be seen as something more *sui generis*.

The ambiguity surrounding civil partnership may explain why it has come to be seen by some – *notwithstanding* the rights and responsibilities – as a socially 'more liberal' or 'less traditional' alternative to marriage that should now be open to all. For example, the litigants in *Steinfeld and Keidan* were an unmarried opposite-sex couple with a conscientious objection to marriage but who wished for legal recognition.[22] While the Supreme Court identified the inequality of treatment that they faced, contrary to Article 14 ECHR (prohibiting discrimination in the enjoyment of ECHR rights) in conjunction with Article 8 (protecting private and family life), with "being denied the range of choice available to same sex couples";[23] it also accepted Briggs LJ's point from the Court of Appeal that since those in the litigants' position had *no* basis for obtaining legal recognition, they might in some circumstances (for example, the death of one partner) suffer financial disadvantage.[24] In consequence, the legislature now faces a choice between abolition and extension of civil partnership. If it is opened up to opposite-sex couples, the UK will have two types of partnership that are near-identical in their legal terms,[25] but that are seen as distinct on a social basis: an interesting example of popular perception moving the understanding of an institution beyond the intentions of at least some of its creators.

France introduced 'alternative partnership' (point (*e*)) in 1999 in the form of the highly distinctive PACS, but moved to 'equal marriage' (with the retention of the PACS) following the opening of marriage, including the right to adopt, to same-sex couples by legislation in 2013.[26] The PACS was established in an environment in which opposite-sex marriage and cohabitation had traditionally been viewed, in both social and legal terms, as wholly distinct from one another, notwithstanding gradual assimilation in the legal treatment of unmarried and married opposite-sex partners.[27] Martin and Théry describe it, given this background and in a situation in which LGBTQ activists were campaigning for legal recognition of same-sex partnerships, as allowing for law reform while avoiding the need to talk *exclusively* of protecting same-sex couples, instead permitting their interests to be catered for *in tandem with* those of the large number of 'modern-minded' opposite-sex couples who were disinclined to engage in 'traditional' marriage.[28] The PACS represented "a kind of 'neither – nor' politics":[29] it was available to two persons of the same

20 *Wilkinson* (n 17), para [122].

21 Government Equalities Office, *Equal civil marriage: a consultation* (2012), paras 1.9.i. and 1.10. See also Maria Miller MP, 'Ministerial foreword', HM Government, *Equal marriage: The Government's response* (2012), 4: "same-sex couples are [still] excluded from marriage" (also paras 2.4, 7.8 and 3.18).

22 *Steinfeld* (n 13), para [6].

23 *Steinfeld* (n 13), para [40] (Lord Kerr); see also paras [48] and [50]. At Court of Appeal level (*Steinfeld and Keidan v Secretary of State for Education* [2017] EWCA Civ 81) see paras [138], [147], [164] (Beatson LJ), and [62], [101] (Arden LJ, dissenting).

24 *Steinfeld* (n 13), para [52], citing Briggs LJ (n 23), paras [167]–[169], [173] (supported by Beatson LJ at para [147]).

25 Divorce may be one point of difference given the need for legislative reform in this area too: see *Owens v. Owens* [2018] UKSC 41.

26 Loi numero 2013–404 du 17 Mai 2013 ouvrant le marriage aux couples de personnes de même sexe.

27 Martin and Théry (n 8), 141–6.

28 Martin and Théry (n 8), 138–41, 148–9.

29 Martin and Théry (n 8), 150.

or opposite sex, but excluded relatives; it was entered into by registration of a contract, without the contents being subject to scrutiny; it could be terminated immediately by the marriage of either party or by agreement, and three months after unilateral official repudiation by one party; the contract governed property relations between the parties, who also determined the distribution of property on termination, with the general legal regime of co-ownership (rather than that governing marriage) applying in default and the court determining distribution; the parties were treated as partners for social security purposes; there were no succession rights except to tenancies, but after three years the parties' income was taxed as if they were married; and there was no right to adopt children.[30] Martin and Théry summarise the PACS as "neither a legal union nor a simple property contract. It is neither public nor private. It is neither [specifically] for couples nor for pairs of friends. It is neither a legal recognition of same-sex couples nor is it non-recognition".[31] While the *Conseil constitutionnel* resolved that only two persons cohabiting as a couple could conclude a PACS, it was distinct from both marriage and simple cohabitation, and in social terms different couples (or members of a couple) could easily view a PACS differently, either as 'almost being married' or 'almost simply cohabiting'.[32]

In Martin and Théry's words, the PACS was thus a "'French way' of giving rights to same-sex couples":[33] a jurisdiction-specific method for dealing with same-sex partnerships in the prevailing national social and legal circumstances of 1999. Against this background, the later opening of marriage might almost seem like a 'standardising' move. While the PACS operates in a more clearly stand-alone way than civil partnerships in the UK, it is however interesting to see that both France and the UK felt the need for a registration-only period for same-sex couples before recognising equal marriage.

In the US, the Supreme Court's decision in *Obergefell v. Hodges*[34] recognised 'equal marriage' in the constitution (point (*a*)), although civil unions are also still permitted in some US States, allowing 'LGBTQ partnership', (*d*), or 'alternative partnership', (*e*), to enter into the picture depending on their terms. *Obergefell* held that State laws excluding same-sex couples from marriage on the same terms and conditions as opposite-sex couples violated the Due Process and Equal Protection Clauses of the Fourteenth Amendment: couples could exercise the fundamental right to marry in all US States.[35] This followed the Court's earlier determination in *United States v. Windsor* that the 1996 Defense of Marriage Act (DOMA) – which defined 'marriage' in federal law to mean a legal union of a man and a woman and 'spouse' as a person of the opposite sex – was an unconstitutional deprivation of liberty under the Due Process Clause of the Fifth Amendment (such liberty containing within it an equal protection element).[36] The two decisions highlight the Supreme Court's decisive role in allowing same-sex couples to marry, but as Kennedy J noted in *Obergefell*, more local recognition had already been accomplished through legislation in many US States and cities.[37]

30 Loi numero 99–944 du 15 Novembre 1999 relative au pacte civile de solidarité; for discussion, see Martin and Théry (n 8), 150–1.
31 Martin and Théry (n 8), 150.
32 Martin and Théry (n 8), 151–2.
33 Martin and Théry (n 8), 146.
34 (2015) 135 S Ct 2584.
35 *Obergefell* (n 34), 2604–5, 2607–8.
36 (2013) 133 S Ct 2675, 2695.
37 *Obergefell* (n 34), 2597, 2605, Appendix B. *Windsor* (n 36), 2692–3, para [24] illustrates the role of one such initiative.

In both cases, Kennedy J emphasised the constitutional importance of equality and dignity. In *Obergefell*, he noted:

> [T]he challenged laws . . . are in essence unequal: same-sex couples are denied all the benefits afforded to opposite-sex couples and are barred from exercising a fundamental right. Especially against a long history of disapproval of their relationships, this denial . . . works a grave and continuing harm. The imposition of this disability on gays and lesbians serves to disrespect and subordinate them.[38]

Furthermore, constitutional "principles and traditions" highlighted that "the reasons marriage is fundamental under the Constitution apply with equal force to same-sex couples".[39] First, personal choice was inherent in the notion of individual autonomy. Choices concerning marriage were "among the most intimate that an individual can make"[40] and involved dignity regardless of sexual orientation. Second, marriage supported a two-person union unlike any other in its importance to those involved. It offered "the hope of companionship and understanding and assurance that while both still live there will be someone to care for the other".[41] Third, marriage safeguarded children and families, and the hundreds of thousands of children being raised by same-sex couples would be stigmatised by the exclusion of their parents from marriage. Fourth, marriage was "a keystone of our social order",[42] and through exclusion same-sex couples were symbolised as "unequal in important respects . . . lock[ed] . . . out of a central institution of the Nation's society".[43] In *Windsor*, Kennedy J had similarly highlighted the "dignity and status" associated with marriage.[44] State law had granted a "lawful status" to same-sex couples who wished to marry, a "far-reaching legal acknowledgement" of a relationship "deemed . . . worthy of dignity in the community equal with all other marriages".[45] DOMA's purpose and effect was, by contrast, to impose a lesser status or stigma on those marriages, which would be "treated as second-class" and deemed "unworthy of federal recognition".[46]

These judgments might, like developments in France and the UK, be seen as reflecting local constitutional norms – here, the role of judicial review of legislation. Kennedy J stressed in *Obergefell* that "individuals need not await legislative action before asserting a fundamental right . . . An individual can invoke a right to constitutional protection when he or she is harmed, even if the broader public disagrees and even if the legislature refuses to act".[47] However, the references in both cases to pre-existing legislative or judicial recognition of same-sex marriage at lower levels raises the question whether the Supreme Court majority would have been as confident *without* such examples. The cases can certainly be seen as demonstrating the central role of judicial decision-making about partnership rights in a constitution with judicial review of legislation,

38 *Obergefell* (n 34), 2604.
39 *Obergefell* (n 34), 2599; see also 2602.
40 *Obergefell* (n 34), 2599.
41 *Obergefell* (n 34), 2599–600; see also 2607–8.
42 *Obergefell* (n 34), 2601.
43 *Obergefell* (n 34), 2602.
44 *Windsor* (n 36), 2692, para [22]; see also 2689, 2692–5.
45 *Windsor* (n 36), 2692, para [24]; see also 2693–4, 2396.
46 *Windsor* (n 36), 2393–4.
47 *Obergefell* (n 34), 2605 (note the preceding qualification, however).

but they might also be said to highlight the importance of legislative initiatives in *encouraging* the majority's position to emerge.[48]

South African law offers wider choice among strong protection mechanisms: it offers 'partnership' (point (*c*)), with supporting elements of 'equal marriage', (*a*), and 'alternative marriage', (*b*). In *Minister of Home Affairs v. Fourie*, the Constitutional Court determined that the existing opposite-sex definition of marriage in common law and section 30(1) of the Marriage Act 1961 was under-inclusive by excluding same-sex couples, and violated the rights to equality and freedom from discrimination under section 9 of the Constitution and dignity under section 10.[49] A judicial finding of unconstitutionality does not necessarily invalidate a legal provision in South Africa, but may instead oblige the legislature to revisit the area. The Court's declaration of invalidity was suspended for one year in *Fourie* to allow Parliament to legislate.[50] Sachs J suggested that the litigants' equality claim was best served "by respecting the separation of powers and giving Parliament an opportunity to deal appropriately with the matter . . . [T]here are different ways in which the legislature could legitimately deal with the gap that exists in the law" and it should have the chance "in the first place to decide how best the equality rights at issue could be achieved". Provided constitutional equality principles were not "trimmed", legislation was likely to produce greater public acceptance and "the more will the achievement of equality be promoted."[51]

As Pierre de Vos notes, "the Court did not give Parliament a wide discretion on the manner in which this defect in the law had to be fixed".[52] In fact, Sachs J's judgment provided detailed guidance,[53] and the resulting Civil Union Act 2006 provided for marriage and civil partnerships for both same-sex and opposite-sex couples, each with the same rights and status, the title of the arrangement to be chosen by the partners.[54] However, the Marriage Act 1961 *also* continued to operate, allowing opposite-sex couples who wished to continue to use the 'traditional' format to do so. De Vos suggests that the 2006 statute was not an unreflective response to *Fourie*: political debate and compromise was involved. For instance, the initial Bill proposed same-sex-only civil partnerships that were to be distinct from marriage.[55] Furthermore, while the maintenance of the 1961 Act alongside the 2006 Act might look like an inelegant outcome, de Vos argues that a hitherto unthinkable legitimacy might in fact have been bestowed on same-sex relationships through the legislative process: an outcome "little short of revolutionary" in political terms.[56]

The legislative outcome – offering all couples the same legal status and rights, but also flexibility in the title and (for opposite-sex couples) the model – would not have been possible without the South African Constitution's distinctive remedial scheme. Another influential local factor was seemingly the country's legacy of category-based inequality. *Fourie* unequivocally denounced the

48 In addition, the Supreme Court's relatively rapid shift, against the background of changing social attitudes, may attract comparisons with the emphasis sometimes placed by the European Court of Human Rights on the evolving 'consensus': see section 2.

49 Case CCT 60/04, 2006 (1) SA 524 (CC), paras [79], [82], [114], [117], [118], [120] (Sachs J); see also [164] (O'Regan J). For analysis, see Pierre de Vos, 'A Judicial Revolution – A Court-Led Achievement of Same-Sex Marriage in South Africa' (2008) 4 *Utrecht L Rev* 162.

50 *Fourie* (n 49), paras [118], [132], [135]; note also [167]–[173] (O'Regan J, dissenting as to remedy).

51 *Fourie* (n 49), para [139]; see also paras [136], [138], [154]–[156], [161].

52 De Vos (n 49), 166.

53 *Fourie* (n 49), paras [149]–[153].

54 Ss 1 and 13; see also De Vos (n 49), 170.

55 De Vos (n 49), 169.

56 De Vos (n 49), 174.

idea of separate legal regimes for same-sex and opposite-sex couples. Sachs J noted the "isolation to which the law has long subjected same-sex couples" through non-recognition,[57] that the "impact of the legal void in which same-sex couples are compelled to live is real, intense and extensive",[58] and that "[a]t the heart of legal disabilities afflicting same-sex life partnerships . . . is the lack of general recognition by the law of their relationships".[59] The exclusion of same-sex couples represented "a harsh if oblique statement" that they "are outsiders, and that their need for affirmation and protection of their intimate relations as human beings is somehow less than that of heterosexual couples", as was "their capacity for love, commitment and accepting responsibility".[60] These are, of course, akin to points made by Kennedy J in *Windsor* and *Obergefell*, but in the South African context they need specifically to be seen in the light of that jurisdiction's concern to build a more equal and inclusive society following the end of *apartheid*.

The four national level case studies thus highlight the different forms of legal recognition potentially available and routes by which it may be achieved. In addition, they show how local factors – constitutional, political and social – play a strong or overwhelming part in shaping the form or route employed. While it would be mistaken to see courts or legislatures as playing an exclusive role, at least in the UK, US and South Africa, the respective roles of each have varied. Interestingly, though, analogous arguments about equality and dignity are visible in the US and South African cases.

International legal requirements

Since international human rights law is not a unified concept, consisting instead of many treaties of varying generality and geographical coverage,[61] this section focuses on the major bodies of law and tribunals that have considered same-sex partnerships.[62] The ECHR has offered the most detailed consideration, seemingly becoming more open to claims over time, but – in line with the International Covenant on Civil and Political Rights (ICCPR) – it does not yet formally acknowledge a right to legal recognition. However, the American Convention on Human Rights (ACHR) has gone further, recognising a right of equal access. By contrast, the African Court on Human and Peoples' Rights has not yet issued any decision concerning sexual orientation discrimination in relation to the African Charter on Human and Peoples' Rights.[63]

The United Nations Human Rights Committee held in *Joslin v. New Zealand* that states are not required to allow same-sex couples to marry.[64] Article 23 of the Covenant refers to the right

57 *Fourie* (n 49), para [155]; see also De Vos (n 49), 165.

58 *Fourie* (n 49), para [62].

59 *Fourie* (n 49), para [117].

60 *Fourie* (n 49), para [71]. See also paras [72]–[75], [155]. This reasoning builds on the Constitutional Court's earlier decision in *National Coalition for Gay and Lesbian Equality v. Minister of Home Affairs*, CCT 10/99, 2000 (2) SA 1 (CC), para [57]; see also paras [32], [36], [40], [42], [49], [53], [54], [56], [59], [86], [97].

61 Andrew Legg, *The Margin of Appreciation in International Human Rights Law: Deference and Proportionality* (Oxford University Press, 2012), 2.

62 How international norms are received into national law depends on the treaty and jurisdiction. Compare the South African Constitutional Court and the UN Human Rights Committee: *Fourie* (n 49), paras [99]–[105].

63 McGoldrick (n 1), 643–6.

64 Communication no 902/1999, 17 July 2002, CCPR/C/75/D/902/1999. For argument that *Joslin* should now be overturned, see Paula Gerber, Kristine Tay and Adiva Sifris, 'Marriage: A Human Right for All?' (2014) 36 *Sydney L Rev* 643.

of men and women to marry, rather than the right of every human being to do so, and this had "consistently and uniformly" been understood as confining the obligation to recognise marriage to opposite-sex unions.[65] Furthermore, no claim of impermissible discrimination on the basis of 'other status' was possible under Article 26. However, the Committee also ruled in *Young v. Australia*[66] and *X v. Colombia*[67] that the denial of a dependent's pension to an unmarried same-sex partner constituted (in the absence of reasonable and objective supporting criteria) impermissible sexual orientation discrimination contrary to Article 26. Since then, both the UN Committee on Economic, Social and Cultural Rights[68] and the UN High Commissioner for Human Rights[69] have recommended that states provide legal recognition for same-sex partnerships. In part given the growing number of states to have subsequently recognised same-sex marriage, critics have argued that the "semantic interpretation" of Article 23 in *Joslin* should be discarded using a 'living instrument' approach whereby the Covenant is interpreted in the light of current circumstances.[70] However, this may be unduly optimistic. As Dominic McGoldrick points out, the total percentage of UN member states to have recognised same-sex marriage stood in May 2016 at only 11 per cent,[71] and a "substantial body of States do not accept" freedom from sexual orientation discrimination either as "an 'existing' right . . . based on a living instrument interpretation" or "a 'new' right".[72]

McGoldrick suggests that in terms of "regional and international human rights systems" the developments in the ECHR "have been the most remarkable".[73] The Council of Europe, which oversees the ECHR and the enforcement of European Court of Human Rights (ECtHR) judgments, has through its Parliamentary Assembly repeatedly called on signatories to ensure legal recognition of same-sex partnerships.[74] Meanwhile, ECtHR case law contains a sustained evaluation of the ECHR's requirements for the treatment of same-sex partnerships at national level, and a relatively rapid evolution in judicial thinking has been evident. Relevant cases have involved Article 8, generally in conjunction with Article 14, and sometimes Article 12 (the right of men and women to marry), and have concerned access to marriage or registered partnership, succession to accommodation held by a deceased partner,[75] access to partnership-related social

65 *Joslin* (n 64), para 8.2.

66 Communication no 941/2000, 6 August 2003, CCPR/C/78/D/941/2000, para 10.4.

67 Communication no 1361/2005, 14 May 2007, CCPR/C/89/D/1361/2005, para 7.2.

68 *Consideration of reports submitted by States parties in accordance with articles 16 and 17 of the Covenant: Concluding observations of the Committee on Economic, Social and Cultural Rights*, E/C.12/SVK/CO/2, 8 June 2012, para 10; *Concluding observations on the combined fourth and fifth reports of Bulgaria, adopted by the Committee at its forty-ninth session*, E/C.12/BGR/CO/4–5, 11 December 2012, para 17.

69 *Discrimination and violence against individuals based on their sexual orientation and gender identity* (n 1), para 79(h).

70 Paula Gerber, Kristine Tay and Adiva Sifris (n 64), 646.

71 McGoldrick (n 1), 653.

72 McGoldrick (n 1), 657.

73 McGoldrick (n 1), 633.

74 Parliamentary Assembly of the Council of Europe, Recommendations 1470 (2000), 1474 (2000), 1547 (2007) and CM/Rec(2010)5, and Resolution 1728 (2010), esp. para 16.9, some or all of which were discussed in *X v. Austria*, application no 19010/07, 19 February 2013 (Grand Chamber), para 54; *Vallianatos v. Greece*, application nos 29381/09 and 32684/09, 7 November 2013 (Grand Chamber), paras 27–30, 91; *Oliari v. Italy*, application nos 18766/11 and 36030/11, 21 July 2015 (Fourth Section Chamber), paras 56–61, 166; *Pajic v. Croatia*, application no 68453/13, 23 February 2016 (Second Section Chamber), paras 31–4. Note also the Council's *Good Practice Guide on Values Based Campaigning for Legal Recognition of Same-Sex Partnerships* (2015), https://rm.coe.int/manual-on-values-based-campaigning-/1680766c87.

75 *Karner v. Austria*, application no 40016/98, 24 July 2003 (First Section Chamber); *Kozak v. Poland*, application no 13102/02, 2 March 2010 (Fourth Section Chamber).

security benefits,[76] the allocation of parental responsibility for[77] or adoption of children,[78] and the difference between maintenance obligations imposed on former partners.[79] The 'margin of appreciation' – the link often highlighted by the ECtHR between ECHR requirements and developing 'consensus' in national practice – has played an important role.

Formally, the ECtHR maintains that Articles 8 and 14 cannot be read as imposing an obligation to grant access to marriage,[80] and that where a state "chooses to provide same-sex couples with an alternative means of legal recognition" such as registered partnership, "it enjoys a certain margin of appreciation as regards the exact status conferred".[81] However, the durability of this position is questionable given that the ECtHR has become more sympathetic in its treatment of same-sex partnerships. As recently as 2001, *Estevez v. Spain* held that long-term same-sex partnerships did not fall within the 'family life' limb of Article 8 – just the more individualised notion of 'private life' – and that a wide margin applied.[82] Similarly, in *Fretté v. France*, concerning the denial of authorisation to a single gay man to adopt, a wide margin was applied.[83]

However, later decisions, often invoking the *changing* consensus among Convention signatories, have discarded these positions.[84] In *Schalk and Kopf v. Austria*, the First Section Chamber held – contrary to *Estevez* – that a cohabiting same-sex couple living in a stable *de facto* partnership fell within the 'family life' limb of Article 8.[85] The Grand Chamber confirmed this in *Vallianatos v. Greece*.[86] Furthermore, the ECtHR started in both cases from the premise that same-sex and opposite-sex couples were equally capable of entering into stable, committed relationships, generating a relatively similar need for legal recognition and protection.[87] In addition, in many Article 14-plus-Article 8 contexts involving same-sex partnerships, the ECtHR now holds that the margin available to states is narrow[88] and that "particularly serious reasons" are needed to justify

76 *PB and JS v. Austria*, application no 18984/02, 22 July 2010 (First Section Chamber).

77 *Salgueiro Da Silva Mouta v. Portugal*, application no 33290/96, 21 December 1999 (Fourth Section Chamber).

78 *Fretté v. France*, application no 36515/97, 26 February 2003 (Former Third Section Chamber); *Gas and Dubois v. France*, application no 25951/07, 15 March 2012 (Fifth Section Chamber); *X v. Austria* (n 74).

79 *JM v. United Kingdom*, application no 37060/06, 28 September 2010 (Fourth Section Chamber).

80 *Schalk and Kopf v. Austria*, application no 30141/04, 24 June 2010, (First Section Chamber), para 101; *Gas and Dubois* (n 78), para 66; *X v. Austria* (n 74), para 106; *Hamalainen v. Finland*, application no 37359/09, 16 July 2014 (Grand Chamber), para 71.

81 *X v. Austria* (n 74), para 106, reiterating *Schalk and Kopf* (n 80), para 108. See also *Gas and Dubois* (n 78), para 66; *Oliari* (n 74), para 177.

82 *Estevez v. Spain*, admissibility decision no 56501/00, 10 May 2001. In *Karner* (n 75), para 33, it was deemed unnecessary to determine whether 'private life' or 'family life' was in issue.

83 *Fretté* (n 78), paras 39–41.

84 On consensus generally, see *Schalk and Kopf* (n 80), para 98; *Oliari* (n 74), para 162.

85 There was a difference of view within *EB v. France*, application no 43546/02, 22 January 2008 (Grand Chamber) as to whether *Fretté* (n 78) was being distinguished on the facts or overturned: compare para 71 with the Dissent of Judge Costa, joined by Judges Turmen, Ugrekhelidze and Jociene, para 3 and the Dissent of Judge Loucaides. Note also *JM* (n 79), para 50.

86 *Vallianatos* (n 74), paras 73, 74 and 78. See also *Oliari* (n 74), paras 103, 165 and 169; *Pajic* (n 74), paras 61–8. Less specifically, see *Hamalainen* (n 80), paras 85–6.

87 *Schalk and Kopf* (n 80), para 99; *Vallianatos* (n 74), para 78. See also *Oliari* (n 74), para 165. This does not preclude the possibility that relationships or statuses may not be found to be directly analogous for particular purposes or in certain contexts: see, eg, *Gas and Dubois* (n 78), paras 68 and 69; *X v. Austria* (n 74), paras 109, 112, 131 and 134, and Judge Spielmann (concurring), paras 1 and 2.

88 *Karner* (n 75), para 41; *X v. Austria* (n 74), paras 99, 139–40; *Kozak* (n 75), para 99; *JM* (n 79), para 54; *Alekseyev v. Russia*, application nos 4916/07, 25924/08 and 14599/09, 21 October 2010 (First Section Chamber), para 108; *Genderdoc-M v. Moldova*, application no 9106/06, 12 June 2012 (Third Section

differences of treatment based on sexual orientation.[89] (This does not always apply, however: the First Section Chamber invoked a wide margin in relation to same-sex marriage in *Alekseyev v. Russia.*[90]) Also, notwithstanding the formal position concerning Articles 8 and 14, the cases highlight practical situations in which same-sex couples *do* gain some form of recognition. In *Vallianatos*, the Grand Chamber avoided treating the case as being about a *general*, positive obligation to legislate for same-sex partnerships, focusing instead on the need to avoid discrimination when enacting a national law establishing civil unions (on the facts, by excluding same-sex couples).[91] In *Oliari*, the *complete* absence of national recognition for same-sex marriage *or any other* type of civil union, and the gap between national law and social reality, were crucial factors. The two cases seemingly suggest that for so long as the formal position persists, it will not be allowed to justify a *total* absence of legal protection or discriminatory treatment.[92]

The *rate of change* has also assumed a central role in measuring 'consensus'. *Schalk and Kopf* highlighted that after *Estevez*, "a rapid evolution of social attitudes towards same-sex couples has taken place in many member States", with a "considerable number" now providing legal recognition.[93] However, a majority had not yet done so, and despite the "emerging European consensus" towards it, there was "no established consensus", and a margin applied concerning the timing of legislative changes and the exact nature of any alternative status.[94] In *Vallianatos*, the Grand Chamber stressed that the state must take into account "changes in the perception of social and civil-status issues and relationships"[95] and show that it was necessary to *exclude* those in same-sex relationships from national civil union legislation.[96] Despite the absence of consensus, "a trend is currently emerging with regard to the introduction of forms of legal recognition of same-sex relationships".[97] Nine states now provided for same-sex marriage and seventeen for civil partnership, so that "the trend emerging . . . is clear".[98] Greece was one of only two exceptions to the inclusion of same-sex couples in new registered partnership legislation.[99] Furthermore, *Oliari* emphasised that the "movement towards legal recognition . . . has continued to develop

---

Chamber), para 51; *X v. Turkey*, application no 24626/09, 9 October 2012 (Second Section Chamber), para 50; *Vallianatos* (n 74), para 77; *Oliari* (n 74), para 162; *Pajic* (n 74), para 59. These points borrow from *Dudgeon v. United Kingdom*, application no 7525/76, 22 October 1981), para 52, *Smith and Grady v. United Kingdom*, application nos 33985/96 and 33986/96, 27 September 1999 (Third Section Chamber), paras 89–90, and *Lustig-Prean and Beckett v. United Kingdom*, application nos 31417/96 and 32377/96, 27 September 1999 (Third Section Chamber), para 82.

89 *Karner* (n 75), para 37. See also *EB* (n 85), para 91; *Kozak* (n 75), para 99; *Schalk and Kopf* (n 80), para 97; *JM* (n 79), para 54; *Alekseyev* (n 88), para 108; *Gas and Dubois* (n 78) para 59; *Genderdoc-M* (n 88), para 51; *X v. Turkey* (n 88), para 50; *X v. Austria* (n 74), paras 99, 139–40; *Vallianatos* (n 74), paras 77, 85; *Hamalainen* (n 80), para 109; *Pajic* (n 74), para 59.

90 *Alekseyev* (n 88), para 83. See also, in relation to economic or social strategy, *Burden* (n 17), para 60; *Schalk and Kopf* (n 80), para 97; *Gas and Dubois* (n 78), para 60; *Hamalainen* (n 80), para 109; *Pajic* (n 74), para 58 (concerning immigration).

91 *Vallianatos* (n 74), para 75.

92 It is perhaps also worth noting here the ECtHR's developing position in relation to authorization to adopt children: compare *Fretté* (n 78) with *EB* (n 85), esp para. 71. Note also, in *EB*, Judges Costa, Turmen, Ugrekhelidze and Jociene (dissenting), para 3; Judge Loucaides (dissenting).

93 *Schalk and Kopf* (n 80), para 93.

94 *Schalk and Kopf* (n 80), paras 105, 108, 109.

95 *Vallianatos* (n 74), para 84. See also *Kozak* (n 75), paras 98–9.

96 *Vallianatos* (n 74), para 85.

97 *Vallianatos* (n 74), para 91.

98 *Vallianatos* (n 74), para 91.

99 *Vallianatos* (n 74), para 92.

rapidly" since *Schalk and Kopf*: twenty-four signatories now had legislation,[100] and the conclusion that Article 8 had been violated was tied to the "changing conditions" at national level.[101] Such reasoning clearly suggests that the ECtHR's conclusions may develop further depending upon national trends.

Article 12 is still held to enshrine the "traditional concept of marriage as being between a man and a woman", with no "obligation . . . to grant access" to same-sex couples.[102] *Schalk and Kopf* explained this by reference to the Article's drafting[103] and to 'consensus': marriage had "undergone major social changes", but only six out of forty-seven states allowed same-sex marriage.[104] Interestingly, though, the ECtHR conceded that it would "no longer consider" that Article 12 "must in all circumstances" be limited to opposite-sex marriage.[105] The ECtHR's reasoning leaves open what would happen should a stronger consensus emerge supporting same-sex marriage – a point reinforced by its willingness to base its reading of Article 12 in relation to gender reassignment on social change in *Christine Goodwin v. United Kingdom*.[106]

All EU Member States are within the Council of Europe and have signed the ECHR, but not all Council states are EU members. EU law – when it is 'directly effective' – takes priority over national law and may thus appear more peremptory in its force than the ECHR,[107] but differs in its scope:[108] the ECHR applies to all actions of its signatory states,[109] but EU law's requirements *only* apply when EU institutions exercise powers conferred under the EU Treaties and when member states implement EU law.[110] This includes guarantees of free movement between member states and non-discrimination within the workplace. EU institutions are obliged to act to combat discrimination based on sexual orientation,[111] and such discrimination is also prohibited, under the Employment Equality Directive, in employment, occupation, working conditions and training.[112] Viewed in the abstract, these requirements do not *directly* concern any obligation to formally *recognise* same-sex marriage, although their interpretation sometimes has consequences for the extent to which employment-related benefits can be denied to same-sex partners.[113]

100 *Oliari* (n 74), para 178; note, however, para 163. Consensus generated a different result in relation to marriage following gender reassignment in *Hamalainen* (n 80), paras 72–75.
101 *Oliari* (n 74), para 186.
102 *Hamalainen* (n 80), para 96. See also *Schalk and Kopf* (n 80), para 63; *Gas and Dubois* (n 78), para 66; *X v. Austria* (n 74), para 106; *Oliari* (n 74), paras 191, 192.
103 *Schalk and Kopf* (n 80), para 55.
104 *Schalk and Kopf* (n 80), para 58. *See also Oliari* (n 74), para 192.
105 *Schalk and Kopf* (n 80), para 61; *Oliari* (n 74), para 191.
106 Application no 28957/95, 11 July 2002 (Grand Chamber), para 100, distinguished without detailed explanation in *Schalk and Kopf* (n 80), paras 52, 59. Further uncertainty may arise from the treatment of civil partnership in *Burden* (n 17).
107 See, e.g., Case 26/62, *Van Gend en Loos v. Nederlandse Administratie der Belastingen* [1963] ECR 1, Case 6/64, *Costa v. ENEL* [1964] ECR 585, Case C-213/89, *R v. Secretary of State for Transport, ex p Factortame* [1990] ECR I-2433.
108 For the European Court of Justice's exposition of the differences, see *Opinion 2/13 of the Court (Re accession to the European Convention on Human Rights)* [2015] 2 CMLR 21.
109 And sometimes generates positive obligations: Alastair Mowbray, *The Development of Positive Obligations under the European Convention on Human Rights by the European Court of Human Rights* (Hart Publishing, 2004).
110 See, principally, TEU Arts 3–6, 13, TFEU Arts 1–6.
111 TFEU Articles 10 and 19 [2012] OJ C 326/47.
112 Council Directive 2000/78/EC of 27 November 2000, establishing a general framework for equal treatment in employment and occupation, Arts 1–3 [2000] OJ L 303/16.
113 Case C-267/06, *Maruko v. Versorgungsanstalt der deutschen Bühnen* [2008] ECR I-1757; Case C-147/08, *Romer v. Freie und Hansestadt Hamburg* [2011] ECR I-3591; Case C-267/12, *Hay v. Credit agricole mutuel de*

However, Article 9 of the Charter of Fundamental Rights of the EU (with the same 'legal value' as provisions of the Treaties[114]) talks of the right to marry without explicit reference to men and women, albeit as "guaranteed in accordance with the national laws governing the exercise of these rights".[115] The legally binding Commentary by the EU Network of Independent Experts on Fundamental Rights notes that "it may be argued that there is no obstacle to recognize same-sex relationships in the context of marriage", but that Article 9 also contains "no explicit requirement that domestic law should facilitate such marriages".[116] Importantly, the ECtHR suggested in *Schalk and Kopf* that Article 9 "deliberately dropped" Article 12's reference to men and women, and "leaves the decision whether or not to allow same-sex marriage to the States".[117] Furthermore, the Family Reunification Directive[118] and the Citizens' Rights Directive – the latter concerning free movement between and residence in Member States by EU citizens and their family members[119] – explicitly protect same-sex registered partners alongside spouses as 'family members'. However, registered partners are only covered by the Citizens' Rights Directive "if the legislation of the host Member State treats registered partnerships as equivalent to marriage and in accordance with the conditions laid down in the relevant legislation",[120] opening the door to litigation concerning the meanings of 'equivalence'[121] and 'spouse'.[122]

The Inter-American Court of Human Rights (IACtHR) determined in *Atalo Riffo v. Chile* that the loss of child custody to a mother in a lesbian relationship breached the rights to privacy (ACHR Article 11)[123] and equality (ACHR Article 24),[124] in conjunction with the general obligation under ACHR Article 1(1) to respect rights and freedoms without discrimination, including due to "any other social condition" – held to include sexual orientation.[125] In reaching this conclusion the court stressed the role of the ACHR as a 'living instrument'[126] and noted resolutions against sexual orientation discrimination passed by the General Assembly of the Organization of American States, alongside the determination of the Committee on Economic, Social, and Cultural Rights and some ECtHR case law.[127] However, the IACtHR went

Charente-Maritime et des Deux-Sevres, 12 December 2013. See, generally, Nicholas Bamforth, 'Discrimination on the Grounds of Sexual Orientation and Gender Identity', ch 20 in Alan Bogg, Cathryn Costello and ACL Davies (eds), *Research Handbook on EU Labour Law* (Edward Elgar, 2016); Colm O'Cinneide, 'The Constitutionalization of Equality within the EU Legal Order: Sexual Orientation as a Testing Ground' (2015) 22 *MJ* 370; Robert Wintemute, 'In Extending Human Rights, which European Court is Substantively "Braver" and Procedurally "Fitter"? The Example of Sexual Orientation and Gender Identity Discrimination', ch.10 in Sonia Morano-Foadi and Lucy Vickers (eds), *Fundamental Rights in the EU: A Matter for Two Courts* (Hart Publishing, 2015).

114 TEU, Article 6(1).

115 Article 21 CFR [2012] OJ C 326/91.

116 *Commentary of the Charter of Fundamental Rights of the European Union* (2006), http://ec.europa.eu/justice_home/cfr_cdf/index_en.htm, at 102.

117 *Schalk and Kopf* (n 80), para 60. See also paras 61 and 62.

118 Council Directive 2003/86/EC, 22 September 2003, Article 4(3).

119 Council Directive 2004/38/EC, 29 April 2004, Article 2.

120 Council Directive 2004/38/EC (n 119), Article 2(2)(b).

121 See Wintemute (n 113), 185.

122 See Case C-673/16, *Coman v. Inspectortatul General pentru Imigrări*, Advocate-General's Opinion, 11 January 2018.

123 *Atala Riffo v. Chile*, Inter-American Court of Human Rights Series C 239, 24 February 2012, paras 135–40.

124 *Atala Riffo* (n 123), para 146.

125 *Atala Riffo* (n 123), paras 85, 91.

126 *Atala Riffo* (n 123), para 83.

127 *Atala Riffo* (n 123), paras 86–91.

beyond the ECtHR, rejecting the state's argument that a lack of consensus concerning sexual orientation as a prohibited ground of discrimination could be considered "a valid argument to deny or restrict" sexual minorities' rights "or to perpetuate and reproduce the historical and structural discrimination" that they had suffered. The "controversial" nature of the issue and possible absence of consensus could not "lead this Court to abstain from issuing a decision".[128] In a later Advisory Opinion, the IACtHR held that the ACHR *required* equal access to marriage for same-sex couples.[129]

We have thus seen that while there is currently no requirement to recognise same-sex marriage under the ICCPR and EU law, it cannot be ruled out as a future possibility. The ECtHR maintains the formal position that there is no right of access, but its treatment of claims has seemingly become more sensitive in response to a shifting 'consensus', and *Vallianatos* and *Oliari* involve context-specific qualifications to the formal position. To date, the IACtHR has gone furthest, recognising a requirement and arguably adopting a more ambitious stance than the ECtHR by refusing to be constrained by the limits which a 'consensus'-driven approach may entail.

Discrimination and conflicts of rights

The formal recognition of same-sex marriages or registered partnerships may not afford complete *practical* protection. In employment and the provision of goods, facilities and services, same-sex couples sometimes encounter adverse treatment, and adherents to religious faiths whose doctrines denounce homosexuality and lesbianism have argued that the right to manifest religion should exempt them from providing otherwise generally available services. Consideration of the law's treatment of same-sex partners must thus include analysis of such situations.[130]

Both *Fourie* and *Obergefell* emphasised that religious faith cannot alone drive the interpretation of constitutional rights. In *Fourie*, Sachs J stated that while "religion provides support and nurture and a framework for individual and social stability and growth", free expression of religious beliefs was distinct from employing them when interpreting the constitutional right to partnership-recognition.[131] In *Obergefell*, Kennedy J stated that

> [m]any who deem same-sex marriage to be wrong reach that conclusion based on decent and honorable religious or philosophical premises . . . But when that sincere, personal opposition becomes enacted law and public policy, the necessary consequence is to put the imprimatur of the State itself on an exclusion that soon demeans or stigmatizes those whose own liberty is then denied.[132]

At a more day-to-day level, many courts have considered calls for religious believers to be exempted from non-discrimination requirements. In the UK, statutory non-discrimination

128 *Atala Riffo* (n 123), para 92.

129 Opiniøn Consultiva OC-24/17 de 24 de Noviembre de 2017, Solicitada Por La Repüblica De Costa Rica, Identidad De Género, E Igualdad Y No Discriminaciøn A Parejas Del Mismo Sexo.

130 See John Corvino, Ryan T. Anderson and Sherif Girgis, *Debating Religious Liberty and Discrimination* (Oxford University Press, 2017), 2; Rex Ahdar and Ian Leigh, *Religious Freedom in the Liberal State* (2nd edn, Oxford University Press, 2013), 158; Robert Wintemute, 'Accommodating Religious Beliefs' (2014) 77 *MLR* 223, 224.

131 *Fourie* (n 49), para [89]. See also paras [90]–[92], [95].

132 *Obergefell* (n 34), 2602. See also 2594, 2607. The decision's relationship with *Burwell, Secretary of Health and Human Services v. Hobby Lobby Stores Inc* (2014) 134 S Ct 2751 is open to argument.

protections apply to civil partnership or marital status.[133] In *Bull v. Hall*, the Supreme Court held that a refusal by Christian hotel-keepers, who believed sexual relations outside opposite-sex marriage to be sinful, to provide a double-bedded room to same-sex civil partners to be unlawful direct discrimination.[134] The hoteliers had applied the criterion that the couple was not legally married, and marriage at the time was confined to opposite-sex couples – a factor indistinguishable from sexual orientation.[135] Furthermore, they lacked a justification for indirect discrimination.[136] Baroness Hale emphasised that it was an "affront" to the dignity of lesbians and gays to deny them "the possibility of fulfilling themselves through relationships with others", and noted the ECtHR's requirement for very weighty reasons to justify discrimination.[137] The decision did not replace "legal oppression" of one community by that of another:[138] if civil partners "ran a hotel which denied a double room to [Christian hoteliers], whether on the ground of their Christian beliefs or on the ground of their sexual orientation, they would find themselves in the same situation."[139]

In *Ladele v. United Kingdom* and *McFarlane v. United Kingdom*, the ECtHR found the dismissals of a Christian marriage registrar and Christian marriage guidance counsellor for refusing to provide services to same-sex couples to have been proportionate by reference to the freedom to manifest religious belief under Article 9 and/or to Article 14.[140] In *Ladele*, it noted that the local authority employer's requirement that all registrars act as civil partnership registrars had a detrimental impact on the claimant due to her religious beliefs,[141] but also that differences in treatment based on sexual orientation needed to be justified by particularly serious reasons.[142] Although the claimant had lost her job, the local authority was aiming to secure the rights of others, and the state had not exceeded its margin of appreciation in striking a balance between the competing rights.[143] In *McFarlane*, the counsellor's knowledge of the employer's equal opportunities policy when he accepted employment was not decisive but had to be considered when assessing whether a fair balance had been struck[144] – in relation to which the state had not exceeded the wide margin it enjoyed in balancing the right to manifest beliefs against the employer's interest in securing the rights of others.

Meanwhile, Kennedy J suggested, *obiter dicta*, in *Masterpiece Cakeshop v. Colorado Civil Rights Commission* that while "religious and philosophical objections" to same-sex marriage are protected forms of expression, they "do not allow business owners . . . to deny protected persons equal access to goods and services under a neutral and generally applicable public accommodations law".[145] Nonetheless, "a member of the clergy who objects to gay marriage on moral and

133 Equality Act 2010, s 8. However, note the religious exemptions relating to civil partnerships and same-sex marriages: Equality Act 2010, Schedule 9; Marriage (Same Sex Couples) Act 2013, s 2.

134 *Bull* (n 16).

135 *Bull* (n 16), para [30].

136 *Bull* (n 16), paras [45]–[51].

137 *Bull* (n 16), para [53].

138 *Bull* (n 16), para [54].

139 *Bull* (n 16), para [54].

140 *Eweida, Chaplin, Ladele and McFarlane v. United Kingdom*, applications nos 48420/10, 59842/10, 51671/10 and 36516/10, 15 January 2013 (Fourth Section Chamber).

141 *Eweida, Chaplin, Ladele and McFarlane* (n 140), para 104.

142 *Eweida, Chaplin, Ladele and McFarlane* (n 140), para 105.

143 *Eweida, Chaplin, Ladele and McFarlane* (n 140), para 106.

144 *Eweida, Chaplin, Ladele and McFarlane* (n 140), paras 109, 110: technically, this was a positive obligation claim.

145 (2018) 584 US, 4 June 2018, p 9. For similar facts, see *Lee v. McArthur and McArthur and Ashers Baking Company Ltd* [2016] NICA 39 and 55 (Northern Ireland Court of Appeal, currently on appeal to UK Supreme Court).

religious grounds could not be compelled to perform the ceremony without denial of his or her right to religion".[146]

Key to the balancing exercises in play is the comparative weights attached to freedom from sexual orientation discrimination and freedom to manifest religious belief.[147] On the one hand, in the *Marriage Commissioners Reference* case, the Saskatchewan Court of Appeal held that permission for marriage commissioners to refuse due to religious belief to solemnise same-sex marriages would contravene the Canadian Charter. Richards JA noted that LGBTQ citizens would be subject to negative and differential treatment and caused offence and personal hurt[148] and that the measures would reinforce historical marginalisation and mistreatment,[149] while Smith JA suggested that an affront to dignity would result.[150] Similarly, Wintemute notes that

> [a]part from the immediate denial of equal access to a service . . . it is insulting for the employee to tell the customer, orally or using a sign, that the employee does not serve persons of the customer's sex, race, religion or sexual orientation.[151]

Non-discrimination protections are a "'package deal' consisting of reciprocal rights and duties",[152] and equality of opportunity in relation to access to a service means access for *all* customers to the same service, in the same place and on the same terms. On the other hand, section 6 of the South African Civil Union Act 2006 exempts marriage officers from solemnising same-sex civil unions on the ground of "conscience, religion and belief",[153] following *Fourie*'s acknowledgement that recognition of same-sex marriage was not inconsistent with the right of religious organisations not to celebrate such marriages.[154]

Arguments about the legal recognition of same-sex partnerships help illustrate the broader clashes between claims that people should be free from discrimination due to sexual orientation and that they should be free to act on the basis of religious beliefs that favour the adverse treatment of lesbians and gay men. At a more specific level, they clearly show that the granting of a legal partnership status may not be enough, on its own, to secure equal treatment: a factor distinct to same-sex – as opposed to opposite-sex – partnerships.

146 *Masterpiece Cakeshop* (n 145), 9.

147 See, e.g., MacDougall, Bonthuys, Norrie and van den Brink (n 4); Chai R. Feldblum, 'Moral Conflict and Liberty: Gay Rights and Religion' (2006) 72 *Brooklyn L Rev* 61. Note also Andrew Koppelman's call for a continuing 'conversation' – 'You Can't Hurry Love – Why Antidiscrimination Protections for Gay People Should Have Religious Exemptions' (2006) 72 *Brooklyn L Rev* 125 – and Carl F. Stychin's context-specific approach: 'Faith in the Future: Sexuality, Religion and the Public Sphere' (2009) 29 *OJLS* 729.

148 *Marriage Commissioners Reference*, 2011 SKCA 3, paras [39], [41], [95]–[98].

149 *Marriage Commissioners Reference* (n 148), paras [45], [94].

150 *Marriage Commissioners Reference* (n 148), para [107].

151 Wintemute (n 130), 241. See also Feldblum (n 147), 119.

152 Wintemute (n 130), 249. Note that Wintemute's arguments apply to discrimination by individuals, not organisations.

153 In *Fourie* (n 49), Sachs J had canvassed the possibility that the "principle of reasonable accommodation" might exempt marriage officers with "sincere religious exceptions" from solemnising same-sex unions: para [159]; De Vos suggests that s 6 "clearly endorses sexual orientation discrimination by state officials" and is thus constitutionally fragile: De Vos (n 49), 172.

154 *Fourie* (n 49), paras [96]–[98], [108], [113]. Note also Kennedy J's observation in *Obergefell* (n 34), 2607 (see also 2594, 2602); Ahdar and Leigh (n 130), 157; Feldblum (n 147), 104–5.

Conclusion

This chapter has shown that legal recognition of same-sex partnerships is a developing trend among countries in the global north and west, but that the form(s) of recognition and the mechanism(s) used to achieve it have been heavily dependent upon the legal (including constitutional) and political conditions in different jurisdictions. Interestingly, though, analogous constitutional arguments relating to dignity and equality have been invoked in South Africa and the US.

To see the complete picture, we must nonetheless acknowledge Kees Waaldijk's observation that while "a very large part of the western world now recognizes same-sex partnership[s] . . . and there is a clear trend towards further recognition", it is "as yet (very) limited in some jurisdictions, while remaining (highly) controversial in many".[155] The United Nations High Commissioner for Human Rights has reported that "[w]hile some progress has been made since . . . 2011, the overall picture remains one of continuing, pervasive, violent abuse, harassment and discrimination affecting LGBT and intersex persons in all regions" of the world.[156] McGoldrick notes that as of May 2016, seventy-four states retained laws that discriminated on the basis of sexual orientation or gender identity, of which thirty-four were African states and twenty-three were Asian states.[157] As might be expected, the states concerned are hostile to same-sex partnerships: Nigeria, for example, enacted a Same Sex Marriage (Prohibition) Act in 2014.

National-level hostility also illustrates, in some contexts, limits to the reach of international requirements: as McGoldrick observes, although the Council of Europe "is in the vanguard" in protecting LGBTQ rights, "even then some significant signs of opposition remain, particularly in States such as the Russian Federation, Moldova and Ukraine".[158] Russia is actively hostile to LGBTQ citizens and same-sex partnerships,[159] and a federal law enacted in 2015 and judicially applied empowers its Constitutional Court to disregard ECtHR judgments if they are found to contradict the Russian Constitution.[160] A direct clash with the ECtHR in relation to same-sex partnerships is a clear possibility. Furthermore, in 2009, Lithuania – a member state of the EU and the Council of Europe – enacted a statute apparently prohibiting the communication to minors of information concerning homosexuality and same-sex relationships,[161] and the

155 'Same-Sex Partnership, International Protection' in *Max Planck Encyclopedia of Public International Law* (Oxford University Press, 2013) Oxford Public International Law, http://opil.ouplaw.com, para 8. A similar point emerges in relation to the treatment of LGBTQ citizens more generally: see McGoldrick (n 1).

156 *Discrimination and violence against individuals based on their sexual orientation and gender identity* (n 1), para 76.

157 McGoldrick (n 1), 649.

158 McGoldrick (n 1), 659. On difficulties faced by same-sex couples in eastern Europe, see Adam Bodnar and Anna Sledzinska-Simon, 'Between Recognition and Homophobia: Same-Sex Couples in Eastern Europe' in Daniele Gallo, Luca Paladini and Pietro Pustorino (eds), *Same-Sex Couples before National, Supranational and International Jurisdictions* (Springer, 2014); Frederik Swennen and Sven Eggermont, 'Same-Sex Couples in Central Europe: Hop, Step and Jump' and Monika Jagielska, 'Eastern European Countries: From Penalisation to Cohabitation or Further?' in Katharina Boele-Woelki and Angelika Fuchs (eds), *Legal Recognition of Same-Sex Relationships in Europe: National, Cross-Border and European Perspectives* (2nd edn, Intersentia, 2012).

159 For example, legislation prohibiting the promotion among minors of 'homosexual propaganda' or 'non-traditional sexual relations' has been held to be constitutionally valid: see McGoldrick (n 1), 654–5.

160 Law Library of Congress, Global Legal Monitor, 'Russian Federation: Constitutional Court Allows Country to Ignore ECHR Rulings', 18 May 2016, www.loc.gov/law/foreign-news/article/russian-federation-constitutional-court-allows-country-to-ignore-echt-rulings.

161 European Union Agency for Fundamental Rights, *Homophobia, transphobia and discrimination on grounds of sexual orientation and gender identity in the EU Member States: Summary of Findings, Trends, Challenges and Promising Practices* (Fundamental Rights Agency, 2010), 17–18 and European Union Agency for

post-2013 Hungarian Constitution confines the definition of marriage to opposite-sex couples. The EU Fundamental Rights Agency notes that "given the various differences in recognising same-sex partnerships", a same-sex couple's "civil status acquired in one Member State", for example through marriage, "is not necessarily 'portable' to another, with all the consequences that this implies".[162] Even within western parts of Europe, areas of social conservatism remain: survey evidence highlights, for example, the level of on-going hostility to LGBTQ citizens in Italy (providing interesting background to *Oliari*).[163]

We saw in the previous section that conferring a formal status upon same-sex partnerships may not be enough to protect couples from adverse treatment in practice. More generally, we can now see that the absorption of international legal requirements at national level clearly depends upon a complex multiplicity of factors. Legislation following national debate, or judicial interpretation of national constitutional rights, may therefore seem like preferable routes for securing legal recognition of same-sex partnerships, but it needs to be kept in mind that legal change by any route may not immediately prompt social acceptance.

Bibliography

Ahdar, R., and Leigh, I., *Religious Freedom in the Liberal State* (2nd edn, Oxford, UK: Oxford University Press, 2013).

Bamforth, N., 'Discrimination on the Grounds of Sexual Orientation and Gender Identity', in Bogg, A., Costello, C., and Davies, A.C.L. (eds), *Research Handbook on EU Labour Law* (Cheltenham, UK: Edward Elgar, 2016).

Beilfuss, C.G., 'All or Nothing: The Dilemma of Southern Jurisdictions' in Boele-Woelki, K., and Fuchs, A. (eds), *Legal Recognition of Same-Sex Relationships in Europe: National, Cross-Border and European Perspectives* (2nd edn, Cambridge, UK: Intersentia, 2012).

Bodnar, A., and Sledzinska-Simon, A., 'Between Recognition and Homophobia: Same-Sex Couples in Eastern Europe' in Gallo, D., Paladini, L., and Pustorino, P. (eds), *Same-Sex Couples before National, Supranational and International Jurisdictions* (Berlin: Springer, 2014).

Corvino, J., Anderson, R.T., and Girgis, S., *Debating Religious Liberty and Discrimination* (Oxford, UK: Oxford University Press, 2017).

Council of Europe, *Good Practice Guide on Values Based Campaigning for Legal Recognition of Same-Sex Partnerships* (2015), https://rm.coe.int/manual-on-values-based-campaigning-/1680766c87.

De Freitas, T.F., and Tega, D., 'Judicial Restraint and Political Responsibility: A Review of the Jurisprudence of the Italian, Spanish and Portuguese High Courts on Same-Sex Couples' in Gallo, D., Paladini, L., and Pustorino, P. (eds), *Same-Sex Couples before National, Supranational and International Jurisdictions* (Berlin: Springer, 2014).

De Vos, P., 'A Judicial Revolution – A Court-Led Achievement of Same-Sex Marriage in South Africa' (2008) 4 *Utrecht L Rev* 162.

Fundamental Rights, *Homophobia, transphobia and discrimination on grounds of sexual orientation and gender identity: 2010 Update* (Fundamental Rights Agency, 2010), 34–5.

162 *Homophobia, transphobia and discrimination on grounds of sexual orientation and gender identity in the EU Member States: Summary of Findings, Trends, Challenges and Promising Practices* (n 161), 30.

163 See, e.g., Ufficio Nazionale Antidiscriminazioni Razzoli (UNAR), *National Strategy to Prevent and Contrast Discrimination on Grounds of Sexual Orientation and Gender Identity 2013–2015* (UNAR, 2013), 12. In relation to Italy and other 'southern' EU states, see Tiago Fidalgo de Freitas and Diletta Tega, 'Judicial Restraint and Political Responsibility: A Review of the Jurisprudence of the Italian, Spanish and Portuguese High Courts on Same-Sex Couples' and Spyridon Drosos and Aristoteles Constantinides, 'The Legal Situation of Same-Sex Couples in Greece and Cyprus' in Gallo, Paladini and Pustorino (eds) (n 158); Cristina Gonzalez Beilfuss, 'All or Nothing: The Dilemma of Southern Jurisdictions' in Boele-Woelki and Fuchs (eds) (n 158).

Department of Trade and Industry, Women and Equality Unit, *Civil Partnership: A framework for the legal recognition of same-sex couples* (2003).

Department of Trade and Industry, Women and Equality Unit, *Responses to Civil Partnership: A framework for the legal recognition of same-sex couples* (2003).

Drosos, S., and Constantinides, A., 'The Legal Situation of Same-Sex Couples in Greece and Cyprus' in Gallo, D., Paladini, L., and Pustorino, P. (eds), *Same-Sex Couples before National, Supranational and International Jurisdictions* (Berlin: Springer, 2014).

Eekelaar, J., 'Perceptions of Equality: The Road to Same-Sex Marriage in England and Wales' (2014) 28 *International Journal of Law, Policy and The Family* 1.

EU Network of Independent Experts on Fundamental Rights, *Commentary of the Charter of Fundamental Rights of the European Union* (2006), http://ec.europa.eu/justice_home/cfr_cdf/index_en.htm.

European Union Agency for Fundamental Rights, *Homophobia, transphobia and discrimination on grounds of sexual orientation and gender identity in the EU Member States: Summary of Findings, Trends, Challenges and Promising Practices* (Fundamental Rights Agency, 2010).

European Union Agency for Fundamental Rights, *Homophobia, transphobia and discrimination on grounds of sexual orientation and gender identity: 2010 Update* (Fundamental Rights Agency, 2010).

Feldblum, C.R., 'Moral Conflict and Liberty: Gay Rights and Religion' (2006) 72 *Brooklyn L Rev* 61.

Gerber, P., Tay, K., and Sifris, A., 'Marriage: A Human Right for All?' (2014) 36 *Sydney L Rev* 643.

Harper, M., Downs, M., Landell, K., and Wilson, G., *Civil Partnership – The New Law* (Bristol, UK: Jordan Publishing, 2005).

HM Government, Government Equalities Office, *Equal Civil Marriage: A Consultation* (2012).

HM Government, Government Equalities Office, *Equal Marriage: The Government's Response* (2012).

Jagielska, M., 'Eastern European Countries: From Penalisation to Cohabitation or Further?' in Boele-Woelki, K., and Fuchs, A. (eds), *Legal Recognition of Same-Sex Relationships in Europe: National, Cross-Border and European Perspectives* (2nd edn, Cambridge, UK: Intersentia, 2012).

Koppelman, A., 'You Can't Hurry Love – Why Antidiscrimination Protections for Gay People Should Have Religious Exemptions' (2006) 72 *Brooklyn L Rev* 125.

Law Library of Congress, Global Legal Monitor, 'Russian Federation: Constitutional Court Allows Country to Ignore ECHR Rulings', 18 May 2016, www.loc.gov/law/foreign-news/article/russian-federation-constitutional-court-allows-country-to-ignore-echt-rulings.

Legg, A., *The Margin of Appreciation in International Human Rights Law: Deference and Proportionality* (Oxford, UK: Oxford University Press, 2012).

MacDougall, B., Bonthuys, E., Norrie, K. McK, and van den Brink, M., 'Conscientious Objecting to Creating Same Sex Unions: An International Analysis' (2012) 1 *Can J Hum Rights* 127.

McGoldrick, D., 'The Development and Status of Sexual Orientation Discrimination under International Human Rights Law' (2016) 16 *HRLR* 613.

Mallender, P., and Rayson, J., *The Civil Partnership Act 2004: A Practical Guide* (Cambridge, UK: Cambridge University Press, 2005).

Martin, C., and Théry, I., 'The PACS and Marriage and Cohabitation in France' (2001) 15 *International Journal of Law, Policy and The Family* 135.

Mowbray, A., *The Development of Positive Obligations under the European Convention on Human Rights by the European Court of Human Rights* (Oxford, UK: Hart, 2004).

O'Cinneide, C., 'The Constitutionalization of Equality within the EU Legal Order: Sexual Orientation as a Testing Ground' (2015) 22 *MJ* 370.

Stychin, C.F., 'Faith in the Future: Sexuality, Religion and the Public Sphere' (2009) 29 *OJLS* 729.

Swennen, F., and Eggermont, S., 'Same-Sex Couples in Central Europe: Hop, Step and Jump' in Boele-Woelki, K., and Fuchs, A. (eds), *Legal Recognition of Same-Sex Relationships in Europe: National, Cross-Border and European Perspectives* (2nd edn, Cambridge, UK: Intersentia, 2012).

Ufficio Nazionale Antidiscriminazioni Razzoli, *National Strategy to Prevent and Contrast Discrimination on Grounds of Sexual Orientation and Gender Identity 2013–2015* (UNAR, 2013).

United Nations High Commissioner for Human Rights, *Discrimination and violence against individuals based on their sexual orientation and gender identity. Report of the Office of the United Nations High Commissioner for Human Rights*, A/HRC/29/23, 4 May 2015.

Waaldijk, K., 'Same-Sex Partnership, International Protection' in *Max Planck Encyclopedia of Public International Law* (Oxford, UK: Oxford University Press, 2013) Oxford Public International Law.

Wintemute, R., 'Conclusion', in Wintemute, R., and Andenaes, M. (eds), *Legal Recognition of Same-Sex Partnerships: A Study of National, European and International Law* (Oxford, UK: Hart, 2001).
Wintemute, R., 'Accommodating Religious Beliefs' (2014) 77 *MLR* 223.
Wintemute, R., 'In Extending Human Rights, which European Court is Substantively "Braver" and Procedurally "Fitter"? The Example of Sexual Orientation and Gender Identity Discrimination', in Morano-Foadi, S., and Vickers, L. (eds), *Fundamental Rights in the EU: A Matter for Two Courts* (Oxford, UK: Hart Publishing, 2015).

3

Customary marriages

Thandabantu Nhlapo

Introduction

In South Africa, the customary law of marriage today draws on both customary law and the provisions of the Recognition of Customary Marriages Act 120 of 1998 (RCMA or "the Act"). Section 1 of the Act defines "customary law" as "the customs and usages traditionally observed among the indigenous African peoples of South Africa and which form part of the culture of those peoples". Customary law is now understood to have at least two manifestations: "official" and "living". The official version represents the rigid, distorted, and discredited set of rules resulting from state interference through colonial and *apartheid* court systems and bureaucracy. Living customary law is seen as mirroring the daily lives of traditional communities – adaptable, legitimate, and responsive to socioeconomic changes. Since the recognition of customary law by section 211(3) of the South African Constitution (Constitution of the Republic of South Africa, 1996) it has been made quite clear by the Constitutional Court of South Africa that the version of customary law it recognises is the "living" version, difficult though it may be to ascertain.[1]

Customary law continues to be relevant despite the enactment of the RCMA, because section 3(1)(b) of the Act bases the validity of a customary marriage on the observance of certain customary requirements, and because the language of the statute requires interpretation by the courts on many customary-law-related issues ranging from *lobolo* to polygamy.[2] Polygamy is the marriage system in which a married person, whether male or female, can have more than one spouse. "Polygyny" describes the marriage of a man to more than one wife, but "polygamy" is preferred in this chapter because of its widespread use in South Africa.

1 See *Certification of the Constitution of the Republic of South Africa* 1996 (4) SA 744 (CC); *Alexkor Ltd and Another v. Richtersveld Community and Others* 2004 (5) 460 (CC); *Bhe and Others v. Magistrate Khayelitsha and Others* 2005 (1) SA 580 (CC); *Shilubana and Others v. Nwamitwa* 2009 (2) SA 66 (CC). See further on living customary law, Heaton, J. and Kruger, H. *South African Family Law* (Durban, LexisNexis, 4th edn, 2015) 222 note 42 and the materials cited therein.

2 *Lobolo* is defined in the Act as

> the property in cash or in kind, whether known as lobolo, bogadi, bohali, xuma, lumalo, thaka, ikhazi, magadi, emabheka, or by any other name, which a prospective husband or the head of his family undertakes to give to the head of the prospective wife's family in consideration of a customary marriage.

Before the coming into operation of the RCMA, customary marriages were not recognised in South African law because of their potentially polygamous nature. This had disastrous consequences for family relations. The most egregious of these consequences were: spouses in customary marriages were not regarded as husband and wife (and thus no duty of support existed between them), their children were considered "illegitimate", and a subsequent civil marriage by the husband to someone else erased the customary marriage, leaving the first wife and her offspring discarded.[3] As a result of these consequences, some limited recognition was accorded to customary marriages in certain specified circumstances.[4] Customary marriage was also, in essence, outside the ambit of state law, being considered a contract between two kinship groups who, as a result, had total control over its formation and its dissolution.[5]

Legal requirements for a valid customary marriage

In recognising customary marriages, section 2 of the RCMA distinguishes between marriages entered into before the date of commencement of the Act (15 November 2000), and marriages concluded after that date. The section recognises customary marriages, monogamous and polygamous, in the following terms:

> (1) A marriage which is a valid marriage at customary law and existing at the commencement of this Act is for all purposes recognised as a marriage.
> (2) A customary marriage entered into after the commencement of this Act, which complies with the requirements of this Act, is for all purposes recognised as a marriage.
> (3) If a person is a spouse in more than one customary marriage, all valid customary marriages entered into before the commencement of this Act are for all purposes recognised as marriages.
> (4) If a person is a spouse in more than one customary marriage, all such marriages entered into after the commencement of this Act, which comply with the provisions of this Act, are for all purposes recognised as marriages.

Broadly speaking, to be valid, marriages concluded before the date of commencement have to comply with customary law, while those contracted thereafter are valid only if they satisfy the requirements stipulated in the Act.

Marriages concluded before 15 November 2000

The requirements for validity for marriages concluded before the date of commencement of the Act are to be sought in customary law. In KwaZulu-Natal, this law is partly codified; in the rest of the country it is not. The KwaZulu Act on the Code of Zulu Law 16 of 1985

3 Dlamini, C.R.M. "The Ultimate Recognition of the Customary Marriage in South Africa" (1999) 20 *Obiter* 14 at 60. See also Himonga, C. and Nhlapo, T. (eds) *African Customary Law in South Africa: Post-Apartheid and Living Law Perspectives* (Cape Town, Oxford University Press Southern Africa, 2014) 93.

4 A duty of spousal support was recognised in s. 31 of the Black Laws Amendment Act 76 of 1963; s. 5(6) of the Maintenance Act 23 of 1963 granted rights to spousal maintenance; and s. 1 of the Income Tax Act 58 of 1962 recognised the spouses as married for purposes of income tax.

5 Himonga and Nhlapo (eds), *supra* note 3 at 92.

and the Natal Code of Zulu Law Proclamation 151 of 1987 ("Codes") set out the essentials as follows:

(a) The consent of the father or the guardian of the intended wife (if she is a minor), which may not be withheld without good reason;
(b) The consent of the father or guardian of the prospective husband (if he is a minor); and
(c) A declaration in public by the prospective wife to the official witness[6] at the wedding ceremony that she voluntarily submits to the marriage and gives her consent.

Interestingly, there is no mention of *lobolo* in this list, although elsewhere (in sections 43, 47, 51 and 52, and chapter 8) the Codes do regulate the practice in terms of what it may consist of, where it is sourced, and how much is payable.

In the rest of South Africa, uncodified customary law applies, with its attendant problems of ascertainment. The official customary law position, as distilled from many sources,[7] gives the requirements for a valid customary marriage in most systems of customary law as:

(a) the consent of the father or guardian of the prospective husband under certain circumstances;
(b) the consent of the guardian of the prospective wife;
(c) the consent of the prospective husband;
(d) the consent of the prospective wife;
(e) the handing over of the prospective wife to the family group of the prospective husband or the prospective husband himself as the case may be; and
(f) an agreement that *lobolo* will be delivered.

Even as a representation of the "official" customary laws of a bygone era, it is doubtful whether this list ever reflected the actual practice of traditional communities.[8] Additionally, the parties must be of "marriageable age" and the couple should not be related within the prohibited degrees of relationship.[9]

The "shape" of a customary marriage and the role of *lobolo*

Without claiming uniformity of customary law systems in South Africa, it is still possible to describe a general framework into which customary marriage and its preliminaries fall for the vast majority of traditional societies in the country. The key concepts in this framework are: family

6 Though appearing to be introduced for the first time by the Codes, the idea of an official witness is consonant with the notion of the chief's messenger (*umgijimi*), well known in certain Nguni communities, a functionary who attended local events on behalf of the chief.

7 E.g., Bekker, J.C. *Seymour's Customary Law in Southern Africa* (Cape Town, Juta, 5th edn, 1989); Olivier, N.J.J. et al. "Indigenous Law" in Joubert, W.A. (ed.) *The Law of South Africa*, Vol. 32 (Durban, LexisNexis 2nd edn 2009 by Church, J. et al.); Sinclair, J.D. assisted by Heaton, J. *The Law of Marriage* Vol. 1 (Cape Town, Juta, 1996); South African Law Commission (SALC). *Report on Customary Marriages, Project 90: The Harmonisation of the Common Law and the Indigenous Law* (Pretoria, 1998); Jansen, R.M. "Customary Family Law" in Rautenbach, C. and Bekker, J.C. (eds) *Introduction to Legal Pluralism in South Africa* (Durban, LexisNexis, 2014) 97–101.

8 Himonga and Nhlapo (eds), *supra* note 3 at 100–102.

9 Jansen, *supra* note 7 at 101.

involvement, negotiation, *lobolo*, and procreation.[10] The family seeking a wife, approaches the family of the bride they wish to marry: they make an offer of *lobolo*, which then becomes the subject of negotiation in a process that aims to forge a relationship in which the procreation of legitimate offspring is a shared objective.[11]

Marriage negotiations are normally initiated by the man's family or the man himself, but may also be instigated by the woman's family.[12] Central to African customary law is the notion of marriage as a desirable state and an indispensable milestone in everyone's journey of life.[13] There is therefore a high tolerance of deviation from mainstream courtship models, which accommodates a variety of irregular entry points into married status.[14] *Ukuthwala*, prevalent in the Eastern Cape and KwaZulu-Natal, is one such irregular mode among others. Literally, meaning "to carry off", the custom has features of a mock abduction of a girl, ideally of marriageable age and with her consent, although abuses of the practice are rife. In the case of *Jezile v. S*,[15] a man's conviction for human trafficking, assault, and rape was upheld and a sentence of twenty-two years confirmed. He had abducted an under-age girl from her home and had claimed in his defence that he had married her in terms of customary law.[16]

Lobolo is the core element in the process of marrying a wife, regardless of whether the initial approach was deemed regular or irregular.[17] Indeed, the commencement of *lobolo* negotiations is the gateway to regular marriage, and marks the centrality of the woman's family in the process. Himonga and Nhlapo[18] argue that this role of the woman's family as the people who determine which suitor to negotiate *lobolo* with is key to determining who can marry in terms of customary law. In their view, "the inescapable conclusion is that a white man can marry into a black family, while neither a black man nor a white man would be able to marry into a white family in terms of the RCMA".[19] A lot has been written about the legal and social role, function, and status of *lobolo*.[20] For the purposes

10 Himonga and Nhlapo (eds), *supra* note 3 at 97–98; Nhlapo, T.R. "The African Family and Women's Rights: Friends or Foes" 1991 *Acta Juridica* 135; Nhlapo, T.R. *Marriage and Divorce in Swazi Law and Custom* (Mbabane, Websters, 1992) 44; SALC, *supra* note 7 at 40.

11 See Phillips, A. (ed.) *Survey of African Marriage and Family Life* (New York, Oxford University Press, 1953) xi–xvii. See also Olivier et al., *supra* note 7 at para. 86. While customary law is accommodating on the question of non-marital children, legitimacy is prized, as reflected in the elaborate link between *lobolo* and children. See the discussion of *lobolo* below.

12 Jansen, *supra* note 7 at 93.

13 Himonga and Nhlapo (eds), *supra* note 3 at 92.

14 Ibid.

15 2016 (2) SA 62 (WCC).

16 See South African Law Reform Commission (SALRC). *Project 138: The Practice of Ukuthwala, Revised Discussion Paper 132* (Pretoria, 2015) 5–10.

17 Jansen, *supra* note 7 at 103–104; Himonga and Nhlapo (eds), *supra* note 3 at 97–98; Himonga, C. and Moore, E. *Reform of Customary Marriage, Divorce and Succession in South Africa: Living Customary Law and Social Realities* (Cape Town, Juta, 2015) 58–68.

18 *Supra* note 3 at 96.

19 At 97.

20 See e.g., Hlophe, J.M., "The KwaZulu Act on the Code of Zulu Law, 6 of 1981– A Guide to Intending Spouses and Some Comments on the Custom of Lobolo" (1984) 17 *The Comparative and International Law Journal of Southern Africa* 163; Dlamini, C.R.M. "The Modern Legal Significance of Ilobolo in Zulu Society" (1984) 1 *De Jure* 148; Dlamini, C.R.M. "Should Ilobolo be Abolished? A Reply to Hlophe" (1985) 18 *The Comparative and International Law Journal of Southern Africa* 361; Chigwedere, A.S. *Lobolo: The Pros and Cons in relation to Emancipation of Women in Zimbabwe* (Harare, Books for Africa, 1988); Chinyenze, M. "A Critique of Chigwedere's Book *Lobolo: The Pros and Cons in relation to the Emancipation of Women in Zimbabwe*" (1983–4) 1 and 2 *Zimbabwe Law Review* 229; Himonga and Moore, *supra* note 17 at 63–74.

of this chapter, it merits mention that the recurring themes in discussions of *lobolo* are its traditional functions of:

(a) the legitimation of children;
(b) a guarantee of good conduct within the marriage;
(c) a resource to the woman's father for her support in case it is needed; and
(d) a resource to the woman's family to acquire a wife for one of her brothers to "balance" the reproductive capacity lost by her departure.[21]

Whatever the reasons, *lobolo* remains popular and the custom is invariably observed even in respect of civil marriages by black persons.[22]

The failure of the RCMA to include *lobolo* among the requirements for validity has been met with some dismay which, with respect, in my view is overstated. The permissive nature of section 3(1)(b) ensures that no violence is done to the marriage processes of those communities whose customary law regards *lobolo* as an essential requirement, whilst refraining from imposing it on those systems that do not.[23]

The law in respect of requirements for validity has been amplified by numerous judicial decisions. In *Ndlovu v. Mokoena and Others*,[24] it was made clear that *lobolo* on its own does not validate a marriage; in *Mabuza v. Mbatha*,[25] a Swazi ritual long considered central to the formation of a marriage was said to be capable of being waived by mutual consent of the two families. Similarly, the court in *Maluleke v. Minister of Home Affairs*[26] was persuaded that the actual performance of a ritual accepted by both families to be essential could, likewise, be dispensed with by agreement. In *Mabena v. Letsoalo*,[27] a mother's ability to negotiate and receive *lobolo* for her daughter unassisted by a man was confirmed. *Raisiba Maria Mathaba v. Minister of the Home Affairs and Others*[28] confirmed a variation of popular expectations about *lobolo* when the court ruled that its terms must be determined according to the specific contract concluded by the parties. Notably, the latter case reveals that while the agreement about *lobolo* is crucial in most systems of customary law in South Africa, the completion of its payment is much less so. Where it was stipulated that it must be paid in full before the marriage could be concluded, failure to comply invalidated the attempted marriage. In *PSC v. LPM*,[29] the court viewed a digital video disk of a children's party to determine whether the function captured on camera amounted to an official integration of the bride into her new family. The decision in *Mxiki v. Mbata, In Re: Mbata v. Department of Home Affairs and Others*[30] illustrates the growing challenge. In the matter of a disputed customary marriage where *lobolo* had been negotiated and paid in part, the lower court had declared the marriage valid on this basis. This was reversed on appeal, on the basis that there had been no

21 Olivier et al., *supra* note 7 at para. 113; Jansen, *supra* note 7 at 103.
22 See Jansen, *supra* note 7 at 104. On the co-existence of a customary marriage and a civil marriage or civil union, see Heaton and Kruger, *supra* note 1 at 234–237.
23 SALC, *supra* note 7 at para. 4.1.13.
24 2009 (5) SA 400 (GNP).
25 2003 (4) SA 218 (C).
26 *Maluleke (in her Capacity as Representative of the Estate of the Late Dumakude Patrick Mtshali) and Others v. Minister of Home Affairs and Another (02/24924)* [2008] ZAGPHC 129 (9 April 2008).
27 1998 (2) SA 1068 (T).
28 [2013] JOL 30820 (GNP).
29 [2013] JOL 29847 (GNP).
30 Unreported, A844/2012, 23 October 2014.

handing over of the bride. *Mmutle v. Thinda and Another*[31] again involved a contested marriage where the couple were cohabiting and *lobolo* had been paid in part. The court considered these circumstances to be sufficient to confirm the marriage, in the face of objections that *lobolo* had not been paid in full (according to Tswana custom), that there had been no exchange of gifts, and no handing over of the bride. *Southon v. Moropane*[32] found a contested marriage proven on the basis of payment of *lobolo* in the face of attempts to impugn the marriage for non-performance of a slate of minor rituals. (An appeal against this decision was dismissed by the Supreme Court of Appeal in 2014.)[33]

The inescapable conclusion from these cases is that it is now unsafe to be dogmatic about the essentials of a customary marriage in the context of the need to furnish the court with evidence of the living customary law in each case. This may reflect the challenges inherent in the whole question of ascertainment, now that the customary law applicable in the courts is living customary law.[34] However, Himonga and Moore conclude that the *lobolo* agreement and the handing over of the bride have emerged as the two essential requirements for validity in living customary law.[35]

Marriages concluded after 15 November 2000

Section 3(1) of the RCMA sets out the requirements for the validity of a customary marriage concluded after the coming into operation of the Act:

> (a) The prospective spouses –
> (i) must both be above the age of 18 years, and
> (ii) must both consent to be married to each other under customary law, and
> (b) the marriage must be negotiated and entered into or celebrated in accordance with customary law.

These requirements have attracted strong criticism from scholars who believe that what has been created is a distortion of customary marriage as known by millions of South Africans who practice customary law.[36] The fluid state of the customary law essentials for a valid marriage appears to bear out the SALC's caution. Section 3(1)(b) has generated the most comment in its attempt to avoid prescribing precise procedures and rituals for all customary law communities in the country, an approach which, in my view, is amply explained by the SALC (now the SALRC) in its *Report on Customary Marriages.*[37] The case of *Mayelane v. Ngwenyama*[38] in the North Gauteng High Court in 2010 introduced some temporary uncertainty in the area of marriage essentials when the court ruled that failure by a husband to comply with the requirements of section 7(6) of the RCMA invalidated the subsequent marriage he was attempting. Section 7(6) is an attempt

31 (20949/2007) [2008] ZAGPHC 352 (23 July 2008).

32 (14295/10) [2012] ZAGPJHC 146 (18 July 2012).

33 *Moropane v. Southon* (755/2012) [2014] ZASCA 76 (29 May 2014).

34 Himonga and Nhlapo (eds), *supra* note 3 at 100–102.

35 *Supra* note 17 at 315–328.

36 E.g., Maithufi, I.P. and Bekker, J.C. "The Recognition of Customary Marriages Act of 1998 and Its Impact on Family Law in South Africa" (2002) 35 *The Comparative and International Law Journal of Southern Africa* 182 at 195–197; Mqeke, R.B. "The 'Rainbow Jurisprudence' and the Institution of Marriage with Emphasis on the Recognition of Customary Marriages Act 120 of 1998" (1999) 20 *Obiter* 52 at 59 ff.

37 *Supra* note 7 at para. 4.1.13.

38 Reported as *MM v. MN and Another* 2010 (4) SA 286 (GNP).

to deal with the property of a polygamous (or soon-to-be polygamous) household and it sets out procedures for the husband to follow, the most important of which is to apply to a court for approval of a written contract regulating the future matrimonial property regime of his marriages. It was not meant as an additional requirement for validity, a point made by the Supreme Court of Appeal when it overruled the High Court decision.[39] The position as it stands is thus that a husband's failure to comply with section 7(6) does not invalidate the subsequent marriage. But the case continues to be relevant to the issue of marriage essentials, in that the Constitutional Court in *Mayelane v. Ngwenyama*[40] in 2013 invalidated the marriage in question, though on a different ground: namely, that the husband should have obtained the consent of his wife in order to marry a second wife. Although all this was in the context of Xitsonga customary law, the court's grounding of the consent requirement on the constitutional rights of equality and dignity hints at the possibility of this requirement being mandatory in all future polygamous marriages.[41]

Section 3(2), read with section 10(1) of the RCMA, prevents couples from going through both a customary marriage and civil marriage unless the marriages are between the same parties.

Section 3(6) of the RCMA stipulates that the issue of prohibited degrees of relationship is to be decided according to customary law.

A duty is placed upon spouses to register their marriage but section 4(9) confirms that failure to register the marriage will not result in its invalidity.[42] Section 4(3)(a) of the RCMA provides that marriages concluded before the commencement of the Act should be registered within twelve months of that date or within any other longer period as determined by the Minister. In similar vein, section 4(3)(b) provides that marriages entered into after the commencement date have to be registered within three months of the wedding or any other longer period determined by the Minister. Section 4(4)(a) ensures that the registering officer must record "the identity of the spouses, the date of the marriage, any *lobolo* agreed to and any other particulars prescribed" if he or she is satisfied of the existence of the marriage. Section 4(5)(a) and (b) provides that a party with "a sufficient interest" in the matter may apply to enquire into an unregistered marriage, and if the registering officer is satisfied that such a marriage exists or existed, he or she must register the marriage and issue a certificate. Section 4(7) provides that a court may be approached for an order registering any customary marriage or cancelling or rectifying any registration already made. Section 4(8) guarantees that a registration certificate is prima facie evidence of the existence of the marriage.

Proprietary consequences of marriage

The legal consequences of a customary marriage, always elaborate, have been rendered even more complex by the enactment of the RCMA. Section 7(1) of the Act states that the proprietary consequences of a customary marriage concluded before the date of commencement of the Act continue to be governed by customary law – a statement that now needs drastic revision since

39 *MN v. MM and Another* 2012 (4) SA 527 (SCA).

40 Reported as *MM v. MN and Another* 2013 (4) SA 415 (CC).

41 Himonga, C. and Pope, A. "Mayelane v Ngwenyama and Minister for Home Affairs: A Reflection on Wider Implications" 2013 *Acta Juridica* 318 at 323; Heaton, J. "Family Law" in Botha, N. et al. (eds) *Annual Survey of South African Law* (Lansdowne, Juta, 2013) 425 at 465; Maithufi, I.P. "Modjadji Florah Mayelane v Mphephu Maria Ngwenyama [2013] ZACC 14" (2013) 46 *De Jure* 1078 at 1087; Heaton and Kruger, *supra* note 1 at 219.

42 The SALC consulted widely on the matter, reaching the conclusion that it was untenable to place another hurdle in the recognition of solidly grounded customary marriages, where invalidity often had negative consequences for women. See SALC *supra* note 7 at paras 4.5.1–4.5.19.

the cases of *Gumede v. President of the Republic of South Africa and Others*[43] in 2009 and *Ramuhovhi and Another v. President of the Republic of South Africa and Others*[44] in 2016. Before these decisions, customary law proprietary consequences applied to all pre-RCMA marriages, regardless of whether they were monogamous or polygamous, while, according to section 7(2), monogamous customary marriages concluded after the date of commencement of the Act were in community of property unless this regime was excluded by antenuptial contract.[45] The decision in *Gumede* altered the rule in section 7(1) by extending community of property to pre-RCMA marriages that were monogamous. The Constitutional Court concluded that depriving women in pre-RCMA monogamous marriages of the benefits of section 7(2) simply because of the date of their marriage amounted to unfair discrimination on grounds of gender. Section 7(1) was therefore unconstitutional and invalid in respect of monogamous customary marriages contracted before the coming into effect of the Act.[46] Turning its attention to section 7(2), the court struck down the words "entered into after the commencement of this Act" as unconstitutional. The result was to make section 7(2) applicable to all customary marriages that were *de facto* monogamous, regardless of the date on which they were concluded. *Polygamous* customary marriages entered into before the RCMA continued to be governed by customary law in terms of section 7(1).

This position stood until the decision in *Ramuhovhi*, which declared section 7(1) unconstitutional and invalid in respect of *polygamous* customary marriages as well. The application was brought by the biological children of one Joseph Netshituka, now deceased, who during his lifetime had entered into polygamous customary marriages with their mothers. The deceased left a will in which he bequeathed his "half share of the joint estate" to his respective wives, including the Fourth Respondent, and all his children. The Fourth Respondent was listed among the beneficiaries and was also named the executrix of the estate. At the time of her husband's death, the Fourth Respondent was the registered owner of an undivided share in fixed property on which a shopping centre was situated. In his will, the deceased indicated that he was married to the Fourth Respondent in community of property. This civil marriage, contracted in January 1997, had in fact been declared null and void by the Supreme Court of Appeal in the case of *Netshituka v. Netshituka and Others*.[47] The reason for the annulment was that Netshituka was already married to two other women by customary rites at the time of the purported civil marriage to the Fourth Respondent. The applicants' submission was that,

> due to the application of section 7(1) of the RCMA and the applicable Venda customary law, their mothers were excluded from ownership of the estate amassed by the deceased. This, in turn, was due to the discriminatory nature of these provisions, which caused prejudice to the deceased's wives and children.

Amongst the findings of the court were the following:[48]

> 1 The provisions of section 7(1) of the Recognition of Customary Marriages Act 120 of 1998 discriminate unjustifiably against women in polygamous customary marriages on

43 2009 (3) *SA* 152 (CC).

44 2016 (6) SA 210 (LT).

45 Section 7(2) of the RCMA. Section 7(3) applies ch. III and ss. 18, 19, 20, and 24 of ch. IV of the Matrimonial Property Act 88 of 1984 to such marriages.

46 Heaton and Kruger, *supra* note 1 at 221–222.

47 2011 (5) SA 453 (SCA).

48 Para. 75.

the basis of gender, race and ethnic or social origin, and are thus inconsistent with the Constitution, and must be declared invalid.

2 In order to ensure effective protection of the rights of women in polygamous customary marriages, a direct approach is required instead of a piecemeal, slow development of customary law, but this direct approach should retain any positive developments in the living customary law.

3 The persons in need of protection should not have to suffer the burden of unfairness and discrimination any longer and an interim remedy is necessary in order to extend protection to them pending the required legislative processes.

4 The interim remedy should ensure that the rights already provided for in terms of the Bill of Rights, the RCMA, the Matrimonial Property Act and any other legislation can indeed find application and can be exercised.

5 The parties to old polygamous customary marriages should enjoy equal rights in and over the matrimonial property.

6 Any rights and protection of women in old polygamous customary marriages, provided for in terms of living customary law should not be removed, but applied.

7 The core nature of polygyny should be retained, in that the rights of the parties to old polygamous customary marriages should be qualified to ensure that the rights are exercised for the benefit of the family unit.

8 The differentiation between family property, house property and personal property should be retained to promote the sustainability of the family unit.

The court issued the following order:[49]

1 Section 7(1) of the Recognition of Customary Marriages Act 120 of 1998 is declared inconsistent with the Constitution and invalid.

2 Until such time as Parliament enacts legislation to govern the matrimonial property regimes of persons who are parties to polygamous customary marriages concluded before the Recognition of Customary Marriages Act 120 of 1998 came into operation, the following regime shall apply to such marriages:

(a) The wives who are parties to such marriages shall have joint and equal rights of management and control over and in the marital property to their husbands, and these rights shall be exercised as follows:

(i) In respect of all house property, by the husband and the wife of the house concerned, jointly and in the best interest of the family unit.

(ii) In respect of all family property, by the husband and all the wives, jointly and in the best interest of the family unit.

(b) In respect of personal property, a party shall retain exclusive rights to [his] or her personal property.

(c) In the event of any disputes arising from this order, any party to such a marriage may approach the court for an order regulating the matrimonial property regime on a just and equitable basis . . . .

In a decision rendered after the due date for this chapter, the Constitutional Court largely confirmed the order, which means that there is now no difference in the proprietary regimes of

49 Para. 76.

customary marriages concluded before the Act.[50] The decision further erodes the relevance of pre-RCMA customary law of matrimonial property, especially in respect of polygamous marriages. However, for reasons of completeness, the basic principles of customary law merit a brief mention here.

In customary law, generally, the matrimonial property regime in polygamous marriages is characterised by the establishment of a "house" for each of the wives, together with its separate house property, and the system of the ranking of wives. As Himonga and Nhlapo state,[51] "each customary marriage constitutes a house in which both the house and the wife belonging to it are ranked according to the customary law of the indigenous community concerned". Although ranking according to the date of the marriage is prevalent, the rules differ from community to community, and the systems are often categorised as simple or complex.[52] Amongst the Swazi for instance, rank is determined both by date and by clan seniority; a bride from a royal family outranks the other wives regardless of the date of her marriage. As Jansen observes, "[the husband] is the family head of all the houses regardless of which form of ranking system applies to the particular family group".[53] As such, he controls all house property and family property and must use it generally in the interests of the family.[54]

In KwaZulu-Natal, the proprietary consequences of polygamous customary marriages were governed by sections 20 and 22 of the Codes, which generally confirmed the basics of the complex ranking system by providing that the husband owns and controls all the family and house property, and that all members of the household are under his control and owe allegiance to him.

The matrimonial property regime of polygamous customary marriages concluded after the commencement of the RCMA is governed by sections 7(6) to (8) of the Act. Section 7(6) requires a husband who seeks to marry another wife to apply to a court to approve a written contract that will regulate the property regime of his future marriage(s). Section 7(7)(a)(i) to (iii) provides that the court is required to terminate the existing regime (if it is either in community of property or out of community with accrual) and effect a division of the property, ensure an equitable division of the property, and pay attention to all relevant circumstances which might affect the family groups involved if the application is granted. Section 7(7)(b) ensures that the court may allow further amendments to the terms of the contract or grant the order subject to any conditions it may deem just; it may also refuse the application if it is not satisfied that the proposed contract adequately protects the interests of the other parties involved. Joinder of all persons "having a sufficient interest in the matter", including the applicant's spouse(s), is required by section 7(8).

Criticisms of the mechanisms created by the provisions discussed above have included the fact that the Act is silent on the consequences of non-compliance with these processes.[55] This has become especially pronounced since the decision in *Mayelane*, where the Constitutional Court was confronted squarely with the question of a husband who had not complied with the

50 *Ramuhovhi and Others v. President of the Republic of South Africa and Others* (CCT 194/16) [2017] (30 November 2017), 2018 (2) SA 1 (CC). The Constitutional Court afforded Parliament 24 months to remedy the unconstitutionality in s. 7(1). In the interim, a similar regime to the one set out in the text above applies. A draft Bill dealing with the requisite changes to the section was published in April 2018: see Draft Recognition of Customary Marriages Amendment Bill, 2018.

51 At 129, citing Cronjé, D.S.P. and Heaton, J. *South African Family Law* (Durban, LexisNexis Butterworths, 3rd edn by Heaton, J., 2010) 210–211.

52 Heaton, *supra* note 41 at 210–211.

53 *Supra* note 7 at 108.

54 See also Bekker, *supra* note 7 at 71; Mqeke, *supra* note 36 at 63 ff.

55 See, e.g., Jansen, *supra* note 7 at 110; Heaton and Kruger, *supra* note 1 at 224.

requirements of section 7(6). The court supported the interpretation of the Supreme Court of Appeal in *Mayelane v. Ngwenyama*[56] that the section was not intended as a validity requirement and that non-compliance with it simply rendered subsequent marriages as marriages out of community of property. Heaton and Kruger endorse this interpretation, referring to complete separation of property as "the only viable matrimonial property system in a polygynous customary marriage".[57] Jansen proposes that the possibility of declaring such marriages putative marriages should be explored.[58]

Dissolution of marriage

Prior to the enactment of the RCMA, customary law treated the dissolution of marriage (as it did its formation) as a private matter involving only the families concerned and outside the ambit of state institutions. Where a marriage was dissolved through the fault of one of the parties, there were known, generally elastic, grounds on which a termination occurred. Himonga and Nhlapo refer to these grounds as "reasons" or "justifications".[59] The death of one of the spouses did not necessarily terminate a customary marriage.[60]

Dissolution by divorce

Grounds

Since the coming into effect of the RCMA, the dissolution of customary marriages has been governed by section 8(1) of the Act, which prescribes that "a customary marriage may only be dissolved by a court by a decree of divorce". The sole ground is irretrievable breakdown of the marriage,[61] which section 8(2) of the Act defines as the point at which "the marriage relationship between the parties to the marriage has reached such a state of disintegration that there is no reasonable prospect of the restoration of a normal marriage relationship between them". It is needless to say that the traditional grounds for divorce continue to be relevant when a court is assessing irretrievable breakdown.[62] For most traditional communities in South Africa, the list of grounds (not all necessarily available to both spouses equally) would include: adultery by the wife, desertion by her with the intention not to return, and incest; availing the wife would be assault and general ill-treatment, including abandonment by the husband, eviction from the family home, and impotence of the husband. This is not a closed list and each case is decided on its merits. Many circumstances and misdemeanours such as an unexplained pregnancy, refusal of

56 *Supra* note 38.

57 *Supra* note 1 at 224.

58 *Supra* note 7 at 110, citing Monareng, K. "Black Women, Are You Aware that You Are Concubines?: The Legal Implications of South African Family Law" 2007 *Agenda* 122 at 124–128.

59 *Supra* note 3 at 149–150.

60 Maithufi and Bekker, *supra* note 36 at 264; Jansen, *supra* note 7 at 115.

61 The impression needs to be corrected that the ground of irretrievable breakdown is an unthinking importation of civil marriage values from the Divorce Act. In fact, the description is a very apt rendition of the customary law position, which has always maintained that marital strife sometimes reaches a point where the two families involved decide that no further efforts at reconciliation should be made. See Jansen, *supra* note 7 at 111; Bekker J.C., "Grounds for Divorce in African Customary Marriages in Natal" (1976) 9 *The Comparative and International Law Journal of Southern Africa* 346 at 355; Himonga and Nhlapo (eds), *supra* note 3 at 149 note 8.

62 Jansen, *supra* note 7 at 111.

sexual privileges, infertility, or gross disrespect may or may not ground a termination, depending on frequency, provocation, intensity, and a host of other factors. The customary law of divorce is founded on compromise and pragmatism. It usually serves no purpose to predict an outcome based on certain behaviours. Even the mutual amity between in-laws may be a factor in how stringently or leniently the applicable rules are applied.[63]

Consequences of divorce

Children

Section 8(3) of the RCMA imports the provisions of Mediation in Certain Divorce Matters Act 24 of 1987 and section 6 of the Divorce Act 70 of 1979 into the process of dissolving a customary marriage. Generally, the former statute avails the services of family advocates and family counsellors to the courts and the parties in cases that involve the welfare of children; the latter, likewise, protects the interests of the children in respect of maintenance, custody and guardianship. This places the children of a customary marriage in an identical position as the children of a civil marriage in divorce, marking a departure from customary law, where, generally, the custody and guardianship of children is determined by *lobolo* and their maintenance by whether they return with the mother to their maternal grandmother's home, or remain with their father.[64]

Patrimonial consequences

Section 8(4)(a) gives the court hearing a divorce in respect of a customary marriage powers as found in sections 7 to 10 of the Divorce Act and section 24(1) of the Matrimonial Property Act. This again erases the distinction between customary law consequences and the law applicable to civil marriages. A court may thus grant post-divorce maintenance to a spouse, confirm and incorporate a settlement agreement into the divorce order, or order a redistribution of assets or forfeiture of matrimonial benefits.[65]

Polygamous marriages are catered for by section 8(4)(b), which requires the court to consider all relevant factors, including any arrangements made pursuant to section 7(4) to (7) of the RCMA, and to make any equitable order it deems just. The provisions in this section are concerned with changes to the matrimonial property regime, joinder of interested parties in the proceedings, and approval of a contract regulating a future property system in case of a husband entering into further marriage(s).

The issue of the redistribution of assets in terms of the powers granted to the court by section 8(4)(a) of the RCMA was sharply contested before the decision in *Gumede v. President of the Republic of South Africa*.[66] The debate was about whether the incorporation of section 7(3) of the Divorce Act allowed a court hearing a divorce in respect of a pre-2000 customary marriage to redistribute assets as it would in the case of a civil marriage. In one view, this could not be done since the regime in such marriages was not one of complete separation of assets as required by section 7(3); the counter position was that the use of section 7(3) for this purpose was apt and equitable precisely because, in practice, the customary marital regime is one of complete

63 Himonga and Nhlapo (eds), *supra* note 3 at 150–153; Nhlapo 1992, *supra* note 10 at 76.
64 Jansen, *supra* note 7 at 112.
65 Heaton and Kruger, *supra* note 1 at 229–230.
66 *Supra* note 43.

separation of assets. Supporters of the former view included Van Schalkwyk.[67] Cronjé and Heaton espoused the latter view.[68] The matter was eventually resolved by the judgment in *Gumede*,[69] which, endorsing the latter view, ruled that the court's power to redistribute assets in terms of section 8(4)(a) applied to all customary marriages whatever the date of the conclusion and whatever matrimonial property regime operated therein. As Heaton and Kruger conclude: "In customary marriages, unlike civil marriages, redistribution of assets can therefore be invoked regardless of the matrimonial property system which operates in the marriage."[70]

The powers of the court extend to ordering post-divorce maintenance of one spouse by the other. When making a maintenance order, section 8(e) requires the court to "take into account any provision or arrangement made in accordance with customary law". Arguably, this allows a court to consider customary payments such as *isondlo* and *lobolo*.[71]

Return of *lobolo*[72]

Traditionally, the process of divorce involved the return of *lobolo* to the husband's family, though this rule was by no means universal. For example, return of *lobolo* was never a rule among the Zulu.[73] In line with the notion of customary marriage, as a private affair between kinship groups, the return of *lobolo* was negotiated between the two families when efforts at reconciling the spouses had been abandoned. Among the considerations taken into account by the negotiators were the following important questions:[74]

(a) whose fault (solely or primarily) caused the breakup?
(b) did the wife bear children in her marital home?
(c) was *lobolo* delivered and, if so, how much?

By far the most compelling considerations were the question of fault and the issue of children. Generally, *lobolo* was forfeited if the breakup was the husband's fault, and returnable if the wife was to blame. It is returned in full or subject to allowable deductions in respect of children born of the marriage.[75] The principle of deductions for children produced by the wife provides striking corroboration for the notion that procreation is the central objective of a customary marriage, although the rules vary from community to community. Among the Swazi, for instance, a deduction of two beasts for each girl up to a total of four beasts was the rule, with one beast for each boy up to a total of two. The higher consideration in respect of girls was based on their

67 Van Schalkwyk, L.N. "Kommentaar op die Wet op Erkenning van Gebruiklike Huwelike 120 van 1998" (2000) 63 *Tydskrif vir Hedendaagse Romeins-Hollandse Reg* 479 at 496.

68 *Supra* note 51 at 195.

69 *Supra* note 43 at para. 43.

70 *Supra* note 1 at 230.

71 Bennett, T.W. *Customary Law in South Africa* (Cape Town, Juta, 2004) 221, 227.

72 The return of *lobolo* is not a requirement of the RCMA, as s. 8 provides for judicial divorce. This area is thus largely about pre-RCMA customary marriage law and, today, would be relevant only to ascertain whether a marriage was properly dissolved before the Act came into effect. See Bennett, *supra* note 71 at 274, who provides a comprehensive review of the official law jurisprudence on the issue.

73 Jansen, *supra* note 7 at 114.

74 See Jansen ibid. at 113. Bennett, *supra* note 71 at 277–278 cites examples of traditional communities who make deductions for notable services by the wife to her marital home, as well as those groups who deduct *lobolo* if the husband was guilty of assault or was impotent.

75 Jansen, *supra* note 7 at 114.

marriageability and consequent capacity to attract *lobolo* cattle into the family coffers.[76] Official customary law recognised deductions for adulterine children[77] and for miscarriages.[78]

Lobolo is not part of the matrimonial property of the spouses since it is based on a private contract between the groom and the bride's family. The wife's father should be joined in the proceeding if a *lobolo* dispute is involved.[79]

Dissolution by death

In uncodified customary law,[80] the death of one of the spouses does not necessarily terminate a customary marriage since the agreement is between the families and not the individuals.[81] In the case of the death of the husband, the marriage may continue through the device of the levirate, also known as *ukungena* (Zulu), *kungena* (Swazi), and *kenela* (Sotho). Levirate requires the widow to cohabit with the brother or other male relative of the deceased for the purpose of raising an heir.[82] Because of this purpose, the pressure on the widow to accept the arrangement will increase if she is still young (and therefore capable of bearing more children), or if she is childless or has only borne female children.[83] It appears that the widow is not forced into the arrangement, but that her refusal to participate invariably spells her eviction from the household. However, and in line with the flexibility of customary law, a widow might decline the levirate with no untoward consequences, depending on several factors, including the esteem in which she is held by the family, which might in turn result from the warmth of her relationship with the deceased during his lifetime.

In the case of the death of a wife, the matrimonial "house" she established, is not extinguished. The practice of the sororate, also known as *inhlanti* (Swazi) and *seantlo* (Tswana), may be invoked by the husband in order to raise children for the deceased's house, especially if she died childless.[84] Depending on the traditional community involved, this invocation of the sororate by the husband's family may take the form of a marriage in which *lobolo* is transferred or, if he accepts a younger sister or cousin of the deceased provided by her family, a surrogate relationship in which no *lobolo* changes hands. Children born to the "seed-raiser" are regarded as children of the deceased spouse.[85] According to section 36(1) of the Codes of Zulu Law, the death of a spouse terminates the marriage.

Bibliography

Bekker, J.C. *Seymour's Customary Law in Southern Africa* (Cape Town, Juta, 5th edn, 1989).
Bekker, J.C. "Grounds for Divorce in African Customary Marriages in Natal" (1976) 9 *The Comparative and International Law Journal of Southern Africa* 346.

76 Nhlapo 1992, *supra* note 10 at 80.
77 *Gqozi v. Mntengwane* 1960 NAC 26 (S).
78 *Mayeki v. Kwababa* 4 NAC 193.
79 Heaton and Kruger, *supra* note 1 at 232; Jansen, *supra* note 7 at 115.
80 In KwaZulu-Natal, the Codes provide in s. 36(1) that the death of a spouse terminates the marriage. Jansen, *supra* note 7 at 116 considers the failure of the RCMA to rule on the issue of the death of a spouse and whether it dissolves the marriage "a serious shortcoming". See also Heaton and Kruger, *supra* note 1 at 233, who refer to the same situation as "[a] significant shortcoming".
81 Maithufi and Bekker, *supra* note 36 at 264; Jansen, *supra* note 7 at 115; Nhlapo 1992, *supra* note 10 at 75.
82 Jansen, *supra* note 7 at 115.
83 Himonga and Nhlapo (eds), *supra* note 3 at 154.
84 Jansen, *supra* note 7 at 115–116.
85 Jansen, *supra* note 7 at 115; Himonga and Nhlapo (eds), *supra* note 3 at 151; see also Nhlapo 1992, *supra* note 10 at 76.

Bennett, T.W. *Customary Law in South Africa* (Cape Town, Juta, 2004).

Chigwedere, A.S. *Lobolo: The Pros and Cons in relation to Emancipation of Women in Zimbabwe* (Harare, Books for Africa, 1988).

Chinyenze, M. "A Critique of Chigwedere's Book *Lobolo: The Pros and Cons in relation to the Emancipation of Women in Zimbabwe*" (1983–4) 1 and 2 *Zimbabwe Law Review* 229.

Cronjé, D.S.P. and Heaton, J. *South African Family Law* (Durban, LexisNexis Butterworths, 3rd edn by Heaton, J., 2010).

Dlamini, C.R.M. "The Ultimate Recognition of the Customary Marriage in South Africa" (1999) 20 *Obiter* 14.

Dlamini, C.R.M. "The Modern Legal Significance of Ilobolo in Zulu Society" (1984) 1 *De Jure* 148.

Dlamini, C.R.M. "Should Ilobolo be Abolished? A Reply to Hlophe" (1985) 18 *The Comparative and International Law Journal of Southern Africa* 361.

Heaton, J. "Family Law" in Botha, N., Van Wyk, J. and Schulze, C. (eds) *Annual Survey of South African Law* (Lansdowne, Juta, 2013) 425.

Heaton, J. and Kruger, H. *South African Family Law* (Durban, LexisNexis, 4th edn, 2015).

Himonga, C. and Moore, E. *Reform of Customary Marriage, Divorce and Succession in South Africa: Living Customary Law and Social Realities* (Cape Town, Juta, 2015).

Himonga, C. and Nhlapo T. (eds) *African Customary Law in South Africa: Post-Apartheid and Living Law Perspectives* (Cape Town, Oxford University Press Southern Africa, 2014).

Himonga, C. and Pope, A. "Mayelane v Ngwenyama and Minister for Home Affairs: A Reflection on Wider Implications" 2013 *Acta Juridica* 318.

Himonga, C., Nhlapo, T., Maithufi, I.P., Weeks, M.S., Mofokeng, L. and Ndima, D. *African Customary Law in South Africa: Post-apartheid and Living Law Perspectives* (Cape Town, Oxford University Press Southern Africa, 2014).

Hlophe, J.M. "The KwaZulu Act on the Code of Zulu Law, 6 of 1981 – A Guide to Intending Spouses and Some Comments on the Custom of Lobolo" (1984) 17 *The Comparative and International Law Journal of Southern Africa* 163.

Jansen, R.M. "Customary Family Law" in Rautenbach, C. and Bekker, J.C. (eds) *Introduction to Legal Pluralism in South Africa* (Durban, LexisNexis, 2014).

Maithufi, I.P. "Modjadji Florah Mayelane v Mphephu Maria Ngwenyama [2013] ZACC 14" (2013) 46 *De Jure* 1078.

Maithufi, I.P. and Bekker, J.C. "The Recognition of Customary Marriages Act and its Impact on Family Law in South Africa" (2002) 35 *The Comparative and International Law Journal of Southern Africa* 182.

Mqeke, R.B. "The 'Rainbow Jurisprudence' and the Institution of Marriage with Emphasis on the Recognition of Customary Marriages Act 120 of 1998" (1999) 20 *Obiter* 52.

Nhlapo, T.R. "The African Family and Women's Rights: Friends or Foes" 1991 *Acta Juridica* 135.

Nhlapo, T.R. *Marriage and Divorce in Swazi Law and Custom* (Mbabane, Websters, 1992).

Olivier, N.J.J., Bekker, J.C. and Olivier, W.H. "Indigenous Law" in Joubert, W.A. (ed.) *The Law of South Africa*, Vol. 32 (Durban, LexisNexis 2nd edn 2009 by Church, J., Olivier, N.J.J., Mqeke, R.B., Mwambene, L., Bekker, J.C., Olivier, W.H., Du Plessis, W. and Rautenbach, C.).

Phillips, A. (ed.) *Survey of African Marriage and Family Life* (New York, Oxford University Press, 1953).

Sinclair, J.D. assisted by Heaton, J. *The Law of Marriage* Vol. 1 (Cape Town, Juta, 1996).

South African Law Commission. *Report on Customary Marriages, Project 90: The Harmonisation of the Common Law and the Indigenous Law* (Pretoria, 1998).

South African Law Reform Commission. *Project 138: The Practice of Ukuthwala, Revised Discussion Paper 132* (Pretoria, 2015).

Van Schalkwyk, L.N. "Kommentaar op die Wet op Erkenning van Gebruiklike Huwelike 120 van 1998" (2000) 63 *Tydskrif vir Hedendaagse Romeins-Hollandse Reg* 479.

Part II
Divorce

4
Divorce

Barbara Stark

Introduction

Divorce is the legal process through which a marriage is ended. While some divorces may involve property distribution, support, child custody, and child support,[1] other divorces do not. All divorces, however, change the parties' status from 'married' to 'single'. They have no further legal obligations to each other, except as set out in the judgment of divorce.

The availability of divorce, and the ease or difficulty with which it can be obtained, reflects the role of marriage in a particular society. Where marriage is a means of forming alliances among families, for example, divorce may be rare or prohibited. When marriage is perceived as serving a larger societal purpose, the couples' interests are less important. Where companionate marriage is the norm, that is, when people marry for their own reasons, rather than those of their families or communities, divorce becomes easier because there are fewer overarching societal interests at stake.

The married couple is at the heart of the family,[2] and the family is often viewed as a microcosm of the state. As Sir Robert Filmer explained in the eighteenth century, just as the citizen was subject to the feudal lord, and the lord to the king; the children were subject to the parents, and the wife to the husband. The hierarchy of the state was replicated in the hierarchy of the family. Children learn their place in hierarchal families, which prepares them to accept their roles in hierarchical societies. Families are more equal in more equal societies. Gendered social roles, similarly, are likely to be replicated in the family. The family is where children first learn about these roles. A related but distinct idea is that children learn how to be citizens through their experience in the family.[3]

1 These are discussed in other chapters in this volume, although in many states these matters are decided as part of the divorce.

2 There are several family forms, however, in which this is not the case. Single-parent families, especially single-mother families, are an increasingly important exception. Polygamous families are another significant exception. While polygamy is still legal in some countries, it is increasingly rare and has been repeatedly condemned by the Committee on the Elimination of Discrimination against Women. See, e.g., Concluding Observations of the Committee on the Elimination of Discrimination against Women: Indonesia (urging state to "(i) prohibit polygamy." Id. at 48(b).)

3 See, e.g., Linda McClain, *The Place of Families* (Harvard University Press 2006).

If the family is a microcosm of the state, and the married couple the core of the family, divorce is a regime change, if not a revolution.[4] Divorce often affects others besides the couple, moreover, including children or other dependents, such as aged parents. Finally, divorce, like marriage, has symbolic significance, and high rates of divorce may be viewed as an indication of instability in family relations, perhaps contributing to broader social instability.

The concerns and objectives of the individuals seeking a divorce may be very different from those of the state or the community, as well as from each other. Individuals want to divorce because they want to leave a troubled relationship; or they want to remarry; or to have children with a new partner; or to resolve and dispose of property issues fairly. They want clarity and certainty as to their status and with respect to their legal rights and obligations. Individuals want to divorce to make a 'clean break' with an old life, and to begin a new one.

If there are children, parents want to make sure that they will be provided for and cared for. In some countries, the responsibility for children is governed by custom or religion. In others, customs and religion have been replaced or supplemented by relatively recent legal regimes. The state may also favor clarity and certainty. But if the children are not provided for, they may become the state's responsibility. The state, accordingly, may focus on care and support for dependent children. Some states are also concerned with the future support of dependent spouses. In addition, some communities want community norms affirmed, whether the norm is the husband's authority over the household, or family privacy, or gender equality.

The first part of this chapter sets out the substantive legal requirements for divorce, which may be established by national law, state or other local law, or religious law. These requirements range from specific acts attested to by witnesses, to a unilateral determination by one of the parties that the marriage is over. The chapter next explains the range of procedures required, which may consist of filing a note in the family registry, at one extreme, to a formal judicial proceeding, at the other. It concludes by discussing the recognition of foreign divorces. While an international treaty has been drafted to address this, only twenty states have become parties.[5]

The availability of divorce, the procedures required to effectuate it, and its recognition by foreign states, are all shaped by powerful, often conflicting, norms. These include religious norms, cultural norms, and norms grounded in human rights, especially non-discrimination and gender equality. Even in Western states, where divorce is generally subject to the authority of the secular state, religious and cultural norms are often influential. Even in Islamic states, where divorce is generally governed by religious law, national laws and international norms may play a significant role.

Substantive requirements for divorce

Marriage

The first prerequisite for divorce is the existence of a marriage. If the state does not recognize a marriage, or a particular form of marriage, divorce may not be available. This has serious consequences for women in customary or polygamous marriages, which many states refuse to recognize. Even in those states that address issues of property distribution and support absent

4 See Marianne Blair et al., *Family Law in the World Community* 197 (Carolina Academic Press 3rd edn 2015) (noting revolutions in France, the Soviet Union and Germany, in which divorce law was radically reformed).

5 Convention of 1 June 1970 on the Recognition of Divorces and Legal Separations, entered into force, Aug. 8, 1975, status report available at www.hcch.net/en/instruments/conventions/status_table/?cid=80.

an extant marriage, the rules and principles applied are usually different from those applied at divorce.

In some states, the availability of divorce means better protections for the economically vulnerable party, usually the woman, although these protections may be minimal. That is, divorce is conditioned upon the husband's ability to support the wife or the wife's ability to support herself. In other states, those concerned with the welfare of economically vulnerable women have sought to make divorce harder to obtain, on the theory that women were likely to be better off economically if they remain married.

If there is no valid marriage, there is generally no divorce. If the parties are ineligible to marry each other because of incest, for example, the marriage is void; that is, nonexistent, and no action is necessary.[6] Incest is a common bar, although the degree of relationships prohibited varies. In Morocco, for example, even if a man satisfies the other requirements allowing him to take a second wife, he may not be married to sisters at the same time, or to a woman and her aunt.[7]

Other impediments to marriage, such as the ages of the parties, merely make the marriage voidable. Such marriages are treated like other marriages until and unless they are declared void by a court or other appropriate tribunal.[8] In New York, for example, a marriage entered into while the parties are under the age of consent (18, without parental or judicial approval) may be annulled if either of the parties brings an action for that purpose before attaining majority. If no action is brought before that time, the parties are considered to have ratified the marriage and it can no longer be challenged on that basis.

Basis for divorce

With the exception of *talaq*,[9] divorce requires a basis, a justification for the termination of the marriage. Some jurisdictions require a showing of fault by one of the parties; that is, one party asserts that the other is responsible for the end of the marriage. Fault grounds have been criticized, however, as a simplistic understanding of the marital relationship. All of the grounds for divorce occur in some enduring marriages; those that do break up do so because the parties are unable or unwilling to continue the marriage. In addition, spouses can grow apart without either being at fault.

Some jurisdictions, accordingly, have replaced traditional fault grounds with no-fault divorce. Others have simply added no-fault to their pre-existing fault grounds. This section concludes by describing various approaches to no-fault divorce, which has become increasingly widespread in the West.

Fault-based grounds for divorce

This section first sets out some common fault-based grounds for divorce. As noted above, the distribution of the parties' post-divorce property, as well as any post-divorce obligations

6 Parties sometimes seek a divorce even if none is necessary, however, either in order to eliminate any ambiguity about the existence of a marriage or to avail themselves of the benefits of divorce law, such as the availability of spousal support or distribution of marital property.

7 The Moroccan Family code (Moudawana) of 2004, Art. 39.

8 See Maehb Harding, Chapter 1 "Marriage", in this volume (discussing void and voidable marriages).

9 See text accompanying notes 31–51, *infra*.

(such as spousal maintenance), are usually resolved, at least initially, at the time of divorce. In some jurisdictions, the marital fault of the parties is considered in the context of these determinations. That is, an economic penalty is imposed for marital fault even if fault is not required for divorce.

Adultery. Adultery is grounds for divorce everywhere fault-based divorce is recognized. In heterosexual marriages, adultery by the wife may raise questions about the paternity of marital children. If a purpose of marriage is to assure certainty in inheritance and succession, adultery by a wife undermines that purpose. If a purpose of marriage is to assure support for dependent children, similarly, adultery by a wife may raise questions about a husband's obligations. If marriage is a contractual agreement between the parties, requiring each to be faithful to the other, adultery by either party is a breach of that agreement.

In the West, fault grounds for divorce are historically grounded in the idea that the party responsible for the end of the marriage should bear the costs. At a time when wives were typically dependent upon their husbands for support, this meant that an innocent wife would be entitled to support from her adulterous husband.[10] But an adulterous wife would not be entitled to support from her innocent husband.

Although adultery is the most widely recognized ground, 'adultery' is defined differently in different states and by different authorities. Under traditional Islamic law, for example, a husband can marry as many as four wives.[11] Under customary laws in Zambia, similarly, a husband may have more than one wife.[12] Sexual relations with women to whom he is not married, however, are not permitted.[13] In Turkey, adultery is defined as sexual intercourse by either spouse with another person, except that a husband's sexual intercourse with a prostitute is not considered adultery.[14]

The consequences of adultery also vary widely. Marital fault may be taken into account for spousal support in the Netherlands, for example, but it is usually less important than the need of one spouse and the ability to pay of the other.[15] A similar approach can be found in contemporary Turkey, where post-divorce maintenance is available for 'destitute' spouses who are found to be less responsible than their spouses for the failure of the marriage.[16]

Other fault grounds. Other common grounds for divorce, in addition to adultery, include desertion, cruelty, drunkenness, and failure to support. In Algeria, for example, a wife can apply for a judicial divorce if she can show that her husband has failed to support her, is impotent, or has been sentenced to a long prison term.[17] Under some forms of Islamic law, the wife's disobedience is also a ground. Historically, in some American jurisdictions, if both parties could show fault, both complaints would be denied, and the parties would remain married.

10 Glendon, cited in Blair et al. *supra* note 4 at 167.

11 Id. at 119.

12 Cynthia Grant Bowman & Akua Kuenyehia, *Women and Law in Sub-Sahara Africa*, 11–12 (2003).

13 Id.

14 *Esin* Örücü, "Turkish Family Law Facing the Principles of European Family Law," in *Juxtaposing Legal Systems and the Principles of European Family Law on Divorce and Maintenance* 183, 205 (Esin Örücü & Jane Mair eds 2007).

15 Bea Verschraegen, Chapter 5, "Divorce," *International Encyclopedia of Comparative Law, Vol. IV, Persons and Family* 64 (2007).

16 Örücü, *supra* note 14.

17 Verschraegen, *supra* note 15 at 64.

Turkey has retained its traditional fault grounds for divorce, despite the addition of no-fault, or 'irretrievable breakdown', as a basis for divorce.[18] In addition to adultery, fault grounds include extreme cruelty; committing a 'humiliating crime' (including theft, fraud, or 'helping in illegal abortions'); or leading a 'dishonorable life' (including drunkenness, gambling, and homosexuality); desertion for a period of six months; or insanity.[19]

No-fault divorce

Under no-fault divorce laws, responsibility for the breakup of the marriage need not be established in court. Rather, all that must be established is that the marriage is 'irretrievably broken' or that the parties have 'irreconcilable differences'. Misconduct need not be proven unless required to show the breakdown of the marriage, or if such misconduct is relevant to the issue of child custody or support. As noted above, some states have pure no-fault laws while others have added no-fault, or 'incompatibility' grounds, to their pre-existing law.

The meaning of 'irretrievable breakdown' varies, however. Under the Matrimonial Causes Act 1973 in England, for example, irretrievable breakdown is the only ground for divorce, but it must be shown by one of five specific facts; that is, a) adultery by the respondent where the petitioner 'find[s] it intolerable to live with the respondent'; b) that the respondent has behaved in such a way that the petitioner cannot reasonably be expected to live with the respondent; c) desertion for at least two years; d) two years separation and the respondent consents to the divorce; or e) five years separation.[20] Most divorces are based on adultery or unreasonable behavior to avoid the extended waiting periods required under the alternative grounds.[21]

Some states have developed mechanisms to assure support, especially for those who, through no fault of their own, would otherwise be left destitute by divorce. Samoa, for example, adopted an exclusive no-fault system in 2010.[22] Like other states which have adopted no-fault, concerns about economically vulnerable spouses were addressed by simultaneous reforms regarding the financial aspects of divorce.[23] Such reforms recognize that while social norms may change the cost should not be borne by one spouse.

The trend in the West is clearly toward no-fault divorce. This reflects the understanding referred to above, that marriages may end without fault or endure notwithstanding fault. It also reflects falling rates of marriage, and its decreasing importance in general, especially in Western states where women may be able to support themselves and their children, and where out-of-wedlock births have become increasingly common, and accepted. While it is also widely recognized that a marriage cannot survive if one of the parties no longer wants to be married, some states still treat unilateral petitions for divorce differently than joint petitions.

18 Örücü, *supra* note 14 at 190.
19 Id. at 191–192.
20 Verschraegen, *supra* note 15 at 12.
21 Id. at 15.
22 Lalotoa Mulitalo & Jennifer Corrin, "Reform of Maintenance and Divorce Laws in Samoa: Appropriate for the 'AIGA'?" *2012 International Survey Fam. L.* 283.
23 When New York adopted no-fault, for example, it implemented a presumptive formula for maintenance when one spouse earns less than two-thirds of the other spouse's income. Barbara Stark, "Maintenance," in *Family Law in New York* (Barbara Stark & Joanna Grossman eds 2016).

Malta prohibited divorce until 2011.[24] Divorce was viewed as "incompatible with Maltese culture and religious tradition which is founded deeply in Roman Catholicism".[25] Marriage in Malta could be ended only by death, annulment, or by registering a foreign judgment of divorce until Act XIV came into effect.[26] Maltese citizens with foreign spouses, who were able to file for divorce in their home states, as well as Maltese citizens with the means to temporarily establish residence elsewhere, were able to divorce.

Even if divorce is not available, other legal mechanisms may be used to clarify the parties' status and their obligations to each other. In Malta, for example, a party could be awarded spousal maintenance or child support in the context of a separation proceeding.[27]

Procedure

In general, the procedure for obtaining a divorce may be judicial or administrative; that is, a divorce is not simply a private matter between the parties, but a change in status requiring some form of public recognition, if not approval. (*Talaq*, as practiced in some states, is a conspicuous exception, as discussed below.) These procedures may be simple and quick or complicated and time-consuming, although simple, quick procedures may require mediation taking months and waiting periods may extend what could have been a straightforward dissolution into a process lasting years. This section sets out some of the major approaches, ranging from those requiring the least involvement by the state, religious or other authority, to those requiring the most. These correlate, roughly, to the time required for a divorce to become effective, with some notable exceptions.

As a practical matter, divorce is much easier to procure in some countries than in others. In Sweden, for example, a childless couple who want a divorce can obtain one "immediately".[28] In Ireland, in contrast, a similarly situated couple must have lived separate and apart for four of the preceding five years.[29] In addition, the court must be satisfied that "there is no reasonable prospect of reconciliation" and "such provision as the court considers proper having regard to the circumstances exists or will be made for the spouses, any children of either or both of them and any other person prescribed by law".[30]

In order of the degree to which authorities, religious or secular, are involved in the divorce process, from the least participation by the authorities to the most, these procedures are: extra-judicial divorce (*talaq*); consensual divorce (administrative and judicial); contested divorce; and dual system divorces (civil and religious). The last includes 'limping' divorces, in which civil legal ties are dissolved, but religious ties remain, effectively precluding remarriage under religious law.

24 Ruth Farrugia, "A Divorce Law for Malta; Act XIV 2011," *Int'l Fam. L.* 192 (2012).

25 Ruth Farrugia, "The Position in Malta Juxtaposed to the Principles of European Family Law: Divorce and Maintenance" in *Juxtaposing Legal Systems and the Principles of European Family Law*, *supra* note 14 at 102 (Esin Örücü & Jane Mair eds 2007).

26 Id.

27 Id. at 110.

28 Verschraegen, *supra* note 15 at 32.

29 Family Law (Divorce) Act of 1996, §5, reprinted in Blair et al. *supra* note 4 at 187.

30 Id.

Extrajudicial divorce

Talaq

Under *Sharia*, the religious laws that govern Islamic family law as well as other matters, the husband has a unilateral right of divorce, *talaq*.[31] This is accomplished by pronouncing the word '*talaq*' (which means 'release, set free, or let go', in Arabic) three times.[32] The husband does not need any reason for the divorce. The wife, on the other hand, can only divorce her husband under Islamic law by obtaining a decree from a Muslim judge (*khul*). In order to be granted the divorce, moreover, she must convince a court that the marriage is over.

The ease and speed of *talaq* is at the wife's expense. Since the husband does not need any justification for the divorce, the wife cannot stop it, and they do not need to agree regarding distribution of marital property or spousal or child support. *Talaq* often leaves women with no means of support and no recourse. As Professor Javaid Rehman observes, "attempts to redress the balance in favor of women have a long and enduring history".[33]

Re-considering *talaq*

Several Muslim states have re-considered *talaq*, or unilateral divorce by the husband,[34] following de-colonization after World War II. These reforms often represent a signal, to the outside world as well as to national constituencies, that a regime is turning to 'modernity', human rights, or the West. The effectiveness of these reforms, similarly, reflects the broader political climate in which they are undertaken.

Tunisia. Following independence in 1956, Tunisia adopted a Personal Status Law barring *talaq* and polygamy and requiring that "divorce shall only take place in court".

Morocco. In Morocco, as in Egypt, family law is the only area of the law that is based on *Sharia*.[35] Moroccan family law was reformed by King Muhammad in 2004, in response to a terrorist attack in 2003. The King wanted to offer an alternative to the radical Islamic views of the terrorists.[36] Under the new law *talaq* is conditioned upon the court's approval.[37] This approval requires the husband to pay the wife whatever the court determines he owes her, which may include outstanding sums for dower, a "consolation gift", and maintenance during the *iddah*, or waiting period.[38] Under the new law, divorce is equally available to women and men.[39] Divorce

31 Javaid Rehman, "The Sharia, Islamic Family Laws and International Human Rights Law: Examining the Theory and Practice of Polygamy and Talaq," 21 *International J. L., Policy, & Fam.* 1, 9 (2007).

32 "Interpreting Women's Right of Divorce in Present Day Islamic Family Laws: Trans-National and Cross-Cultural Development in the Law of Divorce," in *Interpreting Divorce Laws in Islam,* 19, 24 (Rubya Medhi et al. eds DJØF Publishing Copenhagen 2012).

33 Rehman, *supra* note 31 at 10. See also note 81, *infra* (explaining the relationship between a *khul* and a *mahr.*)

34 *Talaq* is discussed further text accompanying notes 35–51, *infra.*

35 Yakare-Oule Jansen, "Muslim Brides and the Ghost of the Shari'a: Have the Recent Law Reforms in Egypt, Tunisia and Morocco Improved Women's Position in Marriage and Divorce, and Can Religious Moderates Bring Reform and Make It Stick?" 5 *Northwestern Journal of International Human Rights* 181, 202–203 (2007).

36 Id. at 202.

37 Id. at 204.

38 Id.

39 Id. at 203.

in Morocco has declined by 46.2% since the adoption of the new law.[40] One commentator attributes this to the widely held belief that the new law makes divorce more expensive for husbands. This includes the erroneous perception that the new law gives wives the right to half of their husbands' property.[41]

Egypt. In 1979, Egyptian President Anwar Sadat introduced laws requiring the *talaq* to be registered and holding it ineffective until the wife was notified.[42] The 1979 Act also gave the wife a right to divorce if the husband failed to obtain her permission before marrying additional wives. The Egyptian Supreme Court rejected these reforms as unconstitutional in 1985.[43] The 1985 Law of Personal Status required the wife to show harm as a result of the husband's marriage before she could file for divorce.[44]

Pakistan. The Muslim Family Law Ordinance, enacted by Pakistan in 1961, requires the husband to give written notice of *talaq* to the Union Council and the wife. The marriage remains in effect until he does so.[45] In *talaq-e-tafweez*, a Muslim man delegates his right of divorce to his wife in the marriage contract.[46] In some states, this option is included in the marriage forms.[47] Under the Hanafi School, the *talaq* can be pronounced without notice to the wife.[48] Failure to register a divorce pursuant to civil law may subject a wife who believes she is in fact divorced to prosecution for *zina*, or unlawful intercourse, with a subsequent husband. The Women Protection Act of 2006 was enacted in Pakistan to protect women from prison, stoning, or flogging following the Islamization of criminal laws.[49]

India. On August 22, 2017, the Supreme Court of India held that *talaq*, or 'instant divorce', was unlawful. Three of the judges on the five-judge panel held that *talaq* was unconstitutional and one held that it violated Islamic law.[50] Religious leaders note that it is not authorized by the *Quran*.[51]

Consensual divorce

Consensual divorce, prohibited as 'collusive' fifty years ago, is now widely accepted throughout the West. Divorce by mutual consent is relatively fast and simple because the parties have resolved their differences, if any, regarding grounds for divorce, support, division of property, and, where there are minor children, custody and child support, prior to their request for a divorce. The process through which agreement is reached, however, is often protracted and difficult. The

40 Rachel Newcomb, "Justice for Everyone? Implementation of Morocco's 2004 *Mudawana* Reforms," in *Interpreting Divorce Laws in Islam* (Rubya Mehdi et al. eds DJØF Publishing Copenhagen 2012).
41 Id.
42 Id. at 10.
43 Id.
44 Id.
45 Id. at 11.
46 Id. at 26.
47 Id.
48 Rehman, *supra* note 31 at 108, 117.
49 "Interpreting Women's Right to Divorce," *supra* note 32 at 29.
50 Jeffrey Gettleman & Suhasini Raj, "India Strikes Down 'Instant Divorce' for Muslims," *New York Times*, Aug. 23, 2017 at A5. See also Aziza Ahmed, Chapter 16 "Theories of state and family", in this volume.
51 Gettleman & Raj, *supra* note 50.

registration of the divorce, in an administrative divorce, or the issuance of a judgment, in a judicial divorce, is merely a formality.

The simplified procedures for consensual divorce, while superficially similar, operate in a wide range of economic and social contexts. This is reflected in the waiting periods, like those recently adopted in Korea;[52] or extrajudicial dispute resolution procedures, such as mediation, like that required in Japan;[53] or the requirement of explicit grounds, like those required under English law; or increasingly, the absence of such requirements in no-fault divorce, that accompany them.

Judicial divorce

Many states have adopted streamlined procedures for divorce by mutual consent, while maintaining a requirement of judicial supervision. In Switzerland, for example, the spouses must both appear before the judge, who hears them individually as well as together. The judge must be certain that the parties agree on the divorce, the terms of the settlement, and that the court can approve the settlement.[54] In Belgium, similarly, divorce by mutual consent is available if the parties agree on the divorce and the terms of the settlement. The judge reviews the agreement, especially the provisions regarding custody and support of any minor children, which must be officially recognized by the court.[55]

In Poland, where access to divorce is limited, a simplified procedure is available if both parties want the divorce and there are no minor children.[56] Even in such cases, however, the court must determine that there has been an "irretrievable and total breakdown of the marriage".[57]

Administrative divorce

In Korea, roughly 80% of all divorces are consensual divorces.[58] Before reforms enacted in 2007, couples seeking a consensual divorce appeared in family court and requested certification of their intent to divorce. The judge would then question the parties to confirm that they in fact agreed to divorce. If the judge was satisfied, the certificate was issued. The couple would then file the divorce with the mayor of the city in which their family registry was kept. The divorce was effective upon filing.

Some argued that this system, in which same-day divorce was quite possible, encouraged ill-considered divorces. Following a lengthy period of study by a specially-appointed committee, accordingly, and review of the proposals by the Ministry of Justice and the legislature, a series

52 Jinsu Yune, "The Reform of the Consensual Divorce Process and the Child Support Enforcement System in Korea," 11 *J. Korean L.* 247 (2012).

53 See text accompanying notes 61–62, *infra*.

54 Ingeborg Schwenzer, "Ten Years Divorce Reform in Switzerland," *2011 International Survey Fam. L.* 397, 400.

55 Jehanne Sosson, "Recent Evolutions (Or Revolutions) in Belgian Family Law," *2010 International Survey Fam. L.* 51, 56.

56 Anna Stepien-Sporek et al., "Divorce Law in Poland: A New Regime Needed?" *2013 International Survey Fam. L.* 321, 324.

57 Id. at 326.

58 Yune, *supra* note 52 at 249.

of experimental waiting periods were adopted by the Seoul Family Court in 2007. Waiting periods of one month were imposed for couples with no minor children. Waiting periods of three months were imposed for couples with minor children, or couples expecting a baby.[59] In addition, in the latter case, issues regarding custody, access, and child support had to be resolved, by the parties or by the court, before the certificate would be issued. The waiting period can be waived, if necessary, as in cases of domestic violence.[60] The new law changes consensual divorce from an administrative procedure to more of a judicial proceeding, at least where there are minor children.

France has adopted a new procedure for consensual divorce, which no longer requires that the parties appear before a judge. Rather, as of January 1, 2017, if the parties have agreed to the divorce and specific provisions regarding distribution of property, spousal support, and the custody and support of any minor children, they may enter into a written agreement, which is then signed by their respective lawyers. The parties then have fifteen days in which to withdraw. If neither does, they appear before a *notaire* who enters the written agreement into her minutes. The agreement is binding and enforceable as of that date.[61]

Contested divorces

In contested divorces, either or both parties seek a divorce before a recognized authority, a claim is filed, a hearing is held, and a judgment is entered.

Unilateral divorce

Divorce may be sought by one party over the objection of the other. This is known as 'unilateral divorce'. Under some laws, divorce may not be granted until the specific terms of support, custody, and property is determined by the parties or the court. In some states, this allows the objecting party to effectively deny the divorce, or at least to delay it for months or even years. In Japan, for example, the parties are required to attend court-sponsored divorce mediation sessions, assisted by court-appointed mediators. These sessions are often scheduled at lengthy intervals. Sessions every six months, for example, are not uncommon. By refusing to agree to terms, the reluctant party can delay the divorce for years.

Other contested divorces

The parties may both want a divorce, while agreeing on little else. They may seek the divorce on different grounds. Even where there are no direct legal consequences, it may be psychologically or socially important to either or both of the parties to be granted the divorce. While the number of divorces may have increased in many countries, adversarial divorces seem to be declining as less formal methods of dispute resolution, such as mediation, become increasingly popular. In Korea, for example, only 20% of divorces are adversarial.[62]

59 Id. at 251.

60 Id. at 250.

61 *Notaires de France*, Differents (sic) types of divorce, www.notaires.fr/en/differents-types-divorce, last visited March 27, 2017.

62 Id.

Recognition of foreign divorces

In some states, divorce is viewed as a question of status. Any court having jurisdiction over the party seeking the divorce can grant it. Whether the divorce will be recognized by other states is another matter.

Recognition of a foreign divorce depends on the law of the state in which such recognition is sought. This may be governed by treaties, such as those discussed below, to which the state is a party. In determining whether to recognize a foreign divorce, a civil law country will generally look to the national law of the spouses. In common law countries, the threshold question is whether the court which granted the divorce had jurisdiction to do so.[63]

If marriage is subject to religious law, as it is in the Catholic Church, where it is considered a sacrament, or as it is in Islamic states and in Israel, where religious norms govern marriage and divorce, divorce may not be available, at least for some parties.

The availability of divorce for same-sex couples has been problematic in the United States and in the European Union. In the United States, this was resolved by the Supreme Court's decisions in *Windsor, infra* and in *Obergefell v. Hodges.*[64] It remains problematic in the European Union.

The Convention on the Recognition of Divorces and Legal Separations, concluded June 1, 1970,[65] applies only to the recognition of a foreign state's determination dissolving marital status. It does not extend to findings of fault or property or support awards. The objective of the Convention is to facilitate the recognition of marriage dissolution among contracting states. It does so by providing that recognition depends upon specified links between the spouses, or either of them, and the state in which the divorce or separation was granted. As of June 4, 2014,[66] there were twenty states parties to this Convention.

In the European Union

Under rules promulgated by the European Commission, if a divorce involves two or more European Union countries, the parties may file joint or separate applications. Jurisdiction may be exercised by any state in which both parties live; in which they last lived together (if one party still lives there); or, if they are filing a joint application, in which one of them lives; where the respondent lives; where petitioner lives, and has lived for six months prior to filing and of which he or she is a national; or any state of which both parties are nationals. If petitions have been filed in two courts, either of which may exercise jurisdiction, the court in which the first petition is filed has jurisdiction. Jurisdiction regarding parental responsibility is limited to a court of the country in which the child lives.[67] A divorce or a legal separation granted in one European Union country will be recognized automatically by every other member of the European Union.

The law that governs the divorce is not necessarily the law of the country where the petition has been filed. Sixteen European Union countries have agreed on a single set of rules to determine which law should apply to cross-border divorces. These countries are: Austria, Belgium, Bulgaria, France, Germany, Greece, Hungary, Italy, Latvia, Lithuania, Luxembourg, Malta,

63 Lynn Wardle, "International Marriage and Divorce Regulation and Recognition: A Survey," 29 *Fam L.Q.* 498, 503–505 (1995), reprinted in Blair et al. *supra* note 4 at 296–297.

64 135 S. Ct. 1039 (2015).

65 The Convention on the Recognition of Divorces and Legal Separations, 978 U.N.T.S. 393 (1970) entered into force Aug. 24, 1975.

66 This is the date of the last official update on the Hague Conference on Private International Law website: www.hcch.net/en/home.

67 http://europa.eu/youreurope/citizens/family/couple/divorce-separation . . . (last visited 8/28/17.)

Portugal, Romania, Slovenia, and Spain. The rules they have accepted are known as the Rome III Regulation. Under Rome III, the parties in any of the sixteen countries set out above can agree to apply the divorce laws of: the country where they live; the country where they last lived together – if one of them still lives there; the country of which either of them is a national; or the country where they are filing for divorce. If the parties do not agree, courts in these sixteen countries will first apply the laws of the country where they live; second, the country where they last lived together – provided they still lived together there one year prior to filing the petition; third, the country of which both are nationals; or fourth, the country where they are filing their petition.

Denmark has opted out of all of the foregoing rules. The other Member States of the European Union are not participating, but may opt in if they later decide to do so pursuant to the "enhanced cooperation" mechanism set out in Article 20 of the Treaty on European Union (TEU).[68] As Professor Katharina Boele-Woelki observes, enhanced cooperation is available only when Union-wide agreement cannot be achieved. Two additional requirements must be met to trigger enhanced cooperation, however, and Boele-Woelki makes a persuasive case that neither has actually been satisfied here. First, the conflict of law rules adopted in connection with divorce and legal separation must "further the objectives of the Union". Second, they must "protect its interests and reinforce its integration process".[69] Neither the 'objectives' of the Union nor its interests and integration process are furthered by these rules, she argues. Rather, she suggests, "the area of international divorce law is too broad, and in fact too insignificant, to allow Europe to give up the unanimity which, to date, has always been achieved in cross-border family law matters".[70] Other commentators have also been critical of Rome III, noting that, "the European Union has in the end found a compromise – with the adoption of choice of law rules at European Union level without correspondent choice of court rules which does not achieve the purpose of simplifying European Union citizens' lives".[71]

In the United States

Comity

The general rule in the United States is that recognition of a foreign judgment is a matter of comity, which

> is neither a matter of absolute obligation, on the one hand, nor of mere courtesy and good will, upon the other. But it is the recognition which one nation allows within its territory to the legislative, executive or judicial acts of another nation, having due regard both to international duty and convenience, and to the rights of its own citizens or of other persons who are under the protection of its laws.[72]

United States courts have denied comity to foreign divorces where the foreign divorce has been found to offend public policy. Under this standard, courts have denied comity where the issuing

68 Katharina Boele-Woelki, "For Better or for Worse: the Europeanization of International Divorce Law," 12 *Yearbook of Private Int'l L.* 1, 6 (2010).

69 Id.

70 Id.

71 Ilaria Queirolo & Laura Carpaneto, "Party Autonomy Under the Rome III Regulation: An Unsatisfactory Compromise," *The European Legal Forum*, 29, 31 (2014).

72 *Hilton v. Guyot* 159 U.S. 113, 16 S.Ct. 139 (1895).

court lacked jurisdiction over the parties under the Due Process Clause of the United States Constitution because neither party was domiciled there, especially if the parties were United States domiciliaries at the time. The courts have done so even where the nation issuing the divorce did not require that either party be domiciled there.[73] Nor, if neither party is domiciled in the rendering state, will United States courts recognize unilateral *ex parte* divorces where the defendant does not appear or where neither party appears (even, in the latter case, if both parties consent to the divorce.)

When the foreign court has personal jurisdiction over the parties, in contrast, American courts are likely to recognize them. As Professor Ann Laquer Estin has pointed out, however, the question of comity in divorce cases may not be resolved by a determination that United States due process and jurisdictional requirements have been met:

> Substantive differences in the divorce laws of different countries, particularly where these differences suggest important problems of gender equality, may also factor into this decision. These questions are less important where the issue is whether to recognize a change in parties' marital status . . . and more important where the issue involves property, support, and other consequences of a divorce decree.[74]

The public policy of the state in which recognition is sought has also been offended where a Pakistani husband claimed to have divorced his wife by *talaq*, where the wife had already filed for divorce in Maryland.[75] The Maryland court held that *talaq*, which is the husband's sole prerogative under Islamic law, offended the public policy of Maryland. Comity will also be denied if the foreign decree was obtained by fraud.

Full faith and credit

Divorce is a matter of state law, rather than federal law, in the United States. Under the United States Constitution, every state must give "full faith and credit" to the judgment of every other state.[76] There is no "public policy" exception to the full faith and credit clause for divorces entered in other states of the United States.

The tension between domestic states recognizing the rights of same-sex couples to marry and divorce,[77] and states that did not, was anticipated by Congress, which enacted the Defense of Marriage Act (DOMA) in 1996.[78] DOMA had two major provisions. First, no state was required to "give effect to any marriage between persons of the same sex . . . or to any right or claim arising from such a relationship".[79]

Second, DOMA established that for purposes of federal law, marriage was limited to heterosexual couples. This meant that same-sex couples could not avail themselves of federal benefits enjoyed by opposite-sex couples, such as the exemption from federal estate tax upon the death

73 Blair et al., *supra* note 4 at 308–309 (citing *Williams v. North Carolina*, 325 U.S. 226 (1945)).

74 Ann Laquer Estin, "Toward a Multicultural Family Law," 38 *Fam. L.Q.* 501, 512 (2004).

75 *Alaem v. Alaem* 947 A.2d 489 (Md. 2008) (cited in Blair et al., *supra* note 4 at 309).

76 United States Constitution, Art. IV, §1 ("Full faith and Credit shall be given in each State to the public Acts, Records and Judicial Proceedings of every other state.")

77 In 2003, Massachusetts became the first state to recognize same-sex marriage as a constitutional right under the state constitution. *Goodridge v. Department of Public Health*, 798 N.E. 2d 941 (Mass. 2003).

78 DOMA (Pub. L. 104–199, 110 Stat. 2419, 1 U.S.C.§ 7 and 28 U.S.C. §1738 C.

79 Id.

of a spouse. When Edith Windsor's wife died, she challenged the second provision of DOMA under the equal protection clause of the federal Constitution. The Supreme Court agreed with her, striking down the provision limiting marriage to heterosexual couples for purposes of federal law, affirming the principle that, "[t]he Constitution's guarantee of equality 'must at the very least mean that a bare congressional desire to harm a politically unpopular group cannot' justify disparate treatment of that group."[80] Two years later, in *Obergefell*, the United States Supreme Court struck down the other provision of DOMA as unconstitutional. This means that every state must recognize same-sex marriages and allow same-sex couples access to their courts for divorce, from other states as well as from other countries.

'Limping' marriages

These are marriages that have been dissolved under the secular law of the state, but that have not been dissolved under the parties' religious law. This leaves the parties in marital limbo; they are single under state law, but unable to remarry under their own religious law. In order for them to do so, they must be freed of the bonds of matrimony under their respective religious laws. For Catholics, a 'canonical annulment', in which the church states that in fact there was no valid marriage, allows the parties to marry again. For Jews, if the husband refuses to give the wife a *get*, as explained below, her options under religious law are limited. Muslim women are similarly dependent on their husbands' agreement to the divorce, although some may be able to obtain a *mahr*.[81]

Under Jewish law, as accepted by Conservative, Orthodox, and Hasidic Jews, a marriage is a contract between the spouses, recognized by the community in a religious ceremony. The specific terms of the marriage contract are set out in the *ketubah*. For members of these groups, divorce requires a *get*, which can only be obtained by the husband, and which the wife must accept voluntarily. If the husband refuses to give the wife a *get*, she can petition the *Beth Din*, or rabbinical court, for assistance. This will only be granted under certain conditions, including the husband's impotence or refusal to support the wife. If the wife refuses to accept the *get*, on the other hand, the husband can initiate a special procedure (the permission of 100 rabbis), which is not an option for the wife. If the wife remarries without having obtained a *get*, she is an *agunah*, a 'chained women', and she cannot remarry under Jewish law. Any children she has with her new husband are regarded as illegitimate under Jewish law. Like their mother, they cannot marry under Jewish law, nor can their children.

A few jurisdictions have enacted legislation to assist such women. In New York, for example, the "Removal of barrier to remarriage" statute provides in pertinent part:

> 3. No final judgment of annulment or divorce shall thereafter be entered unless the plaintiff shall have filed and served a sworn statement: (i) that, to the best of his or her knowledge, he or she has, prior to the entry of such final judgment, taken all steps solely within his or her power to remove all barriers to the defendant's remarriage following the annulment or divorce, or (ii) that the defendant has waived in writing the requirements of this subdivision.[82]

80 *U.S. v. Windsor*, 133 S.Ct. 2675 (2013).

81 See Adelaide Madera, "Civil and Religious Law Concerning Divorce: The Condition of Women and Their Empowerment," 12 *J.L. & Fam. Stud.* 365 (2010) (examining efforts to accommodate religious practices in different legal contexts.) The *mahr* is the wife's dower, which the husband is required to pay in *talaq*. The *khul* is an agreement to allow the dissolution of marriage, if the wife seeks it, by making a payment to the husband. The payment is usually made by the wife relinquishing her claim to *mahr*. See *Interpreting Divorce Laws in Islam*, *supra* note 40 at 25.

82 N.Y. Domestic Relations Law, Art. 13§253.

As Professor Blair explains, courts have withheld divorce decrees in England and Wales, similarly, where one spouse has failed to remove an impediment to remarriage of the other, and courts in France and Canada have awarded compensatory damages to *agunahs*.[83]

Conclusion

This chapter has explained the substantive legal requirements for divorce, including a legal marriage and some basis, or justification, for the divorce. It has described the procedures through which states as well as religious authorities dissolve marriages, including extrajudicial divorce, consensual divorce, and contested divorce. Finally, it has discussed the circumstances under which foreign divorces are likely to be recognized and the problems created by 'limping' marriages, when divorce is recognized by one jurisdiction and not by another, as in the situation when a secular divorce is not recognized by a religious authority.

Bibliography

Ahmed, Aziza. Chapter 16. "Theories of state and family" (this volume).

Blair, Marianne, Merle H. Weiner, Barbara Stark, & Solangel Maldonado. *Family Law in the World Community* (Durham, NC: Carolina Academic Press, 3rd edn, 2015).

Boele-Woelki, Katharina. "For Better or for Worse: The Europeanization of International Divorce Law," 12 *Yearbook of Private Int'l L.* 1 (2010).

Farrugia, Ruth. "A Divorce Law for Malta; Act XIV 2011," *Int'l Fam. L.* 192 (2012).

Farrugia, Ruth. "The Position in Malta Juxtaposed to the Principles of European Family Law: Divorce and Maintenance," in *Juxtaposing Legal Systems and the Principles of European Family Law on Divorce and Maintenance* (Esin Örücü & Jane Mair eds, Cambridge, UK: Intersentia, 2007).

Gettleman, Jeffrey & Suhasini Raj. "India Strikes Down 'Instant Divorce' for Muslims," *New York Times*, Aug. 23, 2017 at A5.

Grant Bowman, Cynthia & Akua Kuenyehia. *Women and Law in Sub-Sahara Africa* (Acra, Ghana: Sedco Publishing, 2003).

Harding, Maehb. Chapter 1. "Marriage" (this volume).

Jansen, Yakare-Oule. "Muslim Brides and the Ghost of the Shari'a: Have the Recent Law Reforms in Egypt, Tunisia and Morocco Improved Women's Position in Marriage and Divorce, and Can Religious Moderates Bring Reform and Make It Stick?" 5 *Northwestern J. International Human Rights* 181 (2007).

Laquer Estin, Ann. "Toward a Multicultural Family Law," 38 *Fam. L.Q.* 501 (2004).

McClain, Linda. *The Place of Families: Fostering Capacity, Equality, and Responsibility*. (Cambridge, MA: Harvard University Press 2006).

Madera, Adelaide. "Civil and Religious Law Concerning Divorce: The Condition of Women and Their Empowerment," 12 *J.L. & Fam. Stud.* 365 (2010).

Mulitalo, Lalotoa & Jennifer Corrin. "Reform of Maintenance and Divorce Laws in Samoa: Appropriate for the 'AIGA'?" *2012 International Survey Fam. L.* 283.

Newcomb, Rachel. "Justice for Everyone? Implementation of Morocco's 2004 *Mudawana* Reforms," in *Interpreting Divorce Laws in Islam* (Rubya Mehdi et al. eds, Copenhagen: DJØF Publishing, 2012).

Örücü, Esin. "Turkish Family Law Facing the Principles of European Family Law," in *Juxtaposing Legal Systems and the Principles of European Family Law on Divorce and Maintenance* (Esin Örücü & Jane Mair eds, Cambridge, UK: Intersentia, 2007).

Queirolo, Ilaria & Laura Carpaneto. "Party Autonomy Under the Rome III Regulation: An Unsatisfactory Compromise," 29 *The European Legal Forum* (2014).

Rehman, Javaid. "The Sharia, Islamic Family Laws and International Human Rights Law: Examining the Theory and Practice of Polygamy and *Talaq*," 21 *International J. L., Policy, & Fam.* 1 (2007).

Schwenzer, Ingeborg. "Ten Years Divorce Reform in Switzerland," *2011 International Survey Fam. L.* 397.

83 Blair et al., *supra* note 4 at 214.

Sosson, Jehanne. "Recent Evolutions (Or Revolutions) in Belgian Family Law," *2010 International Survey Fam. L.* 51.

Stark, Barbara. "Maintenance," in *Family Law in New York* (Barbara Stark & Joanna Grossman eds, Durham, NC: Carolina Academic Press, 2016).

Stepien-Sporek, Anna, P. Stoppa, & M. Ryznar. "Divorce Law in Poland: A New Regime Needed?" *2013 International Survey Fam. L.* 324.

Verschraegen, Bea. Chapter 5, "Divorce," *International Encyclopedia of Comparative Law, Vol. IV, Persons and Family* (Dordrecht, The Netherlands: Marthinus Nijhoff Publishers, 2007).

Wardle, Lynn. "International Marriage and Divorce Regulation and Recognition: A Survey," 29 *Fam L.Q.* 498 (1995), reprinted in Blair et al. at 296.

Yune, Jinsu. "The Reform of the Consensual Divorce Process and the Child Support Enforcement System in Korea," 11 *J. Korean L.* 247 (2012).

5

Post-divorce maintenance for spouses

Geoffrey Shannon

Introduction

The issue of spousal support post-divorce is a divisive one. Following marital breakdown, the upkeep of two households undoubtedly results in a fall in both parties' standard of living and the payment of periodical maintenance by the earning spouse to the dependent spouse is often a necessary occurrence. In considering the general concept of maintenance post the granting of a decree of divorce, it is appropriate to first set out the contrasting rationales underpinning the ordering of post-divorce support, dissecting their strengths and weaknesses. This will involve a comprehensive review of the legal authorities in this area. It will then be necessary to review the applicable legislation in the area of maintenance. This necessitates consideration of the mandatory statutory criteria that the courts are to consider in determining whether to make a maintenance order and the appropriate level of any order ultimately made. Finally, it is appropriate to assess the duration of spousal support and the ability to subsequently vary maintenance orders made upon divorce.

Rationales for maintenance post-divorce

In considering the payment of maintenance as between ex-spouses, it is helpful to review the function and purpose for such support, assessing what maintenance in the context of divorce is designed to achieve. Such an assessment is informative when looking at how the judiciary exercises its discretion and reaches proper provision between the parties to a divorce. Is the ultimate aim to allow a "clean break" for the former spouses? Or is the provision of long-term support for the financially weaker spouse preferable? Should maintenance be seen as a form of compensation for the dependent spouse or is there a rehabilitative aim in ordering such support? Ultimately, it is submitted that neither a "clean break" nor the indefinite provision of support should be the desired objective or overarching concept governing the provision of support between former spouses. A preferable middle-ground is advocated for, namely the promotion of the use of maintenance provisions in facilitating an ordered and smooth transition from dependence to economic independence for the spouse who is in the more vulnerable position financially. This serves to encourage self-sufficiency, rather than long-term dependence and, while not guaranteeing a "clean break" between the parties, gives some hope of finality for ex-spouses. Whatever the rationale, what cannot be disputed is that the issue of financial provision upon divorce is a contentious one. This is particularly so in light of the economic reality for most families where two separate household units are required to be supported out of one pool of resources. This results in a decrease to all parties' standard of living, leaving both spouses less financially secure post-divorce.

Clean break

Over time, the concept of a "clean break" has emerged as a legitimate aim in fixing spousal support obligations. This has developed in light of the no-fault basis for divorce in many jurisdictions, as well as the general trend towards equality of the sexes and the promotion of self-sufficiency. The "clean break" principle gathered momentum in the United States in the 1970s and 1980s where, typically, it was employed by courts in ordering the sale of the marital assets, dividing the proceeds between the spouses. The "clean break" approach is arguably the most superficially attractive option upon the breakdown of a marriage. It facilitates finality and certainty between former spouses, meaning that once the parties are divorced and their assets reordered, they cannot be subject to a claim by the other person into the future. As the marriage is over and the divorce granted, the orders made by the court upon divorce are viewed as a final settlement and neither spouse therefore has any continuing financial obligations to the other.

The advantages of operating a "clean break" jurisdiction in divorce proceedings are therefore clear. It is "simple, clear and final"[1] and equates well with our notions of equality. Certainty is an obvious benefit and as stated by Denham J, a former Irish Chief Justice, "certainty and finality can be as important in [family law] as in other areas of the law".[2] The "clean break" approach enables the parties to establish a new life unencumbered by the former marriage and it enables each spouse to become self-sufficient, not dependent on ongoing contributions from the other spouse. Thorpe LJ in *Mawson v. Mawson*[3] held that it provided the ex-spouses with "peace of mind". He stated: "In the end I would only observe that peace of mind will be the benefit for [the wife in the case] and her former husband when the financial dependency between the parents is brought to termination."[4]

While simplicity, certainty and finality are attractive qualities, the "clean break" option only applies as between former spouses. It will not govern financial obligations between parents and their children. Thus, even in cases where a "clean break" is established between the parties, no such approach will be applicable to the maintenance obligations of a parent toward a dependent child of the family. Maintenance payments for the benefit of a child are discharged upon the cessation of the child's dependency.[5] There are a number of disadvantages in using the "clean break" principle as a general aim for all maintenance obligations. Arguably, it is not a practical solution at all and the notional aspirations of the rhetoric has outstripped the reality. In many marriages, women assume the major responsibility for domestic life and child rearing. As a result, they suffer major economic disadvantages and loss of employment opportunities within their marriage. It is therefore of paramount importance that maintenance for the economically vulnerable

1 D. Byrne, Former Irish Attorney General, "Foreword" in G. Shannon *The Divorce Act in Practice* (Dublin, Round Hall, 1999) viii.

2 *F. v. F. (Judicial Separation)* [1995] 2 IR 354. See also *D.T. v. C.T.* [2002] 3 IR 334.

3 [1994] 2 FLR 985; [1995] Fam Law 9.

4 At 991.

5 See s. 2 of the Irish Family Law (Divorce) Act 1996 (Number 33 of 1996).

spouse, often the woman, be kept on the public agenda until women are no longer disadvantaged financially by marriage itself. Weitzman stated that the "clean break" approach frequently causes the family home to be sold, leading to the "feminisation of poverty".[6] Eekelaar and Maclean similarly noted that there is a general movement into poverty by separated spouses with children, referencing the existence of child care responsibilities as having a significant economic impact on a couple's financial circumstances post-divorce.[7]

The emerging picture from the aforementioned research, therefore, demonstrated that the majority of separated or divorced women worked in sex-segregated, low-paid, insecure employment with limited sick-pay and pension entitlements and carried the twin burdens of the direct and opportunity costs of child care. The major argument against the "clean break" approach is thus that it fails to compensate the homemaker and caregiver for the economic disadvantages that have resulted for her and will continue beyond the separation of the spouses. Commenting on the "clean break" ideal, therefore, a former Irish Attorney General remarked:

> It could be said that [the "clean break" option] is in fact only useful for couples who have assets which may be sold and divided, for those couples where both parties are economically active outside the home, for those couples who are on an equal footing in terms of bargaining power and – in particular – for those couples who do not have children.[8]

Thus, the above statement indicates the difficulty with a "clean break" in many situations and that it may only be useful to certain divorcing spouses who are on an equal footing in terms of bargaining power. For many others, it will not be an option. A further disadvantage of the principle of a "clean break" is that it can only address events up to the time of the separation or divorce. It is not concerned about the future. In this regard, it fails to recognise the more vulnerable financial position that the custodial parent will be in post-divorce. The need for on-going care for any children of the marriage will curtail the already impaired earning capacity of the custodial spouse and therefore her capacity for self-support. A "clean break" will not account for this. Ultimately, therefore, it can be seen that there are benefits and difficulties with a "clean break" approach. This is not to say that the "clean break" option should not be one of the options for the court to choose from in divorce cases, but it certainly should not be the definitive approach.

Long-term payment of maintenance

In complete contrast to the "clean break" ideal, an alternative rationale underpinning financial relief upon the breakdown of marriage is the principle that spouses have a long-term obligation to maintain one another, dissolution of the marriage notwithstanding. This envisages the indefinite provision of periodical payments from one spouse to the other, in recognition of the recipient spouses' more vulnerable financial position. The long-term provision of maintenance addresses some of the foregoing concerns with the "clean break" doctrine. Such a continuing obligation of support recognises that one spouse within the marriage may have suffered a loss of opportunity and ability to make economic gains by virtue of his or her role within the marriage – a loss that cannot be rectified post-divorce in light of, for instance, the parties' age or lack of

6 L.J. Weitzman, "Alimony: Its Premature Demise and Recent Resurgence in the U.S." in L.J. Weitzman and M. Maclean (eds), *The Economic Consequences of Divorce* (Oxford, Clarendon Press, 1992) 247.

7 J. Eekelaar and M. Maclean, *Maintenance after Divorce* (Oxford, Clarendon Press, 1984) 60.

8 Byrne in Shannon *supra* note 1 at viii–ix.

future employment opportunities. Furthermore, it enables recourse to be made to the courts in the future where circumstances have changed, or hardship is endured, thereby taking into account the unpredictable nature of life and adapting to any developments that take place. There is no severing of ties with the divorce decree. This approach, however, can also result in injustice. It fails to recognise that a divorce is the cessation of the marriage contract and that the rights and duties attendant upon that contract should thus similarly cease. It prevents spouses from moving on, gaining independence and having finality in their affairs.

Ireland is a good example of a jurisdiction that, in its divorce legislation, allows for the long-term payment of maintenance. An order for periodical payments made upon a divorce pursuant to section 13 of the Family Law (Divorce) Act 1996 may continue indefinitely, despite the fact that the union between the parties is no longer recognised. The order will cease, however, upon the remarriage or death of the recipient spouse. Only if either significant event occurs will the debtor spouse be definitively relieved of his or her obligations. Thus, the dissolution of a marriage does not result in a corresponding alteration to the law governing maintenance as an ancillary relief. While there is no provision for a "clean break" in Irish legislation, and while the Irish legal regime allows for financial support to continue between former spouses post-divorce, a "clean break" has been recognised as a desired objective by the Irish judiciary. This is discussed below.

Irish courts' approach to a "clean break"

The issue as to whether or not a "clean break" is facilitated by Ireland's divorce legislation has been addressed in a number of Supreme Court judgments, most importantly in the cases of *K. v. K.*[9] and *T. v. T.*[10] It was first, however, discussed at length by the High Court in *J.D. v. D.D.*[11] In that case, the question arose

> whether it is open to the court to endeavour to create a situation of finality, what is commonly called a 'clean break', by making a sizeable lump sum order in favour of the wife and making no order for periodic maintenance.[12]

This case involved the ending of a 30-year-long marriage, where there were considerable financial resources available for distribution. Considering the provisions of the Irish Family Law (Maintenance of Spouses and Children) Act 1976, McGuinness J. noted that since its enactment, it has not been possible to make an order that severs the right of a spouse to apply for maintenance. Notwithstanding the payment of a large lump sum, a spouse could still apply for a periodical order into the future or seek to vary any such order. Therefore, no "clean break" could be made upon granting the dissolution of a marriage. The court stated:

> Just as the payment of a large capital sum for an annuity could not prevent the wife, in certain circumstances, from applying for further maintenance in the future, so also it could not prevent the husband, if he fell on hard times, from applying for maintenance to be paid to him by the wife, thus reducing her annuity income.[13]

9 [2001] 3 IR 371.
10 *Supra* note 2.
11 [1997] 3 IR 64.
12 At 88.
13 Ibid.

The Irish High Court went on to consider specifically the provisions of both the Family Law Act 1995 and the Family Law (Divorce) Act 1996, querying whether in cases where there are ample resources, the policy of the court should be to provide a "clean break" and finality as between the parties. She concluded that such finality was clearly not the intention of the *Oireachtas* (that is the Irish legislature), as it had legislated to permit repeated applications to court concerning ancillary relief. McGuinness J. thus held:

> It appears to me that by the subsequent enactment of the Family Law Act, 1995 and the Family Law (Divorce) Act, 1996, the Oireachtas has made it clear that a "clean break" situation is not to be sought and that, if anything, financial finality is virtually to be prevented . . . The court, in making virtually any order in regard to finance and property on the breakdown of a marriage, is faced with the situation where finality is not and never can be achieved. This also appears to mean that no agreement on property between the parties can be completely final, since such finality would be contrary to the policy and provisions of the legislation. The statutory policy is, therefore, totally opposed to the concept of a "clean break".[14]

Confirming that a "clean break" was not possible, McGuinness J. then proceeded to determine the appropriate level of maintenance payable in the particular circumstances of the case where ample financial resources were available. The court considered the factors set out in section 20(2) of the Family Law (Divorce) Act 1996, but noted that they were subject to the overall discretion of the court. She held that in cases such as this, where there are considerable family assets, the court is not limited to providing for the dependent spouse's actual immediate needs through a periodic maintenance order. The court may seek to ensure that the applicant will continue to enjoy the lifestyle to which she was accustomed into the future through the making of a lump sum order. In this case, the court found the fact that the wife was a "stay at home" wife who had played an equal, albeit non-income producing, role in the marriage to be a very relevant consideration. She thus concluded as follows:

> On a practical level this marriage was a lengthy partnership of complementary roles and it seems to me that it should result in a reasonably equal division of the accumulated assets. I will therefore order the payment of a lump sum by way of maintenance of £200,000 by the husband to the wife in addition to his financing of the wife's residence.[15]

The lump sum order of £200,000 was granted in addition to a periodical maintenance order of £20,000 per annum. While this case concerned judicial separation proceedings as opposed to proceedings under the Divorce Act, McGuinness J. referred to the breakdown of the marriage throughout and made no distinction between maintenance payable under the Family Law (Maintenance of Spouses and Children) Act 1976 or the Divorce Act.

The concept of a "clean break" was subsequently considered by the Irish Supreme Court in *K. v. K.*[16] In this case, the court considered an appeal against a decision of Lavan J. in the High Court, in which he had directed that the applicant wife was entitled to half of the respondent husband's income together with a lump sum of £1.5 million, which represented approximately

14 Ibid. at 89.
15 Ibid. at 95.
16 *Supra* note 9.

half of the respondent's assets. The Supreme Court remitted the case back to the High Court, as the trial judge had not given reasons for the manner in which he had exercised his discretion under section 20 of the 1996 Irish Divorce Act. In the course of her judgment, McGuinness J. reviewed developments in English case law, in particular the House of Lords decision in *White v. White.*[17] In that case, the decades of English jurisprudence in which ancillary orders were made based on the "reasonable requirements" standard which had prevailed in big-money cases was swept away. The House of Lords stated that there was nothing in existing statute to indicate that once the applicant's needs were met, any surplus of matrimonial assets were to remain with the other party. This "reasonable requirements" approach was found to be discriminatory in its nature, based on the erroneous assumption that a party who made money was making a greater contribution than the party who undertook a domestic role. Instead, a "yardstick of equality" was emphasised by the court. The House of Lords held that while there was no statutory presumption of equal division of assets, equality should not be departed from unless there was good reason for so doing.

McGuinness J. stated that the concept of a single capital payment to the wife in a divorce case in order to meet her "reasonable requirements" for the remainder of her life was not a concept that had ever formed part of Irish law. She took the view that a lump sum payment of that kind was inevitably a part of a "clean break" settlement, which was "neither permissible nor possible" under the Irish Family Law Divorce Act of 1996.[18] She also emphasised that the approach of the Irish courts in accordance with article 41.2 of the Irish Constitution and the statutory guidelines has been to give full credit to the wife's contribution through her work in the home and as a mother to her children. McGuinness J. referenced the considerable discretion of the court in determining proper provision in divorce cases. She emphasised, however, that this discretion must be exercised having regard to the mandatory statutory guidelines, and stated that the court is obliged to consider each factor set out in section 20 of the Irish 1996 Divorce Act, measuring their relevance and weight according to the facts of each individual case. Ultimately, in *K. v. K.*, the Supreme Court therefore emphasised fairness as a guiding principle, and stressed that a "clean break" approach was impossible in light of the provisions of Ireland's divorce legislation.

In the later case of *T. v. T.*,[19] the Supreme Court again considered the issue of whether or not a "clean break" is facilitated by Irish divorce legislation. This case concerned a decision of Lavan J. in the High Court in which, in divorce proceedings, he had awarded the respondent wife a lump sum of £5 million (€6.35 million), in three instalments, together with maintenance in the sum of £800 per month for the youngest dependent child of the marriage. The parties had been married for 22 years and there were three children of the marriage. The applicant husband had emphasised in the proceedings that 80% of his assets had been acquired after the date of the parties' separation. In granting the lump sum relief, Lavan J. reviewed the factors set out in section 20 of the 1996 Act, noting the ample assets of the parties and that in the later years of their married life, they had enjoyed an exceptional standard of living. He did not view his decision to make such substantial lump sum payments as introducing the concept of "clean break" into Irish law. He saw these payments as making provision for the financial security of the respondent. The court reviewed the House of Lords decision in *White v. White*[20] and endorsed the view of Mance L.J. in *Cowan v. Cowan*[21] to the effect that the assessment of assets must take place at the date of the trial or appeal.

17 [2000] 3 FLR 555.
18 At 16.
19 *Supra* note 9, at 383.
20 *Supra* note 17.
21 [2001] 2 FLR 982.

On appeal to the Supreme Court, the decision of Lavan J. in relation to the lump sum orders granted to the respondent wife was affirmed. The Supreme Court held that in determining proper provision, the totality of the factors set out in the 1996 Act must be taken into account and applied and in certain cases, in particular "ample resources" cases, the appropriate manner of making proper provision may be to order the payment of a substantial lump sum from one spouse to the other. The court, by a majority of four to one, held that the absence of a "clean break" principle in Irish divorce law did not prevent the payment of a lump sum order as part of the proper provision for a spouse, even where no order for periodic payments by way of maintenance has been made. Denham J. commented:

> There is nothing in the Constitution or legislation which prohibits a lump sum as part of a financial ancillary order . . . The fact that . . . a lump sum order may exclude or greatly limit any further order by a court does not make the provision improper or the order unfair. The underlying principle of the Act of 1996 is fairness.[22]

In this vein, the court made reference to section 20(5) of the 1996 Act, which provides that the court shall not make orders for ancillary relief unless it would be in the interests of justice to do so.

Keane C.J., in his judgment, stated that he did not believe that the *Oireachtas* intended that the courts should exclude the possibility of achieving certainty and finality when financially reordering the assets upon divorce. He disagreed with the view of McGuinness J. in *J.D. v. D.D.*[23] that Irish legislative policy is opposed to the concept of a "clean break" and he stated that the trial judge in the particular case

> appears to have effected a "clean break" between the parties in financial terms insofar as that is permissible having regard to the constitutional and legal provisions; and, given the desirability of avoiding future litigation between spouses whose marriages have irretrievably broken down, I have no doubt that this was the correct approach for him to have adopted.[24]

The judgment of Keane C.J. in *T. v. T.* necessarily overrides the abovementioned High Court decision in *J.D. v. D.D.* and the contrasting interpretation of the relevant statutory provisions contained therein. Evidently, the Irish Supreme Court judgment in *T. v. T.* marks a significant departure from previous judicial interpretation of Irish maintenance legislation. This decision undoubtedly allows for a "clean break" to be facilitated in certain big money cases in so far as this is permitted by the Constitution and the 1996 Act. In particular, it appears that lump sum orders can be utilised to achieve a "clean break".

In two further authorities, the concept of a "clean break" in the context of divorce was raised. In *B. v. B.*,[25] the High Court considered whether a "clean break" could be facilitated as between the husband and wife. In this case, while the financial resources of the parties were significant, much of those resources had been re-invested into additional business ventures. This restricted the capital available for distribution and Abbott J. thus took the view that the case could not, at that point in time, be described as being one of ample resources. The court, however, determined that there was a likelihood of the business ventures being realized into the future which would

22 *Supra* note 2, at 382.
23 *Supra* 2, at 372.
24 *Supra* note 2, at 372.
25 [2007] IEHC 491.

result in a sizeable windfall. Three potential courses of action were therefore considered by the High Court in order to properly provide for each of the parties.

The court first considered assessing the present finances of the parties, making provision because of these finances. Either party then could seek further provision in the future by bringing an application in the event of a change of circumstances. The second option was to adjourn the matter to enable the parties to seek further relief in the future in the event of the business assets improving. Abbott J. ultimately applied the third option in the case, namely to provide a means by which the assets that may be realized in the medium term (five years in this case) would be calculated – setting parameters thereto. He thus ordered that the husband hold 90% of his shares representing his 50% shareholding in the business in question on trust to the benefit of the wife. The wife was in a position to hold or dispose of same, but not during the first five years following the making of the order. Whilst the wife was to be entitled to the dividends in respect of the shareholding, she was not entitled to call for the vesting of the shares, thereby enabling the husband to retain control in the business. The court concluded that if the shares realized in excess of €5 million, the case would be regarded as an "ample resources" case and such lump sum payment to the wife would be regarded in full and final settlement of all matters between the parties, in addition to the further orders granted to ensure financial provision.

In *Y.G. v. N.G.*,[26] the parties had entered into a separation agreement in 1996 pursuant to which the respondent husband provided a capital sum, maintenance, health insurance and a house for the applicant wife. Contained within the separation agreement was a "full and final settlement" clause, purporting to be a final settlement of all matters arising between the parties, to be incorporated into any court decree of separation or divorce. Subsequently, the applicant wife sought a decree of divorce and sought additional provision to that which was agreed within the separation agreement. At the time of the parties' divorce, the husband's net wealth was approximately €21 million, while the wife had suffered an illness which rendered her unfit to work. In the High Court, a decree of divorce was granted. The court also made substantial additional provision for the wife. On appeal to the Irish Supreme Court, the court considered whether the trial judge had given proper weight to the separation agreement and the terms set out therein. In allowing the husband's appeal, the Supreme Court discussed at length the general principles to be applied to cases where there had been a previous settlement agreement. Of note, the court held that Irish law did not establish a right to a "clean break". It stated, however, that this was a legitimate aspiration. The Supreme Court cited the judgment of Keane C.J. in *T v. T*,[27] emphasising that in appropriate circumstances, a court could seek to achieve certainty and finality.

The abovementioned authorities from Ireland's superior courts indicate that divorce legislation in Ireland does not provide for a "clean break". There is provision in Irish law for spouses to seek variations of orders into the future whatever orders the court granted upon divorce, and the legal obligation to maintain a former spouse after the granting of a decree is clear within the relevant legislation. Nevertheless, the decision in *T. v. T.* and subsequent case law serve to indicate that a "clean break" is a possibility in cases where there are "ample resources". The fear and concern with this line of jurisprudence is the creation of a two-tier system of divorce in Ireland. On the one hand, there will be those parties with significant financial resources available to them, who may be able to achieve finality and certainty through lump sum orders. On the other hand, however, there will be the majority of citizens who, even post-divorce, will have to live under the continued threat of repeated court applications for maintenance, never achieving a definitive end to their financial obligations in respect of their former spouse.

26 [2011] 3 IR 717.
27 *Supra* note 2.

Maintenance to rehabilitate or compensate?

As is demonstrated in the foregoing discussion, both the "clean break" and long-term payment of maintenance rationales have their difficulties. Neither represents a flawless approach to the provision of maintenance. There is therefore a necessity to consider other motivations that may be employed to govern the provision of maintenance post-divorce. One such option is to allow for "rehabilitative maintenance". This would essentially involve the appropriate division of the marital assets, with periodical maintenance payments being made on a short-term basis only to the former dependent spouse. In this regard, the economically more vulnerable spouse is provided with a short-term support cushion, thereby giving him or her time to seek to establish himself or herself in the working environment. It can be described in some ways as a "clean break with a cushion". Clearly, the period in which the maintenance would be payable would vary with the facts of each individual case. The rehabilitative maintenance model was considered by the Scottish Law Commission in its *Report on Aliment and Financial Provision* and now forms part of the Family Law (Scotland) Act, 1985.[28] The objective of this model was cited as "to award such sums as were necessary to assist a divorced spouse to regain an independent role in society and to relieve hardship during the rehabilitative process."[29]

The concept of "rehabilitative maintenance" as a formula for financial provision upon divorce has been subject to criticism. This approach often fails to compensate for the reality of post-divorce situations, where dependent spouses – who have been dependent for all their married life, working within the family home – will suffer in any attempt to re-enter the workforce. They will most likely fail to ever realize their full earning capacity because of their long-term absence from employment, and a short-term cushion will not rectify this. Furthermore, the term "rehabilitative" is far from an ideal adjective to govern maintenance post-divorce – bringing to mind the notion that the non-earning spouse is in need of rehabilitation following on from his or her life within the home. Such a troublesome phrase has no place in already contentious divorce litigation. A rehabilitation approach is based on providing limited support to allow the dependent spouse to become self-sufficient. As pointed out by Eekelaar and Maclean,[30] however, this is essentially another manifestation of the "needs" approach – the approach abandoned in England which provides that once the dependent spouse's financial needs are met, the remaining surplus of assets should remain with the earning spouse. This was based on the assumption that the party who makes money is making a greater contribution than the party who undertakes a domestic role.

A preferable option for the provision of maintenance after divorce is a compensation model – viewing maintenance as a way to compensate a spouse, as opposed to rehabilitate him or her. This is perhaps the most desirable option in that it provides a rationale that is both fair and workable. It allows for a spouse to be compensated for the losses and sacrifices made by him or her in favour of the other spouse during the course of the marriage. In this case, the formulation of maintenance amounts would not be an arbitrary procedure but rather would be founded upon actual events and spousal behaviour during the marriage. Maclean, Weitzman and Eekelaar recommend a "compensatory" role for spousal maintenance, arguing that if women are expected to put their earning capacities on hold while they care for children during marriage, then it is only fair to recognise and compensate them for the impairment and dependency which that creates.[31] The

28 Scottish Law Commission, *Report on Aliment and Financial Provision*, No. 67 of 1981.

29 At 87, para. 3.50.

30 See Eekelaar and Maclean *supra* note 7.

31 *Supra* notes 6 and 7.

compensation model views marriage as a partnership. In this regard, there has been a renewed interest in maintenance for wives as the legal mechanism that balances the inequalities of divorce and honours the partnership ideals of the marriage contract. The Californian Appeal Court in *Re Marriage of Brantner* graphically articulated this aim:[32]

> A woman is not a breeding cow to be nurtured during her years of fecundity, then conveniently converted into cheap steaks when past her prime . . . [T]he husband simply has to face up to the fact that his support responsibilities are going to be of extended duration – perhaps for life. This has nothing to do with feminism, sexism, male chauvinism or any other trendy, social ideology. It is ordinary common sense, basic decency and simple justice.

In the House of Lords decision of *Miller v. Miller: McFarlane v. McFarlane*,[33] support can be seen for the concept of compensation as a rationale behind the provision of maintenance. In this case, the court emphasised three principles that it said should guide the court when making financial awards upon divorce – need, compensation and sharing. Specifically, in relation to compensation, this was promoted as a basis for recognising relationship-generated disadvantage as the wife in these proceedings had given up a potentially lucrative career to care for the parties' children. The husband had continued in his employment and enjoyed a vast income, with plenty of surplus income after the parties' ongoing needs had been met. Instead of determining that the wife had a need for some of the surplus income to provide for her retirement, the House of Lords held that she was entitled to be compensated for the loss she had suffered arising out of the relationship. In the later case of *S.A. v. P.A. (Pre-marital agreement: Compensation)*,[34] however, a more limited view of compensation was taken. Mostyn J. held that compensation should be restricted to cases where there is "almost near certainty" that a claimant was giving up a very high earning career and otherwise would have enjoyed remuneration of at least equivalent to that of the respondent.[35]

Ireland: an example of a long-term payment of maintenance regime

In June 1996, the Fifteenth Amendment to the Constitution Bill was signed by the President of Ireland. Following a narrow referendum, article 41.3.2 was introduced into the Irish Constitution (*Bunreacht na hÉireann*), providing for the dissolution of marriage for the first time in Irish law. It allows a court to grant a divorce in specific stringent circumstances and legislative provision for divorce was subsequently made under the Family Law (Divorce) Act 1996. The 1996 Act commenced on 27 February 1997. Pursuant to section 5 thereof, an Irish court can only grant a decree of divorce where it is satisfied that at the date of the institution of proceedings, the spouses have lived separate and apart from one another for a period of at least four years during the previous five years; that there is no reasonable prospect of reconciliation between the spouses; and that such provision as the court considers proper exists or will be made for the spouses and any dependent members of the family. Evidently, therefore, the constitutional and legislative provisions in respect of divorce require that "proper provision" be made for both spouses and any dependent members of the family upon the granting of a divorce decree.

32 67 Cal. App. 3d 4lb at 419–420 (1977).
33 [2006] UKHL 24.
34 [2014] EWHC 392 (Fam).
35 At 1040.

Part III of the Family Law (Divorce) Act 1996 sets out a comprehensive range of ancillary reliefs that are available in the context of divorce, including pension adjustment orders, financial compensation orders and property adjustment orders. The court uses the range of measures provided for in Part III to ensure that proper provision is made as between the spouses, regulating the parties' financial affairs and assets following the end of their marriage. Maintenance orders are a necessary part of this ancillary regime and may be made under section 13 of the 1996 Act. This may include periodical payments orders, lump sum orders and secured periodical payments orders. While, therefore, there is a general duty in law upon each spouse to maintain each other according to the Irish Social Welfare (Consolidation) Act 1993, the 1996 Act makes it clear that this obligation of support continues post-divorce and it specifically enables the court to make maintenance orders as between ex-spouses.

Maintenance under the Family Law (Divorce) Act 1996

There exists a common law duty upon spouses to maintain one another, whether or not they continue to reside with one another or live separately and apart. This duty is preserved in legislation, as demonstrated in the Social Welfare (Consolidation) Act 1993, and survives throughout the marital relationship, continuing even after its termination. Liability to a former spouse only ceases when the recipient spouse dies or remarries. Pursuant to section 13 of the Family Law (Divorce) Act 1996, upon granting a decree of divorce, or at any time thereafter, the court may make:

- a periodical payments order, that is, an order that either spouse shall make to the other spouse for his or her benefit or for the benefit of a dependent member of the family such periodical payments of such amount, during such period and at such times as may be specified in the order;
- a secured periodical payments order, requiring the debtor spouse to secure such periodical payments to the satisfaction of the court;
- a lump sum payments order requiring either spouse to make to the other spouse a lump sum payment or payments of such amount or amounts at such time or times as may be specified.

While section 13 does not provide for the making of retrospective maintenance orders to take account of the non-payment of maintenance prior to the institution of the proceedings, the court may direct that a lump sum be paid to one spouse by the other to discharge any liabilities or expenses reasonably incurred prior to the issuing of the application. Maintenance orders can be enforced by seeking an attachment of earnings order, meaning that periodical payments are made directly to the recipient spouse by the maintenance debtor's employer. Following the granting of a divorce decree, section 2(2)(c) of the Irish Divorce Act provides that a reference to a "spouse" includes a reference to a person who is a party to a marriage that has been dissolved under the Divorce Act for the purposes of the rights and remedies available to him or her under this Act. It is clear, therefore, that the obligation to maintain your spouse is an ongoing one in Irish law, which continues post-divorce and may only cease upon death or re-marriage.

Factors considered in making maintenance orders

In Ireland, in divorce cases, the court is charged with ensuring that proper provision exists and will be made, having regard to the circumstances, for the spouses and any dependent members of the family pursuant to section 5(1)(c) of the 1996 Divorce Act. Section 2(1) of the Act defines a dependent member of the family as any child of either or both of the spouses under the age of 18, or under the age of 23 if the child is in full-time education. Securing "proper provision" will therefore be the basis for the court's order and inform any maintenance order it decides to make. The court, however, has a wide discretion in determining what is "proper" in the overall circumstances of each particular case. This discretion is exercisable within a framework of specific statutory criteria. Section 20(1) of the 1996 Act provides that the court, in deciding whether to make ancillary orders, including those under section 13 regarding maintenance, and in determining the provisions of such an order, must ensure that, having regard to the circumstances, proper provision exists or will be made for the spouses and any dependent member of the family concerned. Without prejudice to the generality of subsection 1, section 20(2) sets out those specific factors to which the court is to have regard in deciding whether to make orders for ancillary relief on the granting of a decree of divorce. The twelve factors included in subsection 2(a) to (l) are as follows:

(a) the income, earning capacity, property and other financial resources which each of the spouses concerned has or is likely to have in the foreseeable future;
(b) the financial needs, obligations and responsibilities which each of the spouses has or is likely to have in the foreseeable future (whether in the case of the remarriage or registration in a civil partnership of the spouse or otherwise);
(c) the standard of living enjoyed by the family concerned before the proceedings were instituted or before the spouses commenced to live apart from one another, as the case may be;
(d) the age of each of the spouses, the duration of their marriage and the length of time during which the spouses lived with one another;
(e) any physical or mental disability of either of the spouses;
(f) the contributions which each of the spouses has made or is likely in the foreseeable future to make to the welfare of the family, including any contribution made by each of them to the income, earning capacity, property and financial resources of the other spouse and any contribution made by either of them by looking after the home or caring for the family;
(g) the effect on the earning capacity of each of the spouses of the marital responsibilities assumed by each during the period when they lived with one another and, in particular, the degree to which the future earning capacity of a spouse is impaired by reason of that spouse having relinquished or foregone the opportunity of remunerative activity in order to look after the home or care for the family;
(h) any income or benefits to which either of the spouses is entitled by or under statute;
(i) the conduct of each of the spouses, if that conduct is such that in the opinion of the court it would in all the circumstances of the case be unjust to disregard it;
(j) the accommodation needs of either of the spouses;
(k) the value to each of the spouses of any benefit (for example, a benefit under a pension scheme) which by reason of the decree of divorce concerned, that spouse will forfeit the opportunity or possibility of acquiring;
(l) the rights of any person other than the spouses but including a person to whom either spouse is remarried.

This is clearly a comprehensive list of matters which the court must consider and there is no hierarchy to these factors. It is for the trial judge to decide what weight, if any, is to be given to each of them having regard to the circumstances of the particular case. The trial judge must, however, consider all of the factors set out in section 20. This was emphasised by McGuinness J.

in *K. v. K.*,[36] where she stated that full regard must be paid to the guidelines set out in section 20 when calculating the appropriate ancillary relief to be made.

While the court must be satisfied that proper provision is made for each spouse and any dependent member of the family, "proper provision" is not defined in the 1996 Act. Each case will be decided on its own facts and the court will determine what constitutes proper provision in the circumstances. The reference to "all the circumstances" means that a subjective view will be taken of each family's situation and there are no standards or guidelines in place as to what constitutes proper provision in general. This was made clear in the Supreme Court decision of *T. v. T.*,[37] where all five members of the court agreed that the trial judge has an overriding discretion in determining what constitutes proper provision in the circumstances of a particular case.

Duration and variation of maintenance orders

A maintenance order made by the court will order one spouse to make to the other spouse such periodical payments, lump sum payments or secured periodical payments of such amount, during such period and at such times as may be specified in the order. Sections 13(4) and (5) of the 1996 Act set out the circumstances when financial obligations between the spouses will definitively terminate with no possibility of resurrection, namely upon the death of either spouse or on the remarriage of the recipient, or beneficiary, spouse. Orders for periodic and secured periodic payments under section 13 of the Irish Divorce Act thus automatically stop operating on the death of either spouse or the remarriage of the receiving spouse. Support obligations after divorce therefore have the capacity to continue for the lifetime of the spouses, save in very limited circumstances.

In some orders made upon a divorce, the court may specifically determine, as part of granting proper provision, that maintenance will cease at a particular point in time – for instance upon the retirement of the debtor spouse. This occurred in the English decision of *H. v. H.*[38] and, in some ways, this can be viewed as a "deferred clean break". Here, the husband had been paying an annual maintenance sum to his first wife. He later remarried and had two young children with his second wife. Unfortunately, his second wife was diagnosed with terminal cancer and he intended to retire from his employment upon her death. He thus applied to court to discharge a maintenance order in favour of his first wife. Considering the first wife's financial position and income needs for the rest of her life, the court ordered that the maintenance order would cease upon the retirement of the husband. At that stage, he was ordered to pay a lump sum to the wife of almost three years' maintenance to discharge entirely his maintenance obligations. While there is no "clean break" in some jurisdictions such as Ireland, often the retirement of the debtor is borne in mind by all parties to divorce proceedings and settlements reached often include provisions for the reduction or cessation of maintenance upon retirement. In many cases, pension adjustment orders are granted in favour of the recipient spouse to replace maintenance in the event of retirement.

Pursuant to section 22 of the Irish Divorce Act, orders – including maintenance orders – may be varied, suspended, reviewed or discharged upon the application of either spouse, once the court is satisfied that it is proper to do so. The court will only alter an order if there is either a change in circumstances or any new evidence has come to light. The effect of section 22 is to

36 *Supra* note 9.
37 *Supra* note 2.
38 [2014] EWHC 760 (Fam).

permit the variation of previously granted ancillary orders into perpetuity. Lump sum orders that are not being paid in instalments, however, cannot be varied. Maintenance as a concept therefore is always reviewable under Irish divorce law. As maintenance may be altered and the amount increased or decreased depending on the circumstances, the assessment of earning capacity in considering proper provision in section 20(2) of the 1996 Irish Divorce Act is limited to the current and reasonably foreseeable future.

Conclusion

It is evident that the issue of spousal support post-divorce is a divisive one. Following marital breakdown, the upkeep of two households undoubtedly results in a fall in both parties' standard of living and the payment of periodical maintenance by the earning spouse to the dependent spouse is often a necessary occurrence. A number of competing rationales are proffered to govern the concept of maintenance ordered upon divorce – namely, to provide a "clean break" for the former spouses; to ensure the long-term financial support for the dependent spouse; to rehabilitate; or to compensate. In Ireland, for example, it is clear that there is an absence of legislative provision for a "clean break". Nevertheless, where the resources of the parties allow for it, the Supreme Court has emphasised that the possibility of achieving certainty and finality is not excluded from the options available to the courts. Irish law, however, does specifically allow for the long-term provision of maintenance, and maintenance orders made upon divorce may continue in operation indefinitely, only ceasing when the recipient spouse dies or remarries.

What is clear from the foregoing is that no single concept alone can definitively govern the provision of maintenance post-divorce in any legal system. Where possible, the payment of maintenance between former spouses should seek to facilitate a smooth transition from dependence to economic independence for the financially vulnerable spouse – enabling certainty to be achieved at some point between the parties, but ensuring the dependent spouse is provided for until such time as he or she is self-sufficient. Despite the obvious benefits of such an approach, it will not be appropriate in every case and ultimately each case must be determined in light of its own specific and individual set of circumstances. Our courts should be tasked with providing "proper provision" as between the spouses and this, therefore, should be the overriding consideration of the judiciary in making any ancillary orders upon divorce, including maintenance.

Bibliography

Eekelaar, J. and Maclean, M. *Maintenance after Divorce* (Oxford, Clarendon Press, 1984).

Scottish Law Commission. *Report on Aliment and Financial Provision*, No. 67 of 1981.

Shannon, G. *The Divorce Act in Practice* (Dublin, Round Hall, 1999).

Weitzman, L.J. "Alimony: Its Premature Demise and Recent Resurgence in the U.S." in L.J. Weitzman and M. Maclean (eds) *The Economic Consequences of Divorce* (Oxford, Clarendon Press, 1992) 247.

6

Distribution of property on divorce

Bill Atkin

Introduction: no uniformity

The internationalisation of family law has been with us for some time. It plays out in the context of matrimonial property because of the greater mobility of families, the greater capacity to invest in property overseas, and, with the contemporary level of relationship breakdown, the greater number of disputes with cross-border factors. In short, the chances that a case will involve property in more than one jurisdiction or parties living in different jurisdictions are not insignificant. It is therefore increasingly important to have an understanding of the general approaches to property division.

Internationalisation also suggests that we should be aiming for harmonisation of the law especially in relation to private international law rules, but unfortunately this may be wishful thinking. We need only look to Europe, where harmonisation is a common goal for the law in general but where progress on matrimonial property has taken a long time. When looking at the global picture, the lack of uniformity stands out. While a few more patterns are discernible in the civil law jurisdictions, this is hardly true of the common law ones. Beyond the Western world, the law is influenced by religious and cultural traditions. On the whole, matrimonial property law is dominated by the internal domestic laws of each country and these vary enormously.

The topic "distribution of property on divorce" may be a slight misnomer. Depending on the country concerned, the rules relating to matrimonial property may operate only on divorce, or at an earlier stage, which is when parties separate. A property system may also operate from the time of marriage, as opposed to divorce. This chapter will inevitably be a little flexible on these points. However, three topics are excluded. First, the law on de facto relationships or unmarried cohabitation is not covered unless passing mention is made. Likewise, coverage does not include civil partnerships (known by a variety of names), where a marriage-like status is created primarily for same-sex partners. Third, the law on distribution of property on death is not dealt with, as this raises a massive range of other issues that go beyond the current brief.[1]

1 It is worth noting however that in some jurisdictions the law on matrimonial property may include claims by survivors, but there is likely to be a coexisting inheritance law as well: see the author's own country, New Zealand and the Property (Relationships) Act 1976 as amended in 2001.

The chapter looks first at underlying concepts, which introduces many of the competing forces in play. Then it covers more of the details of the systems that can govern matrimonial property, some notes on private international law, and developments including harmonisation. Inevitably, the discussion includes a certain amount of generalisation, and examples are selective.

Underlying concepts

Despite the enormous differences between jurisdictions, some underlying concepts or themes can be discerned. While there are synergies, we also find tensions and competing forces. History and human nature play their parts.

Traditional view of marriage

In the history of both common law and civil law countries, traditional marriage was significant. The two spouses became one, but coupled with this was the concept of male headship. Thus, the language of "union" and "community" emerged but with the husband as the controlling force. Wives had little or no control over the property, which was in the name of the husband and under his management. The wife might have some "pin money" to pay for minor purchases at the shop, but that was of no great consequence. More importantly, the other side of the coin was the husband's obligation to maintain his wife and provide for her daily needs. The traditional view operated in an era when divorce was very hard to obtain and rare. In a very different age and different understanding of relationships, the traditional view needs radical updating. However, this is far less true in those parts of the world where religion still prevails, such as the Islamic nations.[2]

A refashioned concept of marriage

In the West in particular but also in a number of emerging nations, developments in human rights have led to a far-less gendered concept of marriage. This can be captured by the word "partnership" or, especially in Europe, "solidarity". The "two" do not become "one" but remain as two, operating together as part of the marital enterprise. How exactly this works out during the course of a marriage varies, but on separation or divorce the law will recognise the joint efforts of both parties. In so doing, the focus will not be solely on financial contributions but, just as significantly, also on non-financial ones such as child care, home management and so forth. Under the notion of solidarity, the family including children may play a role but here jurisdictions part company: some will emphasise the division of property between the two adults, while others make orders that can favour the party with ongoing child care responsibilities over the other. This leads to some more diverging concepts.

Equality versus equity; rules versus discretion

The notion that marriage is a partnership is often accompanied by the principle of equal division. So, the most common regime found in Europe is one where on divorce the property acquired by joint efforts during the period of living together is divided equally or recognised by an equivalent monetary payment, often referred to as a community of acquests regime. Thus, the equal but different contributions of both parties are reflected in an equal share of the common property.

2 Very generally, see C. Mallat and J. Connors *Islamic Family Law* (Graham & Trotman, London, 1990) for example at 156 and S.S. Ali *Modern Challenges to Islamic Law* (Cambridge University Press, Cambridge, 2016).

Two challenges are made to this. The first is that it does not take account of the children and their needs. This may lead, instead of a focus on equality, to statutory provisions as in Australia and England that give the courts discretionary powers to make flexible awards to take account of a variety of circumstances.[3] This discretionary approach is in contrast to the rule-based approach of community property regimes.

The second challenge is an argument that the theory of equal division is not matched by the reality, and thus equality is not necessarily equitable or fair. Another way of putting this is that marriage can financially disadvantage one party in favour of the other. This can happen where a party, often a wife, has put a career on hold to bring up the children, or to enable the other party to get better qualified and have enhanced employment opportunities. The ongoing income positions of the two parties are therefore far from equal. Thus, some countries such as Scotland and New Zealand have provisions that are designed to enable the courts to address these economic advantages and disadvantages (discussed later).

Capital versus income

The difference between jurisdictions that follow a rules-based system, usually accompanied by equal division, and those that have a form of discretionary distribution with no equality imperative is sometimes mirrored in the distinction between capital and income. The community property regimes in all their variety are essentially about assets. Separate provisions deal with income needs, described as income support, maintenance, or alimony. Ongoing payments will not be made according to strict rules such as equal division but will depend on a range of factors including the parties' needs and means. The approach in countries such as England and Australia is in effect to combine capital and income, and to determine the division of property on the basis of a list of factors including income support needs (with maintenance payments also possible). When contributions during cohabitation and future needs are meshed together, a discretionary approach is almost inevitable. This may lead to uncertainty and it can be hard to advise parties on likely outcomes. In Australia, the courts have offered little in the way of guidance,[4] while in England the courts have a yardstick of equality, which can however be departed from.[5] Wider factors such as income earning differences may also come into play, socially, in awarding ongoing maintenance in addition to a share of the property.[6] So, the effect is that capital and income are intermingled, both for the purposes of property orders and ongoing income maintenance payments. To some eyes used to keeping the capital and income apart, this spells confusion.

Clean break

It is sometimes said that an aim of property division law is to ensure a clean break between the parties.[7] By dividing the property cleanly and, if possible swiftly, the parties can get on with their new lives, with some financial backing that may enable them to obtain new accommodation and support a new family. This aim is arguably better serviced by a rule-based scheme that enables

3 Family Law Act 1975 (Aust.) and Matrimonial Causes Act 1973 (England and Wales).

4 B. Fehlberg, R. Kaspiew, J. Millbank, F. Kelly, and J. Behrens, *Australian Family Law: The Contemporary Context* (2nd edn, Oxford University Press, Melbourne, 2015) at 492.

5 *White v. White* [2000] UKHL 54, [2001] 1 AC 596.

6 *Miller v. Miller; McFarlane v. McFarlane* [2006] UKHL 24, [2006] 2 AC 618.

7 See for example *Minton v. Minton* [1979] AC 593, noted in *Miller v. Miller; McFarlane v. McFarlane* [2006] UKHL 24, [2006] 2 AC 618 at [35].

the division to be determined without too much dispute. Arguably, community regimes may fit this goal better because there is more certainty about the outcome but Australia has codified the principle for property and maintenance orders.[8]

The reality belies the goal. Where there are children, a clean break is a somewhat forlorn prospect in many instances. This could be because of ongoing financial support or support in other ways such as where one of the parties continues to occupy the family home. Even a community of acquests system, which sounds relatively easy when described, is in fact far from immune from dispute. Arguments can arise for example in working out what the pre-marriage property is and thus what the common property is that forms the basis of division or financial adjustment.

No-fault divorce

The traditional model of marital relationships incorporated the concept of fault. This usually referred to classic misdemeanours such as adultery and desertion. Its existence could affect entitlements in relation to property and support, and conduct in this general sense is still a matter that can be taken into account in some jurisdictions. For example, section 25(2)(g) of the Matrimonial Causes Act 1973 of England and Wales refers to "the conduct of each of the parties, if that conduct is such that it would in the opinion of the court be inequitable to disregard it". In many parts of the world now, divorce is obtainable on a no-fault basis and so the presence of fault in a property division statute looks rather out-of-place. However, arguably this is truer of community property regimes and ones that create entitlements to the common property rather than discretionary regimes, where a share of property beyond legal and equitable title remains a matter of discretion.

There are however different kinds of fault that can still be highly relevant. This is, for example, where the fault relates to the property itself or is conduct that hampers the process of litigation and settlement of disputes. The first kind can occur where property is transferred to someone else with the object of defeating the other party's claims. Section 37 of the Matrimonial Causes Act 1973 of England and Wales enables the court to set aside the disposition subject to the rights of bona fide third parties. A rebuttable presumption of malevolent intent is created for dispositions made during the three years prior to the application to set a disposition aside.

A variant on the theme of misconduct in relation to property is found in section 18C of the New Zealand Property (Relationships) Act 1976. The court has power to award compensation where "the relationship property has been materially diminished in value by the deliberate action or inaction of one spouse or partner". While the Court of Appeal has interpreted the notion of deliberateness narrowly,[9] it nevertheless exemplifies how fault can still play a part in property division on divorce.

To illustrate misconduct relating to process, the landmark judgment of the United Kingdom Supreme Court in *Prest v. Petrodel Resources Ltd*[10] is worth noting. In many ways it is something of a reality check – we can have grand ideas about equality and equity but they can be confounded by some of the practicalities of litigation. The husband's assets were calculated as being worth £37.5 million but one problem was that he had been very obstructive in providing information

8 Family Law Act 1975 (Aust.), s. 81: "the court shall, as far as practicable, make such orders as will finally determine the financial relationships between the parties to the marriage and avoid further proceedings between them".

9 *G.F.M. v. J.A.M.* [2013] NZCA 660, [2013] NZFLR 418. The Supreme Court refused leave to appeal: *G.F.M. v. J.A.M.* [2014] NZSC 32, [2014] NZFLR 599.

10 [2013] UKSC 34, [2013] 2 AC 415.

about his financial dealings. His conduct was "characterised by persistent obstruction, obfuscation and deceit, and a contumelious refusal to comply with rules of court and specific orders".[11] The wife was entitled to £17.5 million plus periodical payments. Her problem however was that the wealth was tied up in seven companies that owned property in the United Kingdom (it appears that the husband also had business interests in other parts of the world including Nigeria). Was there a way of overcoming the technical nature of the property ownership along with the husband's misconduct and lack of co-operation? After rejecting the application of the so-called doctrine of lifting the corporate veil and also finding that the broad powers in sections 24 and 25 of the Matrimonial Causes Act 1973 to make property adjustment orders were of no avail, the Supreme Court held that it could draw adverse inferences against the mendacious husband and conclude that the properties in question were held by the companies on the basis of resulting trusts in the husband's favour. Given the husband's beneficial interest in the properties, an order transferring his interest to the wife was legally possible. This represented a major victory for the wife but one of the judges, Lady Hale, was not optimistic that it could be given practical effect because of the mortgages that "apparently" encumbered the properties.[12]

The Supreme Court found a way to handle fault of an informational and procedural kind. However, Lord Sumption noted that the outcome was "highly fact-specific"[13] and thus would not be achievable in other situations. It also relies on trust concepts that are foreign to non-common law jurisdictions. The real fault was tackled indirectly but would it not be better if there was a direct power to address the kind of problem we are considering? An award of costs can sometimes achieve this but not in the *Prest* situation where the husband was essentially defaulting.[14]

Autonomy and agreements

The concept of the individual's freedom of choice is endemic in current Western thinking. It can significantly enhance human rights and in so doing secure progress for various groups such as the gay and lesbian community. It nevertheless cuts against the concepts of partnership and solidarity, and may clash with other rights such as those of children, which are inevitably connected to the interests of others such as parents.

The history of women's rights in the common law world is somewhat telling of the position of women. The Married Women's Property Act 1882 (UK)[15] converted the system based on marriage as a union into one of separate property. Wives were entitled to hold property in their own names, something that was seen as a great victory for the women's movement of the day. The difficulty was that women rarely had separate property of their own except that gained through inheritance or otherwise via family wealth. The separate property system came therefore to be seen as massively disadvantageous to most women. Following World War II and the marriage upsets that ensued, it dawned on policy-makers that the law failed to take account of the real contributions, tangible and intangible, that wives made to the marriage. This is where the discretionary approach of the Matrimonial Causes Act 1973 (UK) can be seen as a major, though arguably inadequate, inroad into the separate property system. It represents a swing away from autonomy and individual property rights in the traditional sense and towards a form of solidarity.

11 At [4]. Another expression used was "persistent obstruction and mendacity" at [43].
12 At [96].
13 At [52].
14 See [56] for the court's imposition of costs against some of the companies.
15 Replicated elsewhere such as in New Zealand with the Married Women's Property Act 1884 and similar laws passed in Australia.

In recent times, another major debate about autonomy has occurred. This concerns the extent to which parties can determine their matrimonial property matters by agreement.[16] Rather different attitudes to this form of autonomy abound. At one end of the spectrum contracts that assume that a marriage may end have been regarded as against public policy: marriages were intended to be life-long on this theory. A more modern concern is that the ability to contract out of a statutory scheme can affect the protection that such schemes offer. Autonomy assumes two equally empowered parties who can negotiate a fair agreement. Under the English law, considerable scepticism abounded about contracts and indeed they were void and unenforceable.[17] This was reversed by the *Radmacher* decision of the Supreme Court[18] and the Law Commission of England and Wales has made recommendations in favour of proper statutory provision for agreements.[19]

At the other end of the spectrum, parties may have a relatively free ability to enter into property agreements. These would not be limited to any particular time – they could be antenuptial, postnuptial, during cohabitation, or by way of settlement of disputes after the parties have separated or divorced. The New Zealand scheme illustrates this. Under Part 6 of the Property (Relationships) Act 1976, the parties may contract out of the standard statutory scheme and provide for the status, ownership and division of their property. In short, the terms of the agreement are entirely a matter of choice for the parties. There are however three constraints. First, each party must obtain independent legal advice. Second, the ordinary rules of the law of contract apply. Third and more importantly, the court can set aside an agreement if it finds that the agreement would cause serious injustice.[20] It is possible for example for an agreement made some years earlier to have become out-of-date by later events and it would be unfair on one of the parties to miss out on entitlements that were not originally contemplated. Alternatively, if it is found that the disadvantaged was taken advantage of or manipulated, there could be grounds for setting the agreement aside and falling back on the statutory scheme. There may thus be substantive or procedural unfairness.[21]

In between these two approaches are systems that contain a default regime but at the same time provide alternative regimes that parties can opt into. South Africa is an example of this.[22] Community of property, whereby property at the date of marriage forms part of the joint estate along with subsequent acquisitions, is the default regime. However, prior to marriage the parties can by agreement opt out of community of property. The accrual or acquests approach applies automatically if the parties are "out of community" unless they choose the separate property

16 The major text on this is J. Scherpe (ed.) *Marital Agreements and Private Autonomy in Comparative Perspective* (Hart, Oxford, 2012). Among other writings, see S. Thompson *Prenuptial Agreements and the Presumption of Free Choice Issues of Power in Theory and Practice* (Hart, Oxford, 2015) and K. Boele-Woelki et al. *Principles of European Family Law Regarding Property Relations between Spouses* (Intersentia, Cambridge, 2013) at 9 and following.

17 See for example J. Miles "Marital Agreements and Private Autonomy in England and Wales" in J. Scherpe (ed.) *Marital Agreements and Private Autonomy in Comparative Perspective* (Hart, Oxford, 2012) at 89, 97.

18 *Radmacher v. Granatino* [2010] UKSC 42, [2011] 1 AC 534.

19 Law Commission *Matrimonial Property, Needs and Agreements* (Law. Com. No. 343, The Stationery Office, London, 2014).

20 Property (Relationships) Act 1976, s. 21J.

21 J. Scherpe (ed.) *Marital Agreements and Private Autonomy in Comparative Perspective* (Hart, Oxford, 2012) at 15 and 517.

22 See for example J. Heaton (ed.) *The Law of Divorce and Dissolution of Life Partnerships in South Africa* (Juta, Cape Town, 2014).

alternative. The South African law thus promotes autonomy by offering some limited choices, but does not go as far as New Zealand, which has a largely untrammelled approach. The traditional approach of the common law may be said to have had no truck with these incarnations of autonomy. Of course, private ordering tends not to be the norm. While the alternative regimes in South Africa are said to be popular,[23] the number of agreements in New Zealand is unknown. The majority of couples will not have signed one: it is more likely to occur where parties are entering a subsequent marriage and desire to preserve some of their pre-existing property for the children of their earlier marriage; or where one of the parties has significant pre-marital wealth which that party wishes to keep apart from the marriage.

Colonialism and custom

The question of principles and policies for property division takes on a very different hue when we consider the effect of colonialism on the shape of the law. The principle at work is a very different one from the grand ideals that we have been discussing. It is the principle of inheritance. Many nations have inherited systems from their colonial powers. In some instances, the colonial influence has left a reasonably coherent regime, as the examples of Latin America and some of the states of the United States illustrate: community property in some form or another has been exported seemingly satisfactorily.

The position is far less true of many British Commonwealth countries, especially the small nation states. Typically, British law at the relevant date has been enshrined in the local law, without provision necessarily for changes in the originating country to affect the outcome of a case. Many of these countries have been slow to legislate for themselves and thus to incorporate provisions that are appropriate to local conditions. A good example is Kenya.[24] Prior to the Matrimonial Property Act 2013, the Married Women's Property Act 1882 of England applied even though it had been repealed in England. The new statute treats marriage as a partnership and divides property according to contributions, including non-monetary ones.

A different story occurred in Samoa.[25] At one point, the law was "very unclear", as no statutory law of an external country appeared to apply, giving rise to uncertainty. It even appeared that the common law of England may have governed, making things even more confusing. A dramatic change was ushered in with the Divorce and Matrimonial Causes Amendment Act 2010. This allows the court to make orders altering property rights if just and equitable to do so. While a number of factors such as contributions are to be taken into account, there is a rebuttable presumption that the parties have contributed equally. In this respect, Samoa has gone further than England and Australia but not as far as New Zealand, the country with which it has been most closely associated in recent times. A reality check must be noted. The vast proportion of

23 Ibid. at 59.

24 F. Banda "Changing the Constitution and Changing Attitudes: Recent Developments in Kenyan Family Law" in B. Atkin (ed.) *The International Survey of Family Law* (Jordans, Bristol, 2014) at 261–267.

25 J. Corrin "Getting a Fair Share: Financial Relief on Breakdown of Marriage in Samoa" in B. Atkin (ed.) *The International Survey of Family Law 2008 Edition* (Jordans, Bristol, 2008) at 309–314 and L. Mulitalo and J. Corrin "Reform of Maintenance and Divorce Laws in Samoa: Appropriate for the 'Aiga'" in B. Atkin (ed.) *The International Survey of Family Law 2012 Edition* (Jordans, Bristol, 2012) 288–289. On Pacific countries more generally, see J. Corrin and D. Paterson *Introduction to South Pacific Law* (4th edn, Intersentia, Cambridge, 2017) ch. 7.

land in Samoa is inalienable customary land.[26] Thus, legislation that "is a vast improvement"[27] may in practice have less effect than desired.

The question of custom and pluralistic cultural mores also becomes an important principle to consider alongside colonialism. In the Solomon Islands for example the law relating to ancillary relief does not apply to unregistered customary marriages.[28] Customary practices are very important in a country such as the Solomon Islands but the true position is hard to define, as customary practices differ in different parts of the country and legal recognition is not consistent. If we return to Kenya, we see pluralism at work in two other ways. First, provision is made for polygamous marriages.[29] This can obviously have its complexities when it comes to division between different wives.[30] Second, the Matrimonial Property Act 2013 states that adherents of Islam "may" be governed by Islamic law.[31] Thus, a country with a British heritage provides some very un-British approaches to property division.

Digging a little deeper, we can note a tension between customary and religious practices on the one hand and other human rights on the other.[32] For example, while there is a right to practise one's religion, how do we reconcile this with laws relating to property on divorce that impact unfairly on women? Ultimately this is beyond the scope of this chapter.

The systems in more detail

What property is covered?

This question is deceptive as it in fact contains a variety of subsidiary issues: Is it necessary to ask about property at all? What is "property"? What property is included and what is excluded from the jurisdiction of the court?

The "property" question is vital for all jurisdictions that have a full-scale matrimonial property regime. It is less relevant in places such as England and Australia where there is no sophisticated "system" and where income maintenance is blurred with the division of property. For example, in Australia in exercising its powers, the court must take account of the parties' "financial resources" as well as their income and property.[33] This means that the court can have regard to resources going beyond "property".

Nevertheless, even in Australia, the question of what amounts to "property" can be crucial. The large number of family trusts there has created problems for the fair distribution of property

26 Note that, in New Zealand, indigenous Maori land is excluded from the Property (Relationships) Act 1976: s. 6. However, unlike Samoa, Maori land forms a very small amount of the land in New Zealand.
27 Ibid at 289.
28 J. Corrin and B. Teng "Negotiating the Pluralistic Family Law Regimes in the Solomon Islands" in B. Atkin (ed.) *The International Survey of Family Law 2016 Edition* (Jordans, Bristol, 2016) at 453–454.
29 F. Banda "Changing the Constitution and Changing Attitudes: Recent Developments in Kenyan Family Law" in B. Atkin (ed.) *The International Survey of Family Law* (Jordans, Bristol, 2014) at 264.
30 Note that under s. 52(3) of the Matrimonial Causes Act 1973 (England and Wales) "marriage" includes void and voidable marriages, among them being bigamous and polygamous ones. In New Zealand, the Property (Relationships) Act 1976 recognises the possibility of "polygamous" de facto relationships or the coexistence of a marriage and a de facto relationship: see ss. 52A and 52B.
31 Banda discusses the odd use of "may" in this context: ibid at 265.
32 B. Stark *International Family Law An Introduction* (Ashgate, Aldershot, 2005) at 133. On issues relating to dowry and "dowry abuse" especially in India, see P. Patel et al. "Emerging Issues for International Family Law: Part 3: Transnational Marriage Abandonment and the Dowry Question" [2016] *Fam Law* 1443.
33 Family Law Act 1975, s. 79(4)(c), which refers to s. 75(2): see especially s. 75(2)(b).

on divorce, because the transfer of family assets to a trust can put those assets outside the court's reach. In contrast, this is not an issue in many jurisdictions such as continental Europe where the trust is a foreign concept.

There are various mechanisms to overcome the problem of trusts but, if a property interest held by one or both of the parties can be discerned despite the existence of the trust, then the assets or their monetary equivalent can be the subject of a matrimonial property award. A landmark decision of the High Court of Australia, *Kennon v. Spry*,[34] held that the husband's control of the trust and the wife's right as a beneficiary to due administration of the trust amounted to a property interest, rendering the whole of the trust property or the right to enjoy it property of the parties. In another landmark judgment, the Supreme Court of New Zealand followed *Kennon v. Spry*, noting that the powers of the husband in that case were more extensive than those of Dr Spry.[35] Among the factors that influenced the New Zealand court were the broad definition of "property" in the Act that included "any other right or interest",[36] thus going well beyond ordinary notions of real and personal property, and the legislative goals to ensure proper recognition of the equal contribution of the parties to their marriage. While much turned on the precise terms of the trust, the tenor of the court's reasoning shows a willingness to find a solution to the trust problem.

Some jurisdictions expressly address these points. For example, section 4(1) of the Ontario Family Law Act 1990 defines "property" to include "property over which a spouse has, alone or in conjunction with another person, a power of appointment exercisable in favour of himself or herself". Likewise, section 84(3) of the Family Law Act 2011 of British Columbia refers to vested beneficial interests in a trust, the power to transfer trust property to oneself, and the power to terminate a trust with the property reverting to that party. A clear legislative instruction has some attractions rather than leaving the courts to wrestle with these issues.

Aside from the issue of "property", a key question is what property can be the subject of some kind of order. The answer varies considerably depending on the kind of regime that a jurisdiction has in place. In the case of community of acquests, the property is largely determined by the assessment of what has been acquired as a result of the marriage. In Germany for example, as described by Pintens,[37] a distinction is drawn between the "initial" and the "final property". The former is the net assets of each party owned before marriage plus gifts and inheritances during marriage. The final property of the spouses refers to all the assets that they hold at the end of the marriage subject to deductions for things such as debts, but including gains on pre-marriage acquired property.[38] These two figures enable the gains of each party or the "surplus" during the marriage to be calculated, with the person with the greatest gain being required to make an equalising payment to the other spouse. In other countries such as Belgium, France, Portugal and

34 *Kennon v. Spry* [2008] HCA 56, (2008) 238 CLR 366.

35 *Clayton v. Clayton (Vaughan Road Property Trust)* [2016] NZSC 29, [2016] 1 NZLR 551. In a decision given at the same time involving the same parties, the Supreme Court invoked a somewhat antiquated power in s. 182 of the Family Proceedings Act 1980 to make orders with respect to antenuptial and postnuptial settlements: *Clayton v. Clayton (Claymark Trust)* [2016] NZSC 30, [2016] 1 NZLR 590. This power applies only on divorce and not on separation and is not governed by the same principles as the Property (Relationships) Act 1976. For a discussion of "property" in this context, see B. Atkin "What Kind of Property Is 'Relationship Property?'" (2016) 47 *V.U.W.L.R.* 345.

36 Property (Relationships) Act 1976, s. 2.

37 W. Pintens "Matrimonial Property Law in Europe" in K. Boele-Woelki et al. *The Future of Family Property in Europe* (Intersentia, Cambridge, 2011) at 30.

38 Pintens ibid says of this latter point: "This is an expression of a rather extreme understanding of matrimonial solidarity" (at 30).

Spain, plus middle and eastern European countries the position on divorce is not dissimilar. Items such as clothing, personal effects, and compensation for personal injury are excluded. In short, the system sets out the way in which each party's personal property and the community property are to be calculated so that the gains of the marriage can be shared. The community of acquests approach has a certain symmetry about it, but it also depends on evidence of who owned what assets and when, which may not necessarily be free from dispute. Determining what are acquests or community assets is "often easier said than done".[39]

The approach in the Canadian provinces tends to be rather different, although in some respects the end result is not so dissimilar.[40] For example, in Ontario "net family property" covers the value of all property a spouse owns at the date of valuation but with two important qualifications.[41] First, a deduction is made for debts and pre-marital property as valued at the date of marriage. Second, some categories of property are "excluded", including gifts, inheritances, damages for personal injuries, and proceeds from life insurance policies. However, the matrimonial home is not deducted or excluded, and this marks the regime out from the European model. Another notable feature is that the onus of proof is expressly on the party claiming a deduction or an exclusion, meaning that property is presumed to be part of the family property unless the contrary is proven.[42] British Columbia used to have an interesting exclusion for business assets unless the non-owning party had contributed to them.[43] The law was reformed and now treats family property as all real and personal property that the parties have a legal or beneficial interest in at the date of separation subject, as in Ontario, to some exclusions.[44] The legislation expressly refers to "a share or an interest in a corporation" and "an interest in a partnership, an association, an organization, a business or a venture". Thus, the distinction between family and business assets has been abandoned. Arguably, this makes sense because business assets may have been generated during the course of the marriage and may represent the core of some families' wealth.

In New Zealand, the distinction between "relationship" and "separate property" is the subject of a number of complex rules.[45] Echoing the law in Ontario, the main rule is that property acquired during the marriage is relationship property but the family home and family chattels are always relationship property irrespective of when or how they were acquired. Enhancements in separate property as a result of the use of relationship property or the contributions of the other party are clawed into the pool of relationship property. An exception applies for inheritances and gifts unless they are the home or chattels or have been "intermingled" with relationship property. Pension schemes (known as "superannuation policies") are a fraught topic in some parts of the world but are expressly listed in New Zealand at least in so far as they were contributed to during the marriage.[46] The more difficult issue is valuing such policies, as future contingent interests are to be taken into account.

39 J. Scherpe *European Family Law* (Edward Elgar, Cheltenham, 2016) Vol. III, ch. 5 at 146.

40 See J.D. Payne and M.A. Payne *Canadian Family Law* (4th edn, Irwin Law, Toronto, 2011) ch. 12.

41 Family Law Act 1990 (Ont) s. 4.

42 This is also true of other systems, for example in Germany the burden of proof is on the party to prove that assets were "initial": J. Scherpe *European Family Law* (Edward Elgar, Cheltenham, 2016) Vol. III ch. 5 158. In Norway the onus is on the party arguing that the pre-marital assets, gifts etc. are not excluded whereas the other Nordic countries place the onus on the party seeking an exemption: J. Scherpe (ed.) *Marital Agreements and Private Autonomy in Comparative Perspective* (Hart, Oxford, 2012) at 157.

43 Family Relations Act 1996 (BC) (repealed), s. 59.

44 Family Law Act 2011 (BC) Part 5 especially ss. 84 and 85.

45 Property (Relationships) Act 1976, ss. 8–10.

46 On the position in the United States, see M. Brinig "Marital Property" in B. Atkin (ed.) *The International Survey of Family Law 2016 Edition* (Jordans, Bristol, 2016) at 521.

Division

Under community property regimes, the basic rule is that of equalisation of the gains that the parties have made. As in Germany, this may involve a monetary payment by one party to the other. In other jurisdictions an order may be made expressly distributing property between the parties. This may be affected by an accompanying order relating to the interim occupation of the home, for example while the children are still growing up. There may be exceptions to equalisation as in Ontario where the court can depart from equal sharing if it would be unconscionable not to do so. Among the grounds of unconscionability are failure to disclose debts and liabilities, debts "recklessly" incurred, "intentional or reckless depletion of his or her net family property", and "any other circumstance relating to the acquisition, disposition, preservation, maintenance or improvement of property".[47]

In the countries with discretionary powers, no statutory rule about equal division will exist. This is often because property and maintenance are combined and the calculation is inevitably flexible. In England, the courts have developed various concepts such as "the yardstick of equality",[48] described by Miles and Scherpe as "revolutionary".[49] Australia has eschewed even this with commentators referring to a "lack of conceptual clarity and coherence that continues to exist in this area, reflective of a broader lack of social consensus on these issues".[50] In the United States where most states follow an equitable distribution system rather than community property one, several start with a presumption of equal division. Brinig observes that the two systems have actually been converging.[51]

A middle approach can be found in Scotland, where the court can make a range of orders including the payment of a capital sum or the transfer of property.[52] The first principle that the court must apply is that the net value of matrimonial property should be shared "fairly", but this occurs "when it is shared equally or in such other proportions as are justified by special circumstances". At the same time, "fair account should be taken of any economic advantage derived by either party from contributions by the other, and of any economic disadvantage suffered by either party in the interests of the other party or of the family", thus providing an illustration of the kind of situation that justifies a non-equal division. In New Zealand, where there is a strong rule of equal sharing, the courts can nevertheless order "compensation" where one party, on separation, suffers from an "economic disparity" caused by the marriage.[53] This has given rise to a lot of litigation especially over the way in which the compensation is to be calculated. The courts have approached this crucial issue in two ways: some adopt a formulaic calculation, aided by actuarial evidence;[54] others adopt a "broad brush" approach and endeavour to find a figure

47 Family Law Act 1990 (Ont), s. 5(6).

48 *White v. White* [2000] UKHL 54, [2001] 1 AC 596.

49 J. Miles and J. Scherpe "The Legal Consequences of Dissolution: Property and Financial Support between Spouses" in J. Eekelaar and R. George *Routledge Handbook of Family Law and Policy* (Routledge, Oxford, 2014) at 143.

50 B. Fehlberg, R. Kaspiew, J. Millbank, F. Kelly, and J. Behrens *Australian Family Law: The Contemporary Context* (2nd edn, Oxford University Press, Melbourne, 2015) at 492.

51 M. Brinig "Marital Property" in B. Atkin (ed.) *The International Survey of Family Law 2016 Edition* (Jordans, Bristol, 2016) at 509, 530. See also J.T. Oldham "Economic Consequences of Divorce in the United States: Recent Developments" in J. Eekelaar (ed.) *Family Law in Britain and America in the New Century Essays in Honor of Sanford N Katz* (Brill Nijhoff, Leiden, 2016).

52 Family Law (Scotland) Act 1985, especially s. 9 and following. See K. McK. Norrie "Marital Agreements and Private Autonomy in Scotland" in J. Scherpe (ed.) *Marital Agreements and Private Autonomy in Comparative Perspective* (Hart, Oxford, 2012) at 289.

53 Property (Relationships) Act 1976 s. 15, inserted in 2001.

54 *X. v. X.* [2010] 1 NZLR 601 (CA).

that is about right on the facts of the case.[55] It involves grafting a discretion onto a rule-based regime, and, in the light of future income earnings, adjusts what would otherwise be the equal division of the property.

Summary

While the predominant form of matrimonial property regime is one based on "the fruits of joint labour"[56] or an equal sharing of the assets accrued during the marriage, the above discussion shows that internationally a great variety of approaches are in place. Some of them are "loose", others more rigid. Alongside this, most but not all jurisdictions allow parties to enter prenuptial contracts or settlement agreements that tailor outcomes to suit their own situations.

Private international law

Matrimonial property cases are not always limited to a single jurisdiction. With increased mobility and globalisation, parties may well have property located outside their own country, province or state. This is even more likely to be so in a country such as the United States where each state has its own legal system. The potential for conflicting laws to apply to the same items of property is real. The private international law on matrimonial property is as varied as are the domestic regimes that we have already touched on. It raises questions of jurisdiction, choice of law and recognition of overseas orders and agreements. The answers to these questions are often murky. In the next section on harmonisation we note some attempts at clarification, but major divides continue to exist.

The civil law countries usually rely on the connecting factors of habitual residence and nationality. The new European regulation, discussed in the next section on "Harmonisation", does so as well.

The common law world tends to make use of the distinction between immovables and movables,[57] land being a classic example of the former. Scotland illustrates how this distinction operates. Rights in relation to immovables are determined according to the *lex situs*, that is the law of the country where the property is situated, whereas movables are determined according to the parties' "domicile".[58] If the parties have different domiciles, they "shall be taken to have the same rights to such property as they had immediately before the marriage".[59] These are ostensibly choice of law rules in contrast to New Zealand, which states the position from the jurisdiction perspective: a New Zealand court has jurisdiction over immovables if they are situated in New Zealand, thus by implication excluding overseas immovables, and over movables, whether in the

55 *Jack v. Jack* [2014] NZHC 1495.

56 J. Miles and J. Scherpe "The Legal Consequences of Dissolution: Property and Financial Support between Spouses" in J. Eekelaar and R. George *Routledge Handbook of Family Law and Policy* (Routledge, Oxford, 2014) at 144.

57 See Lord Collins et al. *Dicey, Morris, and Collins The Conflict of Laws* (15th edn, Thomson Reuters, London, 2012) at [22–004].

58 Family Law (Scotland) Act 2006, s. 39. Scotland uses the spelling "immoveable" and "moveable". "Domicile" is a technical concept know to the common law and is a person's permanent home country, but need not coincide with the country where the person happens to reside. Murphy criticises *lex situs* "in that it can lead to juridical fragmentation" because the various items may be subject to different regimes, and he considers domicile to be "chauvinistically determined": J. Murphy *International Dimensions in Family Law* (Manchester University Press, Manchester, 2005) at 169.

59 Family Law (Scotland) Act 2006, s. 39(3).

country or overseas, where one of the parties has a New Zealand domicile.[60] In South Africa, in the absence of an antenuptial agreement, domicile by marriage determines conflicts issues, irrespective of the immovable/movable distinction.[61]

If the court in New Zealand has jurisdiction, the *lex fori* will govern the question of which law will apply. This is true in England as well, which Miles describes as "what might unflatteringly be called its parochial attitude towards the resolution of financial and property disputes following divorce that have a foreign connection".[62] She also notes the Brussels approach of "a simple, but blunt, first-seised rule" and an allied point that Europe generally refuses to accept the common law approach of *forum non conveniens*.[63] This is the concept that, although a court has jurisdiction to hear a case, it may nevertheless stay proceedings on the basis that another country or state is a clearly more appropriate place for the case to be heard.[64]

The trend in the Canadian provinces is to take a line more in sympathy with that found in the civil law countries. In Ontario, rights to marital property "are governed by the internal law of the place where both spouses had their last habitual residence or, if there is no place where the spouses had a common habitual residence, by the law of Ontario".[65]

British Columbia has a much more detailed regime. From the private international law point of view, the two most important grounds for jurisdiction are that one of the spouses is habitually resident in the province or "a real and substantial connection" is shown between the province and the facts of the proceedings.[66] The location of the property in British Columbia and the most recent common habitual residence being in the province are bases for presuming a real and substantial connection. Jurisdiction will however mean that the court can make orders relating to "extraprovincial" property even if it is immovable, but alternatively it may substitute British Columbian property or order compensation to be paid.[67] The *forum non conveniens* doctrine is also spelt out.

The British Columbian rules on choice of law are specified in some detail but it is worth noting the concept of the "proper law of the relationship", which is prima facie "the internal law of the jurisdiction in which the spouses had their most recent common habitual residence".[68] Overarching

60 Property (Relationships) Act 1976, s. 7.

61 C. Schulze "Conflict of Laws" in J. Heaton (ed.) *The Law of Divorce and Dissolution of Life Partnerships in South Africa* (Juta, Cape Town, 2014) at 648.

62 J. Miles "Marital Agreements and Private Autonomy in England and Wales" in J. Scherpe (ed.) *Marital Agreements and Private Autonomy in Comparative Perspective* (Hart, Oxford, 2012) at 114.

63 At 115 and following. See also M. Thorpe "Financial Consequences of Divorce England versus the Rest of Europe" in K. Boele-Woelki et al. *The Future of Family Property in Europe* (Intersentia, Cambridge, 2011) at 6.

64 *Spiliada Maritime Corp v. Cansulex Ltd* [1986] UKHL 10, [1987] AC 460. Australia uses a standard that simply asks whether Australia is a clearly inappropriate forum without entering into a comparison of the two competing fora: *Oceanic Sun Line Special Shipping Company Inc v. Fay* [1988] HCA 32, (1988) 165 CLR 197 and *Voth v. Manildra Flour Mills Pty Ltd* [1990] HCA 55, (1990) 171 CLR 538. In other common law jurisdictions, *Spiliada* tends to be followed, as in the New Zealand case *Gilmore v. Gilmore* [1993] NZFLR 561. Note also that there may be bilateral agreements determining which forum has jurisdiction, for example the Trans-Tasman Agreement between Australia and New Zealand.

65 Family Law Act 1990 (Ont), s. 15. In South Africa, the main rule is that the *lex domicilii* governs both movables and immovables in the absence of an antenuptial contract to the contrary: C. Schulze "Conflict of Laws" in J. Heaton (ed.) *The Law of Divorce and Dissolution of Life Partnerships in South Africa* (Juta, Cape Town, 2014) at 648.

66 Family Law Act 2011 (BC), s. 106.

67 S. 109.

68 S. 107(a).

the choice of law rules is the ability of the parties to make an agreement, with the only limitation being any restrictions imposed by the proper law of the relationship.[69] The effect of an overseas agreement receives varying treatment in other countries. Australia's Family Law Act 1975 for example has no provisions on such agreements,[70] while New Zealand recognises overseas written agreements that are valid according to the law of the overseas country, were made at or before the marriage began, and are not contrary to justice or public policy.[71] In South Africa, the essential validity of an antenuptial contact is determined by the husband's domicile for movables and the *lex situs* for immovables, but the *lex loci contractus* governs the formalities.[72] These examples underlie the need for a more uniform approach to be adopted at a global level to private international law questions.

Harmonisation

The quest for harmonisation of matrimonial property laws has been stuttering. The Nordic countries achieved it in around 1920.[73] In 2010 France and Germany entered an agreement for an optional regime of joint ownership of acquired property. This will assist German/French "binational" couples but others may opt for it as well. This is "the first time in Europe uniform substantive family law will apply in two states" and has the potential to become a multilateral agreement.[74] In the United States, the Uniform Marriage and Divorce Act 1970[75] played a large role in state reforms so that there is now an element of convergence among the states, the distinction between community and equitable distributions states nevertheless remaining.[76]

In March 2016 the European Commission proposed a Regulation on jurisdiction, applicable law and the recognition and enforcement of decisions in matters of matrimonial property regimes.[77] The European Parliament approved it on 23 June 2016. In summary, where there is no agreement on which jurisdiction should apply, the usual basis is

> the habitual residence of the spouses, their last habitual residence if one of them still resides there or the habitual residence of the respondent; these widely used criteria frequently coincide with the location of the spouses' property. A final criterion is the common nationality of the spouses.[78]

69 S. 108(3) and (4).

70 O. Jessup "Marital Agreements and Private Autonomy in Australia" in J. Scherpe (ed.) *Marital Agreements and Private Autonomy in Comparative Perspective* (Hart, Oxford, 2012) 41.

71 Property (Relationships) Act 1976, s. 7A.

72 C. Schulze "Conflict of Laws" in J. Heaton (ed.) *The Law of Divorce and Dissolution of Life Partnerships in South Africa* (Juta, Cape Town, 2014) at 650–651.

73 W. Pintens "Matrimonial Property Law in Europe" in K. Boele-Woelki et al. *The Future of Family Property in Europe* (Intersentia, Cambridge, 2011) at 45.

74 N. Dethloff and A. Maschwitz "Courts Strengthening Equality and New Ways in Cross-Border Matrimonial Property Questions" in B. Atkin (ed.) *The International Survey of Family Law 2011 Edition* (Jordans, Bristol, 2011) at 207–208 and Centre de Droit de la Famille "A Chronicle of French Family Law" in B. Atkin (ed.) *The International Survey of Family Law 2013 Edition* (Jordans, Bristol, 2013) at 131–132. The quoted portion appears in Dethloff and Maschwitz above at 207.

75 National Conference of Commissioners on Uniform State Laws.

76 I.M. Ellman "Marital Agreements and Private Autonomy in the United States" in J. Scherpe (ed.) *Marital Agreements and Private Autonomy in Comparative Perspective* (Hart, Oxford, 2012) at 406 and M. Brinig "United States: Marital Property" in B. Atkin (ed.) *The International Survey of Family Law 2016 Edition* (Jordans, Bristol, 2016) 509, at 521.

77 COM (2016) 106 final 2016/0059 (CNS). For some earlier history, see Lord Collins (gen. ed.) *Dicey, Morris, and Collins The Conflict of Laws* (15th edn, Thomson Reuters, London, 2012) at [28–006].

78 See "Comments" on arts. 6 and 7.

The applicable law, that is choice of law, applies to all property, whether movable or immovable, and the rules on the applicable law reflect those for jurisdiction. In the absence of agreement, typically at the time of marriage (so long as the agreement refers to an applicable law that has some connection to the parties' real situation or history (article 22)), the primary connecting factor for determining the applicable law is the spouses' first common habitual residence, their common nationality on marriage, or the state with which the parties had the closest connection on marriage (article 26). Chapter IV of the Regulation provides for the recognition of orders by the courts of other states without the need for any special procedure.

The Regulation is an effort to harmonise European private international law as opposed to substantive law and thus tackles only one aspect of the wider issue of conflicting regimes. In so far as it goes, it is a considerable advance but with the forthcoming Brexit (the exit of Britain from the European Union), one may wonder to what extent these efforts at harmonisation will truly work and have any influence on other parts of the world. What is really needed is a genuinely international effort, most likely through the Hague Conference. In 1978 a Hague Convention on matrimonial property was indeed produced but only three countries have ratified it: France, Luxembourg, and the Netherlands.[79] It is thus in effect a dead letter. Commentators refer to a tension between The Hague and Brussels, the difference between international versus regional unification.[80] Will a common European approach genuinely point the way for the rest of the world, or will it simply entrench existing positions? Obtaining international agreement is drawing quite a long bow: not only do we have to factor in the differences between the common law world and the civil law, but we also need to recall the deep religious and cultural divisions mentioned earlier in this chapter. For example, how easy is it to rationalise the values that have driven the West with the drivers behind Islam and indigenous mores?

Final word

One author has noted a change in international family law cases from those involving mega-wealthy couples to ones arising at all levels of society.[81] He suggests that the growing number of "international families" who have an increasing number of disputes deserve better than the current "xenophobic hotchpot of conflicting laws".[82] Even if we can discern that a majority of countries have some form of community of accrued gains, worldwide the range of schemes varies enormously. Given the different histories, values, religions, customary practices, and concepts of fairness, it is hard to see global agreement on the main aspects of the substance of the law on matrimonial property distribution on divorce. This is all the more so when we factor in property disputes involving unmarried couples and the growing recognition of the rights of indigenous peoples. Maybe developments in Europe will give fresh impetus to a more universal convention

79 The Convention on the Law Applicable to Matrimonial Property Regimes, concluded 14 March 1978 and in force from 1 September 1992. It allows spouses to choose which country's laws will apply, with the default position being the state of the couple's first habitual residence. See H. Baker and M. Groff "The Impact of the Hague Conventions on European Family Law" in J. Scherpe *European Family Law* (Intersentia, Cambridge, 2016) Vol. I at 188.

80 D. Martiny "The Impact of the EU Private International Law Instruments on European Family Law" in J. Scherpe *European Family Law* (Intersentia, Cambridge, 2016) Vol. I at 274–275 and M. Jänterä-Jareborg "Unification of International Family Law in Europe – A Critical Perspective" in K. Boele-Woelki (ed.) *Perspectives for the Unification and Harmonisation of Family Law in Europe* (Intersentia, Antwerp, 2003) 199.

81 D. Hodson *The International Family Law Practice 2015–2016* (4th edn, Family Law, Bristol, 2015) at [29.5].

82 At [29.6].

on private international law issues, though Brexit will doubtless be a major distraction. An aspect of this could be the wider use by individuals of binding agreements entered into prior to or during marriage. In addition, we may see more use of mediation and arbitration to solve cross-border disputes. For sure, many challenges lie ahead.

Bibliography

Ali, S.S. *Modern Challenges to Islamic Law* (Cambridge, Cambridge University Press, 2016).

Atkin, B. "What Kind of Property Is 'Relationship Property?'", (2016) 47 *V.U.W.L.R.* 345.

Baker, H. and Groff, M. "The Impact of the Hague Conventions on European Family Law", in J. Scherpe *European Family Law* (Cambridge, Intersentia, 2016) Vol. I 143.

Banda, F. "Changing the Constitution and Changing Attitudes: Recent Developments in Kenyan Family Law", in B Atkin (ed.) *The International Survey of Family Law* (Bristol, Jordans, 2014) 255.

Boele-Woelki, K., Ferrand, F., González Beilfuss, C., Jänterä-Jareborg, M., Lowe, N., Martiny, D. and Pintens, W. *Principles of European Family Law Regarding Property Relations between Spouses* (Cambridge, Intersentia, 2013).

Brinig, M. "United States: Marital Property", in B. Atkin (ed.) *The International Survey of Family Law 2016 Edition* (Bristol, Jordans, 2016) 509.

Centre de Droit de la Famille "A Chronicle of French Family Law", in B. Atkin (ed.) *The International Survey of Family Law 2013 Edition* (Bristol, Jordans, 2013) 119.

Collins, Lord of Mapesbury (gen. ed.) *Dicey, Morris, and Collins The Conflict of Laws* (London, Thomson Reuters, 15th edn, 2012).

Corrin, J. and Paterson, D. *Introduction to South Pacific Law* (Cambridge, Intersentia, 4th edn, 2017).

Corrin, J. and Teng, B. "Negotiating the Pluralistic Family Law Regimes in the Solomon Islands", in B. Atkin (ed.) *The International Survey of Family Law 2016 Edition* (Bristol, Jordans, 2016) 427.

Corrin, J. "Getting a Fair Share: Financial Relief on Breakdown of Marriage in Samoa", in B. Atkin (ed.) *The International Survey of Family Law 2008 Edition* (Bristol, Jordans, 2008) 297.

Dethloff, N. and Maschwitz, A. "Courts Strengthening Equality and New Ways in Cross-Border Matrimonial Property Questions", in B. Atkin (ed.) *The International Survey of Family Law 2011 Edition* (Bristol, Jordans, 2011) 199.

Ellman, I. M. "Marital Agreements and Private Autonomy in the United States", in J. Scherpe (ed.) *Marital Agreements and Private Autonomy in Comparative Perspective* (Oxford, Hart, 2012) 403.

Fehlberg, B., Kaspiew, R., Millbank, F., and Behrens, J. *Australian Family Law: The Contemporary Context* (Melbourne, Oxford University Press, 2nd edn, 2015).

Heaton, J. (ed.) *The Law of Divorce and Dissolution of Life Partnerships in South Africa* (Cape Town, Juta, 2014).

Hodson, D. *The International Family Law Practice 2015–2016* (Bristol, Family Law, 4th edn, 2015).

Jänterä-Jareborg, M. "Unification of International Family Law in Europe – A Critical Perspective", in K. Boele-Woelki (ed.) *Perspectives for the Unification and Harmonisation of Family Law in Europe* (Antwerp, Intersentia, 2003) 194.

Jessup, O. "Marital Agreements and Private Autonomy in Australia", in J. Scherpe (ed.) *Marital Agreements and Private Autonomy in Comparative Perspective* (Oxford, Hart, 2012) 17.

Law Commission *Matrimonial Property, Needs and Agreements* (Law. Com. No. 343, London, The Stationery Office, 2014).

Mallat, C. and Connors, J. *Islamic Family Law* (London, Graham & Trotman, 1990).

Martiny, D. "The Impact of the EU Private International Law Instruments on European Family Law", in J. Scherpe *European Family Law* (Cambridge, Intersentia, 2016) Vol. I 261.

Miles, J. and Scherpe, J. "The Legal Consequences of Dissolution: Property and Financial Support between Spouses", in J. Eekelaar and R. George *Routledge Handbook of Family Law and Policy* (Oxford, Routledge, 2014) 138.

Miles, J. "Marital Agreements and Private Autonomy in England and Wales", in J. Scherpe (ed.) *Marital Agreements and Private Autonomy in Comparative Perspective* (Oxford, Hart, 2012) 89.

Mulitalo, L. and Corrin, J. "Reform of Maintenance and Divorce Laws in Samoa: Appropriate for the 'Aiga'", in B. Atkin (ed.) *The International Survey of Family Law 2012 Edition* (Bristol, Jordans, 2012) 69.

Murphy, J. *International Dimensions in Family Law* (Manchester, Manchester University Press, 2005).

Norrie, K. McK. "Marital Agreements and Private Autonomy in Scotland", in J. Scherpe (ed.) *Marital Agreements and Private Autonomy in Comparative Perspective* (Oxford, Hart, 2012) 289.

Oldham, J.T. "Economic Consequences of Divorce in the United States: Recent Developments", in J. Eekelaar (ed.) *Family Law in Britain and America in the New Century Essays in Honor of Sanford N Katz* (Leiden, Brill Nijhoff, 2016) 55.

Patel, P., Handa, R., Anitha, S. and Jahangir, S. "Emerging Issues for International Family Law: Part 3: Transnational Marriage Abandonment and the Dowry Question" (2016) *Fam Law* 1443.

Payne, J.D. and Payne, M.A. *Canadian Family Law* (Toronto, Irwin Law, 4th edn, 2011).

Pintens, W. "Matrimonial Property Law in Europe", in K. Boele-Woelki, Miles, J. and Scherpe, J.M. *The Future of Family Property in Europe* (Cambridge, Intersentia, 2011) 19.

Scherpe, J. (ed.) *Marital Agreements and Private Autonomy in Comparative Perspective* (Oxford, Hart, 2012).

Scherpe, J. *European Family Law* (Cheltenham, Edward Elgar, 2016) Vol. III.

Schulze, C. "Conflict of Laws", in J. Heaton (ed.) *The Law of Divorce and Dissolution of Life Partnerships in South Africa* (Cape Town, Juta, 2014) 631.

Stark, B. *International Family Law: An Introduction* (Aldershot, Ashgate, 2005).

Thompson, S. *Prenuptial Agreements and the Presumption of Free Choice Issues of Power in Theory and Practice* (Oxford, Hart, 2015).

Thorpe, M. "Financial Consequences of Divorce England versus the Rest of Europe", in K. Boele-Woelki, Miles, J. and Scherpe, J.M.. *The Future of Family Property in Europe* (Cambridge, Intersentia, 2011) 3.

7

International family mediation

Recent developments

Nuria Gonzalez-Martin

Introduction: international family and cross-border mediation

Families in a globalised world currently are biracial, bireligious, binational, bilingual and, last but not least, bicultural.[1] Nowadays there is an increase in international families, that is, those formed by individuals who are under different countries' jurisdictions. In Mohamed Keshavjee's words, "the global family is an expatriate family, a migrant family and frequently more and more families are experiencing difficulties resulting from parental child abduction as well as managing contact and bends [sic] across national boundaries".[2]

Global or international families are not exempt from suffering crises, hence the increase in cross-border family conflicts that implicate issues such as child custody, child support, alimony, etcetera. We are being confronted with an alarming increase in the number of international child abductions by parents in cases where intimate partner relationships are terminated.[3] The main international treaty that covers these matters is the Hague Convention on the Civil Aspects of International Child Abduction[4] ("1980 Hague Convention"), a treaty that facilitates the prompt return to their country of habitual residence of children wrongfully removed to, or retained in,

1 Mohamed Keshavjee, "Keynote Address on Key Principles and Promising Practices for International Family Mediation Processes", Power Point Presentation, *Cross Border Child Protection. International Conference & Workshop*, Geneva, 21 Oct. 2015, available at www.iss-ssi.org/index.php/en/conference-2015#2-4-speakers (last accessed 23 July 2016).

2 Ibid.

3 On this topic, see Paul R. Beaumont and Peter E. McEleavy, *The Hague Convention on International Child Abduction* (Oxford, Oxford University Press, 1999) 88 and further; Peter McEleavy, "The New Child Abduction Regime in the European Union: Symbiotic Relationship or Forced Partnership?", 1 *J. Private Int'l. L.* 5 (2005); Peter McEleavy, "Evaluating the Views of Abducted Children: Trends in Appellate Case Law", 20 *Child & Fam. L. Q.* 230 (2008); Sarah Vigers, *Mediating International Child Abduction Cases: The Hague Convention* (Oxford and Portland, Bloomsbury, 2011) 11–12.

4 The Hague Convention of 25 Oct. 1980 on the Civil Aspects on International Child Abduction. The full text of the Convention is available at www.hcch.net (under "Specialized Sections" and "Child Abduction Section") (last accessed 24 March 2017).

any Contracting State.[5] This is a treaty with a high level of cooperation where we can see how important it is to promote agreements facilitating amicable resolutions of disputes in family law.[6]

With this in mind, we can appreciate, on the one hand, that there are several reasons to implement alternative dispute resolution mechanisms such as mediation in respect of issues concerning cross-border family disputes. On the other hand, there are several implications of, and challenges relating to, international family mediation because we need to work harder in order to:

(1) have the best international family mediators with a superior understanding of cultural diversity, religious law and the notion of family in different contexts; and
(2) develop different models of mediation.[7]

Beyond doubt, mediation is an appropriate and useful dispute resolution mechanism in most countries worldwide. In fact, we have a series of international treaties, especially from The Hague Conference on Private International Law, in this field.[8] However, even with respect to the 1980,[9] 1996[10] and 2007[11] Hague Conventions where mediation has been considered, legal and practical issues persist.

International family mediation has numerous challenges. In this chapter I focus on highlighting a few of them such as the latest approaches to or thoughts about recognition and enforcement of cross-border agreements in family matters involving children, the collaborative process on international family mediation, and the principles in international family mediation processes. I end with some conclusions.

5 Nuria Gonzalez Martin, "Non Exceptional Exceptions: The latest on The United States of America and Mexico Supreme Courts' Hague Abduction Decisions (Lozano and Direct Amparo under Revision 903/2014)", 19 *Spanish Yearbook of International Law* 23–33 (2015), available at www.sybil.es/archive/vol-19-2015/.

6 Arts. 7 and 10 of the 1980 Hague Convention *inter alia* provide: "Central Authorities . . . shall take all appropriate measures . . . to secure the voluntary *return of the child* or to bring about an *amicable resolution* of the issues", and "[t]he Central Authority of the State where the child is shall take or cause to be taken all appropriate measures in order to obtain the *voluntary return* of the child" (emphasis added). On the practical operation of the 1980 Hague Convention, see Hague Conference on Private International Law, *Guide to Good Practice under the Hague Convention of 25 October 1980 on the Civil Aspects of International Child Abduction, Mediation* (The Hague, 2012), available at www.hcch.net/upload/guide28mediation_en.pdf. See also Nuria Gonzalez Martin, "International Parental Child Abduction and Mediation: An Overview", 48 *Fam. L. Q.*, 319–350 (Summer 2014) and "International Parental Child Abduction and Mediation", XV *Anuario Mexicano de Derecho International* 353–412 (2015).

7 Mohamed Keshavjee, "Keynote Address on Key Principles and Promising Practices for International Family Mediation Processes", Power Point Presentation, *Cross Border Child Protection. International Conference & Workshop*, Geneva, 21 Oct. 2015, available at www.iss-ssi.org/index.php/en/conference-2015#2-4-speakers (last accessed 23 July 2016).

8 Also see the 1989 Inter-American Convention on the International Return of Children of the regional forum, the Organization of American States, available at www.oas.org/juridico/english/treaties/b-53.html (last accessed 19 Sept. 2016).

9 The Hague Convention on the Civil Aspects of International Child Abduction: see note 4 above.

10 The Hague Convention of 19 Oct. 1996 on Jurisdiction, Applicable Law, Recognition, Enforcement and Co-operation in Respect of Parental Responsibility and Measures for the Protection of Children, available at www.hcch.net/en/instruments/conventions (last accessed 24 March 2017).

11 The Hague Convention of 23 Nov. 2007 on the International Recovery of Child Support and other Forms of Family Maintenance, available at www.hcch.net/en/instruments/conventions (last accessed 24 March 2017).

Key matters under discussion

Cross-border enforcement and recognition of voluntary agreements

The Achilles heel of the 1980 Hague Convention and mediation in family matters involving children's issues is the recognition and enforcement of those voluntary agreements.

In order to study and try to find solutions, especially when it is necessary to recognise and enforce the agreements reached through mediation, the Permanent Bureau of The Hague Conference on Private International Law, by a mandate of the Hague Conference's Council on General Affairs and Policy that took place in March 2012, requested "the identification of the nature and extent of the legal and practical problems, including jurisdictional issues and [evaluation of] the benefit of a new instrument, whether binding or non-binding, in this area",[12] that is, cross-border family issues. It created an Experts' Group on Cross-border Recognition and Enforcement of Voluntary Agreements in Family Matters involving Children that, at the time of writing this chapter, had held two meetings[13] – one from 12 to 14 December 2013 and the other from 2 to 4 November 2015. Subsequent to the first meeting of the Experts' Group, the Council on General Affairs and Policy, at a meeting held from 8 to 10 April 2014, requested our Experts' Group

> to consider further the role that existing Hague Family Law Conventions play in cross-border recognition and enforcement of agreements in international child disputes, as well as the impact that an additional instrument might have on the practical use and "portability" of these agreements across borders. . . .[14]

In its report after its second meeting, the Experts' Group proposed, among its Conclusions and Recommendations,[15] two instruments: (1) a non-binding instrument, in order to explain the possibilities and operations of existing conventions (that is, the 1980, 1996,[16] and 2007 Hague Conventions) and thus to facilitate the recognition and enforcement of voluntary cross-border agreements in family disputes; and (2) a binding instrument, that is, a traditional international convention, since current instruments are not sufficient to enable the recognition and enforcement of these "packages" of agreements (that is, family agreement packages relating to matters such as child support, visits, travel costs, languages, education and religion).

With respect to these proposals, on the one hand, it would be important to bear in mind that the idea to promote a new binding instrument, a new convention or international treaty,

12 Council on General Affairs and Policy of the Conference, "Conclusions and Recommendations Adopted by the Council" (17–20 Apr. 2012), para. 7, available at assets.hcch.net/upload/wop/gap2012concl_en.pdf (last accessed 24 Jan. 2017).

13 The third meeting took place from 14–16 June 2017 (i.e. after the due date of this chapter). The 2017 "Conclusions and Recommendations" of the Experts' Group are available at assets.hcch.net/docs/1c688fd7-631d-4bb3-9597-e2c7a975839a.pdf. They were presented to the Council of General Affairs and Policy of the Hague Conference on Private International Law at its meeting in March 2018.

14 Council on General Affairs and Policy of the Conference, "Conclusions and Recommendations Adopted by the Council" (8–10 April 2014), para. 5, available at assets.hcch.net/upload/wop/genaff2014concl_en.pdf (last accessed 24 Jan. 2017). The author of this paper participated at the first meeting of the Experts' Group.

15 *Report of the Experts' Group Meeting on Cross-border Recognition and Enforcement of Agreements in Family Matters involving Children*, The Hague, 2–4 Nov. 2015, available at assets.hcch.net/docs/e4ee1bfd-27ab-4e0a-9ab2–9b784db5534a.pdf (last accessed 24 Jan. 2017).

16 It is important to highlight that the 1996 Hague Convention had not been signed by an important number of States and, for this reason, the Experts' Group encouraged non-contracting States to the 1996 Hague Conventions to ratify it or accede to it.

was considered because it would not be possible to amend, and consequently update, the three existing Hague Family Law Conventions. With this in mind, the Experts' Group in 2015 stated:

> [I]t is possible to create a new instrument that would build on and supplement the existing Hague Family Law Conventions by providing for a less complicated and more cost-effective way of making family agreements enforceable in and portable to different States.[17]

On the other hand, let us not forget that a new convention depends on political will and, in this sense, the Conclusions and Recommendations of the Experts' Group acknowledged that "a new binding instrument is a complex process and may take a long time to achieve widespread ratification".[18]

Finally, considering the Conclusions and Recommendations by the Experts' Group, the Council on General Affairs and Policy, in a meeting that took place from 15 to 17 March 2016, stated:

> 17 The Council decided to mandate the Permanent Bureau to develop a non-binding "navigation tool" to provide best practices on how an agreement made in the area of family law involving children can be recognized and enforced in a foreign State under the 1980, 1996 and 2007 Hague Conventions. The work shall be carried out *in consultation* with members of the Experts' Group; if necessary, a meeting of the Group may be convened.
>
> 18 The need for and feasibility of developing a binding instrument in this field will be revisited by Council in 2017, based on further information which will result from the work on the navigation tool.[19]

These statements can, clearly, be interpreted as a rejection of the stance taken by the Experts' Group during their second meeting, regarding the creation of a new binding convention (Hard Law) and the acceptance of the creation of a non-binding instrument (Soft Law), which is what The Hague Conference on Private International Law is working on.

In fact, at a meeting that took place from 14 to 16 March 2017, the Council on General Affairs and Policy stated:

> The Council welcomed the oral update on the development of a non-binding "navigation tool" to provide best practices on how an agreement in the area of family law involving children can be recognized and enforced in a foreign State under the 1980 Child Abduction, 1996 Child Protection, and 2007 Child Support Conventions. This draft "navigation tool" will be discussed at the next Experts' Group meeting, to be held in June 2017. The Permanent Bureau will report to the Council in 2018.[20]

From the above discussion, there is evidence that a great deal of resources has been devoted to finding optimal solutions in this matter, which is perfectly understandable because, in cross-border

17 *Report of the Experts' Group Meeting on Cross-border Recognition and Enforcement of Agreements in Family Matters involving Children*, The Hague, 2–4 Nov. 2015, para. 18, available at assets.hcch.net/docs/e4ee1bfd-27ab-4e0a-9ab2–9b784db5534a (last accessed 24 Jan. 2017).

18 Ibid. at para. 29.

19 Council on General Affairs and Policy of the Conference, "Conclusions & Recommendations Adopted by the Council" (15–17 March 2017) paras. 17–18 (emphasis added), available at assets.hcch.net/docs/679bd42c-f974–461a-8e1a-31e1b51eda10.pdf (last accessed 24 March 2017).

20 Council on General Affairs and Policy of the Conference, "Conclusions & Recommendations Adopted by the Council" (14–16 March 2017), para. 11, available at assets.hcch.net/docs/77326cfb-ff7e-401a-b0e8–2de9efa1c7f6.pdf (last accessed 24 March 2017).

voluntary agreements, recognition and enforcement are the foundation of a truly solid child protection framework.[21]

Collaborative process on international family mediation

With respect to a non-binding instrument, a Soft Law instrument, along with the work of the Experts' Group and the 2016 and 2017 Council's "Conclusions and Recommendations", the community of experts in the field detected the necessity to act. A good example of subsequent action is the intervention of non-governmental organisations, in particular, the International Social Service (ISS) which implemented the Collaborative Process on International Family Mediation ("the collaborative process").

This collaborative process entailed several steps. The first was the publishing of the handbook *Resolving Family Conflicts. A Guide to International Family Mediation*,[22] with assistance from experts in this field. As part of the second step, a questionnaire was distributed[23] on the standards and challenges for cross-border family mediation practice around the globe. Based on the responses received, an enlarged international group of family mediation practitioners, 55 to be precise, met in Geneva, from 21 to 23 October 2015,[24] and discussed a "Charter for

21 For the author's stance on these matters, see Nuria Gonzalez Martin, "Mexico and Civil, Family and Commercial Mediation: A Search for Complementary Routes to the State Courts", in *New Developments in Civil and Commercial Mediation. Global Comparative Perspectives Ius Comparatum – Global Studies in Comparative Law Vol.* 6 (Carlos Esplugues and Louis Marquis (eds), Heidelberg New York Dordrecht London, Springer International Publishing AG, 2015) 475.

22 ISS, *Resolving Family Conflicts. A Guide to International Family Mediation* (Geneva, 2014), available at www.ifm-mfi.org.

23 See "Feedback from Enquiry 1. Regarding Training, Competence and Qualification for Mediators", internal working document that is not publicly available. The analysis of the 26 responses received provided a sound basis to address and deepen the discussions that took place during a meeting in Geneva in Oct. 2015. (On the meeting, see further the next footnote below.) A distinction was proposed between key principles and promising practices in the Charter: (1) The adoption of a series of key principles determines a number of rules to be followed during international family mediation processes. Hence, adherence to the Charter invites all actors involved to scrupulously respect these principles. (2) Examples of promising practices serve as guidance to mediation practitioners across the world. The selected set of practices have also proven to be useful and relevant tools for international family mediation practice: see ISS, "Summary of Feedback Shared through 1st Enquiry Professional Consultation on the Charter for International Family Mediation Processes", internal working document that is not publicly available ("Professional Consultation"). Among others, aspects such as the multi-partiality concept; qualifications of mediators (education, hours of training, number of mediations conducted under supervision or co-mediation), continuous training, affiliation to a professional mediation structure, cultural awareness and sensitivity of mediators, decision-making by the parties, and international family mediation being centred on the interests of the child were mentioned. See Geneva 21–23 Oct. 2015 Workshop Docs (Eng.), internal working document that is not publicly available.

24 In Geneva, Switzerland, 21–23 Oct. 2015, at the Ecumenical Centre, two connected and simultaneous events took place under the auspices of The Hague Conference on Private International Law, International Social Services and the University of Geneva among others. The general title was "Cross Border Child Protection. Conference and Workshop".

The first event, entitled "Cross Border Child Protection: Legal and Social Perspectives – Towards a Better Protection of Children Worldwide – The 1996 Hague Child Protection Convention in Practice", brought more than 190 experts from many world regions together. Fifty-five international family mediators representing 24 countries from all continents attended the second meeting, a workshop entitled "Consultation on the Charter for International Family Mediation Processes". The author of this chapter was invited as an international family mediator linked to the Law Research Institute of the National Autonomous University of Mexico (IIJ-UNAM): see Nuria Gonzalez Martin, "Relatoria: 'Cross Border Child Protection. Conference and Workshop'", *Revista de Derecho Privado* no. 10 (2016), available at revistas.juridicas.unam.mx/index.php/derecho-privado/article/viewFile/10605/12771.

International Family Mediation Processes. A Collaborative Process".[25] As a result of this work, a Charter with ten core principles was produced in 2017. I shall comment on the Charter in the next section. A set of promising practices[26] was also compiled to initiate a discussion on training, competence and qualification requirements for mediators specialising in cross-border family conflicts,[27] that is, expectations regarding the development of specialised training.[28] A Draft Proposal on Best Practices for International Family Mediation Process was also prepared.

The ISS continues to work on the creation of a global network of specialised mediators. The larger scope of the discussion was to start a brainstorm regarding the creation of an international network of specialised mediators.[29] The next step was a meeting that took place in Geneva, from 7 to 9 May 2017 with a group of 30 experts well versed and experienced in training, network building and cooperation with State Authorities. Most of them, including the author of this chapter, have been participating in the collaborative process initiated in 2015 for the drafting of the Charter.

During the 2017 meeting we worked on:

(1) the idea to visualise international family mediation practices which were not included in the Charter. An online interactive platform was developed by the ISS to present practices in an accessible and easy-to-use format and to offer mediators who wish to extend their scope and

25 The Charter consists of core principles and a set of best practices. "While the respect of all core principles is a requirement for international family mediation practice, the best practices provide guidance to mediation practitioners to fulfil the principles": ISS, Draft Charter for International Family Mediation Processes. A Collaborative Process, March 2016 ("ISS Draft Charter") which was made available to the group of international mediators listed in the final document entitled *How to Use the Charter. A Manual for State Authorities and Family Mediators*, available at ifm-mfi.org/sites/default/files/CHARTER/ENGLISH/How_to_Use_EN.pdf. Thus, a few topics had to be developed: practices useful to facilitate the mediation process; practices useful when working with legal and administrative bodies; practices useful to take the best interest of the child into account; practices to nurture cross-cultural awareness and sensitivity; practices to ensure mediators' competencies; public awareness; and general trends: see ISS, "Draft Proposal Best Practices for International Family Mediation Processes. A Collaborative Process" Working Document, 19 May 2016, internal working document that is not publicly available. Since 22 March 2016 a group of international family mediators has been working with the ISS to draft the final version of the Charter for International Family Mediation Processes. The author of this chapter was part of this Experts' Group. The final version of the Charter was published after submission of this chapter. It is available at www.ifm-mfi.org/sites/default/files/CHARTER/ENGLISH/IFM%20Charter_ENG.pdf.

26 "Recommendations of the ISS Collaborative Project on International Family Mediation, Geneva, 21–23 October 2015", available at www.iss-ssi.org/images/Conf-MFI/Recommendations_ENG.pdf (last accessed 21 Jan. 2017).

27 "Collaborative Process on International Family Mediation. Summary of Discussions. Training, Competence and Qualification for International Family Mediators", the final document is available at www.ifm-mfi.org (last accessed 21 Jan. 2017).

28 The International Family Mediation training content deals with the following topics: (1) international legal framework, understanding and knowledge of national law; (2) co-mediation with mediators of psychosocial and legal backgrounds, bilingual, woman/man, binational, etc.; (3) consideration of the children's interests; (4) drafting agreements to mediate; (5) dealing with domestic violence; (6) mediation at a distance; (7) cultural awareness and sensitivity; and (8) child-focused and child-inclusive mediation: internal working document that is not publicly available.

29 "Draft Proposal about Best Practices for International Family Mediation Process. A Collaborative Process", internal working document that is not publicly available.

practices with their peers from around the world "a virtual, multilingual and collaborative workplace".[30]

> [T]he platform's main objectives are information sharing and networking. The features of this tool allow users to download documents, to discuss practices, to publish events on specialized training and conferences. A "Demo" version was presented to the participants of the 2017 Meeting and a questionnaire helped identify in detail the needs and expectations of the participants;[31]

(2) mediator profiles involving individual practitioners from different contexts and cultures who have demonstrated proven mediation practices by highlighting their strength and value, as well as a number of lessons learned from their own experience. The presentation of mediator profiles within mediator networks allowed international family mediation practitioners represented in the collaborative process to share their experience, knowledge and approaches;[32]
(3) challenges relating to the creation of a global network and the development of a certification procedure. The participatory workshop gave the opportunity to share the participants'

> views on what was said and on their own experiences. They were asked to imagine the conception and elaboration of an effective global network. Participants reflected on the preparatory work, on network strategy and operation, and on recognition and networking.[33]

As I indicated above, the ISS gathered an international group of international family mediation practitioners from all continents to discuss the relevance of creating a worldwide network of mediators specialising in cross-border family conflicts. After two days of substantial discussions on competence and qualification, and the use of a network, the group decided on an action plan over 12 months, putting in place an international steering committee dedicated to elaboration of terms of references and a modus operandi. The ISS was tasked with the coordination of this steering committee. The objective of the meeting was to discuss opportunities to continue this process, in particular with the conception of an international affiliation procedure to a centralised network of mediators specialising in cross-border family conflicts and the setting up of a structure hosting such a network.

We are absolutely convinced that this collaborative process creates significant value because it enables:

(1) professionalisation of international family mediation practice;
(2) better access to professional mediation for many more people; and
(3) is essential for better recognition of a global effort (synergy).

Principles in international family mediation processes

Fortunately, around the world there is great similarity at the core of mediation. This is why we can talk about, more or less, common principles, skills and processes. For this reason and thinking about international mediation in family matters it is important to comment on some aspects

30 "Summary of Discussions. 2nd Meeting of the Collaborative Process. Towards a Global Network of International Family Mediators", Geneva, 7–9 May 2017, accessible only by the participants.
31 Ibid.
32 Ibid.
33 Ibid.

relating to principles and the latest advances in this field. Mediation principles constitute the basis for mediation; a basis in constant evolution that is also affected by cultural influences.

Once again talking about international parental child abduction and its connection with mediation, it must be said that the main goal or objective is the protection of children living separated and far from one of their parents. Undoubtedly, a multicultural upbringing and environment is enriching and helps children preserve relations with and develop affection for both of their parents, notwithstanding the distance that may separate them.

> While preserving all rights of persons involved, international family mediation empowers the participants to assume ownership and drive discussions over custody and parenting and agree on arrangements that can be made legally binding and enforced. The power of this process depends on a secured and neutral place for discussions to take place, offering participants a space to "tell their story" and share their experience as well as recognise each other's effort to pursue their role as a parent. Open dialogue and free expression are the driving forces for the whole process.[34]

This is where the principles are acknowledged as

> a basic and fundamental requirement to conduct international family mediation processes, each and every one being of equal importance. As they are inter-related, these principles provide a solid basis for the larger framework in which they are meant to be applied and practiced.[35]

In respect of international family mediation, in particular in cases of international parental child abduction, it becomes apparent that additional principles are needed over and above the "classic ones" such as voluntariness, confidentiality, neutrality, among others. The principles that are discussed below are set out in the ISS's Charter. They reflect fundamental values,[36] specifically for mediation in cross-border family conflicts. The Charter's

> *raison d'être* is to unite and engage mediation professionals across cultures and nations in identifying 10 core principles to be observed and respected when practising international family mediation. . . . It [that is, the Charter] was drafted with the mindful objective of protecting children who may be living separated and afar from one of their parents.[37]

The ten principles are basic and fundamental requirements for conducting international family mediation processes, which are all of equal importance. The adoption of ten core principles, which now constitute the Charter for International Family Mediation Processes, is a great path to take in international family mediation. The principles are the following:

34 ISS Draft Charter, preamble.

35 Ibid.

36 After the Geneva meeting that took place in Oct. 2015 (see note 24), the ISS proposed a set of principles in accordance with the discussions and feedback gained during the meeting. Specific points of discussion arose from the Geneva meeting. It was decided that the principle of "Party-driven and party-empowered process" would rather be highlighted in the preamble to the Charter. Furthermore, two proposed principles were still subject to discussion: (1) flexibility (or adaptability) of settings for cross-border family mediation; and (2) transparency of mediation processes. Many mediators agreed that these two principles could in fact feature as promising practices in the dedicated section: ISS Draft Charter.

37 ISS Draft Charter, preamble.

1. Voluntary participation. Mediation, including international family mediation, is a voluntary process through which participants in a cross-border family dispute jointly try to reach agreement in respect of their conflict, arrangements for their children, and related matters. Therefore, mediation cannot succeed if it is not voluntary; however, we cannot discard mandatory mediation.[38] It is important to highlight that in some countries mediation can be mandatory, even though the mediation process itself is voluntary and each participant needs to freely adhere to the process.

The parties should attend a first introductory session in order to be informed about the process.[39] For example: Lawyers and bureaucrats tend to handle international cases. Parties usually do not get involved directly. If parties attend a first meeting, at least they can evaluate the advantages and disadvantages of an amicable process.[40] Some authors are of the view that there may nevertheless be an encouragement or a requirement to attend an information or assessment meeting with a professional family mediator in order to consider mediation in cases of cross-border disputes over arrangements for children and related matters before or while making an application to a court or filing for an international procedure.[41]

Finally, participants as well as the mediator may suspend or terminate the mediation process at any time if they no longer consider it suitable or if no progress can be made towards agreement.[42]

2. Suitability of mediation. The welfare, safety and security of all participants engaging in mediation are of paramount concern for skilled and responsible mediators. Depending on how the mediation is arranged, the mediator may initially meet with each party separately to explore whether mediation or another dispute resolution process is suitable in the circumstances and, if mediation seems appropriate, whether both parties are willing to take part. International family mediation is not suitable for all situations.

The initial conversation revolves around three main questions:[43]

(1) consideration of the personal safety of participants;
(2) capacity to participate in mediation; and
(3) consideration of judicial and administrative proceedings.

3. Decision-making by the participants. Mediators do not have any decision-making power and are not supposed to influence the participants.[44] However, they will intervene when it is clear that certain decisions made by the participants are likely to fall outside the law. The participants should be assisted by the mediators to reach well-informed agreements that are realistic, acceptable

38 Professional Consultation, answer from Mexico.

39 ISS, Charter Questionnaire of the Drafting of the Charter for International Family Mediation Processes, answer from Mexico provided by the author of this chapter. The answer states that, unfortunately, in Mexico City there is no mandatory remission to the first informative session.

40 Professional Consultation, answer from Mexico.

41 ISS Draft Charter.

42 Ibid.

43 Ibid.

44 Ibid. The mediator is simply a facilitator who helps the parties to improve their communication skills and negotiating approach. If the agreement is the result of the most intimate conviction of the parties, the likelihood of compliance is very high. If the third party intervenes excessively, the likelihood of compliance diminishes drastically.

to all concerned, and take into account the wellbeing of the children.[45] This principle is sacrosanct. In spite of this, the mediator and the parties must be aware of judicial and administrative measures that have been taken. They cannot overlook the law governing the case; for example, if custody rights have already been granted to a parent, the margins of negotiation may be narrowed.[46]

On the other hand, it must be noted that there is a thin line between intervening when decisions fall outside the law and telling the parties what the law is. This seems to be an old debate. Is educating the parties about legal matters the same as providing legal advice? Mediators must be very careful not to give the parties legal advice.[47]

4. Access to independent legal advice. International family mediation processes often take place in a judicial context. Mediation agreements usually need to be given legal effect and decisions need to be recognised or made enforceable in all jurisdictions applicable to the dispute. Hence, equal access to independent legal advice for each participant is important to ensure informed decision-making on any joint settlement proposals and to verify whether these settlement proposals are enforceable in all jurisdictions. Mediators are not supposed to give legal advice, but they should inform the participants of the importance of the legal framework in cross-border family disputes. To safeguard the independence of the process, they might also encourage participants to keep in mind the wellbeing of the children when speaking to their legal advisers.[48] I must highlight that assistance by a lawyer does not imply his or her interference with the decisions parties have made in a mediation process.[49]

5. Confidentiality. Confidentiality is one of the most important characteristics of mediation. The participants and the mediator must not disclose any information obtained during the mediation, unless exceptional circumstances are present.[50]

Mediators must not disclose any information obtained during the mediation process without the participants' consent, unless there are indications of child abuse or a child being at risk of harm. The information that a participant reveals to the mediator in a separate meeting must also remain confidential, but the mediator may terminate the mediation process if a criminal offence is revealed. Mediators cannot voluntarily testify, nor can they be subpoenaed to testify in later civil proceedings as to any statement or any conduct that occurred during the mediation. A written settlement agreement resulting from mediation can be admissible in court or can otherwise be disclosed, but only if all parties sign the agreement and the agreement includes a statement that it is binding or it is enforceable in court.

Administrative and legal authorities may have to be informed about the outcome of the mediation, but they should not require access to information on what was said or done during the mediation process. Participants are informed by the mediators that what is said during the

45 ISS Draft Charter.

46 Professional Consultation, answer from Mexico.

47 ISS Draft Charter; Professional Consultation, answer from Mexico.

48 Ibid. The answer from Mexico pointed out that lawyers tend to claim that they are pursuing their client's best interest. This is not necessarily true: they want to win the case, and they are often not really interested in achieving the best for their client.

49 Professional Consultation, answer from Mexico. Lately, in Mexico, there has been an increasing trend to simulate mediation processes. Many people get easily certified as mediators, but they lack supervision. Ultimately, these "mediators" (basically, lawyers) actually sell judicial resolutions (mediation agreements are *res judicata*) to the parties. In truth, they give advice to the parties regarding what they deem to be best for them. Simulation is dangerous.

50 ISS Draft Charter.

process should remain confidential and not be repeated to the extended family, friends or communities. Lawyers or legal advisers will also be informed about the principle of confidentiality when participants seek independent legal advice.

Mediators and participants usually sign an "Agreement to Mediate", which can include and explain the issue of confidentiality and privilege, including exceptions to it.

6. Independence. Mediators must work independently. If mediators work for a State or court-related structure, the principle of independence guarantees the independent status of the mediator during the process. International family mediation processes can take place alongside administrative and judicial proceedings, but must be clearly distinguished from such processes and during communications with administrative and legal authorities.[51]

7. Impartiality. The process is seen to be fair, when mediators give equal attention and support to each participant, as well as to the needs of any child concerned. I prefer the term "multi-partiality" to "impartiality", because it is very difficult to be impartial when different parties are involved. The idea is to be equally connected with everyone, to be partial toward all parties in trying to ensure that their interests are met. It is important to highlight that mediators are trained and skilled to be "multi-partial", that is, they manage the mediation process in a balanced and even-handed way, without taking sides or building alliances with one of the participants. The mediator guiding the mediation must maintain the proceedings free of favouritism, partiality or personal preferences that imply conceding advantages to any of the parties. At the same time, the mediator must not have any conflict of interest or personal interest in the outcome of the mediation.[52]

8. Consideration of the rights and the interests of the child. This principle groups together many different aspects:

(1) Recognition of the rights of the child. The United Nations Convention on the Rights of the Child states that children have the right to express their views on decisions and arrangements that affect their lives, and that these views should be given due weight in accordance with the children's age and maturity. International family mediation processes are underpinned by the four principles of the rights of the child reflected in the Convention on the Rights of the Child (participation, protection, survival and development, and non-discrimination).[53]

(2) Consideration of the needs and wellbeing of the child. Fulfilling the needs and ensuring the wellbeing of the child must be a priority in any mediation process. International family

51 ISS Draft Charter; Professional Consultation, answer from Mexico. This answer indicated that although mediators can be public servants, as in Mexico City's High Court, it is preferable that they act as freely as private professionals do. For example: Judges may unduly interfere with public mediators arguing public interest in a certain case. This does not necessarily happen, but it is less likely that judges would exert pressure on private mediators. In Mexico City, for instance, many mediators work for the High Court, but they have always been independent – even in cases where the judge has asked them to identify the party that has not been cooperating in the mediation process. The principle of confidentiality has always been honoured.

52 ISS Draft Charter; Professional Consultation, answer from Mexico. The answer pointed out that impartiality of mediators can be challenged if they are public employees. In some cases where politicians or famous people are involved in a cross-border case, political and/or diplomatic pressure is unavoidable.

53 ISS Draft Charter; Professional Consultation, answer from Mexico. This answer indicated that parents must be aware of children's rights, but that these rights can be approached in a non-legal language; for instance, on many occasions, parents tend to think that they "own" their children. They have to know that children are the ones who have a right to care by their parents.

mediation processes must give special regard to the needs and wellbeing of children involved in the conflict. Mediators will therefore encourage parents to focus on the developmental interests of their children as well as on their own needs. Particular attention will be given to the importance of children maintaining relationships with both parents whenever safe, with regular virtual and physical contact where possible, given the geographic distance.[54]

(3) The voice of the child in mediation. Including the children's voice in accordance with their age and maturity requires specialised skills and additional resources. In addition, children's inclusion is subject to careful evaluation. International family mediation processes should be child-focused but not necessarily be child-inclusive. Consequently, whenever child-inclusive mediation is appropriate, children may be consulted within or alongside the mediation process. This can only happen with the consent of the parents, the children themselves, or a person appointed to represent the children. The objective of child participation is to voice views and feelings, not to take sides or decisions. Normally children are heard by a trained mediator separately from their parents, or, depending on the country and mediation practice, by a trained child specialist who will carefully bring the children's voice and developmental needs into the mediation processes for consideration. With the approval and skilful support of the mediator, adolescents of sufficient age and maturity may, if they actively seek to do so, share their views directly with their parents during the mediation process.[55]

9. Qualifications of international family mediators. International family mediators must be trained, experienced and accredited family mediators and must gain additional competencies to become international family mediators, including specific knowledge of the international legal framework for cross-border family disputes and cross-cultural awareness.[56] From the author's perspective, continuous bilingual, bicultural and advanced training should be contemplated.[57]

10. Cultural awareness and sensitivity of mediators. Intercultural awareness and respect for cultural differences are at the centre of international family mediation processes. Skilled

54 ISS, Draft Charter.

55 Ibid.

56 ISS Draft Charter; Professional Consultation, answer from Mexico. As this chapter was being written, the author led the first certification training program in the State of Hidalgo, Mexico.

57 An individual who intends to become a mediator must be trained thoroughly as such by senior mediators. From our perspective, the program can be divided into two parts: (1) theoretical learning (no more than 150 hours and at least one semester under the supervision of a qualified mediator); and (2) educational degree(s) and/or professional license(s) appropriate to the applicant's field of expertise, and current membership in a relevant business, trade, or professional association(s). The responsibilities inherent in the role of a mediator include: (a) Continuing mediator education and training: Involvement in continuing education and training activities designed to enhance mediator skills and knowledge; (b) Mediative capacity: Appropriate temperament (i.e. unbiased, patient, and professional); commitment to multi-partiality and objectivity. (c) Mediation skills: Ability to manage the mediation process; ability to foster collaboration, communication, and get to mutually acceptable resolutions; (d) Reputation (i.e. held in the highest regard by peers for integrity, fairness, and good judgment; dedicated to upholding the Model Standards of Conduct for Mediators); (e) Commitment to the alternative dispute resolution process (i.e. willingness to devote time and effort when selected to serve, in accordance with the needs of the parties; willingness to commit to speed, economy, and a just resolution; willingness to support efforts to best serve the field of alternative dispute resolution. All mediators should be well-trained in the art of asking relevant and pertinent questions to the parties, so that they can discover their real interests and abandon their positions. These views are available at www.adr.org/aaa/ShowPDF?doc=ADRSTG_003882 (last accessed 27 Jan. 2017).

mediators are conscious of the parties' cultural background and the context of the parties' upbringing, environment and beliefs even though they do not know each culture in detail. They will ensure that individuals are treated with equal respect regardless of their culture. Respect for individuals of all cultures is crucial.[58] Beliefs, cultural norms and values should be understood and taken into account. The mediation process is flexible and allows for the participation of religious or community leaders and extended family members where necessary and appropriate. Equally important, mediators have the capacity to detach from their own cultural background and history during mediation and to show openness and respect for all cultures while managing multiple divorce patterns, ensuring an appropriate gender balance.[59]

Conclusions

Undoubtedly, cooperation is a key component of Private International Law. Cooperation between different stakeholders – governmental and non-governmental organisations, academics and practitioners – is important in order to link theoretical and practical experience. Making use of the complementary nature of the work and progress of the various stakeholders by way of a collaborative process can be the key to implementing a good instrument, or several instruments, and may result in a successful method of resolving matters that concern families and children around the world, especially the recognition and enforcement of cross-border voluntary agreements.

As I mentioned above, we are concerned with families across different cultural, linguistic, and jurisdictional contexts, with conflicts and challenges that require appropriate solutions, aimed at protecting minors who are involuntarily immersed in painful disagreements. The implementation of a collaborative process is an extremely useful tool to cater for international family disputes. This process can be envisioned through the numerous advancements mentioned in this chapter.

A collaborative process is possible because there are good initiatives in place. From the deliberations emerge simple and practical ideas. However, cooperation is still necessary in at least two different ways:

(1) promoting information on international family mediation practice; and
(2) dedicating personnel from the Permanent Bureau of The Hague Conference on Private International Law or non-governmental organisations to coordinate goals with every single State through their Central Authority.

We need mediators in whom the parties can have the utmost confidence – individuals with whom the organisation (court or any other institution) has a strong and positive relationship and whose selection is based primarily on caseload needs and user preferences.

Bibliography

Beaumont, Paul R. and McEleavy, Peter E. *The Hague Convention on International Child Abduction* (Oxford, Oxford University Press, 1999).

Gonzalez Martin, Nuria. "International Parental Child Abduction and Mediation: An Overview", 48 *Fam. L. Q.* 319 (Summer 2014).

58 ISS Draft Charter; Professional Consultation, answer from Mexico. This answer included an example in order to understand the interests of the parties, namely that mediators must be acquainted with the culture of the party who is not residing in his or her own country. If other people's cultural traits are not understood, communication might be truncated.

59 ISS Draft Charter.

Gonzalez Martin, Nuria. "International Parental Child Abduction and Mediation", XV *Anuario Mexicano de Derecho International* 353 (2015).

Gonzalez Martin, Nuria. "Mexico and Civil, Family and Commercial Mediation: A Search for Complementary Routes to the State Courts", in Carlos Esplugues and Louis Marquis (eds) *New Developments in Civil and Commercial Mediation. Global Comparative Perspectives Ius Comparatum – Global Studies in Comparative Law Vol.* 6 (Heidelberg New York Dordrecht London, Springer International Publishing AG, 2015) 475.

Gonzalez Martin, Nuria. "Non Exceptional Exceptions: The latest on The United States of America and Mexico Supreme Courts' Hague Abduction Decisions (Lozano and Direct Amparo under Revision 903/2014)", 19 *Spanish Yearbook of International Law* 23 (2015).

Gonzalez Martin, Nuria. "Relatoria: 'Cross Border Child Protection. Conference and Workshop'", *Revista de Derecho Privado*, no. 10 (2016).

Hague Conference on Private International Law. *Guide to Good Practice under the Hague Convention of 25 October 1980 on the Civil Aspects of International Child Abduction, Mediation* (The Hague, 2012).

McEleavy, Peter. "Evaluating the Views of Abducted Children: Trends in Appellate Case Law", 20 *Child & Fam. L. Q.* 230 (2008).

McEleavy, Peter. "The New Child Abduction Regime in the European Union: Symbiotic Relationship or Forced Partnership?", 1 *J. Private Int'l. L.*, 5 (2005).

Vigers, Sarah. *Mediating International Child Abduction Cases: The Hague Convention* (Oxford and Portland, Bloomsbury, 2011).

Part III
Children

8

Child custody and cognate concepts

The challenges

Elaine E. Sutherland

Introduction

Many legal systems have long used the term "custody" to denote having overall responsibility for a child, sometimes distinguishing legal custody, the right to make decisions about the child's life, from physical custody, the right to have the child in one's care. The word has unmistakable possessory overtones and reflects an adult-centred approach to family relationships. In disputed cases, it is burdened by the historical baggage of commodifying children as a prize to be fought over, with parents being cast in the role of winners and losers, something that does nothing to encourage co-operative parenting in the future.

For these reasons, many jurisdictions have abandoned the term altogether, preferring a discourse that talks of "parental responsibility" (or "parental responsibilities") or "guardianship". These terms will be used in this chapter, alongside "custody", to reflect its comparative nature. Where the child's parents live together with the child in what is known as an "intact family", the divisible nature of custody or parental responsibility is not usually significant, separability acquiring greater importance in respect of never-together or separated parents.

Custody and the cognate concepts do not tell the whole story since parents and others who do not have custody of a child may still have a legally recognised role in the child's life through visitation, contact or parenting time and, while they are discussed in depth elsewhere in this volume,[1] mention will be made of them here. As ever with international comparisons, similar terminology may mask differences in the content of the concepts at play and, of course, the law must be understood in the social, political and economic context in which it is operating.

Set against the backdrop of international standards, this chapter addresses how domestic legal systems allocate custody of a child, in the first instance, before moving on to examine the resolution of disputes. Different approaches will be illustrated by the use of selective examples and particular attention will be devoted to issues that are controversial or challenging in many jurisdictions.

1 See Frederik Swennen, "Personal relations and contact concerning children" in this volume.

The international context

Any international examination of a child-related issue necessarily begins with the United Nations Convention on the Rights of the Child (CRC),[2] the gold standard for children's rights, ratified by all the countries of the world except the United States (US).[3] Three of its general principles are of particular importance for our present enquiry: Article 3, according primacy to the child's best interests; article 12, guaranteeing the child's right to participate in the decision-making process; and article 2, prohibiting discrimination on a range of grounds, including the child's or the parent's birth or other status.[4]

Beyond these principles, the CRC recognises the important role of parents and, sometimes, the wider family group, in providing direction and guidance to the child in a manner consistent with the child's evolving capacity,[5] noting the common responsibilities of both parents for the child's upbringing.[6] Anticipating the possibility of parental separation, the Convention emphasises the child's right to maintain personal relations and direct contact with both parents, save where such a course would be contrary to the child's best interests.[7] In addition, states are placed under an obligation to protect the child from all forms of physical or mental violence.[8]

Given its child-centred nature, it is unsurprising that the CRC does not use the term "custody", although it is found in other international instruments including the Hague conventions governing international co-operation in respect of child abduction[9] and on jurisdiction, and enforcement of parental responsibility.[10]

Numerous regional instruments are relevant to child custody in the countries where they apply. For the member states of the Council of Europe, the European Convention on Human Rights is of particular importance despite making no express mention of children or parents. Unsurprisingly, it is regional instruments dedicated to children, such as the African Charter on the Rights and Welfare of the Child,[11] the European Convention on the Exercise of Children's Rights[12] and the European Convention on Contact concerning Children,[13] that are most explicit in addressing many of the issues explored in this chapter.

2 1577 U.N.T.S. 3; (1989) 28 I.L.M. 1448, in force 2 Sept. 1990. For a discussion of how children's rights play out in specific contexts, see Geraldine Van Bueren, "Children's rights in the family" in this volume.

3 This is not the place for a discussion of the peculiar position of the US. Suffice to say that it has signed the Convention and many of the values embodied therein are respected in the law of the various US jurisdictions.

4 *General Comment No 5: General Measures of Implementation of the Convention on the Rights of the Child* (2003), CRC/GC/2003/5, para. 12.

5 Art. 5.

6 Art. 18(1). Reflecting the era in which it was drafted, the Convention proceeds on the basis of a child having two parents, not anticipating the recognition of multiple parents, discussed below.

7 Art. 9(3). See also art. 8(1), where preservation of family relations is one of the facets of the child's identity mentioned expressly.

8 Art. 19(1).

9 Hague Convention on the Civil Aspects of International Child Abduction 1980, H.C.C.H., No. 28.

10 Hague Convention on Jurisdiction, Applicable Law, Recognition, Enforcement and Co-operation in Respect of Parental Responsibility and Measures for the Protection of Children 1996, H.C.C.H., No. 34.

11 O.A.U. Doc. CAB/LEG/24.9/49 (1990), in force 29 Nov. 1999.

12 E.T.S. No. 160 (1996), in force 1 July 2000.

13 E.T.S. No. 192 (2003), in force 1 Sept. 2005.

The starting point

Many legal systems have long since abandoned the notion of the *paterfamilias* with almost unfettered authority over his children and, often, his wife.[14] Spousal equality is now the order of the day and custody and parental responsibility now vest in both married, different-sex parents in the intact family. Despite legal parity, mothers continue to provide more childcare than do fathers,[15] something that may become significant in the event of future parenting disputes. The child's participation rights, guaranteed by article 12 of the CRC, apply to the family setting as they do elsewhere,[16] but the extent to which they are respected, in law or in fact, varies between legal systems and, in all probability, between families.[17]

So much for married, genetic parents, but what of unmarried parents, same-sex parents, other family members and the challenges posed by assisted reproductive technology (ART)?

Non-marital fathers

Historically, legal systems expressed societal disapproval of extra-marital sex by drawing a distinction between children born to married parents and those who were not, with the latter facing discrimination. As the proportion of non-marital births increased – now exceeding 50% in many countries[18] – and moral policing abated, legal discrimination diminished.[19] Negative perception of non-marital fathers persisted and, while they have achieved equality with mothers and married fathers in some jurisdictions, that approach is far from universal.[20] They may continue to face challenges, first, in establishing paternity and, second, in the additional test they must pass in order to gain responsibility.

14 Mary Ann Glendon, *The Transformation of Family Law: State, Law and Family in the United States and Western Europe* (University of Chicago Press, Chicago, 1989) 97–98.

15 *Global Gender Gap Report 2016* (World Economic Forum, Geneva, 2016), 31–32, available at www.oecd.org/gender/data/balancingpaidworkunpaidworkandleisure.htm.

16 United Nations Committee on the Rights of the Child, *General Comment No 12: The Right of the Child to be Heard* (2009), CRC/C/GC/12, paras. 92–96.

17 *Law Reform and Implementation of the Convention of the Rights of the Child* (UNICEF Innocenti Research Centre, Florence, 2007) (concluding that "laws that expressly recognise the right of children to be heard in the context of the family are rare" since only three of the 52 countries surveyed – the Czech Republic, Romania and Scotland – had such laws in place). There are other examples, including Germany, Hungary, Finland, Norway, Portugal, South Africa, Sweden and Russia. See further, Elaine E. Sutherland, "Listening to the Child's Voice in the Family Setting: From Aspiration to Reality", *Child & Family Law Quarterly* 26, no. 2 (2014) 152.

18 The Organisation for Economic Cooperation and Development (OECD) reported that, in 2014, just under 40% of births in its 35 member countries occurred outside of marriage. Individual countries showed marked variations, the proportion being below 10% in Greece, Israel, Japan, Korea and Turkey and over 50% in Belgium, Chile, Denmark, Iceland, Estonia, France, Mexico, Norway, Slovenia, and Sweden. See OECD Family Database, Chart SF2.4.A, available at www.oecd.org/els/family/SF_2_4_Share_births_outside_marriage.pdf.

19 Exceptions remain. For example, while the Succession to the Crown Act 2013 removed gender discrimination in respect of the monarchy in the UK, it had no effect on birth status, nor on succession to aristocratic titles.

20 For recent developments in particular jurisdictions, see Luise Hauschild, "Germany: Reforming the Law on Parental Responsibility" and Ingerborg Schwenzer & Tomie Keller, "New Rules on Parental Responsibility in Switzerland", both in *The International Survey of Family Law* (Bill Atkin ed., Jordans, Bristol, 2014) 145 and 457, respectively.

A married man customarily benefits from the (usually rebuttable) legal presumption that he is the father of his wife's child.[21] In some jurisdictions, male cohabitants benefit from a similar presumption[22] and there are often simple administrative procedures for acknowledging paternity where the parents agree.[23] In the absence of such provisions and the requisite maternal co-operation, the father may have to establish paternity in court and DNA testing facilitates that process, provided that the mother agrees to the child being tested or the court has the power to authorise the test.[24]

Assuming he can establish paternity, the non-marital father has the same custodial or parental responsibilities as mothers and married fathers in some jurisdictions.[25] In others, he may have to demonstrate that he is worthy of equal treatment. Echoing the words of the US Supreme Court from some two decades earlier,[26] the European Court of Human Rights, in 2005, articulated the position as follows:

> The Court does not agree . . . that a mere biological kinship, without any further legal or factual elements indicating the existence of a close personal relationship, would be regarded as sufficient to attract the protection of Article 8.[27]

There is a plentiful body of European Court case law on fathers who did[28] or did not[29] pass that test. In South Africa, blanket paternal equality has been rejected on the basis that a "nuanced and balanced consideration of a society in which the factual demographic picture and parental relationships are often quite different from those upon which 'first-world' western societies are premised"[30] justified a different approach.

Donor children

Development in the various techniques falling under the umbrella of ART, combined with their increased use, has created new challenges for legal systems, posing fundamental questions about the very meaning of parentage.

21 See, for example, Family Law Act 1995, s. 69P (Australia); Uniform Child Status Act 2010, s. 4(1) (Canada); Children Act 1981, §3 (Norway); Law Reform (Parent and Child) (Scotland) Act, 1986, s. 5(1)(a); Children's Act 38 of 2005, s. 20(1) (South Africa).

22 See, for example, Family Law Act 1995 s. 69Q (Australia); Uniform Child Status Act 2010, s. 4(1) (Canada); Children's Act 38 of 2005, s. 21(1) (South Africa).

23 See, for example, Family Law Act 1995, s. 69R (Australia); Uniform Child Status Act 2010, s. 4(1) (Canada); Children Act 1981, §4 (Norway); Law Reform (Parent and Child) (Scotland) Act 1986, s. 5(1)(b); Children's Act 38 of 2005, s. 21(1) (South Africa).

24 In Scotland, for example, the court has no power to overrule maternal refusal to have the child tested, allowing her to block or, at least, impede the father's progress: Law Reform (Parent and Child) (Scotland) Act 1986, s. 6. In contrast, in Norway, the mother has no such latitude: Children Act 1981, §§ 5 and 25.

25 See, for example, Care of Children Act 2004, s. 18 (New Zealand); Children (Scotland) Act 1995, s. 3.

26 *Lehr v. Robertson* 463 US 248, 262 (1983). See further, Serena Mayeri, "Foundling Fathers: (Non-)Marriage and Parental Rights in the Age of Equality", *Yale Law Journal* 125, no. 8 (2016) 2292.

27 *Lebbink v. Netherlands* (2005) 40 E.H.R.R. 18, [37]. Art. 8 of the European Convention on Human Rights guarantees respect for private life and family life.

28 *Sahin v. Germany* (2003) 36 E.H.R.R. 43 (the father had lived with his daughter for the first year of her life and continued to have contact with her thereafter for some time) and *Zaunegger v. Germany* (2010) 50 E.H.R.R. 38 (unmarried parents had lived together for the first three years of the child's life and the father had cared for his daughter for the two years following their separation).

29 *Söderbäck v. Sweden* (1998) 29 E.H.R.R. 95, [32] (father's contact with the child had been "infrequent and limited in character").

30 *Fraser v. Children's Court, Pretoria North* 1997 (2) SA 261 (CC), [29].

Even before the advent of statutory regulation of ART, where a married woman gave birth to a child using donor gametes, her husband benefitted from the statutory presumption of paternity, the donor was excluded, custody vested in the couple and they could conceal the circumstances of conception from the world and, indeed, from the child, if they chose to do so.[31] For other couples, the position was less clear and disputes were resolved on a case-by-case basis.

Surrogacy was always more controversial,[32] in part, due to its commercial associations[33] and the scope for surrogates to be exploited,[34] and it is banned in a number of jurisdictions.[35] While it is permitted in most US states, two early surrogacy cases illustrate the consequences of a lack of statutory regulation. In 1988, the New Jersey Supreme Court refused to enforce a traditional surrogacy agreement,[36] but gave custody of the child to the intended parents, nonetheless, on the basis of the child's best interests.[37] Just five years later, the California Supreme Court upheld a gestational surrogacy agreement.[38] While model legislation governing the whole range of ART techniques is available for adoption by the various US states,[39] they vary in the extent and manner of regulation.

While same-sex couples were sometimes obstructed in accessing ART in the past, it is now widely available to them.[40] Recognition of the child's second parent can involve a complex intersection of their opportunity to formalise their own relationship, whether they do so, the consequences of that for parental recognition and the regulation of ART itself.[41] That problem is

31 Deception of the child implicates arts. 7 and 8 of the CRC. In some jurisdictions mandatory disclosure to the adult child of the fact of donor conception, combined with disclosure of the donor's identity, addresses the problem. See Eric Blyth & Lucy Frith, "Donor-Conceived People's Access to Genetic and Biographical History: An Analysis of Provisions in Different Jurisdictions Permitting Disclosure of Donor Identity", *International Journal of Law, Policy and the Family* 23, no. 2 (2009) 174 and Petra Nordqvist, "The Drive for Openness in Donor Conception Disclosure and the Trouble with Real Life", *International Journal of Law, Policy and the Family* 28, no. 3 (2014) 321.

32 See Philipp Reuss, "Surrogacy" in this volume.

33 In India, a favourite destination for foreigners seeking a commercial surrogate, if the Surrogacy (Regulation) Bill 2016 passes, commercial surrogacy would become illegal and altruistic surrogacy would only be permitted where the surrogate is a member of the (married) intending parents' family and subject to a range of other conditions. See the Surrogacy (Regulation) Bill 2016, available at www.prsindia.org/billtrack/the-surrogacy-regulation-bill-2016-4470/.

34 Melanie G. Fellowes, "Commercial Surrogacy in India: The Presumption of Adaptive Preference Formation, the Possibility of Autonomy and the Persistence of Exploitation", *Medical Law International* 17, no. 4 (2017) 249.

35 While surrogacy is prohibited in some European jurisdictions, this has not prevented the European Court of Human Rights protecting the child's art. 8 right to respect for private and family life: *Labassée v. France* Application No. 65941/11 and *Mennesson v. France* Application No. 65192/11, both judgments of the Fifth Section, 26 June 2014. See also, *Paradiso and Campanelli v. Italy* (2017) 65 E.H.R.R. 2.

36 "Traditional" surrogacy involves a surrogate being impregnated using donor sperm, often that of the man who plans to raise the resulting child, making the surrogate the child's genetic mother. In "gestational surrogacy" the surrogate is an unrelated host, with the embryo being the product of gametes provided by the intended parents or donors.

37 *In the Matter of Baby M.* 109 N.J. 396; 537 A.2d 1227 (N.J. 1988).

38 *Johnson v. Calvert* 5 Cal.4th 84, 851 P. 2d 776 (Cal. 1993).

39 Uniform Parentage Act 2017 which, at the time of writing, has been adopted in the state of Washington. The earlier, 2002 version regulated ART and has been adopted in a number of states.

40 See Nicholas Bamforth, "Same-sex marriages and civil or registered partnerships" in this volume.

41 An illustration of this intersection at play can be found in the *per curiam* opinion of the US Supreme Court in *Pavan v. Smith* 137 S.Ct. 2075 (2017), where it applied its own reasoning in its landmark decision in *Obergefell v. Hodges* 136 S.Ct. 2584 (2015), in holding the refusal of the state of Arkansas to register the birth mother's wife as the child's second parent, despite the fact that it did so for husbands of married women who have children in similar circumstances, to be unconstitutional. The court refused to revisit this issue when it denied the petition for writ of certiorari sought in *McLaughlin v. McLaughlin* 138 S.Ct. 1165.

avoided in the many jurisdictions where the legislation in place governing the parentage of donor children includes same-sex couples.

The United Kingdom (UK) provides a good example of an attempt at comprehensive regulation of ART. While the first statute, passed in 1990, provided for determining the legal parentage of donor children, it was shamelessly heteronormative in character.[42] Happily, its 2008 successor is very much more inclusive,[43] and provides that the woman who gives birth is treated as the child's mother. Her (male or female) spouse or (female) civil partner is treated as the child's other parent. Where the birth mother is not married or civilly enpartnered, the provisions are more complex but, in essence, as long as treatment was undertaken in the UK by a provider licensed under the statute and the mother consents, the child's second parent will be the person who agrees to take on that role and gives the requisite formal notice. Thereafter, parental responsibility flows from recognition as a parent for spouses and civil partners, and from registration as a parent for other second parents.[44] Surrogacy is accommodated by a form of expedited adoption which, subject to a host of conditions, including the consent of the surrogate, allows for recognition of the intended parents. It will be clear from the above summary that this system of bright line rules and state oversight is designed to facilitate the child having two parents and the exclusion of donors.

Challenging the dyad

Thus far, this discussion has been premised on a child having, at most, two custodial parents. Yet legal systems have long provided for more than two people playing significant roles in a child's life in the context of open adoption; through recognition of *de facto* parents; and by permitting other persons such as step-parents, grandparents and the child's siblings to seek custody or specific responsibilities.[45]

When ART challenged traditional notions of parentage, it focussed attention on a more radical option: the possibility of a child having three or more parents. 2007 was a landmark year for multiple parentage, with courts in Ontario[46] and Pennsylvania[47] embracing it, and reports of a similar decision in Brazil in 2014.[48] More recently, legislatures in British Columbia[49] and California[50] have also taken this path. It is a reflection of the controversy surrounding multiple parentage that the Canadian model statute, available for adoption by the provinces, makes provision for multiple parentage in the context of ART,[51] while its equivalent in the US applies the concept more generally and offers states alternative provisions, one allowing for the possibility of multiple parents and the other preserving the dyad.[52]

42 Human Fertilisation and Embryology Act 1990 (UK).
43 Human Fertilisation and Embryology Act 2008 (UK).
44 Children (Scotland) Act 1995, s. 3.
45 Haim Abraham, "A Family Is What You Make It? Recognition and Regulation of Multiple Parents", *American University Journal of Gender Social Policy & Law* 25, no. 4 (2017) 405.
46 *A.(A.) v. B.(B.)* (2007) 278 D.L.R. (4th) 519 (Ont. C.A.).
47 *Jacob v. Shultz-Jacob* 923 A.2d 473 (Pa. Super. Ct. 2007).
48 "Brazilian Baby Registered with Three Parents", *BBC News*, 13 Sept. 2014, available at www.bbc.co.uk/news/world-latin-america-29195890.
49 Family Law Act 2011, SBC, ss. 29 and 30.
50 Cal.Fam.Code § 7612. See also Me. Rev. Stat. tit. 19-a, § 1853(2).
51 Uniform Child Status Act 2010, s. 9 (Canada).
52 Uniform Parentage Act 2017, § 613(c) (US).

Multiple parentage can bring multiple benefits. The child acquires an additional, legally recognised, champion (or champions) and there may be pecuniary rewards in terms of financial support and inheritance rights. The adults secure legal recognition and all that goes with it and have the opportunity to share responsibility.[53] The disadvantage is that there are more adults who may find themselves in dispute, creating the potential for more – and more complex – litigation.

Resolving disputes

Most parting and never-together parents resolve issues over the future care of their children by agreement or, sometimes, by default, with one parent simply ceasing to be a part of the child's life. Whatever they decide, it is to be hoped that they prioritise the child's best interests and respect the child's participation rights. As with decision-making in intact families, the extent to which that is the case will, necessarily, depend on the family in question.

It has long been accepted that courts may not be the optimum setting in which to resolve disputes over the future care of children. The cost and time involved are among the shortcomings commonly cited, but the principal criticism is the potential of (particularly adversarial) litigation to generate or exacerbate acrimony. Various forms of alternative dispute resolution (ADR), including mediation, collaborative law and arbitration, have been embraced in the family law context.[54] Such is the enthusiasm for ADR, in some jurisdictions, that couples are required to attempt to resolve difference in that way before they can take a dispute to court, with exceptions usually being made for urgent cases and those involving domestic abuse.[55] ADR is not, however, a panacea and the fact that the parents have reached agreement does not necessarily mean that their solution is in the child's best interests,[56] nor that the child's participation rights have been respected.[57]

The best interests test

Some parenting disputes are not amenable to negotiation and it falls to the courts to resolve them. Consistent with the CRC, in most jurisdictions the courts apply the "best interests test", sometimes known as the "welfare test", in reaching decisions and, indeed, in many of them its use predates the CRC. The Janus-like quality of the test, combining the virtue of flexibility with the vice of vagueness, has long been recognised.[58] Its flexibility enables courts to engage

53 Abraham, *supra* note 45 at 420–425; Susan F. Appleton, "Parents by the Numbers", *Hofstra Law Review* 37, no. 1 (2008) 11; Lois Harder & Michelle Thomarat, "Parentage Law in Canada: The Numbers Game of Standing and Status", *International Journal of Law, Policy and the Family* 26, no. 1 (2012) 62.

54 See Nuria Gonzalez-Martin, "International family mediation: recent developments" in this volume for a discussion of a number of the forms of ADR used in family disputes.

55 See, for example, Family Law Act 1995, s. 60I (Australia); Children and Families Act 2014, s. 10(1) (England and Wales); Marriage Act 1991, s. 26 (Norway).

56 Eva Ryrstedt, "Mediation regarding Children – Is the Result Always in the Best Interests of the Child: A View from Sweden", *International Journal of Law, Policy and the Family* 26, no. 2 (2012) 220.

57 For promising developments, see Jennifer McIntosh *et al.*, "Child-Focused and Child-Inclusive Mediation: A Comparative Study of Outcomes", *Journal of Family Studies* 10, no. 1 (2004) 87 (Australia) and Deb Inder, "A Comparison of Child Inclusive and Child Focused Mediation Models, their Benefits and Relevance in the Context of Family Law Practice in New Zealand", *New Zealand Family Law Journal* 8, no. 4 (2014) 69.

58 See further Elaine E. Sutherland, "Article 3 of the UN Convention on the Rights of the Child: The Challenges of Vagueness and Priorities", in *Implementing Article 3 of the United Nations Convention on the Rights of the Child: Best Interests, Welfare and Well-Being* (Elaine E. Sutherland & Lesley-Anne Barnes Macfarlane eds, Cambridge University Press, Cambridge, UK, 2016) 21, 36.

in individualised decision-making, assessing what will serve the interests of the particular child. The price of flexibility is uncertainty and long ago Robert Mnookin famously described the best interests test as "vague and indeterminate",[59] opening the door to, almost unlimited, judicial discretion.[60] Since indeterminacy leads to unpredictability, it is argued, the incentive for the parties to negotiate a settlement is reduced, resulting in increased resort to litigation.[61]

The challenge lies in identifying the content of "best interests". What is relevant in assessing what is beneficial or detrimental to a child? Many jurisdictions have sought to clarify the content of the concept and to curtail judicial discretion by devising statutory welfare checklists, enumerating the factors that are relevant. A sufficiently broad-ranging checklist can provide guidance to a court without diminishing the scope for individualised assessment,[62] but whether checklists limit judicial discretion has been doubted and they have been criticised for being incomplete and for failing to attach relative weight to different factors or prioritise potentially conflicting factors.[63]

These criticisms did not trouble the United Nations Committee on the Rights of the Child (UNCRC) when it recommended the use of a "non-exhaustive and non-hierarchical list of elements that could be included in a best-interests assessment",[64] something it saw as accommodating flexibility and individualised assessment. It went on to provide full discussion, not only of the elements it saw as central,[65] but also of how the assessment and determination should be carried out, requiring evaluation to be by means of a "transparent and objective formal process"[66] that incorporates "child-friendly procedural safeguards".[67]

Presumptions – and a rule

While they are sometimes incorporated into welfare checklists, presumptions depart from the ethos of the UNCRC recommendations. Whereas a checklist operates with "the weight of each element depending on the others",[68] a presumption – even one that is rebuttable – starts from the assumption that one factor outweighs other considerations. While that may not render all presumptions incompatible with the CRC, it suggests that they warrant particular scrutiny.

Two issues dominate legal and political discourse on parenting disputes. The first is ensuring that both parents continue to be involved in the child's life, an approach endorsed by the CRC.[69]

59 Robert H. Mnookin, "Child Custody Adjudication: Judicial Functions in the Face of Indeterminacy", *Current Legal Problems* 39, no. 3 (1976) 226, 229. For a reappraisal of his earlier thoughts, see Robert Mnookin, "Child Custody Revisited", *Law and Contemporary Problems* 77, no. 1 (2014) 249.

60 Helen Reece, "The Paramountcy Principle: Consensus or Construct?", *Current Legal Problems* 49 (1996) 267, 273; Stephen Parker, "The Best Interests of the Child – Principles and Problems", *International Journal of Law and the Family* 8, no. 1 (1994) 26.

61 Mnookin (1979), *supra* note 59 at 262; Reece, *supra* note 60 at 273.

62 Robert A. Warshak, "Parenting by the Clock: The Best Interests of the Child Standard, Judicial Discretion, and the American Law Institute's 'Approximation Rule'", *University of Baltimore Law Review* 41, no. 1 (2011) 83, 98.

63 John Eekelaar, *Regulating Divorce* (Clarendon Press, Alderley, 1991) 125.

64 *General Comment No. 14 on the Rights of the Child to Have his or her Best Interests Taken as a Primary Consideration* (2013), CRC/C/GC/14, para. 50.

65 Ibid., paras. 52–79.

66 Ibid., para. 87.

67 Ibid., paras. 85–99.

68 Ibid., para. 80.

69 Arts. 5, 8, 9 and 18.

Presumptions favouring joint custody and shared parenting have emerged in many legal systems in response to this imperative and I shall return to each presently.

The second dominant issue is the need to protect children from exposure to domestic abuse, something identified long ago as harmful to children, leading to problems with behaviour, in school and in forming relationships[70] and, in some cases, to post-traumatic stress disorder.[71] More recent research has highlighted the impact of trauma on children and the long-term impact of witnessing domestic abuse on brain development.[72] As we have seen, the CRC places states under an obligation to protect the child from all forms of physical or mental violence.[73]

These two imperatives – continuing parental involvement and protection from domestic abuse – pose a significant challenge to legal systems. Their intersection has resulted in, sometimes ferocious, lobbying and debate that often takes on a very gendered dynamic with groups supporting (largely female) abuse victims clashing with fathers' rights organisations. Presumptions that operated in the past are noted below before the various modern presumptions that seek to secure continuing parental involvement in the child's life are assessed.

Historical presumptions

In the past, parenting by separated and never-together parents often proceeded on the basis of one parent being given custody of the child while the other was awarded visitation or access. The older presumption that gave the married father primacy, post-divorce, disappeared. In some jurisdictions, it was replaced, for a time, either in law or in practice, by a maternal preference, particularly where the child was of "tender years". The explicit gender bias embodied in that presumption resulted in its consignment to the history books as well.[74]

Another approach that found favour in a small number of US states in the 1980s is the, facially gender-neutral, "primary caretaker presumption" under which the parent who discharged parenting functions in the past was preferred in awarding custody of the child, always provided that parent was deemed "fit".[75] While it has been criticised as a backward-looking, thinly-disguised maternal preference,[76] it lives on as one factor in welfare checklists in some states.[77]

70 Peter G. Jaffe *et al.*, *Child Custody and Domestic Violence: A Call for Safety and Accountability* (Sage Publications, Thousand Oaks, 2003) 23.

71 Sandra A. Graham-Berman & Alytia A. Levendosky, "Traumatic Stress Symptoms in Children of Battered Women", *Journal of Interpersonal Violence* 13, no. 1 (1998) 111; Peter Lehmann, "The Development of Posttraumatic Stress Disorder in Children who Witnessed Mother Abuse", *Journal of Family Violence* 12, no. 3 (1997) 241.

72 Areti Tsavoussis *et al.*, "Child-witnessed Domestic Violence and its Adverse Effects on Brain Development: A Call for Societal Self-examination and Awareness", *Frontiers in Public Health* 2 (2014) 178; Robert F. Anda *et al.*, "The Enduring Effects of Abuse and Related Adverse Experiences in Childhood: A Convergence of Evidence from Neurobiology and Epidemiology", *European Archives of Psychiatry & Clinical Neuroscience* 256, no. 3 (2006) 174.

73 Art. 19(1).

74 Warshak, *supra* note 62 at 90–93.

75 The presumption was famously articulated in *Garska v. McCoy* 167 W.Va. 59; 278 S.E.2d 357 (W.Va. 1981). See Richard Neely, "The Primary Caretaker Parent Rule: Child Custody and the Dynamics of Greed", *Yale Law and Policy Review* 3, no. 1 (1984) 168.

76 Sheri A. Ahl, "A Step Backward: The Minnesota Supreme Court Adopts A 'Primary Caretaker' Presumption in Child Custody Cases: *Pikula v Pikula*", *Minnesota Law Review* 70, no. 6 (1986) 1344.

77 See, for example, Ore. Rev. Stat. § 107.137(1).

Joint custody

At first glance, joint custody is the most conceptually unambiguous way to endorse continuing parental involvement in the child's life. Like custody itself, it may mean different things depending on the jurisdiction in question, and the extent to which parental involvement is equal may vary. It usually anticipates shared or joint parental decision-making, at least in respect of significant decisions, with courts often having the power to allocate authority over specific decisions to one parent. It may also denote the right to determine the child's residence. As one US commentator observed, "the joint custody-sole custody distinction is best viewed along a continuum, not as a sharp divide".[78]

Joint custody emerged in the US in the 1970s, becoming the preferred option in many states in the 1980s. In the constantly shifting tableau of state laws, generalisations should be offered with caution, but all states now permit joint custody, with some having a presumption in its favour.[79] Parental consent is often, but not always, a prerequisite. Following the 1990 Congressional resolution supporting a statutory presumption against giving custody of a child to a spouse-abusing parent,[80] all states now require domestic abuse to be considered in the context of custody decisions, with many having a presumption against joint custody where it is present.[81]

Sweden embraced joint custody earlier than many other European jurisdictions and provides a good example of it being adjusted to meet emerging concerns. In 1976, married and unmarried parents were given the option of joint parental responsibility, with the court acquiring the power to impose it, despite the opposition of one parent, in 1998.[82] It is anticipated that parents will take all major decisions (everything beyond everyday care) jointly, although the court retains the power to determine residence and contact. In 2006, the law was amended further to take account of the parents' ability to co-operate, and the need to protect children from domestic abuse and to reinforce the child's participation rights.[83] Denmark and Norway followed the Swedish approach and have their own local variations.[84]

Shared parenting – and the element of time

Shared parenting seeks to ensure the continuing involvement of both parents in the child's life, something supported wholeheartedly by the CRC, provided that course is in the child's best interests. While proponents of shared parenting claim that it is beneficial to children,[85] others present a more nuanced picture, highlighting the importance of the child's developmental stage and the degree of parental co-operation or conflict.[86]

78 J. Herbie DiFonzo, "From the Rule of One to Joint Parenting: Custody Presumptions in Law and Policy", *Family Courts Review* 52, no. 4 (2014) 213, 217.

79 Linda Elrod, *Child Custody Practice and Procedure* (Thomson Reuters, Eagan, 2017) § 5.1.

80 136 Cong. Rec. H11777 (1990).

81 Elrod, *supra* note 79 at § 5.14.

82 Anna Singer, "Parenting Issues after Parental Separation: A Scandinavian Perspective", in *Routledge Handbook of Family Law and Policy* (John Eekelaar & Rob George eds Routledge, Oxford, 2014) 235, 236–237.

83 Maria Eriksson, "Contact, Shared Parenting and Violence: Children as Witnesses of Domestic Violence in Sweden", *International Journal of Law, Policy and the Family* 25, no. 2 (2011) 165.

84 Singer, *supra* note 82 at 237.

85 Linda Nielsen, "Re-examining the Research on Parental Conflict, Coparenting, and Custody Arrangements", *Psychology, Public Policy and Law* 23, no. 2 (2017) 211.

86 Jennifer McIntosh *et al.*, "Post-separation Parenting Arrangements", *Family Matters* 86 (2011) 40.

What distinguished some current law reform initiatives from the CRC and the UNCRC recommendations lies in the preoccupation with the amount of time each parent spends with the child, with some fathers' rights groups calling for equal – that is, a 50–50 division of – parenting time. Allocation of time is about quantity and discloses nothing about the quality of the resulting child – parent interaction,[87] leading commentators to warn that "a preoccupation with time as such might reflect parental feelings of entitlement rather than benefits for children".[88]

With the exception of the approximation rule, discussed below, statutory models for shared parenting do not normally quantify the time to be spent with each parent. There is reference in some of the academic literature to the child spending at least 35% of the time with each parent.[89] That figure is significant in some jurisdictions in calculating child support liability,[90] raising questions over the motive of some parents in seeking extensive time with the child.[91]

Australia is often cited as the poster child for shared – or, erroneously, for equal – parenting time. The 2006 reforms there created a presumption of "equal shared parental responsibility".[92] When it became apparent that this had resulted in inadequate protection against the child being exposed to domestic abuse,[93] the legislation was amended further, in 2011, emphasising that the presumption does not apply to cases where child abuse or family violence is present.[94] Abuse and violence aside, courts are directed to do no more than "*consider* whether the child spending equal time with each of the parents would be in the best interests of the child" and practicable.[95] There is no presumption of equal parenting time. It seems, however, that the legislative developments created very real confusion in the country, with many people believing that "equal or shared care was the default presumption".[96] Recent research demonstrates that courts ordered equal parenting time in only 3 to 10% of disputed cases in the years following the reforms.[97]

Shared parenting has found academic support in Europe[98] and, while many European jurisdictions provide for separated parents to have shared responsibilities, there is reluctance to legislate for the amount of time the child should spend with each parent. For example, despite extensive lobbying by fathers' rights groups in England and Wales in support of a presumption of equal parenting time, the 2014 reforms there secured nothing more than the addition of a rebuttable

87 Mary Jean Dolan & Daniel J. Hynan, "Fighting over Bedtime Stories: An Empirical Study of the Risks of Valuing Quantity over Quality in Child Custody Decisions", *Law and Psychology Review* 38 (2014) 45.
88 Bruce Smyth *et al.*, "Legislating for Shared-Time Parenting after Parental Separation: Insights from Australia?", *Law and Contemporary Problems* 77, no. 1 (2014) 109, 145.
89 Nielsen, *supra* note 85 at 211; Smyth *et al.*, *supra* note 88 at 125.
90 See Margaret Brinig, "Child support" in this volume.
91 See Karen Czapanskiy, "The Shared Custody Child Support Adjustment: Not Worth the Candle", *Family Law Quarterly* 49, no. 3 (2015) 409 (US); Courtney Palmer, "Child Support and Shared Parenting in Canada: A Reality Cheque", *Dalhousie Journal of Legal Studies* 22 (2013) 101; and Smyth *et al.*, *supra* note 88 at 125–126 (Australia).
92 Family Law Act 1975, s. 61DA, as amended by the Family Law Amendment (Shared Parental Responsibility) Act 2006.
93 Richard Chisholm, *Family Courts Violence Review* (Attorney-General's Department, 2009); *Social Policy Research Centre, Shared Care Parenting Arrangements since the 2006 Family Law Reforms* (Social Policy Centre University of New South Wales, Sydney, 2010).
94 Family Law Act 1975, s. 61DA, as amended by the Family Law Legislation Amendment (Family Violence and Other Measures) Act 2011. See Smyth *et al.*, *supra* note 88 at 120.
95 Ibid., s. 65DAA(1) (emphasis added).
96 Smyth *et al.*, *supra* note 88 at 119.
97 Ibid., 135–140.
98 Katharina Boele-Woelki *et al.*, *Principles of European Family Law Regarding Parental Responsibilities* (Intersentia, Antwerp, 2007), Principle 3.10.

presumption that parental involvement in the child's life "will further the child's welfare", subject to an exception where such involvement would put the child at risk of suffering harm.[99] "Involvement" is defined as "involvement of some kind, either direct or indirect, but *not any particular division of a child's time*".[100] This reluctance to mandate equal parenting time may be no more than a reflection of the fact that families are infinitely varied and that individualised decision-making requires a degree of flexibility. In contrast, calls for a presumption of "equal parenting time" continue in a number of US states and, to date, they have had mixed success.[101]

The approximation rule

The American Law Institute sought to provide parents and courts with a predictable method of calculating how parenting might be shared when it proposed the "approximation rule", allocating custodial responsibility "so that the proportion of custodial time the child spends with each parent approximates the proportion of time each parent spent performing caretaking functions" in the past.[102] It differs from the older primary caretaker presumption, since it allocates time *between* the parents, rather than "time spent" being the tie-breaker in a custody decision. The drafters made clear that their goal was "to clarify and define the best-interests standard rather than to eliminate it",[103] albeit some commentators question that this is the effect of their proposals.[104]

The rule permits of a host of exceptions, *inter alia*: to permit the child to have a relationship with each parent; to accommodate the firm and reasonable preferences of a child who has reached a specific age; to keep siblings together; to avoid an allocation of custodial responsibility that would be extremely impractical or that would interfere substantially with the child's need for stability.[105] Other exceptions address abuse of the child by the parent, domestic abuse, parental drug or alcohol abuse and persistent interference with the other parent's access to the child.[106]

Supporters of the approximation rule argue that it serves the child's need for stability and continuity.[107] Others raise many of the criticisms that were levelled at the primary caretaker standard: the conflation of quantity and quality of time spent with the child; its backward-looking nature; and its potential for gender bias.[108] While one commentator condemned it as representing a "19th century mechanistic view of the universe",[109] something that is the antithesis of

99 Children Act 1989, s. 1(2A) and (6), as amended by the Children and Families Act 2014.

100 Ibid., s. 1(2B), emphasis added.

101 In Arkansas, the court is empowered to award joint custody, that being defined as "the approximate and reasonable equal division of time with the child by both parents": Ark. Code Ann. § 9–13–101(a)(5). In Florida, equal parenting time legislation passed by the legislature was vetoed by the governor: Alexandra Fernandez, "Florida Legislature Passes Bill on Shared Parenting", *WUFT-FM*, 16 March 2016, available at www.wuft.org/news/2016/03/16/florida-legislature-passes-bill-on-shared-parenting/. See also Michigan House Bill No. 4691, introduced in 2017 (presumption favouring "substantially equal parenting time", meaning not in excess of 200 nights with either parent) and Kansas Senate Bill 257, introduced in 2018 (creating a presumption that equal or approximately equal time with each parent is in the best interests of the child).

102 American Law Institute, *Principles of the Law of Family Dissolution: Analysis and Recommendations* (2002), § 2.08(1).

103 Ibid., § 2.02.

104 Warshak, *supra* note 62 at 118.

105 *Principles of the Law of Family Dissolution*, *supra* note 102 at § 2.08(1).

106 Ibid., § 2.11(1).

107 Katherine T. Bartlett, "Prioritizing Past Caretaking in Child-Custody Decisionmaking", *Law and Contemporary Problems*, 77, no. 1 (2014) 29, 33.

108 Warshak, *supra* note 62 at 110–111.

109 Ibid., 162.

individualised decision-making, another observed that considerable judicial discretion is introduced by the exceptions.[110] The rule was adopted first in Virginia and it is under active consideration in a number of other states.[111]

Continuing challenges

As we have seen, legal systems increasingly support the involvement of both parents in a child's life, sometimes employing presumptions to secure that end. Most are alert to the danger of exposing children to domestic abuse, and seek to protect them from it, again using presumptions, this time against giving custody of children to an abuser or by making special mention of abuse as a factor that might warrant departure from other presumptions.[112] Yet the intersection of these two issues continues to be problematic for legal systems, with lobbying for law reform often taking on a very gendered dynamic.

As a wealth of case law in numerous jurisdictions demonstrates, some parents, motivated by nothing other than resentment or anger stemming from their own relationship with the child's other parent, seek to damage or destroy the child's relationship with that parent, obstructing their attempts to maintain involvement in the child's life. While it is sometimes associated with the largely discredited work of late Richard Gardner,[113] there is no denying the existence of what is variously known as "parental alienation" or "implacable hostility".[114] Two qualifications are important to note in this context. First, children sometimes evince what appear unduly negative attitudes toward one parent for a range of reasons, some having more to do with the dynamic of family breakdown than with the conduct of the other parent.[115] Respecting the child's rights requires that legal systems listen to the child rather than assuming a particular cause for the child's position.

Second, one parent's opposition to the continuing involvement of the other may be motivated by the valid desire to protect the child (and herself) from the very real dangers posed by further

110 Robert J. Levy, "Custody Laws and the ALI Principles: A Little History, a Little Policy and Some Very Tentative Judgments", in *Reconceiving the Family: Critique of the American Law Institute's Principles of the Law of Family Dissolution* (Robin Fretwell Wilson, ed., Cambridge University Press, Cambridge, UK, 2006) 67, 76–77.

111 W. Va. Code § 48–9–101 *et seq.*

112 For a fresh examination of how such cases can be managed, see Peter G. Jaffe *et al.*, "A Framework for Addressing Allegations of Domestic Violence in Child Custody Disputes", *Journal of Child Custody* 6, no. 3 (2009) 169.

113 In his self-published work, *The Parental Alienation Syndrome: A Guide for Mental Health and Legal Professionals* (2nd edn, Creative Therapeutics, Cresskill, 1998), he described what he claimed was a "syndrome" whereby mothers so denigrated the child's father that the child developed an irrational hostility towards, or fear of, the father and refused to have contact with him. His assertions have been rejected by numerous commentators. For an overview, see Joan S. Meier, "A Historical Perspective on Parental Alienation Syndrome and Parental Alienation", *Journal of Child Custody* 6, nos. 3–4 (2009) 232. The American Psychiatric Association never accepted the existence of the so-called syndrome. Its highly influential *Diagnostic and Statistical Manual of Mental Disorders* (5th edn, American Psychiatric Association Publishing, Arlington, 2013) 715–716 discusses "Parent-Child Relational Problem" and "Child Affected by Parental Relationship Distress".

114 *V. v. V. (Contact: Implacable Hostility)* [2004] 2 F.L.R. 851 (England).

115 Joan B. Kelly & Janet R. Johnston, "The Alienated Child: A Reformulation of Parental Alienation Syndrome", *Family Court Review* 39, no. 3 (2001) 249; Nicholas Bala, *et al.*, "Alienated Children and Parental Separation: Legal Responses in Canada's Family Courts", (2007) *Queen's Law Journal* 33, no. 1 (2007) 79.

exposure to domestic abuse. Domestic abuse is not solely a male-on-female phenomenon, sometimes being perpetrated by women against men and in same-sex relationships, but that is how it manifests most frequently. Respect for equality is rightly valued highly, but that is no reason to ignore reality. Nor should legal systems be blind to the inherently controlling nature of domestic abusers[116] who use presumptions favouring the continuing involvement of both parents in the child's life to ensure that they remain present in the lives of their children and, thereby, their adult victims long after parental separation.[117]

There is emerging evidence of abusers who create a narrative that uses the allegation of abuse itself as evidence that the survivor is engaging in parental alienation: that is, to characterise the survivor "as a pathological or vengeful liar who is severely 'emotionally abusing' her children by falsely teaching them to hate and fear their father".[118] A recent empirical pilot study in the US found that abusers have employed this tactic successfully, with some courts appearing to show bias against mothers who report abuse and sympathy for fathers who claim parental alienation,[119] findings that are consistent with earlier qualitative research in England.[120]

Another way in which domestic abusers exploit the legal system is by misuse of the legal process, a phenomenon that has attracted growing academic attention comparatively recently. This manifests itself when the abuser uses the courts or other state agencies as a means of continuing to harass the survivor, and tactics include "filing frivolous lawsuits, making false reports of child abuse, and taking other legal actions as a means of exerting power, forcing contact, and financially burdening their ex-partners".[121] Again a facet of the coercive control dynamic at play in domestic abuse, it is also known as "abusive litigation",[122] "paper abuse",[123] "custody stalking"[124] and, rather more dramatically, "judicial terrorism".[125] While much of the research and scholarship comes from the US, the issue has garnered attention in Canada[126] and a recent study from New Zealand highlighted the problem there.[127]

116 Evan Stark, *Coercive Control: The Entrapment of Women in Personal Life* (Oxford University Press, New York, 2007).

117 Allen M. Bailey, "Prioritizing Child Safety as the Prime Best-Interests Factor", *Family Law Quarterly* 47, no. 1 (2013–2014) 35 (US); Adrienne Barnett, "Contact at all Costs? Domestic Violence and Children's Welfare", *Child and Family Law Quarterly* 26, no. 4 (2014) 439 (England).

118 Joan S. Meier & Sean Dickson, "Mapping Gender: Shedding Empirical Light on Family Courts' Treatment of Cases Involving Abuse and Alienation", *Law & Inequality* 35, no. 2 (2011) 311, 317.

119 Meier & Dickson, *supra* note 118 at 331–332.

120 Barnett, *supra* note 117 at 450–451.

121 Susan L. Miller & Nicole L. Smolter, "'Paper Abuse': When All Else Fails, Batterers Use Procedural Stalking", *Violence Against Women* 17, no. 5 (2011) 637, 637–638.

122 David Ward, "In Her Words: Recognizing and Preventing Abusive Litigation against Domestic Abuse Survivors", *Seattle Journal for Social Justice* 14, no. 2 (2015) 429. See also Emmaline Campbell, "How Domestic Violence Batterers Use Custody Proceedings in Family Court to Abuse Victims, and How the Courts Can Put a Stop to It", *UCLA Women's Law Journal* 24, no. 1 (2017) 41.

123 Miller & Smolter, *supra* note 121 at 637.

124 Vivienne Elizabeth, "Custody Stalking: A Mechanism of Coercively Controlling Mothers following Separation", *Feminist Legal Studies* 25, no. 2 (2017) 185.

125 Nancy J. King, "Naming the Judicial Terrorist: An Exposé of an Abuser's Successful Use of a Judicial Proceeding for Continued Domestic Violence", *Tennessee Journal of Race, Gender & Social Justice* 1, no. 1 (2012) 153, 153.

126 Esther L. Lenkinski *et al.*, "Legal Bullying: Abusive Litigation within Family Law Proceedings", (2003) *Canadian Family Law Quarterly* 22, no. 3 (2004) 337.

127 Elizabeth, *supra* note 124 at 198–199.

Conclusions

Making generalisations about legal systems is a perilous, if not foolhardy, business. These concluding observations simply highlight some of the key themes to emerge from this chapter using the CRC as the lens.

When they allocate responsibility for a child, legal systems should accord primacy to the best interests of the child, the fundamental principle that sits alongside the child's equality and participation rights. Identifying what will serve the interests of children generally is challenging, but most will benefit from the involvement of both – or sometimes more – parents and other family members in their lives. In a dispute case, however, the court is not making a decision about an abstract, general child. It is addressing the needs of a particular child, something that warrants individualised assessment of that child's circumstances and listening to that child's views.

Respecting equality is important, of course, but it requires no more than treating what is the same in a like manner. It does not require treating different situations in the same way. In this context, it is crucial not to conflate adult equality rights with those of children. Sometimes the two coincide and legal systems are increasingly appreciating that the gender, marital status and sexual orientation of parents are not significant markers. Parental hostility and domestic abuse create a different dynamic since the presence of either can have a negative impact on the child. If presumptions are to be employed in decision-making, they must be crafted carefully in order to accommodate important distinctions.

In the past, children were too often commodified, with their time being given to adults on the basis of custody and visitation. Employing a presumption that favours equal parenting time risks repeating that mistake by portioning out the child's time in a manner that is deemed fair to the parents. It is only by having a child-centred focus – putting the child's best interests first, examining the impact on the child of a particular course of action and listening to the child – that legal systems will meet their obligations to children.

Bibliography

Abraham, Haim. "A Family Is What You Make It? Recognition and Regulation of Multiple Parents", *American University Journal of Gender Social Policy & Law* 25, no. 4 (2017) 405.

Ahl, Sheri A. "A Step Backward: The Minnesota Supreme Court Adopts a 'Primary Caretaker' Presumption in Child Custody Cases: *Pikula v Pikula*", *Minnesota Law Review* 70, no. 6 (1986) 1344.

American Law Institute. *Principles of the Law of Family Dissolution: Analysis and Recommendations* (2002).

Anda, Robert F., Felitti, Vincent J., Bremner, J. Douglas, Walker, John D., Whitfield, Charles, Perry, Bruce D., Dube, Shanta R. & Giles, Wayne H. "The Enduring Effects of Abuse and Related Adverse Experiences in Childhood: A Convergence of Evidence from Neurobiology and Epidemiology", *European Archives of Psychiatry & Clinical Neuroscience* 256, no. 3 (2006) 174.

Appleton, Susan F. "Parents by the Numbers", *Hofstra Law Review* 37, no. 1 (2008) 11.

Bailey, Allen M. "Prioritizing Child Safety as the Prime Best-Interests Factor", *Family Law Quarterly* 47, no. 1 (2013–2014) 35.

Bala, Nicholas, Fidler, Barbara-Jo, Goldberg, Dan & Houston, Claire. "Alienated Children and Parental Separation: Legal Responses in Canada's Family Courts", *Queen's Law Journal* 33, no. 1 (2007) 79.

Bamforth, Nicholas. "Same-sex marriages and civil or registered partnerships" (this volume).

Barnett, Adrienne. "Contact at all Costs? Domestic Violence and Children's Welfare", *Child and Family Law Quarterly* 26, no. 4 (2014) 439.

Bartlett, Katherine T. "Prioritizing Past Caretaking in Child-Custody Decisionmaking", *Law and Contemporary Problems*, 77, no. 1 (2014) 29.

Blyth, Eric & Frith, Lucy. "Donor-Conceived People's Access to Genetic and Biographical History: An Analysis of Provisions in Different Jurisdictions Permitting Disclosure of Donor Identity", *International Journal of Law, Policy and the Family* 23, no. 2 (2009) 174.

Boele-Woelki, Katharina, Ferrand, Frédérique, González Beilfuss, Cristina, Jänterä-Jareborg, Maarit, Lowe, Nigel, Martiny, Dieter & Pintens, Walter. *Principles of European Family Law Regarding Parental Responsibilities* (Intersentia, Antwerp, 2007).
Brinig, Margaret. "Child support" (this volume).
Campbell, Emmaline. "How Domestic Violence Batterers Use Custody Proceedings in Family Court to Abuse Victims, and How the Courts Can Put a Stop to It", *UCLA Women's Law Journal* 24, no. 1 (2017) 41.
Chisholm, Richard. *Family Courts Violence Review* (Attorney-General's Department, 2009).
Czapanskiy, Karen. "The Shared Custody Child Support Adjustment: Not Worth the Candle", *Family Law Quarterly* 49, no. 3 (2015) 409.
DiFonzo, J. Herbie. "From the Rule of One to Joint Parenting: Custody Presumptions in Law and Policy", *Family Courts Review* 52, no. 4 (2014) 213.
Dolan, Mary Jean & Hynan, Daniel J. "Fighting over Bedtime Stories: An Empirical Study of the Risks of Valuing Quantity over Quality in Child Custody Decisions", *Law and Psychology Review* 38 (2014) 45.
Eekelaar, John. *Regulating Divorce* (Clarendon Press, Alderley, 1991).
Elizabeth, Vivienne. "Custody Stalking: A Mechanism of Coercively Controlling Mothers following Separation", *Feminist Legal Studies* 25, no. 2 (2017) 185.
Elrod, Linda. *Child Custody Practice and Procedure* (Thomson Reuters, Eagan, 2017).
Eriksson, Maria. "Contact, Shared Parenting and Violence: Children as Witnesses of Domestic Violence in Sweden", *International Journal of Law, Policy and the Family* 25, no. 2 (2011) 165.
Fellowes, Melanie G. "Commercial Surrogacy in India: The Presumption of Adaptive Preference Formation, the Possibility of Autonomy and the Persistence of Exploitation", *Medical Law International* 17, no. 4 (2017) 249.
Gardner, Richard. *The Parental Alienation Syndrome: A Guide for Mental Health and Legal Professionals* (2nd edn, Creative Therapeutics, Cresskill, 1998).
Glendon, Mary Ann. *The Transformation of Family Law: State, Law and Family in the United States and Western Europe* (University of Chicago Press, Chicago, 1989).
Gonzalez-Martin, Nuria. "International family mediation: recent developments" (this volume).
Graham-Berman, Sandra A. & Levendosky, Alytia A. "Traumatic Stress Symptoms in Children of Battered Women", *Journal of Interpersonal Violence* 13, no. 1 (1998) 111.
Harder, Lois & Thomarat, Michelle. "Parentage Law in Canada: The Numbers Game of Standing and Status", *International Journal of Law, Policy and the Family* 26, no. 1 (2012) 62.
Hauschild, Luise. "Germany: Reforming the Law on Parental Responsibility", *The International Survey of Family Law* (Bill Atkin ed., Jordans, Bristol, 2014) 145.
Inder, Deb. "A Comparison of Child Inclusive and Child Focused Mediation Models, their Benefits and Relevance in the Context of Family Law Practice in New Zealand", *New Zealand Family Law Journal* 8, no. 4 (2014) 69.
Jaffe, Peter G., Crooks, Claire V. & Bala, Nicholas. "A Framework for Addressing Allegations of Domestic Violence in Child Custody Disputes", *Journal of Child Custody* 6, no. 3 (2009) 169.
Jaffe, Peter G., Lemon, Nancy, K.D. & Poisson, Samantha E. *Child Custody and Domestic Violence: A Call for Safety and Accountability* (Sage Publications, Thousand Oaks, 2003) 23.
Kelly, Joan B. & Johnston, Janet R. "The Alienated Child: A Reformulation of Parental Alienation Syndrome", *Family Court Review* 39, no. 3 (2001) 249.
King, Nancy J. "Naming the Judicial Terrorist: An Exposé of an Abuser's Successful Use of a Judicial Proceeding for Continued Domestic Violence", *Tennessee Journal of Race, Gender & Social Justice* 1, no. 1 (2012) 153.
Lehmann, Peter. "The Development of Posttraumatic Stress Disorder in Children who Witnessed Mother Abuse", *Journal of Family Violence* 12, no. 3 (1997) 241.
Lenkinski, Esther L., Orser, Barbara & Schwartz, Alana. "Legal Bullying: Abusive Litigation within Family Law Proceedings", (2003) *Canadian Family Law Quarterly* 22, no. 3 (2004) 337.
Levy, Robert J. "Custody Laws and the ALI Principles: A Little History, a Little Policy and Some Very Tentative Judgments" in *Reconceiving the Family: Critique of the American Law Institute's Principles of the Law of Family Dissolution* (Robin Fretwell Wilson ed., Cambridge University Press, Cambridge, 2006) 67.
Mayeri, Serena. "Foundling Fathers: (Non-)Marriage and Parental Rights in the Age of Equality", *Yale Law Journal* 125, no. 8 (2016) 2292.
McIntosh, Jennifer, Long, Caroline & Moloney, Lawrie. "Child-Focused and Child-Inclusive Mediation: A Comparative Study of Outcomes", *Journal of Family Studies* 10, no. 1 (2004) 87.

McIntosh, Jennifer, Smyth, Bruce, Kelaher, Margaret, Wells, Yvonne & Long, Caroline. "Post-separation Parenting Arrangements", *Family Matters* 86 (2011) 40.
Meier, Joan S. & Dickson, Sean. "Mapping Gender: Shedding Empirical Light on Family Courts' Treatment of Cases Involving Abuse and Alienation", *Law & Inequality* 35, no. 2 (2011) 311.
Meier, Joan S. "A Historical Perspective on Parental Alienation Syndrome and Parental Alienation", *Journal of Child Custody* 6, nos. 3–4 (2009) 232.
Miller, Susan L. & Smolter, Nicole L. "'Paper Abuse': When All Else Fails, Batterers Use Procedural Stalking", *Violence Against Women* 17, no. 5 (2011) 637.
Mnookin, Robert. "Child Custody Revisited", *Law and Contemporary Problems* 77, no. 1 (2014) 249.
Mnookin, Robert H. "Child Custody Adjudication: Judicial Functions in the Face of Indeterminacy", *Current Legal Problems* 39, no. 3 (1976) 226.
Neely, Richard. "The Primary Caretaker Parent Rule: Child Custody and the Dynamics of Greed", *Yale Law and Policy Review* 3, no. 1 (1984) 168.
Nielsen, Linda. "Re-examining the Research on Parental Conflict, Coparenting, and Custody Arrangements", *Psychology, Public Policy and Law* 23, no. 2 (2017) 211.
Nordqvist, Petra. "The Drive for Openness in Donor Conception Disclosure and the Trouble with Real Life", *International Journal of Law, Policy and the Family* 28, no. 3 (2014) 321.
Palmer, Courtney. "Child Support and Shared Parenting in Canada: A Reality Cheque", *Dalhousie Journal of Legal Studies* 22 (2013) 101.
Parker, Stephen. "The Best Interests of the Child – Principles and Problems", *International Journal of Law and the Family* 8, no. 1 (1994) 26.
Reece, Helen. "The Paramountcy Principle: Consensus or Construct?", *Current Legal Problems* 49 (1996) 267.
Reuss, Philipp. "Surrogacy" (this volume).
Ryrstedt, Eva. "Mediation regarding Children – Is the Result Always in the Best Interests of the Child: A View from Sweden", *International Journal of Law, Policy and the Family* 26, no. 2 (2012) 220.
Schwenzer, Ingerborg & Keller, Tomie. "New Rules on Parental Responsibility in Switzerland", *The International Survey of Family Law* (Bill Atkin ed., Jordans, Bristol, 2014) 457.
Singer, Anna. "Parenting Issues after Parental Separation: A Scandinavian Perspective" in *Routledge Handbook of Family Law and Policy* (John Eekelaar & Rob George eds Routledge, Oxford, 2014) 235.
Smyth, Bruce, Chisholm, Richard, Rodgers, Bryan & Son, Vu, "Legislating for Shared-Time Parenting after Parental Separation: Insights from Australia?", *Law and Contemporary Problems* 77, no. 1 (2014) 109.
Social Policy Research Centre. *Shared Care Parenting Arrangements since the 2006 Family Law Reforms* (Social Policy Centre University of New South Wales, Sydney, 2010).
Stark, Evan. *Coercive Control: The Entrapment of Women in Personal Life* (Oxford University Press, New York, 2007).
Sutherland, Elaine E. "Article 3 of the UN Convention on the Rights of the Child: The Challenges of Vagueness and Priorities" in *Implementing Article 3 of the United Nations Convention on the Rights of the Child: Best Interests, Welfare and Well-Being* (Elaine E. Sutherland & Lesley-Anne Barnes Macfarlane eds, Cambridge University Press, Cambridge, UK, 2016) 21.
Sutherland, Elaine E. "Listening to the Child's Voice in the Family Setting: From Aspiration to Reality", *Child & Family Law Quarterly* 26, no. 2 (2014) 152.
Swennen, Frederik. "Personal relations and contact concerning children" (this volume).
The American Psychiatric Association. *Diagnostic and Statistical Manual of Mental Disorders* (5th edn, American Psychiatric Association Publishing, Arlington, 2013).
Tsavoussis, Areti, Stawicki, Stanislaw P.A., Stoicea, Nicoleta & Papadimos, Thomas J. "Child-witnessed Domestic Violence and its Adverse Effects on Brain Development: A Call for Societal Self-examination and Awareness", *Frontiers in Public Health* 2 (2014) 178.
UNICEF. *Law Reform and Implementation of the Convention of the Rights of the Child* (UNICEF Innocenti Research Centre, Florence, 2007).
Van Bueren, Geraldine. "Children's rights in the family" (this volume).
Ward, David. "In Her Words: Recognizing and Preventing Abusive Litigation against Domestic Abuse Survivors", *Seattle Journal for Social Justice* 14, no. 2 (2015) 429.
Warshak, Robert A. "Parenting by the Clock: The Best Interests of the Child Standard, Judicial Discretion, and the American Law Institute's 'Approximation Rule'", *University of Baltimore Law Review* 41, no. 1 (2011) 83.

9
Child support

Margaret F. Brinig

The duty to support one's offspring during their minority follows from biological and social imperatives. Except for largely philosophical discourses, such as Plato's, and some limited experimentation (such as in the group rearing of the Nazi state), it is universally held today, at least as a first principle.[1] This said, the chapter will note some divergence on how far the duty (and reciprocal right) extend, how large a role the state plays in accepting some part of the parental duty, and how much duty adult children owe in return to their parents. The duties are not coextensive with those due upon the death of the parent (inheritance law), when children need not be treated equally and a surviving spouse may inherit a greater portion.[2]

While the duty to support children pertains during the parents' marital or other relationship, and may be enforced then through child protective (neglect) or even criminal law (nonsupport)

1 Thus Art. 27 of the United Nations Convention on the Rights of the Child (ratification and accession by General Assembly resolution 44/25 of 20 November 1989; entry into force 2 September 1990, in accordance with Art. 49) provides:

> 1 States Parties recognize the right of every child to a standard of living adequate for the child's physical, mental, spiritual, moral and social development.
> 2 The parent(s) or others responsible for the child have the primary responsibility to secure, within their abilities and financial capacities, the conditions of living necessary for the child's development.
> 3 States Parties, in accordance with national conditions and within their means, shall take appropriate measures to assist parents and others responsible for the child to implement this right and shall in case of need provide material assistance and support programmes, particularly with regard to nutrition, clothing and housing.
> 4 States Parties shall take all appropriate measures to secure the recovery of maintenance for the child from the parents or other persons having financial responsibility for the child, both within the State Party and from abroad. In particular, where the person having financial responsibility for the child lives in a State different from that of the child, States Parties shall promote the accession to international agreements or the conclusion of such agreements, as well as the making of other appropriate arrangements.

2 For examples, see Inheritance (Provision for Family and Dependants) Act 1975 (UK); NY Estate and Probate Code § 4–1.1.

or for reimbursement of public assistance paid to indigent parents, the great majority of legal cases are brought when parents separate. In the context of separating or divorcing parents, child support has increasingly become a political issue closely interwoven with the sharing of parental responsibility and time.

This chapter proceeds in four parts. Part I considers where the duty to support lies. This considers the function of the state in supplanting part or most of the duty. It also discusses which adults are expected to shoulder the duty: whether it extends to parents who never married, whether to children in state or third party care, whether to step-parents or other "de facto" parents, whether to other relatives such as grandparents. It also will treat the question of whether persons with the duty may contract out of it, either through premarital agreements or upon separation or divorce.

Part II analyses the extent of the duty: how much support is due. It will distinguish the usual concept (consistent, as far as possible, with the standard of living established during the relationship) from the alimentary obligation in civil law or necessaries/family support doctrine in common law societies where support is limited to a minimal standard needed for survival or to keep the child off public assistance. This section will also discuss the increasing role of Child Support Guidelines, particularly in Anglo-American countries. It will continue with the concept of imputation of income for under-employed or non-employed parents who might have other assets or obtain employment (and the duty of unrelated adults in subsequent relationships with the parent to furnish the support). The section will also discuss what kinds of income can be considered in allocating or reaching support, for example, income from federal pensions or that granted to compensate for disabilities or injury. It will also discuss the rather hotly contested relationship (theoretical and practical) between time spent with the child and the duty to pay support. The role of the UN Convention on the Rights of the Child will also be considered, as will the parents' duty to pay for college or other post-secondary education, particularly when the child has now reached majority age but is still dependent.

Part III will discuss enforcement of the duty to pay support, both in terms of domestic and international procedural mechanisms such as those under The Hague Convention and various nations' reciprocal agreements. In federal countries such as the US, agreements between states on the establishment and collection of support also need to be considered. The mechanisms for collecting support, such as garnishment of income, tax interceptions, the withholding of licenses and passports, and shaming will be mentioned here. Some cases discuss standing issues (whether children or other non-parent caretakers can enforce the parents' duty) and the ability of parents to evade collection through seeking bankruptcy or through self-help.

In Part IV the reader will find discussions of when child support duties terminate. This generally happens when the child reaches majority age, but may be extended if the child remains disabled and incapable of self-support. It may occur sooner if the child becomes legally emancipated, typically when marrying or sometimes when entering military service, but occasionally when living outside the parental home in a lifestyle the parent does not support. The duty to pay support may also terminate during minority when the child begins to live with the obligor parent, but usually this requires a court action as well. Still less frequently, it may end when the child is removed from parental custody and/or adopted by another.

A brief conclusion follows, stressing what seem to be universal principles and highlighting the systemic differences and some current problems.

Part I. Who has the duty?

(a) Community or private duty

In every contemporary society, the duty to furnish support to minors rests first in the child's parents.[3] However, depending upon the extent of publicly supplied benefits, this duty may be delegated in part.[4] The largest delegation is typically to a system of public education.[5] This is guaranteed by many national or subsidiary constitutions and is typically funded by taxation. In some countries, such as Canada, they would be locally funded through property and income taxation set for a province-level area rather than by school district,[6] while in the US, education funding occurs primarily through property taxation and is administered at the state level with substantial funding provided by the local authorities.[7]

Another large portion of support comes through expenditures for medical care. Again, in many countries medical care is provided through national systems funded by income taxation.[8] In the US, medical care of this kind is currently paid to children of very poor families under Medicaid, and the Affordable Care Act (Obamacare) extends such benefits to a larger group of children under a public insurance scheme. Most children in the US continue to enjoy medical care provided through their parents' private health insurance schemes funded through their employers. However, the duty to furnish medical care remains with the parents, and failure to provide care can subject them to actions for neglect or even abuse in extreme cases. Many of the reported cases deal with parents who could afford medical care but do not provide it because of religious beliefs or because they prefer less standard medical care.[9] Some deal with minors who choose not to receive life-saving medical care. The latter subjects are dealt with in another chapter.

Some governments, particularly in the EU, also provide for some sort of child allowance.[10] This allowance may supplement or replace parental income and may be available even in intact

3 See UNCRC Art. 27, *supra* note 1; The Organisation for Economic Co-operation and Development (OECD), Family Database PF1.5 (2010), available at www.oecd.org/els/family/database.htm.

4 For a comprehensive discussion of the difference between community and private support, see Marsha Garrison, "An Evaluation of Two Models of Parental Obligation," *California Law Review* 86, no. 1 (1998): 41.

5 In general, see Organisation for Economic Co-operation and Development (OECD), Family Database Part 3, Public Policies for Families and Children (2010), available at www.oecd.org/els/family/database.htm, PF1.2, showing expenditures averaging 4.5% of GDP (with the highest amounts of over 6% of GDP in Denmark and Norway).

6 Juliana Herman, "Canada's Approach to School Funding: The Adoption of Provincial Control of Education Funding in Three Provinces," available at www. Americanprogress.org (May, 2013).

7 See, for example, Alana Semuels, "Good School, Rich School; Bad School, Poor School" *The Atlantic*, August 25, 2016.

8 For recent international profiles of 15 developed countries, see Elias Mossialos et al. (eds) *International Profiles of Health Care Systems* 2014 (2015), Table 1, available at www.commonwealthfund.org/~/media/files/publications/fund-report/2015/jan/1802_mossialos_intl_profiles_2014_v7.pdf.

9 See, for example, Margaret F. Brinig, "Religion and Child Custody," *University of Illinois Law Review* 2016, no. 4: 1369.

10 See OECD Family Database, *supra* note 5, PF1.3. Urging universal basic income grant rather than targeting for children in South Africa, see June Sinclair and Trynie Davel, "Poverty, Welfare and the Family: South Africa's Miracle Transition at Risk," *International Survey of Family Law* (2007 ed., William Atkin, ed., London): 455. The inequalities driven by the South African system, where cash grants to children in foster care far exceed those cared for informally by family members, see Ann Skelton, "Kinship Care and Cash Grants: In Search of Sustainable Solutions for Children Living with Members of Their Extended Families in South Africa," *International Survey of Family Law* (2012 ed., William Atkin, ed., London): 333.

For Lithuania, see Inga Kudinavičiūtė-Michaelovienė and Aušra Malauskaitė, "Children's Maintenance Fund in Lithuania: Legal and Sociological Aspects of its Activities," *International Survey of Family Law* (2016 ed., William Atkin and Fareda Banda, eds., London): 305.

parental relationships. Most countries, but not the US, additionally afford generous compensated family leave for fairly extensive periods.[11] Paid leave available to mothers averages 37.5 weeks, with paid leave specific to or reserved for fathers typically shorter (on average, just over eight weeks). In the US, less generous cash support is available on a temporary basis under the Temporary Assistance to Needy Families legislation.[12] The system requires parents to work[13] or complete their education and is generally limited to a five-year lifetime benefit.[14] States are encouraged under this system to recoup benefits paid under this program from non-custodial parents. Other programs such as SNAP (food stamps) and the FHA (housing) provide subsidies to low income families. As of this writing, all these US programs are threatened with elimination (health care) or budget cuts (public education, housing, food, and cash assistance).[15] Parental leave required in most US states cases is uncompensated[16] and for short periods of time. Some employers offer more generous policies.

(b) Private responsibilities to support children

Increasingly, to the extent that private parental duties to support remain,[17] they do not rely upon the parents' marital status. That is, children born to married or unmarried parents are equally entitled to their parents' support during their minority.[18] This duty to provide support to all one's

11 Gretchen Livingston, "Among 41 Nations, U.S. is the Outlier When it Comes to Paid Parental Leave," Facttank, (Washington, D.C. Pew Research Center), September 26, 2016, available at www.pewresearch.org/fact-tank/2016/09/26/u-s-lacks-mandated-paid-parental-leave/. Data comes from OECD Family database, *supra* note 5, available at www.oecd.org/els/family/database.htm, table PF2.1, Paid Maternity Leave (2016). For a recent graph, see OECD, PF2.1A, Paid maternity leave, 2016.

12 Personal Responsibility and Work Opportunity Reconciliation Act of 1996 (PRWORA)(Pub. L. 104–193). The laws appear in Title IV of the Social Security Act, 42 USCA §§ 401–479B.

13 42 USCA § 407.

14 There may be up to a 20% deviance in special cases, such as when the recipient was the victim of domestic violence. See US Department of Health and Human Services, Administration of Children and Families, Office of Family Assistance. See TANF Final Rule Executive Summary, April 12, 1999, available at www.acf.hhs.gov/ofa/resource/exsumcl (Time Limits). The rules appear in §§ 264.1–264.3 of 64 CFR Fed. Reg. 17845–9, 17896–7. However, states may (and some do) limit enrollment to shorter time periods. Arizona, under SB 1479 (2015) set its lifetime limit at 12 months.

15 See Yamiche Alcindor, "Trump Budget Cuts Programs for Poor While Sparing Many Older People," *New York Times*, May 22, 2017.

16 In five states, including California, parents may be eligible for temporary medical disabilities. See Barbara Gault et al., "Paid Parental Leave in the United States," (Washington, DC: Institute for Women's Policy Research 2014), Appendix; US Department of Health and Human Services, Administration for Children and Families, Office of Family Assistance, TANF Final Rule Executive Summary, April 12, 1999, available at www.acf.hhs.gov/ofa/resource/exsumcl.

17 This is changing, even in countries that used to rely extensively on private (family) support. For one example, see the Korean Act on the Guarantee and Support of the Performance of the Child Support [Yangyugbi Ihaenghwagbo Mit Jiwone Gwanhan Beoblyul], enacted 24 March 2014 effective 25 March 2015. This introduced an advance payment system for children and established a special agency to support this and other processes regarding the performance and enforcement of child support. For a description of the legislation, see Donjin Lee, "Recent Developments in Korean Family Law: Divorce, Adoption, Parental Responsibility, and Family Support," *International Survey of Family Law* (2015 ed., William Atkin and Fareda Banda, eds., London): 193, 208.

18 According to the OECD, the exceptions are for Cyprus, Germany and Poland, OECD, *supra* note 5, Child Support, Table PF1.5.1. In Germany, special provisions appear in Subtitle 2 of the German Civil Code § 1615. It is not clear from looking at the statute how these are treated differently, though unmarried mothers generally receive full custody and their duty to support is met through their care. See Civil Code § 1612a. These apparently retain different systems for children born to unmarried

children seems to be nearly universal today.[19] It may be found not only in industrialized nations but in the third world (at least in principle).[20] To some extent, private duties for support are taking over some more community-minded legislation.[21]

Under civil law systems, the duty was extended beyond parents to grandparents and other "ascendant" relatives,[22] though this duty may be limited to the provision of necessities rather than to the extent of parental lifestyles based upon their income. There are cases (and some legislation) in the common law systems where grandparents have been required to support their minor children's children. For example, in the US, this has for many years been the rule in the state of Wisconsin and has also been part of the TANF legislation. The idea here was that parents might provide more guidance to their minor children about the wisdom of having children if the parents were responsible for their upkeep.[23] While the teen birth rate in the US has decreased, some evidence suggests that this is due to better contraceptives rather than the design of the welfare system.[24]

A more common problem in countries where remarriage occurs regularly or where children may be born to parents who ultimately marry others involves the duty of step-parents to pay for children's support, especially if the biological parent does not pay at all or cannot provide enough

---

parents. Unmarried parents are also responsible for supporting children in Namibia under sec. 3(3) of the Maintenance Act of 2003, and for Hindu parents in India. See Anil Malhotra and Ranjit Malhotra, "Maintenance, Non-Resident Indians and the Law," *International Survey of Family Law* (2016 ed., William Atkin and Fareda Banda, eds., London): 213, 244: Minor children in India are entitled to be maintained under two sets of laws, their personal law, and (ii) the secular Law Code of Criminal Procedure 1973. Under the Hindu Marriage Act 1955 Sec. 20 Adoptions and Maintenance Act: a Hindu is bound to maintain his or her legitimate or illegitimate children plus a daughter who is unmarried and unable to maintain herself out of own earnings (as well as the expenses of marriage).

19 For a comprehensive discussion of EU policies, see European Parliament, Directorate-General for Internal Policies, Child Maintenance Systems in EU Member States from a Gender Perspective (Brussels: 2014), available at www.europarl.europa.eu/RegData/etudes/note/join/2014/474407/IPOL-FEMM_NT(2014)474407_EN.pdf.

20 For example, see Sec. 3(3) of the Maintenance Act of 2003 (Namibia). See generally Manfred O. Hinz and Clever Mapaure, "Legal Pluralism and the Apartheid Past: Challenges to Namibian Family Law Reform and Development," in *International Survey of Family Law* (2009 ed., William Atkin, ed., London): 301, 303.

21 William Atkin, "New Zealand: Whose Responsibility Are Our Children?" in *International Survey of Family Law* (1997 ed., William Atkin, ed., London): 309. Under the New Zealand Code of Social and Family Responsibility a form of contract is set between a welfare recipient and the State. This seems to extend a shift "from the State's having a major role to a minimalist one in the care of children. State responsibility is replaced by an individualist philosophy, with the State's task being to police rather than to share the burden."

22 For example, see the [Czech] New Civil Code Sec. 915 (Act No. 89/2012 Co.), that came into effect January 1, 2014. German Civ. Code § 1603(b). More generally, see Zdeňka Kráčková, "New Family Law in the Czech Republic: Back to Traditions and Towards Modern Trends," *International Survey of Family Law* (2014 ed., William Atkin, ed., London): 71. See also *Petersen v. Maintenance Officer, Simon's Town Maintenance Court*, 2004 (2) SA 56 (C) [South Africa]. For a discussion of why this obligation extends to grandchildren born outside marriage, see Robbie Robinson, "South Africa, Family and Child Law in South Africa: Common Law v. Constitutional Norms and Values," *International Survey of Family Law* (2007 ed., William Atkin, ed., London): 271, 282.

23 Tommy G. Thompson, "W-2, Wisconsin Works," (Madison: Wisconsin Division of Economic Support 1996): 12, available at content.wisconsinhistory.org/cdm/ref/collection/tp/id/49207.

24 See, for example, Eileen Patten and Gretchen Livingston, "Why is the Teen Birth Rate Falling?" *Fact-tank* (Washington, DC: Pew Research Center, April 29, 2016), available at www.pewresearch.org/fact-tank/2016/04/29/why-is-the-teen-birth-rate-falling/.

support to make ends meet. For these situations there seem to be two rules applicable to married step-parents only, and a third that may apply to either situation.[25] The first rule is that the step-parent is responsible if he or she has taken on a role of parent to the child.[26] In an extreme case, this might prevent the biological parent from intervening over the other parent/step-parents' objection to seek any kind of parental rights. The second rule is that the step-parent may be responsible, but only so long as the marriage to the biological parent remains intact.[27] The third rule, and that applicable to unmarried subsequent relationships in any case, is that the step-parent assumes no duty to support, which always rests with the biological noncustodial parent.

Biology usually governs the duty to make support payments, even where there is no underlying "relationship" between the parents (as in the case of unmarried parents where a man was allegedly or admittedly tricked into conception).[28] If the child is conceived through consensual assisted reproductive technology and the donor of egg, sperm or both is anonymous, the parent or parents, particularly if married, who intended the child's conception and consented to it will be held responsible. This will be true even if the underlying marriage or relationship ceases before the birth of the child and even if the child turns out to be disabled. If a donor is known, he or she may also have a duty to support (and a corresponding ability to enjoy custodial or other parental rights with the child).

While these are general, or default, rules, the question remains whether parents can contract out of their support obligations. Most often they cannot, particularly at the beginning of a marriage where the parties make a premarital agreement.[29] Sometimes there are also legislative prohibitions on waiving support obligations at the time of separation as well (for example, in exchange for disallowing visitation rights). Some parents do, for tax or other reasons, combine child support and spousal maintenance into a unitary payment. This is usually allowed since the tax benefits may encourage the obligor to comply with an agreement or court order. There are also occasional cases where the obligor furnishes services in exchange for direct financial support. For example, the parent's interest in the marital home may be given to the custodial parent, promoting household stability and relieving cash flow problems at the time of divorce, and courts may allow this in exchange for a periodic support payment. Some low-income parents may furnish items needed by the child (diapers, formula, clothing) rather than cash, or may provide child care services while the primary custodial parent is working. These non-standard exchanges may well not be recognized in the US as equivalent to the financial support obligation, particularly if the custodial parent is receiving public assistance.

25 For a general discussion, see Margorie Engel, "Stepfamily Tribulations Under US Laws and Social Policies," *International Survey of Family Law* (2005 ed., William Atkin, ed., London): 529.

26 In the case of Zambia, step-parents who have taken on parental roles have for many years been held responsible for their support. Local Court (Amendment) Act No. 8 of 1991.

27 See, for example, Olga Cvejic Jancic, "Maintenance Obligations under the Family Act of Serbia," *International Survey of Family Law* (2009 ed., William Atkin, ed., London): 425.

28 For an example, see *In the Matter of Pamela P. v. Frank S.*, 449 N.E.2d 713 (N.Y. 1983). The duty to pay exists even if the father would have chosen to abort the child. *In the Interest of S.P.B.*, 651 P. 2d 1213 (Colo. 1982). For discussions of the rule involving marital presumptions of legitimacy (and the duty to support), see June Carbone and Naomi Cahn, "The Past, Present and Future of the Marital Presumption," *International Survey of Family Law* (2003 ed., William Atkin, ed., London): 287.

29 See, for example, Uniform Premarital and Marital Agreements Act (Denver: National Conference of Commissioners on Uniform State Laws, 2012) § 10(a) declares unenforceable a term adversely affecting a child's right to support. Comments to the section cite *In re Marriage of Best*, 901 N.E.2d 967, 970–71 (Ill. App. 2009).

Part II. How much support is due following a separation or divorce?

To answer this question, we must first distinguish between the alimentary duties in civil law (or family support in common law countries) and the special obligations for supporting one's child. The alimentary obligations extend to relatives in the vertical or ascendant chain: specifically one's parents, children, grandparents and grandchildren who are in need. They are generally set at a threshold designed to keep the dependent relative from falling on public support or charity, and may be spread among all other persons in the chain. The duty does not extend, as child support may, to persons related through marriage (except one's spouse), nor, in general, to adult siblings. In the US this duty is typically set by statute and generally is triggered by suits brought by third party creditors for provision of "necessaries" such as medical care.[30] Child support is not in theory fixed at a certain minimal amount, or even at "the standard of living of the marriage," but may fluctuate with the circumstances of the child or the obligor parent. This difference from even periodic spousal support occurs because a child's relationship with a parent, unlike a spouse's, is not curtailed by separation or divorce. For example, the child may need more as he or she reaches teen years (or attends college), requires special education or support in some athletic or artistic endeavor, or requires orthodontic or psychiatric treatment. If, post-divorce, a parent's income increases substantially (as with some professional athletes or entertainers, for example), the child, but not the spouse, is entitled to share in the higher standard of living. (Of course, many if not most parents are financially strapped at the time of divorce so that support will not even permit achievement of the marital standard of living once they need to form two households.)

Because of felt injustice in the setting of support by judges, either because support was systematically set too low (as in Canada)[31] or was unpredictable because of differences between judges' ideas of what children needed or parents could provide, many countries set at least a prima facie amount by the use of guideline formulas, which may be advisory only or quite rigid. The OECD collects information on member states' child support initiatives, and notes in its Family Database that the US, Britain, Australia, Canada, Denmark and Norway were of the more rigid variety in 2010, while Austria, Belgium, France, Germany and Sweden tended to fix payment rates through courts operating with discretion.[32]

In the US, for example, Guidelines have been set in every state since 1987 when this became a condition for the state to receive substantial federal funding under the Social Security Act.[33] The Guidelines are simply tables based upon the number of children subject to the order and the incomes of one (primary obligor states) or both (income share states) parents.[34] The basic amount in the tables reflects sophisticated calculations stemming from the cost of adding an additional person to a household, updated every four years. These basic amounts are adjusted downward for parents who must support other children under court orders (or are raising them in their household), for payment toward child care or health insurance for the child, and, in some states,

30 For example, see *Forsyth Memorial Hospital v. Chisholm*, 467 S.E.2d 88 (N.C. 1996).

31 See, for example, Paul Miller & Anne H. Gauthier, "What Were They Thinking? The Development of Child Support Guidelines in Canada," *Canadian Journal of Law and Society* 17, no. 1 (2002): 139.

32 OECD, *supra* note 5, at Table PF1.5A.

33 42 USCA § 667.

34 See generally Douglas W. Allen and Margaret F. Brinig, "Child Support Guidelines: The Good, the Bad, and the Ugly," 45 *Family Law Quarterly* 45, no. 2 (2011): 135. Illinois changed from a primary obligor to an income shares model effective July, 2017. Ill PA 99–0764 (enacted 8/12/2016); 750 ILCS 5/505 (a)(1)(D).

to reflect reductions in the custodial parents' cost of raising the child because of substantial time (sometimes overnights) in the payor parents' home.[35] They may be adjusted upward for "extraordinary expenses" incurred by the child or, under some systems, for children over age ten.[36] Most states reserve some minimum amount for the self-support of the payor parent.[37] (This is usually some proportion of the poverty level.) In many jurisdictions, but not in Canada, the tables also reflect the diminishing proportion of income that is paid for varying purchases such as food as income increases.[38] And in many places the tables "top out" at some amount reflecting high income(s), since "no child requires three ponies."[39] The range of average payments, converted to US dollars, was computed for 14 OECD countries based on 2004 data. The range was from a mean of 9.2% of net income (Denmark, with average payments per child amounting to $131.6 dollars per month) to a high of 35.1% of net disposable income (Switzerland, with payments of $657.10).[40]

Because most divorce issues are resolved by written agreements, in some places such as the US parents may modify the amount otherwise due under the Guidelines.[41] The court setting the final order must ensure that the agreed amount reflects the "best interests of the child,"[42] and must typically give written reasons for major deviations from the guidelines. (In many cases, the deviations are small and reflect rounding of amounts to the nearest $10 USD increment or child-related concessions made elsewhere in the agreement or deviations to $0 because the amount due is so small that the costs of collection would exceed it.)

One of the problems of calculating child support, even under Guideline systems, is establishing the incomes of the parents. These are relatively easy to determine if the parent is employed and receiving a recorded amount from the employer (such as a W-2 form for tax purposes in the US). If a parent receives no income because he or she cannot work (because ill or totally disabled), attributing a zero income becomes possible. However, there are cases in which a parent may be receiving unreported income (especially when self-employed, but arguably in cases where the parent is providing "under the table" support in kind to the other parent on public assistance),[43] may be out of the labor force because supported by a new spouse and doing child care for a subsequent family, or even may elect to be underemployed because of a distaste for paying child support.[44]

35 For a criticism of this rule, see Karen Czapanskiy, "Child Support and Visitation: Rethinking the Connections," *Rutgers Law Journal* 20 (1989): 619.

36 For a description of Arizona and Indiana's guidelines, see Margaret F. Brinig, "Result Inequality in Family Law," *Akron Law Review* 46, no. 2 (2016): 471.

37 Setting aside a self-support reserve for the payor but not the payee parent is criticized, especially for poor parents, in Marsha Garrison, "Child Support Guideline Review: Problems and Prospects," in *International Survey of Family Law* (2001 ed., William Atkin, ed., London): 437, 440. In general, see Jane C. Venohr, "Child Support Guidelines and Guidelines Reviews: State Differences and Common Issues," *Family Law Quarterly* 47, no. 3 (2015): 327, 340–41.

38 Canada's system is described in Allen and Brinig, *supra* note 34.

39 *Strahan v. Strahan*, 953 A.2d 1219, 1224 (N.J. App. Div. 2007) (quoting from *In re Patterson*, 22 Kan. App.2d 522, 920 P. 2d 450, 455 (1996)).

40 OECD Family Database, *supra* note 5, at Table PF1.5.C.

41 They may agree to provide for things that exceed guideline amounts. For an example involving expensive private school tuition, see *Salomond v. Ball*, 470 S.E.2d 159 (Va. 1996).

42 See, for example, *Watson v. Watson*, 436 S.E.2d 193 (Va. App. 1993).

43 Maria Cancian and Daniel R. Meyer, "Fathers of Children Receiving Welfare: Can They Provide More Child Support?" *Social Service Review* 78 no. 2 (2004): 179.

44 In general see Ira Mark Ellman and Tara Ellman, "The Theory of Child Support," *Harvard Journal of Legislation* 45, no. 1 (2008): 107.

In these cases, courts and agencies typically impute income to the parent.[45] In the case of no reported (but suspected) income, this may be at the level of minimum wage, or, for the parent doing childcare, it may be at the level earned before gainful employment ceased. States may also impute income (or not) in the case of incarcerated parents, though there are certainly arguments that the accumulated arrearage by the time of release adds almost impossible burdens to the former inmate.[46] Recent studies in the US of unmarried low-income fathers suggest that imputation of income is especially burdensome for this group, overrepresented by persons of color.

Generally, income that is designed to compensate for earnings is subject to child support. However, parents sometimes receive income from personal injury settlements or disability payments under Social Security that does not compensate for lost earnings but rather from lost personal support or for pain and suffering. These amounts are generally not subject to the Guidelines.

One of the hotly contested questions in the field of child support continues to be the role of shared custody. Some parents and advocates contend that parents ask for more custodial time than they actually will exercise because of the deductions from the amount of child support they would otherwise need to pay.[47] Some recipient parents and academics contend that the set-offs under the Guidelines are unrealistic and unjust because their expenses (for rent, heat, cable television, a larger car) are not actually reduced by the time spent with the paying parent. In the case where the receiving parents are just meeting their budgets while the payor parent is a very high earner, the reductions (frequently by half, sometimes to zero) may put them into poverty or cause severe financial distress. To meet these concerns, a few states divide expenses into fixed and variable categories – the fixed expenses (rent, childcare or tuition and so forth) that will not change with additional overnights and the variable expenses (primarily food) that will.

On the other side, some payor (noncustodial) parents object to paying large sums or large proportions of their incomes to the other parent since these inevitably have the effect, since money is fungible, of raising the standard of living for the custodial parent.[48] While some jurisdictions explicitly disregard this concern (attempting to match the standard of living of the two households),[49] others have taken it seriously. For example, the state of Illinois equates the penalties for nonpayment of child support and interfering with custodial time.[50] Other states consider the income of custodial parents' spouses in determining the "need" of the child. The concerns have also added financial to other injuries, fueling the push to more equal parenting time, discussed in another chapter.

45 For some US examples, see *Pencovic v. Pencovic*, 287 P2d 500 (Cal 1955); *Hur v. Virginia Dept of Social Servs*, 409 SE2d 454 (Va 1991); *Goldberger v. Goldberger*, 624 A2d 1328 (Ct App Md 1993). Recently, see *Miller v. Miller*, 72 NE3d 952 2017 WL 1130980 (Ind. 2017)). Polish laws also allow imputation of income under the Family and Guardianship Code Arts 135 §1 and 136.

46 For a survey of state approaches, see *Lambert v. Lambert*, 861 NE2d 1176, 1177–79 (Ind 2007) (declining to impute income).

47 These problems are discussed and examined empirically in Margaret F. Brinig, "Chickens and Eggs: Does Custody Move Support, or Vice-Versa?" *Journal of the American Academy of Matrimonial Lawyers* 29, no. 2 (2017): 269.

48 For one such problem in Britain, where recipients now must pay to get enforcement, see Polly Toynbee, "Why the Silence on the Scandal of Unpaid Child Maintenance," *The Guardian*, June 16, 2016, available at www.theguardian.com/commentisfree/2016/jun/16/silence-scandal-unpaid-child-maintenance.

49 This seemed to be true in Canada. See Allen and Brinig, *supra* note 34, see also Miller and Gauthier, *supra* note 31.

50 Italy, in Art. 155 par. 3 of the Civil Code adopted a system allowing direct provision of day-to-day expenses by parents sharing custody (who presumably live in the same neighborhood). Virginia Zambrano, "Allocating Child Shared Custody to Separating or Divorcing Couples: Law 54/2006 (Italy)," *International Survey of Family Law* (2008 ed., William Atkin, ed., London): 203, 210.

The obligation of parents to provide tertiary (college) education is not universally recognized. In some places, particularly for parents who themselves are college-educated, courts enforce such duties for divorcing or separating parents with qualified children, reasoning that had the parents remained together they likely would have provided such support (sometimes reasoning further that children of divorce are disadvantaged by their parents' divorce and should at least not be impeded by losing education).[51] In others, because children past high school are likely of majority age, divorce courts are not held to have jurisdiction over the matter unless the parents have agreed between them to provide for the college education.[52] In other places, where tuition for public facilities is minimal, such payments are rarely at issue.[53] In contrast, if divorcing parents had already enrolled their children in private elementary or secondary schools and can afford to maintain tuition after separation, courts may order that the wealthier parent pay for or at least contribute to, continuing such education often separate from and in addition to Guidelines amounts. However, continuing such payments, as opposed to basic child support, may be conditioned on the young adult student's remaining in good standing and maintaining at least a civil relationship with the parent paying tuition.[54]

Part III. How will child support be enforced?

While parents who remain together have many incentives to provide for their children, once they separate, these incentives decrease. The numbers of parents in this situation has increased since 1960 not only because of an increasing divorce rate worldwide but also because of the increasing number of parents who never marry (and whose relationships are less stable than marriage).[55] The distaste may be because the payor parent no longer enjoys a close relationship with the child and feels simply like a "pocketbook,"[56] or because he or she distrusts the custodial parent's motivations in spending the money,[57] because the custodial parent inevitably benefits as well from the receipt of money,[58] or because the payor has a subsequent family who must also be supported

51 See, for example, *In re Marriage of Crocker*, 971 P. 2d 469 (Ore. 1998); *Rohn v. Thuma*, 408 N.E.2d 578 (Ind. App. 1980) (limiting the duty under an ambiguous parental separation agreement to expenses at the state's public universities while children had enrolled in much more expensive private schools); see also Iowa Code Ann § 598.21F (2016) (limiting duty to in-state public institution and splitting it in thirds for the two parents and the child).

52 See, for example, *Curtis v. Kline*, 666 A.2d 265 (Pa. 1995).

53 This was the case in the Ukraine. Irina Zhylinkova, "Juvenile Property Rights in Ukraine," *International Survey of Family Law* (2000 ed., William Atkin, ed., London): 369, 372 (2000).

54 See, for example, *Milne v. Milne*, 556 A.2d 854, 859 (Pa. Super. 1989).

55 For recent statistics from 17 countries in Europe and the US, see W. Bradford Wilcox and Laurie DeRose, "The Cohabitation-Round: Cohabitation and Family Instability Across the Globe, available at "worldfamilymap.ifstudies.org/2017/files/WFM-2017-FullReport.pdf. The OECD, *supra* note 5, in Table PF1/5.B, lists the percentage of sole parents in 2004. It has substantially increased since then in the US, from 21.5% to 41%, according to the Bureau of the Census.

56 See Brinig, *supra* note 47, at 275 & N.24.

57 See, for example, Judith A. Seltzer et al., "Family Ties after Divorce: The Relationship between Visiting and Paying Child Support," *Journal of Marriage and the Family* 51, no. 4 (1989): 1013; Yoram Weiss and Robert Willis, "Children as Collective Goods in Divorce Settlements," *Journal of Labor Economics* 3, no. 3 (1985): 268. Enforcement in the US generally is discussed in Andrea H. Beller and John W. Graham, "Small Change: The Economics of Child Support" (New Haven, CT: *Yale University Press*, 1993).

58 See Ira Ellman et al., "Child Support Judgments: Comparing Public Policy to the Public's Policy," *International Journal of Law, Policy and Family* 28 (2014): 274.

and for whom the incentives to pay are higher.[59] Collection of the full amounts due (or even any support due) has been problematic for many years.

The problems are compounded when parents are indigent and the custodial parent (payee) receives public support so the payor is simply reimbursing the welfare authorities, never seeing resources going directly to the child. They are also compounded in a global society where the parent may not simply move further away within the jurisdiction (or to another state) but outside the country where the original order was obtained. Because child support may be modified in the future, the older US interstate cases were plagued by payor state claims that the amounts due were unrealistic according to the standards of their laws and simply modifying the amounts retroactively or certainly for the future. States were only bound by the Full Faith and Credit clause of the Constitution to final orders. If a parent could simply evade enforcement by moving across a state line (especially in multiple state metropolitan areas such as those surrounding New York, Boston, Chicago, St. Louis, Philadelphia and Washington), recovering past due child support could quickly become a nightmare for payee parents. Beginning in 1979, even before the Guideline era, states enacted reciprocal enforcement laws to eliminate, or at least reduce, these problems.[60] The Hague Convention on the International Recovery of Child Support and Other Forms of Family Maintenance, as of this writing ratified by 35 nations,[61] extends these enforcement authorities worldwide. The list of applicable remedies, while it does not include incarceration of the noncompliant debtor, otherwise closely resembles those remedies included in the requirements of the US federal laws concerning enforcement,[62] which also now require that states give full faith and credit to other states' awards.[63]

Garnishment, available both in the US and under The Hague Convention, also proved problematic at first. Employers were reluctant to issue two paychecks and were naturally supportive of their employees rather than estranged former spouses. They were also concerned about the stigmatization that might ensue. However, garnishment has proven the most effective method of

59 See, for example, Mary Campbell, "Can't Pay, or Won't Pay? Fathers are Protesting Too Loudly at their Child Support Agency Bills," *Independent*, February 1, 1994.

60 The original formulation was the Uniform Reciprocal Enforcement of Support Act (URESA), succeeded by the Revised Reciprocal Enforcement of Support Act (RURESA). These were replaced by the Uniform Interstate Family Support Act (UIFSA), formulated in 1992 and revised in 1996.

61 See Hague Convention of 23 November 2007 on the International Recovery of Child Support and Other Forms of Family Maintenance, available at www.hcch.net/en/instruments/conventions/status-table/?cid=131 (includes Albania, Bosnia and Herzegovina, the EU, Montenegro, Norway, Turkey, Ukraine and the US as of December, 2016). It was not ratified by Burkina Faso, Belarus and Canada. The Convention requires each state to designate a central authority to cooperate with the other such authorities, transmit and receive applications for enforcement, to help locate debtors, facilitate ongoing enforcement, collection and transfer of payments, establish parentage where necessary, provide for free legal assistance in respect of child support payments, and so forth. While the procedures are quite detailed (constituting 65 Articles and some Annexed forms), enforcement takes place in accordance with the law of the debtor's State, and may include wage withholding, garnishment, deductions from social security payments, liens, tax refund withholding, withholding or attachment of pension benefits, and denial suspension or revocation of various licenses. The use of mediation or similar procedures to bring about voluntary compliance is also included in Art. 34 on enforcement measures and elsewhere in procedural sections.

62 42 USC § 666. State enforcement agencies were required by 42 USCA § 654; and garnishment or wage withholding by 42 USCA § 659, 661, 665 (federal and District of Columbia employees, and members of the military).

63 1984 Child Support Enforcement Amendments, 42 USCA § 666(a)(9).

collecting enforcement and was eventually mandated by US legislation.[64] As already mentioned, wage withholding or garnishment are the first listed remedies under The Hague Convention as well.[65]

The Hague Convention and the provisions of many states allow withholding of various licenses, including drivers' licenses, hunting and fishing permits, and licenses for some professions. States have also employed a variety of techniques other than incarceration that stigmatize so-called "deadbeat dads." These include publication on the internet of "most wanted" photos, names, descriptions and the amount of support owed, using social media,[66] and the "booting" of debtors' automobiles with devices that identify the child support enforcement authority. The Convention and US rules allow for tax refund intercepts and the filing of liens.

In the US, but not according to the Convention, substantial child support debtors may be found guilty of contempt and sentenced to terms of incarceration that increase each time and may be deferred to give the (theoretical for low wage earners or unemployed) opportunity to regain compliance. Typically, these contempt orders provide for release upon payment of some amount, which may vary from several hundred to several thousand dollars. While incarceration was shown in the late 1970s to be effective in communities where personal reputation was important,[67] it retains a large but ineffective role in communities where incarceration is commonplace, where payors have multiple families subject to orders, or where employment is not forthcoming.[68] States cannot constitutionally condition the right to marry (or remarry) on keeping child support current.[69]

In countries where personal bankruptcy is available, such as the US and Canada, debts for child support are not subject to relief.[70] However, the relief of other debt may free income to pay for current or past due support.

64 There is still some income that cannot be garnished. There may also be provisions in private employment contracts that disallow income from reach by creditors. Nor can income paid for disability under SSI, nor a second spouse's income. Workers' compensation benefits that replace income may or may not be garnishable, depending upon state law.

65 See also (Hong Kong) Marriage and Children (Miscellaneous Amendments) Ordinance 1997, No. 69 of 1997.

66 See, for example, Nick Statt, "Arizona is Shaming 'Deadbeat' Dads on Social Media," *The Verge*, January 12, 2016, available at www.theverge.com/2016/1/12/10757320/deadbeat-dad-arizona-public-shaming-child-support (use of governor's Twitter account). Single moms in Kenya are also apparently using such an approach. *Mommyish*, September 19, 2014, available at www.mommyish.com/2014/09/19/facebook-page-dead-beat-kenya-shames-parents-into-paying-child-support/.

67 David Chambers, *What Makes Fathers Pay?* (Chicago, IL: University of Chicago Press, 1979).

68 For a discussion of these problems, some data, and mention of December, 2016, changes to the US Office of Child Support Enforcement's final rules (suggesting that diversion and employment programs may be more effective), as well as a number of state diversion programs see National Conference for State Legislatures, Child Support and Incarceration (Denver: February 2016), available at www.ncsl.org/research/human-services/child-support-and-incarceration.aspx.

Since the Supreme Court case of *Turner v. Rogers*, 564 U.S. 431 (2011), a state must provide safeguards (but not necessarily appointed counsel) to reduce the risk of erroneous deprivation of liberty in civil contempt child support cases. This would include notice that "ability to pay" is a critical issue, the use of a form to elicit relevant financial information and an opportunity to respond at the hearing to statements and questions about his financial status and, finally, an express finding by the court that the defendant does have the ability to pay. *Turner*, 564 U.S. at 546–48.

69 *Zablocki v. Redhail*, 434 U.S. 374 (1978).

70 Bankruptcy Abuse Prevention and Consumer Protection Act of 2005. Debts "in the nature of support" are not subject to discharge. The Canadian provision is Bankruptcy & Insolvency Act, Sec. 178(1)(b)(c). A bankrupt individual will be obligated to continue to make ongoing payments. In the UK, child maintenance payments are called "non-provable debts" and are not discharged. See 4.6; www.gov.uk/government/publications/guide-to-bankruptcy.

Child support enforcement actions are usually brought by the creditor parent, though sometimes with the assistance of a child support enforcement agency. When child support recoupment is sought after payment (or advancement) by a public social agency, the creditor parent may assign the right to receive payments to the agency, and only appear nominally in court enforcement pleadings.[71] While the child is the object of the payments, since how it is spent it is generally subject to the complete discretion of the creditor parent, the child will not have legal standing to bring an enforcement action.[72] In most of the cases of this type, the debtor parent has actually paid the creditor but the child has been residing with a third party like a grandparent, who has no legal standing either.

While circumstances may change, the duty to pay child support and the amount owed cannot be reduced except by a return to court to demonstrate a substantial and continuing change of circumstances.[73] Self-help cannot be used to modify child support, nor can the obligations be modified by agreement of the parties out of court, because the court retains an interest in protecting the best interests of the child. In some states, "substantial change" is determined by demonstration of a deviation in what the Guidelines would specify by more than 20%.[74] More often, it is shown by such matters as increased expenses, increased needs of the children (balanced against the parent's ability to provide for them), increased or decreased financial ability of the debtor parent (weighed against the standard of living of the marriage, and considering whether a change of employment was made in good faith), a change in relative parenting responsibilities including a complete change of custody, emancipation of a child,[75] and, occasionally, the resources of the child (such as receipt of a large inheritance). Remarriage of either parent will not automatically trigger such a change.[76]

Part IV. Termination of child support duties

Most often, child support terminates when the child reaches the age of majority (or achieves the greater age specified in a parental agreement). In most OECD countries, the age of majority is 18, but a number of nations, including Australia, Ireland, Greece and Mexico extend that time if the child is still pursuing full-time education.[77] Other nations, including the Czech Republic, Japan and New Zealand specify that the duty ceases when the child reaches economic independence, and Korea specifies that it ceases at 20 unless a parental agreement provides otherwise.[78] In the US, where it is subject to varying state laws, the time ranges between age 16 (also the age in the UK)

71 This is the requirement of the US cash assistance program (TANF) under 42 USC § 608(a)(3).

72 *Drake v. Drake*, 455 N.Y.S .2d 420 (App. Div. 1982; *Chen v. Chen*, 893 A.2d 87 (Pa. 2006); *Yarborough v. Yarborough*, 290 U.S. 202 (1933).

73 See, for example, Indiana Code § 31–16–8–1 (either showing a substantial change of circumstances or by a showing of deviation of 20% or more from the guidelines from an order at least 12 months old).

74 See, for example, 750 Ill. Comp. Stat. § 5/510(a).

75 The birth of a child to the debtor's daughter did not emancipated her according to *Filippone v. Lee*, 700 A.2d 384, 388 (N.J. App. Div. 1997), citing many other cases, but her brother's lack of continued successful schooling did emancipate him when he had reached age 18, id. at 389, even though a year later he incurred a serious disability.

76 See, for example, *Ball v. Minnick*, 648 A.2d 1192 (Pa. 1994).

77 See also Switzerland: If on attaining majority child has not yet completed suitable education, parents must pay for his or her maintenance, to the extent that this can be expected in the overall circumstances (Art. 277, par. 2, SCC). This is not limited to maintenance in kind but also includes a financial contribution (Art. 276, par. 2).

78 OECD, *supra* note 5, Child Support Table PF1.5.A.

and age 25, if completing education. Arrearages will continue to be owed, and the now adult child may bring an action for payments that should be made toward tuition or to keep life insurance in force. In the case of a child so disabled that self-support is impossible, the parent may be required to continue to provide support so that the disabled person does not become a public charge, though this duty seems to end in Poland at age 24 according to the OECD table.

Sometimes, custody situations change, ending child support. For example, a father originally expected to pay child support may become the primary caretaker of one or more children, so that his duty to pay ceases (and perhaps the mother's duty to pay begins under a new order). While parents with children in care still owe duties to pay support, this will cease upon termination of parental rights and a court order terminating support.[79] Similarly, should a step-parent adopt the children of an earlier relationship, the biological father's duty to pay will cease. Since court orders are involved with these situations, attempted self-help in terminating child support will be unlikely.

In rare cases, the child will become independent before reaching the age of majority.[80] This can happen when the supported child marries or enters the armed forces. Occasionally a child can be declared emancipated by a court if no longer living with the parent or under the parent's control and capable of self-support. In these situations, the debtor parent must usually obtain a court order before legally ceasing to make payments.

The payor or debtor parent has no legal ability to cease making child support payments if the payee or creditor parent does not comply with visitation orders. Courts faced with such situations reason that since the child is supposed to benefit, the child should not be doubly punished by loss of a relationship with the noncustodial parent and loss of support income.[81]

The only occasions in which a child's attitudes or time with the debtor parent seem to matter are those in which the child is now legally an adult and scorns, mocks or abuses the parent helping the child attend college.[82]

Conclusions

The problems and issues with child support are relatively constant worldwide, though they do differ based upon the wealth of the nation at issue and the degree to which the community (state) has assumed what would otherwise be parental duties. They also seem to be politicized in many countries.

79 For example, see *In re Beck*, 488 Mich. 6, 793 N.W.2d 752 (2010), in which the Michigan Supreme Court ruled that termination of parental rights does not automatically end a child support obligation and that payments continue until the support order is specifically terminated by a court with proper jurisdiction.

80 For a discussion, see Carol Sanger and Eleanor Willemsen, "Minor Changes: Emancipating Children in Modern Times," *Michigan Journal of Law Reform*, 25 (1991): 239.

81 For a general discussion of the problem, see Karen Czapanskiy, "Child Support and Visitation: Rethinking the Connections," 20 *Rutgers Law Journal* 619 (1989). For a Macedonian law, Art. 87, par. 2 of the Family Law Act, that seems to run afoul of this principle, though from another direction, cutting off visitation if child support is not paid for more than three months, see Dejan Mickovik & Angel Ristov, "The Exercise of Parental Rights After Divorce in Macedonian Family Law," *International Survey of Family Law* (2013 ed., William Atkin, ed., London): 251, 261 (2013). If the non-resident parent has not provided maintenance for child for more than 3 months, the Centre of Social Work may decide to limit his right to maintain personal relations and direct contact with the child. Art. 87, par. 2 of the Family Law Act.

82 For an example, see *Milne v. Milne*, 556 A.2d 854 (Pa. Super. 1989).

Some clearly require more thought and more study. For example, the problems with imputed income in some ways resemble those of racial profiling, casting doubt on the fairness of the whole legal system. The ACLU website notes about profiling that, "[j]ust as importantly, racial profiling is ineffective. It alienates communities from law enforcement, hinders community policing efforts, and causes law enforcement to lose credibility and trust among the people they are sworn to protect and serve."[83] Imputing income to indigent parents who cannot obtain work and causing their arrearages to mount astronomically is counterproductive, particularly if they then disappear to avoid enforcement and cannot at least maintain relationships with their children.

In the US, still more should be done to relieve the problems of obligors who are incarcerated for failure to pay support or who have child support obligations but cannot pay existing child support obligations. My own recent work with Marsha Garrison indicates there does not seem to be any deterrence from having additional children with other mothers, and failure of the system is problematic.[84]

Finally, more study should be given to tradeoffs between visitation/shared custody and the collection of child support. There is little recent evidence that it works, and substantial evidence that custodial families may be impoverished because of direct connections between visitation/shared custody and child support guidelines.

Bibliography

Alcindor, Yamiche. "Trump Budget Cuts Programs for Poor While Sparing Many Older People," *New York Times*, May 22, 2017.

Allen, Douglas W. and Margaret F. Brinig. "Child Support Guidelines: The Good, the Bad, and the Ugly," *Family Law Quarterly* 45, no. 2 (2011): 135.

Atkin, Bill. "New Zealand: Whose Responsibility Are Our Children?" in *International Survey of Family Law* (1997 edn, William Atkin, ed., London): 309.

Bailey, Martha. "Canada: Children, Same-Sex Marriage and Cohabitation," *International Survey of Family Law* (2003 edn, William Atkin, ed., London): 81.

Beller, Andrea H. and John W. Graham. *Small Change: The Economics of Child Support* (New Haven, CT: Yale University Press, 1993).

Brinig, Margaret F. "Chickens and Eggs: Does Custody Move Support, or Vice-Versa?" *Journal of the American Academy of Matrimonial Lawyers* 29, no. 2 (2017): 269.

Brinig, Margaret F. "Result Inequality in Family Law," *Akron Law Review* 46, no. 2 (2016): 471.

Brinig, Margaret F. "Religion and Child Custody," *University of Illinois Law Review* 2016, no. 4: 1369.

Campbell, Mary. "Can't Pay, or Won't Pay? Fathers are Protesting Too Loudly at their Child Support Agency Bills," *Independent*, Febr. 1, 1994.

Cancian, Maria and Daniel R. Meyer. "Fathers of Children Receiving Welfare: Can They Provide More Child Support?" *Social Service Review* 78 no. 2 (2004): 179.

Carbone, June and Naomi Cahn., "The Past, Present and Future of the Marital Presumption," *International Survey of Family Law* (2003 edn, William Atkin, ed., London): 287.

Chambers, David. *What Makes Fathers Pay?* (Chicago, IL: University of Chicago Press, 1979).

83 See www.aclu.org/issues/racial-justice/race-and-criminal-justice/racial-profiling. See also the debates about enforcement of Jim Crow laws promoting racial segregation, against civil disobedience, for example J.L. LeGrande, "Nonviolent Civil Disobedience and Police Enforcement Policy," *Journal of Criminal Law and Criminology*, 58 (1968): 393, 399.

84 See, for example, *Bannatyne v. Bannatyne*, 2003 (2) BCLR 111 (CC), CCT 18/02 (S.A. Constitutional Court, 2002) (confinement for contempt should only be issued sparingly and after exhaustion of less drastic measures), and, see generally Chuma Himonga, "(South Africa) Transforming the Family Law Landscape: The Role of the Courts," in *International Survey of Family Law* (2004 edn, William Atkin, ed., London): 421, 434.

Czapanskiy, Karen. "Child Support and Visitation: Rethinking the Connections," *Rutgers Law Journal* 20 (1989): 619.

Ellman, Ira, Steve McKay, Joanna Miles and Caroline Bryson "Child Support Judgments: Comparing Public Policy to the Public's Policy," *International Journal of Law, Policy and Family* 28 (2014): 274.

Ellman, Ira Mark and Tara Ellman. "The Theory of Child Support," *Harvard Journal of Legislation* 45, no. 1 (2008): 107.

Engel, Margorie. "Stepfamily Tribulations Under US Laws and Social Policies," *International Survey of Family Law* (2005 edn, William Atkin, ed., London): 529.

European Parliament, Directorate-General for Internal Policies, Child Maintenance Systems in EU Member States from a Gender Perspective: In Depth Analysis for the FEMM Committee (Brussels, 2014), www.europarl.europa.eu/RegData/etudes/note/join/2014/474407/IPOL-FEMM_NT(2014)474407_EN.pdf.

Garrison, Marsha. "An Evaluation of Two Models of Parental Obligation," *California Law Review* 86, no. 1 (1998): 41.

Garrison, Marsha. "Child Support Guideline Review: Problems and Prospects," in *International Survey of Family Law* (2001 edn, William Atkin, ed., London): 437.

Gault, Barbara, Heidi Hartmann, Ariane Hegewisch, Jessica Milli and Lindsey Reichlin Cruse, "Paid Parental Leave in the United States" (Washington, DC: Institute for Women's Policy Research 2014), Appendix.

Hague Convention of 23 November 2007 on the International Recovery of Child Support and Other Forms of Family Maintenance, www.hcch.net/en/instruments/conventions/status-table/?cid=131.

Herman, Juliana. "Canada's Approach to School Funding: The Adoption of Provincial Control of Education Funding in Three Provinces," www. Americanprogress.org (May, 2013).

Himonga, Chuma. "(South Africa) Transforming the Family Law Landscape: The Role of the Courts," in *International Survey of Family Law* (2004 edn, William Atkin, ed., London): 421.

Hinz, Manfred O. and Clever Mapaure. "Legal Pluralism and the Apartheid Past: Challenges to Namibian Family Law Reform and Development," in *International Survey of Family Law* (2009 edn, William Atkin, ed., London): 301.

Jancic, Olga Cvejic. "Maintenance Obligations under the Family Act of Serbia," *International Survey of Family Law* (2009 edn, William Atkin, ed., London): 425.

Kráčková, Zdeňka. "New Family Law in the Czech Republic: Back to Traditions and Towards Modern Trends," *International Survey of Family Law* (2014 edn, William Atkin, ed., London): 71.

Kudinavičiūtė-Michaelovienė, Inga and Aušra Malauskaitė. "Children's Maintenance Fund in Lithuania: Legal and Sociological Aspects of its Activities," *International Survey of Family Law* (2016 edn, William Atkin and Fareda Banda, eds, London): 305.

Lee, Donjin. "Recent Developments in Korean Family Law: Divorce, Adoption, Parental Responsibility, and Family Support," *International Survey of Family Law* (2015 edn, William Atkin and Fareda Banda, eds, London): 193.

Livingston, Gretchen. "Among 41 nations, U.S. is the outlier when it comes to paid parental leave," *Facttank* (Washington, D.C. Pew Research Center), Sept. 26, 2016, www.pewresearch.org/fact-tank/2016/09/26/u-s-lacks-mandated-paid-parental-leave/.

Malhotra, Anil and Ranjit Malhotra. "Maintenance, Non-Resident Indians and the Law," *International Survey of Family Law* (2016 edn, William Atkin and Fareda Banda, eds, London): 213.

Mickovik, Dejan and Angel Ristov. "The Exercise of Parental Rights After Divorce in Macedonian Family Law," *International Survey of Family Law* (2013 ed., William Atkin, ed., London): 251.

Miller, Paul and Anne H. Gauthier, "What Were They Thinking? The Development of Child Support Guidelines in Canada," *Canadian Journal of Law and Society* 17, no. 1 (2002): 139.

Mossialos, Elias and Martin Wenzl. "International Profiles of Health Care Systems 2014" (2015), www.commonwealthfund.org/~/media/files/publications/fund-report/2015/jan/1802_mossialos_intl_profiles_2014_v7.pdf.

National Conference for State Legislatures, Child Support and Incarceration (Denver: Feb. 2016), www.ncsl.org/research/human-services/child-support-and-incarceration.aspx.

Organisation for Economic Co-operation and Development (OECD), Family Database Part 3, Public Policies for Families and Children (2010), www.oecd.org/els/family/database.htm.

Patten, Eileen and Gretchen Livingston. "Why is the Teen Birth Rate Falling?" *Facttank*, (Washington, DC: Pew Research Center, April 29, 2016), www.pewresearch.org/fact-tank/2016/04/29/why-is-the-teen-birth-rate-falling/.

Robinson, Robbie. "South Africa, Family and Child Law in South Africa: Common Law v. Constitutional Norms and Values," *International Survey of Family Law* (2007 edn, William Atkin, ed., London): 271.

Sanger, Carol and Eleanor Willemsen. "Minor Changes: Emancipating Children in Modern Times," *Michigan Journal of Law Reform*, 25 (1991): 239.

Seltzer, Judith A., Nora Cate Schaeffer and Hong-Wen Chang, "Family Ties after Divorce: The Relationship between Visiting and Paying Child Support," *Journal of Marriage and the Family* 51, no. 4 (1989): 1013.

Sinclair, June and Trynie Davel. "Poverty, Welfare and the Family: South Africa's Miracle Transition at Risk," *International Survey of Family Law* (2007 edn, William Atkin, ed., London): 455.

Skelton, Ann. "Kinship Care and Cash Grants: In Search of Sustainable Solutions for Children Living with Members of Their Extended Families in South Africa," *International Survey of Family Law* (2012 edn, William Atkin, ed., London): 333.

Thompson, Tommy George. "W-2, Wisconsin Works," (Madison: Wisconsin Division of Economic Support 1996): 12, http://content.wisconsinhistory.org/cdm/ref/collection/tp/id/49207.

Uniform Premarital and Marital Agreements Act (Denver: National Conference of Commissioners on Uniform State Laws, 2012).

United Nations Convention on the Rights of the Child (ratification and accession by General Assembly resolution 44/25 of 20 November 1989; entry into force 2 September 1990, in accordance with article 49).

US Department of Health and Human Services, Administration of Children and Families, Office of Family Assistance. TANF Final Rule Executive Summary, April 12, 1999, www.acf.hhs.gov/ofa/resource/exsumcl.

Venohr, Jane C. "Child Support Guidelines and Guidelines Reviews: State Differences and Common Issues," *Family Law Quarterly* 47, no. 3 (2015): 327.

Weiss, Yoram and Robert Willis. "Children as Collective Goods in Divorce Settlements," *Journal of Labor Economics* 3, no. 3 (1985): 268.

Wilcox, W. Bradford and Laurie DeRose. "The Cohabitation-Round: Cohabitation and Family Instability Across the Globe," worldfamilymap.ifstudies.org/2017/files/WFM-2017-FullReport.pdf.

Zambrano, Virginia. "Allocating Child Shared Custody to Separating or Divorcing Couples: Law 54/2006 (Italy)," *International Survey of Family Law* (2008 edn, William Atkin, ed., London): 203.

Zhylinkova, Irina. "Juvenile Property Rights in Ukraine," *International Survey of Family Law* (2000 edn, William Atkin, ed., London): 369.

10

Personal relations and contact concerning children

Frederik Swennen

Introduction

This chapter sets out to investigate the international law governing substantive and private international law aspects of personal relations and contact concerning children.

In the past, this chapter's title would have been "Visitation and Access", reflecting an approach whereby children were considered to be the objects of one-way rights of other persons to visit, and to have access to, them.[1] The United Nations (UN) Convention on the Rights of the Child has (at least apparently, see below) has caused a paradigm shift. Under articles 9(3) and 10(2) of the Convention, children themselves, too, are considered holders of rights to personal relations and direct contact with their parents. The Council of Europe (COE) Convention on Contact Concerning Children has broadened this right towards contact with non-parents as well. The terminology in this chapter should therefore reflect such two-way legal relationship.[2]

The relevant international legal sources on personal relations and contact concerning children mostly coincide with those on custody. On the one hand, personal relations and contact are considered to be the normal corollary of custody.[3] On the other hand, personal relations and contact with non-custodial parents and non-parents are also separately governed by the same sources. This chapter will limit itself to the particularities concerning personal relations and contact, as Chapter 8 deals with custody.

As is the case for custody, the relevant legal sources are increasingly concerned with transfrontier (cross-border) personal relations and contact, given increasing international

1 Estin, A.L. *International Family Law Desk Book* (American Bar Association Publishing, 2013) 127.

2 As is the case in the COE Convention on Contact Concerning Children: see the Preamble and the Explanatory Report, para. 3. Also see Boele-Woelki, K. et al. *Principles of European Family Law Regarding Parental Responsibilities* (Cambridge, Intersentia, 2007) Comment 1 on Principle 3:25.

3 Recital 3 to the COE European Convention on Recognition and Enforcement of Decisions Concerning Custody of Children and on Restoration of Custody of Children. Also see Kodilinye, L. "Is Access the Right of the Parent or the Right of the Child? A Commonwealth View", (1992) 41 *International and Comparative Law Quarterly* 190, 191.

family mobility.[4] Article 10 of the UN Convention on the Rights of the Child and article 10(2)(b) of the COE Convention on Contact Concerning Children, for example, specifically deal with transfrontier personal relations and contact, as do several private international law instruments. The underlying principles are nonetheless comparable to those for domestic cases.

Personal relations and contact concerning children are governed on three interwoven levels. First, some aspects are governed *ex lege*, as default rules. Second, those rules subsequently influence the conclusion of agreements between children, parents and non-parents. Different sources explicitly incentivise agreements, for example in the context of recognition and enforceability in private international law.[5] Third, court intervention is considered to be a last resort. Agreements are also incentivised on the latter level, for example through (in-court) mediation or court confirmation of agreements, unless they are contrary to the rights of the child.[6]

Substantive law

This section is devoted to substantive law aspects of personal relations and contact concerning children. After having determined the various rights holders, the content and enforcement of personal relations and contact are dealt with.

Rights holders

The determination of the rights holders of personal relations and contact concerning children is somewhat of a conundrum.

The child

As already mentioned, most of the relevant instruments, from the UN Convention on the Rights of the Child onwards,[7] consider children themselves (too) to be rights holders of personal

4 Hague Conference on Private International Law, *General Principles and Guide to Good Practice. Transfrontier Contact Concerning Children* (Bristol, Family Law, 2008) 4; Explanatory Report to the COE Convention on Contact Concerning Children, para. 1; Detrick, S. *A Commentary on the United Nations Convention on the Rights of the Child* (Leiden and Boston, Martinus Nijhoff Publishers, 1999) 170; Explanations to the European Union (EU) Charter of Fundamental Rights, 25; Doek, J.E. "Article 8 The Right to Preservation of Identity. Article 9 The Right Not to be Separated from his or her Parents", in *A Commentary on the United Nations Convention on the Rights of the Child* (Alen, A. et al. eds., Leiden and Boston, Martinus Nijhoff Publishers, 2006) para. 3.

5 Arts. 2(b) and 7 of the COE Convention on Contact Concerning Children and Explanatory Report, para. 27; Explanatory Report to the COE European Convention on the Exercise of Children's Rights, para. 8; Hague Conference on Private International Law, *General Principles and Guide to Good Practice. Transfrontier Contact Concerning Children*, *supra* note 4 at 6 ff. Also see Principle 3:27 of the Commission on European Family Law (CEFL) Principles of European Family Law Regarding Parental Responsibilities, available at ceflonline.net/wp-content/uploads/Principles-PR-English.pdf (accessed 20 June 2017).

6 For example in art. 8(2) of the COE Convention on Contact Concerning Children; Principle 3:27(2) of the CEFL Principles of European Family Law Regarding Parental Responsibilities.

7 And even before: see the Government's submissions in ECtHR, *R. v. United Kingdom* (1987), paras. 79 and 83.

relations and contact with their parents[8] and with non-parents.[9] The only exception is article 3(b) of the Hague Convention on Jurisdiction, Applicable Law, Recognition, Enforcement and Co-Operation in respect of Parental Responsibility and Measures for the Protection of Children. The term "access" has been retained there "both for reasons of convenience and in order to take into account the still numerous legal systems which continue to conceive of parental responsibility as a linkage based on authority".[10]

A *first* consequence of such approach is that – in a Hohfeldian analysis[11] – a duty to maintain personal relations and contact with the child/rights holder rests upon other (adult) persons. However, enforcement *manu militari* on adults is much more difficult to conceive, let alone justify, than on children.[12] Some legal systems therefore consider the adults, rather than the children, to be the rights holders. *Second*, minors lack capacity to legally enforce their rights in many legal systems. Absent representation ad hoc by a public or private institution, it would therefore often be up to an adult desiring to obtain or maintain personal relations with the child to start proceedings based on an own right and to put flesh on the bones of such claim by referring to the child's own right to obtain or maintain personal relations with the claimant. This is odd, for the claimant usually cannot be considered the child's representative. *Third*, and most importantly, if the child is considered to be the rights holder, awarding personal relations and contact with a child should require a threshold showing of positively serving the child's best interests. Under such rule, the "simple fact of being a parent"[13] would not be sufficient to justify personal relations and contact, even though parents are considered to be the persons who are primarily responsible for the development of the child.[14] The way out of this conundrum has been to formulate children's rights from the perspective of others', particularly parents', rights, for example article 9(3) of the UN Convention on the Rights of the Child states:

> States Parties shall respect the right of the child who is separated from one or both parents to maintain personal relations and direct contact with both parents on a regular basis, except if it is contrary to the child's best interests.

In other words, the child's right is formulated in a way to best serve an interest of his or her parents or certain non-parents – which seems, at the very least, contradictory.[15]

8 Arts. 9(3) and 10(2) of the UN Convention on the Rights of the Child; art. 4(1) of the COE Convention on Contact Concerning Children; art. 24(3) of the EU Charter of Fundamental Rights; art. 19(2) of the Organization of African Unity (OAU) African Charter on the Rights and Welfare of the Child. Besides, the right to respect for one's private and family life is also relevant as generic provision: see art. 24(1) of the UN International Covenant on Civil and Political Rights and UN Human Rights Committee, *General Comment No. 17*, para. 6; art. 16 of the UN Convention for the Rights of the Child; art. 8 of the COE Convention for the Protection of Human Rights and Fundamental Freedoms; art. 7 of the EU Charter of Fundamental Rights.

9 Boele-Woelki et al., *supra* note 2, Comment 2 on Principle 3:25; Kodilinye, *supra* note 3; Stark, B. *International Family Law: An Introduction* (Aldershot, Ashgate, 2005), 160 and 170.

10 Explanatory Report, para. 20.

11 Compare Finegan, T. "An Unmarried Father's Right to Guardianship of his Child and a Child's Right to the Support of his/her Father: A Hohfeldian View of the Irish Constitution", (2010) 32 *Dublin University Law Journal* 320.

12 Boele-Woelki et al., *supra* note 2, Comment 3 on Principle 3:25.

13 Kodilinye, *supra* note 3 at 196.

14 Art. 18 of the UN Convention for the Rights of the Child.

15 Also see Olsen, F. "Children's Rights: Some Feminist Approaches to the United Nations Convention on the Rights of the Child", (1992) 6 *International Journal of Law and the Family* 192, 198 ff and 204 ff.

All in all, it makes sense to determine personal relations and contact reciprocally from the perspective of both the children and the other persons concerned, as is the case in article 4 of the COE Convention on Contact Concerning Children.[16] Particular importance is to be attached to the best interests of the child, which may be,[17] but are not necessarily,[18] sufficient to override the interests of other persons. When balancing the other persons' interests, a distinction is usually drawn between parents on the one hand, and non-parents on the other. Non-parents are furthermore divided into persons with existing family ties and persons with (potentially) close personal ties. A hierarchy applies, whereby personal relations with parents are protected more strongly than those with non-parents with existing family ties, which in turn are more strongly protected than those with other persons.[19]

Parents

Parents[20] and children have a fundamental right to personal relations and regular contact with each other, either under specific provisions[21] or under the generic right to respect for one's family life.[22] Article 16 of the Organization of American States (OAS) Protocol of San Salvador moreover particularly protects the mother – child bond. Parental personal relations and contact are presumed to serve the children's best interest.[23] Only very serious grounds in another (higher)

16 Preamble to the COE Convention on Contact Concerning Children. See already ECtHR, *R. v. United Kingdom* (1987), paras. 79 and 83, where the court found that qualifying the child as a rights holder does not exclude the parent from also qualifying as a rights holder. Also see Hague Conference on Private International Law, *General Principles and Guide to Good Practice. Transfrontier Contact Concerning Children*, *supra* note 4 at 5; Boele-Woelki et al., *supra* note 2, Comment 4 on Principle 3:25.

17 ECtHR (Grand Chamber), *Sahin v. Germany* (2003), para. 66.

18 ECtHR, *K.B. and Others v. Kroatia* (2017), para. 143.

19 Arts. 4 and 5 of the COE Convention on Contact Concerning Children and Explanatory Report, paras. 49 and 51; Principle 3:25 of the CEFL Principles of European Family Law Regarding Parental Responsibilities.

20 The relevant provisions in the UN Convention on the Rights of the Child and the COE Convention on Contact Concerning Children explicitly refer to *both* parents. In some legal systems, a child can have more than two parents, and the provisions should then apply accordingly, as is the case for non-parents in whom parental rights have vested. On multi-parenthood, with a comparative overview, see Dutch Government Committee on the Reassessment of Parenthood, *Child and Parents in the 21st Century*, (The Hague, 2016), available at www.government.nl/documents/reports/2016/12/07/child-and-parent-in-the-21st-century (accessed 20 June 2017). See also "Child custody and cognate concepts: the challenges" in this volume. On non-parents as holders of parental responsibilities, see Explanatory Report to the Hague Convention on the Civil Aspects of International Child Abduction, para. 79; art. 1(2) of the Hague Convention on Jurisdiction, Applicable Law, Recognition, Enforcement and Co-Operation in respect of Parental Responsibility and Measures for the Protection of Children and Explanatory Report, paras. 14 and 22; art. 2(b) of the COE Convention on the Exercise of Children's Rights and Explanatory Report, para. 24; art. 2.7 of the EU Council Regulation (EC) No 2201/2003 concerning jurisdiction and the recognition and enforcement of judgments in matrimonial matters and the matters of parental responsibility (EU Brussels IIa Regulation).

21 Arts. 9(3) and 10(2) of the UN Convention on the Rights of the Child; art. 4(1) of the COE Convention on Contact Concerning Children and Explanatory Report, para. 40. Also see Hague Conference on Private International Law, *General Principles and Guide to Good Practice. Transfrontier Contact Concerning Children*, *supra* note 4 at 4. Also see the references in note 7 above, from the perspective of the child.

22 Estin, *supra* note 1 at 127 and 129; Stark, *supra* note 9 at 160.

23 ECtHR (Grand Chamber), *Sahin v. Germany* (2003), para. 92; ECJ, *Detiček v. Scueglia* (2009), para. 54. Also see Doek *supra* note 4 at para. 13.

interest of the child could justify restricting, let alone excluding,[24] these ties.[25] The European Court of Human Rights (ECtHR) applies strict scrutiny to domestic authorities' decisions in this regard.[26] The protection of the morals and health of the child constitutes such ground for restriction or exclusion,[27] as does "a history of physical or other abuse of the child, in addition to situations where physical abuse or other abuse of the primary carer has meant that the relationship between the contact parent and the child is too damaged".[28]

Whereas the opposition of the custodial parent would not constitute a serious argument,[29] the purpose of keeping the child away from conflict between the parents could.[30] The refusal by children may also be a relevant factor,[31] depending on their ability to form and articulate an opinion, taking into account their maturity,[32] loyalty conflicts, and their exposure to alienating behaviour of one parent.[33] It is, however, an obligation of means for the authorities to address the causes of such resistance.[34]

In summary, instead of having to positively serve the child's best interest, personal relations and contact with parents may not negatively (create a risk of) harm (to) the child.[35]

Non-parents

Two categories of non-parents are distinguished when determining their right to personal relations and contact with children. For neither category is it statutorily presumed that the exercise of such rights would serve the best interest of the child. In other words, the onus of proof that personal relations and contact would positively serve the best interest of the child is put on the non-parent.

A *first* category of non-parents are persons with *de jure* or *de facto* family ties with the child. One the one hand, near *de jure* relatives of the child, such as his or her grandparents or siblings,[36] are often statutorily protected.[37] Regarding ties with grandparents, the ECtHR has pointed out

24 ECtHR, *R. v. United Kingdom* (1987), para. 64; ECtHR (Grand Chamber), *Scozzari and Giunta v. Italy* (2000), para. 170; ECtHR (Grand Chamber), *Sahin v. Germany* (2003), para. 65.
25 Art. 4(2) of the COE Convention on Contact Concerning Children and Explanatory Report, paras. 8 and 24; ECJ, *Detiček v. Scueglia* (2009), paras. 58 and 59.
26 ECtHR, *Anayo v. Germany* (2010), para. 66.
27 Explanatory Report to the COE Convention on Contact Concerning Children, para. 8.
28 Hague Conference on Private International Law, *General Principles and Guide to Good Practice. Transfrontier Contact Concerning Children, supra* note 4 at 4 and 5.
29 UN Human Rights Committee, Communication No. 201/1985, *Hendriks v. The Netherlands*.
30 ECnHR, *Hendriks v. The Netherlands* (1982), para. 121; ECtHR (Grand Chamber), *Sahin v. Germany* (2003), para. 67.
31 Stark, *supra* note 9 at 160.
32 ECtHR (Grand Chamber), *Sommerfeld v. Germany* (2003), para. 58.
33 ECtHR, *K.B. and Others v. Kroatia* (2017), para. 143.
34 Ibid., para. 144.
35 ECtHR (Grand Chamber), *Sahin v. Germany* (2003), para. 66; ECtHR, *K.B. and Others v. Kroatia* (2017), para. 143; ECtHR, *Petrov and X. v. Russia* (2018), para. 100.
36 Art. 2(d) of the COE Convention on Contact Concerning Children.
37 Explanatory Report to the Hague Convention on the Civil Aspects of International Child Abduction, para. 79; Hague Conference on Private International Law, *General Principles and Guide to Good Practice. Transfrontier Contact Concerning Children, supra* note 4 at xxvi; Explanatory Report to the COE Convention on Contact Concerning Children, paras. 9 and 47; European Commission, *Practice Guide for the Application of the Brussels IIa Regulation* (2014), available at ec.europa.eu/justice/civil/files/brussels_ii_practice_guide_en.pdf (accessed 28 December 2017), 43. For the US, see *Troxel v. Granville*, 530 US 57, 63 (2000). Also see Doek *supra* note 4 at para. 11.

that "[r]espect for family life . . . implies an obligation for the State to act in a manner calculated to allow these ties to develop normally".[38] This seems almost to amount to a presumption in favour of near relatives that parents would have to rebut.[39] On the other hand, protection applies to persons who have *de facto*, but not *de jure*, family life with the child.[40] This is usually the case for persons with whom the child has shared a household, such as foster parents, step-parents or commissioning parents in cases of artificial insemination with donor sperm.[41] The family of origin, with whom the legal relation is terminated by an adoption, would also qualify under this category, even if the Hague Convention on Protection of Children and Co-operation in Respect of Intercountry Adoption does not accommodate them in that regard. For this category, contact *may* be established with children, subject to the latter's best interest.[42] Contrary to parents, there is no right.

The *second* category of non-parents consists of all other persons with whom the child may have strong personal links now or in the future. Current strong personal ties may exist between a child and a teacher.[43] Potential future ties are protected under non-parents' right to respect for their intended family life or their right to respect for their private life. For example, the ECtHR has considered that adoptive parents, who had never seen their children because the foreign authorities refused to execute the adoption judgments, had a right to respect for their intended family life under article 8 of the COE Convention for the Protection of Human Rights and Fundamental Freedoms.[44] Even more far-reaching, a violation of biological fathers' right to respect for their private life was found in two cases where the national courts had not assessed *in concreto* whether claimed contact with (and information on) their child would be in the latter's best interest, because "a child born out of wedlock and the child's biological father, . . . are inalterably linked by a natural bond".[45] One should wonder what this approach might mean for claims made by donors in assisted reproduction.[46] For this category of non-parents, States are free to extend the provisions on contact with persons having family ties and are free to decide what aspects of contact shall apply.[47]

Even with the onus of proof on the claimant, the European approach of awarding non-parental claims even against the will of the parents is "breathtakingly broad"[48] compared to other legal systems. The United States (US) Supreme Court has found such approach to be an unconstitutional infringement on the parents' role as primary decision-makers about which personal relations and contact with non-parents would serve their child's best interest.[49]

38 ECtHR (Grand Chamber), *Scozzari and Giunta v. Italy* (2000), para. 221.

39 In this regard, see *Troxel v. Granville*, 530 US 57, 69 (2000).

40 Art. 2(d) of the COE Convention on Contact Concerning Children; Hague Conference on Private International Law, *General Principles and Guide to Good Practice. Transfrontier Contact Concerning Children*, *supra* note 4 at 5.

41 E.g. ECtHR (Grand Chamber), *X., Y. and Z. v. United Kingdom* (1997), para. 37. Also see Explanatory Report to the COE Convention on Contact Concerning Children, paras. 9, 34 and 47.

42 Art. 5, para. 1 of the COE Convention on Contact Concerning Children. Compare Principle 3:25(2) of the CEFL Principles of European Family Law Regarding Parental Responsibilities.

43 Explanatory Report to the COE Convention on Contact Concerning Children, para. 51.

44 ECtHR, *Pini and Others v. Romania* (2004), para. 148.

45 ECtHR, *Anayo v. Germany* (2010), para. 60; ECtHR, *Schneider v. Germany* (2010), para. 84.

46 Olsen, *supra* note 15 at 201.

47 Art. 5, para. 2 of the COE Convention on Contact Concerning Children. Compare Principle 3:25(3) of the CEFL Principles of European Family Law Regarding Parental Responsibilities.

48 *Troxel v. Granville*, 530 US 57, 67 (2000).

49 Ibid. Also see the Explanatory Report to the COE European Convention on the Exercise of Children's Rights, para. 8 and on further cultural variations, see Stark, *supra* note 9 at 160 and Boele-Woelki et al., *supra* note 2, Comments 5–6 on Principle 3:25.

Personal relations and contact

Rather than juxtaposing personal relations and contact, contact should be considered the instrument to achieve the objective of the right to maintain personal relations between the child and other rights holders.[50] In most relevant instruments, contact (formerly, visitation or access) is considered an aspect of parental responsibilities,[51] and is usually[52] juxtaposed[53] with custody, which concerns decision-making power. Contact can be exercised directly or indirectly. It can be restricted if unrestricted contact would be contrary to the best interest of the child.

Contact

Contact can be maintained either face-to-face, through direct communication or, indirectly, though the provision of information. The latter two means can either supplement or replace face-to-face contact.[54]

The default position regarding contact is that a child and other rights holders should be able to enjoy each other's company,[55] hence, that contact should be face-to-face.[56] Contact can consist in meeting the child or having him or her stay for a limited period of time at a place other than his or her usual residence.[57] Agreements or court orders should also deal with the modalities of contact,[58] such as the responsibility for transport and the costs thereof.[59] The term "direct contact" is also used for face-to-face contact, even though direct contact can be exercised through other means, too.

Various instruments recognise the maintenance of contact between the child and other rights holders through any means of communication.[60] Formerly, reference was made to

50 Boele-Woelki et al., *supra* note 2, Comment 1 on Principle 3:25.

51 Art. 1(3) of the COE European Convention on the Exercise of Children's Rights and Explanatory Report, para. 24; arts. 1(2) and 2(7) of the EU Brussels IIa Regulation. Also see Principle 3:1(b) of the CEFL Principles of European Family Law Regarding Parental Responsibilities.

52 In some instruments, it is considered an aspect of the right to custody though: art. 1(c) of the COE European Convention on Recognition and Enforcement of Decisions Concerning Custody of Children and on Restoration of Custody of Children. Also see Estin, *supra* note 1 at 129.

53 Art. 5(b) of the Hague Convention on the Civil Aspects of International Child Abduction; art. 3(b) of the Hague Convention on Jurisdiction, Applicable Law, Recognition, Enforcement and Co-Operation in respect of Parental Responsibility and Measures for the Protection of Children. Also see the sources in note 46 above.

54 Explanatory Report to the COE Convention on Contact Concerning Children, para. 22.

55 ECtHR, *R. v. United Kingdom* (1987), para. 64; ECtHR (Grand Chamber), *Scozzari and Giunta v. Italy* (2000), para. 169; ECtHR *Z.J. v. Lithuania* (2014), para. 92; ECtHR, *K.B. and Others v. Kroatia* (2017), para. 144.

56 Explanatory Report to the COE Convention on Contact Concerning Children, paras. 22 and 45.

57 Art. 5(b) of the Hague Convention on the Civil Aspects of International Child Abduction; art. 3(b) of the Hague Convention on Jurisdiction, Applicable Law, Recognition, Enforcement and Co-Operation in respect of Parental Responsibility and Measures for the Protection of Children; art. 2(a)(i) of the COE Convention on Contact Concerning Children and Explanatory Report, para. 22; art. 2(10) of the EU Brussels IIa Regulation and European Commission, *Practice Guide for the Application of the Brussels IIa Regulation*, *supra* note 32 at 43; art. 3(b) of the OAS Inter-American Convention on the International Return of Children. Also see Principle 3:26(1) of the CEFL Principles of European Family Law Regarding Parental Responsibilities.

58 Art. 48 of the EU Brussels IIa Regulation and European Commission, *Practice Guide for the Application of the Brussels IIa Regulation*, *supra* note 37 at 46.

59 Art. 10(2)(a) of the Convention on Contact Concerning Children. Also see Estin, *supra* note 1 at 129.

60 Art. 2(a)(ii) of the COE Convention on Contact Concerning Children; Principle 3:26(1) of the CEFL Principles of European Family Law Regarding Parental Responsibilities. Also see Boele-Woelki et al., *supra* note 2, Comment 2 on Principle 3:26.

telephone, letters and faxes,[61] whereas currently email and different social media would be more relevant.[62]

Some instruments consider the one-way[63] or two-way[64] provision of information on the child and other rights holders also to be contact. It should rather be considered another means to maintain personal relations.[65] This aspect encompasses essential information on the whereabouts of absent persons,[66] as well as information about the child's personal situation[67] "e.g. sending recent photographs, school reports, medical reports etc.".[68]

Restrictions

Restrictions usually refer to direct, face-to-face contact.[69] Nonetheless, they can also apply to other forms of contact or to the provision of information.

Restrictions on contact or information should be justified in the best interest of the child, with a view to protecting the child from actual harm[70] in case of "e.g. domestic violence, danger of abuse, risk of abduction of the child, parent who has not seen the child for a long time, etc.".[71] Restrictions can only be applied insofar and for as long as needed.[72] Strict scrutiny applies.[73]

Restrictions can, first, concern the frequency or the nature of contact.[74] Whereas regular contact between the child and his or her parents is the rule,[75] contact can be made irregular, for example be limited to important events such as birthdays.[76] It could also be limited to indirect contact through telephone or social media.[77]

61 Explanatory Report to the Hague Convention on Jurisdiction, Applicable Law, Recognition, Enforcement and Co-Operation in respect of Parental Responsibility and Measures for the Protection of Children, para. 20.

62 Explanatory Report to the COE Convention on Contact Concerning Children, para. 22; European Commission, *Practice Guide for the Application of the Brussels IIa Regulation*, 43. Also see Doek *supra* note 4 at para. 14; Welsh, D. "Virtual Parents: How Virtual Visitation Legislation is Shaping the Future of Custody Law", (2008) 11 *Journal of Law and Family Studies* 215.

63 As a right of the parent: ECtHR, *Schneider v. Germany* (2010), para. 95 and Principle 3:29 of the CEFL Principles of European Family Law Regarding Parental Responsibilities.

64 Art. 2(a)(iii) of the COE Convention on Contact Concerning Children.

65 Boele-Woelki et al., *supra* note 2, Comment 2 on Principle 3:29.

66 Art. 9(4) of the UN Convention for the Rights of the Child; art. 19(3) of the OAU African Charter on the Rights and Welfare of the Child. Also see Doek *supra* note 4 at para. 15.

67 Principle 3:29 of the CEFL Principles of European Family Law Regarding Parental Responsibilities.

68 Explanatory Report to the COE Convention on Contact Concerning Children, paras. 22 and 45.

69 Ibid., para. 45.

70 Principle 3:28 of the CEFL Principles of European Family Law Regarding Parental Responsibilities. Also see Stark, *supra* note 9 at 159.

71 Explanatory Report to the COE Convention on Contact Concerning Children, paras. 44 and 76.

72 Ibid., para. 44.

73 ECtHR (Grand Chamber), *Sahin v. Germany* (2003), para. 65; ECtHR (Grand Chamber), *Sommerfeld v. Germany* (2003), para. 63; ECtHR, *Schneider v. Germany* (2010), para. 94.

74 Stark, *supra* note 9 at 160.

75 Arts. 9(3) and 10(2) of the UN Convention on the Rights of the Child; art. 4(1) of the COE Convention on Contact Concerning Children and Explanatory Report, para. 2; art. 24(3) of the EU Charter of Fundamental Rights and Explanations, 25; ECJ, *Detiček v. Scueglia* (2009), para. 54; art. 19(2) of the OAU African Charter on the Rights and Welfare of the Child.

76 Explanatory Report to the COE Convention on Contact Concerning Children, para. 42.

77 Art. 3 of the COE Convention on Contact Concerning Children.

Second, restrictions can refer to the premises where contact takes place.[78] Contact could be limited to safe places, such as neutral premises or premises from where child abduction is not possible.[79]

Furthermore, restrictions can imply the presence or absence of certain persons.[80] It can be required that other persons be present for supervision[81] during visits or conversations with a child, such as a custodial parent, another person of confidence, or professional support services.[82]

Other restrictions can consist in safeguards and guarantees, such as the supervision of correspondence, the provision of financial or property securities or the surrender of documents, and undertakings or stipulations to the court, to avoid abduction or non-return.[83]

Enforcement

States not only have a negative obligation to abstain from preventing rights to personal relations and contact from being exercised. Positive obligations also rest upon them, to take all necessary steps that can reasonably be demanded in the special circumstances of each case, to facilitate the exercise of those rights.[84]

Insofar as the rights holder is concerned, facilitation consists in providing access to a speedy and effective procedure. "Speedy" means that the overall length of the procedure, including the implementation of the measures, may not exceed a reasonable time, taking into account the necessary careful examination of the situation.[85] "Effective" means that it should result in the proper application of coercive measures[86] to carry the right into effect.[87]

The appropriate measures are usually aimed at the custodial parent(s), with a view to overcoming their unlawful obstruction of contact rights,[88] whereas they should actually enable and support the rights holders, particularly the child.[89] Possible measures are

- supervision of contact;
- the obligation for a person to provide for the travel and accommodation expenses of the child and, as may be appropriate, of any other person accompanying the child;

78 Stark, *supra* note 9 at 160.
79 Explanatory Report to the COE Convention on Contact Concerning Children, para. 76.
80 Stark, *supra* note 9 at 160.
81 Arts. 3 and 10(2)(a) and (b) of the COE Convention on Contact Concerning Children and Explanatory Report, paras. 42, 44 and 76.
82 Doek *supra* note 4 at para. 12, 129.
83 Art. 10(2)(a) and (b) of the Convention on Contact Concerning Children and Explanatory Report, paras. 83 and 84; Explanatory Report to the Hague Convention on the Civil Aspects of International Child Abduction, para. 128.
84 ECtHR, *Hokkanen v. Finland* (1994), para. 55; ECtHR, *Nuutinen v. Finland* (2000), para. 128; ECtHR, *Ignaccolo-Zenide v. Romania* (2000), para. 94; ECtHR, *Bondavalli v. Italy* (2015), para. 72; ECtHR, *K.B. and Others v. Kroatia* (2017), para. 142. Also see Doek *supra* note 4 at para. 12.
85 Art. 7 of the COE European Convention on the Exercise of Children's Rights; Explanatory Report to the COE Convention on Contact Concerning Children, para. 70; ECnHR, *Hendriks v. The Netherlands* (1982), para. 137; ECtHR, *Hokkanen v. Finland* (1994), para. 72; ECtHR, *Nuutinen v. Finland* (2000), para. 120; ECtHR, *Ignaccolo-Zenide v. Romania* (2000), para. 102; ECtHR, *Bondavalli v. Italy* (2015), para. 73; ECtHR, *K.B. and Others v. Kroatia* (2017), para. 142.
86 Explanatory Report to the COE Convention on Contact Concerning Children, para. 69.
87 Arts. 9 and 10(2) of the COE Convention on Contact Concerning Children; ECtHR, *Ignaccolo-Zenide v. Romania* (2000), para. 91. Also see Boele-Woelki et al., *supra* note 2, Comment 2 on Principle 3:39.
88 Preamble to the COE European Convention on the Exercise of Children's Rights; Principle 3:39 of the CEFL Principles of European Family Law Regarding Parental Responsibilities. Also see ECtHR, *Bondavalli v. Italy* (2015), para. 82.
89 Boele-Woelki et al., *supra* note 2, Comment 3 on Principle 3:25.

- a security to be deposited by the person with whom the child is usually living to ensure that the person seeking contact with the child is not prevented from having such contact;
- a fine to be imposed on the person with whom the child is usually living, should this person refuse to comply with the contact order.[90]

Children should be protected particularly in the framework of enforcement. On the one hand, States should take preparatory measures in case immediate reunification is not desirable.[91] On the other hand, coercion on children would rarely serve their best interest, particularly in cases where they are considered mature enough to refuse to collaborate.[92] It should not, however, be ruled out.[93]

Specific categories of rights holders should benefit from specific measures of facilitation. This applies, for example, to rights holders who are deprived of their personal liberty.[94]

Private international law

Scope

One regional instrument particularly regulates transfrontier contact rights: the COE Convention on Contact Concerning Children of 2003. Other international private international law instruments that govern transfrontier parental responsibilities in general are applicable to issues concerning transfrontier personal relations and contact concerning children, too. These issues are addressed either as a separate category, besides custody issues,[95] or as an aspect thereof.[96] In light of the stronger protection of custody rights,[97] particularly in the context of the return of a child after wrongful removal or retention, qualification of personal relations and contact rights *as custody rights* may be relevant (see below).

Jurisdiction, applicable law, recognition and enforcement, and international co-operation are briefly dealt with below.

Jurisdiction

Ever since the Hague Convention Concerning the Powers of Authorities and the Law Applicable in respect of the Protection of Infants of 1961, the child's habitual residence at the time the authorities are seized of the matter has been the main connecting factor for

90 Art. 10(2)(a) of the COE Convention on Contact Concerning Children.

91 ECtHR, *Nuutinen v. Finland* (2000), para. 128; ECtHR, *Ignaccolo-Zenide v. Romania* (2000), para. 94; ECtHR, *Bondavalli v. Italy* (2015), para. 72; ECtHR, *K.B. and Others v. Kroatia* (2017), para. 144.

92 ECtHR, *Nuutinen v. Finland* (2000), para. 128; ECtHR, *Ignaccolo-Zenide v. Romania* (2000), para. 94; ECtHR, *Hokkanen v. Finland* (1994), paras. 58 and 61. Also see Boele-Woelki et al., *supra* note 2, Comment 3 on Principle 3:39.

93 ECtHR, *Ignaccolo-Zenide v. Romania* (2000), para. 106.

94 Art. 37(c) of the UN Convention on the Rights of the Child; ECtHR, *Messina v. Italy (No. 2)* (2000), paras. 62 and 73; art. 30 of the OAU African Charter on the Rights and Welfare of the Child. Also see Doek *supra* note 4 at para. 12.

95 Art. 5 of the Hague Convention on the Civil Aspects of International Child Abduction; art. 3(b) of the Hague Convention on Jurisdiction, Applicable Law, Recognition, Enforcement and Co-Operation in respect of Parental Responsibility and Measures for the Protection of Children; art. 1(2)(a) of the EU Brussels IIa Regulation; art. 3 of the OAS Inter-American Convention on the International Return of Children.

96 Art. 1(c) of the COE European Convention on Recognition and Enforcement of Decisions Concerning Custody of Children and on Restoration of Custody of Children and Explanatory Report, para. 17.

97 See however Explanatory Report to the Hague Convention on the Civil Aspects of International Child Abduction, para. 61: "access rights are treated more favourably".

jurisdiction.[98] Interestingly, the European Union (EU) Brussels IIa Regulation retains the jurisdiction of the authorities of a child's former habitual residence for three months, with a view to determining the contact rights of the rights holder remaining in that State.[99] The different instruments also provide for prorogation of jurisdiction[100] and for jurisdiction of, among other, States' authorities who are better placed to assess the best interest of the child,[101] or for urgent[102] or provisional[103] measures.

Applicable law

As was already the case under article 2 of the 1961 Hague Convention Concerning the Powers of Authorities and the Law Applicable in respect of the Protection of Infants, article 15(1) of the 1996 Hague Convention on Jurisdiction, Applicable Law, Recognition, Enforcement and Co-Operation in respect of Parental Responsibility and Measures for the Protection of Children refers to the law of the authorities having jurisdiction as applicable law. Those authorities may however take into consideration the law of another State with which the case has a substantial connection.[104]

Recognition and enforcement

The various international instruments offer a particularly strong fourfold protection for rights holders in transfrontier contact cases.[105]

First, Contracting or Member States' decisions on personal relations and contact shall be recognised in all other Contracting or Member States without any special procedure being

98 Art. 1 of the Hague Convention Concerning the Powers of Authorities and the Law Applicable in respect of the Protection of Infants; art. 5(1) of the Hague Convention on Jurisdiction, Applicable Law, Recognition, Enforcement and Co-Operation in respect of Parental Responsibility and Measures for the Protection of Children; art. 8(1) of the EU Brussels IIa Regulation. On those instruments, see Blair, D.M. et al. *Family Law in the World Community: Cases, Materials, and Problems in Comparative and International Family Law* (Durham, NC, Carolina Academic Press, 2009) 542–43 and 547; Estin, *supra* note 1 at 144–45 and 152.

99 Art. 9(1) of the EU Brussels IIa Regulation.

100 Art. 10 of the Hague Convention on Jurisdiction, Applicable Law, Recognition, Enforcement and Co-Operation in respect of Parental Responsibility and Measures for the Protection of Children; art. 12 EU Brussels IIa Regulation.

101 Arts. 3 and 4 of the Hague Convention Concerning the Powers of Authorities and the Law Applicable in respect of the Protection of Infants; arts. 8 and 9 of the Hague Convention on Jurisdiction, Applicable Law, Recognition, Enforcement and Co-Operation in respect of Parental Responsibility and Measures for the Protection of Children; arts. 13 and 15 of the EU Brussels IIa Regulation.

102 Arts. 8 and 9 of the Hague Convention Concerning the Powers of Authorities and the Law Applicable in respect of the Protection of Infants; art. 11 of the Hague Convention on Jurisdiction, Applicable Law, Recognition, Enforcement and Co-Operation in respect of Parental Responsibility and Measures for the Protection of Children; art. 20 of the EU Brussels IIa Regulation, as interpreted in ECJ, *Detiček v. Sgueglia* (2009), para. 39.

103 Art. 12 of the Hague Convention on Jurisdiction, Applicable Law, Recognition, Enforcement and Co-Operation in respect of Parental Responsibility and Measures for the Protection of Children; art. 20 of the EU Brussels IIa Regulation.

104 See hereto Blair et al., *supra* note 98 at 543.

105 See, in general, Blair et al., *supra* note 98 at 543 ff; Estin, *supra* note 1 at 128 and 145 ff.

required.[106] Non-recognition is limited to particular grounds that are restrictively listed in those instruments and do not allow a review as to the substance of the decision.[107]

Second, decisions that are enforceable in the State of origin, should also be made enforceable in the other Contracting or Member States, subject to the same exceptions that apply in the case of recognition.[108] However, the EU Brussels IIa Regulation offers stronger protection.[109] According to article 41:

> 1. The rights of access . . . granted in an enforceable judgment given in a Member State shall be recognised and enforceable in another Member State without the need for a declaration of enforceability and without any possibility of opposing its recognition if the judgment has been certified in the Member State of origin . . .

and

> 3. Where the rights of access involve a cross-border situation at the time of the delivery of the judgment, the certificate shall be issued ex officio when the judgment becomes enforceable, even if only provisionally. If the situation subsequently acquires a cross-border character, the certificate shall be issued at the request of one of the parties.

Third, the actual enforcement of decisions on personal relations and contact is guaranteed through a machinery comparable to return proceedings, and which allows the rights holder to turn to the Central Authority, which has extensive competence to "fix or adapt the conditions for its implementation, as well as any safeguards or guarantees attaching to it, if necessary for facilitating the exercise of this contact, provided that the essential elements of the order are respected".[110] Adaptations of conditions may be necessary, for example, to take into account the timing of school holidays.[111]

Finally, rights holders sometimes benefit from the same enforcement procedure that applies to a child's return. This is the case under article 21 of the OAS Inter-American Convention on the International Return of Children. The US Supreme Court has also found that the *ne exeat* right of a parent with visitation rights is to be considered a custody right in the sense of the

106 Art. 21(1) of the EU Brussels IIa Regulation. The same applies under art. 7 of the Hague Convention Concerning the Powers of Authorities and the Law Applicable in respect of the Protection of Infants; arts. 7 and 11(1) of the COE European Convention on Recognition and Enforcement of Decisions Concerning Custody of Children and on Restoration of Custody of Children and art. 14(1) of the COE Convention on Contact Concerning Children.

107 Arts. 23(2) and 27 of the Hague Convention on Jurisdiction, Applicable Law, Recognition, Enforcement and Co-Operation in respect of Parental Responsibility and Measures for the Protection of Children; art. 10 of the COE European Convention on Recognition and Enforcement of Decisions Concerning Custody of Children and on Restoration of Custody of Children; arts. 23 ff of the EU Brussels IIa Regulation.

108 Arts. 7 and 11(1) of the COE European Convention on Recognition and Enforcement of Decisions Concerning Custody of Children and on Restoration of Custody of Children and art. 14(1) of the COE Convention on Contact Concerning Children.

109 European Commission, *Practice Guide for the Application of the Brussels IIa Regulation, supra* note 37 at 41.

110 Art. 15 of the COE Convention on Contact Concerning Children. Also see art. 21 of the Hague Convention on the Civil Aspects of International Child Abduction; art. 11(2) of the COE European Convention on Recognition and Enforcement of Decisions Concerning Custody of Children and on Restoration of Custody of Children; art. 48 of the EU Brussels IIa Regulation.

111 Explanatory Report to the COE European Convention on Recognition and Enforcement of Decisions Concerning Custody of Children and on Restoration of Custody of Children, para. 59.

Hague Convention on the Civil Aspects of International Child Abduction, making a return order possible at the parent's request.[112] The EU Court of Justice (ECJ) however found under the EU Brussels IIa Regulation that removal or retention by a mother cannot be considered wrongful if the child's unmarried father is required under national law to apply to court for custody rights, but has not yet done so.[113]

International co-operation

The different instruments place a strong emphasis on co-operation between the Central Authorities of Contracting or Member States,[114] with a view of both safeguarding the personal relations and contact rights of the various rights holders and securing the return of children to their custodial parents after those rights have been exercised. Co-operation is foreseen both in the preparatory phase – for example, to gather information and deliver a certificate on the desirability and conditions of contact – and in the phase of actual exercise – for example, to remove any obstacles to the exercise.[115]

Bibliography

Blair, D.M., Weiner, M.H., Stark, B. and Maldonado, S. *Family Law in the World Community: Cases, Materials, and Problems in Comparative and International Family Law* (Durham, NC, Carolina Academic Press, 2009).

Boele-Woelki, Katharina, Ferrand, Frédérique, González Beilfuss, Cristina, Jänterä-Jareborg, Maarit, Lowe, Nigel, Martiny, Dieter and Pintens, Walter. *Principles of European Family Law Regarding Parental Responsibilities* (Cambridge, UK, Intersentia, 2007).

Detrick, S. *A Commentary on the United Nations Convention on the Rights of the Child* (Leiden and Boston, MA, Martinus Nijhoff Publishers, 1999).

Doek, J.E. "Article 8 The Right to Preservation of Identity. Article 9 The Right Not to be Separated from his or her Parents" in *A Commentary on the United Nations Convention on the Rights of the Child* (Alen, A., Lanotte, J.V., Verhellen, E., Ang, F., Berghmans, E. and Verheyde, M. eds, Leiden and Boston, MA, Martinus Nijhoff Publishers, 2006).

Estin, A.L. *International Family Law Desk Book* (American Bar Association Publishing, 2013).

European Commission. *Practice Guide for the Application of the Brussels IIa Regulation* (2014).

Finegan, T. "An Unmarried Father's Right to Guardianship of his Child and a Child's Right to the Support of his/her Father: A Hohfeldian View of the Irish Constitution", (2010) 32 *Dublin University Law Journal* 320.

Government Committee on the Reassessment of Parenthood. *Child and Parents in the 21st Century* (The Hague, 2016).

Hague Conference on Private International Law. *General Principles and Guide to Good Practice. Transfrontier Contact Concerning Children* (Bristol, UK, Family Law, 2008).

112 *Abott v. Abott*, 560 US 1 (2010).

113 ECJ, *J. McB v. L.E.* (2010) and European Commission, *Practice Guide for the Application of the Brussels IIa Regulation*, *supra* note 37 at 53.

114 Arts. 6–7 and 21 of the Hague Convention on the Civil Aspects of International Child Abduction; arts. 29 ff, particularly art. 35, of the Hague Convention on Jurisdiction, Applicable Law, Recognition, Enforcement and Co-Operation in respect of Parental Responsibility and Measures for the Protection of Children; arts. 11 and 13 of the COE Convention on Contact Concerning Children and Explanatory Report, paras. 1–2; Chapter IV of the EU Brussels IIa Regulation.

115 Explanatory Report to the Hague Convention on the Civil Aspects of International Child Abduction, para. 125; Explanatory Report to the Hague Convention on Jurisdiction, Applicable Law, Recognition, Enforcement and Co-Operation in respect of Parental Responsibility and Measures for the Protection of Children, paras. 146–147. Also see Blair et al., *supra* note 98 at 548.

Kodilinye, L. "Is Access the Right of the Parent or the Right of the Child? A Commonwealth View", (1992) 41 *International and Comparative Law Quarterly* 190.
Olsen, F. "Children's Rights: Some Feminist Approaches to the United Nations Convention on the Rights of the Child", (1992) 6 *International Journal of Law and the Family* 192.
Stark, B. *International Family Law: An Introduction* (Aldershot, UK, Ashgate, 2005).
Welsh, D. "Virtual Parents: How Virtual Visitation Legislation is Shaping the Future of Custody Law", (2008) 11 *Journal of Law and Family Studies* 215.

11
Adoption

Barbara Stark[1]

Introduction

When parents cannot or will not care for their infants or children, another member of the family or community usually steps up. Historian Peter Conn has shown that adoption is ancient and ubiquitous.[2] But legal adoption by strangers, in which all ties to the family of origin are severed, was rare until the nineteenth century. Intercountry adoption, the legal adoption of children and babies born in one country by strangers in another, is even more recent, beginning after World War II, and peaking in 2004 with 45,000 adoptees placed in foreign countries.[3]

Part I of this chapter offers a brief historical overview of adoption, up through the entry into force of the Hague Convention on Intercountry Adoption (the Adoption Convention).[4] Part II discusses the human rights issues raised by intercountry adoption, from the perspectives of the adoptees, the adoptive and biological parents, and the larger communities of which they all are a part. Part III examines the legal framework and standards set out in the Adoption Convention, along with recent responses to the human rights challenges discussed in Part II and widespread financial abuses. Part IV concludes with an analysis of the global decline of intercountry adoption, and some of the responses to this decline.

1 This chapter draws on the author's earlier work on intercountry adoption, including "When Genealogy Matters: Intercountry Adoption, International Human Rights, and Global Neoliberalism," 51 *Vand. J. Int'l L.* 159 (2018).
2 See Peter Conn, *Adoption: A Brief Social and Cultural History* 27 (2013) (providing anecdotal accounts of adoption dating back to 1772 BCE, and noting that it is found in most human societies as well as over 120 mammalian and 150 avian species.)
3 Marianne Blair et al., *Family Law in the World Community* 803 (3rd edn 2015).
4 Convention on Protection of Children and Co-operation in Respect to Intercountry Adoption, opened for signature 29 May 1993, 1870 U.N.T.S. at 182; see also G. Parra-Aranguren, Explanatory Report on the Convention on Protection of Children and Co-operation in respect of Intercountry Adoption (1994), available at www.hcch.net/e/conventionsl/expl33e.html.

I. Brief historical overview

Adoption is an evolving institution, changing over time as cultures change and conceptions of childhood, and the roles of nature and nurture, change. Cultures, and their approaches to adoption, also change as they come into contact with other cultures. As Professor Marianne Blair notes, the main purpose of adoption in ancient Rome, Babylonia, and China was to "ensure the continuity of the family."[5] But the Church disapproved of childless men of property who adopted heirs, and adoption became virtually unknown in Europe. The importance of blood ties, and the maintenance of family registries discouraged adoption throughout Asia, with the exception of India.[6] Adoption is prohibited under Islamic law; orphans are the responsibility of relatives under *kafalah*,[7] in which ties are retained to the family of origin.

Adoption on the national level

Domestic adoption has been used to formalise step-parent relationships, clarify rights of inheritance, and legitimise children born to unmarried parents. It has also served broader legal and political purposes. Adoption has been used to compel the assimilation of indigenous people and racial minorities, as well as to hide Jewish children from the Nazis and eliminate traces of the "disappeared" in Argentina.

This Part first addresses domestic adoption; that is, adoption on the national level, where it first developed. This section shows how adoption was shaped by national laws and politics. The second section explains the origins of intercountry adoption. It describes the process through which sometimes conflicting domestic objectives were dealt with in the Adoption Convention.

In the United States

Professor Barbara Melosh has suggested that modern adoption is an American invention:

> The emergence of modern adoption required a radically different understanding of family, one that overturned deeply held beliefs about blood and nurture, obligation and love, choice and chance. It was no accident that the United States was the crucible of this kind of adoption: in its repudiation of the past and its confidence in social engineering, adoption is quintessentially American.[8]

Adoption by strangers became widespread in the United States in the 1850s, as an alternative to indentured servitude or apprenticeship for orphans.[9] Orphan Trains carried over 250,000 children from the crowded slums of the eastern cities to Midwest and Western farms, where they could acquire practical skills, while providing farmers with cheap labour.[10] By the middle

5 Blair et al., *supra* note 3 at 754.

6 "When Genealogy Matters," *supra* note 1 at 165.

7 "[W]hile it forbids adoption, the Quran expressly commends the care of orphans. These children should be valued, protected, and treated in all respects except name and inheritance as a non-adoption son or daughter. Thus, Kafalah is the model proposed by Sharia law in this respect." Conn, *supra* note 2 at 55.

8 Barbara Melosh, *Strangers and Kin: The American Way of Adoption* 15 (2002).

9 David Ray Papke, "Pondering Past Purposes: A Critical History of American Adoption Law," 102 *W. Va. L. Rev.* 459, 461 (1999).

10 Conn, *supra* note 2, at 75–82.

of the twentieth century, the conventional wisdom was that babies should be "matched" with adoptive families, to simulate biological families. Social workers conducted interviews and home visits in order to place children in appropriate homes. Native American children were placed with white families, however, in order to promote their assimilation in the majority white culture.

Adoption in America has been transformed during the past few decades, reflecting an increase in births to unmarried white women, the decreasing stigma for such births, easier access to contraception, the greater autonomy of birth mothers, and an increase in "open" adoptions.[11] In open adoptions, either or both birth parents are known to the adopting parents, and often expect to have some kind of ongoing relationship with the child. During this same period, growing numbers of black children have entered the foster care system.[12] New federal law made them available for adoption on an accelerated basis. The Multiethnic Placement Act of 1994[13] made them available for adoption by white parents, notwithstanding the opposition of the National Association of Black Social Workers.[14]

The Indian Adoption Project

In 1881, Congress decided that Native American children should be taken from their tribes and sent to government boarding schools or mission schools to become "civilised."[15] This was intended to solve the "Indian problem," as the Commissioner of Indian Affairs explained:

> It is admitted by most people that the adult savage is not susceptible to the influence of civilization, and we must therefore turn to these children, that they might be taught to abandon the pathway of barbarism and walk with a sure step along the pleasant highway of Christian civilization . . . They must be withdrawn, in tender years, entirely from the camp and taught to eat, to sleep, to dress, to play, to work, to think after the manner of the white man.[16]

Professor Lila George describes how Native American children were taught that their own cultures were "immoral, inferior and contemptible."[17] Their clothes were replaced by uniforms, their languages by English, their beliefs by Christian doctrine, and their customs by rigid rules, often enforced by corporal punishment, which Native Americans rarely used.[18]

11 See, e.g., Lisa Belkin, "Now Accepting Applications for My Baby," *N.Y. Times Mag.*, 5 Apr. 1998, at 58 (describing the process through which a birth mother selected the parents of the child she was surrendering.)
12 See *Placing Black Children with White Families, infra.*
13 P.L. 103–382 amending Title IV-E of the Social Security Act.
14 National Association of Black Social Workers Position Statement on Trans-Racial Adoptions, Sept. 1972.
15 Lorie M. Graham, "The Past Never Vanishes: A Contextual Critique of the Existing Indian Family Law Doctrine," 23 *Am. Indian L. Rev.* 1, 13–18 (1995–1999) (describing the role of boarding schools in United States assimilationist policies.)
16 Lila George, "Why the Need for the Indian Child Welfare Act?" in *The Challenge of Permanency Planning in a Multicultural Society* 165, 169 (Gary R. Anderson et al. eds 1997).
17 Id.
18 Id. Graham, *supra* note 15, at 26–27 (explaining how rejection of corporal punishment by Native American families was later criticised as "too permissive" by social workers, and relied upon, in connection with other practices – such as leaving children with relatives – as a basis for removing children from their home).

Canada and Australia took similar measures to assimilate indigenous people by removing their children.[19]

In the 1930s, when the Indian Reorganization Act restored some autonomy to the tribes, the boarding schools began closing. The Social Security Act, which was passed in 1935, included Aid to Dependent Children (ADC), which was administered by the states. This allowed state social workers to decide whether Indian children were being properly cared for by their often unmarried Indian mothers, or other members of their extended families.[20] In the 1950s, care by single parents or other relatives was viewed as inferior to care provided by a stay-at-home mother in a nuclear family. Boarding schools and foster care were too expensive.[21] Adoption was proposed as a solution to the "Indian problem."

The Indian Adoption Project, initiated in 1958 and ending in 1968, placed children "far from the reservation, geographically as well as culturally."[22] The Project placed 395 Indian children with white families,[23] but its purpose was more ambitious; that is, "to stimulate the adoption of American Indian children on a nation-wide basis."[24] It worked. The Project could not handle the demand for adoptees, so agencies in the children's home states arranged for their adoptions. By the early 1970s, between 25% and 35% of Native American children had been legally adopted by white families.[25]

The children and their families were devastated by these adoptions. As Congress found when it passed the Indian Child Adoption Welfare Act of 1978 (ICWA),[26]

> there is no resource that is more vital to the continued existence and integrity of Indian tribes than their children . . . [A]n alarmingly high percentage of Indian families are broken up by the removal, often unwarranted, of their children from them by nontribal public and private agencies and . . . an alarmingly high percentage of such children are placed in non-Indian foster and adoptive homes and institutions.[27]

In *Mississippi Band of Choctaw Indians v. Holyfield*,[28] the Supreme Court examined the jurisdictional provisions "[a]t the heart of the ICWA."[29] *Holyfield* involved the adoption of twin illegitimate infants whose parents, both members of the tribe, "went to some efforts to see that they were born outside the reservation."[30] Although the babies were never physically present on the

19 See, e.g., Douglas Martin, "Doris Pilkington Garimara, Aboriginal Novelist, Dies at 76," *N.Y. Times*, 2 July 2018 (author of *Follow the Rabbit-Proof Fence*, which describes the Australian government's removal of Aboriginal children from their families in the 1930s); Ian Austen, "Trudeau Apologizes for Abuse and 'Profound Cultural Loss' at Indigenous Schools," *N.Y. Times*, 24 Nov. 2017 (Prime Minister apologises and Canadian government settles a class action lawsuit for 50 million Canadian dollars for a residential school programme that separated indigenous children from their families and cultures from the nineteenth century until 1996.)

20 The Bureau of Indian Affairs (BIA) reported that "many children had been passed from family to family on a reservation." David Fanshel, *Far From the Reservation* 36–37 (1972).

21 See Graham, *supra* note 15, at 7.

22 George, *supra* note 16, at 169.

23 Id.

24 Fanshel, *supra* note 20, at 35.

25 George, *supra* note 16, at 172–173.

26 25 U.S.C.A §1901 *et seq.*

27 Id. at §1901. Id. at (5).

28 490 U.S. 30 (1989).

29 Id. at 36.

30 Id. at 30.

reservation, and the parents voluntarily surrendered them to the non-Indian adoptive parents, the court held that the ICWA established exclusive jurisdiction in the tribal courts over Indian children domiciled there, and that the "domicile of origin" for Indian babies was that of their mother.[31]

In a recent decision, *Adoptive Couple v. Baby Girl*,[32] however, the Supreme Court held that the ICWA did not bar the adoption of an Indian baby by non-Indians where her Indian father had never had physical or legal custody of her.[33] As Justice Sotomayer noted in her dissent, the ICWA "protects not only Indian parents' interests but also those of Indian tribes."[34] In *Adoptive Couple*, the Supreme Court discounted the importance of children to their tribes, explicitly set out in the ICWA and confirmed in *Holyfield*.

Placing black children with white families

When slavery was legal in the United States, from the founding of the country to the end of the Civil War, black children, like their mothers, were considered the property of their owners. As Professor Peggy Cooper Davis has shown, enslaved families coped with their inability to claim legal ties to parents and children through fictive kin and extended caregiving networks.[35]

Davis explains how black parents, no longer slaves after the Civil War, tried to reunite families that had been torn apart by slavery.[36] White southerners claimed that the black children in their households were not slaves, but "apprentices," who were better off with them than they would be with their free, but destitute, biological families.[37] The placement of black children in white homes, purportedly for their own good, has had a painful history.

In the 1950s, white southerners pointed to unwed black mothers to detract from the respectability projected by Martin Luther King Jr. and other civil rights activists in suits and ties. It was an effective strategy and established a pattern of blaming black mothers for black poverty.[38] In 1954, Congress amended the Social Security Act to allow agricultural and domestic workers to qualify for Aid to Families with Dependent Children (AFDC). Black women and children in the South were then eligible for welfare under federal law.[39] Southern states quickly enacted state-wide rules banning benefits for "immoral" or "unsuitable" households, striking thousands of "illegitimate" children from state welfare rolls. In 1964, the Mississippi legislature debated a bill, expressly aimed at black women,[40] making it a felony to "bear or beget" an illegitimate child, punishable by sterilisation or three years in prison.[41]

31 See Solangel Maldonado, "Race, Culture, and Adoption: Lessons from Mississippi Band of Choctaw Indians v. Holyfield," 17 *Colum. J. Gender & L.* 1, 27 (2008).

32 133 S. Ct. 2552 (2013).

33 Id.

34 Id. at 2583–2584.

35 Peggy Cooper Davis, *Neglected Stories: The Constitution and Family Values* 4 (1997).

36 Id. at 144.

37 Id.

38 Or, as Daniel Patrick Moynihan put it, the "tangle of pathology." See Daniel Patrick Moynihan, *The Negro Family: The Case for National Action* (1965).

39 Laura Briggs, *Somebody's Children: The Politics of Transracial and Transnational Adoption* 7, 39 (2012).

40 See id. (quoting a sponsor of the bill: "The negro woman, because of child welfare assistance, [is] making . . . a business . . . of giving birth to illegitimate children . . . . The purpose of my bill was to try to stop, or slow down, such traffic at its source." Id.)

41 Id. at 39.

In response, Arthur Fleming, the Secretary of Health, Education and Welfare, promulgated a rule requiring states cutting such benefits to provide foster care or orphanages for the affected children (at much greater cost to the state.)[42] But the Fleming Rule backfired. Instead of discouraging states from denying benefits to single black mothers, it discouraged these mothers from applying for benefits, since by doing so they risked losing their children.[43]

In 1996, Congress passed the Personal Responsibility and Work Opportunity Reconciliation Act,[44] which promised, as then-President Bill Clinton put it, "to end welfare as we know it."[45] AFDC was replaced by Temporary Assistance to Needy Families (TANF), which put a federal lifetime cap of five years on welfare, although states were allowed to set even shorter limits.[46] A year later, in 1997, Clinton signed the Adoption and Safe Families Act (ASFA),[47] which aimed "to double the number of foster children adopted annually to 54,000 by 2002."[48] When a child is put in foster care, the new law requires a permanency hearing to be held within a year. If the child is still in foster care three months later (with specific exemptions for relative care, the agency's failure to make reasonable efforts at reunification, or some other "compelling reason"), the agency is expected to commence termination proceedings. The federal government also pays states bonuses for children adopted above the state baseline, determined by average adoptions between 1995 and 1997.[49] In 1999 there were 46,000 adoptions and states received $20 million in adoption bonuses.[50] As Professor Dorothy Roberts notes, the "number of children in foster care . . . doubled . . . from 262,000 in 1982 to 568,000 in 1999."[51] By 2000, 42% of the children in foster care were black, even though only 17% of American children were black.[52]

In Poland and Argentina

During World War II, many Jewish children were informally adopted by non-Jews in Poland after their parents were captured by the Nazis.[53] Some of these children later reclaimed their Jewish identities.[54] A few were reunited with their parents.[55]

As Professor Laura Oren has documented, during Argentina's "dirty war" in the 1970s and early 1980s, thousands of dissidents were "disappeared."[56] Hundreds of children of the

42 Enacted as Public Law 87–31, Public Service Amendments of 1962.
43 Briggs, *supra* note 39 at 42.
44 Public Law 104–193, 22 Aug. 1996; 110 Stat. 2105 104th Cong., H.R. 3734.
45 See, e.g., Alana Semuels, "The End of Welfare as We Know It," *Atlantic*, 1 Apr. 2016.
46 "When Genealogy Matters," *supra* note 1 at 172.
47 Pub. L. 105–189, 19 Nov. 1997, III Stat. 2115.
48 Dorothy Roberts, *Shattered Bonds: The Color of Child Welfare* 105 (2002).
49 Id.
50 Id. at 111.
51 Id. at 8.
52 Id.
53 See, e.g., "Ass'n of Hidden Children of the Holocaust in Poland, Children of the Holocaust Association in Poland," available at www.dzieciholocaustu.org.pl/szab51.php?s=index3.php (last visited 2 July 2018) (containing home page of organisation of children saved by Poles, with membership of 750 in 1999). Nahum Bogner, "The Convent Children: The Rescue of Jewish Children in Polish Convents During the Holocaust," *Yad Vashem Studies* XXVII, 235 (Naftali Greenwood trans., Yad Vashem Martyrs' and Heroes' Remembrance Auth. 1999) (describing children who survived the Holocaust in Polish convents).
54 See "Ass'n of Children of the Holocaust in Poland," *supra* note 53.
55 Bogner, *supra* note 53, at 284.
56 Laura Oren "Righting Child Custody Wrongs: The Children of the 'Disappeared' in Argentina," 14 *Harv. Hum. Rts. J.* 123, 127–128 (2001).

"disappeared," including infants born while their mothers were in police custody, were adopted. As many as 450 children were adopted by military or police families.[57] Most of these children were never found. But some were tracked down and returned to their families of origin.[58] The results were mixed.[59] While some of the children adjusted readily to their new families, others were conflicted. Some adoption professionals pressed for reunification, others were concerned that the children's interests were being subordinated to those of the group.[60]

In 1986, Poland joined with Argentina to propose that the Convention on the Rights of the Child[61] (CRC) require states to assist any child "fraudulently deprived of . . . his identity."[62] Article 7 of the CRC provides in pertinent part that "[t]he child shall be registered immediately after birth and shall have the right to know and be cared for by his or her parents." Article 8 requires states to assist any child "illegally deprived of some or all of the elements of his or her identity." As noted in the Explanatory Report, the right of the child to obtain information was undisputed because of the CRC.[63] Unrestricted access, however, raised issues under Article 7(2) of the CRC regarding the privacy rights of the parents.[64] The result was a carefully worded compromise, assuring access to information, "under appropriate guidance."[65]

Intercountry adoption

Children in crisis

International adoption began after World War II with Pearl Buck's work to save children in China from the chaos of the revolution, poverty, and communism.[66] After adopting seven children herself, Buck opened her own agency, Welcome House, when she was unable to place two mixed-race children with any of the existing agencies.[67] Harry and Berthe Holt, similarly, adopted eight South Korean children after the Korean War.[68] There were many mixed race children, fathered by American troops, and they were discriminated against in South Korea. The evangelical Holts were not only saving the children from poverty and rejection, they felt that they were saving the children spiritually, by raising them in Christian homes. Buck and the Holts were part of a triumphant, prosperous, post-war America that was ready to save the world.

57 Id. at 124.

58 Id. at 125. Of 200 documented kidnapped children, forty-two were found. Nineteen of these were reunited with their biological families, twelve stayed with their adoptive families (while resuming their original names and developing ties with their families of origin), six cases were pending, and five of the children were dead. Id. at 164.

59 Id. at 162.

60 In 1987, Argentina established a National Genetic Bank to enable families to establish the true identities of children of the disappeared. Francisco Goldman, "Children of the Dirty War," *New Yorker*, 19 March 2012.

61 U.N. Doc. A/44/49 (1989).

62 D. Marianne Brower Blair, "The Impact of Family Paradigms, Domestic Constitutions, and International Conventions on Disclosure of an Adopted Person's Identities and Heritage: A Comparative Examination," 22 *Mich. J. Int'l. L.* 587, 648 (2001). Polish law did not allow adult adoptees access to identifying information until 1995. Id.

63 Explanatory Report *supra* note 4 at para. 512.

64 Id.

65 Art. 30(2) of the Adoption Convention, *supra* note 4.

66 Briggs, *supra* note 39 at 39.

67 See Conn, *supra* note 2 at 117 ("[I]n the sixty-plus years since Welcome House and similar organizations began their work, upwards of 800,000 children have come to the U.S. for adoption.")

68 Briggs, *supra* note 39.

Welcome House and the Holt Agency were established to rescue children in crisis. More recently, missionaries attempted to "rescue" Haitian children after the 2010 earthquake.[69] But most children in crisis (including the Haitians), are only temporarily separated from parents, or other family members, who will care for them once they are reunited. As the United Nations High Commissioner on Refugees explains, since "most unaccompanied children are not orphans, what they need is suitable interim care with a view toward possible reunification with their families, not adoption."[70]

Westerners seeking children

Intercountry adoption surged in the 1990s, much of it driven by American and other Western would-be parents unable or unwilling to adopt domestically.[71] Intercountry adoption enabled these parents to adopt babies or toddlers, usually without ever meeting the birth parents. International adoption became more appealing for some, and the only option for many. The numbers of babies and young children adopted increased steadily after the end of the Cold War, peaking in 2004, when the numbers began to decline.[72]

As set out in the Explanatory Report,[73] international adoptions, "had become a worldwide phenomenon involving migration of children over long distances and from one society and culture to another very different environment."[74] This presented serious and unprecedented problems, including children procured through fraud, duress, and money; adoptions that were not in a child's best interest; the absence of legally binding standards; and the obvious need for a multilateral approach. But the Hague Conference was reluctant to address these issues because many states of origin were not members of the Conference, and would not be participating in the project. The Secretary General contacted inter-governmental and non-governmental organisations (NGOs), officials of non-Member States, private organisations, and scholars. The response was positive and non-Member States agreed to join in the work. This was further facilitated by the Secretary General's subsequent suggestion to allow the Spanish-speaking countries to participate in Spanish, rather than in English or French. After multiple meetings, drafts, and revisions,[75] the resulting Adoption Convention was finally examined in two full Plenary Sessions and unanimously approved on 28 May 1993. The substance of the Convention is discussed in Part III, *infra*.

II. Human rights and intercountry adoption

Adoption is governed by national law, and, in some cases, regional law. Under the African Charter on the Rights and Welfare of the Child,[76] for example, intercountry adoption is limited to those countries that are either parties to the African Charter on the Rights of the Child or

69 John Seabrook, "The Last Babylift," *New Yorker*, 10 May 2010.

70 UNHCR, UNHCR Policy on Adoption of Refugee Children (1995); Daniel Steinbock, "Unaccompanied Children in Comparative and International Law," in Everett M. Ressler, Neil Boothby and Daniel J. Steinbock, *Unaccompanied Children: Care and Protection in Wars, Natural Disasters, and Refugee Movements* 269 (1988).

71 See, e.g., text accompanying nn. 10–14, *supra*.

72 Blair et al., *supra* note 3 at 803.

73 *Supra* note 4.

74 Explanatory Report, *supra* note 4 at para. 6(i).

75 See, e.g., Explanatory Report, *supra* note 4 at para. 27 (describing twenty-one sessions, 201 working documents, and innumerable sub-groups at the Second Commission Alone.)

76 African Charter on the Rights and Welfare of the Child, OAU Doc. CAB/LEG/24.9/49 (1990) (entered into force 29 Nov. 1999).

to the CRC.[77] Different national laws are coordinated by the Adoption Convention. But the Convention is only binding when both the sending and the receiving states are parties. Even if both states are parties, moreover, the Convention provides minimal human rights protection. In general, adoption laws protect the rights of biological families, and adoptive parents, from subsequent claims by requiring the freely-given consent of the biological parents. But the Adoption Convention does not purport to subject the adoption to human rights law.

Intercountry adoption raises human rights issues for the surrendering parents, the community of which they are a part, the adoptive parents, and the adoptee herself. Intercountry adoption raises these issues not only at the time of the adoption, but over the life span of the adoptee, as well as both her biological and her legal parents. The major human rights instruments applicable in the context of intercountry adoption are: the International Covenant on Civil and Political Rights (the Civil Covenant),[78] the International Covenant on Economic, Social and Cultural Rights (the Economic Covenant),[79] the CRC,[80] and the Convention on the Elimination of All Forms of Discrimination Against Women (the Women's Convention.)[81]

While intercountry adoption advocates agree that the child must be "properly" separated from both biological parents and that the child should be placed with appropriately screened parents, the Adoption Convention does not require consideration of the violations of the parents' human rights that may have led to the surrender of the child. When babies were abandoned by Chinese parents subject to the one-child policy, for example, the obvious coercion did not preclude Hague adoptions.[82] Nor does the Adoption Convention discourage adoptions when children are surrendered because of discrimination on the basis of race, gender or disability, whether on the part of the parents' community, the state, or the parents themselves. Finally, the Adoption Convention does not require consideration of the parents' (or the mother's) economic situation.

Adoptees' human rights

The human rights issues that arise most frequently in the context of intercountry adoption – gender, racial, or other forms of discrimination and the denial of economic rights – are well known in both sending and receiving states. The prohibition against racial discrimination is a *jus cogens* norm, from which no derogation is permitted.[83] Gender discrimination and economic rights, if less well-entrenched, are not only included in the International Bill of Rights (this refers to the Universal Declaration, the ICCPR, and the ICESCR), but in a growing number of national constitutions.[84] The focus of non-discrimination, like that of economic, social, and cultural rights, may well change as the adoptee matures. A child whose surrender may have been triggered by

77 Id. at Art. 24(b).

78 International Covenant on Civil and Political Rights (ICCPR), 23 March 1976, 999 U.N.T.S. 171.

79 International Covenant on Economic, Social and Cultural Rights (ICESCR), 3 Jan. 1976, 993 U.N.T.S. 3.

80 *Supra* note 61.

81 1249 U.N.T.S 13 entered into force in 1981.

82 China became a party to the Hague Convention in 2006. The one-child policy was rescinded in 2015. Chris Buckley, "China Ends One-Child Policy, Allowing Families to Have Two Children," *N.Y. Times*, 29 Oct. 2015.

83 Antonio Cassesse, "A Plea for Global Community Grounded in a Core of Human Rights," in *Realizing Utopia: The Future of International Law* 37, 139 (2012).

84 David Law and Mila Versteeg, "The Declining Influence of the United States Constitution," 87 *N.Y.U.L. Rev.* 3 (2013).

the difficulties of raising a biracial, half-white child in her country of origin, for example, may find herself discriminated against in an American suburb because she is half-Asian.

As the adoptee matures, other human rights may be triggered, including the child's right to know her parents and her culture, to be part of a community, and to be part of a country.[85] The child's right to belong is important socially, psychologically, and politically. There is growing literature on this subject, ranging from personal accounts to nascent movements, including initiatives by Korean adoptees to find birth parents and reclaim their culture.[86]

Birth parents' human rights

Economic rights matter in intercountry adoption because parents who lack these rights, including the reproductive rights that are part of the right to health,[87] may be forced to abandon or surrender children they cannot support. Without an education,[88] and work,[89] mothers and fathers cannot provide for their families. Without an adequate standard of living,[90] including food, shelter, and clothing for themselves and their children, parents – especially single mothers – are forced to make desperate choices, "surrendering" a child for adoption in order to feed her siblings.

Recent studies indicate that most of the poorest people in the world live in middle-income countries, which are probably able to assure the basic needs of their nationals.[91] It is not clear whether parents compelled to surrender their children for adoption are in this group,[92] although many of the major sending states are in fact middle-income countries.

Adoptive parents' human rights

There is, of course, no right to a child. But the European Court of Human Rights has held that there is a right to be able to adopt without illegal discrimination under Article 14 of the European Convention on Human Rights[93] (prohibition of discrimination) in conjunction with Article 8 (right to respect for family life). These rights were violated in *E.B. v. France*,[94] where the court found that domestic administrative authorities, and domestic courts, had rejected the applicant's request for authorisation to adopt because there was no "father" in the household and because she was a lesbian.

In *A.H. and Others v. Russia*,[95] similarly, the court held that these Articles had been violated when Russia abruptly terminated adoptions, including those in the final stages, purely on the basis

85 CRC, *supra* note 61.

86 See, e.g., Marie Tae McDermott, "Trying to Fill in Blanks, Adopted Koreans Find Hope in a Cotton Swab," *N.Y. Times*, 28 Aug. 2016 (explaining how "DNA testing offers a way around the bureaucratic hurdles and flawed records.")

87 Art. 12 of the ICESCR, *supra* note 79. See also "When Genealogy Matters," *supra* note 1 at text accompanying nn. 197–200.

88 Arts. 13 and 14 of the ICESCR, *supra* note 79.

89 Id. at Arts. 7 and 8.

90 Id. at Art. 11.

91 Andy Sumner, *Global Poverty and the New "Bottom Billion" Revisited: Exploring the Paradox That Most of the World's Extreme Poor No Longer Live in the World's Poorest Countries*, 14 May 2012, available at www.ids.ac.uk/files/dmfile/AndySumnerGlobalPoverty14May2012.pdf.

92 Id.

93 European Convention for the Protection of Human Rights and Fundamental Freedoms, 4 Nov. 1950, Europ. T.S. No. 5, 213 U.N.T.S. 221.

94 22 Jan. 2008 (Grand Chamber).

95 17 Jan. 2017.

of the prospective parents' "nationality." The court criticised the Russian government's action because it was retroactive and did not take the circumstances of the 27 individual children into account.

In *Frette v. France*, in contrast, the court found no violation of these rights where the homosexual applicant's request for authorisation had been rejected on the basis of the "interests of children eligible for adoption," rather than the applicant's sexual orientation. Nor did the court find any violation where the application of one woman to adopt the child of the woman with whom she was cohabiting was denied. The court found that they had been treated the same as a heterosexual couple who were not married.[96] The court also held that there was no violation of Article 8 where a French national was denied permission to adopt an Algerian baby in her care under *kafalah*, or guardianship under *Sharia* law.[97] Rather, the court concluded, this reflected a "fair balance" between the public interest in cultural pluralism and the applicant's interest in severing the child's legal ties to Algeria, her country of origin.

Once an adoption has been finalised, the adoptive parents have the same rights as biological parents. So the Greek government's refusal to recognise the United States adoption of his nephew by a monk violated Articles 8 and 14.[98] A single adoptive mother in Turkey, similarly, had the right to have her forename entered on the documents for her adopted son.[99]

The Adoption Convention versus the CRC

Most intercountry adoption advocates concede that in-country placement with a family is the first preference for a child, although Professor Bartholet argues that preference be given to the first available placement instead.[100] But the Adoption Convention and the CRC take different approaches to intercountry adoption and in-country "care," which may include institutionalisation. The Adoption Convention privileges the human right to a family and the CRC privileges the human right to a broader culture.[101] Under the Convention, if in-country adoption or other "family" care is not feasible, international adoption is preferred over in-country institutionalisation.[102] Under the CRC and the Banjul Charter, in contrast, in-country foster care or other "suitable" care – including institutionalisation – is preferred over intercountry adoption.[103]

Those who favour the Adoption Convention approach argue that it will always be better for an individual child or baby to be raised in the affluent West, even if she is raised in a family and community where she is the only child of colour. As Professor Bartholet notes,

> [t]he empirical studies that have focused on international adoption provide no basis for concern as to the welfare of the vast majority of international adoptees and their families . . . The studies show that adoption has for the most part been extraordinarily successful in enabling

96 *Gas and Dubois v. France*, 15 March 2012.

97 *Harroudi v. France*, 4 Oct. 2012. See also *Chbihi Ludoudi and Others v. Belgium*, 16 Dec. 2014 (no violation of Art. 8 when Belgium refused the adoption application of a child already in *kafalah* guardianship.)

98 *Negrepontis-Giannisis v. Greece*, 3 May 2011.

99 *Gözüm v. Turkey*, 15 Jan. 2015.

100 Elizabeth Bartholet, "International Adoption: The Human Rights Issues," in *Baby Markets: Money and the New Politics of Creating Families* 94, 106, 107 (Michele Bratcher Goodwin ed. 2010).

101 *Supra* note 61.

102 Elizabeth Bartholet, "The Debate" in Judith L. Gibbons and Karen Smith Rotabi eds, *Intercountry Adoption: Policies, Practices and Outcomes* 234–235 (2012).

103 See Art. 20(3) of the CRC, *supra* note 61, 21; "When Genealogy Matters," *supra* note 1 at 178.

> even those children who have suffered extremely severe forms of deprivation and abuse in their early lives, to recover and flourish.[104]

But adoptees from Korea have described the racism confronting them in white suburbs and the white parents reluctant to acknowledge it.[105] Black adoptees have described their sense of isolation, and their difficulties "fitting in" with black as well as white communities.[106]

III. The international legal framework and standards

The Adoption Convention

Like many private international law treaties, the Adoption Convention focuses on procedural requirements and minimum standards. Like the Hague Abduction Convention,[107] the Adoption Convention requires states parties to establish Central Authorities responsible for its administration, including compliance. The Central Authority can outsource some of these responsibilities to either "accredited bodies" or "approved persons" under Article 22. (This is a nod to the United States practice of non-agency, "independent" adoptions.) The state must file a declaration pursuant to Article 22(2) that such persons "meet the requirements of integrity, professional competence, experience and accountability of that State."[108] Other contracting states may declare that the adoption of children from their territory will be limited to states that do not outsource these responsibilities.[109]

Under the Adoption Convention, adoption can take place in either the sending or the receiving country. Article 4 of the Convention sets out strict requirements for obtaining the consent of those "whose consent is necessary for adoption." Consent must be given "freely, in the required legal form, and expressed or evidenced in writing."[110] Article 4(4) prohibits the inducement of consent "by payment or compensation of any kind."[111]

In addition, a competent government authority must confirm that these requirements have been met and that intercountry adoption is in the best interest of the child, taking available domestic placement options into account.[112] The Adoption Convention further requires identifying information to be obtained from the birth parents and sent, along with the child's medical records, to the receiving country.[113] Whether this information is disclosed is left to the law of the

104 Elizabeth Bartholet, "International Adoption: Propriety, Prospects and Pragmatics," 13 *J. Am. Acad. Matr. Lawyers* 181, 201–203 (1996).
105 Blair et. al., *supra* note 3 at 815–819.
106 Id. at 813–815.
107 Hague Convention on the Civil Aspects of International Child Abduction, 25 Oct. 1980, 1343 U.N.T.S. 89.
108 The United States later enacted the Universal Accreditation Act of 2012 (UAA), which holds all adoption service providers to the same federal standard. 22 CFB 96.2 *et seq.* In 2010, a Special Commission had recommended prohibiting independent adoptions. Experts' Report, *infra* note 123 (citing 2010 recommendation, at 14, para. 62). The Report explicitly refers to the UAA as an example of an effort to impose Hague standards on non-Hague adoptions, observing that, "in practice, this is very often not done." Id. at 15, para. 64.
109 Art. 22 of the Adoption Convention, *supra* note 4, 1870 U.N.T.S. at 188–189. See also Blair et al. *supra* note 3 at 838.
110 Art. 4(c) of the Adoption Convention, *supra* note 4, 1870 U.N.T.S. at 184. This Article also requires that such persons "have been counseled as may be necessary." Art. 4(d)(3), 1870 U.N.T.S. at 184.
111 Art. 4(d)(3), 1870 U.N.T.S. at 184.
112 Blair et al., *supra* note 3 at 842.
113 Adoption Convention, *supra* note 4.

country where the child and her adoptive parents will reside.[114] This reflects both the recognition that general medical information may be useful, even critical, and the lack of consensus regarding the use of specific identifying information, that is, the actual identities of the biological family. Identifying information is unlikely to be available in most countries where there is still a stigma on unwed births.

Financial abuses

In poor countries such as Vietnam, where the annual income was under $800 in the mid-2000s, Western agencies offering $10,000 for "facilitating" adoptions or as "finders' fees" promoted baby-selling.[115] There were no social safety nets to assure that families had food, shelter or healthcare. There were no regulations governing orphanages or adoption services, no standards to which those purporting to provide such services could be held. In Cambodia, for example, investigators described a shack with a handwritten sign, "Orphanage," and babies lying in their own waste in rusty cribs.[116]

As Nigel Cantwell, an expert on child welfare and adoption systems in Eastern Europe and Central Asia, explained:

> There are simply not enough healthy, adoptable infants to meet Western demand. And there's too much Western money in search of babies. As a result, many international adoption agencies work not to find homes for needy children but to find children for Western homes.[117]

Asked how many healthy babies would be available for international adoption if money never exchanged hands, Cantwell replied, "I would hazard a guess at zero."[118]

The disparity between supply and demand led to widespread trafficking in sending countries, including Cambodia, Guatemala, Nepal, Vietnam, India, and, on a smaller scale, in Haiti, Sierra Leone, Congo, and Uganda.[119] In addition, there have been allegations of corruption in China, Russia, and South Korea.[120] Some of these cases involved agencies lying to parents, telling them, for example, that their children would be educated in America, and would send for their parents when they were older.[121] In other cases, children were simply abducted.[122]

114 Id. Art. 16–2.

115 Blair et al. *supra* note 3 at 828. These fees, modest by Western standards, "induce local officials or bureaucrats to engage in dubious practices." E. J. Graff, "The Lie We Love: Foreign Adoption Seems Like a Win – Win Arrangement. Unfortunately, Those Bundles of Joy May Not be Orphans at All," *Foreign Policy*, May – June 2009, available at www.utne.com/politics/international-adoption-lies-orphans-myths.aspx.

116 Marianne Blair, "Safeguarding the Interests of Children in Intercountry Adoption: Assessing the Gatekeepers," 34 *Cap. U. L. Rev.* 349, 368 (2005).

117 Graff, *supra* note 115.

118 "When Genealogy Matters," *supra* note 1 at 178.

119 David M. Smolin, "The Corrupting Influence of the United States on a Vulnerable Intercountry Adoption System: A Guide for Stakeholders, Hague and Non-Hague Nations, NGOs, and Concerned Parties," 2013 *Utah L. Rev.* 1065; Peter Selman, "The Rise and Fall of Intercountry Adoption in the 21st Century: Global Trends from 2001 to 2010," in Judith L. Gibbons and Karen Smith Rotabi eds, *Intercountry Adoption: Policies, Practices and Outcomes* 7 (2012).

120 Blair et al., *supra* note 3 at 31.

121 Id.

122 Id. at 82.

The experts' groups

In response, the Council on General Affairs and Policy of the Hague Conference recommended that an Experts' Group be convened to address the issue of costs in intercountry adoption. A group consisting of the Central Authorities of states of origin and receiving states, representing a range of regions and legal systems, international organisations and NGOs, was convened in The Hague in October 2012. The group produced a cogent but comprehensive report, *Note on the Financial Aspects of Intercountry Adoption* (Experts' Report).[123]

The Experts' Report notes the impact of global inequality on intercountry adoption and suggests policies to be avoided as well as promoted to reduce illicit practices. The wide variation in adoption costs from some states was criticised. In India, for example, costs ranged from 3,500 euros to 17,000 euros; in Colombia, similarly, costs ranged from 4,000 euros to 21,000 euros.[124] The Report suggests that ceilings for fees be set and made public. Transparency in general is encouraged. The Report cites with approval the American requirement, applicable to accredited agencies as well as "approved bodies," that prospective parents be provided with a written schedule of fees. Adoptive parents, the Report recommends, should request receipts for all payments. These should state the purpose for which the fee was paid.[125] Private development aid was strongly discouraged because of the absence of standards for such aid and the risks of influencing the process, creating expectations, and encouraging competition.[126] This includes "donations [which] should never be given to biological families of adoptable children." Development aid through official channels, on the other hand, is considered "appropriate,"[127] as are "small, well thought-through projects of accredited bodies designed for a specific community."[128]

The Reports' conclusions are merely advisory; actual enforcement is left to the states. This, too, encompasses a broad range, from fines, to loss of professional licenses, to prison. Some states refuse to recognise an adoption involving illicit practices.[129] The experts have reservations about such refusals, however, because of the possible consequences for adopted children.

Two years later, another Group was convened, which produced a short report.[130] The Group "recognized that the lack of adequate policies on the regulation of financial matters" remained a major cause of illicit practices, welcomed the tools set out in the earlier Note, and emphasised the need for coordination between the two Groups,[131] before setting out its own recommendations. These included: drafting and posting fact sheets on "illicit practices, inadequate policies and risky activities;" and developing a model procedure; resources for victims; and a spectrum of responses.[132] A further report was to be submitted in 2018.

123 June 2014, available on the Conference website – www.hcch.net under "Intercountry Adoption Section."
124 Id. at 22, para. 99.
125 Id. at 30, para. 145.
126 Id. at 26, paras. 118–123.
127 Id. at 28, para 135.
128 Id. at 29, para. 138.
129 Id. at 36, para 169.
130 *Conclusions and Recommendations of the Working Group on Preventing and Addressing Illicit Practices in Intercountry Adoption*, Meeting of 13–15 Oct. 2016, available on the Conference website – www.hcch.net under "Intercountry Adoption Section."
131 Id. at 2, para. 10.
132 Id. at 3, paras. 17–20.

IV. The decline of intercountry adoption

As abuses were exposed, programmes were shut down, or put on hold. Some receiving states imposed moratoria, refusing to accept children from states that did not comply with the Adoption Convention standards.[133] Adoption programmes have also been shut down for political reasons. Russia halted adoptions by Americans in 2012, for example, to retaliate against a United States law barring Russians accused of violating human rights from travelling to the United States or owning real estate in the United States.[134] Some critics argue that the Adoption Convention, and the rigorous implementation of its standards,[135] make it too difficult for poor countries to comply.[136]

Some would-be adoptive parents may have been deterred by widespread publicity about the same problems that triggered the moratoria; that is, corruption, child abduction, and babies and families falling through the cracks. Others, including LGBT people, have been explicitly prohibited from adopting in some sending states, such as China.

There are also other options, for those seeking children, at least for those who can afford them. Gestational surrogacy, in which a fertilised egg is implanted in a woman whose job it is to carry the baby to term and give birth, is an increasingly appealing option for infertile couples and gay men.[137] The bans on commercial surrogacy enacted throughout Europe and China produced booming businesses in less regulated states, including Thailand and, until 2015, India.[138]

Intercountry adoptions have steadily decreased since 2004, according to Professor Peter Selman. Based on data provided by receiving states, his tables show that, in 2016, there were 11,102 intercountry adoptions.[139] In 2017, there were only 4,714 intercountry adoptions in the United States.[140]

There is no question that too many children have inadequate care, or no care at all. And many would concede that hundreds, perhaps thousands, of children might have better lives were it not for the Adoption Convention and the reluctance of states (and would-be adoptive parents) to cut

133 Termination was often abrupt, leaving would-be adoptive parents in limbo. See, e.g., Rachel L. Swarns, "A Family for a Few Days a Year," *N.Y. Times*, 8 Dec. 2012 (describing the Carrs, who travelled multiple times to Guatemala, trying to expedite the adoption of Geovany, who they met as a toddler). Several states objected to Guatemala's accession to the Hague Convention on the ground that it was unable to comply with its requirements. See Guatemala at Adoption Convention Status Report, Table (noting objections of five states), available at www.hcch.net/en/instruments/status-table [perma.cc/W224-KDN9] (archived 12 Jan. 2018).

134 See, e.g., David M. Herszenhorn and Andrew Roth, "In Russia, Calls for a Halt to Adoptions by Americans," *N.Y. Times*, 19 Dec. 2012. See note 95 *supra* (*A.H. and Others v. Russia.*)

135 See, e.g., *The Experts' Groups*, *supra*.

136 Mark Montgomery and Irene Powell, "International adoptions have dropped 72% since 2005 – here's why," The Conversation, 28 Feb. 2018, available at theconversation.com/international-adoptions-have-dropped-72-percent-since-2005-heres-why-91809.

137 See Barbara Stark, "Transnational Surrogacy and International Human Rights Law," 18 *ILSA J. Int'l & Comp. L.* 369 (2012).

138 Bans are usually justified on the ground that surrogacy commodifies women. See Arlie Hochschild, "Childbirth at the Global Crossroads," 20 *American Prospect*, 19 Sept. 2009, at 25, 27 (stating that surrogacy is banned in China, New York and much of Europe), available at prospect.org/article/childbirth-global-crossroads-0 (last visited 13 March 2012); Joanna Sugden, "India Restricts Foreigners' Access to Surrogate Mothers," *Wall St. J.* 29 Oct. 2015.

139 Peter Selman, "Global Statistics for Intercountry Adoption: Receiving States and States of Origin 2004–2016," available at HCCH Adoption Section – Annual Adoption Statistics, 3 May 2018.

140 United States State Department, Intercountry Adoption Statistics, available at travel.state.gov/content/travel/en/Intercountry-Adoption/adopt_ref/adoption-statistics.html.

corners. No one claims that intercountry adoption is a "solution" for the poor children of the world, but it can certainly help some.

It cannot do so, however, by putting other babies and children at increased risk. The purpose of the Adoption Convention is to assure that babies and children who are voluntarily surrendered are placed in in-country adoption or other "family" care, or, if the only available in-country care is institutionalisation, with a foreign family. A system that stretches "voluntarily surrendered" to include children given up by parents temporarily in crisis, or defrauded parents, or children abducted, or even children of uncertain origin, certified as adoptable by corrupt local officials, is not a "partial" solution, but a contributing cause to these practices.

Bibliography

Austen, Ian. "Trudeau Apologizes for Abuse and 'Profound Cultural Loss' at Indigenous Schools," *N.Y. Times*, 24 Nov. 2017.

Bartholet, Elizabeth. "International Adoption: Propriety, Prospects and Pragmatics," 13 *J. Am. Acad. Matr. Lawyers* 181, 201–203 (1996).

Bartholet, Elizabeth. "International Adoption: The Human Rights Issues," in *Baby Markets: Money and the New Politics of Creating Families* 94, 106 (Michele Bratcher Goodwin ed., Cambridge, UK: Cambridge University Press, 2010) 107.

Bartholet, Elizabeth. "The Debate," in *Intercountry Adoption: Policies, Practices and Outcomes* 234–235 (Judith L. Gibbons and Karen Smith Rotabi (eds), New York: Routledge, 2012).

Belkin, Lisa. "Now Accepting Applications for My Baby," *N.Y. Times Mag.*, 5 Apr. 1998.

Blair, Marianne D., Weiner, Merle H., Stark, Barbara and Maldonado, Solangel. *Family Law in the World Community: Cases, Materials, and Problems in Comparative and International Family Law* (Durham, NC: Carolina Academic Press, 3rd edn, 2015).

Blair, Marianne. "Safeguarding the Interests of Children in Intercountry Adoption: Assessing the Gatekeepers," 34 *Cap. U. L. Rev.* 349, 368 (2005).

Bogner, Nahum. "The Convent Children: The Rescue of Jewish Children in Polish Convents During the Holocaust," in *Yad Vashem Studies* XXVII, 235 (David Silberklang (ed.), Naftali Greenwood trans., Jerusalem: Yad Vashem Martyrs' and Heroes' Remembrance Authority, 1999).

Briggs, Laura. *Somebody's Children: The Politics of Transracial and Transnational Adoption* 7, 39 (Durham, NC: Duke University Press, 2012).

Brower Blair, Marianne D. "The Impact of Family Paradigms, Domestic Constitutions, and International Conventions on Disclosure of an Adopted Person's Identities and Heritage: A Comparative Examination," 22 *Mich. J. Int'l. L.* 587, 648 (2001).

Buckley, Chris. "China Ends One-Child Policy, Allowing Families to Have Two Children," *N.Y. Times*, 29 Oct. 2015.

Cassesse, Antonio. "A Plea for Global Community Grounded in a Core of Human Rights," in *Realizing Utopia: The Future of International Law* (Antonio Cassesse ed., Oxford, UK: Oxford University Press, 2012) 37, 139.

Conn, Peter. *Adoption: A Brief Social and Cultural History* 27 (New York: Palgrave Macmillan, 2013).

Cooper Davis, Peggy. *Neglected Stories: The Constitution and Family Values* (New York: Hill & Wang, 1997).

Fanshel, David. *Far From the Reservation* 36–37 (Metuchen, NJ: Scarecrow Press, 1972).

George, Lila. "Why the Need for the Indian Child Welfare Act?" in *The Challenge of Permanency Planning in a Multicultural Society* 165,169 (Gary R. Anderson, Angela Shen Ryan and Bogart R. Leashore eds, New York: Routledge, 1997).

Goldman, Francisco. "Children of the Dirty War," *New Yorker*, 19 March 2012.

Graham, Lorie M. "The Past Never Vanishes: A Contextual Critique of the Existing Indian Family Law Doctrine," 23 *Am. Indian L. Rev.* 1, 13–18 (1995–1999).

Herszenhorn, David M. and Roth, Andrew. "In Russia, Calls for a Halt to Adoptions by Americans," *N.Y. Times*, 19 Dec. 2012.

Hochschild, Arlie. "Childbirth at the Global Crossroads," 20 *American Prospect*, 19 Sept. 2009.

Law, David and Versteeg, Mila. "The Declining Influence of the United States Constitution," 87 *N.Y.U.L. Rev.* 3 (2013).

Maldonado, Solangel. "Race, Culture, and Adoption: Lessons from Mississippi Band of Choctaw Indians v. Holyfield," 17 *Colum. J. Gender & L.* 1, 27 (2008).

Martin, Douglas. "Doris Pilkington Garimara, Aboriginal Novelist, Dies at 76," *N.Y. Times*, 2 July 2018.
Melosh, Barbara. *Strangers and Kin: The American Way of Adoption* 15 (Cambridge, MA: Harvard University Press, 2002).
Moynihan, Daniel Patrick. *The Negro Family: The Case for National Action* (Washington, DC: US Department of Labor, 1965).
Oren, Laura. "Righting Child Custody Wrongs: The Children of the 'Disappeared' in Argentina," 14 *Harv. Hum. Rts. J.* 123, 127–128 (2001).
Papke, David Ray. "Pondering Past Purposes: A Critical History of American Adoption Law," 102 *W. Va. L. Rev.* 459 (1999).
Parra-Aranguren, G. Explanatory Report on the Convention on Protection of Children and Co-operation in respect of Intercountry Adoption (The Hague: HCCH Publications, 1994).
Roberts, Dorothy. *Shattered Bonds: The Color of Child Welfare* (New York: Basic Books, 2002).
Seabrook, John. "The Last Babylift," *New Yorker*, 10 May 2010.
Selman, Peter. "Global Statistics for Intercountry Adoption: Receiving States and States of origin 2004–2016, available at HCCH Adoption Section – Annual Adoption Statistics," 3 May 2018.
Selman, Peter. "The Rise and Fall of Intercountry Adoption in the 21st Century: Global Trends from 2001 to 2010," in *Intercountry Adoption: Policies, Practices and Outcomes* 7 (Judith L. Gibbons and Karen Smith Rotabi eds, New York: Routledge, 2012).
Semuels, Alana. "The End of Welfare as We Know It," *Atlantic*, 1 Apr. 2016.
Smolin, David M. "The Corrupting Influence of the United States on a Vulnerable Intercountry Adoption System: A Guide for Stakeholders, Hague and Non-Hague Nations, NGOs, and Concerned Parties," 2013 *Utah L. Rev.* 1065.
Stark, Barbara. "Transnational Surrogacy and International Human Rights Law," 18 *ILSA J. Int'l & Comp. L.* 369 (2012).
Stark, Barbara. "When Genealogy Matters: Intercountry Adoption, International Human Rights, and Global Neoliberalism," 51 *Vand. J. Int'l L.* 159 (2018).
Steinbock, Daniel "Unaccompanied Children in Comparative and International Law," in Everett M. Ressler, Neil Boothby and Daniel J. Steinbock, *Unaccompanied Children: Care and Protection in Wars, Natural Disasters, and Refugee Movements* 269 (New York: Oxford University Press, 1988).
Sugden, Joanna "India Restricts Foreigners' Access to Surrogate Mothers," *Wall St. J.* 29 Oct. 2015.
Swarns, Rachel L. "A Family for a Few Days a Year," *N.Y. Times*, 8 Dec. 2012.
Tae McDermott, Marie. "Trying to Fill in Blanks, Adopted Koreans Find Hope in a Cotton Swab," *N.Y. Times*, 28 Aug. 2016.

Part IV

Human rights within and affecting the family

12

Children's rights in the family

*Geraldine Van Bueren QC**

The family

The family is recognised in many international and regional human rights instruments. "The family is the natural and fundamental group unit of society and is entitled to protection by society and the State" according to the Universal Declaration of Human Rights (UDHR),[1] the International Covenant on Civil and Political Rights (ICCPR),[2] and the American Convention of Human Rights (ACHR),[3] and there is similar language in the Convention on the Rights of the Child (CRC),[4] the International Covenant on Economic, Social and Cultural Rights (ICESCR),[5] and the African Charter on Human and Peoples' Rights (ACHPR). The CRC itself has many references to "family" and "parents",[6] as does the African Charter on the Rights and Welfare of the Child (ACRWC).[7] Originally the protection of children's rights was linked to the protection of mothers' rights as in article 25(2) of the UDHR, article 7 of the American Declaration of the Rights and Duties of Man (ADRDM)[8] and article 18(3) of the ACHPR.[9] Article 30 of the ACRWC makes specific provision for the children of imprisoned mothers – an approach followed by the Constitutional Court of South Africa in *President of the Republic of South Africa and Another v. Hugo*,[10] although not without criticism.

* I am grateful to Alison Bryony Winstanley for her research assistance.

1 UDHR (adopted 10 Dec. 1948) UNGA Res. 217 A(III), art. 16(3).

2 ICCPR (adopted 16 Dec. 1966, entered into force 23 March 1976) 999 U.N.T.S. 171, art. 23(1).

3 ACHR (adopted 22 Nov. 1969, entered into force 18 July 1978) 1144 U.N.T.S. 123, art. 17(1).

4 CRC (adopted 20 Nov. 1989, entered into force 2 Sept. 1990) 1577 U.N.T.S. 3, preamble.

5 ICESCR (adopted 16 Dec. 1966, entered into force 3 Jan. 1976) 993 U.N.T.S. 3, art. 10(1).

6 CRC, arts. 2(1), 2(2), 3(2), 5, 7(1), 8(1), 9(1), 9(3), 9(4), 10(1), 10(2), 14(2), 16(1), 18(1), 18(2), 18(3), 19(1), 20(1), 21(a), 21(b), 22(1), 22(2), 23(2), 23(3), 24(2)(e), 24(2)(f), 27(2), 27(3), 27(4), 29(1)(c), 37(c), 40(2)(b)(ii), 40(2)(b)(iii).

7 There are express references to "parents" and/or families in the ACRWC, arts. 3, 9(2), 9(3), 10, 11(4), 11(5), 14(2)(f), 14(2)(h), 17(3), 18(1), 18(3), 19(1), 19(2), 19(3), 19(4), 20(1), 20(2)(a), 20(2)(b), 20(2)(c), 23(1), 23(2), 23(3), 24(a), 24(b), 25(1), 25(2)(a), 25(2)(b), 25(3), 29(a), 30(1)(f), 31(a).

8 ADRDM O.A.S. Res. XXX adopted by the Ninth International Conference of American States (1948), reprinted in Basic Documents Pertaining to Human Rights in the Inter-American System O.E.A./Ser. L/V/II.82 Doc. 6 Rev. 1 at 17 (1992).

9 To be precise, art. 18(3) of the ACHPR refers to "the rights of the woman and the child" rather than "the mother".

10 (CCT11/96) [1997] ZACC 4, 1997 (4) SA 1 (CC).

There is no express treaty definition of "family",[11] although there are references to "family life"[12] and "family environment"[13] in international human rights law instruments. The expanding definition of "family" has evolved through national and regional jurisprudence and through General Comments of the treaty bodies. This chapter will concentrate on the rights of the child in the family as defined by the CRC Committee.

Many of the provisions regarding children and family life are in the form of obligations on the state not to interfere with family life.[14] Article 17 of the ICCPR imposes an obligation on the state not to subject an individual's privacy and family to "arbitrary or unlawful interference"; article 11(2) of the ACHR protects against "arbitrary or abusive interference"; and article 5 of the ADRDM against "abusive attacks". But states also have expanding supportive and positive obligations to protect children's rights in the private sphere, in particular within the family. One of the reasons the United States (US) has not ratified the CRC is the claim that the CRC would alter US laws regarding parental rights,[15] changing the balance from parental rights to parental responsibilities. This, however, is an insufficient reason as a number of states, including Poland, have entered reservations and declarations protecting, as they would see it, the more traditional approach to family governance. The Holy See has made a reservation that it will interpret the CRC "in a way which safeguards the primary and inalienable rights of parents". Poland and Kiribati have made declarations that CRC rights "shall be exercised with respect for parental authority", and Singapore has declared that CRC rights "shall be exercised with respect for the authority of parents".[16] The CRC Committee has said that it disapproves of such reservations or declarations.[17]

Best interests

Although many countries favour parental authority over children's autonomy there is, I would argue, universal acceptance of the concept in article 3(1) of the CRC, namely that "[i]n all actions concerning children . . . the best interests of the child shall be a primary consideration",[18] although there is debate about what those best interests actually are.[19]

It is not always clear in which circumstances the child's best interests should be *paramount* rather than *a primary* consideration. Within the CRC only article 21, concerning adoption, states that the child's best interests are to be the paramount consideration. In its General Comment on article 3(1) the CRC Committee said that "the best interests of the child are to be the

11 Geraldine Van Bueren, *The International Law on the Rights of the Child* (The Hague/Boston/London, Martinus Nijhoff Publishers, 1998) 68.

12 ADRDM, art. 5; European Convention for the Protection of Human Rights and Fundamental Freedoms (ECHR), as amended by Protocols Nos. 11 and 14 (adopted 4 Nov. 1950, entered into force 3 Sept. 1953) E.T.S. 5 (ECHR), art. 8.

13 CRC, preamble, arts. 20(1), 22(2); ACRWC, preamble, arts. 23(3), 25(1), 25(2)(a).

14 Privacy and the family are linked in art. 17 of the ICCPR, private life and family in art. 11 of the ACHR, and private and family life in art. 5 of the ADRDM and art. 8 of the ECHR.

15 Bruce C. Hafen and Jonathan O. Hafen, "Abandoning Children to Their Autonomy: The United Nations Convention on the Rights of the Child" (1996) 37 *Harvard International Law Journal* 449.

16 "Declarations and Reservations", available at treaties.un.org/Pages/ViewDetails.aspx?src=TREATY&mtdsg_no=IV-11&chapter=4&clang=_en (accessed 1 Nov. 2017).

17 See for example CRC Committee, "Concluding Observations on the Combined Third and Fourth Periodic Reports of Poland" (30 Oct. 2015) U.N. Doc. CRC/C/POL/3–4, para. 7.

18 There are no reservations to this article. See "Declarations and Reservations", *supra* note 16.

19 John Eekelaar, "The Role of the Best Interests Principle in Decisions Affecting Children and Decisions about Children" (2015) 23 *International Journal of Children's Rights* 3.

determining factor when taking a decision on adoption, but also on other issues", but does not explain what those other issues should be.[20] The second principle of the United Nations General Assembly's (UNGA) 1959 Declaration of the Rights of the Child is that "[t]he child shall enjoy special protection . . . the best interests of the child shall be the paramount consideration".[21]

"Evolving capacities"

The CRC's four general principles are contained in article 2 (non-discrimination),[22] article 3 (best interests of the child to be a primary consideration),[23] article 6 (right to life, survival and development)[24] and article 12 (right to be heard).[25] Regarding children's rights within the family article 5 provides:

> States Parties shall respect the responsibilities, rights and duties of parents or, where applicable, the members of the extended family or community as provided for by local custom, legal guardians or other persons legally responsible for the child, to provide, in a manner consistent with the evolving capacities of the child, appropriate direction and guidance in the exercise by the child of the rights recognized in the present Convention.

The CRC Committee's General Comment on adolescents' rights[26] cites one of the four general principles as the "[r]ight to development",[27] and the only article of the CRC cited in the body of the text under that heading is article 5 rather than article 6.[28]

When should a child be capable of consenting to something independently of parents or other family members? In its General Comment on Adolescents' Rights the CRC Committee says that there should be flexibility regarding age limits concerning "health services or treatment, consent to adoption, change of name or applications to family courts", and comments that "the right of any child below that minimum age and able to demonstrate sufficient understanding to be entitled to give or refuse consent should be recognized".[29] This flexibility is required, otherwise a strict age minimum could result in a presumption of immaturity.

The committee also states that "[t]he voluntary and informed consent of the adolescent should be obtained whether or not the consent of a parent or guardian is required for any medical treatment or procedure".[30] Consideration should be given to "the introduction of a legal presumption that adolescents are competent to seek and have access to preventive or time-sensitive sexual and reproductive health commodities and services", and that there should be

20 CRC Committee, "General Comment No 14 (2013) on the Right of the Child to have his or her Best Interests Taken as a Primary Consideration (art 3 para 1)" (29 May 2013) U.N. Doc. CRC/C/GC/14 ("General Comment on the Child's Best Interests"), para. IV A 4.

21 UNGA, "Declaration of the Rights of the Child" (20 Nov. 1959) U.N. Doc. A/RES/1386(XIV).

22 "General Comment on the Child's Best Interests", *supra* note 20, para. IV B 1.

23 Ibid., para. I A.

24 Ibid., para. IV B2.

25 Ibid., para. IV B3.

26 CRC Committee, "General Comment No 20 (2016) on the Implementation of the Rights of the Child during Adolescence" (6 Dec. 2016) U.N. Doc. CRC/C/GC/20 ("General Comment on Adolescents' Rights").

27 Ibid., para. IV A.

28 Ibid., paras. 15–20.

29 Ibid., para. 39.

30 Ibid.

no age limit on an adolescent's "right to have access to confidential medical counselling and advice without the consent of a parent or guardian".[31] The committee does propose a minimum age of 18 for activities involving a certain "degree of associated risk and harm", such as "marriage, recruitment into the armed forces, involvement in hazardous or exploitative work and the purchase and consumption of alcohol and tobacco".[32] Regarding sexual activity, the Committee suggests an "acceptable" age of consent, but avoids specifying it, instead calling upon states to "take into account the need to balance protection and evolving capacities" and to "avoid criminalizing adolescents of similar ages for factually consensual and non-exploitative sexual activity".[33]

When does a child acquire rights inside the family?

Does a child acquire rights before or after birth? The CRC is not clear. The preamble of the CRC repeats exactly the words in the preamble of the Declaration of the Rights of the Child on the need for "special safeguards and care, including appropriate legal protection, before as well as after birth", but does not say that this "appropriate legal protection" includes the right to life. Article 1 of the CRC only states when a person ceases to be a child (18 "unless under the law applicable to the child, majority is attained earlier"). The different interpretations by states on this question are expressed in several declarations to the CRC. Argentina and Guatemala declare that article 1 of the CRC applies from the moment of conception; the Holy See has declared that the CRC "will safeguard the rights of the child before as well as after birth"; and Ecuador has declared that "the need to protect the unborn child . . . should be borne in mind" in interpreting the CRC, particularly in article 24, which addresses "the right of the child to the enjoyment of the highest attainable standard of health".[34] In contrast, France, Luxembourg and Tunisia have declared that article 6 (the right to life, survival and development) is not an obstacle to their legislation/regulation on abortion; and the United Kingdom (UK) has declared that the CRC only applies "following a live birth".[35]

Article 4(1) of the ACHR says that the right to life applies "in general, from the moment of conception". Because of this contrast the CRC has been perceived by some as pro-abortion, and this perception has been given as one of the reasons for the refusal of the US to ratify the CRC, although abortion is lawful under US constitutional law.[36] But the Inter-American Commission of Human Rights, in *Baby Boy v. United States*[37] (brought by US petitioners), found that the phrase "in general" allowed for legislation permitting abortion (and that, even if it did not, this would not bind the US, which had not accepted or ratified the ACHR, but had only signed the ADRDM).[38] The issue is not only of concern in relation to abortion but also in relation to inheritance. There are *dicta* from the now disbanded European Commission of Human Rights that rights acquired in the womb include inheritance.

31 Ibid.
32 Ibid., para. 40.
33 Ibid.
34 "Declarations and Reservations", *supra* note 16.
35 Ibid.
36 Lainie Rutkow and Joshua T. Lozman, "Suffer the Children: A Call for United States Ratification of the United Nations Convention on the Rights of the Child" (2006) 19 *Harvard Human Rights Journal* 161, 186.
37 Case of 2141 Report No. 23/81 O.E.A./Ser. L/V/II.54 Doc. 9 Rev. 1 (1981).
38 Ibid., paras. 14 (under "Summary of the Case"), 30, 31 (under "Whereas").

The child's right to health advice and treatment

A child's right to medical advice and treatment is often subject to restrictions by parents and the state, particularly regarding contraception and abortion. Some states have made declarations to maintain parental control over such medical information. Argentina's declaration to article 24(2)(f) of the CRC says that it "considers that questions relating to family planning are the exclusive concern of parents",[39] while the Holy See has made a reservation saying that article 24(2) concerns "only those methods of family planning which it considers morally acceptable, that is, the natural methods of family planning".[40]

The CRC Committee's guidance regarding children's access to health advice and treatment is not clear as to what should happen if a child wants a medical treatment but the parent or guardian disapproves. In the General Comment on Adolescents' Rights the Committee urged states to decriminalise abortion and to "review legislation with a view to guaranteeing the best interests of pregnant adolescents and ensure that their views are always heard and respected in abortion-related decisions",[41] but this does not clearly state the circumstances in which a child should be able to have an abortion without parental consent. In its 2016 Concluding Observations on Slovakia, the Committee urged the State Party to "remove the parental consent requirement for abortions and contraceptives requested by adolescent girls above the age of sexual consent",[42] but did not say whether that would also apply to any girl below that age.

The child's right to religious choice

Article 18(1) of the ICCPR guarantees the "freedom to have or to adopt a religion or belief of his choice", and article 18(2) prohibits "coercion which would impair his freedom to have or to adopt a religion or belief of his choice". Article 12(1) of the ACHR includes the "freedom to maintain or to change one's religion or beliefs" and article 12(2) prohibits "restrictions that might impair his freedom to maintain or to change his religion or beliefs". Article 9(1) of the ECHR also includes the "freedom to change his religion or belief and freedom". But article 18(4) of the ICCPR and article 13(3) of the ICESCR protect parents' and legal guardians' ability "to ensure the religious and moral education of their children in conformity with their own convictions", and similar words are used in article 12(4) of the ACHR. Article 2 of protocol 1 to the ECHR[43] protects parents' rights to ensure their children are educated and taught "in conformity with their own religious and philosophical convictions". Article 14(1) of the CRC (right of the child to freedom of thought, conscience and religion) does not contain an express right for children to choose or change their religion, but article 14(2) requires States Parties to "respect the rights and duties of the parents and, when applicable, legal guardians, to provide direction to the child in the exercise of his or her right in a manner consistent with the evolving capacities of the child". Article 9(1) of the ACRWC guarantees children "the right to freedom of thought conscience and religion". Article 9(2) imposes on parents and legal guardians "the duty to provide guidance and direction in the exercise of these rights having regard to the evolving capacities, and best

39 "Declarations and Reservations", *supra* note 16.

40 Ibid.

41 "General Comment on Adolescents' Rights", *supra* note 26, para. 60.

42 CRC Committee, "Concluding Observations on the Combined Third to Fifth Periodic Reports of Slovakia" (20 July 2016) U.N. Doc. CRC/C/SVK/CO/3-5 ("Concluding Observations on Slovakia"), para. 41 c.

43 Protocol 1 to the ECHR (adopted 20 March 1952, entered into force 18 May 1954) E.T.S. 9.

interests of the child", and article 9(3) requires States Parties to respect that duty "subject to the national laws and policies". Article 11(4) of the ACRWC requires States Parties to respect the right of parents and legal guardians "to ensure the religious and moral education of the child in a manner consistent with the evolving capacities of the child".

Disagreement over the extent of a child's right to freedom of religion (including freedom to choose religion) is clear from the declarations and reservations relating to article 14 of the CRC. There are a wide range of both specific and more general religiously motivated declarations and reservations to the CRC as a whole. Several states have made general reservations to the CRC to the extent they deem it incompatible with Islamic law (Iran, Kuwait, Mauritania, Saudi Arabia, Somalia and Syria[44]). Syria's reservation is addressed to article 14 "in particular", and gives reasons, including "the extent to which the right in question might conflict with the right of parents and guardians to ensure the religious education of their children".[45]

Among the Islamic states with reservations specific to article 14, Algeria interprets article 14(1) and (2) in conformity with the Algerian Family Code, "which stipulates that a child's education is to take place in accordance with the religion of its father".[46] Iraq's reservation states that "allowing a child to change his or her religion runs counter to the provisions of the *Islamic Shariah*",[47] and Jordan's reservation says that "the right to freedom of choice of religion" for a child is "at variance with the precepts of the tolerant Islamic Shariah".[48] Oman has a reservation that it is "not committed" to article 14 for the child "until he reaches the age of maturity".[49] The reservation by the United Arab Emirates provides that they are "bound by the tenor of this article to the extent that it does not conflict with the principles and provisions of Islamic law".[50] Bangladesh has entered a reservation to article 14(1), and Brunei Darussalam, the Maldives, Qatar and Somalia have entered reservations to article 14 generally.[51]

On 19 October 2006, Morocco withdrew its reservation to article 14 of the CRC, and instead has a declaration that it interprets article 14(1) in light of its constitutional provision "that Islam, the State religion, shall guarantee freedom of worship for all", and of its Family Code stipulation "that parents owe their children the right to religious guidance and education based on good conduct".[52]

The reservation by the Holy See stating that it interprets the CRC "in a way which safeguards the primary and inalienable rights of parents", also says that this interpretation applies "in particular" to article 14 (together with articles 13, 15, 16 and 28).[53] Poland's declaration concerning "parental authority" applies "in particular" to articles 12 to 16.[54] Singapore's declaration concerning "the authority of parents" applies to "in particular the rights defined in article 12 to 17".[55]

In contrast, Belgium has declared that "the right of the child to freedom of thought, conscience and religion implies also the freedom to choose his or her religion or belief".[56] Similarly,

44 "Declarations and Reservations", *supra* note 16.
45 Ibid., endnote 59.
46 "Declarations and Reservations", *supra* note 16.
47 Ibid. (original emphasis).
48 Ibid.
49 Ibid.
50 Ibid.
51 Ibid.
52 Ibid., endnote 46.
53 Ibid.
54 Ibid.
55 Ibid.
56 Ibid.

the Netherlands has interpreted the right to include "the freedom of a child to have or adopt a religion or belief of his or her choice as soon as the child is capable of making such choice in view of his or her age or maturity".[57] In the US article 14 has been interpreted as limiting parents' rights to raise children according to parental religious convictions, and this is one of the reasons given by opponents to the US's ratification of the CRC.[58]

In its General Comment on Adolescents' Rights the CRC Committee said that "it is the child who exercises the right to freedom of religion, not the parent, and the parental role necessarily diminishes as the child acquires an increasingly active role in exercising choice throughout adolescence".[59] In its Concluding Observations on the UK, the CRC Committee expressed concern about the restrictions on children's ability to withdraw from daily religious worship in state schools without parental consent,[60] and called upon the UK to "ensure that children can independently exercise the right to withdraw from religious worship at school".[61]

Discrimination against non-marital children

Several Islamic states have made declarations and reservations regarding article 2 of the CRC, which proscribes discrimination on grounds including "birth or other status". This has a long history, as one of the reasons for the abstention by Saudi Arabia to the UDHR was its prohibition of discrimination against children born outside marriage. Article 25(2) of the UDHR says that "[a]ll children, whether born in or out of wedlock, shall enjoy the same social protection".

Although many Islamic states continue to express reservations specifically regarding article 2 (such as Malaysia and Qatar[62]), on 23 September 2008, Tunisia gave notice of withdrawal of its reservation, which had read that article 2 "may not impede implementation of the provisions of its national legislation concerning personal status, particularly in relation to marriage and inheritance rights".[63]

As well as general anti-discrimination provisions in international human rights instruments, there are some that deal specifically with discrimination against non-marital children. Article 17(5) of the ACHR guarantees "equal rights for children born out of wedlock and those born in wedlock", and article 18(3) of the ACRWC provides that "[n]o child shall be deprived of maintenance by reference to the parents' marital status".

The child's right to know birth parents

Article 7(1) of the CRC says that a child has "as far as possible, the right to know and be cared for by his or her parents", and article 8(1) says that a child also has the right "to preserve his or her identity, including nationality, name and family relations as recognized by law without unlawful interference". For the first time the CRC established the child's right to know parents' identity

57 Ibid.
58 Hafen and Hafen, *supra* note 15, 470.
59 "General Comment on Adolescents' Rights", *supra* note 26, para. 43.
60 CRC Committee, "Concluding Observations on the Fifth Periodic Report of the United Kingdom of Great Britain and Northern Ireland" (12 July 2016) U.N. Doc. CRC/C/G/BR/CO/5 ("Concluding Observations on the UK"), para. 35.
61 Ibid., para. 36.
62 "Declarations and Reservations", *supra* note 16.
63 Ibid., endnote 61.

while still a child, and not just later as an adult[64] (the right of an adult to know one's origins had been established under other international instruments).

This right was not universally welcomed. Czechoslovakia (as it then was) made a declaration to the CRC regarding article 7(1) in cases of adoption and artificial fertilisation that "the non-communication of a natural parent's name or natural parents' names to the child is not in contradiction with this provision".[65] Luxembourg's reservation to article 7 says that it "presents no obstacle to the legal process in respect of anonymous births, which is deemed to be in the interest of the child, as provided under article 3". The UK made a declaration that "parents" means "only those persons who, as a matter of national law, are treated as parents".[66] Poland made a reservation to article 7 to "enable adoptive parents to maintain the confidentiality of the child's origin", but in 2013 gave notice of its intention to withdraw it.[67]

The CRC Committee has expressed concern about the use of "baby boxes" or "baby flaps", used in Austria,[68] Germany[69] and Slovakia,[70] for abandoning babies anonymously. In its Concluding Observations on Slovakia the Committee accepted "as a last resort, the possibility of confidential hospital births"[71] because the Committee was concerned that if confidentiality were to be prohibited there was a risk of both child abandonment and infanticide.

The child's right to a relationship with parents after separation

Articles 7, 8 and 9 of the CRC provide some rights to a child after parents separate. In particular, article 9(1) provides that a child is not to be forcibly separated from a parent "except when competent authorities subject to judicial review determine, in accordance with applicable law and procedures, that such separation is necessary for the best interests of the child", and article 9(3) guarantees "the right of the child who is separated from one or both parents to maintain personal relations and direct contact with both parents on a regular basis, except if it is contrary to the child's best interests".

But decisions made about a child after parental separation often are based on the gender of the child's parents and the age of the child, rather than what is in the best interests of the child. One crucial decision following parental separation is about which parent the child will live with, often described as the "custody" of the child.

Adoption and *kafalah*

The only CRC article in which the child's best interests are *expressly* stated to be the *paramount* consideration is article 21, concerning "States Parties that recognize and/or permit the system of adoption". Both adoption and *kafalah* are described in article 20(3) as alternative care options for children "deprived of a family environment" (article 21(1)). Although article 21 is only

64 Ibid., 139 (citation omitted).

65 "Declarations and Reservations", *supra* note 16, endnote 7.

66 "Declarations and Reservations", *supra* note 16.

67 Ibid., endnote 50.

68 CRC Committee, "Concluding Observations on the Combined Third and Fourth Periodic report of Austria, adopted by the Committee at its Sixty-First Session (17 September – 5 October 2012)" (3 Dec. 2012) U.N. Doc. CRC/C/AUT/CO/3–4, para. 29.

69 CRC Committee, "Concluding Observations on the Combined Third and Fourth Periodic Reports of Germany" (25 Feb. 2014) U.N. Doc. CRC/C/DEU/CO/3–4, para. 30.

70 "Concluding Observations on Slovakia", *supra* note 42, para. 20.

71 Ibid., para. 21.

addressed to states that recognise and/or permit adoption, several states that do not recognise or permit adoption have made reservations or declarations regarding the article. These are principally Islamic states, namely Bangladesh, Jordan, Kuwait, the Maldives, Somalia and the United Arab Emirates.[72] Canada also has a reservation to article 21.[73]

The reason for Islamic states' reservations and declarations regarding article 21 is that the concept of adoption is inconsistent with Islamic law, which instead approves the practice of *kafalah*. Under *kafalah* a child is usually placed in a family that is as closely related to his or her birth family as possible,[74] and the child's family name is not changed.[75] But several Islamic states have withdrawn or modified their reservations to article 21. Notifications of withdrawal have been given by Egypt (31 July 2003),[76] Syria (13 June 2012)[77] and Oman (9 December 2014).[78] On 10 August 2015, the Government of Brunei Darussalam gave notice of its intention to withdraw its reservations to article 21(a) of the CRC while leaving in place its reservation to article 21(b) to (e), which concerns intercountry adoption.[79]

One important distinction regarding adoption is the difference between "full" and "simple" adoptions: in the former, the original parent – child relationship is terminated; in the latter it is not, although parental responsibilities for the child are transferred to the adoptive parents.[80] It also is important that there is potential for a *kafalah* child to be disadvantaged by the fact that such a child has no right to inherit from the guardian,[81] although that could be compensated for by maintaining the right to inherit from birth parents. A child born outside marriage has no right to inherit from the birth father under the Sunni *Fiqa*, and under the Shiah *Fiqa* has no right to inherit from either parent.[82] But a third of a person's estate can be passed on to a *kafalah* child by way of will or gift, so that in practice such a child can have an inheritance through testamentary succession.

Intercountry adoption

Some of the countries that have withdrawn reservations to article 21(a) have maintained reservations to the remainder of the article, which concerns intercountry adoption. Argentina's reservation to subparagraphs (b) to (e) of article 21 of the CRC says that "before they can be applied a strict mechanism must exist for the legal protection of children in matters of intercountry adoption, in order to prevent trafficking in and the sale of children".[83] The CRC Committee has said that the Hague Convention on Protection of Children and Cooperation in respect of Intercountry Adoption is such a "strict mechanism",[84] and recommends that states

72 "Declarations and Reservations", *supra* note 16.
73 See text to note 44.
74 Usang S. Assim and Julia Sloth-Nielsen, "Islamic *Kafalah* as an Alternative Care System for Children Deprived of a Family Environment" (2014) 14 *African Human Rights Law Journal* 322, 330.
75 Ibid., 331.
76 "Declarations and Reservations", *supra* note 16, endnote 9.
77 Ibid., endnote 60.
78 Ibid., endnote 49.
79 Ibid., endnote 27.
80 Assim and Sloth-Nielsen, *supra* note 74, 335.
81 Ibid., 404.
82 Ibid., 408.
83 "Declarations and Reservations", *supra* note 16.
84 Hague Convention on Protection of Children and Cooperation in respect of Intercountry Adoption (adopted 29 May 1993, entered into force 1 May 1995) 33.

ratify it.[85] The ACRWC also has provisions specifically concerned with intercountry adoption in article 24(b) to (f).

The CRC, the Hague Convention and the ACRWC take somewhat different approaches. Article 21(b) of the CRC requires states to

> [r]ecognize that inter-country adoption may be considered as an alternative means of child's [sic] care, if the child cannot be placed in a foster or an adoptive family or cannot in any suitable manner be cared for in the child's country of origin.

Article 24(b) of the ACRWC uses similar language, but adds the words "as the last resort". In contrast, the preamble to the Hague Convention says "intercountry adoption may offer the advantage of a permanent family to a child for whom a suitable family cannot be found in his or her State of origin". The Hague Convention thus clearly accords preference to intercountry adoption over institutional care in a child's country of origin, but the same cannot be said of the text of the CRC and ACRWC.[86]

The CRC Committee has given mixed messages over whether intercountry adoption or institutional care is "the last resort".[87] The Committee described institutional care as the last resort under the CRC in at least two of its recent Concluding Observations. It urged Samoa to ensure that "institutionalization is used as a last resort"[88] and encouraged ratification of the Hague Convention on Intercountry Adoption.[89] It urged Romania to "[e]nsure that children who could not be placed with families domestically have access to inter-country adoption".[90]

The Constitutional Court of South Africa considered the adoption by US citizens of a South African child in *A.D. and Another v. D.W. and Others*.[91] One significant factor in the case was that the child had lived with the US couple for nearly three years and was thus "deeply embedded" in that family.[92]

Whether adoption is in-country or intercountry, regard must be had to the child's evolving capacities under article 5 and the right to express his or her views under article 12 of the CRC. The CRC Committee has urged flexibility over age limits for child consent to adoption,[93] and has, in its Concluding Observations, criticised states where children under ten do not have a right to be heard in adoption cases.[94]

85 See for example CRC Committee, "Concluding Observations on the Combined Third to Fifth Periodic Reports of the Democratic Republic of Congo" (28 Feb. 2017) U.N. Doc. CRC/C/COD/CO/3–5 ("Concluding Observations on the DRC"), para. 33 c; "Concluding Observations on the Combined Second and Third Periodic Reports of Saint Vincent and the Grenadines" (13 March 2017) U.N. Doc. CRC/C/VCT/CO/2–3, para. 42; "Concluding Observations on the Combined Fourth and Fifth Periodic Report of Lebanon" (22 June 2017) U.N. Doc. CRC/C/LBN/CO/4–5, para. 27.

86 Benyam Dawit Mezmur, "'Acting Like a Rich Bully'?: Madonna, Mercy, Malawi and International Children's Rights Law in Adoption" (2012) 20 *International Journal of Children's Rights Law* 24, 37.

87 Ibid., 37–38.

88 CRC Committee, "Concluding Observations on the Combined Second to Fourth Periodic Reports on Samoa" (12 July 2016) U.N. Doc. CRC/C/WSM/CO/2–4, para. 35 a.

89 Ibid., para. 37 c.

90 CRC Committee, "Concluding Observations on the Fifth Periodic Report of Romania" (13 July 2017) U.N. Doc. CRC/C/ROU/CO/5 ("Concluding Observations on Romania"), para. 30 c.

91 (CCT 48/07) [2007] ZACC 27, 2008 (3) SA 183 (CC).

92 Ibid., para. 30.

93 See text to note 29.

94 CRC Committee, "Concluding Observations on the Combined Second to Fourth Periodic Reports of Albania, adopted by the Committee at its Sixty-First Session (17 September – 5 October 2012)" U.N. Doc. CRC/C/ALB/CO/2–4 (7 Dec. 2012), para. 56 a; "Concluding Observations on the Combined Third to Fifth Periodic Reports of Tajikistan" (29 Sept. 2017) U.N. Doc. CRC/C/TJK/CO/3–5 ("Concluding Observations on Tajikistan"), para. 16.

Early marriage

The CRC has no definition of a minimum age for marriage, unlike article 21(2) of the ACRWC, which sets it at 18. A joint General Recommendation/Comment by the CRC Committee and the CEDAW Committee in 2014 said that child marriage caused

> early and frequent pregnancy and childbirth, resulting in higher than average maternal morbidity and mortality rates, . . . infant mortality, . . . limited decision-making power in relation to [girls'] own lives, higher rates of school dropout, . . . forced exclusion from school and an increased risk of domestic violence, in addition to limiting the enjoyment of the right to freedom of movement.[95]

Despite these consequences of child marriage, the CRC Committee and the CEDAW Committee recommended that "a marriage of a mature, capable child below 18 years of age may be allowed in exceptional circumstances, provided that the child is at least 16 years of age".

In contrast, only two years later, in its 2016 General Comment on Adolescents' Rights, the CRC Committee stated that "the minimum age limit should be 18 years for marriage . . . in view of the degree of associated risk and harm",[96] with no mention of exceptions to take into account evolving capacities and autonomy. In its 2016 Concluding Observations on the UK, the CRC Committee recommended that the UK both "raise the minimum age of marriage to 18 years",[97] and that it adopt "effective measures to ensure that marriage of children aged 16 and 17 years takes place only in exceptional circumstances and is based on the full, free and informed consent of the concerned children".[98] In recent Concluding Observations on other states, the Committee has said that the minimum age for marriage should be 18 with no exceptions.[99] The CRC Committee does not stipulate 18 as a minimum age for sexual consent, but encourages States Parties to "take into account the need to balance protection and evolving capacities, and define an acceptable minimum age", and that[100] "States should avoid criminalizing adolescents of similar ages for factually consensual and non-exploitative sexual activity".[101]

Physical punishment

Article 19 of the CRC provides a child's right to protection from physical and mental violence, injury, abuse, neglect, negligent treatment, maltreatment, exploitation and sexual abuse, and article 37 of the CRC provides a right to protection from torture or other cruel, inhuman or degrading

95 CEDAW Committee and CRC Committee, "Joint General Recommendation No 31 of the Committee on the Elimination of Discrimination Against Women/General Comment No 18 of the Committee on the Rights of the Child on Harmful Practices" (14 Nov. 2014) U.N. Doc. CEDAW/C/GC/31-CRC/C/GC/18, para. 22.

96 "General Comment on Adolescents' Rights", *supra* note 26, para. 40.

97 "Concluding Observations on the UK", *supra* note 60, para. 20.

98 Ibid., para. 47(a).

99 For example, "Concluding Observations on Tajikistan", *supra* note 94, para. 13; CRC Committee "Concluding Observations on the Second Periodic Report of Barbados" (3 March 2017) U.N. Doc. CRC/C/BRB/CO/2, ("Concluding Observations on Barbados"), para. 20; CRC Committee, "Concluding Observations on the Second Periodic Report of the Central African Republic" (8 March 2017) U.N. Doc. CRC/C/CAF/CO/2, ("Concluding Observations on the Central African Republic"), para. 23.

100 Ibid.

101 Ibid.

treatment or punishment. Singapore has made a declaration in this relation which says that these provisions do not proscribe "the judicious application of corporal punishment in the best interest of the child".[102]

The CRC Committee is clear, however, that all forms of physical punishment of children are impermissible, defining physical punishment as "any punishment in which physical force is used and intended to cause some degree of pain or discomfort, however light".[103] The committee has also condemned "other non-physical forms of punishment that are also cruel and degrading and thus incompatible with the Convention", including by way of example "punishment which belittles, humiliates, denigrates, scapegoats, threatens, scares or ridicules the child".[104] The committee has frequently criticised states for their failure to prohibit all forms of physical punishment of children, including the UK for its maintenance of the "reasonable chastisement" defence.[105] There is growing international support for the prohibition of physical punishment of children within the family. Beginning with Sweden in 1979, 53 states have legislated against all physical punishment of children,[106] with Scotland recently announcing that it plans to do so,[107] and the High Court of South Africa has ruled that the common law defence of "reasonable chastisement" to a charge of assault on a child was unconstitutional.[108]

The child's right to privacy in the family

Deference to parental rights to privacy has often hindered protection of children's rights within the family. Children also have rights to privacy, which can protect them and their families from an intrusive state, and also protect children themselves from intrusive parents or other family members. But a child's right to privacy is still an under-developed right. There is nothing particularly child-focused about article 16 of the CRC, which has wording almost identical to that

102 "Declarations and Reservations", *supra* note 16.

103 CRC Committee, "General Comment No 8 (2006): The Right of the Child to Protection from Corporal Punishment and Other Cruel or Degrading Forms of Punishment (arts. 19; 28, para. 2; and 37, inter alia)" (2 March 2007) U.N. Doc. CRC/C/GC/8, para. 11.

104 Ibid.

105 "Concluding Observations on the UK", *supra* note 60, para. 41 a. See also, for example, "Concluding Observations on the Second to Fourth Periodic Reports of Vanuatu" (29 Sept. 2017) U.N. Doc. CRC/C/VUT/CO/2–4 ("Concluding Observations on Vanuatu"), para. 25 a; "Concluding Observations on Tajikistan", *supra* note 94, para. 22 a; "Concluding Observations on the Fifth Periodic Report of the Democratic People's Republic of Korea" (29 Sept. 2017) U.N. Doc. CRC/C/PRK/CO/5, para. 27 a.

106 Global Initiative to End All Corporal Punishment of Children, "States which have Prohibited All Corporal Punishment", available at www.endcorporalpunishment.org/progress/prohibiting-states/ (accessed 27 Oct. 2017). The following states are listed: Sweden (1979), Finland (1983), Norway (1987), Austria (1989), Cyprus (1994), Denmark (1997), Latvia (1998), Croatia (1999), Germany, Israel and Bulgaria (2000), Turkmenistan (2002), Iceland (2003), Romania and Ukraine (2004), Hungary (2005), Greece (2006), Togo, Spain, Venezuela, Uruguay, Portugal, New Zealand and the Netherlands (2007), Liechtenstein, Luxembourg, Republic of Moldova and Costa Rica (2008), Albania, Republic of Congo, Kenya, Tunisia and Poland (2010), South Sudan (2011), Cabo Verde, Honduras and The Former Yugoslav Republic (Macedonia) (2013), Andorra, Estonia, Nicaragua, San Marino, Argentina, Bolivia, Brazil and Malta (2014), Benin, Ireland and Peru (2015), Mongolia, Montenegro, Paraguay and Slovenia (2016), and Lithuania (2017).

107 BBC News Scotland, "Smacking to be Banned in Scotland" (19 October 2017), available at www.bbc.co.uk/news/uk-scotland-scotland-politics-41678797 (accessed 27 Oct. 2017).

108 *Y.G. v. S.* [2017] ZAGPJHC 290, 2018 (1) SACR 64 (GJ).

of article 17 of the ICCPR, providing everyone with the right against "arbitrary or unlawful interference with his or her privacy, family, home or correspondence" and "unlawful attacks on his or her honour and reputation", and article 10 of the ACRCW is very similar.

The Committee of the CRC has not explained what the right to privacy means for children, and several reservations elevate parental authority above children's privacy and there is urgent need for a general comment on this and which ought to include the privacy rights of the child within a family. The Holy See's reservation to the CRC preserves "the primary and inalienable rights of parents", and is particularly concerned with the article 16 right to privacy, and other rights.[109] Kiribati and Poland have made declarations regarding "parental authority", and Singapore's declaration upholds "the authority of parents".[110]

Child privacy rights have had little attention in the Concluding Observations of the CRC Committee. Out of the 21 published so far,[111] 11 make no mention of children's privacy or private life at all, let alone in the context of the family.[112] Five mention privacy, but not in connection with the family.[113] The only Concluding Observations where the child's right to privacy within the family was covered in any detail were those on Mongolia, where the CRC Committee expressed concern regarding "the undue interference with this right by parents . . . leading in some cases to suicide", and recommended that Mongolia "establish clear guidelines for parents . . . to ensure that they fully understand and respect the right of the child to privacy".[114]

Conclusion

The rights of the child within the family are affected by factors that do not apply, or at least do not apply with the same force, to the rights of the child in the public sphere. One legal factor is that some child rights, such as the right to education, are formulated, or at least have been interpreted in the past, as rights of the parent (as in the right to education in the First Protocol to the ECHR). Another legal factor is that the right to privacy in most international human rights

109 "Declarations and Reservations", *supra* note 16.

110 Ibid.

111 The date of writing is 1 November 2017.

112 "Concluding Observations on the DRC", *supra* note 85; "Concluding Observations on Barbados", *supra* note 99; "Concluding Observations on the Central African Republic", *supra* note 99; CRC Committee, "Concluding Observations on the Combined Third to Fifth Periodic Reports of Malawi" (6 March 2017) U.N. Doc. CRC/MWI/C/CO/3–5; "Concluding Observations on the Fourth Periodic Report of Georgia" (9 March 2017) U.N. Doc. CRC/C/GEO/CO/4 2017); "Concluding Observations on the Combined Third and Fourth Periodic Reports of Qatar" (22 June 2017) U.N. Doc. CRC/C/QAT/C/CO/3–4; "Concluding Observations on the Combined Third to Fifth Periodic Reports of Cameroon" (6 July 2017) U.N. Doc. CRC/C/CMR/CO/3–5; "Concluding Observations on Vanuatu", *supra* note 105; "Concluding Observations on Tajikistan", *supra* note 94; "Concluding Observations on the Fifth and Sixth Periodic Reports of Ecuador" (29 Sept. 2017) U.N. Doc. CRC/C/ECU/CO/5–6; "Concluding Observations on the Fifth Periodic Report of Denmark" (26 Oct. 2017) U.N. Doc. CRC/C/DNK/CO/5.

113 CRC Committee, "Concluding Observations on the Combined Second and Third Periodic Reports of Serbia" (7 March 2017) U.N. Doc. CRC/C/SRB/CO/2–3, para. 17 b; "Concluding Observations on the Combined Second to Fourth Periodic Reports of Estonia" (8 March 2017) U.N. Doc. CRC/C/EST/CO/2–4, para. 48 c; "Concluding Observations on the Combined Second to Fourth Periodic Reports of Antigua and Barbuda" (30 June 2017) U.N. Doc. CRC/C/ATG/2–4, para. 15 c; "Concluding Observations on the Combined Third to Fifth Periodic Reports of Bhutan" (5 July 2017) U.N. Doc. CRC/C/BTN/CO/3–5, para. 10 b; "Concluding Observations on Romania", *supra* note 90, para. 22.

114 CRC Committee, "Concluding Observations on the Fifth Periodic Report of Mongolia" (12 July 2017) U.N. Doc. CRC/C/MNG/CO/5, para. 21.

instruments includes the right to family privacy, as well as the right to individual privacy. This can be interpreted as establishing a "jurisdiction" of the family that limits the "intrusion" of the state to empower children with rights. This "off limits" approach may be reinforced by the characterisation of the rights of the child as dependent on the "evolving capacity" of the child, which, in the first instance, may make child rights dependent upon parental recognition of the state of the child's capacity.

Despite these factors, international human rights law has evolved in recognition of the rights of the child within the family. Increasingly, children have rights not to be subject to physical punishment within the family, following on from the prohibition of judicially ordered corporal punishment and corporal punishment in both state and private schools.

The child's right to autonomy includes the rights to choose and change religion, even in the face of parental opposition. A child right to autonomy of expression remains to be developed by interpretation.

The physical right to autonomy of a child now includes the right to seek medical advice and treatment, independently of parental supervision. This is particularly significant in medical matters such as sex education, contraception and abortion, that often involve religious convictions.

The right of a child born outside a legal marital relationship not to be discriminated against has long been established. What is emerging is the right of a child to know the identity of birth parents. The right of a child to have a relationship with parents, whether birth or adoptive, cannot be determined by the gender or sexual orientation of the parent. Of course, this right of the child is a correlative of the rights of parents not to be discriminated against on grounds of gender or sexual orientation.

The best interests of the child are the paramount consideration regarding adoption, whether in-country or intercountry, and in relation to *kafalah*, as they should be in making any decisions regarding children. A child's right to autonomy is increasingly being recognised, at least in being heard in the determination of the best interests of a child in particular situations. An emerging right of autonomy is a child's right to privacy, both informational and physical, and both within society and within the family. It is now very clear that parental rights, many of which in reality are not rights but parental responsibilities, can only be interpreted in a way that upholds the dignity of children in the family.

Bibliography

Assim, Usang S. and Sloth-Nielsen, Julia. "Islamic Kafalah as an Alternative Care System for Children Deprived of a Family Environment" (2014) 14 *African Human Rights Law Journal* 322.

Eekelaar, John. "The Role of the Best Interests Principle in Decisions Affecting Children and Decisions about Children" (2015) 23 *International Journal of Children's Rights* 3.

Hafen, Bruce C. and Hafen, Jonathan O. "Abandoning Children to Their Autonomy: The United Nations Convention on the Rights of the Child" (1996) 37 *Harvard International Law Journal* 449.

Mezmur, Benyam Dawit. "'Acting Like a Rich Bully'?: Madonna, Mercy, Malawi and International Children's Rights Law in Adoption" (2012) 20 *International Journal of Children's Rights Law* 24.

Rutkow, Lainie and Lozman, Joshua T. "Suffer the Children: A Call for United States Ratification of the United Nations Convention on the Rights of the Child" (2006) 19 *Harvard Human Rights Journal* 161.

Van Bueren, Geraldine. *The International Law on the Rights of the Child* (The Hague/Boston/London, Martinus Nijhoff Publishers, 1998).

13

Reproductive rights

Rachel Rebouché

Introduction

There are many ways to address the topic of "reproductive rights" in an edited collection on international family law. One could attempt to cover the field – canvassing and describing the range of issues that constitute reproductive rights. Such a chapter might dedicate subparts to abortion, birth control, prenatal and postnatal care, sex education, sterilisation, just to name a few topics. But another approach is to understand the treatment of "reproductive rights" at the level of international policy and advocacy. For the latter, a case study can explore how reproductive rights circulate in international law, and this chapter takes just that tack.

The case study I offer focuses on abortion law reform, and I chose that focus for a couple of reasons. First, abortion has proved a controversial topic for courts and legislatures around the world. The progress made by reproductive rights advocates in decriminalising termination services (particularly early in pregnancy or for certain grounds) highlights the increasing influence of reproductive rights arguments. Second, the human rights claims that underpin abortion law reform often support other issues, such as access to contraceptives, sexual education, and prenatal or postnatal care. Women's rights to equality, dignity, health and autonomy have helped make the global case for accessible and affordable reproductive health care.

The basis for this chapter's analysis is a 2016 decision of the First Chamber of the Supreme Court of Brazil.[1] A panel of five justices found that clandestine abortion providers, performing terminations with the consent of pregnant women in violation of the penal code, could not be detained pre-trial. Brazil criminalises all abortion, punishing both providers and patients, except in cases of rape and danger to the pregnant woman's life.[2] Two previous decisions of the Supreme

1 S.T.F., Habeas Corpus No. 124.306, Relator: Min. Marco Aurélio, Supremo Tribunal Federal Jurisprudencia [S.T.F.J.], 29.11.2016, 1, para. 20 (Braz.); English translation available at www.iconnectblog.com/wp-content/uploads/2017/03/Brazilian-Abortion-Ruling-Translation.pdf.

2 Art. 124 and Art. 126 provide for detention of the pregnant women (from one to three years) and of the third party inducing the abortion (from one to four years). Decreto-Lei n. 2.848/1940 – Código Penal. *Diário Oficial da República,* 31 dez. 1940, available at www.planalto.gov.br/ccivil_03/decreto-lei/Del2848compilado.htm.

Court expanded abortion permission: one authorised the development of stem cell research in Brazil (in 2010) and one granted the right to abortion in cases of anencephaly (in 2012).[3]

Writing for the majority of the panel, Justice Luís Roberto Barroso held that not only was pre-trial detention inappropriate given the potential sentences and lack of criminal records of the defendants, but also that criminalisation of early pregnancy termination was incompatible with women's fundamental rights and failed to meet the requirements of proportionality.[4] Although the panel did not strike down the existing criminal penalties for abortion, the opinion establishes a precedent that lower courts can follow, and it may have opened the door for a similar decision by the entire Supreme Court. Indeed, the panel suggests, and as Part II explains, decriminalisation of first-trimester terminations is in step with the laws of the "developed and democratic" world. The opinion's syllabus, for instance, lists as examples the abortion laws of the United States (US), Germany, the United Kingdom, Canada, France, Italy, Spain, Portugal, and the Netherlands (in that order).[5]

The panel's decision – that punishing first trimester abortion violates women's fundamental human rights – is no doubt an important affirmation and advancement of Brazilian women's reproductive rights. The panel's reasoning, in embracing women's equality and empowerment, tracks the understanding of reproductive health and decision-making as expressed by human rights bodies and documents. The panel's affirmation of "reproductive rights as human rights" places the court in conversation with international human rights bodies and advocacy groups.[6] Specifically, abortion rights, early in pregnancy or on limited grounds, though contested, are now fixtures of human rights law.

In three parts, this chapter will draw from the Brazilian decision to explore three arguments that have supported reproductive rights at the international level.[7] First, the decision reflects the intersecting influences (and importance) of the universal values that underpin human rights. Second, the opinion relies on a comparative consensus among other countries, mostly located in the global North. And, third, it offers justifications for reform in terms of protecting women's health and resisting state policies that would seek to advance foetal rights. Similar arguments, rooted in universalism and consensus, have been crucial in advancing the field of international family law more generally. From campaigns for marriage equality between wives and husbands to marriage equality for couples of the same sex, universal or fundamental human rights and consensus-minded comparative projects resist treating abortion as a solely local issue or personal choice.[8] This is no small feat given states' historic treatment of family law as a purely national or

3 Debora Diniz, "The Architecture of a Constitutional Case in Three Acts – Anencephaly at the Brazilian Supreme Court," 1 *U. Brasília L.J.* (2016). See also Luís Roberto Barroso, "Bringing Abortion into the Brazilian Public Debate: Legal Strategies for Anencephalic Pregnancy," in *Abortion Law in Transnational Perspective: Cases and Controversies* 258–278 (Rebecca J. Cook et al. eds, 2014).

4 Habeas Corpus n. 124.306, supra note 1, para. 7. Justice Barroso served as the *pro bono* lawyer, before he was appointed as a justice, to prepare petitions to the Supreme Court in previous abortion litigation. Debora Diniz, "The Brazilian Litigation on Abortion: Zika Epidemic and Beyond" (2017), at 8, available at www.law.nyu.edu/sites/default/files/upload_documents/Diniz_March.pdf.

5 Habeas Corpus n. 124.306, supra note 1, paras. 8–10.

6 See, e.g., Rachel Rebouché, "Abortion Rights as Human Rights," 25 *Soc. Leg. Stud.* 765, 771–774 (2016); Rachel Rebouché, "Reproducing Rights: The Intersection of Reproductive Justice and Human Rights," 7 *U.C. Irvine. L. Rev.* 579, 584–585 (2017).

7 Portions of Parts I and II of this chapter draw from Rachel Rebouché, "Reproducing Rights: The Intersection of Reproductive Justice and Human Rights," 7 *U.C. Irvine L. Rev.* 579 (2017).

8 See Barbara Stark, "When Globalization Hits Home: International Family Law Comes of Age," 39 *Vand. J. Transnat'l L.* 1551, 1556–1557 (2006) (arguing that human rights and gender equality (as well as globalisation and labour mobility) have contributed to the development of international family law).

domestic concern.[9] But despite the international attention given to reproductive rights, political contestation and contextual differences among countries suggest that approaches rooted in rights and consensus have limits. The chapter concludes by reflecting on how international reproductive rights advocates might respond to the resistance that reproductive rights can engender.

I. Fundamental (human) rights and abortion rights

One need only look at human right documents – spanning conventions drafted in the 1970s, such as the Convention on the Elimination of all Forms of Discrimination Against Women (CEDAW), to contemporary instruments, such as the 2003 Protocol to the African Charter on the Rights of Women – to see the imprint of reproductive rights on international law.[10] Although women's rights to reproductive health care and decision-making were not originally part of a global agenda for development or a right to health, reproductive rights have received significant attention at international, regional, and national levels as fundamental to women's human rights.[11] This is the product of decades of advocacy by women's rights activists, who helped make reproductive rights, including abortion rights, a priority for human rights bodies and organisations.[12] And, presently, gender equality and women's empowerment are central to international conversations about reproduction, fertility, and population.[13]

Safe and legal abortion has become a priority for a range of international bodies, and features prominently in human rights declarations, though it remains a contentious issue.[14] The panel of the Supreme Court of Brazil identifies the 1994 International Conference on Population and Development (ICPD) and the 1995 Fourth World Conference on Women (FWCW) as two events – "decisive moments" – that advanced the mantra "reproductive rights are human rights."[15] Indeed, most academics and advocates agree that the ICPD and the FWCW were pivotal in advancing an international human rights agenda for reproductive rights.[16] Women's rights advocates were at the centre of ICPD negotiations and drafted guiding principles that focused on gender equality and "the empowerment of women."[17] A year after the ICPD, the FWCW

9 See Janet Halley & Kerry Rittich, "Critical Directions in Comparative Family Law: Genealogies and Contemporary Studies of Family Law Exceptionalism," 58 *Am. J. Comp. L.* 753, 754 (2010).

10 See D. Marianne Blair et al., *Family Law in the World Community: Cases, Materials, and Problems in Comparative and International Family Law* 28–50 (2nd edn 2003) (noting the international instruments that govern family law matters, including reproductive rights).

11 See, e.g., Laura Reichenbach, "The Global Reproductive Health and Rights Agenda: Opportunities and Challenges for the Future," in *Reproductive Health and Human Rights: The Way Forward* 23–24 (Laura Reichenbach & Mindy Roseman eds, 2009).

12 See generally Hilary Charlesworth et al., "Feminist Approaches to International Law: Reflections from Another Century," in *International Law: Modern Feminist Approaches* (Doris Buss & Ambreena Manji eds, 2005).

13 Alma Beltrán y Puga, "Paradigmatic Changes in Gender Justice: The Advancement of Reproductive Rights in International Human Rights Law," 3 *Creighton Int'l & Comp. L.J.* 158, 159–162 (2012).

14 Rebouché, "Abortion Rights as Human Rights," supra note 6, at 767–770 (2016).

15 Habeas Corpus n. 124.306, supra note 1, para. 28.

16 Eva Brems, "Enemies or Allies? Feminism and Cultural Relativism as Dissident Voices in Human Rights Discourse," 19 *Hum. Rts. Q.* 136, 152 (1997); Rhonda Copelon, "Remarks of Rhonda Copelon," 44 *Am. U. L. Rev.* 1253, 1253 (1995); Nancy Northup, "Reproductive Rights at Home and Abroad," 15 *C.U.N.Y. L. Rev.* 265, 265 (2012); Christina Zampas & Jaime M. Gher, "Abortion as a Human Right – International and Regional Standards," 8 *Hum. Rts. L. Rev.* 249, 252 (2008).

17 International Conference on Population and Development, *Report of the International Conference on Population and Development*, Principle 4, U.N. Doc. A/CONF.171/13/Rev.1 (13 Sept. 1994).

brought further attention to women's rights and reproductive rights.[18] Although both stopped short of calling for abortion liberalisation, the ICPD Programme of Action and FWCW Platform for Action were among the first human rights documents that referred to abortion explicitly and have been rallying points for reproductive rights supporters.[19]

Despite significant differences among national laws governing abortion, national courts have looked to human rights texts and the decisions of human rights bodies to translate states' international human rights commitments into domestic interpretations of legislation or constitutional provisions.[20] The Brazil case provides an apt example. The panel's reference to the "nucleus around which a number of fundamental rights of women revolve" draws from the rights announced in international documents (and interpreted by human rights bodies).[21] And these values are framed as universal human rights.

The panel discussed the intersection of international and domestic constitutional rights by stating:

> The history of humanity is the history of the affirmation of the individual in the face of political, economic, and religious power, the latter seeking to define the dominant social morality. The product of this millennial struggle is that of fundamental rights, here understood as the human rights incorporated into the constitutional order.[22]

The panel continued by elaborating on what many would argue is the canonical, traditional (and thus perhaps dated) view of human rights.[23] Justice Barroso wrote:

> After World War II, fundamental rights came to be treated as an emanation of human dignity, following one of the propositions of the Kantian categorical imperative: every person shall be treated as an end unto him or herself, not as a means to satisfy interests of others or collective interests. Dignity means, from the point of view of the person, that every individual has an inherent value and autonomy.[24]

Scholars and advocates writing about sexual and reproductive rights describe human rights in the same way:

> [Human rights] are universal because everyone is born with and possesses the same rights, regardless of where they live, their gender or race, or their religious, cultural or ethnic

18 Fourth World Conference on Women, *Report of the Fourth World Conference on Women*, 2–4, U.N. Doc. A/CONF.177/20/Rev.1, Annex I (15 Sept. 1995).

19 Marge Berer, "The Cairo 'Compromise' on Abortion and its Consequences for Making Abortion Safe and Legal," in *Reproductive Health and Human Rights: The Way Forward* 152–159 (Laura Reichenbach & Mindy Jane Roseman eds, 2009); Adrienne Germain & Theresa Kim, *Expanding Access to Safe Abortion: Strategies for Action* 3–4 (The International Women's Health Coalition ed., 1998); Rebecca J. Cook & Bernard M. Dickens, "Human Rights Dynamics of Abortion Law Reform," 25 *Hum. Rts. Q.* 1, 4 (2003).

20 Rebouché, "Abortion Rights as Human Rights," supra note 6, at 771–774.

21 Habeas Corpus n. 124.306, supra note 1, paras. 1, 31.

22 Id., para. 14.

23 But see Samuel Moyn, *The Last Utopia: Human Rights in History* 210 (2012) (arguing that the origin of modern human rights law was a response to the Cold War: "[T]he rise of human rights in international law occurred . . . due to the ideological changes that set the stage for a moral triumph of human rights – one that in turn gave a whole new relevance to the field's mission.").

24 Habeas Corpus n. 124.306, supra note 1, para. 18.

> background. They are inalienable because people's rights can never be taken away. They are indivisible and interdependent because all rights – political, civil, social, cultural and economic – are equal in importance and none can be fully enjoyed without the others.[25]

From the premise of natural and universal rights, the panel elaborated on which rights comprise the "nucleus" of women's fundamental rights. The decision explained that Brazil's abortion restrictions undermine women's rights to autonomy, physical and psychological integrity, gender equality, sexual expression, and freedom from "social discrimination."[26] Rights to autonomy, integrity and equality play the central roles in reproductive rights, and, reflecting contemporary understandings in the field, the panel highlights freedom of sexual expression and freedom from social discrimination or inequality relating to poverty. Incorporating income disparities as well as sexual expression into a reproductive rights agenda, as I argue below, is bound up in equality rationales.

Taking autonomy rights first, the panel defined autonomy as the "essential core of individual freedom, protected by the principle of dignity."[27] It is an individual's right to liberty and security, which, according to Justice Barroso, implicate negative and positive rights – "certain duties of abstention and action by the State."[28] Rebecca Cook and Bernard Dickens explain the difference between negative and positive rights to liberty: "Negative rights . . . restrain police and other governmental obstruction of abortion procedures of which women can avail themselves, but positive rights require governments to provide women with reasonable access to safe services."[29]

When the panel invoked the negative conception of liberty or autonomy, it spoke to the limits of state power in criminalising all abortion and imprisoning women who seek termination services.[30]

Positive rights to reproductive liberty and autonomy include steps states should take to ensure one's choices are unencumbered, and these guarantees are often phrased in terms of women's empowerment. Paragraph 96 of the 1994 Beijing Platform for Action, for example, urged states to recognise that the "human rights of women include their right to decide freely and responsibly on all matters related to their sexuality, free of coercion, discrimination and violence." The panel similarly embraced a right to autonomy rooted in women's liberation:

> When it comes to a woman, a central aspect of her autonomy is the power to control her own body and to make decisions about it . . . How can the State . . . force a woman, in the early weeks of pregnancy, to carry it to term, as if she were a womb at the service of society, and not an autonomous person, in her full capacity to be, to think, and to live her own life?[31]

Next, and in the same vein, the panel included physical and psychological integrity in the "nucleus of women's fundamental rights." The panel describes physical integrity as freedom from "undue interference and injury to [individuals'] bodies and minds," relating to the "rights of health and

25 Alice M. Miller et al., "Sexual Rights as Human Rights: A Guide to Authoritative Sources and Principles for Applying Human Rights to Sexuality and Sexual Health," 23 *Repro. Health Matters* 16, 21 (2015).
26 Habeas Corpus n. 124.306, supra note 1, paras. 24–31.
27 Id., para. 24.
28 Id., para. 15.
29 Cook & Dickens, supra note 19, at 30.
30 Id. at 31–32 (citing the past imprisonment of women seeking abortions in Nepal, Chile, Ireland).
31 Habeas Corpus n. 124.306, supra note 1, para. 25.

safety."[32] Related to international reproductive rights, a number of human rights bodies have emphasised the health implications of rights to physical integrity.[33] In General Recommendation 24, the CEDAW Committee charges states to "take appropriate legislative, judicial, administrative, budgetary, economic and other measures to the maximum extent of their available resources to ensure that women realize their right to health care." More recently, a 2011 report of the Special Rapporteur on the Right of Everyone to the Enjoyment of the Highest Attainable Standard of Physical and Mental Health stated: "Criminal laws penalizing and restricting induced abortion are the paradigmatic examples of impermissible barriers to the realization of women's right to health and must be eliminated."[34] The Rapporteur recommends that "legal and safe abortion services [be] available, accessible, and of good quality."[35]

The panel also considered how abortion restrictions impair women's psychological integrity because an unwanted pregnancy can result in "the assumption of a lifelong obligation, demanding self-abnegation, as well as dedication and deep commitment to the newborn."[36] The Human Rights Committee has decided cases and issued comments connecting the right to be free from cruel, inhuman or degrading treatment to the mental suffering that abortion restrictions can cause, especially when laws do not provide exceptions for abortion after sexual assault.[37]

Perhaps at the core of a "nucleus" of fundamental rights, the panel focused on how gender equality is advanced by abortion permission. The panel adopts both narrow and expansive views of equality. That is, the decision covered not only how reproductive rights relate to formal equality between men and women and to anti-stereotyping, but also explored how women realize reproductive rights in practice, concentrating on substantive equality (described in the conclusion of this part).

First, the burdens that women bear in pregnancy are the product of "historic, economic and social injustices."[38] In this way, the panel conceives of law's different treatment of pregnant women (as compared to men) as a form of discrimination and an affront to formal equality: abortion laws single out the procreative decisions of women, and not men. International thinking has also evolved to include pregnancy discrimination as a type of sex-based inequality. In its Beyond 2014 ICPD review, the CEDAW Committee issued a statement in support of advancing sexual and reproductive rights, and stated that "criminalisation of some services that only women require is a violation of women's reproductive rights and constitutes discrimination against them."[39]

32 Id., para. 26.

33 See, e.g., ICESCR, Art. 12(1); CEDAW, Art. 12, CRC, Art. 24.

34 United Nations Special Rapporteur, Right of Everyone to the Enjoyment of the Highest Attainable Standard of Physical and Mental Health, para. IV.1.21, U.N. Doc. A/66/254 (3 Aug. 2011).

35 Id., para. IV.1.29.

36 Habeas Corpus n. 124.306, supra note 1, para. 26.

37 See, e.g., *K.L. v. Peru*, Comm. No. 1153/2003, U.N. Doc. CCPR/C/85/D/1153/2003 (2005), para. 6; Human Rights Committee, General Comment No. 20: Article 7 (Prohibition of Torture, or Other Cruel, Inhuman or Degrading Treatment or Punishment), U.N. Doc. HRI/GEN/1/Rev.1 (1994), para. 5.

38 Habeas Corpus n. 124.306, supra note 1, para. 29.

39 CEDAW Committee, "Statement of the Committee on the Elimination of Discrimination against Women on Sexual and Reproductive Health and Rights: Beyond 2014 ICPD Review, 57th Session", at 2 (10–28 Feb. 2014), available at www.ohchr.org/Documents/HRBodies/CEDAW/Statements/SRHR26Feb2014.pdf. See also Joint Statement by United Nations Human Rights Experts, the Rapporteur on the Rights of Women of the Inter-American Commission on Human Rights and the Special Rapporteurs on the Rights of Women and Human Rights Defenders of the African Commission on Human and Peoples' Rights (2015) ("The criminalization of or other failure to provide services that only women require, such as abortion and emergency contraception, constitute discrimination based on sex, and is impermissible.").

The panel then shifts from law's differential treatment of men and women to explain root causes of gender discrimination – stereotypes that promote, as Carol Sanger writes, "maternalistic account[s] of abortion" in which "all women are imagined to be mothers someday."[40] The panel speaks broadly of "exclusionary, stereotypical and discriminatory conceptions of female identity" and links those loosely to "an idealized vision of the experience of motherhood."[41] The Beyond 2014 ICPD statement of the CEDAW Committee similarly stated: "The Committee continuously addresses discriminatory gender stereotypes and harmful practices that contribute to, and perpetuate, these violations."[42]

Stereotypes of women as mothers also embed heteronormative and stilted conceptions of sexuality. In commenting on sexual rights, the panel offered reasoning that advances reproductive rights beyond what is typical in court decisions, though increasingly recognised by international bodies. For one, the decision drew attention to the historic subordination of women's sexuality, stating that "female sexuality alongside women's reproductive rights has suffered millennia of oppression."[43] The panel cited the ICPD as promoting the development of "female sexual freedom."[44] Interestingly, this section of the opinion combined reproductive health and sexual expression – that a right to an "active and fulfilling sexual life" has "always been granted to men" but not women. (One might query whether the panel considered the repression of gay men's sexuality.)

The introduction of sexual rights as part of the constellation of reproductive rights mirrors the thinking of human rights authorities. For example, the World Health Organisation's definition of sexual rights states: "Sexual rights embrace certain human rights that are already recognized in international and regional human rights treaties, supported in consensus documents and found in national laws."[45] United Nations documents also make commitments to the realization of women's and men's sexual rights. The United Nations Economic Commission for Latin America and the Caribbean concluded that states must

> promote policies that enable persons to exercise their sexual rights, which embrace the right to a safe and full sex life, as well as the right to take free, informed, voluntary and responsible decisions on their sexuality, sexual orientation and gender identity, without coercion, discrimination or violence.[46]

Finally, in the last paragraphs detailing women's "fundamental rights," the panel adopted substantive equality in considering how criminalisation disproportionately harms women with limited financial resources – what the court calls "social discrimination."[47] Alice Miller and her colleagues describe the "test of substantive equality" in terms of differently situated people's ability "to access resources, participate and make decisions in public and private life equally and with equal capacity to influence results, and generally enjoy rights in practice."[48] This also implies

40 Carol Sanger, *About Abortion: Terminating Pregnancy in Twenty-First Century America* 188–190 (2017).
41 Habeas Corpus n. 124.306, supra note 1, para. 29.
42 CEDAW Committee, Beyond 2014 ICPD Review.
43 Habeas Corpus n. 124.306, supra note 1, para. 27.
44 Id., para. 28.
45 World Health Organisation, Developing Sexual Health Programmes: A Framework for Action, WHO/RHR/HRP/10.22 (2010).
46 United Nations Economic Commission for Latin America and the Caribbean (UNECLAC). Montevideo: United Nations Economic Commission for Latin America and the Caribbean (15 Aug. 2013).
47 Habeas Corpus n. 124.306, supra note 1, para. 30.
48 Miller et al., "Sexual Rights as Human Rights," supra note 25, at 23.

positive duties: "States' obligations include not only refraining from discriminatory actions, but also taking affirmative action to remove barriers and redress historical legacies of inequality. In such circumstances, such 'positive discrimination' as a temporary special measure is not prohibited."[49]

The panel's reliance on concepts of substantive equality and reference to social discrimination correspond with thinking about the nature of gender inequality at the international level.[50] A recent joint statement of human rights experts begins: "We are deeply concerned by reports of women who . . . experience institutional abuse and discrimination by health service providers as a result of public policies and laws or on grounds of social and economic status."[51] Likewise, the Committee on Economic, Social and Cultural Rights asserts that abortion restrictions disproportionately harm low income women.[52] The panel of the Supreme Court expressed a similar concern by emphasising how criminal laws disproportionately impact poor women, "who neither have access to private doctors and clinics, nor are able to use the public health system to carry out the abortive procedure."[53]

By describing abortion as indivisible from human rights protections, courts such as the Supreme Court of Brazil marry reproductive rights to the protection and promotion of women's equality. And these rights are feminist interventions.[54] They are part of a broader agenda for women's human rights. The strength of human rights argument comes in part from the consensus those values enjoy among signatories to human rights documents. Assessing the depth and breadth of consensus depends on a comparative project, and those comparisons – particularly around countries' treatment of women's rights – have not been without controversy, as the next part makes clear.

II. Transnational consensus and legitimacy

Distinct from universal values such as autonomy or equality, human rights arguments build on shared values that gain legitimacy from consensus among countries. Sally Engle Merry argues that the agreement supporting human rights law confers its own unique culture: it is "a culture of transnational modernity."[55] To defend, to support, or to pass a permissive abortion law signals a state's commitment to women's rights, at least on paper, as well as its affiliation with

49 Id. at 23.

50 United Nations Committee on Economic, Social and Cultural Rights, General Comment No. 16: The Equal Right of Men and Women to the Enjoyment of all Economic, Social and Cultural Rights, UN Doc. E/C. 12/2005/4, (2005); Organisation of American States, General Assembly Resolution: Human Rights, Sexual Orientation and Gender Identity, OAS Doc. AG/RES.2504 (XXXIX-O/09) (2009); Organisation of American States, Human Rights, Sexual Orientation and Gender Identity, Resolution AG/RES. 2653 (XLI-O/11) (2013); Council of Europe, Protocol No. 12 to the Convention for the Protection of Human Rights and Fundamental Freedoms, ETS No. 177 (2000).

51 Joint Statement by United Nations Human Rights Experts, supra note 39, at 2.

52 See Human Rights Watch, "Brief to Argumentation of Noncompliance of Fundamental Precept no 442", at 21 (2017), available at www.hrw.org/news/2017/04/25/amicus-curiae-decriminalization-abortion-brazil-12-weeks.

53 Habeas Corpus n. 124.306, supra note 1, para. 30.

54 Chao-ju Chen, "A Progressive Voice from the South, I-CONnect Symposium: Five Perspectives on the Brazilian Abortion Ruling", *Int'l J. Const. L. Blog*, Mar. 7, 2017, available at www.iconnectblog.com/2017/03/symposium-on-brazilian-abortion-ruling-five-perspectives.

55 Sally Engle Merry, "Human Rights and Transnational Culture: Regulating Gender Violence through Global Law," 44 *Osgoode Hall L.J.* 54, 65 (2006).

other states that have permissive abortion laws, mostly among North American and Western European countries.[56] In turn, consensus about the importance of women's reproductive rights affirms human rights as the way to communicate concerns for global social justice.[57] The panel's decision offers an example: "the dominant view in the democratic and developed world is that the criminalization of voluntary termination of pregnancy seriously affects several fundamental rights of women."[58] The panel highlighted the legal permissions for first trimester abortions in the US, Germany, Belgium, France, Uruguay, and Mexico City as proof of consensus.[59]

Human rights obligations also impose a duty to implement limited abortion rights or to decriminalise terminations even in the face of anti-abortion arguments.[60] The panel cited cases from the US, Germany, and Canada to assert that "protection of the unborn life does not outweigh the fundamental right of the woman to perform an abortion."[61] The Brazilian judgement agreed with international commentary on the subject, which affirms that "negotiating history of the treaties, jurisprudence, and most legal analysis suggest that the right to life, as contemplated in those documents, does not apply before the birth of a human being."[62] The panel referred to pre-termination counselling in Germany, Portugal, France, and Belgium to note how legislatures balance respect for potential life and women's rights.[63] The panel called this "proportionality in the narrow sense," before turning to the state's right to limit post-viability terminations.[64]

The panel's argument for these rights-based claims relied on iconic decisions that are thirty or forty years old – *Roe v. Wade*, *R. v. Morgentaler*, and the pre-unification decision of the Federal Constitutional Court of West Germany.[65] In particular, US abortion law and advocacy featured prominently in the Brazilian opinion. After citing a handful of articles from Brazilian publications, the panel began its discussion of the "violation of the fundamental rights of women" with a lengthy list of journal articles and books written predominantly by US scholars.[66] Indeed, over the last forty years, courts across the world, like in Brazil, consistently have cited *Roe v. Wade* as an example of permissive and progressive abortion law.[67] For instance, the panel cited *Roe* a second time to argue

56 See, e.g., U.N. Dep't of Econ. & Soc. Affairs, Abortion Policies and Reproductive Health Around the World, U.N. Doc. ST/ESA/SER.A/343, U.N. Sales No. E.14.XIII.11 at 1, 6 (2014); see also Reva B. Siegel, "Dignity and Sexuality: Claims on Dignity in Transnational Debates over Abortion and Same-sex Marriage," 10 *Int'l J. Const. L.* 355, 359–360 (2012).

57 Engle Merry, supra note 55, at 56.

58 Habeas Corpus n. 124.306, supra note 1, para. 20.

59 Id. paras. 46–47.

60 "The proponents of right to 'fetal life' are no more automatically shut out of attempts to use rights claims than those of us seeking to use rights claims for decriminalizing access to abortion or rights to information on family planning. The answer to why their claim for 'fetal life' or religious exceptions cannot defeat rights claims to access to abortion or sexual diversity lies within rights." Alice M. Miller et al., "Sound and Fury – Engaging with the Politics and the Law of Sexual Rights," 23 *Reproductive Health Matters* 7, 13 (2015).

61 Habeas Corpus n. 124.306, supra note 1, paras. 39, 46.

62 Human Rights Watch, supra note 52, at 12. But see Grégor Puppinck, "Abortion in European Law: Human Rights, Social Rights, and the New Cultural Trend," 4 *Ave Maria Int'l L.J.* 29, 39–40 (2015) ("In recent years, a growing number of European States are reopening the debate on abortion and reconsidering legislation that would place restrictions on abortion."); Cook & Dickens, supra note 19, at 26–27 ("In several countries, however, the intention to give effect to religious faith as understood in the Roman Catholic tradition is expressed in constitutional provisions or legislation that declare the protection of human life from conception.").

63 Id. para. 41.

64 Id. para. 46.

65 Habeas Corpus n. 124.306, supra note 1, paras. 39, 46.

66 Id. n.8.

67 Rachel Rebouché, "Comparative Pragmatism," 72 *Md. L. Rev.* 85, 124–130 (2012).

that the rights of women outweigh the rights of a foetus.[68] National courts, however, rarely cite post-*Roe* decisions that have upheld various abortion restrictions or undermined constitutional protection for abortion, which might suggest that *Roe* is perhaps a dated and inapt example.[69]

Yet the influence of US reproductive rights is bi-directional. US-based advocates participate in litigation before international treaty bodies and national courts, as seen in this chapter's case study and in subsequent cases before the Supreme Court of Brazil.[70] So on the one hand, US law has influenced international and transnational abortion law reform. On the other hand, US advocates seek to "bring human rights home."[71] Constitutional rights define US abortion law, and some advocates have argued that human rights claims could bolster equal protection and substantive due process arguments under the US Constitution. The latter campaign has met with resistance for a number of reasons – US exceptionalism in international law and the hostility to abortion from state and federal legislators, to name two.[72]

But setting aside the domestic resistance to incorporating human rights, the US investment in and influence over international reproductive rights may undermine, as Cynthia Soohoo and Suzanne Stolz have called it, a "global women's movement."[73] The panel's focus on law reform in the global North – "democratic and developed" states, to use again the panel's description – may privilege ideologies associated with North American and Western European feminisms.

A well-known source of debate among international feminists is how to square universalism with perspectives outside of the global North and with the diversity of the world's women.[74] Post-colonial theorists have challenged women's rights campaigns that target so-called "harmful cultural practices" of the global South and cast women as the victims of their communities and in need of saving by international human rights law.[75] In this vein, post-colonial feminists have

68 Habeas Corpus n. 124.306, supra note 1, para. 46. One might also notice the rhetoric used by the panel echoes a mainstay of US abortion discourse since the Clinton Administration – abortion should be "rare and safe." Id. para. 13.

69 Rebouché, "Comparative Pragmatism," supra note 67, at 124–130. Also, *Roe v. Wade* proved influential in the abortion law reform of different countries in the 1970s and the 1980s. Reva B. Siegel, "The Constitutionalization of Abortion," in *The Oxford Handbook of Comparative Constitutional Law* 1057–1058 (Michel Rosenfeld & András Sajó eds, 2012).

70 See, e.g., "International Campaign for Women's Right to Safe Abortion, Abortion Rights at the Supreme Court: A Public Debate in Brazil," 19 April 2017, available at abortion-news.info/abortion-rights-at-the-supreme-court-a-public-debate-in-brazil/. See also Julia L. Ernst, et al., "The Global Pattern of U.S. Initiatives Curtailing Women's Reproductive Rights: A Perspective on the Increasingly Anti-Choice Mosaic," 6 *U. Pa. J. Const. L.* 752, 763–764, 785 (2004).

71 The Guttmacher Institute's multi-country study of abortion law implementation notes that advocacy groups based in the US, such as Ipas, the Population Council, the Guttmacher Institute, and the Center for Reproductive Rights, played primary roles in educational campaigns, litigation, grant writing, and research in transnational abortion law reform. Guttmacher Institute, *Making Abortion Services Accessible in the Wake of Legal Reforms: A Framework and Six Case Studies* 38 (2012).

72 Miller et al., "Sound and Fury," supra note 60, at 10.

73 Cynthia Soohoo & Suzanne Stolz, "Bringing Theories of Human Rights Change Home," 77 *Fordham L. Rev.* 459, 498 (2008).

74 See Ratna Kapur, "The Tragedy of Victimization Rhetoric: Resurrecting the 'Native' Subject in International/Post-Colonial Feminist Legal Politics," 15 *Harv. Hum. Rts. J.* 1, 6 (2002); Hope Lewis, "Embracing Complexity: Human Rights in Critical Race Feminist Perspective," 12 *Colum. J. Gender & L.* 510, 513 (2003); L. Amede Obiora, "Feminism, Globalization, and Culture: After Beijing," 4 *Ind. J. Global Legal Stud.* 355, 368–369 (1997).

75 See Uma Narayan, "Minds of Their Own: Choices, Autonomy, Cultural Practices, and Other Women," in *A Mind of One's Own: Feminist Essays on Reason and Objectivity* 418 (Louise M. Antony & Charlotte E. Witt eds, 2nd edn 2002); Paula C. Johnson & L. Amede Obiora, "How Does the Universal Declaration of Human Rights Protect African Women?," 26 *Syracuse J. Int'l L. & Com.* 195, 207 (1999); Kapur, supra note 74 at 6–7.

observed that certain issues traditionally have received a disproportionate amount of attention, such as violence against women. As one consequence, issues important to economic distribution of resources, such as making a living wage, have received less attention.[76]

Privileging the global North and the US experience of abortion reform can re-inscribe hierarchies in which the interests of powerful nations shape advocacy agendas. To be sure, reproductive rights materials, like most women's human rights campaigns, refer to the importance of including the voices and experiences of women from the global South. But embracing the rhetoric of diversity without engaging divergent interests can produce essentialist accounts of women who contest and resist rights-based narratives of gender, family, and procreation.[77] Cyra Choudhury, for example, writes that "[t]ransnational collaborations must make space for subaltern agents to speak and act. If they do not, they risk disempowering poor women further and failing to reach the potential of feminist transnational advocacy."[78]

Moreover, the tendency to cite laws from the global North can produce blind spots. For one, the means by which women gain access to abortion outside of the law or through informal means can disappear.[79] Consider how religious and cultural forces shape abortion policies and practices.[80] Local practices may facilitate the early termination of pregnancy, but not because of attachments to women's human rights.[81] More pointedly, rights may not matter as much to projects that seek to improve women's reproductive health in places for which rights are not central to procreative discourses. Women in some communities will not support reproductive rights, especially if that advocacy includes supporting abortion.

The final part considers the role of resistance in reproductive rights advocacy, and first notes how public health studies offer justifications for law reform based on rates of maternal mortality and morbidity. Taking again the Brazil example, the chapter concludes by questioning how public health strategies might address the political contestation of gender, procreation, and sexuality.

III. Reproductive health, politics, and resistance

A third and final aspect of the panel's reasoning also mirrors trends in the field of reproductive rights. Although the decision is dedicated primarily to discussing rights and consensus, it also highlights public health evidence that demonstrates a correlation between restrictive laws and poor health outcomes for women. Unlike rights or comparative examples, public health data provides practical evidence for legal reform and showcases the pitfalls of ignoring reproductive rights. The panel noted, for instance, that 4% of the country's pregnant women die because of

76 Kapur, supra note 74, at 29–32; Obiora, supra note 74 at 369–370 (citing work on "feminist imperialism").

77 Karen Engle described the feminist response to post-colonial critique as "culturally sensitive universalism." Engle writes: "The culturally sensitive universalism . . . failed to respond to the most radical potential of [Third World feminists'] critiques, which was their refusal to separate the cultural from the economic." Karen Engle, "Feminist Governance and International Law: From Liberal Inclusion to Carceral Feminism," in *Governance Feminism: Notes from the Field* 11–12 (Janet Halley et al. eds, 2019).

78 Cyra Akila Choudhury, "Exporting Subjects: Globalizing Family Law Progress through International Human Rights," 32 *Mich. J. Int'l L.* 259, 323 (2011).

79 Rebouché, "Comparative Pragmatism," supra note 67, n. 389.

80 Cf. Kapur, supra note 74, at 29–32 (calling for feminist scholarship that recognises multiple subjectivities and the "peripheral subject" as well as focuses on "moments of resistance" to women's subjugation).

81 Lynn P. Freedman & Stephen L. Isaacs, "Human Rights and Reproductive Choice," 24 *Stud. Fam. Plan.* 18, 27–28 (1993) (noting countries in which the "interplay of state, religious, and customary law" governs abortion and where abortion early in pregnancy is permitted).

complications from unsafe abortions.[82] To offer further proof, the panel cited studies on the worldwide incidence of illegal abortion, published by the World Health Organisation and the US non-profit organisation, the Guttmacher Institute.[83]

Specifically, the panel elaborated on the "social and concrete costs for the health system" of illegal abortion.[84] There are a high number of abortions performed outside of the law's requirements and outside of licensed facilities. According to a census cited by the panel, one in five Brazilian women have an abortion.[85] But, as explained in a 2017 amicus brief submitted to the Supreme Court by Human Rights Watch, "only 37 health services registered by health authorities perform legal abortion in all of Brazil, and . . . seven states do not have any institutions that offer this service."[86] Thus, the majority of the country's abortions, given the shortage of providers and narrow grounds for legal terminations, happen in violation of the law. The panel, in the last pages of the opinion, offered a dire account of clinics operating underground, although seemingly not applicable to the defendants in the case before it: "[P]oor women must resort to either clandestine clinics without any medical infrastructure, or to precarious and primitive amateur procedures, which create high risks of injury, mutilation and death."[87]

In addition to underground clinics, the panel highlighted the "private consumption of pills" to end pregnancy.[88] Decades ago, women in Brazil discovered that Cytotech, an over-the-counter ulcer drug, is misoprostol, which will induce abortion if taken before eight to ten weeks of pregnancy. As in many places, the health effects of self-induced abortion vary, and misoprostol's effectiveness depends on its proper use. In Brazil, maternal mortality rates dropped dramatically with the use of misoprostol.[89] In fact, the prevalence of self-induced abortion prompted the government to take Cytotech off pharmacy shelves.

What emerges from the panel's description of illegal abortion is that Brazil's health care system fails to address women's reproductive health needs, and there are well-known, extra-legal services to meet the demand for termination services. But what is striking about the Brazil opinion, however, are the missing details about the clandestine clinic that police raided or the providers that serviced it. Who were the abortion providers and who were their patients? In reasoning that pre-trial detention was inappropriate, Justice Barroso noted that the defendants were not a flight risk, despite attempting to "flee the scene of the crime," because the defendants "[did] not have any criminal record and are upstanding citizens."[90] That tells the reader little about what this clinic was like: was it makeshift or a permanent fixture of a neighbourhood? Did it meet the sanitary standards of a comparable medical facility or did it present a threat to patient health?

Was the clinic and its providers part of a broader effort to resist the law? Perhaps this clinic was indicative of a well-developed network in a country with changing cultural and religious mores.

82 Habeas Corpus n. 124.306, supra note 1, n. 23.
83 Id. paras. 35–36.
84 Id. para. 44.
85 Debora Diniz et al., "National Abortion Survey 2016", available at www.scielo.br/pdf/csc/v22n2/en_1413-8123-csc-22-02-0653.pdf. The Guttmacher Institute estimates that between 8 to 18% of maternal deaths around the world are due to unsafe abortion, and estimates of the number of abortion-related deaths in 2014 ranged from 22,500 to 44,000. Guttmacher Institute, "Facts on Induced Abortion Worldwide", available at www.guttmacher.org/fact-sheet/facts-induced-abortion-worldwide.
86 Human Rights Watch, supra note 52, at 20.
87 Id. para. 30.
88 Habeas Corpus n. 124.306, supra note 1, para. 36.
89 However, Debora Diniz reports that maternal morbidity rates remain high. Diniz, "The Brazilian Litigation on Abortion", supra note 4, at 5.
90 Habeas Corpus n. 124.306, supra note 1, para. 8.

Opinions about abortion have shifted in Brazil. On the one hand, Brazil has an active anti-abortion lobby: in 2016, there were nineteen bills before the National Congress to revoke grounds for legal abortion or to increase criminal sanctions.[91] On the other hand, polls conducted in 2017 by Catholics for the Right to Decide and a national polling institute revealed that 64% of a representative sample considered that terminating a pregnancy should be the exclusive decision of the woman.[92]

The clinic in controversy and others like it could have been responding to increased demand for abortion because of Zika infections – an epidemic that the panel does not mention. Following the 2015 Zika outbreak in Brazil, there have been 10,867 reported cases of microcephalic births (though only over a fifth of these have been confirmed with half pending evaluation).[93] And the panel's opinion coincides with stakeholders lobbying the legislature to permit pregnancy termination in light of the Zika virus and to decriminalise abortion generally. A 2016 petition asks the Supreme Court of Brazil to provide an exception to criminal abortion laws for pregnant women infected with Zika and in mental distress.[94] In another petition, before the Supreme Court at the time of writing, petitioners (the Socialism and Freedom Party and the Anis Institute of Bioethics) call for the decriminalisation of abortion until the twelfth week of pregnancy.[95] Minister Rosa Weber, a Supreme Court justice on the panel that decided the case discussed in this chapter, was appointed by the court to process this latest petition.[96]

But even the most robust set of rights cannot meet the challenge of accessible services; the problem is one of politics and health policy – how communities and countries decide to allocate social goods and health resources. There is a wellspring of activism in reproductive rights that engages with community and grassroots mobilisation to take on these political considerations.[97] And reproductive rights approaches, working with a commitment to improving low-income women's lives, may not need human rights to accomplish the movement's goals. Although CEDAW and other human rights documents make important statements about autonomy, equality, and dignity, they do not necessarily address deep socio-economic inequality. As Samuel Moyn writes:

> One could imagine one man owning everything – an absolute overlord – and he would not violate the current scheme of human rights, so long as everyone had their basic rights fulfilled. Even perfectly realized human rights are compatible with radical inequality.[98]

91 Diniz, "The Brazilian Litigation on Abortion", supra note 4, at 3. See also Debora Diniz, "A New Ruling in the Brazilian Supreme Court Prior to the Hearing on the Zika Submission," *Abortion News Info*, 6 Dec. 2016, available at abortion-news.info/tag/debora-diniz/ (noting "a number of regressive bills are pending for a final vote" and "as soon as the news of [the panel's] opinions was made public, members of the House of Representatives created a committee whose aims was [sic] to contest the judgment").

92 "International Campaign for Women's Right to Safe Abortion," supra note 70.

93 Id. at 6.

94 In addition, the petition asks the Supreme Court to require the government to provide information on the risks of Zika, distribute family planning methods, guarantee access to transportation to health services, and provide a cash benefit equivalent to the minimum wage to affected households. Diniz, "The Brazilian Litigation on Abortion", supra note 4, at 7–8.

95 See "International Campaign for Women's Right to Safe Abortion," supra note 70.

96 Justice Weber requested arrests, police inquiries, and judicial proceedings under criminal laws be suspended while the current case before the Supreme Court is decided. Id.

97 Reproductive justice materials call for community lawyering that can provide social benefits for low-income women. See Sarah London, "Reproductive Justice: Developing a Lawyering Model," 13 *Berkeley J. Afr.-Am. L. & Pol'y* 71, 80, 97–101 (2011). See, e.g., Jackie Calmes, "Activists Help Pay for Patients' Travel to Shrinking Number of Abortion Clinics," *N.Y. Times*, 27 Nov. 2014, available at www.nytimes.com/2014/11/28/us/advocates-help-pay-for-travel-to-a-shrinking-number-of-abortion-clinics.html.

98 Samuel Moyn, "Human Rights and the Age of Inequality," *OpenDemocracy* (27 Oct. 2015), available at www.opendemocracy.net/openglobalrights/samuel-moyn/human-rights-and-age-of-inequality.

Advocates need to weigh the costs and limits of human rights advocacy. As the conclusion suggests, rights-based approaches sometimes will be the best avenues to change; in other instances, different tactics and frames will be necessary to achieve distributive and social justice goals.

Conclusion

Persuasive justifications for abortion law reform are not necessarily rooted in fundamental rights to autonomy or equality, but in the reality that pregnant women, across class lines and across the country, have contracted Zika with difficult to predict consequences. The current call for safe, accessible abortion in Brazil not only highlights the country's constrained recognition of women's reproductive rights, but it also, and as importantly, highlights the shortcomings of a health system that may be unprepared to provide adequate reproductive health services.

A view of the health care system at work (both the formal and informal services available to women) implicates, too, the many reproductive health issues outside of abortion. So although the focus of this chapter has been abortion law reform, conversations about the termination of pregnancies are bound up in and related to accessible contraceptives, sex education, maternal care – the spectrum of reproductive justice.[99] And to be sure, the panel of the Supreme Court recognised those interconnections in the cases analysed here: the panel lists the variety of ways in which individuals' reproductive health can be protected and promoted, such as better childcare, sex education, free contraceptives.[100] This discussion mirrors the ICPD's call for a stronger social safety net to meet an array of women's and men's reproductive needs.

What may be missing from the panel's opinion is how the various justifications it offers for advancing women's reproductive rights – promoting women's fundamental human rights, aligning with the "democratic and developed world," and protecting women's health – fit together given the context of Brazil's reproductive health infrastructure. Reproductive rights, as articulated by the panel and under the country's current abortion law, may not assist Zika-infected women, who learn late in pregnancy that the foetuses they carry have developed a fatal condition. But perhaps that is the limitation of human rights or transnational consensus. Strategies to address the context in which reproductive rights are exercised, as well as the realities of healthcare provision across income levels and locations, may not need to begin with rights, but rather with the assessment of a country's health policies in practice.[101]

Bibliography

Barroso, Luís Roberto. "Bringing Abortion into the Brazilian Public Debate: Legal Strategies for Anencephalic Pregnancy," in *Abortion Law in Transnational Perspective: Cases and Controversies* (Rebecca J. Cook, Joanna N. Erdmann & Bernard M. Dickens eds, Philadelphia, University of Pennsylvania Press, 2014) 258.

Beltrán y Puga, Alma. "Paradigmatic Changes in Gender Justice: The Advancement of Reproductive Rights in International Human Rights Law," 3 *Creighton Int'l & Comp. L.J.* 158 (2012).

Berer, Marge. "The Cairo 'Compromise' on Abortion and its Consequences for Making Abortion Safe and Legal," in *Reproductive Health and Human Rights: The Way Forward* (Laura Reichenbach & Mindy Jane Roseman eds, Philadelphia, University of Pennsylvania Press, 2009) 152.

Blair, D. Marianne, Weiner, Merle H., Stark, Barbara & Maldonado, Solangel *Family Law in the World Community: Cases, Materials, and Problems in Comparative and International Family Law* (Durham, Carolina Academic Press, 2nd edn 2003).

99 Human Rights Watch, supra note 52, at 25.
100 Habeas Corpus n. 124.306, supra note 1, para. 42.
101 Lindsay F. Wiley, "Health Law as Social Justice," 24 *Cornell J. L. & Pub. Pol'y* 47, 74 (2014).

Brems, Eva. "Enemies or Allies? Feminism and Cultural Relativism as Dissident Voices in Human Rights Discourse," 19 *Hum. Rts. Q.* 136 (1997).

Charlesworth, Hilary, Chinkin, Christine & Wright, Shelley. "Feminist Approaches to International Law: Reflections from Another Century," in *International Law: Modern Feminist Approaches* (Doris Buss & Ambreena Manji eds, Oxford, Hart Publishing, 2005) 17.

Choudhury, Cyra Akila. "Exporting Subjects: Globalizing Family Law Progress through International Human Rights," 32 *Mich. J. Int'l L.* 259 (2011).

Cook, Rebecca J. & Dickens, Bernard M. "Human Rights Dynamics of Abortion Law Reform," 25 *Hum. Rts. Q.* 1 (2003).

Copelon, Rhonda. "Remarks of Rhonda Copelon," 44 *Am. U. L. Rev.* 1253 (1995).

Diniz, Debora. "The Architecture of a Constitutional Case in Three Acts – Anencephaly at the Brazilian Supreme Court," 1 *U. Brasília L.J.* 155 (2016).

Engle, Karen. "Feminist Governance and International Law: From Liberal Inclusion to Carceral Feminism," in *Governance Feminism: Notes from the Field* (Janet E. Halley, Prabha Kotiswaran, Rachel Rebouché & Hila Shamir eds, University of Minnesota Press, 2019).

Ernst, Julia L., Katzive, Laura & Smock, Erica. "The Global Pattern of U.S. Initiatives Curtailing Women's Reproductive Rights: A Perspective on the Increasingly Anti-Choice Mosaic," 6 *U. Pa. J. Const. L.* 752 (2004).

Freedman, Lynn P. & Isaacs, Stephen L. "Human Rights and Reproductive Choice," 24 *Stud. Fam. Plan.* 18 (1993).

Germain, Adrienne & Kim, Theresa. *Expanding Access to Safe Abortion: Strategies for Action* (New York, The International Women's Health Coalition, 1998).

Halley, Janet & Rittich, Kerry. "Critical Directions in Comparative Family Law: Genealogies and Contemporary Studies of Family Law Exceptionalism," 58 *Am. J. Comp. L.* 753 (2010).

Johnson, Paula C. & Obiora, L. Amede. "How Does the Universal Declaration of Human Rights Protect African Women?," 26 *Syracuse J. Int'l L. & Com.* 195 (1999).

Kapur, Ratna. "The Tragedy of Victimization Rhetoric: Resurrecting the 'Native' Subject in International/Post-Colonial Feminist Legal Politics," 15 *Harv. Hum. Rts. J.* 1 (2002).

Lewis, Hope. "Embracing Complexity: Human Rights in Critical Race Feminist Perspective," 12 *Colum. J. Gender & L.* 510 (2003).

London, Sarah. "Reproductive Justice: Developing a Lawyering Model," 13 *Berkeley J. Afr.-Am. L. & Pol'y* 71 (2011).

Merry, Sally Engle. "Human Rights and Transnational Culture: Regulating Gender Violence through Global Law," 44 *Osgoode Hall L.J.* 53 (2006).

Miller, Alice M., Kismödi, Eszter, Cottingham, Jane & Gruskin, Sofia. "Sexual Rights as Human Rights: A Guide to Authoritative Sources and Principles for Applying Human Rights to Sexuality and Sexual Health," 23 *Repro. Health Matters* 16 (2015).

Miller, Alice M., Gruskin, Sofia, Cottingham, Jane & Kismödi, Eszter. "Sound and Fury – Engaging with the Politics and the Law of Sexual Rights," 23 *Reproductive Health Matters* 7 (2015).

Moyn, Samuel. *The Last Utopia: Human Rights in History* (Cambridge, Harvard University Press, 2012).

Narayan, Uma. "Minds of Their Own: Choices, Autonomy, Cultural Practices, and Other Women," in *A Mind of One's Own: Feminist Essays on Reason and Objectivity* (Boulder, Westview Press, Louise M. Antony & Charlotte E. Witt eds, 2nd edn 2002) 418.

Northup, Nancy. "Reproductive Rights at Home and Abroad," 15 *C.U.N.Y. L. Rev.* 265 (2012).

Obiora, L. Amede. "Feminism, Globalization, and Culture: After Beijing," 4 *Ind. J. Global Legal Stud.* 355 (1997).

Puppinck, Grégor. "Abortion in European Law: Human Rights, Social Rights, and the New Cultural Trend," 4 *Ave Maria Int'l L.J.* 29 (2015).

Rebouché, Rachel. "Abortion Rights as Human Rights," 25 *Soc. Leg. Stud.* 765 (2016).

Rebouché, Rachel. "Comparative Pragmatism," 72 *Md. L. Rev.* 85 (2012).

Rebouché, Rachel. "Reproducing Rights: The Intersection of Reproductive Justice and Human Rights," 7 *U.C. Irvine. L. Rev.* 579 (2017).

Reichenbach, Laura. "The Global Reproductive Health and Rights Agenda: Opportunities and Challenges for the Future," in *Reproductive Health and Human Rights: The Way Forward* (Laura Reichenbach & Mindy Jane Roseman eds, Philadelphia, University of Pennsylvania Press, 2009) 21.

Sanger, Carol. *About Abortion: Terminating Pregnancy in Twenty-First Century America* (Cambridge, Harvard University Press, 2017).

Siegel, Reva B. "Dignity and Sexuality: Claims on Dignity in Transnational Debates over Abortion and Same-sex Marriage," 10 *Int'l J. Const. L.* 355 (2012).
Siegel, Reva B. "The Constitutionalization of Abortion," in *The Oxford Handbook of Comparative Constitutional Law* (Michel Rosenfeld & András Sajó eds, Oxford University Press, 2012) 1057.
Soohoo, Cynthia & Stolz, Suzanne. "Bringing Theories of Human Rights Change Home," 77 *Fordham L. Rev.* 459 (2008).
Stark, Barbara. "When Globalization Hits Home: International Family Law Comes of Age," 39 *Vand. J. Transnat'l L.* 1551 (2006).
Wiley, Lindsay F. "Health Law as Social Justice," 24 *Cornell J. L. & Pub. Pol'y* 47 (2014).
Zampas, Christina & Gher, Jaime M. "Abortion as a Human Right – International and Regional Standards," 8 *Hum. Rts. L. Rev.* 249 (2008).

14
Surrogacy

Philipp M. Reuss

Introduction

In recent years, surrogacy has become a focal point of discussion both in academia and by the public. Sparked by media reports on celebrities like Elton John[1] and Kim Kardashian,[2] who have entered into contracts with surrogate mothers to bear their children, and fuelled by reports on cases such as Baby Gammy,[3] where Australian intended parents of twins refused to take responsibility for one twin suffering from Down syndrome, a lively debate on the admissibility of surrogacy practices, their altruistic or commercial nature, and methods of safeguarding the rights of the affected parties has developed. Supporters and opponents of a liberal approach towards surrogacy seem to be fiercely fighting with each other. The amount of academic literature on the matter is enormous.[4]

1 Daily Mail Reporter "Last of the Big Spenders! Elton John 'paid £20,000' to Surrogate Mother for Giving Birth to Second Son Elijah", available at www.dailymail.co.uk/tvshowbiz/article-2265463/Elton-John-paid-20-000-surrogate-mother-giving-birth-second-son-Elijah.html (last accessed 25 Oct. 2017).

2 Nola Ojomu and Joanne Kavanagh "Star Baby. When was Kim Kardashian and Kanye West's Baby Girl Born, Who was their Surrogate and Why's She Named Chicago?", available at www.thesun.co.uk/tvandshowbiz/4411458/kim-kardashian-kanye-west-baby-surrogate-name-date-confirmed/ (last accessed 25 Oct. 2017).

3 Kathy Marks "Baby Gammy: Australian Father who Abandoned Down Syndrome Surrogate Child now Tries to Access Funds Donated for his Care", available at www.independent.co.uk/news/world/australasia/baby-gammy-australian-father-who-abandoned-down-syndrome-surrogate-child-now-tries-to-access-funds-10261916.html (last accessed 25 Oct. 2017).

4 See e.g. recent doctoral theses: Stoll, *Surrogacy Arrangements and Legal Parenthood – Swedish Law in a Comparative Context*, (2013); Bertschi, *Leihmutterschaft – Theorie, Praxis und rechtliche Perspektiven in der Schweiz, den USA und Indien*, (2014); Diel, *Leihmutterschaft und Reproduktionstourismus*, (2014); Lammers, *Leihmutterschaft in Deutschland – Rechtfertigen die Menschenwürde und das Kindeswohl ein striktes Verbot?*, (2016); Lederer, *Grenzenloser Kinderwunsch – Leihmutterschaft im nationalen, europäischen und globalen rechtlichen Spannungsfeld*, (2016); Duden, *Leihmutterschaft im Internationalen Privat- und Verfahrensrecht*, (2015); Thomale, *Mietmutterschaft*, (2015); Voss, *Leihmutterschaft in Deutschland – Rechtliche Folgen und Verfassungsmäßigkeit des Verbotes*, (2015); Sitter, *Grenzüberschreitende Leihmutterschaft – Eine Untersuchung des materiellen und internationalen Abstammungsrechts Deutschlands und der USA*, (2017).

This chapter will examine surrogacy practices in detail. Following a brief overview of the origins of, forms of and recent data on surrogacy practices, the chapter will outline the human rights framework influencing the regulation of surrogacy and the implications for the parties involved. The chapter will further examine existing national approaches towards surrogacy arrangements that take place within national borders and approaches towards the recognition of surrogacy in cross-border settings. Finally, the chapter will take a view on ways to tackle related concerns and problems in the future.

Origins of, forms of and recent data on surrogacy practices

Origins

Surrogacy is not a new phenomenon. Relevant practices can be traced far back in time. Forms of surrogacy even appear in the Bible with respect to the stories of Jacob, Leah and Rachel and their children (Genesis 29, 1–30 and Genesis 30, 1–24) and Abram, Sarai and Hagar (Genesis 16, 1–16),[5] where surrogate mothers helped to overcome (temporary) infertility of the intended mothers and thus secured the family line that was to be continued. In modern times, surrogacy practices have been promoted primarily through achievements in assisted reproductive technology. The first leading cases, such as *Baby M.*[6] and *Baby Cotton*,[7] date back to the 1980s and were decided shortly after the birth of the first in vitro fertilisation (IVF) baby, Louise Brown, in 1978. The possibilities of ovum donation and IVF, in particular, enable women who cannot bear children due to medical reasons to become parents of genetically related children. Furthermore, surrogacy arrangements facilitate the way to parenthood for male same-sex partners and single persons.

Recent data

Although, nowadays, a considerable number of states permit surrogacy practices, it is far from clear how many surrogacy arrangements are undertaken each year. Sound statistical data is absent. Although the number of cases will presumably be significantly lower than the general number of assisted reproductions,[8] the sheer number of cases dealing with the recognition of cross-border surrogacy shows that surrogacy arrangements are far from being marginal. Approximately 10,000 cases are estimated to take place per year (worldwide).[9]

Recent analysis of intended parents' motivations for undertaking surrogacy show that in most cases surrogacy is the last resort to fulfil the intended parents' desire to have children. In many cases, intended parents have undergone a long process of reproductive treatment (7.5 years on average) that has finally proven unsuccessful. In the vast majority of cases, medical reasons are

5 See e.g. Coester, in Mansel et al. (eds), *Festschrift für Erik Jayme*, (2004) 1243. For further historic traces of surrogacy, see Lederer, *Grenzenloser Kinderwunsch – Leihmutterschaft im nationalen, europäischen und globalen rechtlichen Spannungsfeld*, (2016) 31 *et seq.*; Bertschi, *Leihmutterschaft – Theorie, Praxis und rechtliche Perspektiven in der Schweiz, den USA und Indien*, (2014) 5 *et seq.* (Hinduism); Lammers, *Leihmutterschaft in Deutschland – Rechtfertigen die Menschenwürde und das Kindeswohl ein striktes Verbot?*, (2016) 40 *et seq.* (Christianity, Judaism, Hinduism, Islam).

6 *In the matter of Baby M.*, 109 N.J. 396 (N.J. 1988).

7 *Re C. (A Minor) (Wardship: Surrogacy)*, (1985) Fam. Law 191.

8 For figures (that are far from comprehensive), see the publications of the European Society of Human Reproduction and Embryology available at www.eshre.eu (last accessed 27 Oct. 2017).

9 *MüKoBGB*/Wellenhofer, § 1591 para. 31; see Dethloff, *JuristenZeitung* (2014) 922 for further references.

present.[10] Thus, surrogacy nowadays mainly serves persons who cannot have children on their own by fulfilling their deeply rooted desire for parenthood. There is, however, a very small minority of cases where contracts are concluded with surrogate mothers for different reasons (for example the avoidance of detrimental effects on the body due to pregnancy).[11]

Forms of surrogacy

Different forms of surrogacy may be distinguished:[12] First, surrogacy may involve the surrogate mother's ovum being used for the (natural or medically assisted) conception of the child. This form of surrogacy is called *traditional surrogacy*,[13] because the surrogate mother is – as has traditionally been the case, that is, before the above-mentioned methods of assisted reproduction were developed – both the birth mother and the genetic mother of the child. The second form of surrogacy occurs in cases where the birth mother is not genetically related to the child because either the intended mother's ovum or a donor's ovum is used. This form of surrogacy is called *gestational surrogacy*.[14] In this category, the surrogate mother only has a biological link to the child by giving birth to the child. Countries that allow surrogacy practices tend to favour gestational surrogacy over traditional surrogacy as the absent genetic link of surrogate mother and child reduces the risk that the surrogate will refuse to hand over the child after birth.[15]

Categorisation may also be undertaken with respect to the persons who enter into a contract with a surrogate mother to bear their children. These persons are generally called *intended* or *commissioning parents*.[16] Intended parents may be categorised as genetically related or not genetically related to the child. The former is the case if gametes (that is, ovum and semen) of both intended parents are used for the child's conception. The latter is the case if the genetic material is completely supplied by donors. Also, mixed forms exist where only one of the intended parents is genetically related to the child and the other gamete is supplied by a donor or the surrogate mother. This is very likely to happen when same-sex partners enter into a contract with a surrogate mother.

10 MacCullum et al., 18 *Human Reproduction* (2003) 1334, 1336; Blyth, 13 *Journal of Reproductive and Infant Psychology* (1995) 185, 188. See also the report of an intended mother Meyer-Spendler, in Weller and Ditzen (eds), *Leihmutterschaft – Aktuelle Entwicklungen und interdisziplinäre Herausforderungen*, (2018) (forthcoming), 24 *et seq.* For possible medical reasons, see Voss, *Leihmutterschaft in Deutschland – Rechtliche Folgen und Verfassungsmäßigkeit des Verbotes*, (2015) 13 *et seq.*

11 Jadva, in Golombok et al. (eds), *Regulating Reproductive Donation*, (2016) 126, 131; Lederer, *Grenzenloser Kinderwunsch – Leihmutterschaft im nationalen, europäischen und globalen rechtlichen Spannungsfeld*, (2016) 30; Bertschi, *Leihmutterschaft – Theorie, Praxis und rechtliche Perspektiven in der Schweiz, den USA und Indien*, (2014) 90 *et seq.*

12 See Coester, in Mansel et al. (eds), *Festschrift für Erik Jayme*, (2004) 1243; Dethloff, *JuristenZeitung* (2014) 922, 923; Bertschi, *Leihmutterschaft – Theorie, Praxis und rechtliche Perspektiven in der Schweiz, den USA und Indien*, (2014) 7 *et seq.*; Lammers, *Leihmutterschaft in Deutschland – Rechtfertigen die Menschenwürde und das Kindeswohl ein striktes Verbot?*, (2016) 26 *et seq.*; Sitter, *Grenzüberschreitende Leihmutterschaft – Eine Untersuchung des materiellen und internationalen Abstammungsrechts Deutschlands und der USA*, (2017) 32 *et seq.*; Bleisch, 17 *Jahrbuch für Wissenschaft und Ethik* (2012) 5, 8.

13 Jadva, in Golombok et al. (eds), *Regulating Reproductive Donation*, (2016) 126; the German expression is "Ersatzmutter": see Dethloff, *Familienrecht*, (2015) § 10 para. 71; Lederer, *Grenzenloser Kinderwunsch – Leihmutterschaft im nationalen, europäischen und globalen rechtlichen Spannungsfeld*, (2016) 27.

14 Jadva, in Golombok et al. (eds), *Regulating Reproductive Donation*, (2016) 126; the German expression is "Leihmutterschaft": see Dethloff, *Familienrecht*, (2015) § 10 para. 71; Lederer, *Grenzenloser Kinderwunsch – Leihmutterschaft im nationalen, europäischen und globalen rechtlichen Spannungsfeld*, (2016) 28.

15 Funcke, *Neue Zeitschrift für Familienrecht* (2016) 207, 208.

16 Jadva, in Golombok et al. (eds), *Regulating Reproductive Donation*, (2016) 126, 127; the German term is "Wunscheltern".

Human rights and surrogacy practices

Human rights framework

Surrogacy concerns a plurality of different guarantees of human rights laws at national and international level. Not all of them can be examined here in detail. Of great importance, however, are the guarantees of the European Convention on Human Rights and Fundamental Freedoms (ECHR)[17] and the United Nations Convention on the Rights of the Child (CRC)[18] on which some light is shed below.

Protection of private and family life, Article 8 of the ECHR

The legal relationship between parents and their children falls within the ambit of the protection of private and family life in article 8(1) of the ECHR.[19] The relationship is generally covered by the notion of private life, which contains important aspects of one's personal identity.[20]

The parent – child relationship further falls within the notion of family life if a close personal relationship between the parent and the child actually exists.[21] It does not matter whether – besides the existence of such relationship – there is also a genetic or biological link between the parent and the child or whether the parent is also a legal parent. Article 8(1) of the ECHR protects the existing *de facto* family.[22] Furthermore, to apply the notion of family life, a factual family life need not necessarily already exist. Although the European Court of Human Rights (ECtHR) constantly reiterates that article 8(1) of the ECHR presupposes the existence of family life and does not cover family formation,[23] the case law on this question is not entirely consistent. Contrary to

17 European Convention for the Protection of Human Rights and Fundamental Freedoms of 4 Nov. 1950, available at www.echr.coe.int/Documents/Convention_ENG.pdf (last accessed 27 Oct. 2017).

18 United Nations Convention on the Rights of the Child of 20 Nov. 1989, available at www.ohchr.org/EN/ProfessionalInterest/Pages/CRC.aspx (last accessed 27 Oct. 2017).

19 ECtHR, Judgment of 21 Dec. 2010–20578/07 (*Anayo v. Germany*), *Neue Juristische Wochenschrift* (2011) 3565, 3566. See in detail *BeckOGK*/Reuss, § 1598a BGB para. 14; Pintens, *Zeitschrift für das gesamte Familienrecht* (2016) 341. See also Cottier and Wyttenbach, *Die Praxis des Familienrechts* (2016) 75 *et seq.*

20 ECtHR, Judgment of 21 Dec. 2010–20578/07 (*Anayo v. Germany*), *Neue Juristische Wochenschrift* 2011, 3565, 3566; ECtHR, Judgment of 15 Sept. 2011–17080/07 (*Schneider v. Germany*), *Neue Juristische Wochenschrift* (2012) 2781, 2784.

21 ECtHR, Judgment of 21 Dec. 2010–20578/07 (*Anayo v. Germany*), *Neue Juristische Wochenschrift* (2011) 3565, 3566; ECtHR, Judgment of 26 May 1994–16969/90 (*Keegan v. Ireland*), available at hudoc.echr.coe.int/sites/eng/pages/search.aspx?i=001–57881 (last accessed 6 March 2018), 14; ECtHR, Judgment of 27 Oct. 1994–18535/91 (*Kroon et al. v. The Netherlands*), available at hudoc.echr.coe.int/sites/eng/pages/search.aspx?i=001–57904 (last accessed 6 March 2018), 12; ECtHR, Decision of 18 March 2008–33375/03 (*Hülsmann v. Germany*), *Neue Juristische Wochenschrift-RR* (2009) 1585; ECtHR, Judgment of 22 March 2012–23338/09 (*Kautzor v. Germany*), *Neue Juristische Wochenschrift* (2013) 1937; ECtHR, Judgment of 19 Feb. 2013–19010/07 (*X. et al. v. Österreich*), *Neue Juristische Wochenschrift* (2013) 2173; ECtHR, Decision of 7 May 2013–8017/11 (*B. and G.B. v. Germany*), *Zeitschrift für das gesamte Familienrecht* 2014, 97. See also Crowley, in Atkin (ed.), *The International Survey of Family Law* 2015 edn, (2015) 54.

22 ECtHR, Judgment of 21 Dec. 2010–20578/07 (*Anayo v. Germany*), *Neue Juristische Wochenschrift* (2011) 3565; ECtHR, Judgment of 24 June 2010–30141/04 (*Schalk and Kopf v. Österreich*), available at www.refworld.org/cases,ECHR,4c29fa712.html (last accessed 9 March 2018).

23 ECtHR, Judgment of 24 Jan. 2017 – No. 25358/12 (*Paradiso and Campanelli v. Italy*), available at hudoc.echr.coe.int/eng?i=001–170359 (last accessed 8 Oct. 2017); ECtHR, Judgment of 26 Feb. 2002 – No. 36515/97 (*Frette v. France*), available at hudoc.echr.coe.int/eng?i=001–60168 (last accessed 8 Oct. 2017) para. 32; ECtHR, Judgment of 22 Jan. 2008 – No. 43546/02 (*E.B. v. France*), available at hudoc.echr.coe.int/eng?i=001–84571 (last accessed 8 Oct. 2017) para. 41; art. 12 of the ECHR explicitly covers family formation but does not apply to single persons and unmarried couples: see ECtHR, Judgment of 13 Dec. 2007 – No. 39051/03 (*Emonet et al. v. Schweiz*), available at hudoc.echr.coe.int/eng?i=001–83992 (last accessed 8 Oct. 2017) para. 92.

the findings just cited, the notion of family life is also applied to the sphere of assisted reproduction and thus to aspects of family formation.[24] Furthermore, according to the jurisprudence of the ECtHR the notion of family life may also be applicable under certain circumstances where a close personal relationship between the parent and his or her child has not yet been established but its establishment is clearly intended.[25] This leads to the conclusion that the intention to become a parent of a child by establishing close personal ties in the future may also be protected under the notion of family life in article 8(1) of the ECHR. However, the ECtHR recently clarified its jurisprudence in a case concerning cross-border surrogacy. It stated that the intent of parents to create a close personal relationship with a child may, in the absence of biological ties or a recognised legal tie, be regarded as family life only if the factual family life has somehow materialised.[26] Six to eight months of an existing factual parent – child relationship were held not to be sufficient to constitute family life.[27] Therefore, an intended, not-yet-sufficiently-materialised family life between a non-genetic, non-biological or non-legal parent and a child may only be protected under the notion of private life within article 8(1) of the ECHR.

Article 8(1) of the ECHR, among others, protects the interest of the parents and the child to have their respective parent – child relationship legally established.[28] This for example means that the interest of intended parents also to become the legal parents of the child and the interest of the child also to become the legal child of the intended parents are generally safeguarded by article 8(1) of the ECHR (either under the notion of private life or under the notion of family life). This does not mean, however, that states are under all circumstances obliged to allow surrogacy practices at national level or to recognise legal parent – child relationships that have been established under application of foreign laws permitting surrogacy. The protection of private

24 ECtHR, Judgment of 3 Nov. 2011 – No. 57813/00 (*S.H. et al. v. Österreich*), available at hudoc.echr.coe.int/eng?i=001–107325 para. 82. See Coester-Waltjen, in Wiesemann and Simon (eds), *Patientenautonomie*, (2013) 222, 225 for further references.

25 For example: ECtHR, Judgment of 26 May 1994–16969/90 (*Keegan v. Ireland*), available at hudoc.echr.coe.int/sites/eng/pages/search.aspx?i=001–57881 (last accessed 6 March 2018), 15; ECtHR, Decision of 29 June 1999–27110/95 (*Nylund v. Finnland*), available at hudoc.echr.coe.int/sites/eng/pages/search.aspx?i=001–21999 (last accessed 6 March 2018), 14; ECtHR, Judgment of 22 June 2004 – No. 78028/01 et al. (*Pini v. Romania*), available at hudoc.echr.coe.int/eng?i=001–61837 (last accessed 6 March 2018) para. 143; ECtHR, Decision of 18 March 2008–33375/03 (*Hülsmann v. Germany*), *Neue Juristische Wochenschrift-RR* (2009) 1585; ECtHR, Judgment of 21 Dec. 2010–20578/07 (*Anayo v. Germany*), *Neue Juristische Wochenschrift* (2011) 3565; ECtHR, Judgment of 22 March 2012–23338/09 (*Kautzor v. Germany*), *Neue Juristische Wochenschrift* (2013) 1937; ECtHR, Judgment of 5 June 2014 – No. 31021/08 (*I.S. v. Germany*), available at hudoc.echr.coe.int/eng?i=001–146785 (last accessed 5 Sept. 2017); ECtHR, Decision of 19 June 2003 – No. 46165/99 (*Nekvedavcius v. Germany*), available at hudoc.echr.coe.int/eng?i=001–23277 (last accessed 5 Sept. 2017).

26 ECtHR, Judgment of 24 Jan. 2017 – No. 25358/12 (*Paradiso and Campanelli v. Italy*), available at hudoc.echr.coe.int/eng?i=001–170359 (last accessed 8 Oct. 2017). For criticism, see Duden, *Zeitschrift für das gesamte Familienrecht* (2017) 445, 446; the ECtHR will soon rule again on the matter: see accepted request by the French Cour de Cassation for advisory opinion in a surrogacy case, 16 October 2018.

27 For a critique according to the well-established findings of psychological research, see Reuss, *Theorie eines Elternschaftsrechts*, (2018) ch. 3 B.II.1.a.; Sanders, *Neue Juristische Wochenschrift* (2017) 925, 926.

28 ECtHR, Judgment of 18 Feb. 2014 – No. 28609/08 (*A.L. v. Poland*), available at hudoc.echr.coe.int/eng?i=001–140920 (last accessed 6 March 2018), 10; ECtHR, Judgment of 12 Jan. 2006 – No. 26111/02 (*Mizzi v. Malta*), available at hudoc.echr.coe.int/sites/eng/pages/search.aspx?i=001–71983 (last accessed 6 March 2018), 21; similarly ECtHR, Judgment of 15 Sept. 2011–17080/07 (*Schneider v. Germany*), *Neue Juristische Wochenschrift* 2012, 2781; ECtHR, Judgment of 28 Nov. 1984 – No. 9/1983/65/100 (*Rasmussen*), *Neue Juristische Wochenschrift* 1986, 2176; ECtHR, Judgment of 7 May 2009 – No. 3451/05 (*Kalcheva v. Russia*), available at hudoc.echr.coe.int/eng?i=001–92572 (last accessed 5 Sept. 2017) paras. 28–30. See also Singer, in Boele-Woelki et al. (eds), *Family Law and Culture in Europe*, (2014) 137, 139 et seq. (positive right to parents).

and family life may be restricted according to article 8(2) of the ECHR if this is necessary in a democratic society in the interests of national security, public safety or the economic well-being of the country, for the prevention of disorder or crime, for the protection of health or morals, or for the protection of the rights and freedoms of others. With respect to surrogacy, states are awarded a wide margin of appreciation as to how to fulfil their duties under article 8 of the ECHR, because surrogacy practices involve difficult ethical questions and a consensus among the ECHR member states on how surrogacy shall be treated is generally lacking.[29] The ECtHR has not yet ruled on the question of whether there is under certain circumstances a violation of article 8 of the ECHR by generally prohibiting surrogacy at national level. There is, however, some case law on the recognition of legal parent – child relationships in cross-border surrogacy settings.

Two strands of jurisprudence may be distinguished:[30] In cases where at least one intended parent is genetically related to the child, the ECtHR has found that the refusal to recognise the legal parent – child relationship may not be justified and thus violates the private life of the child (not of the parents!).[31] In cases, however, where a genetic link between the intended parents and the child is absent, the Grand Chamber has – without considering the child's interests in detail – denied such violation.[32] Considering the position of the child, the fact of being genetically related to the intended parents seems an arbitrary dividing line. The child has no influence whatsoever on the circumstances of his or her procreation. It is therefore not entirely convincing when the ECtHR considers the *intended parents'* decision to choose a particular way of conceiving the child as having a detrimental effect on the rights of the *child.*[33] Furthermore, the child's interest to have parents in the legal sense, who are willing and able to care for him or her is present regardless of whether the parents are the child's genetic parents or not. From the child's perspective, it is not an option to regard the surrogate mother as the child's legal parent as she normally will not be willing to care for the child.[34] The non-existence of a genetic link thus seems not to be a feasible justification of the interference with the child's rights under article 8(1) of the ECHR.

Best interest of the child, Article 3, Article 18 of the CRC

One of the major concerns of family law in general is the best interest of the child. Children are the weakest parties to family relations and thus have a particular interest in being protected. This is especially true in surrogacy cases, which are mainly focussed on the child's creation. On the

29 ECtHR, Judgment of 26 June 2014 – No. 65192/11 (*Mennesson v. France*), *Zeitschrift für das gesamte Familienrecht* (2014) 1525.

30 See also Duden, *Zeitschrift für das gesamte Familienrecht* (2017) 445, 446. In contrast, see Swiss Federal Supreme Court, Judgment of 14 Sept. 2015–5A 443/2014, *Das Standesamt* (2016) 179.

31 ECtHR, Judgment of 26 June 2014 – No. 65192/11 (*Mennesson v. France*), *Zeitschrift für das gesamte Familienrecht* (2014) 1525; ECtHR, Judgment of 26 June 2014 – No. 65941/11 (*Labassée v. France*), *Zeitschrift für das gesamte Familienrecht* (2014) 1525.

32 ECtHR, Judgment of 24 Jan. 2017 – No. 25358/12 (*Paradiso and Campanelli v. Italy*), available at hudoc.echr.coe.int/eng?i=001–170359 (last accessed 8 Oct. 2017); in contrast, see the chamber judgment of the ECtHR, Judgment of 27 Jan. 2015 – No. 25358/12 (*Paradiso and Campanelli v. Italy*), available at hudoc.echr.coe.int/eng?i=001–150770 (last accessed 8 Oct. 2017). For another surrogacy case, see ECtHR, Decision of 8 July 2014 – No. 29176/13 (*D. et al. v. Belgium*), available at hudoc.echr.coe.int/eng?i=001–155182 (last accessed 10 Oct. 2017).

33 Dethloff, *JuristenZeitung* (2014) 922, 931.

34 Henrich, in Hofer et al. (eds), *Perspektiven des Familienrechts*, (2005) 1141, 1151; Duden, *Leihmutterschaft im Internationalen Privat- und Verfahrensrecht*, (2015) 61 *et seq.*; Duden, *Das Standesamt* (2017) 225, 227.

human rights level, the best interest of the child is highlighted especially by articles 3 and 18 of the CRC, but it is also guaranteed under the ECHR.[35]

Article 3 of the CRC provides that in all actions concerning children the best interest of the child shall be a primary consideration. Consequently, member states are obliged to ensure the child such protection and care as is necessary for his or her well-being, and to take all appropriate legislative and administrative measures to this end. If the best interest of the child is a primary consideration, the question inevitably arises how the term has to be understood.[36] On the one hand, the best interest of the child may be regarded as a *maximal standard* endeavouring the optimal outcome for the child him- or herself. On the other hand, it may be understood as a *minimal standard* protecting the child from grave detriments to his or her well-being (ethical minimum standard).[37] In liberal societies, the best interest of a child may only be understood as the latter.[38] Who else than the individual him- or herself may determine exactly how the optimum shall be framed? There is no such thing as a unified society's optimum that every individual has to strive for.

Articles 3 and 18 of the CRC thus oblige the state to protect the child from grave detriments to his or her well-being. This obligation encompasses, in the first place, ensuring that a child may be cared for by parents. This brings about the necessity of making the establishment of a legal parent – child relationship possible for persons who are willing and able to care for the child.[39] Furthermore, the minimal standard also comprises, as the CRC points out in article 35 and in the Second Optional Protocol to the CRC on the sale of children, child prostitution and child pornography, that a state has to take appropriate measures to prevent the sale of children. Children are not goods that can be sold for any agreed sum by one person to another. When regulating surrogacy practices, it has to be ensured that children are not made subject to contracts.

Right to know one's parents, Article 7 of the CRC and Article 8(1) of the ECHR

Furthermore, surrogacy concerns the right of the child to know his or her genetic origins. As surrogacy practices often involve techniques of assisted reproduction and the use of donor gametes, the persons caring for the child as social parents are not in every case the child's genetic parents. The interest of the child to know who his or her genetic parents are then becomes vital. According to the findings of developmental psychology, knowledge of one's genetic origins

35 For example see ECtHR, Judgment of 5 Dec. 2002 – No. 28422/95 (*Hoppe v. Germany*), available at hudoc.echr.coe.int/eng?i=001–139193 (last accessed 8 Oct. 2017) para.48.

36 See Coester, *Das Kindeswohl als Rechtsbegriff*, (1983) 171, 173 *et seq.* See also with regard to assisted reproduction in general Coester-Waltjen, in Ständige Deputation des Deutschen Juristentages (ed.), *Verhandlungen des 56. Deutschen Juristentages*, (1986) 9, B 45 *et seq.*

37 Deutscher Ethikrat, *Embryospende, Embryoadoption und elterliche Verantwortung*, (2016) 85 *et seq.* See also Wiesemann, in Ach et al. (eds), *wissen.leben.ethik. Themen und Postionen der Bioethik*, (2014) 155, 159 *et seq.*

38 Coester-Waltjen, in Bundesministerium für Gesundheit (ed.), *Fortpflanzungsmedizin in Deutschland*, (2001) 158, 158; Müller-Terpitz, in Spickhoff *Medizinrecht* (2014) comment on art. 6 of the *Grundgesetz* (GG, i.e. the German Constitution) para. 14.

39 Persönliche Leitlinien der Mitglieder des Arbeitskreis Abstammungsrecht des BMJV, *Abschlussbericht – Empfehlungen für eine Reform des Abstammungsrechts*, (2017) 119 (Heinz Kindler); Persönliche Leitlinien der Mitglieder des Arbeitskreis Abstammungsrecht des BMJV, *Abschlussbericht – Empfehlungen für eine Reform des Abstammungsrechts*, (2017) 122 (Thomas Meysen); similarly, Schwenzer, 71 *Rabels Zeitschrift für ausländisches und internationales Privatrecht* (2007) 706, 722 *et seq.*

plays a crucial role in identity formation as it enables the individual to locate him- or herself in a world of interpersonal relationships.[40] Therefore, article 7 of the CRC guarantees the right to know one's parents. This means that the member states to the Convention have to ensure that it is possible for the child to trace his or her origins. Article 8(1) of the ECHR also covers this right.[41] Both guarantees are, however, not absolute and may be restricted.

Although, as yet, there is little case law and interdisciplinary research on the question, it has been argued in the literature that the right to know one's parents should also comprise a right to know one's biological parent, that is, the birth mother.[42] This would mean that the child borne by a surrogate mother would also have a right to know his or her birth mother even if she is not genetically related to him or her. It is not unlikely that the fact of a child being borne by a specific woman who is not his or her genetic mother plays as important a role as the child's genetic origins in the child's identity formation. It thus seems plausible to extend the right to know one's parents also to information about the biological parent.[43]

Further guarantees

Further human rights guarantees are implicated by surrogacy. This is true for example of one's right to life (article 3 of the ECHR), which is especially safeguarded as the child's right to life under article 6 of the CRC. In addition to this, the prohibition of discrimination (article 14 of the ECHR and article 2 of the CRC) becomes relevant especially in so far as access to surrogacy practices of same-sex partners or single persons is concerned. Many additional human rights guarantees and sources of such guarantees may be applicable to surrogacy practices, but due to space restrictions they cannot be discussed here.[44]

Implications of surrogacy for the parties involved

What human rights implications does surrogacy bring about for the parties involved?

Intended parents

The starting point of a surrogacy arrangement is the desire of the intended parents to found a family by becoming parents of a child. This individual interest is protected by the right to procreate and to found a family, which is guaranteed by article 8(1) of the ECHR. States that generally prohibit surrogacy or set decisive limits to it interfere with this right. This interference needs to be justified in accordance with the general rules outlined above.

Surrogate mother

Surrogacy also brings about implications for surrogate mothers. One of the main objections against surrogacy practices in general is that surrogacy violates the human dignity of the surrogate

40 Erikson, *Identität und Lebenszyklus*, (1966).

41 ECtHR *Neue Juristische Wochenschrift* (2011) 3565 (3566) – *Anayo v. Germany*; *Neue Juristische Wochenschrift* (2012) 2781 (2784) – *Schneider v. Germany*.

42 Coester-Waltjen, *Forum Familienrecht* (2017) 224, 228 who cites additional references.

43 See in detail Reuss, *Theorie eines Elternschaftsrechts*, (2018) ch. 5 A.I.1.

44 For a more detailed analysis, see Reuss, *Theorie eines Elternschaftsrechts*, (2018).

mother.[45] It is true that there may be situations where a woman is forced to bear a child under degrading circumstances, where the problematic social or financial situation of the surrogate mother is utilised to induce her consent, where the surrogate mother is not sufficiently informed about the risks that reproductive treatment entail, where the surrogate mother is not awarded a reasonable compensation for her services and is, thus, exploited,[46] or where the surrogate mother is forced to abort[47] or to hand over the child after birth against her will.[48] All these situations may be considered a violation of the surrogate mother's human rights in general and a violation of her inherent human dignity in particular.

However, not all surrogacy arrangements bring about these situations. As long as the law governing surrogacy ensures that the surrogate mother freely and voluntarily consents to the surrogacy arrangement and to handing over the child after birth on an informed basis, her rights are not violated and she is not deprived of her inherent human dignity.[49] With regard to organ donation and prostitution it is well established that an interference with human rights may be justified by the particular person's consent.[50] There is no reason to treat surrogacy differently. This means that surrogacy does not per se violate the surrogate mother's human rights or deprive her of her human dignity. States are, however, obliged under the depicted human rights framework to ensure that the rights of surrogate mothers are respected and taken into account when regulating surrogacy.

45 See e.g. the reasoning of the German lawmaker BT-Drs. 11/5460, 15; for criticism, see also Beck-Gernsheim, in Maio et al. (eds), *Kinderwunsch und Reproduktionsmedizin*, (2013) 337, 350 *et seq.*; Beck-Gernsheim, in Weller and Ditzen (eds), *Leihmutterschaft – Aktuelle Entwicklungen und interdisziplinäre Herausforderungen*, (2018) (forthcoming), 31, 32 *et seq.* For ethical concerns, see Kirchenamt der Evangelischen Kirche in Deutschland (EKD), "EKD-Texte: Zur Achtung vor dem Leben – Maßstäbe für Gentechnik und Fortpflanzungsmedizin", available at www.ekd.de/EKD-Texte/achtungvordemleben_1987.html (last accessed 2 March 2017), Appendix; see also Thomale, *Mietmutterschaft*, (2015) 7 *et seq.*; Voss, *Leihmutterschaft in Deutschland – Rechtliche Folgen und Verfassungsmäßigkeit des Verbotes*, (2015) 253 *et seq.*; Lammers, *Leihmutterschaft in Deutschland – Rechtfertigen die Menschenwürde und das Kindeswohl ein striktes Verbot?*, (2016) 153 n. 854. But see also Bleisch, 17 *Jahrbuch für Wissenschaft und Ethik* (2012) 5 *et seq.*

46 Beck-Gernsheim, in Maio et al. (eds), *Kinderwunsch und Reproduktionsmedizin*, (2013) 337, 347; Thomale, *Mietmutterschaft*, (2015), 10 *et seq.*; Field, *Surrogate Motherhood*, (1990) 25 *et seq.*; Ikemoto, 2 *Journal of Law and the Biosciences* (2015) 112; Bleisch, 17 *Jahrbuch für Wissenschaft und Ethik* (2012) 5, 9 *et seq.*

47 Coester-Waltjen, in Ständige Deputation des Deutschen Juristentages (ed.), *Verhandlungen des 56. Deutschen Juristentages*, (1986) 9, B 89; Thomale, *Mietmutterschaft*, (2015) 13.

48 Dethloff, *Familienrecht*, (2015) § 10 para. 94; Coester-Waltjen, in Ständige Deputation des Deutschen Juristentages (ed.), *Verhandlungen des 56. Deutschen Juristentages*, (1986) 9, B 81. This is not very often the case: see Golombok, *Modern Families*, (2015) 130.

49 Coester-Waltjen, in Ständige Deputation des Deutschen Juristentages (ed.), *Verhandlungen des 56. Deutschen Juristentages*, (1986) 9, B 80; Dethloff, in Weller and Ditzen (eds), *Leihmutterschaft – Aktuelle Entwicklungen und interdisziplinäre Herausforderungen*, (2018) (forthcoming), 41, 53; *MüKoBGB*/Wellenhofer, § 1591 para. 53; Duden, *Leihmutterschaft im Internationalen Privat- und Verfahrensrecht*, (2015) 159, 163, 170 *et seq.*; Bertschi, *Leihmutterschaft – Theorie, Praxis und rechtliche Perspektiven in der Schweiz, den USA und Indien*, (2014) 42 *et seq.*; Lammers, *Leihmutterschaft in Deutschland – Rechtfertigen die Menschenwürde und das Kindeswohl ein striktes Verbot?*, (2016) 156. In contrast, see Thomale, *Mietmutterschaft*, (2015) 10 *et seq.* But see Engel, *Zeitschrift für Europäisches Privatrecht* (2014) 538, 557, who is unsure.

50 *MüKoBGB*/Wellenhofer, § 1591 para. 54; Kress, *Familie Partnerschaft und Recht* (2013) 240, 243; Duden, *Leihmutterschaft im Internationalen Privat- und Verfahrensrecht*, (2015) 163, 169 *et seq.*; Bertschi, *Leihmutterschaft – Theorie, Praxis und rechtliche Perspektiven in der Schweiz, den USA und Indien*, (2014) 42 *et seq.*

Child

Surrogacy also has implications for the child. Some of the human rights guarantees involved have already been outlined above. The major objection against surrogacy with respect to children's rights is also an alleged violation of human dignity and in particular a violation of the right to life.[51] This objection is by no means convincing as it is logically flawed. If life is considered a value in itself,[52] it may not convincingly be argued that it would be better for the child not to be born because, without the conception of the child through a surrogacy arrangement, the child would not exist.[53]

Furthermore, it is also argued that surrogacy practices do not serve the best interest of the child.[54] Recent analyses concerning child development, however, speak against this assumption. Longitudinal studies in the United Kingdom have found that children raised in surrogacy families experience no grave or enduring adjustment difficulties compared to children raised in other families.[55] Furthermore, no detrimental effects on the child's well-being were discovered. It has been noted that these studies are limited with respect to their sample size and thus general assumptions may not be deduced.[56] They show, however, that within a regulated system of surrogacy arrangements positive outcomes with respect to child development may be achieved.[57] Thus it cannot be generally argued that surrogacy is in conflict with the child's best interest.

Finally, it has to be kept in mind that it has to be assured that children are in no way traded for money or money's worth.[58] The sale of children violates the interests of the child and human

51 Cf. e.g. Thomale, *Mietmutterschaft*, (2015) 11 *et seq.*; Voss, *Leihmutterschaft in Deutschland – Rechtliche Folgen und Verfassungsmäßigkeit des Verbotes*, (2015) 213 *et seq.*

52 Coester-Waltjen, in Ständige Deputation des Deutschen Juristentages (ed.), *Verhandlungen des 56. Deutschen Juristentages*, (1986) 9, B 46.

53 Coester-Waltjen, in Wiesemann and Simon (eds), *Patientenautonomie*, (2013) 222, 229 *et seq.*; see also Müller-Terpitz, in Spickhoff *Medizinrecht* (2014) comment on art. 6 of the GG para. 13; Kersten, *Das Klonen von Menschen*, (2004) 308; Dethloff, in Weller and Ditzen (eds), *Leihmutterschaft – Aktuelle Entwicklungen und interdisziplinäre Herausforderungen*, (2018) (forthcoming), 41, 53. See Reuss, *Das Standesamt* (2016) 353; Bertschi, *Leihmutterschaft – Theorie, Praxis und rechtliche Perspektiven in der Schweiz, den USA und Indien*, (2014) 44; Duden, *Leihmutterschaft im Internationalen Privat- und Verfahrensrecht*, (2015) 177 *et seq.* In contrast, see Massie, in Steinbock (ed.), *Legal and Ethical Issues in Human Reproduction*, (2002) 135, 164 *et seq.*; Thomale, *Mietmutterschaft*, 2015, 14; Voss, *Leihmutterschaft in Deutschland – Rechtliche Folgen und Verfassungsmäßigkeit des Verbotes*, (2015) 211; Lammers, *Leihmutterschaft in Deutschland – Rechtfertigen die Menschenwürde und das Kindeswohl ein striktes Verbot?*, (2016) 159.

54 Rauscher, *Familienrecht*, (2008) 663 para. 765 ("Form der Kindeswohlschädigung"); Wohn, *Medizinische Reproduktionstechniken und das neue Abstammungsrecht*, (2001) 121 (without giving reasons); Voss, *Leihmutterschaft in Deutschland – Rechtliche Folgen und Verfassungsmäßigkeit des Verbotes*, (2015) 239.

55 Golombok et al., 47 *Journal of Child Psychology and Psychiatry* (2006) 213, 220; Golombok et al., 47 *Developmental Psychology* (2011) 1579; Golombok et al., 54 *Journal of Child Psychology and Psychiatry* (2013) 653, 657 *et seq.*; Jadva, in Golombok et al. (eds), *Regulating Reproductive Donation*, (2016) 126, 136 *et seq.*; Golombok, *Modern Families*, (2015) 124 *et seq.* Walper et al., in Röthel and Heiderhoff (eds), *Regelungsaufgabe Mutterstellung – Was kann, was darf, was will der Staat?*, (2016) 31, 47 *et seq.* See also Sitter, *Grenzüberschreitende Leihmutterschaft – Eine Untersuchung des materiellen und internationalen Abstammungsrechts Deutschlands und der USA*, (2017), 39 *et seq.*, who does not take the above-mentioned sources into account.

56 Tobin, 63 *International and Comparative Law Quarterly* (2014) 317; Funcke, *Neue Zeitschrift für Familienrecht* (2016) 207; Engel, in Boele-Woelki et al. (eds), *Family Law and Culture in Europe*, (2014) 199, 213.

57 *MüKoBGB*/Wellenhofer, § 1591 para. 52; Duden, *Leihmutterschaft im Internationalen Privat- und Verfahrensrecht*, (2015) 155; Diel, *Leihmutterschaft und Reproduktionstourismus*, (2014) 65.

58 Tobin, 63 *International and Comparative Law Quarterly* (2014) 317; Duden, *Leihmutterschaft im Internationalen Privat- und Verfahrensrecht*, (2015) 180 *et seq.*; Thomale, *Mietmutterschaft*, 2015, 12 *et seq.*, who seems to extend this criticism to all cases of surrogacy. In contrast, see Wade, 29 *Child and Family Law Quarterly* (2017) 113, 121 who cites additional references.

rights laws. Surrogacy does not necessarily involve a sale of the child, especially not in cases where the intended parents are also the genetic parents of the child.[59] However, even in cases where the intended parents lack a genetic bond with the child, the sale of children may be prevented by state regulation, for example the prohibition on paying money exceeding reasonable compensation for the surrogate mother's services etc.[60]

National approaches towards surrogacy

Among the world's jurisdictions, there is no consensus on how to approach surrogacy at national level.[61] Some states clearly oppose such practices and generally prohibit surrogacy arrangements. This is true for example for Germany,[62] France,[63] Austria[64] and Switzerland.[65] Other countries permit altruistic versions of surrogacy. This means that the surrogate mother is allowed to receive reasonable compensation for her services, but payments that go beyond a compensatory nature are prohibited. This is the case for example in Greece,[66] Portugal,[67] Belgium,[68] the

59 For criticism, see Lederer, *Grenzenloser Kinderwunsch – Leihmutterschaft im nationalen, europäischen und globalen rechtlichen Spannungsfeld*, (2016) 162. Cf. for similar questions in adoption, Fenton-Glynn, *Children's Rights in Intercountry Adoption*, (2014) 89 *et seq.* In contrast, see Voss, *Leihmutterschaft in Deutschland – Rechtliche Folgen und Verfassungsmäßigkeit des Verbotes*, (2015) 221 (general violation of human dignity).

60 Coester-Waltjen, in Ständige Deputation des Deutschen Juristentages (ed.), *Verhandlungen des 56. Deutschen Juristentages*, (1986) 9, B 81; *MüKoBGB*/Wellenhofer, § 1591 para. 55; compare Duden, *Leihmutterschaft im Internationalen Privat- und Verfahrensrecht*, (2015) 180.

61 See the study of the European Parliament, *A Comprehensive Study on the Regime of Surrogacy in the EU-Member States*, PE 474.403, available at www.europarl.europa.eu/studies (last accessed 10 Oct. 2017). For Chinese law, see Ding, 2 *Journal of Law and the Biosciences* (2015) 33 *et seq.*

62 § 1 No. 7 *Embryonenschutzgesetz*, § 5 Abs. 3, 4, §§ 13c, 14b *Adoptionsvermittlungsgesetz*.

63 Arts. 16–7 and 16–9 of the *Code Civil* as well as art. 227–12 of the *Code Penal*. See the report of the French Sénat, Michèle André, Alain Milon and Henri de Richemont, "Contribution à la réflexion sur la maternité pour autrui – Rapport d'information n° 421 (2007–2008) fait au nom de la commission des lois et de la commission des affaires sociales", available at www.senat.fr/rap/r07-421/r07-421.html (last accessed 10 Oct. 2017), which is in favour of abolishing the prohibition in some parts. See also Lederer, *Grenzenloser Kinderwunsch – Leihmutterschaft im nationalen, europäischen und globalen rechtlichen Spannungsfeld*, (2016) 47 *et seq.*; De Wolf, in Boele-Woelki and Oderkerk (eds), *(On)geoorloofdheid van het Draagmoederschap in Rechtsvergelijkend Perspectief*, (1999) 89.

64 § 3 *Fortpflanzungsmedizingesetz* (*FMedG*); see Ferrari, in Dutta et al. (eds), *Künstliche Fortpflanzung und europäisches Familienrecht*, (2015) 182, 198.

65 Arts. 4 and 31 of the *FMedG*, cf. Bertschi, *Leihmutterschaft – Theorie, Praxis und rechtliche Perspektiven in der Schweiz, den USA und Indien*, (2014) 25 *et seq.*; Aebi-Müller and Dörr, in Dutta et al. (eds), *Künstliche Fortpflanzung und europäisches Familienrecht*, (2015), 151, 164 *et seq.* On the recognition of cross-border surrogacy, see Swiss Federal Supreme Court, Judgment of 21 May 2015–5A 748/2014, *Zeitschrift für das gesamte Familienrecht* 2015, 1912; Swiss Federal Supreme Court, Judgment of 14 Sept. 2015–5A 443/2014, *Das Standesamt* (2016) 179; Büchler and Maranta, in Atkin (ed.), *The International Survey of Family Law* 2015 ed., (2015) 327 *et seq.*

66 Zervogianni, in Dutta et al. (eds), *Künstliche Fortpflanzung und europäisches Familienrecht*, (2015) 205, 216 *et seq.*

67 Cf. Decreto Regulamentar No. 6/2017 of 31 July 2017, Bergmann-Aktuell: available at www.bergmann-aktuell.de/news/ausfuehrungsverordnung-gesetz-ueber-medizinisch-unterstuetzte-fortpflanzung. See also Oliveira, *Zeitschrift für das gesamte Familienrecht* (2016) 1550, 1553.

68 Pintens, in Dutta et al. (eds), *Künstliche Fortpflanzung und europäisches Familienrecht*, (2015) 105, 121 *et seq.*; De Wolf, in Boele-Woelki and Oderkerk (eds), *(On)geoorloofdheid van het Draagmoederschap in Rechtsvergelijkend Perspectief*, (1999) 89.

Netherlands,[69] England and Wales,[70] Israel[71] and New Zealand.[72] There are, however, also states that allow commercial surrogacy where payment exceeding mere compensatory sums is possible. This is the case in some states of the United States of America[73] such as California,[74] and in British Columbia,[75] Australia,[76] the Ukraine and Russia.[77] In the United States, surrogacy costs up to USD 100,000 – not all of the money is paid to the surrogate mother, however.[78]

The systems of surrogacy laws largely differ among the states that permit surrogacy arrangements. In some countries, the legal parent – child relationship between the child and the intended parents is established by the operation of law, as is the case in British Columbia.[79] When the legal prerequisites are met, the intended parents automatically become legal parents upon the birth of the child. Other jurisdictions demand a (facilitated) adoption procedure. This is the case for example under Dutch law.[80] The intended parents become the legal parents of the child when the court decision allowing the adoption comes into effect. Other systems have special instruments to transfer legal parentage from the surrogate mother to the intended parents. This is the case for example in England and Wales, where section 54 of the Human Fertilisation and Embryology Act 2008 empowers the court to issue a parental order transferring legal parentage from the surrogate mother to the intended parents.

69 Boele-Woelki, in Haager Konferenz für Internationales Privatrecht (ed.), A *Commitment to Private International Law – Essays in Honour of Hans van Loon*, (2013) 47 *et seq.*; Reuss, in Dutta et al. (eds), *Künstliche Fortpflanzung und europäisches Familienrecht*, (2015) 127; Rechtbank Noord-Nederland, Decision of 11 Sept. 2013 – C-17–125959 – FA RK 13–474, www.rechtspraak.nl; Broekhuijsen-Molenaar, in Boele-Woelki and Oderkerk (eds), *(On)geoorloofdheid van het Draagmoederschap in Rechtsvergelijkend Perspectief*, (1999) 33. On the validity of surrogacy agreements, see Nieuwenhuis, *Nederlands Juristenblad* (2001) 1795, 1797.

70 Sec. 1A of the Surrogacy Arrangements Act 1985 and sec. 54 of the Human Fertilisation and Embryology Act 2008.

71 See Dethloff, *JuristenZeitung* (2014) 922, 924 who cites additional references; Lederer, *Grenzenloser Kinderwunsch – Leihmutterschaft im nationalen, europäischen und globalen rechtlichen Spannungsfeld*, (2016) 96 *et seq.*

72 See Powell, 29 *Child and Family Law Quarterly* (2017) 149.

73 See Bertschi, *Leihmutterschaft – Theorie, Praxis und rechtliche Perspektiven in der Schweiz, den USA und Indien*, (2014) 109 *et seq.*; Sitter, *Grenzüberschreitende Leihmutterschaft – Eine Untersuchung des materiellen und internationalen Abstammungsrechts Deutschlands und der USA*, (2017) 53 *et seq.*; Hall, in Weller and Ditzen (eds), *Leihmutterschaft – Aktuelle Entwicklungen und interdisziplinäre Herausforderungen*, (2018) (forthcoming), 55 *et seq.*

74 Dethloff, *JuristenZeitung* (2014) 922, 923.

75 Part 3 of the Family Law Act.

76 See Dethloff, *JuristenZeitung* (2014) 922, 924; Lederer, *Grenzenloser Kinderwunsch – Leihmutterschaft im nationalen, europäischen und globalen rechtlichen Spannungsfeld*, (2016) 91 *et seq.*

77 See *MüKoBGB*/Wellenhofer, § 1591 para. 31 *et seq.*; Dethloff, *JuristenZeitung* (2014) 922, 924; Budzikiewicz, in Boele-Woelki et al. (eds), *Family Law and Culture in Europe*, (2014) 151, 158 *et seq.*; Lederer, *Grenzenloser Kinderwunsch – Leihmutterschaft im nationalen, europäischen und globalen rechtlichen Spannungsfeld*, (2016) 103 *et seq.* (India); Antokolskaya, in Boele-Woelki and Oderkerk (eds), *(On)geoorloofdheid van het Draagmoederschap in Rechtsvergelijkend Perspectief*, (1999) 127. Concerning Swedish law, see Stoll, *Surrogacy Arrangements and Legal Parenthood – Swedish Law in a Comparative Context*, (2013).

78 Field, *Surrogate Motherhood*, (1990) 26; Golombok, *Modern Families*, (2015) 119; *MüKoBGB*/Wellenhofer, § 1591 para. 31. Beck-Gernsheim, in Maio et al. (eds), *Kinderwunsch und Reproduktionsmedizin*, (2013) 337, 347 *et seq.* (who states that up to USD 120,000 is paid; see also Bertschi, *Leihmutterschaft – Theorie, Praxis und rechtliche Perspektiven in der Schweiz, den USA und Indien*, (2014) 133. For numbers concerning the United Kingdom, see Alghrani and Griffiths, 29 *Child and Family Law Quarterly* (2017) 165, 179 (app. £15,000 as compensatory payment).

79 Sec. 29 of the Family Law Act.

80 Reuss, in Dutta et al. (eds), *Künstliche Fortpflanzung und europäisches Familienrecht*, (2015) 127, 147 *et seq.* For a similar situation in New Zealand, see Powell, 29 *Child and Family Law Quarterly* (2017) 149.

The prerequisites which have to be fulfilled to effect legal parentage also differ from state to state. In some jurisdictions, surrogacy arrangements are open only to partners of the opposite sex. This is true for the Netherlands, as the genetic material used for the conception of the child must stem from both intended parents.[81] In contrast to this, English law also enables same-sex partners to apply for a parental order. Section 54(1)(b) of the Human Fertilisation and Embryology Act 2008 demands a genetic link to only one intended parent. Other countries grant access to surrogacy arrangements without the prerequisite of an existing genetic link.

National approaches towards recognition of surrogacy in cross-border cases

Unanimity is also lacking with respect to the recognition of parent – child relationships in cross-border surrogacy settings. The national frameworks for the recognition of foreign parent – child relationships differ strongly. However, nearly all systems apply some sort of public policy test regardless of whether the legal parent – child relationship has been established by operation of law or through a court decision. The outcomes of this test differ, however, from state to state. For example, Austria, a country that prohibits surrogacy arrangements, does not consider surrogacy to be contrary to public policy.[82] A legal parent – child relationship that has been established under foreign surrogacy law may thus be recognised under Austrian law. The same now applies under German law.[83] In contrast to this, Swiss law considers surrogacy a circumvention of the national prohibition on surrogacy and thus a violation of public policy.[84] Intended parents thus have to seek other ways to establish a legal tie to their child, for example through adoption.

Ways forward

The differences in the legal regimes bring about uncertainties for intended parents, surrogate mothers and – this is of particular concern – the children involved. Intended parents have to clarify beforehand where a legal parent – child relationship may be recognised and which prerequisites have to be fulfilled to this end. This is not an easy task for laypersons and – due to the concept of the public policy exception in private international law and international civil procedure – involves a fact-sensitive case-by-case analysis. Thus, there have been suggestions in the literature that the national laws should be altered to facilitate the recognition of parentage in cross-border surrogacy cases.[85] All these approaches will aid the parties with respect to the recognition of the parent – child relationship in the respective country; they may, however, not protect the consequences of the parent – child relationship when the persons involved later move to another country.

An international instrument, for example a surrogacy convention, that sets international standards for surrogacy practices and regulates uniform prerequisites for the recognition of parent – child

81 Boele-Woelki et al., "Commercieel draagmoederschap en illegale opneming van kinderen", available at www.wodc.nl/onderzoeksdatabase/draagmoederschap.aspx (last accessed 6 March 2018), 36.

82 Austrian Constitutional Court, Decision of 14 Dec. 2011 – B 13/11–10, BeckRS 2013, 80296; Lurger, *Praxis des Internationalen Privat- und Verfahrensrechts* (2013) 282.

83 German Federal Supreme Court, Decision of 10 Dec. 2014 – XII ZB 463/13, BeckRS 2014, 23505 and Decision of 5 Sept. 2018 – XII ZB 224/17, BeckRS 2018, 23794.

84 Swiss Federal Supreme Court, Judgment of 21 May 2015–5A 748/2014, *Zeitschrift für das gesamte Familienrecht* (2015) 1912; Swiss Federal Supreme Court, Judgment of 14 Sept. 2015–5A 443/2014, *Das Standesamt* (2016) 179; Büchler and Maranta, in Atkin (ed.), *The International Survey of Family Law* 2015 ed., (2015) 327 *et seq.*

85 See in detail Reuss, *Theorie eines Elternschaftsrechts*, (2018).

relationships may be a sound solution to such problems.[86] It is thus highly welcomed that the Hague Conference on Private International Law has been working on the matter for some time.[87] The work is still at the beginning and currently concentrates on the recognition of court decisions.[88] With respect to the great differences among the states with regard to surrogacy, this seems a feasible starting point to draft and discuss a convention.[89]

Bibliography

Aebi-Müller, Regina and Dörr, Bianka. "Künstliche Fortpflanzung im schweizerischen Recht", in Anatol Dutta, Dieter Schwab and Dieter Henrich (eds), *Künstliche Fortpflanzung und europäisches Familienrecht*, (Bielefeld, Gieseking, 2015) 151.

Alghrani, Amel and Griffiths, Danielle. "The Regulation of Surrogacy in the United Kingdom: The Case for Reform", 29 *Child and Family Law Quarterly* (2017) 165.

Antokolskaya, Masha. "Draagmoederschap naar Russisch recht", in Katharina Boele-Woelki and Marieke Oderkerk (eds), *(On)geoorloofdheid van het Draagmoederschap in Rechtsvergelijkend Perspectief*, (Antwerp, Intersentia, 1999) 127.

Arbeitskreis Abstammungsrecht des BMJV. *Abschlussbericht – Empfehlungen für eine Reform des Abstammungsrechts, Bundesanzeiger*, (Cologne, Bundesanzeiger Verlag, 2017).

Beck-Gernsheim, Elisabeth. "Kinderwunsch ohne Grenzen?", in Giovanni Maio, Tobias Eichinger and Claudia Bozzaro (eds), *Kinderwunsch und Reproduktionsmedizin, Ethische Herausforderungen der technisierten Fortpflanzung*, (Freiburg im Breisgau, Verlag Karl Alber, 2013) 337.

Beck-Gernsheim, Elisabeth. "Ist das Embryonenschutzgesetz anachronistisch geworden? Sollen wir das Verbot von Leihmutterschaft aufheben?", in Marc-Philippe Weller and Beate Ditzen (eds), *Leihmutterschaft – Aktuelle Entwicklungen und interdisziplinäre Herausforderungen*, (Mohr Siebeck, Tübingen, 2018) (forthcoming) 31.

Bertschi, Nora. *Leihmutterschaft – Theorie, Praxis und rechtliche Perspektiven in der Schweiz, den USA und Indien*, (Stämpfli Verlag, Bern 2014).

Bleisch, Barbara. "Leihmutterschaft als persönliche Beziehung", 17 *Jahrbuch für Wissenschaft und Ethik* (2012) 5.

Blyth, Eric. "'Not a Primrose Path': Commissioning Parents' Experiences of Surrogacy Arrangements in Britain", 13 *Journal of Reproductive and Infant Psychology* (1995) 185.

Boele-Woelki, Katharina. "(Cross Border) Surrogate Motherhood: We Need To Take Action Now!", in Haager Konferenz für Internationales Privatrecht (ed.), *A Commitment to Private International Law – Essays in Honour of Hans van Loon*, (Intersentia, Cambridge, UK, 2013) 47.

Broekhuijsen-Molenaar, Anneleen. "Geoorloofdheid van Draagmoederschap naar Nederlands (Wenselijk) Recht", in Katharina Boele-Woelki and Marieke Oderkerk (eds), *(On)geoorloofdheid van het Draagmoederschap in Rechtsvergelijkend Perspectief*, (Antwerp, Intersentia, 1999) 33.

Büchler, Andrea and Maranta, Luca. "Surrogacy and Private International Law in Switzerland", in Bill Atkin (ed.), *The International Survey of Family Law* 2015 edn, (Bristol, Jordans, 2015) 327.

86 Approving Boele-Woelki, in Haager Konferenz für Internationales Privatrecht (ed.), A *Commitment to Private International Law – Essays in Honour of Hans van Loon*, (2013) 47, 57; Bertschi, *Leihmutterschaft – Theorie, Praxis und rechtliche Perspektiven in der Schweiz, den USA und Indien*, (2014) 220 *et seq.* (which includes a regulatory proposal); approving also Sitter, *Grenzüberschreitende Leihmutterschaft – Eine Untersuchung des materiellen und internationalen Abstammungsrechts Deutschlands und der USA*, (2017) 306 *et seq.* But see Engel, in Boele-Woelki et al. (eds), *Family Law and Culture in Europe*, (2014) 199, 211.

87 Cf. Lederer, *Grenzenloser Kinderwunsch – Leihmutterschaft im nationalen, europäischen und globalen rechtlichen Spannungsfeld*, (2016) 216 *et seq.*

88 Report of the Expert Group of Feb. 2017, available at assets.hcch.net/docs/ed997a8d-bdcb-48eb-9672–6d0535249d0e.pdf (last accessed 30 Sept. 2017), 2.

89 For criticism concerning the chances of realising such project, see Helms, in Ständige Deputation des Deutschen Juristentages (ed.), *Rechtliche, biologische und soziale Elternschaft – Herausforderungen durch neue Familienformen*, (2016) F 1, F 56. For a completely drafted proposal, see Bertschi, *Leihmutterschaft – Theorie, Praxis und rechtliche Perspektiven in der Schweiz, den USA und Indien*, (2014) 226 *et seq.*

Budzikiewicz, Christine. "Contracting on Parentage", in Katharina Boele-Woelki, Nina Dethloff and Werner Gephart (eds), *Family Law and Culture in Europe, Developments, Challenges and Opportunities*, (Intersentia, Cambridge, UK, 2014) 151.

Coester, Michael. *Das Kindeswohl als Rechtsbegriff – Die richterliche Entscheidung über die elterliche Sorge beim Zerfall der Familiengemeinschaft*, (Augsburg University, Habilitationsschrift, Augsburg, 1981/82), (Alfred Metzner Verlag, Frankfurt am Main 1983).

Coester, Michael. "Ersatzmutterschaft in Europa", in Heinz-Peter Mansel, Thomas Pfeiffer and Herbert Kronke (eds), *Festschrift für Erik Jayme*, (Munich, Sellier, 2004) 1243.

Coester-Waltjen, Dagmar. "Gutachten B: Die künstliche Befruchtung beim Menschen – Zulässigkeit und zivilrechtliche Folgen", in Ständige Deputation des Deutschen Juristentages (ed.), *Verhandlungen des 56. Deutschen Juristentages, I. Band* (Gutachten), (Munich, Verlag C.H. Beck, 1986) 9.

Coester-Waltjen, Dagmar. "Elternschaft außerhalb der Ehe – Sechs juristische Prämissen und Folgerungen für die künstliche Befruchtung", in Bundesministerium für Gesundheit (ed.), *Fortpflanzungsmedizin in Deutschland, Wissenschaftliches Symposium des Bundesministeriums für Gesundheit in Zusammenarbeit mit dem Robert-Koch-Institut vom 24. bis 26. Mai 2000 in Berlin*, (Baden-Baden, Nomos-Verlagsgesellschaft, 2001) 158.

Coester-Waltjen, Dagmar. "Reproduktive Autonomie aus rechtlicher Sicht", in Claudia Wiesemann and Alfred Simon (eds), *Patientenautonomie. Theoretische Grundlagen, praktische Anwendungen*, (Münster, Mentis, 2013) 222.

Coester-Waltjen, Dagmar. "Das Recht auf (Kenntnis der eigenen) Abstammung", *Forum Familienrecht* (2017) 224.

Cottier, Michelle and Wyttenbach, Judith. "Die Rechtsprechung des Europäischen Gerichtshofes für Menschenrechte zu Art. 8 EMRK und ihr Einfluss auf die Schweiz: ausgewählte jüngere Entwicklungen im Bereich des Familienrechts", *Praxis des Familienrechts* (2016) 75.

Crowley, Louise. "Defining the Family and the Scope of Protection Available – Tensions between National Governance and International Expectations", in Bill Atkin (ed.), *The International Survey of Family Law* 2015 edn, (Bristol, Jordans, 2015) 54.

De Oliveira, Guilherme. "Changes in Portuguese Family Law 2015–2016", *Zeitschrift für das gesamte Familienrecht* (2016) 1550.

De Wolf, Ann. "Draagmoederschap in België en Frankrijk: Een Stand van Zaken", in Katharina Boele-Woelki and Marieke Oderkerk (eds), *(On)geoorloofdheid van het Draagmoederschap in Rechtsvergelijkend Perspectief*, (Antwerp, Intersentia, 1999) 89.

Dethloff, Nina. "Leihmütter, Wunscheltern und ihre Kinder", *JuristenZeitung* (2014) 922.

Dethloff, Nina. *Familienrecht – Ein Studienbuch*, (C.H. Beck, Munich, 31st edn 2015).

Dethloff, Nina. "Leihmutterschaft in rechtsvergleichender Perspektive", in Marc-Philippe Weller and Beate Ditzen (eds), *Leihmutterschaft – Aktuelle Entwicklungen und interdisziplinäre Herausforderungen*, (Mohr Siebeck, Tübingen, 2018) (forthcoming), 41.

Deutscher Ethikrat. *Embryospende, Embryoadoption und elterliche Verantwortung – Stellungnahme*, (Deutscher Ethikrat, Berlin, 2016).

Diel, Alexander. *Leihmutterschaft und Reproduktionstourismus*, (Wolfgang Metzner Verlag, Frankfurt am Main, 2014).

Ding, Chunyan. "Surrogacy Litigation in China and Beyond", 2 *Journal of Law and the Biosciences* (2015) 33.

Duden, Konrad. *Leihmutterschaft im Internationalen Privat- und Verfahrensrecht – Abstammung und ordre public im Spiegel des Verfassungs-, Völker- und Europarechts*, (Mohr Siebeck, Tübingen 2015).

Duden, Konrad. "Anmerkung zu ECtHR, Urt. v. 24.1.2017 – Nr. 25358/12 (Paradiso u. Campanelli/Italy)", *Zeitschrift für das gesamte Familienrecht* (2017) 445.

Duden, Konrad. "Zweifel an der Elternschaft bei internationaler Leihmutterschaft", *Das Standesamt* (2017) 225.

Engel, Martin. "Cross-Border Surrogacy: Time for a Convention?", in Katharina Boele-Woelki, Nina Dethloff and Werner Gephart (eds), *Family Law and Culture in Europe, Developments, Challenges and Opportunities*, (Intersentia, Cambridge, UK, 2014) 199.

Engel, Martin. "Internationale Leihmutterschaft und Kindeswohl", *Zeitschrift für Europäisches Privatrecht* (2014) 538.

Erikson, Erik H. *Identität und Lebenszyklus*, (Suhrkamp Verlag, Frankfurt am Main 1966).

Fenton-Glynn, Claire. *Children's Rights in Intercountry Adoption*, (Intersentia, Cambridge, UK, 2014).

Ferrari, Susanne. "Künstliche Fortpflanzung im österreichischen Recht", in Anatol Dutta, Dieter Schwab and Dieter Henrich (eds), *Künstliche Fortpflanzung und europäisches Familienrecht*, (Bielefeld, Gieseking, 2015) 182.

Field, Martha A. *Surrogate Motherhood*, (Harvard University Press, Cambridge, MA, expanded edn, 1990).
Funcke, Dorett. "Leihmutterschaftsfamilien", *Neue Zeitschrift für Familienrecht* (2016) 207.
Golombok, Susan. *Modern Families – Parents and Children in New Family Forms*, (Cambridge University Press, Cambridge, UK, 2015).
Golombok, Susan, Lucy Blake, Polly Casey, Gabriela Roman and Vasanti Jadva. "Children born through Reproductive Donation: A Longitudinal Study of Psychological Adjustment", 54 *Journal of Child Psychology and Psychiatry* (2013) 653.
Golombok, Susan, Fiona MacCullum, Clare Murray, Emma Lycett and Vasanti Jadva. "Surrogacy Families: Parental Functioning, Parent-Child Relationships and Children's Psychological Development at Age 2", 47 *Journal of Child Psychology and Psychiatry* (2006) 213.
Golombok, Susan, Jennifer Readings, Lucy Blake, Polly Casey, Alex Marks and Vasanti Jadva. "Families Created Through Surrogacy: Mother-Child Relationships and Children's Psychological Adjustment at Age 7", 47 *Developmental Psychology* (2011) 1579.
Hall, Eliza. "From European Theory to American Practice: The United States as a Laboratory for Surrogacy Law", in Marc-Philippe Weller and Beate Ditzen (eds), *Leihmutterschaft – Aktuelle Entwicklungen und interdisziplinäre Herausforderungen*, (Mohr Siebeck, Tübingen, 2018) (forthcoming) 55.
Helms, Tobias. "Gutachten F zum 71. DJT", in Ständige Deputation des Deutschen Juristentages (ed.), *Rechtliche, biologische und soziale Elternschaft – Herausforderungen durch neue Familienformen*, (Munich, C.H. Beck, 2016) F 1.
Henrich, Dieter. "Das Kind mit zwei Müttern (und zwei Vätern) im internationalen Privatrecht", in Sybille Hofer, Diethelm Klippel and Ute Walter (eds), *Perspektiven des Familienrechts, Festschrift für Dieter Schwab zum 70. Geburtstag*, (Bielefeld, Gieseking, 2005) 1141.
Ikemoto, Lisa. "Egg Freezing, Stratified Reproduction and the Logic of Not", 2 *Journal of Law and the Biosciences* (2015) 112.
Jadva, Vasanti. "Surrogacy", in Susan Golombok, Rosamund Scott and John B. Appleby (eds), *Regulating Reproductive Donation*, (Cambridge University Press, Cambridge, UK, 2016) 126.
Kersten, Jens. *Das Klonen von Menschen – Eine verfassungs-, europa- und völkerrechtliche Kritik*, (Humboldt-University, Habilitationsschrift, Berlin, 2004), (Mohr Siebeck, Tübingen, 2004).
Kress, Hartmut. "Samenspende und Leihmutterschaft – Problemstand, Rechtsunsicherheiten, Regelungsansätze", *Familie Partnerschaft und Recht* (2013) 240.
Lammers, Roman. *Leihmutterschaft in Deutschland – Rechtfertigen die Menschenwürde und das Kindeswohl ein striktes Verbot?*, (Peter Lang GmbH, Frankfurt am Main, 2016).
Lederer, Nadine. *Grenzenloser Kinderwunsch – Leihmutterschaft im nationalen, europäischen und globalen rechtlichen Spannungsfeld*, (Peter Lang GmbH, Frankfurt am Main, 2016).
Lurger, Brigitta. "Das österreichische IPR bei Leihmutterschaft im Ausland – das Kindeswohl zwischen Anerkennung, europäischen Grundrechten und inländischem Leihmutterschaftsverbot", *Praxis des Internationalen Privat- und Verfahrensrechts* (2013) 282.
MacCullum, Fiona, Emma Lycett, Clare Murray, Vasanti Jadva and Susan Golombok. "Surrogacy: The Experience of Commissioning Couples", 18 *Human Reproduction* (2003) 1334.
Massie, Ann MacLean. "Regulating Choice: A Constitutional Law Response to Professor John A. Robertson's Children of Choice", in Bonnie Steinbock (ed.), *Legal and Ethical Issues in Human Reproduction*, (Aldershot, UK, Ashgate, 2002) 135.
Meyer-Spendler, Regine. "Leihmutterschaft – Die persönliche Perspektive", in Marc-Philippe Weller and Beate Ditzen (eds), *Leihmutterschaft – Aktuelle Entwicklungen und interdisziplinäre Herausforderungen*, (Mohr Siebeck, Tübingen, 2018) (forthcoming), 24.
Müller-Terpitz, Ralf in Andreas Spickhoff *Medizinrecht.* (Munich, C.H. Beck, 2nd edn. 2014).
Nieuwenhuis, J.H. "Promises, Promises – Over contracten en andere afspraken", *Nederlands Juristenblad* (2001) 1795.
Pintens, Walter. "Künstliche Fortpflanzung im belgischen und französischen Recht", in Anatol Dutta, Dieter Schwab and Dieter Henrich (eds), *Künstliche Fortpflanzung und europäisches Familienrecht*, (Bielefeld, Gieseking, 2015) 105.
Pintens, Walter. "Familienrecht und Rechtsvergleichung in der Rechtsprechung des Europäischen Gerichtshofs für Menschenrechte", *Zeitschrift für das gesamte Familienrecht* (2016) 341.
Powell, Rhonda. "International Surrogacy and Parenthood in New Zealand: Crossing Geographical, Legal and Biological Borders", 29 *Child and Family Law Quarterly* (2017) 149.
Rauscher, Thomas. *Familienrecht*, (C.F. Müller, Heidelberg, 2nd edn, 2008).
Reuss, Philipp. "Künstliche Fortpflanzung im niederländischen Recht", in Anatol Dutta, Dieter Schwab and Dieter Henrich (eds), *Künstliche Fortpflanzung und europäisches Familienrecht*, (Bielefeld, Gieseking, 2015) 127.

Reuss, Philipp. "Muss das Kind einen Vater haben? – Einige Überlegungen zur Elternschaft alleinstehender Frauen durch medizinisch-assistierte Reproduktion", *Das Standesamt* (2016) 353.

Reuss, Philipp. "§ 1598a BGB", in Beate Gsell, Wolfgang Krüger, Stephan Lorenz and Jörg Mayer (eds) *beck-online. GROSSKOMMENTAR.* (Munich, Verlag C.H. Beck, 2017) (cited as *BeckOGK*/Reuss).

Reuss, Philipp. *Theorie eines Elternschaftsrechts*, (Berlin, Duncker & Humblot, 2018).

Sanders, Anne, "Was ist eine Familie? – der ECtHR und die Mehrelternschaft", *Neue Juristische Wochenschrift* (2017) 925.

Schwenzer, Ingeborg. "Zehnte Ernst Rabel Vorlesung: Grundlinien eines modernen Familienrechts aus rechtsvergleichender Sicht", 71 *Rabels Zeitschrift für ausländisches und internationales Privatrecht* (2007) 706.

Singer, Anna. "The Right of the Child to Parents", in Katharina Boele-Woelki, Nina Dethloff and Werner Gephart (eds), *Family Law and Culture in Europe, Developments, Challenges and Opportunities*, (Intersentia, Cambridge, UK, 2014) 137.

Sitter, Sophie Catherine. *Grenzüberschreitende Leihmutterschaft – Eine Untersuchung des materiellen und internationalen Abstammungsrechts Deutschlands und der USA*, (Dissertation), (Duncker & Humblot, Berlin, 2017).

Stoll, Jane. *Surrogacy Arrangements and Legal Parenthood – Swedish Law in a Comparative Context*, (Uppsala University, Uppsala, 2013).

Thomale, Chris. *Mietmutterschaft – Eine international-privatrechtliche Kritik*, (Mohr Siebeck, Tübingen 2015).

Tobin, John. "To Prohibit or Permit: What is the (Human) Rights Response to the Practice of International Commercial Surrogacy?", 63 *International and Comparative Law Quarterly* (2014) 317.

Voss, Solvejg Sonja. *Leihmutterschaft in Deutschland – Rechtliche Folgen und Verfassungsmäßigkeit des Verbotes*, (Kovač, Hamburg, 2015).

Wade, Katherine. "The Regulation of Surrogacy: A Children's Rights Perspective", 29 *Child and Family Law Quarterly* (2017) 113.

Walper, Sabine, Ina Bovenschen, Christine Entleitner-Phleps and Ulrike Lux. "Was kann der Staat? Mutterschaft aus Sicht der Familien-, Kinder- und Jugendforschung", in Anne Röthel and Bettina Heiderhoff (eds), *Regelungsaufgabe Mutterstellung – Was kann, was darf, was will der Staat?*, (Frankfurt am Main, Wolfgang Metzner Verlag, 2016) 31.

Wellenhofer, Marina. "§ 1591", in Franz Jürgen Säcker, Roland Rixecker, Hartmut Oetker and Bettina Limperg (eds) *Münchener Kommentar zum Bürgerlichen Gesetzbuch*, (Munich, C.H. Beck, 7th edn, 2017 (cited as *MüKoBGB*/Wellenhofer).

Wiesemann, Claudia. "Der moralische Status des Kindes in der Medizin", in Johann S. Ach, Beate Lüttenberg and Michael Quante (eds), *wissen.leben.ethik., Themen und Positionen der Bioethik*, (Münster, Mentis, 2014) 155.

Wohn, Annette. *Medizinische Reproduktionstechniken und das neue Abstammungsrecht*, (Bielefeld, Verlag Ernst und Werner Gieseking, 2001).

Zervogianni, Eleni. "Künstliche Fortpflanzung im griechischen Recht", in Anatol Dutta, Dieter Schwab and Dieter Henrich (eds), *Künstliche Fortpflanzung und europäisches Familienrecht*, (Bielefeld, Gieseking, 2015) 205.

15

Fathers' rights

Japan as a different paradigm

Colin P.A. Jones

Introduction

Although its laws and institutions may seem very familiar to Western observers, Japan in the twenty-first century still represents a very different paradigm of family law. This is true not only when it comes to fathers' rights and responsibilities, but the rights and duties of parents of either gender even within a "traditional" (i.e., male – female married couple) family relationship. Moreover, Japanese family law still contains provisions that effectively treat families differently depending on their nationality and the legitimacy of children. Rules on the presumptions of paternity and adoption can also lead to counterintuitive results that may further frustrate the recognition of parental rights in fathers, or their exercise.

Thus, in order to understand the rights and responsibilities (if any) of fathers – as well as who even qualifies for such status – *outside* such traditional relationships, whether in de facto marriages, same-sex couples or in the context of assisted reproduction, it is thus necessary to first understand how the law deals with the traditional paradigm. Moreover, it is necessary to ask a very basic question about family law – who is it for? In the Japanese context, the answer to this question is further complicated by the fact that the interrelationship between family law and identity in Japan is much more closely tied to nationality than in Western countries. The basic rules by which changes in personal and family status are recorded and confirmed are based on a system that assumes everyone is a Japanese citizen, with rules for non-Japanese being a workaround that leads to different treatment, not because of discriminatory motives by the people involved, but because that is the way the system is designed.

Nor have Japanese courts or legislators identified constitutionally protected dimensions to the parent – child relationship. There are no Supreme Court of Japan cases like *Troxel v. Granville* (530 U.S. 57 (2000)) identifying a fundamental right of parents to be an integral part of their children's lives. Nor is there formal law clearly respecting family life and protecting it from excessive interference by government such as Article 8 of the European Convention on Human Rights.

This chapter will seek to prevent a conceptual yet practical overview of some of the differences in the Japanese approach to family law and how they manifest themselves in the sphere of the rights and responsibilities of parents in general, and of fathers in particular.

East meets West: the Hague Convention on Child Abduction

A good starting point for this discussion is the Hague Convention on the Civil Aspects of International Child Abduction (the "Convention"). Japan ratified it in 2014. "Finally," some might be tempted to add, since this development came after years of criticism from the international community about Japan's status as a "black hole" for international child abduction.[1] Children of failed relationships taken to Japan were never returned by the country's courts. Not only that, the Left-Behind-Parent (LBP) might go months or years without being able to even see their children – despite having full custody rights under their home country law or even the acknowledgment by Japanese courts of something that seemed like custodial or access rights.

Western press accounts tended to attribute such inscrutable results to the peculiarities of Japanese culture. However, as this author has tried to show in other publications in both English and Japanese, the international cases were simply the tip of the iceberg, a variant of a deeper, endemic problem that caused – and is still causing – suffering to parents and children in "mundane" domestic custody and access disputes outside the scope of the Convention.[2]

The Convention started primarily as a "Western" instrument of private international law, with relatively few Asian signatories joining until well into the twenty-first century.[3] The treaty is based on what can arguably be described as "Western," rights-based family law concepts: "rights of custody" and "rights of access" (or visitation, in American parlance).[4]

What do these concepts mean in Japan – for fathers or any parent? Since Japan's ratification of the Convention most of the attention in the Western press continues to be on cases of children taken *to* Japan. For purposes of this chapter, however, the more interesting question is how one might go about proving to a foreign court or other authority that one has rights of custody or access under *Japanese* law, when using the Convention to seek the return of a child from a foreign country or assistance in realizing visitation with a child taken *from* Japan. The answer will help inform us about the state of parents' rights in Japan.

The Civil Code and rights of access

The principal source of substantive family law is Part IV of the Japanese Civil Code. This was originally passed in 1898 and substantially revised during the post-war occupation to make it consistent with the equal protection and gender equality guarantees contained in articles 14 and 24 of the current constitution.

Logically Part IV is where one would look for provisions identifying rights of custody or access. Until recently one would have looked in vain for the latter, since Japanese law did not

1 See, e.g., Geraldine Carney, "Disrupt, Support and Document: The Role of Social Media in International Parental Child Abduction Cases Involving Japan," in: *New Voices in Japanese Studies* 8 (2016); Colin P.A. Jones, "In the Best Interests of the Court: What American Lawyers Need to Know about Child Custody and Visitation in Japan," *Asian-Pacific Law & Policy Journal* 8 (2007).

2 Id. See also, Colin P.A. Jones, "Kodomo No Tsuresari Mondaii" [The Child Abduction Problem] (*Heibonsha shinsho*, 2011).

3 See, Colin P.A. Jones, "Will the Child Abduction Treaty become more 'Asian'? A First Look at the Efforts of Singapore and Japan to Implement the Hague Convention," *Denver Journal of International Law and Policy* 42 (2013–2014).

4 As defined in Article 5 of the Convention:
  a) "rights of custody" shall include rights relating to the care of the person of the child and, in particular, the right to determine the child's place of residence;
  b) "rights of access" shall include the right to take a child for a limited period of time to a place other than the child's habitual residence."

contain any references to visitation until 2011, when article 766 of the Code was amended to require divorcing parents to agree upon, *inter alia*, post-divorce contact. The relevant language is set forth below (the underlining reflecting the 2011 amendments) and clearly describes a *duty* rather than a right, and a duty to agree on *something* (including little or no visitation) rather than a right. The best interests of the child is the applicable standard, but nowhere is a presumption in favor of visitation ever articulated.

> (Determination of Matters regarding Custody of Child after Divorce etc.)
>
> Article 766 (1) If parents divorce by agreement, the matters of who will have custody over a child, visitation and other contacts between the father or mother and the child, sharing of expenses required for custody of the child and any other necessary matters regarding custody over the child shall be determined by that agreement. In this case, the child's interests shall be considered with the highest priority.
>
> (2) If the agreement set forth in the preceding paragraph has not been made, or cannot be made, the matters set forth in the preceding paragraph shall be determined by the family court.
>
> (3) The family court may change the agreement or determination under the provisions of the preceding two paragraphs and order any other proper disposition regarding custody over the child, if it finds this necessary.
>
> (4) The rights and duties of parents beyond the scope of custody may not be altered by the provisions of the preceding three paragraphs.

Collectively, article 766 appears to describe visitation as something that exists only if parents formally agree to it or a court makes a determination that it should take place. In practice this often puts the parent seeking visitation in the position of having to prove it will *not* be harmful to the child, which can be a challenge if the parent-in-possession argues it is.

Note also the Code does not describe visitation as a "right." In guidance for litigants in domestic cases the Japanese courts also scrupulously avoid describing visitation as a right.

Nor does the language of Article 766 appear to provide any clear relief if parents separate but do not divorce, or while a divorce proceeding is pending (which may take several years) or if the parents are not married in the first place.

With respect to the former case, court practice has expanded the language to cover pre-divorce separation. As to the latter, article 788 of the Code makes article 766 applicable *mutatis mutandis* to cases involving unmarried couples in which the father has acknowledged paternity of the child. Nonetheless, this very limited language illustrates how limited the formal law providing for visitation is even in the context of traditional (married mother – father pairings) family relationships.[5]

5 Although Japanese family courts have been recognizing visitation as a possible component of post-divorce custody arrangements since the 1960s, not being a common law jurisdiction, a judicially created generally applicable right of visitation has never existed. If anything, what little attention Japan's Supreme Court has paid to the subject of preserving and fostering the parent – child relationship after separation has been limited to: (i) rejecting claims of a general right of visitation based on the constitutional guarantee of the right to the pursuit of happiness (Supreme Court, Second Petty Bench decision of July 6, 1984; hereafter the "1984 Case") , (ii) confirming the authority of family courts to order visitation under article 766 *before* divorce despite language clearly referring only to *post* divorce situations (Supreme Court, First Petty Bench decision of May 1, 2000) notwithstanding the clear "post-divorce" language of Article 766, and (iii) clarifying that visitation was only amenable to judicial enforcement if its terms (time, date, etc.) were sufficiently

As in many other countries, courts and academics reject the possibility of tying visitation to payment of child support. Some custodial mothers often struggle to collect agreed or court-ordered child support and the deficiencies of the system for enforcing civil judgments are evident here, but are nowhere near the hurdles involved in enforcing visitation. In fact, visitation is generally understood to be unenforceable, particularly against an impecunious custodial parent, since the principal remedy for non-compliance is a non-penal fine imposed by the courts. Academics and practitioners have suggested a "good parent rule" be used as a remedy against uncooperative parents. In 2016 a family court ordered a transfer of the child in a case where the custodial mother had denied access to the father for five years, but it was overturned the following year on appeal with the status quo still in place.[6]

The Civil Code and rights of custody

What of "rights of custody?" Here the Civil Code has long had provisions that seem relevant. Not only that, but the Ministry of Foreign Affairs (MOFA) – Japan's "Central Authority" for Convention Purposes – provides specific guidance for parents filling out applications seeking their assistance in obtaining the return of a child taken abroad.[7] The guidance comes in several versions depending on whether court orders are in place or not. Preemptive abductions/retentions by a taking parent (TP) before any court proceedings are even commenced let alone orders in place are a common scenario that arises under the Convention, and for this scenario the MOFA guidance indicates parents should cite two provisions of the Civil Code as the basis for having rights of custody under Japanese law: 818(3) and 820. Translations of both articles from the Japanese government's Japanese Law Translation website[8] are set forth below.

> (Person Who Has Parental Authority)
>
> Article 818 (1) A child who has not attained the age of majority shall be subject to the parental authority of his/her parents.
>
> (2) If a child is an adopted child, he/she shall be subject to the parental authority of his/her adoptive parents.
>
> (3) Parental authority shall be exercised jointly by married parents; provided that if either parent is incapable of exercising parental authority, the other parent shall do so.

---

clearly defined and essentially rejecting a longstanding preference among lower courts for vaguely defined visitation that would supposedly accommodate the child's circumstances but also made it possible for custodial parents to always find a reason to prevent visitation from actually taking place (Supreme Court, First Petty Bench decisions (3) of March 28, 2013). Note that the limited judicial interest in preserving the parent – child relationship seems at odds with Japan's obligations under the UN Convention on the Rights of the Child which requires signatory states to recognize children as having, *inter alia*, rights to know and be cared for by their parents, preserve their identity including family relations, and to continued contact with parents to the extent possible even when separated unless contrary to the child's best interests (articles 7, 8 and 9).

6 "Good Parent' Ditched in Custody Case Reversal," *The Japan Times* (January 27, 2017).

7 Application for assistance (return; English version): www.mofa.go.jp/files/000031336.pdf; Application for assistance (access; English version): www.mofa.go.jp/files/000031347.pdf . Last accessed March 15, 2017. Guide to Application for Assistance in Child's Return (English dated February 14, 2017): www.mofa.go.jp/files/000031335.pdf (Last accessed March 15, 2017).

8 www.japaneselawtranslation.go.jp.

(Right and Duty of Care and Education)

Article 820 A person who exercises parental authority holds the right, and bears the duty, to care for and educate the child for the child's interests.

Interestingly, the MOFA guidance for parents seeking Central Authority assistance in exercising "access rights" in respect of children in foreign countries under the Convention references the same two provisions,[9] despite the lack of any mention of access rights in either provision or elsewhere in the Code except article 766, as described above. Also interesting is that in its guidance for applications for assistance for both returns and access based on Japanese law rights of custody or access, the MOFA does not provide any advice for LBPs who are not or never were legally married to the TP.

The Civil Code and parental authority: the historical context and the Convention

In the view of the author, the two Civil Code provisions cited by the MOFA illustrate some very basic potential pitfalls of comparative law. That said, their use by MOFA in this context is almost certainly based on a conscious awareness of the limitations described below but not disclosed in their guidance.

Let us start with Article 818, which enunciates what likely seems to a Western practitioner a familiar, if slightly vague articulation of where parental authority is vested in various situations. In its historical context, however, it takes on a different meaning. The family law provisions of the Civil Code were drastically revised during the post-war US occupation. This was in part due to the need to reconcile them to the new constitution and its guarantees of equal protection of the law generally (article 14) and gender equality specifically (article 24). Under the pre-war Civil Code parental authority was vested *only* in fathers unless the father was unavailable. Parental authority – the disciplinary aspects of it at least – also extended to *adult* offspring who did not earn their own keep. To a degree therefore, Article 818(1) and (3) thus represent a rejection of prior law.

Similarly, paragraph (3) of article 818 – "parental authority shall be jointly exercised by married parents" – seems to articulate a basic feature of modern family law just about everywhere. Contract lawyers, however, might appreciate that it does not say "jointly *and severally*." It is thus possible to interpret the language as articulating that a married mother and father exercise parental authority jointly *against the rest of the world*, but not necessarily individually as between themselves. This may be closer to the *correct* interpretation; while article 825 specifically protects third parties from conflicting exercises of parental authority, the Code is silent as to what happens between parents unable to agree. As noted by Professor Mariko Shirasu in one of the leading commentaries on Chapter IV of the Civil Code: "(c)urrent law does not provide for any procedures that can be followed in the event that during the marriage the mother and father disagree as to the exercise of parental authority."[10]

This being the case, one would likely search long and hard in Japanese academic and practice literature to find a statement as clear as that of the MOFA to the effect that article 818(3) (or 820) constitutes a basis for demanding visitation with or the return of a child in a strictly domestic case between Japanese parents and not implicating the Convention.

9 Guide to Application for Assistance in Visitation or Contacts with Child, (English version dated February 14, 2017): www.mofa.go.jp/files/000031346.pdf. Last accessed March 15, 2017.

10 *Shinkihon Hō Komentāru Shinzoku (Minpō Dai 725 Jō – Dai 881 Jō* [New Commentaries on Basic Laws: Civil Code Arts 725–881] (Matsukawa & Atsumi eds, 2015; hereafter "*Commentaries*"), at 216.

In fact, the extraordinary thing about the 150 article procedural statute passed by Japan's Diet for the sole purpose of implementing the Convention, is that it uses the terms "rights of custody" and "visitation" without ever clearly defining them, either in reference to the Convention or the Civil Code.[11] The disconnect between this law and the Convention on the one hand and the Civil Code on the other is particularly blatant. The implementing act uses a term "*kango no kenri*" ("rights of custody") that is not used in the Civil Code. Despite the Convention defining such rights as including "rights relating to the care of the person of the child and, *in particular, the right to determine the child's place of residence*" (emphasis added) and article 821 of the Civil Code stating that "[r]esidence of a child shall be determined by a person who exercises parental authority," there is no effort to tie parental authority under the Civil Code with rights of custody under the Convention.

In a similar vein, despite a Convention that clearly speaks of *rights* of access, Japan's implementing statute never refers to visitation as a right. The author's view is that the drafting of the statute reflects a conscious effort on the part of policy-makers to avoid it being the basis for identifying clear rights of custody or access in Japanese law that can be asserted in *domestic* cases, a subject we will revisit later in this chapter.

The family registry system

Here let us consider the very basic question introduced at the beginning of this chapter: who is family law for? In Japan, the answer may be that historically it has been primarily for the government and the rest of society, rather than members within the family unit. This is reflected in the fact that a great deal of Japanese family law is or was devoted to *identifying* the family so that it can be used as a tool for governance and identifying points of intersection in legal dealings between a family and the rest of society.

This aspect of the law becomes apparent in the *koseki*, Japan's family registry system.[12] Marriages, births, adoptions, divorces and other changes in family status are registered in a Japanese person's *koseki*, and an official extract from the registry serves as proof of family status for a wide variety of legal purposes such as inheritance and dealings with government agencies.[13] Until it was revised together with the Civil Code during the US occupation, the *koseki* also identified the "head of household," a heritable legal status (usually vested in the eldest legitimate male) that had numerous enumerated powers to dispose of family property and decide what other members of the family could and couldn't do in matters such as marriage or adoption. The head of household also served as an identifiable nexus of responsibility for the family through whom government authorities could impose policies such as conscription, taxation and education, and creditors could enforce debts.

Until the 1970s a person's *koseki* was essentially a quasi-public document; anyone could view another person's family history meaning divorces and children born out of wedlock were a matter

11 Act for Implementation of the Convention on the Civil Aspects of International Child Abduction, Act No. 48 Of 2013. English translation available at: www.japaneselawtranslation.go.jp/law/detail/?id=2159&vm=&re= (last accessed May 20, 2017). The disconnect between "rights of custody" in this law and the Convention on one hand and the Civil Code on the other is particularly blatant. Article 5 of the Convention defines "rights of custody" as including "rights relating to the care of the person of the child and, in particular, *the right to determine the child's place of residence*" (emphasis added). Article 821 of the Civil Code states clearly that "*[r]esidence of a child shall be determined by a person who exercises parental authority.*"

12 The current family registry system is governed by the Family Register Act, Act No. 224 of 1947. However such registries have existed in various forms in Japan (and other Asian jurisdictions) for centuries.

13 The *koseki* system obviates the need for many judicial probate proceedings because in many cases surviving family members can use *koseki* records to prove conclusively to a bank or the real property registry authority that they represent all possible heirs of the decedent and have estate property disposed of as per their collectively-expressed wishes.

of public record. Even now legal professionals (and of course government authorities) have the ability to access a person's *koseki* for certain purposes.[14] Yet the originally quasi-public character of the *koseki* was more consistent with its purpose in the context of Japanese family law, a means of authenticating to the rest of the world family relationships that have potential legal significance in dealings between the family and third parties. In essence, the *koseki* once offered a functionality analogous to that of a real estate title registry. It showed the legal family relationships recognized by the family code, even if that did not reflect family reality; whether a husband and wife actually lived together (for example) would be evident from a separate system of residence registry.

As for the rights and duties as between members *within* a family unit, the long held traditional view was that the law should not interfere in domestic affairs. The provisions of the Civil Code on these aspects of family law will likely seem sparse to a Western lawyer; here the courts have filled in much of the detail through case law and practice. For example, just as 2011 amendments to the Civil Code saw post-divorce visitation formally acknowledged in statutory form for the first time, the same is true of financial support for children post-divorce. Even now there is no statutory duty to pay anything, though imposing it is a routine practice in family courts and the judiciary has created detailed guidelines for calculating the amount that should be paid.[15]

In essence, therefore, Japanese family law is comprised of two prongs. In fact the author has heard this described by a Japanese attorney as there being two systems of family law: one under the jurisdiction of the Ministry of Justice (i.e., the family register system) and the other under the jurisdiction of the courts.

The former system identifies those legally recognized family relationships that can potentially affect the rest of the world: marital status (through joint claims to property and liability for debts) and parental authority (the authority to manage a child's property and transact on their behalf). More extended family relationships may also be relevant in the inheritance sphere. These relationships are ascertainable from the *koseki*, and because they are part of a system of identification they need to be unambiguous. Article 818(3) allocates it to married parents, article 818(2) allocates it to adoptive parents, and article 819 makes it clear that parental authority is presumed to default solely to the mother of a child born out of wedlock and can only be allocated to one parent after divorce, whether judicial or consensual.[16] These clear, simple rules mean the locus of parental authority will always be clear from a *koseki* extract.

14 Family Register Act, article 10–2.

15 See, e.g., Tokyo Family Court guidelines for calculating child maintenance and spousal support (*Yōikuhi/kon'in hiyō santeihyō*) at: www.courts.go.jp/tokyo-f/vcms_lf/santeihyo.pdf (last accessed May 20, 2017).

16 (Person Who Has Parental Authority in the Case of Divorce or Recognition)

Article 819

(1) If parents divorce by agreement, they may agree upon which parent shall have parental authority in relation to a child.
(2) In the case of judicial divorce, the court shall determine which parent shall have parental authority.
(3) In the case where parents divorce before the birth of a child, the mother shall exercise parental rights and duties; provided that the parties may agree that the father shall have parental authority after the child is born.
(4) A father shall only exercise parental authority with regard to a child of his that he has affiliated if both parents agree that he shall have parental authority.
(5) When the parents do not, or cannot, make the agreements referred to in paragraph (1), paragraph (3), and the preceding paragraph, the family court may, at the request of the father or the mother, make a ruling in lieu of agreement.
(6) The family court may, at the request of any relative of the child, rule that the other parent shall have parental authority in relation to the child if it finds it necessary for the interests of the child.

The latter system of family law – that administered by the courts – could be described as "everything else," and includes many things that do not (and probably should not) affect third parties – at least legally – and thus do not need to be reflected in the *koseki*. In the context of divorce and child custody this would include whether child support is paid and how much, who the children live with, where they go to school and what sort of contact the non-residential parent will have (if any) after separation. In the first instance the parties are free to decide upon whatever they want, which may well include not deciding on anything other than to execute and file the divorce paperwork (including allocation of parental authority over each child of the marriage) at the local municipal office.

Courts only become involved if the parties can't agree on the terms of the separation or one party doesn't want to divorce or surrender parental authority, or if there is no "divorce" to fight over in the first place, but perhaps a long-term relationship involving financial dependency or even children. Even if courts do become involved in such cases, however, they operate under a "conciliation first" principle, reflecting a statutory mandate to conduct court-sponsored conciliation before proceeding with anything adversarial, let alone formal litigation.[17]

Thus, the involvement of a Japanese family court in such disputes usually begins and (more often than not) ends with the court encouraging parents to reach an agreement they could have reached out of court anyways, though perhaps more informed about the likely legal outcome and with neutral judges, mediators and possibly specialist family court investigators offering informed "suggestions" about what might be best for the children. Cases only proceed to formal litigation under the Personal Status Litigation Act of 2003 if the family conciliation process is unsuccessful and if one or both parties persist in their claim. By this point, however, the *status quo* as to any children involved may have become well established through the passage of time (mediation proceedings can drag out for months) but also provisional "pre-trial" dispositions made by the courts in the interests of the child, including those relating to who has (physical) custody, child support payments and visitation (if any). These dispositions may come in the form of a decree expressing the agreement the court *thinks* the parties should have come to, and literally called "decrees in lieu of conciliation" (*chōtei ni kawaru shinpan*).[18] Such dispositions can be revisited at the litigation stage, though of course it will likely be an uphill struggle to convince a judge that these earlier dispositions were misguided.

As for litigation, Japan is odd in that on the one hand consensual divorces are shockingly *easy* to procure,[19] yet litigated divorces are very *hard*. Article 770 of the Civil Code only recognizes limited grounds for divorce suits: infidelity, bad faith abandonment, disappearance, incurable mental disease, and a helpful "other" category that has been interpreted in various ways by courts, with irretrievable breakdown demonstrated by years of separation being increasingly accepted. Moreover, just as parents can only allocate parental authority and have it reflected in the *koseki* at the time of divorce, courts are also generally only able to make decisions about parental authority (or more accurately the "legal custody" aspects of it) at the time it grants a divorce.[20] Marital

17 Domestic Relations Case Procedure Act (Act. No. 52 of 2011, hereafter "DRCPA"), article 257.

18 DRCPA articles 284–287.

19 So easy that one does not even need to be in Japan to get one; Japanese people can conduct *koseki* filings from abroad by mail or through their local consulates. Also so easy that fraudulent filings are a persistent problem, with foreign spouses unable to read Japanese sometimes finding out too late that what they were told they were signing was a kindergarten application (for example) was actually a divorce filing that also surrendered parental authority to the Japanese parent.

20 Civil Code, articles 819(1) and (2).

status affects parental authority and both are reflected in the *koseki*, so absent special circumstances a court will only allocate parental authority at the time it renders a divorce.

Although family courts can theoretically issue a divorce decree at the conclusion of a an unsuccessful divorce conciliation, instances of them actually doing so are exceptionally rare, possibly because they can be readily voided by filing an objection.[21] This leaves parties to commence litigation proceedings or live separately but still as husband and wife at law. For those who do proceed with litigation it can involve a prolonged period of limbo during which the non-custodial parent is still vested with parental authority but may have virtually no access to his or her children or ability to participate meaningfully in their care or education.

Judicial divorces and allocations of parental authority represent a minority of cases brought before the courts, which in turn represent a small minority of divorces overall. Even when the courts *do* grant divorces and allocate parental authority in the form of a judgment, the substance of the decree would be reflected in the parties' *koseki*.[22] Since even a judicial divorce results in the relevant status being reflected in the *koseki*, divorce and custody decrees are never used as proof of identification in the way they are in the United States and other countries where everything is done through the judicial process.

According to Japan's National Institute of Population and Social Security Research, of the 235,406 divorces recorded in 2012, 205,406 were achieved without any judicial involvement at all, by merely filing notifications of divorce with the *koseki* system; 23,616 were resolved through judicial conciliation and only 2,788 – just 1.1% of the total! – resulted from adversarial litigation resulting in a final judgment.[23]

Obeying the law, without knowing it

Having absorbed this information, we can now turn to what may be one of the ways in which the Japanese system differs from that familiar to US lawyers, at least insofar as the parent – child relationship is concerned. That is, the Japanese system is not founded in parties coming to court from the outset and asserting specific, clearly identified rights, whether to a divorce, child support, custody, visitation or anything else. It is based on parties agreeing to whatever they think appropriate (subject to the restraints on what can and can't be reflected in the *koseki*) in the first instance, a court encouraging them to agree on a settlement in the second instance, and a court adjudicating the matter only as a final resort.[24] When it does so it will almost certainly make decisions about the children based on to what may seem to outside observers a completely subjective "best interests" standards and which, given the time involved in obtaining a litigated

21 DRCPA, articles 284, 286(5).

22 Here it is worth noting an important but often overlooked difference between the Japanese system of family law and that of common law countries is that court orders are never used as official proof of status, since this can be accomplished more efficiently with *koseki* extracts. Common law lawyers and judges handling family cases involving a Japanese nexus may overestimate the significance of whether a foreign court order will be "recognized" or "enforced" by Japanese courts.

23 www.ipss.go.jp/syoushika/tohkei/Popular/P_Detail2014.asp?fname=T06-02.htm (last accessed April 22, 2017). A small number of divorces were also achieved through pre-trial decrees, settlement or other procedurally obscure means.

24 Moreover, the litigation stage is likely to involve more efforts by the court to encourage the parties to agree on something, as is suggested by the fact that in 2012 more divorces (3,831) were achieved through settlements reached after litigation was commenced than by judicial decision. Id.

divorce, will almost certainly involve ratifying the status quo, even in situations where one parent has unilaterally taken the child.[25]

Yet it is also worth looking beyond the "best interests of the child standard" to Japanese history. Before Japan opened up and modernized by adopting Western-modeled laws and legal institutions, its system of civil justice was based on supplicants coming before an official *without knowing the law*. In fact there was an official proscription on the dissemination of information about what the law actually was. A Confucian saying from this era illustrates the attitude of the ruling class: "the people do not need to know the law, but they should be made to obey it."[26]

Japanese law is no longer governed by Confucian precedents, of course, but in the views of the author there remains an element of obfuscation in what the law actually is that is part of the essentially authoritarian (but not totalitarian) character of the Japanese system. In any case, unlike common law systems, Japan does *not* have a long tradition of litigants showing up in court and asserting specific rights, nor do its judges or other officials have a long tradition of being told by the common man or woman what they are supposed to do in any particular situation.

Moreover, the freedom the *koseki* system accords to people to change their family relationships without judicial involvement make the Japanese system very different for other reasons as already described. These very basic differences are important yet easy to miss when an American-trained lawyer starts talking to her Japanese counterpart about how to deal with a cross-border divorce or child custody matter, whether under the Convention or otherwise. This is because the Japanese lawyer may offer a description of how Japanese courts deal with family disputes in a way that sounds comfortingly familiar, but is in fact highly misleading if it does not mention that the underlying system assumes court involvement to be an optional extra rather than a central feature and when they *do* become involved there are no clearly identifiable external standards governing what they *must* do in any particular case.

Parental rights as parental duties

Here a Western lawyer might be tempted to interject that even though only a small minority of divorce cases are finally resolved through the courts, the overall system that results in conciliated results and out of court settlements is at least vaguely informed and shaped by those resolutions, which in cases involving children would include the manner in which courts validate and enforce parental rights.

Such an argument would involve a number of assumptions about what, if anything, the concept of "parental rights" means in the Japanese context. Here we should return to the text of article 820 of the Civil Code,[27] which it should be recalled is supposedly the other leg on which

25 On October 21, 2013 Diet member Kazuyuki Hamada submitted a set of questions to the government noting that family courts seemed to be ratifying what were essentially parental child abductions by applying the "principle of continuity" (*keizokusei no gensoku*) and seeking the government's official views on the situation and data such as the number of suicides and arrests that resulted from such cases. www.sangiin.go.jp/japanese/joho1/kousei/syuisyo/185/syuh/s185018.htm. On November 19, the government responded with a demurrer to the effect that it had no data, did not see a need to understand the situation and that such matters were up to the courts. www.sangiin.go.jp/japanese/joho1/kousei/syuisyo/185/touh/t185050.htm. (last accessed March 23, 2017).

26 For a very useful discussion of the constraints imposed on dissemination of legal knowledge in pre-Meiji Japan see chapter 1 of Darryl Flaherty, *Public Law, Private Practice: Politics, Profit and the Legal Profession in Nineteenth-Century Japan* (2013).

27 See 4. The Civil Code and Rights of Custody, supra.

a claim of "rights of custody" or "rights of access" under Japanese law should be asserted in foreign jurisdiction in cases arising under the Convention.

Note, however, that to the extent article 820 at least *appears* to be the source of rights – the right (and duty) to care for and educate children – it recognizes them in a "person having parental authority" rather than "parents" per se. Articles 818 and 819 establish the categories of persons "having parental authority" and for the most part these categories consist of parents, but not *all* of them: unmarried fathers are generally excluded as is one parent after a divorce. And as discussed later in this chapter, the presumptions of paternity contained elsewhere in the Civil Code (and of maternity by the Supreme Court) further restrict who may claim parental authority.

A simple example of what this means in terms of parental rights – or their absence, depending on your perspective – comes up in the practice of post-remarriage adoption. The Civil Code's provisions on adoption accord great flexibility for forming and dissolving adoptive relations through filings with the family registry in much the same manner as marriages and divorces.[28] If a woman remarries after divorce, it is not uncommon for her new husband to adopt the children of the prior marriage (assuming she has parental authority over them). Although the Civil Code (article 798) requires adoptions of minors to be authorized by a family court, there is a specific exception from this requirement "where the person to be adopted is a lineal descendant of either the adoptive parent or the adoptive parent's spouse." The prior husband/biological father has no right to even receive notice of this arrangement, let alone consent to it. This is logical in a way; he no longer has parental authority, while it would be odd for his ex-wife's new husband to lack it despite (presumably) living in the same house with them.[29]

What of parental rights before divorce? Let us return to article 820, which articulates a "right and duty of care and education." Not only does the statutory language refer to "rights," but one of the Chinese characters comprising *shinken* – the Japanese term for "parental authority" is *ken*, which actually means "right" and is used in a wide variety of other legal terms expressing some sort of right. So it seems fairly obvious that to the extent at least *some* parents enjoy parental authority, it involves some parental rights.

Yet what the concept of "rights" entails may involve a number of assumptions that are of questionable applicability in Japan. First, it bears reiterating that Japan is not a common law jurisdiction; which is to say (again) its substantive law has not evolved primarily through the process of parties asserting rights to specific, known categories of judicial relief broadly known to comprise part of the "common" law.[30]

28 In Japan "adoption" means something quite different from what Western readers are likely to associate with the term. Provided for under articles 792 to 817 of the Civil Code, Japanese adoption is common among adults and was long a solution to the problem of (for example) families needing a male to carry on a family business but lacking a son. In standard adoptions, the formation of the adoptive relationship does not terminate the adoptees' relationship with his or her natural parent for inheritance purposes, and in fact generation-skipping adoptions within families are a common estate planning technique. What Americans are likely to associate with adoption – assuming exclusive care and control of a young child in an arrangement that results in the termination of the relationship with the natural parent(s) is in Japan a "special adoption," and covered in articles 817–2 through 817–11, which were only added to the Civil Code in 1987.

29 A social aspect of this dynamic is that in the experience of the author it is rare for Japanese people to self-identify the nitty-gritty details of their family status, and there are not even any commonly used Japanese terms used to refer to "step" or "half" family members.

30 By contrast, prior to the Meiji Restoration, Japanese society was subject to various positive proscriptions on the dissemination of information about the law; parties who sought adjudication of disputes through trial-like proceedings were not supposed to know what the law was. See generally, Flaherty, supra note 25 at 28–88.

Second, it may be necessary to distinguish between "rights" and what I will call for lack of a better term "capabilities." As the preceding discussion has hopefully shown, parental authority is clearly not meaningless – one who has it may (for example) consent to the adoption of their child by a spouse or grandparent, one who does not may not. Parental authority gives those who have it the capability of interacting with government bodies and the rest of society on behalf of the child, in what may essentially be yes/no binary transactions. But is that the same as a *right* of the sort articulated in Article 820?

Third, in their basic essence as legal concepts both rights and duties involve demanding that someone act or refrain from acting in a particular way. Beyond that the difference between the two is largely positional: if I am asserting it against you it is a right, if you are asserting it against me it is a duty. This basic dynamic becomes more complex when asserting rights through a third party – a court or other authority figure – in the context of a dispute over the existence, extent or exercise of the rights. This is because it is possible for the authority to tell one or both parties that they must do something (a duty) without acknowledging a specific right – at least in the parties.

In disputes over children, the modern approach of Japanese courts (and courts elsewhere as well) is likely to cast this in terms of the welfare of the child – or children's rights. This is logical, may seem consistent with what courts in other developed nations are doing and is even arguably consistent with article 3(1) of the UN Convention on the Rights of the Child.[31] Yet it should also be borne in mind that such "best interests" determinations are made absent any clearly articulated legislative or judicial principles,[32] and the results may seem inconsistent with the UNCRC provisions regarding the rights of children to know and be cared for by their parents, to preserve their identity (including family relations), and maintain contact with parents despite separation.[33]

Moreover, the modern Japanese approach is also consistent with the pre-modern Japanese system of dispute resolution described whereby litigants were expected to conciliate without knowing the law or whatever might have been considered as "rights" at the time.[34] Either way, parental *duties* can be defined post facto and tailored to specific circumstances, while minimizing any connection to a priori knowable concrete rights.

This is certainly consistent with Japanese court's approach to visitation. Recall that MOFA suggests that Articles 818 and 820 of the Civil Code form the basis for asserting "rights of access" in connection with the Convention. Having specifically rejected any constitutional foundation

31 "In all actions concerning children, whether undertaken by public or private social welfare institutions, courts of law, administrative authorities or legislative bodies, the best interests of the child shall be a primary consideration."

32 The absence of clear standards of what is presumed best for children; frequent and continuing contact with both parents, absent exceptional circumstances, for example, is consistent within the framework of the "rights/duties" dynamic described earlier in this chapter. Clear a priori knowable standards would increase the number of instances where parties could appear in court and make rights-like *demands* that a court act in a particular way.

33 Articles 7, 8 and 9. This author has also seen at least one case in which a Japanese family court refused to grant the father more than extremely limited visitation in part on the grounds that parental feuding might "inconvenience" schools and other third parties, demonstrably *not* treating the best interests of the child as the primary consideration.

34 "Kenri," the Japanese term for "right" had to be invented in the latter half of the nineteenth century in order to translate Western codes and statutes into Japanese. Some have argued that this indicates the Japanese lacked a concept of "rights" until their exposure to Western writings on the subject. By the same logic, however, Western culture could be said to lack "empathy" until that term was invented around the same time. Susan Lanzoni, *A Short History of Empathy*, The Atlantic, Oct. 15, 2015 (available at: www.theatlantic.com/health/archive/2015/10/a-short-history-of-empathy/409912/).

for a right of visitation as early as 1984,[35] the court referenced both articles when it revisited the subject of visitation again in 2000.[36] However, it did so in the context of ratifying a lower court decision ordering visitation in a case involving parents who were estranged but still married under Article 766 of the Civil Code. That article, by both title and content, only refers to "Determination of Matters regarding Custody of Child *after* Divorce etc." (emphasis added), and the case arose in the form of a challenge by a mother resisting visitation by the father on the grounds the lower court had the authority to apply the provision by analogy in situations where the parties were not yet divorced.

The 2000 case thus did not involve an assertion of rights of custody or visitation but a challenge to the authority of courts to make a particular type of disposition. Unsurprisingly, it was unsuccessful, and in justifying its rejection of the mother's appeal, it referenced articles 818 and 820 only to the extent of declaring that "visitation can be construed as a component of the child custody for either parent not living with the child." Note the use of the word "component," not "right."

In fact, despite the judgment in the 2000 case being quite short, it is generally understood as having resolved the longstanding dispute over whether visitation was a right and if so, of whom. The explanatory memorandum published by the research judge on the Supreme Court who assisted the bench with the 2000 case makes it clear that visitation is not a right of demand, but a right to ask a court to make a disposition in the interests of the child.[37] Whether the court is required to make such a disposition in any particular case is another matter, of course; at least one leading commentator on family court practice has made it clear that visitation is only a "right" when a court says so.[38] Japanese family courts can and do decline to order visitation, even for parents still theoretically vested with full joint parental authority, often on no more basis than that the parent having control over the children is uncooperative or has concerns.

On the subject of "rights" of custody, access or anything else that might be derived from Article 820 (or other provisions of the Civil Code defining the parameters of parental authority) it should be noted that most commentary from mainstream academics and practitioners is almost openly hostile to conceptualizing parental authority in terms of parental "rights." For example, one leading commentary on the "parental authority" provisions of the Civil Code states that:

> Parental authority is the role a parent must play in raising a minor child to be a full member of society. It is referred to as parental "rights" but it has been pointed out that it has been principally of the nature of duties since the age of the Meiji Civil Code. Parental authority must be exercised only for the welfare and benefit of the child, not in furtherance of the parent's own interests. Of course, there is a right-like aspect to it in that persons having parental authority have the right to exclude other parties from the care and education of the child, and there are also aspects of it entailing rights against the child him/herself. However, in place of the traditional explanation of parental authority entailing rights and duties, in recent years there is a view that [article 820] can be interpreted as enunciating parental authority as entailing no rights and only duties [citations omitted].[39]

35 Supreme Court, 2nd Petty Bench decision of July 6, 1984.
36 Supreme Court, First Petty Bench decision of May 1, 2000.
37 This memorandum is discussed in detail in Jones, *supra* note 1, at 242–245.
38 Taichi Kajimura, *Rikon Chōtei Gaidobukku* [Divorce Conciliation Guidebook] (3rd edn, 2008), at 179 ("because *visitation only becomes a concrete right upon the parties agreeing to it or through a court decree in lieu of such agreement,* in family case conciliation it is important to avoid unnecessarily recommending it to parties while indiscriminately declaring 'it's a right, it's a right'"). Emphasis added.
39 Michihiro Tanaka, *Article 820, Commentaries, supra* note 10, at 225. Translation of quote by Jones.

This conceptual erasure of any "parental rights" component of parental authority is a common theme in Japanese academic and professional commentary on the subject of parental authority.

Finally, it should be noted that not only is parental authority overwhelmingly considered to be *duties* of parents – and thus difficult to assert by (as opposed to against) parents – until 2011 it was not even clear to whom these duties were owed. The seemingly obvious "for the child's interests" was not added to article 820 until 2011. In literature pre-dating this change it was not uncommon to see explanations to the effect that parental authority was in part a duty of parents to society in general.[40] This is probably more consistent with views of what *shinken* meant dating back to the process of drafting the original Civil Code at the end of the nineteenth century. For example, debates at the time included when language specifying the duty to pay for education (at a time when the state lacked resources) should be included, if so who should bear that duty (the parents, or the head of the household in which they were registered).[41] Scholarly quotes from the period include descriptions of parental authority as "a duty ordered of fathers and mothers so the state may make good subjects" and "something received from the state, subject to some limitations, interference, and assistance."[42]

Rights of custody and access reconsidered

Readers who have persisted on this circuitous route may now be able to appreciate why it may be difficult for a parent of either gender to assert rights of custody or visitation, even while possessed of parental authority under Japanese law in strictly domestic cases. One may also appreciate why, given their interpretation in domestic cases, using articles 818(3) and 820 of the Civil Code as a basis for asserting "rights of custody" or "rights of access" under Japanese law in *foreign* courts under the Convention might seem to border on mendacity.[43] It may also assist in at least speculating why Japan's statute implementing the Convention defines "rights of custody" and "visitation" without any language tying them to article 818(3), 820 or any other supposedly rights-based provision of Japanese law – because substantively there aren't any.[44]

Thus, to the extent a Japanese court does consider the best interests of the child in a manner similar to that of a common law court, it will do so without being informed (or, depending on your viewpoint, burdened) by the much more deeply rooted practice in common law systems of deriving rules of family law from the recognition and protection of parental rights. In common law

40 See, e.g., Takashi Uchida, *Minpō IV* (2004), at 211 (["the right to raise and educate the child under article 820] should be considered a social responsibility.")

41 Tazuko Hiroi, *Shinken no seiritsu, Meiji minpō no naka no oya, kodomo, kokka [The establishment of parental authority; parents, children and the state in the Meiji Civil Code]*, at 4–5. http://hiroitz.sakura.ne.jp/resources/%E8%AB%96%E6%96%87/parental-right2.pdf (last accessed May 3, 2017).

42 Id. at 8–9. Interestingly, some commentators at the time objected to bringing the state into the equation, reflecting the view of some that the Civil Code was concerned only with "private rights" and that adding a public law element was inappropriate.

43 In fairness to the MOFA, they are technically seeking evidence of rights of custody or access for purposes of evaluating whether a parent is eligible for their assistance as Central Authority in cases under the Convention. At the time of writing their on-line guidance actually went on to state that different assertions regarding the basis for rights of access or custody may need to be made in court proceedings!

44 Act for Implementation of the Convention on the Civil Aspects of International Child Abduction, Act No. 48 of 2013. For example, article 11(1) of this law simply refers to "a person who has the rights of custody of said child under the laws and regulations of Japan" without reference to any provisions of the Civil Code. On the subject of visitation, the law manages to avoid even using the phrase "visitation under the laws and regulations of Japan" and in fact skillfully avoids ever referring to visitation as a "right" at all (despite it being so under the Convention).

systems this manifests itself in a constitutional dimension, as in *Troxel v. Granville* in the United States, or Canada where "It could be said, then, that parents' rights (or, at least, an aspect thereof) are the oldest constitutionalized individual rights in Canadian law."[45] In Japan this background is missing.

Legitimacy and "non-traditional" family structures

The foregoing discussion has focused on the not insignificant hurdles a married parent who has parental authority may face when seeking to assert parental rights – rights of custody or access – against the other parent. The ability of unmarried fathers, grandparents or other persons outside the scope of a traditional family unit to assert rights – access rights, for example – is even more constrained.

We can now turn to another hurdle presented by the Japanese family law system, which is how parents – fathers in particular – are defined and identified. These come primarily in the form of Civil Code presumptions of paternity and legitimacy, which quite literally date back to the nineteenth century. They also come attached to what is now in some parts of the world the "classical" conception of marriage as being between a male and a female, and children as being a byproduct of intercourse between them. This means that for parents in same-sex unions (which are not recognized under Japanese law) rights of custody or access are limited.

One element of this somewhat archaic heritage is that legitimacy remains surprisingly important in Japanese family law. Currently whether a child is born in wedlock or not results in differing treatment as to how the child is registered in the family registry (and in whose), their legal surname (Civil Code, article 790), default allocation of parental authority (article 819(4)) and eligibility for Japanese nationality (Nationality Act, articles 2 and 3). In the past legitimacy also affected inheritance rights and eligibility for head of household status.[46] In 2013 the Supreme Court issued a decision upholding a requirement that parents check a box in a notice of birth filed with the family registry authorities if the child was "illegitimate," notwithstanding the fact that the authorities would be able to ascertain such status from the *koseki* without parents self-reporting.[47]

For children born out of wedlock there are procedures for voluntary or forced (judicial) affiliation.[48] These will result in the affiliating parent's name appearing in the child's *koseki*, and the *mutatis mutandis* application of article 766 to the duty of the parents to decide on matters relating to the *custody* of the child (article 788). Beyond that, affiliation does not appear to result in any additional "rights" on the part of a father doing so.

Presumptions of paternity, assisted reproduction and scientific proof

As for paternity, the Civil Code establishes rigid presumptions of paternity that date back to the nineteenth century. Moreover, in several recent decisions it has made it clear that even when there is conclusive proof that *genetic* parenthood is different from presumed parenthood the latter shall prevail.

45 Katie Sykes, in "Bambi Meets Godzilla: Children's and Parents' Rights in Canadian Foundation for Children, Youth and the Law v. Canada" 51 McGill Law Journal 131, 135 (2006).

46 Until it was found unconstitutional in 2013, article 900 of the Civil Code accorded to those offspring born out of wedlock a share of a decedent's estate that was only half of that received to legitimate children. "Head of household" was a heritable status that was eliminated by the post-war occupation-era amendments to the Code.

47 Supreme Court, 1st Petty Bench decision of September 26, 2013.

48 Civil Code articles 779–788.

For example, in 2013, the Supreme Court ruled it was inappropriate for local family registry authorities to refuse to register as the father of a newborn baby the transgender husband of the child's mother. In 2004 it became possible to change one's legal gender by confirming the completion of various medical procedures through the family courts and the family registry system.[49] A person born (and registered in the family registry) as a woman went through this process and married a woman. They conceived a child through donor sperm, but because the registry authorities could see from the husband's registry details that he had been born biologically as female, they knew that the child was not his. The Supreme Court ruled that this was inappropriate and found in favor of registering the husband as father.

In 2015 the court found that the prohibition on women (only) remarrying within six months after termination of a prior marriage contained in article 233 of the Civil Code was unconstitutional *to the extent the prohibition period exceeded 100 days*. The Civil Code was promptly amended so that the prohibition is now limited to 100 days, but still applies only to women.

In the first case the court's ruling seems (and was touted by some media as) extremely progressive. The second case will likely seem perverse, but certainly not progressive. Both, however, are driven by the court's desire to preserve the doctrinal purity of the presumptions of paternity reflected in article 772 of the Civil Code, which states that:

(1) A child conceived by a wife during marriage shall be presumed to be a child of her husband.
(2) A child born after 200 days from the formation of marriage or within 300 days of the day of the dissolution or rescission of marriage shall be presumed to have been conceived during marriage.

The transgender father case can be understood as a fairly simply application of Paragraph (1). After all, he and his wife were in the same situation as any other couple conceiving through donor sperm, the only difference being the knowledge about his biological past was available to registry officials. Moreover, the Civil Code accords only the husband the right to challenge paternity, and then only within a year of learning of the birth (articles 774 and 777). These provisions were developed at a time when the ability to scientifically confirm, or even deny paternity did not exist and it was deemed desirable to establish extremely firm presumptions to minimize the instances and period of latency of disputes over paternity. It was thus not the place of registry officials to rebut these presumptions simply because they happened to know facts about this particular husband that made paternity particularly implausible.

The remarriage restriction case also makes sense within this framework. The Civil Code essentially assumes a 300-day gestation period during which the presumptions should ideally point to a single person as putative father. The post-dissolution 300-day period during which the presumption runs to the ex-husband reflects this (as well as a possibly unrealistic assumption that couples are likely to have sex the day before registering a divorce).[50] The presumption of paternity in births 200 days AFTER marriage is of a similar provenance, though reflecting a

49 Act on Special Cases in Handling Gender Status for Persons with Gender Identity Disorder, Act. No. 111 of 2003. Note that the article 3 of the law specifically prohibits those who are already married or have minor children from availing themselves of the process.

50 Family courts have developed some "solutions" to remedy the default registration of a child as that of a prior husband; however these typically involve the conciliation process and thus require the cooperation of the ex-husband, meaning they may not be available if he is hostile or the mother fears him due to domestic violence, etc.

compromise in the face of the well-established past practice of waiting for a pregnancy before actually registering a marriage that may have been celebrated in an elaborate ceremony but was nonetheless meaningless for legal purposes until a marriage was registered in the *koseki*.[51]

Combined with a six-month remarriage prohibition on women, the likelihood of overlapping presumptions of paternity was minimized. However, in the 2015 case on the subject, the court pointed out that a 100-day prohibition coupled with 200-day threshold in article 772(2) would accomplish the same goal in a less restrictive way. Hence the oddly precise partial ruling of unconstitutionality; the important thing was that the doctrinal purity of the Civil Code and its nineteenth-century presumptions was preserved, regardless of how things might actually be for Japanese families in the twenty-first century.

Lest anyone doubt the court's preference for nineteenth century rules over twenty-first century reality, in July 2014 the court issued a trio of decisions rejecting the use of DNA to overturn the Civil Code presumptions of paternity.[52] In one case the presumed father was already divorced from the mother, who together with the child was living with the biological father. Such things did not matter to the court, the law was the law, after all. As the court notes:

> Even if it is clear from scientific evidence that there is no biological father – child relationship between a husband and a child, and the husband and the wife have already divorced and started to live separately and the child is presently taken care of by the wife, who has parental authority, the existence of these circumstances does not necessarily deny the necessity to preserve the legal stability of the child's status, and therefore it is appropriate to consider that the existence of the abovementioned circumstances does not preclude the presumption of legitimacy under said Article [772], and the existence of the father – child relationship cannot be challenged by filing an action for a declaratory judgment on the nonexistence of a parent – child relationship. This reasoning could lead to the situation in which the legal father – child relationship is inconsistent with the biological father – child relationship, but the provisions of said Article and Articles 774 through 778 of the Civil Code can be understood as even permitting such inconsistency to take place.[53]

The court had already made a similar refusal to acknowledge modern reproductive technology in 2007 when it refused on public policy grounds to grant comity to a Nevada judgment confirming the genetic Japanese mother and father as the birth parents of a child actually born to a surrogate mother pursuant to a valid Nevada surrogacy contract. In refusing to recognize the genetic parents as parents for legal purposes, the Court reasoned that:

> [a] natural parent – child relationship is the most fundamental relationship concerning a person's status. It is the foundation for various relationships in social life, and in this respect,

51 This practice prevailed well into the post-war period. In 1966 a commercial airliner crashed at Matsuyama airport killing all aboard, including 12 couples on their honeymoon. However, it turned out that *none* of their marriages had been registered, meaning legally the "husbands and wives" were unrelated strangers. In response, the Ministry of Justice conducted an awareness campaign encouraging newlyweds to register their marriages. Colin Jones, "Japan's discriminatory koseki registry system looks ever more outdated," *The Japan Times* (July 10, 2016), available at: www.japantimes.co.jp/community/2016/07/10/issues/japans-discriminatory-koseki-registry-system-looks-ever-outdated/#.WREuKDdUvIU (last accessed May 9, 2017).

52 Supreme Court, 1st Petty Bench Decisions (3) of July 17, 2014.

53 An English translation of this case is available at: www.courts.go.jp/app/hanrei_en/detail?id=1288 (last accessed May 9, 2017). See also, Colin Jones, "Nineteenth Century Rules Over Twenty-First Century Reality – Legal Parentage Under Japanese Law," 49 *Family Law Quarterly* (2015).

> it does not only concern matters between private persons but is also deeply involved in the public interest, and it has a material impact on child welfare. The eligibility for a natural parent – child relationship is an issue concerning the fundamental principle or fundamental philosophy that serves as the basis of the rules of law on personal status in each country. Therefore, the criteria for the eligibility for a natural parent – child relationship should be definite and clear, and the existence or nonexistence of a natural parent – child relationship should be determined uniformly according to such criteria. Consequently, it should be construed that the Civil Code, which forms the rules of law on personal statuses in Japan, will acknowledge a natural parent – child relationship only in the cases set forth therein, while denying the establishment of a natural parent – child relationship in other cases. In conclusion, a judgment rendered by a foreign court acknowledging the establishment of a natural parent – child relationship between the persons who are not eligible for such relationship under the Civil Code, is incompatible with the fundamental principle or fundamental philosophy of the rules of law in Japan, and therefore it should be deemed to be contrary to public policy.[54]

In short, the consistent application of simple black-and-white rules as to parent – child status is more important than biological or social reality in any particular case. That in the surrogacy case this resulted in the twins at issue without legal parents *anywhere in the world* was an unfortunate result (as acknowledged by comments in the judgment to the effect that some sort of adoption proceedings might be appropriate), but apparently necessary to protect the doctrinal purity of the court's jurisprudence.[55]

With even fathers who donated sperm the old-fashioned way being treated thusly by the system, the ability of those in more modern relationships – same sex unions, polygamous or other non-traditional relationships – to be recognized as "parents" let alone assert parental authority or whatever rights or capabilities that come with it can likely be considered non-existent, absent changes to the Civil Code and the family registry system to formally acknowledge such relationships.

Foreigners

This being a handbook on *international* family law, it would be remiss to end this chapter without noting that everything written above assumes the parties are *Japanese*. Another quirk of the Japanese family law system is that it treats family members differently depending on their nationality.

First and foremost, only Japanese nationals are registered in the *koseki* system; citizenship and registration in the *koseki* have a chicken-and-egg like interrelationship, particularly since Japan's Nationality Act is based on the principle of *jus sanguinis*, rather than *jus solis*. Foreigners who marry Japanese nationals will appear in the Japanese party's family register as will children of the marriage, but they do not have registers themselves.[56] Things that Japanese nationals can easily do

54 Supreme Court, 2nd Petty Bench decision of March 23, 2007, English translation available at: www.courts.go.jp/app/hanrei_en/detail?id=883.

55 This case seems to be an example of a court clearly rendering a decision contrary to Japan's treaty obligations under the UNCRC.

56 For purposes of this discussion "foreigner" is used as a distinct term from "non-Japanese" which would also encompass the nation's ethnic Korean population, some of whom have not acquired Japanese nationality despite living in Japan for several generations. Although they are not registered in the *koseki* the government has developed special procedures for them that do not apply to other non-Japanese residents or visitors.

through the family registry system (including accessing the information it contains, particularly after divorce) are difficult or even impossible; to the author's knowledge it is not possible for two foreigners living in Japan to get married except through whatever procedures might be made available by their respective consulates. Marriages in Japan are achieved through a filing with the family registry – if neither party has a *koseki* the transaction cannot occur. Similarly, consensual divorces between a couple in which both parties are foreigners are similarly impossible.

In fact, under Japan's choice of law statute, the law governing personal status in situations involving foreigners is generally the law of their home state (with various exceptions such as divorce or marriage when one party is Japanese).[57] In the case of the parent – child relationship, its formation and contents may also be governed by home country law, or in some cases the law of the child's habitual residence.[58] A family case arising in Japan involving foreigners – particularly one in which *all* parties are foreigners – may thus end up taking a different path due to not being governed by Japanese law. Or rather it *should*; the comparative rarity of such cases means it is questionable whether busy courts will do a thorough job of researching and applying family law as opposed to resolving them in the same way as "normal" cases.[59] In any case, the procedural requirement that parties conciliate first would seem to render it questionable whether any clearly defined "parental rights" (as opposed to parental *status*) under foreign law are likely to be applied and enforced in practice.

Bibliography

Bryant, Tamie L. "Family Models, Family Dispute Resolution and Family Law in Japan," 14 *UCLA Pacific Basin Law Journal* 1–27 (1995).

Bryant, Tamie L. "'Responsible' Husbands, 'Recalcitrant' Wives, Retributive Judges: Judicial Management of Contested Divorce in Japan," 18 *Journal of Japanese Studies* 407–443 (1992).

Bryant, Tamie L. "For the Sake of the Country, for the Sake of the Family: The Oppressive Impact of Family Registration on Women and Minorities in Japan," 39 *UCLA Law Review* 109–168 (1991).

Carney, Geraldine. "Disrupt, Support and Document: The Role of Social Media in International Parental Child Abduction Cases Involving Japan," 8 *New Voices in Japanese Studies* 1–31 (2016).

Endō, Masataka. *Koseki to Kokuseki no Kingendaishi* [The Recent and Modern History of Family Registration and Nationality] (Tokyo, Akashi Shoten 2013).

Flaherty, Darryl. *Public Law, Private Practice: Politics, Profit and the Legal Profession in Nineteenth-Century Japan* (Cambridge, MA, Harvard University Press, 2013).

Fuess, Harald. *Divorce in Japan: Family Gender and the State, 1600–2000* (Redwood City, CA, Stanford University Press, 2004).

Hanrei Minpō 9 – Shinzoku [Civil Code with Case Annotations, Volume Nine, Family Relations] (Tokyo, Daiichihoki, Yoshihisa Nomi & Shintaro Kato eds, 2nd edn, 2009).

Hiroi, Tazuko. *Shinken no seiritsu, Meiji minpō no naka no oya, kodomo, kokka* [The establishment of parental authority; parents, children and the state in the Meiji Civil Code], http://hiroitz.sakura.ne.jp/resources/%E8%AB%96%E6%96%87/parental-right2.pdf.

Jones, Colin P.A. "Nineteenth Century Rules Over Twenty-First Century Reality – Legal Parentage Under Japanese Law," 49 *Family Law Quarterly* (2015).

Jones, Colin P.A. "In the Best Interests of the Court: What American Lawyers Need to Know about Child Custody and Visitation in Japan," 8 *Asian-Pacific Law & Policy Journal* (2007).

Jones, Colin P.A. "Kodomo No Tsuresari Mondai" [The Child Abduction Problem] (*Heibonsha shinsho*, 2011).

Jones, Colin P.A. "Will the Child Abduction Treaty become more 'Asian'? A First Look at the Efforts of Singapore and Japan to Implement the Hague Convention," 42 *Denver Journal of International Law and Policy* 287 (2014).

57 Act on General Rules for Application of Laws, Act No. 78 of 2006, articles 24–33.

58 Articles 28, 29, 31, 32.

59 Although over a decade ago, the author is aware of one case where the evidence of California law of custody offered by counsel for one parent consisted of the table of contents from West's California Digest.

Kajimura, Taichi. Rikon Chōtei Gaidobukku [Divorce Conciliation Guidebook] (Tokyo, Nihonkajo Shuppan, 3rd edn, 2008).

Shinkihon Hō Komentāru Shinzoku *(Minpō Dai 725 Jō – Dai 881 Jō* [New Commentaries on Basic Laws: Civil Code Arts 725–881] (Tokyo, Nihon Hyoronsha, Matsukawa & Atsumi eds, 2015).

Shigenori Matsui, "'Never Had a Choice and No Power to Alter': Illegitimate Children and the Supreme Court of Japan," 44 *Georgia Journal of International and Comparative Law* 577 (2016).

Seishoku iryō to hō [Law and Reproductive Medicine] (Yoshiaki Sakurada, et al., 2012)

Stark, Barbara, "Foreign Fathers, Japanese Mothers, and the Hague Abduction Convention: *Spirited Away*," 41 *North Carolina Journal of International Law* 762 (2016).

Sykes, Katie. "Bambi Meets Godzilla: Children's and Parents' Rights in Canadian Foundation for Children, Youth and the Law v. Canada," 51 *McGill Law Journal* 131, 135 (2006).

Uchida, Takashi. *Minpō IV* [Civil Code, Volume IV] (Tokyo, Tokyo University Press, 2004).

Wada, Mikihiko. "Abolition of the House (ie) Under the Occupation: Or the Two Faces of Koseki: A Janus," 26 *Law in Japan* 99 (Tokyo, Shinzansha, 2000).

Wada, Mikihiko. *Ieseido no Haishi* [The Abolition of the *Ie* System] (2010).

Part V
The family and the state

16

Theories of state and family

Aziza Ahmed

This goal of this chapter is to highlight the role of family law as a site of governance and distribution. Following a brief description of theoretical interventions on family law in this vein, the chapter then turns to the specific case of India where family law is complicated by a system of "personal laws" that creates a system of shared governance between state and religious leadership with regard to families.[1] Focusing on Muslim Personal Law (MPL) the chapter demonstrates how family law not only provides the opportunity for the state and religious authorities to govern the family but also offers a tool to manage religious minorities, in this case, Muslims. Issues of gender are central to the management of family, community, and religion in India where secular and religious law interact to create a complicated interplay of rules that individuals must navigate in the context of marriage and divorce.[2] These rules are produced and maintained in the context of a country that faces high levels of communal violence. In turn, this chapter argues that transformations in MPL in India are not only the product of shifting religious belief and practice but the outcome of broader social, political, and economic contestation. By contextualizing MPL it is possible to see how family law in India not only distributes rights and responsibilities within the family, it also works to regulate the Muslim community.

Regulating through family law

Scholars recognize family law to be a tool of governance. In their work on "family law exceptionalism" Janet Halley and Kerry Rittich craft a genealogy of family law that demonstrates how the family came to occupy a distinct domain of law in the eighteenth century distinguished

1 This is not only specific to Muslim communities in India; this duality exists in other Muslim minority settings. Asifa Quraishi and Najeeba Syeed-Miller, "No Altars: a Survey of Islamic Family Law in the United States," in Lyn Welchman (ed.) *Women's Rights and Islamic Family Law: Perspectives on Reform* (London: Zed Books, 2004), 179.

2 The sections on India in this chapter draw on earlier work. Aziza Ahmed, "Dual subordination: Muslim sexuality in secular and religious legal discourse in India," 4 *Muslim World J. of Hum. Rts.* (2007) and Aziza Ahmed, "No Way Out: The Dual Subordination of Muslim Women in Indian Legal Culture" in Chitra Raghavan and James P. Levine (eds) *Self-Determination and Women's Rights in Muslim Societies* (Brandeis University Press, 2012).

from the law of contract.[3] Drawing on Michel Foucault, they argue that with the turn towards understanding the family as the nuclear affective unit and free from the "individualist ethos of contract," the family became a "tool of society."[4] Central to the delegation of rights and responsibilities to the family or the state is the idea of the public/private divide that relegates the family to the private sphere and the market to the public. In turn, the family became a site of care and dependency where moral and spiritual life would thrive.[5] In her seminal work, Martha Fineman demonstrates that in the American context a myth of self-reliance creates a narrative of autonomy that runs against the recognition of a dependent society in which the state must play an active role in supporting the family.[6] Instead, caretaking is left to the family, often with little or no state support. In keeping with feminist scholarship, women bear the burden of this care. Gender becomes an axis to distribute rights and responsibility within the family.

In a distinct but related literature, scholars describe how families are also managed through the welfare state. The welfare system, as described by David Garland, is a densely woven set of laws and regulations, "involving a multitude of . . . programmes, and agencies – each with its own technical details, legislative history, and interest group politics."[7] Building on earlier social theorists, Garland argues that the welfare state acts as a mode of "social administration" allowing the state to assume some "control over social and economic processes."[8] Family law scholars, including Tonya Brito, have introduced criminal law as a way to see how the state manages, and punishes, the family in the context of the welfare system. Brito's work highlights that in a nexus of criminal, family, and welfare law derivation from legal rules can result in a punitive response to the state. This is exemplified, in her work, through the punitive approach to the failure to pay child support.[9] Central to the administration of rights and responsibilities in the context of child support is, again, the public/private distinction – in this case the idea that the father is the primary financial caretaker of a family and not the state. The regulation of society and state through family law results in the production of communities and individuals that are differentially situated. In their work on family law exceptionalism, Halley and Rittich speak to this productive dynamic driven by family law:

> wherever "the family" and its law do gain distinct categorical status in the social and legal order, that distinctiveness is not only a reflection of reality but a constitutive and productive basis for it. We hypothesize that "the family" and its law are full of ideological and political meaning and do concrete distributional work not only by virtue of specific rules but also by the sheer force of their categorical existence.[10]

Taking Brito's example of child support, we see that the idea that fathers are responsible for the financial care of the family (as opposed to the state) structures a legal regime on child support. In

3 Janet Halley and Kerry Rittich, "Critical Directions in Comparative Family Law: Genealogies and Contemporary Studies of Family Law Exceptionalism," 58 *Am. J. of Comp. L.* (2010). Here Halley and Rittich draw on Duncan Kennedy, "Savigny's Family/Patrimony Distinction and its Place in the Global Genealogy of Classical Legal Thought," 58 *Am. J. of Comp. L.* (2010).

4 Id.

5 Id.

6 Martha Fineman, *The Autonomy Myth: A Theory of Dependency* (The New Press, 2004).

7 David Garland, *The Welfare State: A Very Short Introduction* (Oxford University Press, 2016).

8 Id.

9 Tonya L Brito, "Fathers Behind Bars: Rethinking Child Support Policy Toward Low-Income Noncustodial Fathers and Their Families," 15 *J. Gender Race & Just.* 617 (2012).

10 *Supra* note 3.

turn, the idea that the family is the site of caretaking and fathers are the primary breadwinners is reproduced and governed at the nexus of family, criminal law, and welfare law. The use of criminal law is not limited to the regulation of child support. Feminist scholars and advocates mobilized criminal law to penalize the mistreatment of women in marriage and reset gender norms in the home. The feminist turn towards criminal law as a mode of regulating gender norms is now the subject of critique and contestation in the broader feminist family law literature.[11]

Theories of the state and the family in the context of legal pluralism

Religious law adds yet another dimension to understanding the family as a site of regulation. State legal regimes that incorporate both secular and religious law of the family have primarily been assessed through the lens of legal pluralism described by socio-legal scholar Sally Engle Merry as two or more legal systems in the same "social field" or state.[12] Legally pluralistic jurisdictions are frequently the product of colonization and occupation by ruling states.[13] The governance of society and state through family is complicated by the presence of religious law yet many similarities remain. The division between family law and market, for example, maps onto the public – private divide. In her book *Religious Difference in a Secular Age: A Minority Report*, Saba Mahmood adds in the centrality of religion to the private sphere:

> Family law today is predicated upon the public-private divide – foundational to the modern secular political order – that relegates religion, family, and sexuality to the private sphere, thereby entwining their legal and moral fates. This has invested modern religious identity in the domain of sexuality and family relations in a manner that is historically unique. In this context, minority religious communities that have legal autonomy over family law tend to view any state attempt to reform family law as an illegitimate intervention into communal affairs.[14]

The role of religion in crafting the norms that shape family law in legally plural jurisdictions is central to understanding the role of family law as a mode of governance.

Legally pluralistic regimes differ significantly. In his book *Human Rights under State-Enforced Religious Family Laws in Israel, Egypt and India*, Yüksel Sezgin complicates the notion of formal legal pluralism by describing both the formal and informal manifestations in many family law regimes. In formal jurisdictions, the state incorporates various legal regimes as the final administrator of legal rules. In informal jurisdictions, state and non-state orderings exist in the same legal space but there is no formal incorporation of religious or traditional law by the state.[15]

11 Donna Coker and Ahjane D. Macquoid, "Why Opposing Hyper-Incarceration Should Be Central to the Work of the Anti-Domestic Violence Movement," 5 *University of Miami Race and Social Justice Law Review* 586 (2015); Leigh Goodmark, "Should Domestic Violence Be Decriminalized?" 40 *Harvard Journal of Law and Gender* 53 (2017); Deborah Weissman, "Countering Neoliberalism and Aligning Solidarities: Rethinking Domestic Violence Advocacy," 45 *Southwestern University Law Review* 916 (2016).

12 Sally Engle Merry, "Legal Pluralism," 22 *Law & Soc. Rev.* 869 (1988) [hereinafter Legal Pluralism]; Yüksel Sezgin, *Human Rights Under State-Enforced Religious Family Laws in Israel, Egypt, and India* (Cambridge University Press, 2013) [hereinafter Human Rights]

13 Legal pluralism at 869.

14 Saba Mahmood, *Religious Difference in a Secular Age: A Minority Report* (Princeton University Press, 2016) [hereinafter Religious Difference].

15 Human Rights 19–26 (2013).

While many scholars have focused attention on formerly colonized countries, others argue that all countries are, to some extent, legally pluralistic.[16] As described by Sezgin, family law is often characterized, as it is in the Indian legal system, as a system of "personal laws" that can be understood to be a "system in which members of various ethno-religious communities that are specifically recognized as such by central authorities are subject to jurisdiction of state-sanctioned communal norms and institutions in regard to personal or familial matters such as marriage, divorce, spousal maintenance, and so forth."[17]

The idea of a "personal law system" suggests a distinction between family law and other legal rules pertaining to issues including contracts and corporations. Mahmood offers a genealogy of the term "personal law" in the context of the Middle East and the exception of Egypt that, like India, has an existing personal law system. Mahmood explains that "personal status" referred to one's status in a tribe, group or nation. In the eighteenth century personal status law traveled with the individual. Eventually, the rise of the nation-state resulted in personal laws giving way to national laws. In Egypt, however, and like India in the example that follows, personal law persisted. This was in part the result of colonization in which colonizing countries maintained a personal law system to facilitate the management of the colony.[18]

The treatment of family law as distinct from the broader political and economic context has been problematized by Halley and Rittich, who argue that distinguishing family law as distinct accepts the family unit as natural and transhistorical, disguising its "legal, social, and ideological production."[19] Denaturalizing the family allows for the exploration of the family unit as a tool of governance produced by the regulatory state and the background legal order. In legally pluralistic jurisdictions, such as that of India, the formalization of a separate legal space for matters of the family relegated the family to religious leadership. Thus, the family is further distanced from politics and economics as it is contained not only within its own traditionally private realm, but also within the private realm of religion. In her examination of family law exceptionalism in Arab societies, Lama Abu Odeh adds that traditional practice, including honor killings, frequently work to regulate gender in the home.[20] As the next section demonstrates, this is also the case in India. However, given that Muslim family law in India is a minority practice, family law becomes a tool not only for the governance of gender within the family but also of producing and governing Muslims in India.

The case of Muslim family law in India

This section highlights the governance, regulatory and productive functions of family law in the context of India. In other words, through Muslim Personal Law the state is able to reinforce and shape norms on gender, sexuality, and religion. In turn, family law becomes a tool for distributing rights and entitlements both for a religious community and within families on issues including divorce, alimony, and child support. In the cases presented here, divorce law is central to how religious practice is imagined and, central to this, how women are treated in the context of Muslim Personal Law.

The history of Muslim personal laws in India represents a layering of pre-colonial, post-colonial, and contemporary ideas about religion, state, and the family. Shariat law,[21] or divine law in the

16 Id.

17 Id.

18 *Supra* note 14.

19 *Supra* note 4.

20 Lama Abu Odeh, "Honor Killings and the Construction of Gender in Arab Societies," 58 *Am. J. of Comp. L.* 911 (2010).

21 What is commonly spoken of as Sharia Law is transliterated as Shariat Law in the Indian context.

Muslim religious tradition,[22] was first introduced in India around the twelfth and thirteenth century AD.[23] There are several schools of interpretation of Islamic law including the Hanafi, Maliki, Hanbali, Shafi'i, Zahiri, and Shia.[24] Shias are approximately 10–15 percent of the total Muslim population.[25] Among Muslims there are over 350 regional or ethno-linguistic groups. India's Muslims have maintained many similarities in practice and custom to the broader Hindu community.[26] Today, Muslims make up the country's largest religious minority accounting for 13.4 percent of the Indian population.[27]

Muslims are generally of lower socio-economic status in India. Muslim women in India have lower work participation rates and educational levels compared to other minority groups in India.[28] Further, a political trope about Muslims as "outsiders" galvanized by right-wing parties, including the ruling Bharatiya Janata Party (BJP), resulted in numerous acts of violence against the Muslim community including a pogrom in Gujarat in 2002 widely understood to have been orchestrated by state and non-state actors.[29] The governance of religious minorities is furthered through a rhetoric deployed by the government of the need to modernize the Muslim community vis-à-vis women's rights in the family due to the existence of retrogressive practice. While the need to examine women's rights is plainly necessary given structural inequalities faced by women, the rhetoric of modernization is frequently deployed by the right-wing parties of India to further distance the idea of the Muslim community as part of the broader Indian body politic. Family law is central to this project and the adjudication of Muslim Personal Law in secular courts becomes a site of this contestation.

As I have described in earlier work,[30] the development of Shariat law in India is a product of India's colonial legacy. In *Gender and Community: Muslim Women's Rights in India*, Vrinda Narain argues that the underlying objective of maintaining religious law was to utilize a decentralized power structure vis-à-vis scriptural and religious norms.[31] In doing so, the British were able to maintain the political and economic goals of the colonial state by exploiting existing community

22 Mohammad Hashim Kamali. *Principles of Islamic Jurisprudence* (Cambridge: Islamic Texts Society, 2003).

23 This section of the chapter draws on and updates my prior work in this area. Aziza Ahmed, "Dual Subordination: Muslim Sexuality in Secular and Religious Legal Discourse in India," 4 *Muslim World J. of Hum. Rts.* (2007) and Aziza Ahmed, "No Way Out: The Dual Subordination of Muslim Women in Indian Legal Culture" in Chitra Raghavan and James P. Levine, *Self-Determination and Women's Rights in Muslim Societies* (Brandeis University Press, 2012).

24 Id.

25 Minority Rights Group International, *Muslim Women in India* (United Kingdom: Minority Rights Group, 1999).

26 Flavia Agnes, *Law and Gender Inequality: The Politics of Women's Rights in India* (Delhi: Oxford University Press, 1999).

27 Office of the Registrar General and Census Commissioner, India (Ministry of Home Affairs, accessed 8 November 2017) available from http://censusindia.gov.in/Census_And_You/religion.aspx.

28 *Supra* note 24.

29 People's Union for Democratic Rights. *Maaro! Kaapo! Baalo!* (People's Union for Democratic Rights 2002, accessed 27 November 2017) available from www.pucl.org/Topics/Religion-communalism/2002/maro_kapo_balo.pdf; Human Rights Watch. *We Have No Orders to Save You: State Participation and Complicity in Communal Violence in Gujarat* (Human Rights Watch, 2002, accessed 21 April 2007) available from http://hrw.org/reports/2002/india/.

30 Aziza Ahmed, "Dual Subordination: Muslim Sexuality in Secular and Religious Legal Discourse in India," 4 *Muslim World J. of Hum. Rts.* (2007) and Aziza Ahmed, "No Way Out: The Dual Subordination of Muslim Women in Indian Legal Culture" in Chitra Raghavan and James P. Levine (eds) *Self-Determination and Women's Rights in Muslim Societies* (Brandeis University Press, 2012).

31 Vrinda Narain, *Gender and Community: Muslim Women's Rights in India* (Toronto: University of Toronto Press, 2001).

structures that allowed for existing elite, in this case religious elite, to maintain power.[32] The British codified Islamic family law in India with the Muslim Personal Law (Shariat) Application Act of 1937.[33] Following Mahmood, this relegated issues of religion, family, sexuality, and gender into the private realm and had the effect of empowering religious leaders complicated by the divergent leadership of Muslim sects and the self-appointed nature of many who claim to be religious authorities. Importantly, as Mahmood argues, religious identity became "invested in the domain of family law" in ways that are "primordial but in effect are recent, contingent, and provisional."[34] This important insight helps us to evaluate the role of the Courts and legislature in India in being productive of ideas of what it means to be Muslim in India.

Article 44 of the Indian Constitution includes provision for a Uniform Civil Code (UCC). The UCC would bring family law under the umbrella of civil law and do away with religious laws governing marriage.[35] Through the 1940s, women's rights groups consistently advocated for the eradication of the personal law system and for the UCC. In 1947, following partition of India and Pakistan, the formal proposal to enact the UCC was introduced to the Constituent Assembly. With the possibility of the UCC bandied about by politicians and political parties to gain votes, courts began to take cases that required weighing key questions of how religious law was being implemented redefining the boundaries of religious and secular law. Family law became a key site of negotiating religious minority identity.

A foundational case in the evolution of litigation on Muslim Personal Law is *Mohd. Ahmed Khan v. Shah Bano Begum & Ors (Shah Bano)* decided in the Supreme Court of India in 1985.[36] The case is infamous in India for igniting communal tensions and placing pressure on the ruling Congress Party to protect the rights of Muslim leadership, an important constituency. Shah Bano, a 73-year-old Muslim woman divorced by her husband, brought a petition of maintenance from her husband under Section 125 of the Criminal Procedure Code (CPC) which allows for the criminal prosecution of men who do not pay maintenance (alimony).[37] Muslim scholars argued

32 Id.

33 Muslim Personal Law (Shariat) Application Act of 1937:

> all questions regarding intestate succession, special property of females, including personal property inherited or obtained under contract or gift or any other provision of Personal law, marriage, dissolution of marriage, including talaq, ila, zihar, lian, khula and mabaraat, maintenance, dower, guardianship, gifts, trusts and trust properties, and wakfs (other than charities and charitable institutions and charitable and religious endowments) the rule of decision in cases where the parties are Muslims shall be the Muslim Personal Law (Shariat).

34 *Supra* note 14.

35 The Indian constitution also carves out specific protections for religious minorities. With Articles 26, 27, and 28 of the Indian constitution, for example, minorities have the right to manage their own religious affairs, are not compelled to attend state-funded religious institutions, and receive equal treatment for minority-managed institutions.

36 *Mohd. Ahmed Khan v. Shah Bano Begum & Ors*, 1985 (2) SCC 556.

37 Indian Criminal Procedure Code, Chapter IX, Section 125.

> Order for maintenance of wives, children and parents. (1) If any person having sufficient means neglects or refuses to maintain (a) his wife, unable to maintain herself, or (b) his legitimate or illegitimate minor child, whether married or not, unable to maintain itself . . . (3) If any person so ordered fails without sufficient cause to comply with the order, any such Magistrate may, for every breach of the order, issue a warrant for levying the amount due in the manner provided for levying fines, and may sentence such person, for the whole or any part of each month's allowances remaining unpaid after the execution of the warrant, to imprisonment for a term which may extend to one month or until payment if sooner made.

that she was only entitled to maintenance (alimony) during the *iddat*, the period three months after the divorce that a Muslim woman cannot remarry. The most vocal of these groups was the All India Muslim Personal Law Board (AIMPLB) founded in 1973. They are the self-declared leaders of Muslim Personal Law in India.[38] The organization frequently takes views that counter those of feminist activists.[39]

The Supreme Court overrode the interpretation of the Shariat by Muslim leadership and ruled that under Section 125 of the CPC Shah Bano was entitled to maintenance beyond the period of *iddat*.[40] The Muslim community, led by conservative and orthodox Muslims, protested the decision on the ground that Islam in India was in danger, believing that the court had overstepped its bounds given that the view of Muslim theologians that they alone were able to interpret the Quran.

Following the decision, and largely in response to it, an independent member of parliament introduced the Muslim Women's (Protection of Rights on Divorce) Act, 1986 (MWA) which provided that Section 125 of the CPC does not apply to divorced Muslim women. This carve-out caved to the pressures of the more religious Muslim advocates and ruffled the feathers of the Hindu right who sought to decrease the power of the Muslim leadership rather than embolden it. In turn, an odd political pairing, one that would return in the mid 2010s, including feminists and the Hindu Right unsuccessfully campaigned against the bill.[41] The law allowed the Congress Party to claim deference to Muslim leadership who felt that the regulation of family and gender should be within their purview. Yet, the law engendered confusion with regard to whether a Muslim woman could, in fact, seek aid through a civil court if she was not paid a "reasonable and fair" maintenance as guaranteed by Section 127 of the Muslim Women's (Protection of Rights on Divorce) Act.

In 2001, the Supreme Court revisited the issue of Muslim Personal Law in *Danial Latifi v. Union of India* in order to clarify when Muslim women could seek aid from a civil court to ensure maintenance. The court found that Muslim husbands are liable to their divorced wife for a "reasonable and fair" maintenance. Yet, the court stops short of declaring the law unconstitutional.[42] Finding for women, but in preserving the law, courts were able to balance the communal tensions that might result from striking down the law. Further, while the decision was seen as a victory for women's rights, the court reinforces the traditional roles of women in the household in reflecting on the earlier *Shah Bano* case, demonstrating how the cases serve to regulate gender as well as religion:

> The important feature of the case was that the wife had managed the matrimonial home for more than 40 years and had borne and reared five children and was incapable of taking up any career or independently supporting herself at that late stage of her life – remarriage was an impossibility in that case. The husband, a successful Advocate with an approximate income of Rs.5,000/- per month provided Rs.200/- per month to the divorced wife, who had shared his life for half a century and mothered his five children and was in desperate need of money to survive.

38 The Islamic Shariat Board who also advocated that women not be given maintenance beyond the *iddat* period in the *Danial Latifi* case.

39 *Danial Latifi v. Union of India*, 1985 (2) SCC 556.

40 *Mohd. Ahmed Khan v. Shah Bano Begum & Ors*, 1985 (2) SCC 556.

41 Ratna Kapur and Brenda Crossman, *Subversive Sites: Feminist Engagements with Law in India* (New Delhi: Sage, 1996).

42 South Asian's Citizen's Wire, *Hullaballoo over Triple Talaq in India* (accessed 21 April 2007) available from www.wluml.org/english/newsfulltxt.shtml?cmd%5B157%5D=x-157-64559.

In other words the secular state court rewarded the petitioner in *Shah Bano* (and in turn the plaintiff in *Latifi*) for fulfilling their obligations to reproduce and rear children. Because the petitioner exemplified what it means to be a "good wife and sacrificing mother" she was rewarded with maintenance after divorce.[43] Once again, the care work of the family is relegated and celebrated as within the private realm.[44] Gender became an axis by which to distribute resources.[45]

The most recent high-profile case negotiating the tense boundaries between family, religious, and secular law came in 2016 over the issue of triple *talaq*. Triple *talaq* allows for divorce upon the declaration "*talaq, talaq, talaq*" by a man to his wife. Sharaya Bano, the plaintiff, left her husband due to extreme physical abuse that included being locked in a room, beaten, and drugged. In October 2015, Bano's husband divorced her utilizing triple *talaq*. Bano's case was heard by the Supreme Court. She argued that although the practice was legal under Muslim Personal Law it should be declared unconstitutional by the Supreme Court.[46]

In a comprehensive 394 page decision, a five judge bench engaged in a series of inquiries including a comparison of states that adhere in some way to Muslim family law (including in the Middle East and North Africa, Southeast Asia, and South Asia), potential violations of human rights, the social and political history of religious minority rights in India, and interpretations of the Quran and *hadith* (sayings of the Prophet Mohammed) in order to determine the constitutionality of the law.[47] In a victory for Muslim feminists, the court issued an injunction against the practice of triple *talaq* until the legislature reconsiders the issue. Importantly, they directed the legislators to consider the trend in doing away with the practice of triple *talaq* in jurisdictions that integrate Muslim Personal Law into the law of the family. Three of the five justices stated that the practice of triple *talaq* is unconstitutional. The justices disagreed about how fundamental triple *talaq* is to the religious practice of the Muslim community.[48]

While Bano wins her case, and, in turn, formally alters a deep power imbalance between men and women in the context of Muslim divorce law, the decision itself treads a delicate balance between civil and religious law with the court once again navigating interpretations of Shariat law and in doing so implicitly lending support to particular Muslim practices, despite their stated desire to stay out of regulating the personal laws of religious communities.

The case was complicated by the political context, namely, the rise of the right-wing BJP in India after the 2014 elections, and the election of Narendra Modi as Prime Minister. Right-wing leadership in government resulted in an increase in state and non-state action against religious minorities. This was a predictable outcome of the rhetoric of the BJP and the leadership of Narendra Modi as Chief Minister of Gujarat at the time of widespread communal rioting and targeted violence in the state. For the BJP, altering Muslim Personal Law allowed both for the possibility of highlighting the "backward" ways of the Muslim community and overriding minority rights. In turn, as the Supreme Court described it, the Government of India, respondents on the case, took an "aggressive posture" in arguing for the invalidation of the law. The All India Muslim Personal Law Board felt that the case was an assault on Muslim practice in India. While

43 *Supra* note 40.

44 Courts continued their critique of Muslim Personal Law with *In re, Smt. Amina* decided in the High Court of Bombay in 1991 in which the court articulated that the "Constitutions framers did not intent to exclude personal laws from ambit of Article 13 of the Constitution" which protects fundamental rights. *In re, Smt. Amina.* In the High Court of Bombay. Manu/MH/0039/1992

45 Libby Adler, "The Gay Agenda," 16 *Mich. J. Gender & L.* (2009).

46 *Sharya Bano v. Union of India and others*, 2017 SCC OnLine SC 963.

47 Id.

48 Id.

for Muslim women, the rejection of triple *talaq* would be seen as a step forward, they risked their arguments being hijacked by the right wing who claimed to be supportive of Muslim women's rights. Their supposed support for women's rights was undermined by their long history of igniting communal violence in ways that violently targeted Muslim women.[49]

Both Muslim women and the BJP celebrated the outcome of the triple *talaq* case. Muslim women's rights activists, however, pointed out that the fundamentalist religious values of the BJP and conservative Muslim leadership all failed Muslim women and, importantly, openly acknowledged the political gains for the BJP in stoking communal tensions by highlighting the differences of Muslim divorce law from Hindu practice in India.[50] The BJP claimed a commitment to women's rights, and, perhaps more strategically, a desire to help Muslim women allowing them to counter the accusation of violence against them.

In the course of these groundbreaking family law decisions spanning decades, the Courts both make grand declarations of laws as "un-Islamic" and express reticence to act as religious arbiters. The latter position reveals the Supreme Court's awareness that they play a role in shaping religious practice. Following on the intervention by Halley and Rittich to de-exceptionalize the family, Muslim Personal Law in India becomes a site of governance both for minorities and for the distribution of rights related to gender in the family. In the Indian context, it provides an opportunity not only to shape societal norms but to reify or challenge religious practice deemed out of line with Indian values. The central role of gender in the definition of community, religion, and culture makes women's issues a battleground for competing political interests. In the context of a legally pluralistic state, such as the case of India, family law personal law sits in an uncomfortable relationship with the civil law system – on the one hand as a body of law shaped by religious authority while on the other hand subject to the authority of civil courts which then impacts the rights of individuals within the Muslim family. In turn, while family law is treated politically as though it is a manifestation of religious practice driven by Muslim leadership, in reality, the legal rules that comprise Muslim Personal Law is a settlement between competing political interests. The burden of the negative consequences of this regime typically fall on women who suffer under conservative religious interpretations in formal and informal practice of Islamic Law and whose lives become political fodder in the larger civil and political struggle over religious minorities.

Conclusion

Family law is a mode of governing state and society. Utilizing India as a case study, the chapter highlights how family law shapes norms on gender, sexuality, and religion. In the cases presented here, it is divorce law that sets the stage for the negotiation of Muslim Personal Law in secular, civil courts. Following Halley and Rittich, and building on Mahmood, it is clear that understanding family law as a mode of governance requires denaturalizing the family and thinking through the way the public – private divide shapes the relegation of practices of gender, sexuality, and religion to the family, and in turn family law. Reading the Indian cases in the context of broader political, social, and economic realities demonstrates how family law becomes a way not only to manage a family, but also to regulate religious minorities.

49 Human Rights Watch, *We Have No Orders to Save You: State Participation and Complicity in Communal Violence in Gujarat*, accessed 21 April 2007, available at http://hrw.org/reports/2002/india/.

50 Betwa Sharma, "Why These Muslim Women, Survivors of Triple Talaq, Went Over to the BJP" (*Huffington Post*, accessed 8 November 2017) available at www.huffingtonpost.in/2017/02/28/why-these-muslim-women-survivors-of-triple-talaq-went-over-to_a_21845365/.

Bibliography

Abu Odeh, Lama, "Honor Killings and the Construction of Gender in Arab Societies," *American Journal of Comparative Law* 58 (2010): 911.

Adler, Libby. "The Gay Agenda," *Michigan Journal of Gender and the Law* 16 (2009): 147.

Agnes, Flavia. *Law and Gender Inequality: The Politics of Women's Rights in India* (Delhi: Oxford University Press, 1999).

Ahmed, Aziza. "Dual Subordination: Muslim Sexuality in Secular and Religious Legal Discourse in India," *Muslim World Journal of Human Rights* 4.1 (2007).

Ahmed, Aziza. "No Way Out: The Dual Subordination of Muslim Women in Indian Legal Culture," in Chitra Raghavan and James P. Levine (eds) *Self-Determination and Women's Rights in Muslim Societies* (Waltham, MA: Brandeis University Press, 2012).

Brito, Tonya L. "Fathers Behind Bars: Rethinking Child Support Policy Toward Low-Income Noncustodial Fathers and Their Families," *Journal of Gender, Race, and Justice* 15 (2012): 617.

Coker, Donna and Ahjane D. Macquoid, "Why Opposing Hyper-Incarceration Should Be Central to the Work of the Anti-Domestic Violence Movement," *University of Miami Race and Social Justice Law Review* 5 (2015): 586.

Danial Latifi vs Union of India, 1985 (2) SCC 556.

Human Rights Watch. *We Have No Orders to Save You: State Participation and Complicity in Communal Violence in Gujarat* (Human Rights Watch, 2002, accessed 21 April 2007) available from http://hrw.org/reports/2002/india/.

Indian Criminal Procedure Code, Chapter IX, Section 125.

Fineman, Martha. *The Autonomy Myth: A Theory of Dependency* (New York: The New Press, 2004).

Garland, David. *The Welfare State: A Very Short Introduction* (Oxford, UK: Oxford University Press, 2016).

Goodmark, Leigh, "Should Domestic Violence Be Decriminalized?" *Harvard Journal of Law and Gender* 40 (2017): 53.

Halley, Janet, and Kerry Rittich. "Critical Directions in Comparative Family Law: Genealogies and Contemporary Studies of Family Law Exceptionalism," *The American Journal of Comparative Law* 58.4 (2010): 753–75.

Kamali, Mohammad Hashim. *Principles of Islamic Jurisprudence* (Cambridge, UK: Islamic Texts Society, 2003).

In re, Smt. Amina. In the High Court of Bombay. Manu/MH/0039/1992.

Kapur, Ratna and Brenda Cossman. *Subversive Sites: Feminist Engagements with Law in India* (New Delhi: Sage, 1996).

Kennedy, Duncan. "Savigny's Family/Patrimony Distinction and its Place in the Global Genealogy of Classical Legal Thought," *The American Journal of Comparative Law* 58.4 (2010): 811–41.

Mahmood, Saba. *Religious Difference in a Secular Age: A Minority Report* (Princeton, NJ: Princeton University Press, 2016).

Merry, Sally Engle. "Legal Pluralism," *Law & Society Review* 22.5 (1988): 869–96.

Minority Rights Group International, "Muslim Women in India" (United Kingdom: Minority Rights Group, 1999).

Mohd. Ahmed Khan v. Shah Bano Begum & Ors, 1985 (2) SCC 556.

Muslim Personal Law (Shariat) Application Act of 1937.

Mohd. Ahmed Khan v. Shah Bano Begum & Ors, 1985 (2) SCC 556.

Narain, Vrinda. *Gender and Community: Muslim Women's Rights in India* (Toronto: University of Toronto Press, 2001).

Office of the Registrar General and Census Commissioner, India (Ministry of Home Affairs, accessed 8 November 2017) available from http://censusindia.gov.in/Census_And_You/religion.aspx.

People's Union for Democratic Rights. *Maaro! Kaapo! Baalo!* (People's Union for Democratic Rights 2002, accessed 27 November 2017) available from www.pucl.org/Topics/Religion-communalism/2002/maro_kapo_balo.pdf.

Quraishi, Asifa and Najeeba Syeed-Miller, "No Altars: a Survey of Islamic Family Law in the United States." in Lynn Welchman (ed.) *Women's Rights and Islamic Family Law Perspectives on Reform* (London: Zed Books, 2004), 179.

Sezgin, Yüksel. *Human Rights Under State-Enforced Religious Family Laws in Israel, Egypt, and India* (Cambridge, UK: Cambridge University Press, 2013).

Sharma, Betwa. "Why These Muslim Women, Survivors of Triple Talaq, Went Over to the BJP" (*Huffington Post*, accessed 8 November 2017) available at www.huffingtonpost.in/2017/02/28/why-these-muslim-women-survivors-of-triple-talaq-went-over-to_a_21845365/.

Sharya Bano v. Union of India and others, 2017 SCC OnLine SC 963.

South Asian's Citizen's Wire, *Hullaballoo over triple Talaq in India*, accessed 21 April 2007) available from www.wluml.org/english/newsfulltxt.shtml?cmd%5B157%5D=x-157-64559.

Weissman, Deborah. "Countering Neoliberalism and Aligning Solidarities: Rethinking Domestic Violence Advocacy," *Southwestern University Law Review* 45 (2016): 916.

17

Normative developments on domestic violence against women

Rashida Manjoo

Introduction

The interchangeable use of terminology such as domestic violence, family violence, intimate partner violence, gender-based violence, and violence against women, among others, requires clarity as regards who is being included when such terms are used; who is disproportionately impacted by such violence; and also, what manifestation of violence is being addressed. The term 'domestic violence' can include violence that is experienced by women, men, girls, boys, the elderly, people employed in domestic work; i.e., people working in a family setting; extended family members, and so on. The manifestations of violence can include, among others, physical, sexual, psychological abuse; threats; controlling behaviour; child abuse; and harmful cultural and religious practices, including early and forced marriages and female genital cutting. At a practical level of usage, many of the abovementioned terms and manifestations tend to refer to domestic violence that is experienced primarily by women who are or were in an intimate relationship with a partner or spouse. In such cases the relationship status can include current or prior marriage, cohabitation, legal domestic partnership, or dating relationships. In some instances violence that is inflicted by a family member who is not a partner or spouse is also included under the term 'domestic violence'.[1]

In addition to the interchangeable use of terminology, there have been attempts over the years regarding the categorization of the phenomena of domestic violence against women. In the early years of recognition, such violence was primarily categorized as a social issue. In later years it was discussed as a welfare issue, a criminal justice issue, subsequently as a public health issue, and in more recent times as a human rights violation that disproportionately impacts women and girls.[2] Depending on the categorization, the remedies and responses have ranged from explicit provision of specific powers being given to the police and social welfare workers; enhancing health sector responses; and the development of legal remedies, including civil, criminal and matrimonial remedies. In addition, government and non-governmental responses have included remedies such

1 See generally the reports of the United Nations Special Rapporteur on Violence against Women, different UN organizations such as UN Women and the World Health Organization.

2 Ibid.

as the provision of shelters, counselling services, emergency hotline services, legal aid provision, and perpetrator programmes.[3]

Due to word count limitations this chapter will highlight normative developments on violence against women and the ground-breaking cases on the issue of domestic violence against women as perpetrated by current or former intimate partners. In addition to the introduction, the second section will provide a brief historical mapping of developments with regard to the recognition of violence against women by the international community, especially the 'soft law' development of standards within the United Nations (UN) system. The developments within three regional human rights systems will be discussed in the third section, while some reflections on the gaps and challenges will be discussed in the conclusion.

United Nations developments

The United Nations Universal Declaration on Human Rights (UDHR) in Article 16(3) states that "the family is the natural and fundamental group unit of society and is entitled to protection by society and the State."[4] The singling out and protectionist underpinnings of this articulation has reaffirmed, perpetuated and reinforced the invisibility of the right of women to be considered as individuals with human rights, including the right to a life free of violence. The male domination of the human rights sector and also the male-centric approach in the development of international human rights law,[5] has led to women being seen as synonymous with the 'family' and the family being seen as part of the private sphere. The first UN Special Rapporteur on Violence against Women stated that "the family has been the focus of very little scrutiny under international law. This is largely a consequence of the traditional division between the public and private spheres and the emphasis in human rights discourse on public sphere violations."[6] For a long time, the abovementioned points served to reinforce the view that violence against women that occurs in the family is a private matter and that it should be treated differently from other human rights violations. One of the consequences of such views has been the differential treatment accorded to women's lives, realities and human rights violations, due to both the protection of the family unit, as well as patriarchal notions linked to viewing of women as wives, mothers, victims, and the property of men.[7] Recent developments in the UN system regarding the adoption of resolutions on protection of the family, traditional values, and protection of religion, are giving rise to concerns about the implications of such developments for the promotion and protection of women's human rights broadly and the right of women to be free from all forms of violence in particular.[8]

United Nations World Conferences and meetings

Prior to, and during, the UN Decade for Women, from 1975 to 1985, the issue of violence against women in general, and more specifically domestic violence, was high on the agenda of women's rights activists. Advocacy at the World Conferences on Women, held in Mexico City

3 See generally Dobash, R.E. and R. Dobash; Eekelaar, J.M. and S.N. Katz, eds.; Foakes, J.; Gee, P.W.; Bunch, C.; Levinson, D. and K. Roth.
4 Universal Declaration on Human Rights.
5 See generally Charlesworth H, Chinkin C. and Wright S and Charlesworth H. and Chinkin C.
6 Report of UNSRVAW (1999).
7 Reports of UNSRVAW (1995, 1996 and 1999).
8 Observatory on the Universality of Rights.

in 1975[9] and Copenhagen in 1980,[10] served as a catalyst for the adoption in 1985 of a General Assembly resolution on domestic violence.[11] The Third World Conference on Women, held in Nairobi in 1985,[12] the Expert Group meeting on violence in the family with special emphasis on women, held in Vienna in 1986, and the Expert Group meeting on violence against women held in Vienna in 1991, further highlighted the global nature and concern regarding violence against women.[13] In 1991, the Commission on the Status of Women made a recommendation to the Economic and Social Council regarding the adoption of a framework for an international instrument that would explicitly address violence against women. A resolution on 'Violence against women in all its forms' was adopted by the Economic and Social Council in 1991 in which, among others, it recommended the development of a framework for an international instrument that would explicitly address the issue.[14]

The explicit recognition of violence against women as a human rights violation occurred at the UN World Conference on Human Rights, held in Vienna in 1993. The Vienna Declaration and Programme of Action adopted by the Conference did not specifically define violence against women, but it did call for the

> elimination of violence against women in public and private life, the elimination of all forms of sexual harassment, exploitation and trafficking in women, the elimination of gender bias in the administration of justice and the eradication of any conflicts which may arise between the rights of women and the harmful effects of certain traditional or customary practices, cultural prejudices and religious extremism.[15]

This statement makes it clear that domestic violence is included in the broader understanding and discourse on violence against women through its emphasis on the elimination of violence against women in all areas of life, both public and private, as being central to the attainment of women's human rights. In 1993 the General Assembly adopted the Declaration on the Elimination of Violence against Women,[16] as recommended by the Economic and Social Council, and in 1994, the Commission on Human Rights adopted a resolution establishing the mandate of the Special Rapporteur on Violence against Women, its Causes and Consequences.[17] Further political articulations of commitments by Member States, on the issue of violence against women, emerged in other UN-driven conferences including the 1994 International Conference on Population and Development and its Programme of Action[18] and the 1995 Beijing Declaration and Platform for Action.[19]

United Nations mechanisms

The Commission on the Status of Women has focused on the issue of violence against women and/or girls as a priority theme on three occasions: the theme of gender-based persecution was the focus of its 1998 session; the elimination of all forms of discrimination and violence against

9 UN Report on Mexico conference (1975).
10 UN Report on Copenhagen conference (1980).
11 UN General Assembly resolution (1985).
12 UN Report on Nairobi conference (1985).
13 Report of UNSRVAW (1995).
14 Economic and Social Council resolution (1991).
15 Vienna Declaration and Programme of Action (1993).
16 General Assembly resolution (1993).
17 Commission on Human Rights resolution (1994).
18 UN Report of International Conference on Population and Development (1994).
19 UN Report of Beijing conference (1995).

the girl child was addressed in the 2007 session; and the elimination and prevention of all forms of violence against women and girls was considered at the 2013 session.[20]

As mentioned above, the Commission on Human Rights created the mandate of the Special Rapporteur on Violence against Women, Its Causes and Consequences, in 1994 through a resolution on the question of integrating the rights of women into the human rights mechanisms of the United Nations and the elimination of violence against women. In that resolution, the Commission outlined the main scope of the mandate and invited the Special Rapporteur to carry out the mandate within the framework of the Universal Declaration of Human Rights and all other international human rights instruments, including the Declaration on the Elimination of Violence against Women. Subsequent resolutions by the Commission on Human Rights,[21] and since 2006, by the Human Rights Council,[22] have continued to extend the mandate of the Special Rapporteur, while also expanding the resolutions' substantive content regarding the issue of violence against women. The work and reports of the four UN Special Rapporteurs on Violence against Women over twenty-three years reflect substantive conceptual clarity on manifestations, causes and consequences of gendered violence against women; the development of Model Legislation on Domestic Violence; the refinement of the understandings of State responsibility to act with due diligence; and an expansion of the understanding of violence against women as a barrier to the realization of all human rights and to the exercise of effective citizenship.[23]

The General Assembly's adoption of two resolutions on domestic violence in 1985[24] and 1990[25] was an attempt to articulate a response to a pervasive global problem that had no specific normative standards in international human rights law. The 1985 resolution situates domestic violence within the perspective of crime prevention and criminal justice in the context of socio-economic circumstances; highlights the abuse of alcohol, narcotic drugs and psychotropic substances as exacerbating factors in domestic violence; requests the Committee on Crime Prevention and Control to examine the problem of domestic violence; and invites States to ensure a coordinated response from the health, welfare and justice sectors.[26] The 1990 resolution highlights the serious lack of information and research on domestic violence; recognizes the concern of States about domestic violence as an urgent problem deserving focused attention and concerted action; highlights the need to focus on all victims of domestic violence; notes the long-term effects of domestic violence, including the increased tolerance to violence in society as a whole; and requests the Committee on Crime Prevention and Control to prioritize the topic of domestic violence on the agenda of the Ninth Congress.[27]

The ground-breaking 1993 General Assembly Declaration on the Elimination of Violence against Women[28] was the first internationally adopted document that provided a comprehensive 'soft law' framework in terms of definition, scope, obligations of States to act with due diligence and the role of the United Nations. The Preamble to the Declaration highlights that the root causes of violence against women are patriarchy and the subordination of women, that violence against women is a manifestation of historically unequal power relations between men and

20 Commission on the Status of Women agreed conclusions (1998, 2007 and 2013).
21 Commission on Human Rights resolutions (1994, 1997, 2000 and 2003).
22 Human Rights Council resolutions 2007, 2009, 2010, 2011 and 2013.
23 See generally reports of UNSRVAW in general and 15-year review report (2009 add.5).
24 General Assembly resolution (1985).
25 General Assembly resolution (1990).
26 General Assembly resolution (1985) preamble and para 4.
27 General Assembly resolution (1990) preamble and para 6.
28 General Assembly resolution (1993).

women, and that this has led to domination over and discrimination against women by men and the prevention of the full advancement of women. In articles 1 and 2 the Declaration defines violence against women as any act of gender-based violence resulting in harm to women, including psychological abuse, threats or coercion, whether occurring within the family, the community, at work, in institutions, and violence perpetrated by the State. It also articulates specific recommendations in respect of actions to be taken by States in Article 4 and by the United Nations system in Article 5. It should be noted that the above-mentioned declarations and resolutions serve as consensus statements by Member States. They are not legally binding, but are of persuasive value in influencing international norms with regard to the elimination of violence against women and in providing normative standards for States to follow at the national level.

United Nations treaty system

Within the UN treaty system, there is no binding international law that explicitly and specifically addresses the issue of violence against women generally or domestic violence in particular. Currently, specialized regional treaties on violence against women, and also cases adjudicated by the regional human rights courts, are the only 'hard law' developments to date. In addition to the political articulations noted above, there have been numerous non-legally binding 'soft law' developments within the UN human rights system. Treaty monitoring bodies within the UN system contribute to the 'soft law' developments through their reviews of State Party reports, their interactive dialogues, their concluding observations and recommendations on State Party reports, through the communications procedure and their development of general recommendations and comments. Treaty bodies do not have the power to ensure the enforcement of their findings and recommendations. Furthermore, there is no enforcement mechanism, such as an international human rights court, in the human rights system, to ensure compliance with human rights treaty obligations.

In their interpretative work, numerous treaty bodies have made observations and recommendations regarding the nature of obligations of the State regarding violence against women, whether perpetrated by State or non-State actors. In particular the Committee on the Elimination of all forms of Discrimination against Women, the Human Rights Committee and the Committee against Torture, have demonstrated a willingness to interpret the applicable treaty provisions to include women's experiences of violence.[29] Violence against women is now generally viewed as a matter of State responsibility,[30] primarily due to the expanded understanding of the concept of due diligence.[31] For example, the Human Rights Committee that monitors the International Covenant on Civil and Political Rights[32] addresses States' obligations towards eliminating violence by the creative interpretation of provisions on the right to life, freedom from torture or to cruel, inhuman or degrading treatment, and the right to liberty and security of the person. Under Article 7, which prohibits torture and cruel, inhuman and degrading treatment, and Article 9 (the right to security of the person), the Committee has requested States to report on national laws and practices regarding violence against women, including domestic violence and rape, and has highlighted that States must respond appropriately to patterns of violence, including as experienced by women.[33] The Convention against Torture[34] acknowledges certain

29 See generally Chinkin in Freeman, Chinkin and Rudolf, eds; Edwards A. and Meyersfeld B.

30 See generally Cook, R.

31 Inter-American Court of Human Rights, *Velasquez-Rodriguez* case.

32 International Covenant on Civil and Political Rights.

33 Human Rights Committee, General Comment 28, 31 and 35.

34 International Convention against Torture.

manifestations of violence against women as torture, as per the interpretation of the definition of Article 1 which includes severe pain or suffering. The Committee against Torture has interpreted the treaty to include situations involving non-State actors who are implicated in violence against women situations such as rape, domestic violence, female genital mutilation, and trafficking.[35]

The only specific provision directly linked to violence against women in the Convention on the Elimination of all forms of Discrimination against Women (CEDAW) is Article 6, which requires States Parties to take all appropriate measures, including legislation, to suppress all forms of traffic in women and exploitation of prostitution of women.[36] Due to the absence of specific treaty provisions addressing all forms of violence against women, the CEDAW Committee embarked on a 'soft law' interpretative approach, through the adoption of General Recommendations 12, 19, 30 and 35 to specifically address the issue of violence against women. Most recently, in August 2017, the CEDAW Committee adopted General Recommendation 35 on Gender-Based Violence against Women, which updates General Recommendation 19. General Recommendation 12 urging States to include actions taken to prevent violence against women in their periodic reports.[37] In 1992, the Committee adopted General Recommendation 19 where it defined violence against women as violence that is directed against a woman because she is a woman or that affects women disproportionately, and notes that the term 'violence' is not restricted to physical violence alone, but also includes mental and sexual harm, and even threats of such acts, coercion and other deprivations of liberty.[38] Thus, despite the absence of specific treaty language on violence against women, the Committee in adopting General Recommendation 19 interpreted the definition of discrimination in Article 1 of the CEDAW treaty as encompassing violence against women. The Committee has adopted an interpretation that treats violence against women as a matter of discrimination, and not first and foremost as a human rights violation in and of itself – with discrimination being a cause and a consequence of violence against women. Domestic violence that disproportionately impacts women is part of the CEDAW discourse in its reports and recommendations, but there has been no specific general recommendation on this manifestation of violence against women.

The Optional Protocol to CEDAW allows the Committee to address communications (complaints) that are received. A leading communication on domestic violence addressed by the CEDAW committee is *A.T. v. Hungary*.[39] The petitioner indicated that the State's procedures for protecting her were ineffective, lengthy and did not provide for protection orders. The Committee utilized General Recommendation 19 in finding that the failure to provide a mechanism for protection orders against perpetrators of domestic violence was a violation of CEDAW, due to the State not enacting sufficient legislative measures to combat sex-based stereotypes to eliminate discrimination against women in the family setting. Despite legislative changes made by Hungary, the Committee noted that formal requirements are not necessarily enough to fulfil due diligence requirements and that the obligations set out in Article 2a, b and e of CEDAW "remain unfulfilled and constitute a violation of the author's human rights violations and fundamental freedoms, particularly her right to security of the person."[40]

35 Committee Against Torture, General Comment 2.
36 Convention on the Elimination of All Forms of Discrimination against Women.
37 CEDAW General Recommendation 12.
38 CEDAW General Recommendation 19.
39 CEDAW communication No. 2/2003.
40 Ibid. at para 9.3.

In the *Goekce v. Austria*[41] and *Yildirim v. Austria*[42] cases, the Committee found that the State failed to protect victims who were eventually killed by their husbands. They had filed multiple complaints with the local police and prosecution authorities, with very little success in obtaining effective remedies, thereby giving rise to the violation of their right to equal treatment under the law. In both cases, the Committee referred to Articles 1 and 5 of CEDAW and found that

> in order for the individual woman victim of domestic violence to enjoy the practical realization of the principle of equality of men and women and human rights and fundamental freedoms, the political will that is expressed in the aforementioned comprehensive system of Austria must be supported by State actors, who adhere to the State party's due diligence obligations.[43]

In *V.K. v. Bulgaria*[44] the Committee examined how the Law of Protection against Domestic Violence in Bulgaria defined domestic violence, as measured against Articles 1 and 2 of the CEDAW and also General Recommendation 19. The Committee's finding was that the Bulgarian Courts applied an "overly restrictive definition of domestic violence [focused on physical violence] that was not warranted by the Law and was inconsistent with the obligations of the State party under Article 2 (c) and (d) of the Convention."[45] The Committee also found that the lack of availability of a shelter for a victim of domestic violence, coupled with the Court's refusal to grant a permanent restraining order, violated CEDAW, including by placing an excessively high standard of proof on the victim.[46]

Developments in the regional human rights systems

Unlike at the UN level, three regional human rights systems have adopted treaties that specifically address violence against women and important case law has emerged from the Commissions and Courts established in these systems. The treaties and jurisprudence are considered 'hard law' and some national legal systems have domesticated regional human rights standards.

The Inter-American system

The Inter-American Convention on the Prevention, Punishment and Eradication of Violence against Women (Belém do Pará) was adopted in 1994 and is the first legally binding multilateral treaty concerning violence against women. The Convention is one of the most ratified treaties in the hemisphere of the Organization of American States.[47] The inclusion of detailed definitions, State obligations and enforcement mechanisms linked to other instruments of the Inter-American human rights system, renders this a unique development.[48] It prohibits gendered violence and codifies the right of women to be free from discrimination and violence. It defines violence against women as any act or conduct, based on gender, that causes death or physical, sexual or

41 CEDAW communication No. 5/2005.
42 CEDAW communication No. 6/2005.
43 Ibid. at para 12.1.2.
44 CEDAW communication No. 20/2008.
45 Ibid at para 9.9.
46 Ibid.
47 Center for Justice and International Law.
48 Solon Helal, I.

psychological harm or suffering to women, whether in the public or the private sphere, whether occurring within the family, community, or that is perpetuated by the State.[49]

The issue of State responsibility is clearly articulated in this Convention and includes the obligation to respect the rights and freedoms highlighted and also the obligation to ensure the free and full exercise of such to all who are subject to the jurisdiction of the treaty.[50] The Convention creates specific obligations for States Parties, including to exercise due diligence to prevent, investigate and impose penalties for violence against women.[51] Chapter III of the Convention outlines immediate duties of States Parties, including refraining from direct acts of violence against women, applying due diligence to prevent violence against women by private actors, passing necessary legislation to punish violators and prevent them from further harassing victims, and amending current laws to change cultural or legal practices that sustain the persistence and tolerance of violence against women. Article 8 outlines progressive duties of States Parties, including awareness raising, changing cultural practices harmful to women and attitudes of female inferiority through education, providing training for law enforcement personnel and other individuals involved in the justice process, providing services for victims of violence and gathering data and statistics to increase effectiveness of these policies aimed at prevention, punishment and eradication of violence against women. Article 9 provides for the possibility of an intersectional approach by requiring States Parties to take into account factors such as race, ethnic background, status as migrants, refugees or displaced persons, which can contribute to the vulnerability of women to violence.

Articles 10, 11 and 12 detail the Convention's implementation mechanisms of protection. The Organization of American States supervises and guides the compliance of obligations through the Inter-American Commission on Women, and also the Inter-American Commission on Human Rights and the Inter-American Court of Human Rights (IACHR).[52] States submit a report every two years to the Commission on Women, with the content as prescribed in Article 10. Article 11 provides information on the function and use of IACHR in respect of advisory opinions. Article 12 grants standing to individual and collective groups to file petitions to the IACHR for violations of Article 7. Due to concerns about the high prevalence rates of violence against women, despite the adoption of this specific treaty,[53] the Inter-American system adopted the Mechanism to follow up on Implementation of the Convention (MESECVI) in 2004. The MESECVI is an intergovernmental body that supports parties to the Convention in the implementation of the treaty provisions through reciprocal evaluation, including through forums of exchange of experiences and technical cooperation facilitated by a Committee of Experts.[54] Through this mechanism recommendations are formulated with respect to those areas in which there are legal gaps or in which further progress is necessary. Concerns have been raised about the ability of the Follow-Up Mechanism to review State reports, to engage in substantive dialogues with States, to provide technical assistance, and to make recommendations.[55]

49 Inter-American Convention on the Prevention, Punishment, and Eradication of Violence Against Women (Belém do Pará).
50 Guide to the Application of the Inter-American Convention on the Prevention, Punishment and Eradication of Violence Against Women.
51 Belém do Pará Art. 7.
52 OAS "What is MESECVI?"
53 *Supra* note 48 CEJIL.
54 *Supra* note 53 "What is MESECVI?"
55 *Supra* note 48 CEJIL.

A ground-breaking domestic violence case in the Inter-American Commission is that of *Maria da Penha Maia Fernandes v. Brazil*,[56] where the Commission applied the Belém do Pará Convention for the first time. The case involved the attempted murder of a woman by her husband, rendering her paraplegic. The Commission found Brazil in violation of treaty obligations for failing to exercise due diligence in sanctioning, preventing and eradicating domestic violence, due to the State not acting against the perpetrator for seventeen years. This was in violation of Article 7 and the duty to condemn all forms of violence against women; not addressing the widespread phenomena of domestic violence; and the condonation of the State in respect of judicial inefficiency towards domestic violence cases.[57] The Commission also found violations of articles 8 and 25 due to the judicial delays which resulted in violating the right to prompt and effective remedies provided for in the relevant human rights instruments.[58] The Commission did not examine the duty to investigate or punish as part of the duty to protect the right to life and physical integrity, despite the fact that there was a duty to prevent the violation, and also to address the violation of the right to personal integrity due to the lack of investigation. Instead, the case focused on impunity and a general pattern of violence in Brazil and was notable for its articulation of the due diligence principle in the context of domestic violence, as well as the need for holistic remedies.[59] The Commission also issued a series of recommendations to Brazil to address the individual needs of the victim and also to challenge the pattern of tolerance, including through prompt criminal proceedings against the perpetrator, the performance of impartial and exhaustive investigations to determine responsibilities for irregularities, and a State reform process to end the tolerance of violence against women.[60] In 2006, following consultations between the Brazilian government and civil society, the Maria da Penha Law was passed and it is seen as one of the most progressive laws on domestic violence in the region.[61]

In another domestic violence case *Jessica Lenahan (Gonzales) v. United States*[62] the Commission found the United States in violation of the American Declaration and its due diligence obligations for failing to enforce a restraining order against Jessica Gonzales' estranged husband, which resulted in the death of her three young children.[63] In exhausting her national level remedies, up to the US Supreme Court[64] it was held that the government generally has no duty to protect individuals from private acts of violence. Ms Gonzales approached the Inter-American Commission for relief. In reaching their decision, the Commission took into account the evolving law and practice both regionally and internationally concerning the application of the due diligence standard in cases of violence against women. The Commission found the United States in violation of the American Declaration, due to its failure to protect victims of domestic violence adequately and effectively, due to the lack of enforcement of protection orders.[65] This failure constitutes a form of discrimination against women, who are in the majority as beneficiaries of restraining orders. The Commission concluded that the State had failed to act with due diligence to protect Ms Gonzales and her children from domestic violence.

56 *Maria de Penha* case (2001).
57 Ibid. at 58.
58 Ibid. at 41.
59 Moser, P. T.
60 Celorio, R.
61 *Supra* note 60 Moser.
62 *Jessica Lenahan (Gonzales) v. United States* (2011).
63 Ibid.
64 *Town of Castle Rock v. Jessica Gonzales* (2005).
65 *Supra* note 63 at paras 126, 127.

The African system

The Organization of African Unity (OAU), which was replaced by the African Union in 2002, was created in 1963.[66] The political charter creating the OAU made no reference to human rights, as the main issue on the agenda was to end colonialism and assert the right to self-determination of African States.[67] The creation of the African human rights system in 1981 led to the adoption of several human rights instruments and the setting up of monitoring mechanisms. Applicable human rights instruments that have been adopted since 1981 include the African Charter on Human and Peoples' Rights, the African Charter on the Rights and Welfare of the Child, the Protocol to the African Charter on Human and Peoples' Rights on the Rights of Women in Africa and the Protocol on the Statute of the African Court of Justice and Human Rights. Monitoring bodies include the African Court of Justice and Human Rights and the African Commission on Human and Peoples' Rights, with the latter monitoring the implementation by States of their obligations as set out in, among others, the African Charter and the Protocol on the Rights of Women in Africa. The Commission has the mandate to receive and examine State Party reports, consider communications and fulfil other protective and promotional responsibilities.[68]

The African Charter on Human and Peoples' Rights includes specific references to women in Article 2 which prohibits discrimination, including on the basis of sex, and Article 18(3), which obliges States to eliminate all discrimination against women and to ensure the protection of the rights of women as stipulated in international declarations and conventions. The Charter incorporates principles related to culture, group rights and respect for the family environment. Article 60 of the Charter mandates the African Commission to draw inspiration from international law in its promotion and protection of human rights. The Charter has been criticized by some for being unrealistic and overambitious, and for ignoring women's human rights, while others have praised it for protecting all human rights, both individual and collective.[69]

Concerns about the lack of promotion and protection of women's rights led to lobbying efforts for a specific instrument on women's rights from 1995, largely led by non-governmental organizations (NGOs) working in the field of women's rights. The first Special Rapporteur on Rights of Women in Africa was appointed in 1999 and she supported the efforts of NGOs to develop a protocol to the African Charter on the rights of women. A minimalist approach was adopted by Member States in addressing the inadequacies regarding the human rights of women in the African Charter, with consensus to adopt a protocol, as opposed to a separate treaty with its own monitoring body. The draft protocol was finalized by a team of government experts, and the Protocol to the African Charter on Human and Peoples' Rights on the Rights of Women in Africa (Maputo Protocol)[70] was adopted by the Assembly of the African Union in July 2003. It entered into force in 2005. The Protocol on the Rights of Women calls for States Parties to report to the African Commission on Human and Peoples' Rights regarding their implementation of the Protocol, as no separate monitoring body was created in the Protocol.[71] Reporting guidelines have been issued by the African Commission and the African Court on Human and Peoples' Rights has the authority to interpret the Protocol on the Rights of Women.

66 See generally Heyns, C.; Evans, M. and Murray, R. eds.
67 See the Charter of the Organization of African Unity, in particular Arts 2 and 3.
68 See Arts 30, 45 and 47 of the African Charter on Human and Peoples' Rights.
69 Bondzie-Simpson, E.
70 Protocol to the African Charter on Human and Peoples' Rights on the Rights of Women in Africa (Maputo Protocol).
71 Ibid. Art. 26.

The Maputo Protocol has been signed and ratified by 28 States, with 18 States that have signed but not ratified.[72] It defines discrimination against women as well as violence against women in Article 1. Discrimination is defined as "any distinction, exclusion or restriction or any differential treatment based on sex and whose objectives or effects compromise or destroy the recognition, enjoyment or the exercise by women . . . of human rights and fundamental freedoms in all spheres of life."[73] Violence against women is defined as encompassing a broad array of violence including physical, sexual, psychological and economic harm.[74] Interestingly, the Maputo Protocol is the first regional treaty that specifically refers to violent acts perpetrated during times of war as well as peace.

The Protocol includes provisions on violence against women, based largely on the Declaration on the Elimination of Violence against Women, but with additions that are both context specific and progressive. Article 1 of the Protocol provides a broad definition of violence against women, which includes explicit reference to the deprivation of fundamental freedoms in private or public life, and defines harmful practices as all behaviour, attitudes and/or practices that negatively affect the fundamental rights of women and girls, such as their right to life, health, dignity, education and physical integrity. Article 4 is comprehensive with regard to the legal and non-legal measures to be taken by Member States in addressing violence against women, including the enactment of specific legislation; the imposition of appropriate sanctions/punishment when violence occurs; the provision of adequate budgetary resources; the adoption of public education and awareness-raising measures, including to address negative elements in attitudes, traditions and culture in order to eliminate harmful cultural and traditional practices; and the provision of relevant services, including justice, healthcare and shelters. Importantly, in the preamble of the Protocol it is made explicit that positive African values are based on the principles of equality, freedom, dignity, justice, solidarity and democracy. This clarification is important in the area of violence against women, as research indicates that violence, including wife beating, is considered or perceived to be one of the values of African families in some societies.[75]

Article 4 of the Maputo Protocol articulates the right to life, integrity and security of the person and prohibits all forms of exploitation, cruel, inhuman or degrading punishment and treatment with measures including enacting laws to prohibit violence against women in public or in private, taking legislative, administrative, social and economic measures to ensure prevention, punishment and eradication, identifying causes of violence against women and taking actions to prevent it, providing education to change traditional cultural beliefs that tolerate violence against women, punishing perpetrators and preventing and prosecuting trafficking in women. Article 5 of the Protocol calls for the elimination of harmful practices, such as female genital mutilation, and recommends measures such as public awareness campaigns, legal prohibition and the provision of support services for victims and at-risk women.

The jurisprudence on women's human rights broadly is largely non-existent, and there are no domestic violence decisions from the African Commission or the Court.[76] The *Egyptian Initiative for Personal Rights and INTERIGHTS v. Egypt* case[77] is the first specific violence against women case, decided in 2011. The African Commission found Egypt in violation of Articles 2 and 18(3) of the African Charter, as the Maputo Protocol is not applicable due to Egypt not

72 See website of African Commission.

73 *Supra* note 71 Art. 1(f).

74 Ibid. Art. 1(j).

75 Armstrong, A.

76 A Guide to Using the Protocol on the Rights of Women in Africa for Legal Action.

77 African Commission Communication 323/06.

being a State Party. This case was about four female journalists who were physically and sexually assaulted by police officers and other unnamed attackers. The Commission found that violence against women violates fundamental human rights and is a form of discrimination. The Commission also found a violation of Article 16(1), finding that "[t]he trauma and injuries sustained has affected their physical, psychological and mental health clearly in violation of Article 16(1) of the African Charter."[78]

Despite the existence of the Charter on Human and Peoples' Rights and the Protocol on the Rights of Women in Africa, African states have been criticized not only for their human rights record generally, but also for their treatment of women's human rights specifically.[79] The absence of more cases on women's human rights broadly, and violence against women in particular, is an indicator of the weakness of the African human rights system.

The European system

Since the 1990s the Council of Europe has adopted numerous measures and produced recommendations, indicators, reports and other non-binding documents that set guidelines on achieving progress through legislative and other measures addressing violence against women and domestic violence.[80] In 2009, based on the recommendation of a task force, the Council decided to develop a binding legal instrument that would address prevention, protection and punishment in the area of violence against women, thereby addressing the gap in the regional human rights system. The Convention on Preventing and Combating Violence against Women and Domestic Violence (Istanbul Convention) is the second regional treaty adopted to specifically address violence against women.[81] It was adopted in 2011, and came into effect in 2014.

The Istanbul Convention addresses violence against women as a human rights violation and also as a form of gender-based discrimination, thereby strengthening the obligations imposed on States. The 81 articles in the Convention define the range of integrated legal and other measures that States are required to take in order to meet their obligations to prevent, protect and prosecute violence against women. Those measures include data collection, prevention, protection and support measures, as well as legislative, investigative and prosecutorial measures. The Convention also provides for the establishment of a monitoring mechanism to ensure State accountability. On the whole, the Convention requires States to adopt specific, comprehensive, integrated and coordinated laws, policies and other measures that place the rights of victims at the centre of all measures, and to involve all relevant actors, including government agencies, national, regional and local authorities, civil society organizations and other relevant entities. The Istanbul Convention is open for all to ratify, including non-Council of Europe states.

The Convention has the most detailed definition of violence against women at the regional level. Article 3 defines violence against women, domestic violence, gender, and gender-based violence against women. Its definition of violence against women reflects other standard-setting definitions, such as those contained in CEDAW General Recommendation 19 and the Belém do Pará, but it explicitly labels violence against women as a violation of human rights and also discrimination against women. The Istanbul Convention also includes a broader definition of

78 Ibid. at 265.

79 Heyns, C.

80 See Council of Europe, "Compilation of International Legal Instruments relevant to the Ad Hoc Committee on Preventing and Combating Violence against Women and Domestic Violence".

81 Council of Europe Convention on Preventing and Combating Violence against Women and Domestic Violence (Istanbul Convention).

gender-based violence against women,[82] with gender also being defined more specifically than in other standard-setting documents.[83] However, the treaty is clear that this is a treaty that is referring to gender-based violence against women. As the term 'woman' is not defined in the treaty, it is unclear whether gender-based violence against women would include individuals that are not biologically women. Domestic violence is defined as violence occurring "within the family or domestic unit or between former or current spouses or partners," and this category of violence is applicable to men and women who may be subjected to domestic violence.[84]

The Istanbul Convention provides the most specific list of obligations for States. Article 4 requires States to enshrine the principle of equality between men and women, prohibit discrimination against women and abolish laws that discriminate against women.[85] The treaty also obligates States to "exercise due diligence to prevent, investigate, punish and provide reparation" for actions of private parties.[86] After outlining the general requirement of due diligence, Chapter III of the treaty lays out specific legislative, policy and other measures for States to take in order to prevent violence against women, while Chapter IV provides for a framework on protection and support. In Chapter V the convention provides a framework for substantive laws. This includes civil lawsuits and remedies,[87] and lists specific acts that must be criminalized, including sexual violence and rape,[88] psychological violence,[89] physical violence,[90] forced marriage,[91] female genital mutilation,[92] and forced sterilization or abortion.[93] It further requires that sexual harassment be criminalized or subject to some type of legal sanction.[94] Chapter VI outlines requirements for investigation, prosecution, procedural law and protective measures, with Chapter VII addressing migration and asylum issues; and Chapter VIII, on international cooperation. Chapter IX of the Convention contains detailed provisions concerning the monitoring system necessary for the implementation of the Convention, both nationally and regionally.

With respect to substantive law, States are required: to provide for adequate civil remedies; to ensure that all forms of violence against women and domestic violence are criminalized and appropriately punished; and to recognize in law that being a family member or ex-spouse of a victim of violence against women and domestic violence is an aggravating circumstance that must be taken into consideration in the determination of the penalty. As regards investigation, prosecution and procedural aspects, States must ensure that all forms of violence against women and domestic violence are appropriately punished; ensure that culture, custom, religion or so-called 'honour' are not accepted as justification for any act of violence; ensure that victims have access to special protection measures during investigation and judicial proceedings; implement risk assessment protocols to enhance the protection of victims; ensure that law enforcement agencies respond promptly to calls for assistance and that they manage dangerous situations adequately; and introduce preventive and protective legislation, including emergency barring orders.

82 Ibid. Art. 3(4).
83 Ibid. Art. 3(3).
84 Ibid. Art. 3(2).
85 Ibid. Art. 4(2).
86 Ibid. Art 5(2).
87 Ibid. Art. 29.
88 Ibid. Art. 36.
89 Ibid. Art. 33.
90 Ibid. Art. 35.
91 Ibid. Art. 37.
92 Ibid. Art. 38.
93 Ibid. Art. 39.
94 Ibid. Art. 40.

The relevant case law discussion on domestic violence in the European human rights system emanates from the European Court of Human Rights, based on the Convention for the Protection of Human Rights and Fundamental Freedoms,[95] and subsequent amending protocols.[96] The Court has addressed cases of domestic violence, rape, honour-based violence, female genital mutilation, inhumane treatment in detention, violence in public places, servitude, forced sterilization, and abortion-related violence. Article 2 (right to life), Article 3 (prohibition of torture), Article 8 (right to respect for private and family life), Article 13 (right to an effective remedy) and Article 14 (prohibition of discrimination) are relevant to cases of violence against women. However, complaints concerning violence against women are usually discussed under the broad themes of whether the incidents constitute a violation of Article 8, whether the violence reaches a certain threshold of severity under Article 2, and whether the violence amounts to torture or inhuman or degrading treatment under Article 3. The Court has often discussed cases of violence against women solely under Article 8, and has refrained from considering the relevance of other articles.

Except in one case,[97] the Court has failed to recognize discrimination against women as one of the causes of violence against women, and it has not considered it necessary to examine the complaints under other provisions of the Convention, including Article 14. The ground-breaking case of *Opuz v. Turkey* concerns domestic violence where the alleged perpetrator was not prosecuted after the victims withdrew their numerous complaints as a result of being harassed by the perpetrator. The perpetrator eventually killed the mother of the applicant and was later released from prison pending his appeal and continued to harass the victim. The Court found a violation of Article 2 (the right to life) concerning the murder of the applicant's mother, and a violation of Article 3 (the prohibition of inhuman or degrading treatment) for that State's failure to protect the wife from her husband. The European Court took note of regional and international developments regarding violence against women and stated that "the State's failure – even if unintentional – to protect women against domestic violence breached women's right to equal protection of the law."[98] The Court found, for the first time in a domestic violence case, that there had been a violation of Article 14 (prohibition of discrimination) read in conjunction with Articles 2 and 3 on account of the violence suffered by the applicant and her mother having been gender-based, which amounted to a form of discrimination against women.

In *Eremia and Others v. The Republic of Moldova*,[99] the first applicant suffered domestic violence by her police officer husband, even after obtaining a protection order. The abuse was often in front of, and therefore affected, their two children (the second and third applicant). The Court found that the history of domestic violence and the fear of future assaults "was sufficiently serious to cause the first applicant to experience suffering and anxiety amounting to inhuman treatment within the meaning of Article 3 of the Convention."[100] The Court also found that "the authorities' actions were not a simple failure or delay in dealing with violence against the first applicant, but amounted to repeatedly condoning such violence and reflected a discriminatory attitude towards the first applicant as a woman."[101] The finding of the Court was that there was a violation of Article 14 in conjunction with Article 3 of the Convention in respect of the first applicant. In respect of the children, the Court found a violation in terms of Article 8 stating that

95 European Convention on Human Rights, Art. 46 (2).
96 See Council of Europe, *Collected Edition of the "Travaux Preparatoires"*, vol. I, p. 48.
97 *Opuz v. Turkey* (2009).
98 Ibid. at 5.
99 *Eremia and Others v. The Republic of Moldova* (2013).
100 Ibid. at 4.
101 Ibid. at 5 and 6.

their psychological well-being had been adversely affected by repeatedly witnessing their father's violence against their mother in the family home. This amounted to an interference with the second and third applicants' right to private life and respect for their home within the meaning of Article 8 of the Convention.[102]

Conclusion

As discussed above, normative developments regarding binding obligations on States to act with due diligence to address violence against women exist in the established regional human rights frameworks of the African, Inter-American and European systems. The UN practice has been one of 'soft law' developments through the adoption of resolutions, declarations and general recommendations or comments. Guidance by UN standard-setting documents has led to the issue of domestic violence being acknowledged as a human rights violation, but this has come through a process of normativity without legality.[103]

Furthermore, the jurisprudence on domestic violence in the European and Inter-American system has been ground-breaking and has provided some positive change in a few countries. But, considering the widespread and pervasive problem of domestic violence that exists globally, it is apparent that there is largely a failure to protect against, prevent and eradicate domestic violence in all countries of the world. As regards other regions where there is no established human rights system, or where there is a nascent developing system, it is difficult to comment on the success or challenge inherent therein. For example, the Association of Southeast Asian Nations (ASEAN) has two declarations calling for the prevention and protection of women in trafficking[104] as well as violence against women,[105] but the impact of such developments is unclear.

The normative gap at the international level relating to the lack of a specific treaty on violence against women, and the lack of specific provisions on the issue in CEDAW, have resulted in the absence of legally binding definitions, imposition of State obligations to act with due diligence, and the lack of dedicated and effective monitoring of State actions or inactions regarding gendered violence, among other challenges. The approach of other UN treaties to violence against women is in line with the approach of adopting a general matter for human rights promotion and protection. The lack of specificity and understanding of gendered harms in a more nuanced way further reinforces the argument for an international treaty that holistically addresses all forms of violence against women, including domestic violence experienced by women. The remedies that are needed must include civil, criminal and matrimonial aspects, within an understanding of the causes and consequences of gendered violence.

Bibliography

Armstrong, A. (1998). *Culture and Choice: Lessons from Survivors of Gender Violence in Zimbabwe*. Southern African Research and Documentation Centre.

Association of Southeast Asian Nations (ASEAN). (2004). Declaration against Trafficking in Persons, Particularly Women and Children. Adopted at the 10th ASEAN Summit, Vientiane, Lao People's Democratic Republic. Available at www.asean.org/news/item/asean-declaration-against-trafficking-in-persons-particularly-women-and-children-3 (Accessed 5 December 2016).

Association of Southeast Asian Nations (ASEAN). (2004). Declaration on the Elimination of Violence Against Women in the ASEAN Region (adopted in Jakarta, Indonesia. Available at www.asean.org/

102 Ibid. at 5.

103 UNSRVAW report to Human Rights Council (2014).

104 ASEAN Declaration Against Trafficking in Persons Particularly Women and Children.

105 Declaration on the Elimination of Violence Against Women in the ASEAN Region.

communities/asean-political-security-community/item/declaration-on-the-elimination-of-violence-against-women-in-the-asean-region-2n (Accessed 5 December 2016).

Association of Southeast Asian Nations (ASEAN). (2009). Terms of Reference (TOR) of the ASEAN Commission on the Promotion and Protection of the Rights of Women and Children (ACWC). Adopted at the 15th ASEAN Summit, Hua Hin, Thailand. Available at www.asean.org/images/2012/Social_cultural/ACW/TOR-ACWC.pdf (Accessed 5 December 2016).

Bondzie-Simpson, E. (1988). "A Critique of the African Charter on Human and Peoples' Rights," *Howard Law Journal* 31, 643–665.

Bunch, C. (1990). "Women's Rights as Human Rights: Towards a Revision of Human Rights," *Human Rights Quarterly*, 12, 486–498.

CEDAW Communications available at www.un.org/womenwatch/daw/cedaw/protocol/decisionsviews/CEDAW (Accessed 21 November 2016).

CEDAW Communication No. 2/2003 *Ms. A.T. v. Hungary*, UN Doc. CEDAW/C/36/D/2/2003 (2005).

CEDAW Communication No. 5/2005, *Goekce (deceased) v. Austria*, UN Doc. CEDAW/C/39/D/5/2005 (2007).

CEDAW Communication No. 6/2005 *Yildrin v. Austria. UN* Doc. CEDAW/C/39/D/6/2005 (2007).

CEDAW Communication No. 20/2008 *VK v. Bulgaria*, UN Doc. CEDAW/C/49/D/20/2008 (2011).

CEDAW General Recommendation No. 12 (1989). Violence against women. Available at www.ohchr.org/EN/HRBodies/CEDAW/Pages/Recommendations.aspx (Accessed 5 December 2016).

CEDAW General Recommendation 19 Violence against women (1993) Adopted at Eleventh session, (1992). U.N. Doc. A/47/38 (1993), reprinted in Compilation of General Comments and General Recommendations Adopted by Human Rights Treaty Bodies, U.N. Doc. HRI/GEN/1/Rev.6 at 243 (2003). Available at www.ohchr.org/EN/HRBodies/CEDAW/Pages/Recommendations.aspx (Accessed 5 December 2016).

Celorio, R. (2011). "The Rights of Women in the Inter-American System of Human Rights: Current Opportunities and Challenges in Standard-Setting," *U. Miami L. Rev.* 65, 819.

Center for Justice and International Law (CEJIL). (2006). *Evaluation of the State of the Mechanism to Follow-Up on the Implementation of the Convention of Belém do Pará.* 1st edn. San José, C.R.

Charlesworth, H., Chinkin, C. and Wright, S. (1991). "Feminist Approaches to International Law," *American Journal of International Law*, 85(4), 613–645.

Charlesworth, H. and Chinkin, C. (2000). *The Boundaries of International Law: A Feminist Analysis.* Manchester, UK: Manchester University Press.

Charlesworth, H. and Chinkin, C. (1994). "Violence against Women: A Global Issue," in J. Stubbs (ed.) *Women, Male Violence and the Law 13*. Sydney: Institute of Criminology Monograph Series, No. 6.

Chinkin, C. (2012). "Violence against Women," in M. Freeman, C. Chinkin and B. Rudolf, (eds) *The UN Convention on the Elimination of All Forms of Discrimination against Women: A Commentary*. Oxford, UK: Oxford University Press.

Committee Against Torture. (2007). Implementation of article 2 by States Parties. General Comment 2 U.N. Doc. CAT/C/GC/2/CRP. 1/Rev.4.

Communication 323/06: *Egyptian Initiative for Personal Rights and INTERIGHTS v. Egypt.* Available at www.achpr.org/communications/decision/323.06/ (Accessed 5 December 2016).

Cook, R. (1994). "State Responsibility for Violation of Women's Human Rights," *Harvard Human Rights Journal* 7, 125–175.

Cook, R. (1990). "Reservations to the Convention on the Elimination of All Forms of Discrimination against Women," *VA. J. Int'l L.* 30, 643–709.

Council of Europe. "Compilation of International Legal Instruments Relevant to the Ad Hoc Committee on Preventing and Combating Violence Against Women and Domestic Violence." Available at www.coe.int/t/dghl/standardsetting/convention-violence/CAHVIO/compilation_en.pdf (Accessed 5 December 2016).

Council of Europe Convention on Preventing and Combating Violence Against Women and Domestic Violence, Apr. 7, 2011, C.E.T.S. No. 210 (Istanbul Convention).

Council of Europe. *Collected Edition of the Travaux Preparatoires, vol. I.*

Council of Europe, European Convention for the Protection of Human Rights and Fundamental Freedoms, as amended by Protocols Nos. 11 and 14, 4 November 1950, ETS 5.

Deller-Ross, S. (2008). *Women's Human Rights: The International and Comparative Law Casebook.* Philadelphia, PA: University of Pennsylvania Press.

Dobash, R.E. and Dobash, R. (1980). *Violence against Wives: A Case Against the Patriarchy.* London: Open Books.

Edwards, A. (2011). *Violence against Women under International Human Rights Law.* Cambridge, UK: Cambridge University Press.
Eekelaar, J.M. and Katz, S.N. (1977). *Family Violence: An International and Interdisciplinary Study.* Toronto: Butterworths.
Equality Now. (2011). *A Guide to Using the Protocol on the Rights of Women in Africa for Legal Action.* Available at www.equalitynow.org/sites/default/files/Manual%20on%20Protocol%20on%20Women%20Rights%20in%20Africa_EN.pdf (Accessed 15 December 2016).
Eremia and Others v. The Republic of Moldova Application No. 3564/11 (2013) European Court of Human Rights.
Foakes, J. (1984). *Family Violence: Law and Practice.* London: Hemstal Press.
Gee, P.W. (1983). "Ensuring Police Protection for Battered Women," *Signs: Journal of Women in Culture and Society*, 8, 554–567.
Hellum, A. and Aasen, S.A. (2013). *Women's Human Rights: CEDAW in International, Regional and National Law.* Cambridge, UK: Cambridge University Press.
Heyns, C. (2001). "The African Regional Human Rights System: In Need of Reform?" *African Human Rights Journal* 1(2), 155–174.
Heyns, C. (2003). "African Regional Human Rights System: The African Charter," *Penn St. L. Rev.* 108, 679–692.
Human Rights Committee documents available at https://documents-dds-ny.un.org/doc/UNDOC/GEN/.
Human Rights Committee. (2004). *General Comment 31 (The Nature of the General Legal Obligation Imposed on States Parties to the Covenant).* UN Doc. CCPR/C/21/Rev.1/Add.13.
Human Rights Committee. (2000). *General Comment 28 Equality of Rights between Men and Women.* UN Doc. CCPR/C/21/Rev.1/Add.10, Article 3.
Human Rights Committee. (2013). States Parties Obligations under Article 9 of the International Covenant on Civil and Political Rights, concerning the Right to Liberty and Security of the Person. UN Doc CCPR/C/107/R.3.
Human Rights Institute. (n.d). Commentary on *Jessica Gonzales v. United States of America.* Available at http://web.law.columbia.edu/human-rights-institute/inter-american-human-rights-system/jessica-gonzales-v-us (Accessed 20 December 2016).
Inter-American Court of Human Rights. *Velasquez-Rodriguez*, (1988) ser. C., No.4, 9 Hum. Rts.l.J. 212.
Inter-American Convention on the Prevention, Punishment, and Eradication of Violence Against Women (Belém do Pará) 33 I.L.M. 1534 (1994), adopted June 9, 1994 and entered into force March 5, 1995. Available at www.oas.org/en. (Accessed 20 December 2016).
Inter-American Commission of Women and Follow-up Mechanism to the Belem do Para Convention (MESECVI). (2014). Guide to the Application of the Inter-American Convention on the Prevention, Punishment and Eradication of Violence Against Women. Available at www.oas.org/en/mesecvi/docs/bdp-guiaaplicacion-web-en.pdf (Accessed 20 December 2016).
International Covenant on Civil and Political Rights, G.A. res. 2200A (XXI), 21 U.N. GAOR Supp. (No. 16) at 52. UN Doc. A/6316 (1966), 999 U.N.T.S. 171, entered into force Mar. 23, 1976.
International Convention against Torture and Other Cruel, Inhuman or Degrading Treatment or Punishment, adopted Dec. 10, 1984, G.A. Res. 39/46, UN GAOR, 39th Sess., Supp. No.51, at 197, UN Doc. A/39/51 (1984), 1465 U.N.T.S. 85 (entered into force June 26, 1987).
International Convention on the Elimination of All Forms of Discrimination Against Women, (CEDAW) adopted 18 December 1979, United Nations, Treaty Series, vol. 1249, p. 13 (entered into force 3 September 1981).
Jessica Lenahan (Gonzales) v. the United States. (2011). Inter-American Report No. 80/11, Case 12.626.
Levinson, D. (1989). *Family Violence in Cross Cultural Perspective.* Newbury Park, CA: Sage.
Malcolm, E. and Murray, R. (2008). *The African Charter on Human and Peoples' Rights: The System in Practice 1986–2006.* Cambridge, UK: Cambridge University Press.
Manjoo, R. (2016). Twenty Years of Normativity without Legality – United Nations Developments on Violence against Women, its Causes and Consequences. QMHRR 3(1). Available at www.law.qmul.ac.uk/humanrights/Docs/hrlr/2016/198764.pdf. (Accessed 20 June 2017)
Maria da Penha v. Brazil, Case 12.051, Report No. 54/01, OEA/Ser.L/V/II.111 Doc. 20 rev. at 704 (2001).
Meyersfeld B. (2010). *Domestic Violence and International Law.* Oxford, UK: Hart..
Moser, P.T. (2012). "Duty to Ensure Human Rights and Its Evolution in the Inter-American System: Comparing *Maria de Penha v. Brazil* with *Jessica Lenahan (Gonzales) v. United States*," *American University Journal of Gender Social Policy and Law* 21(2), 437.
OAS. (n.d). "What is MESECVI?". Organization of American States. Available at www.oas.org/en/about/mechanisms.asp (Accessed 20 December 2016).

Observatory on the Universality of Rights Trends Report 2017 "Rights at Risk" published by Association for Women's Rights in Development (Toronto and Mexico City). Available at www.oursplatform.org/ (Accessed 20 June 2017).

Open Society Justice Initiative. (2013). Case Digests: Legal Update on Discrimination. Open Society Case Summaries Digest. Available at www.opensocietyfoundations.org/briefing-papers/case-digests-legal-update-discrimination (Accessed 20 November 2016).

Optional Protocol to the 1979 Convention on the Elimination of All Forms of Discrimination against Women (adopted 6 October 1999, entered into force 22 December 2000) 2131 UNTS 83.

Opuz v. Turkey Application No. 33401/02 (2009) European Court of Human Rights.

Organization of African Unity. (1981). African Charter on Human and Peoples' Rights ("Banjul Charter"), 27 June 1981, CAB/LEG/67/3 rev. 5, 21 I.L.M. 58 (1982).

Pasqualucci, J.M. (2012). *The Practice and Procedure of the Inter-American Court of Human Rights.* Cambridge, UK: Cambridge University Press.

Protocol to the African Charter on Human and Peoples' Rights on the Rights of Women in Africa. (Maputo Protocol). Adopted Sept. 13, 2000 and entered into force Nov. 25, 2005. CAB/LEG/66.6 (Sept. 13, 2000). Available at www.achpr.org/instruments/women-protocol/ (Accessed 2 December 2016).

Report of the International Conference on Population and Development. (1995) A/RES/49/128. Cairo, Egypt. Available at www.un.org/popin/icpd2.htm (Accessed 20 December 2016).

Reports of the United Nations Special Rapporteur on Violence against Women, (UNSRVAW). Available at www.ohchr.org.

Roth, K. (1994). "Domestic Violence as an International Human Rights Issue," in R. Cook (ed.), *Human Rights of Women: National and International Perspectives.* Philadelphia, PA: University of Pennsylvania Press.

Solon Helal, I. (2002). "The UN Declaration on the Elimination of Violence Against Women and the Inter-American Convention on the Prevention, Punishment and Eradication of Violence Against Women," *Jurisfemme* 21(2).

Town of Castle Rock v. Gonzales case 545 U.S.748 (2005).

UN Commission on Human Rights resolutions, available at http://ap.ohchr.org/documents/E/CHR/resolutions/

UN Commission on Human Rights reports of the Special Rapporteur on Violence against women, available at www.ohchr.org.

UN Commission on Human Rights. (1995, 1996, 1999). Reports of the United Nations Special Rapporteur on Violence against Women. Radhika Coomaraswamy. Violence against women in the family. UN Doc E/CN.4/1995/42; E/CN.4/1996/53 and E/CN.4/1999/68.

UN Commission on Human Rights. (1999). Report of the Special Rapporteur on Violence against Women, Its Causes and Consequences, Radhika Coomaraswamy. UN Doc. E/CN.4/1999/68.

UN Commission on Human Rights. (1996). Report of the Special Rapporteur on Violence against Women, Its Causes and Consequences, Radhika Coomaraswamy. UN Doc. E/CN.4/1996/53.

UN Commission on Human Rights. (1995). Report of the Special Rapporteur on Violence against Women, Its Causes and Consequences, Radhika Coomaraswamy. UN Doc. E/CN.4/1995/42.

UN Commission on Human Rights. (1994). Question of Integrating the Rights of Women into the Human Rights Mechanisms of the United Nations and the Elimination of Violence against Women. Resolution 1994/45.

UN Commission on Human Rights. (1997). The Elimination of Violence against Women. Resolution 1997/44.

UN Commission on Human Rights. (2000). The Right to Restitution, Compensation and Rehabilitation for Victims of Grave Violations of Human Rights and Fundamental Freedoms. Resolution 2000/45.

UN Commission on Human Rights. (2003). The Elimination of Violence against Women. Resolution 2003/45.

UN Commission on the Status of Women, Agreed Conclusions on Women and Armed Conflict (1998). UN Doc. E/1998/27-E/CN.6/1998/12). Available at www.un.org/documents/ecosoc/docs/1998/e1998-27.htm (Accessed 20 December 2016).

UN Commission on the Status of Women, Agreed Conclusions on the Elimination of All Forms Of Discrimination and Violence against the Girl Child (2007). UN Doc. E/2007/27-E/CN.6/2007/9). Available at https://unispal.un.org/DPA/DPR/unispal.nsf/0/66718C71F70D7F22852572DB00576287 (Accessed 20 December 2016).

UN Commission on the Status of Women, agreed conclusions on the elimination and prevention of all forms of violence against women (2013). UN Doc. E/2013/27-E/CN.6/2013/11). Available at https://unispal.un.org/DPA/DPR/unispal.nsf/0/76DE014A042884EA85257BDC0050B1C5 (Accessed 20 December 2016).

UN Economic and Social Council. (30 May 1991). Violence against Women in All Its Forms. Resolution 1991/18. Available at http://repository.un.org/handle/11176/186952 (Accessed 5 November 2016).
UN Human Rights Council Resolutions and Reports, available at http://ap.ohchr.org/documents/E/HRC/resolutions/ www.ohchr.org and www.un.org/womenwatch/daw/vaw/v-hrc.htm (Accessed 20 December 2016).
UN Human Rights Council. (2007). Adequate Housing as a Component of the Right to an Adequate Standard of Living. Resolution 6/27.
UN Human Rights Council. (2008). Elimination of Violence against Women. Resolution 7/24.
UN Human Rights Council. (2010). Trafficking in Persons, Especially Women and Children: Regional and Sub-Regional Cooperation in Promoting a Human Rights Based Approach to Combatting Trafficking in Persons. Resolution 14/12.
UN Human Rights Council. (2011). Mandate of the Special Rapporteur on Violence against Women, Its Causes and Consequences. Resolution 16/7.
UN Human Rights Council. (2013). Accelerating Efforts to Eliminate All Forms of Violence Against Women: Preventing and Responding to Rape and Other Forms of Sexual Violence. Resolution 23/25.
UN Human Rights Council. (2010). Accelerating Efforts to Eliminate All Forms of Violence against Women: Ensuring Due Diligence in Prevention. Resolutions 14/12.
UN Human Rights Council. (2009). Accelerating Efforts to Eliminate All Forms of Violence against Women. Resolution 11/2.
UN Human Rights Council. (2014). Report of the United Nations Special Rapporteur on Violence against Women, Rashida Manjoo. "Violence against Women: Twenty Years of Developments within the United Nations," UN Doc A/HRC/26/38 (2014)
UN Human Rights Council. (2009). Report of the United Nations Special Rapporteur on Violence against Women, Yakin Erturk. "15 Years of the United Nations Special Rapporteur on Violence against Women, Its Causes and Consequences (1994–2009): A Critical Review," A/HRC/11/6/Add.5.
UN General Assembly. Universal Declaration of Human Rights, 10 December 1948, 217 A (III).
UN General Assembly Resolutions and Conference Reports, available at www.un.org/documents/ga/res/; www.un.org/womenwatch/daw/beijing/otherconferences/Mexico/Mexico%20conference%20report%20optimized.pdf; www.unwomen.org (Accessed 2 January 2017).
UN General Assembly. (1975). Report of the World conference of the International Women's Year. (Mexico) UN Publication, Sales no. E.76. IV. 1.
UN General Assembly. (1980). Report of the World Conference of the United Nations Decade for Women: Equality, Development and Peace. (Copenhagen). UN Publication, Sales No. E. 80. IV. 3.
UN General Assembly. (1985). Report of the World Conference to Review and Appraise the Achievements of the United Nations Decade for Women: Equality, Development and Peace. (Nairobi). UN Publication Sales No. E. 85. IV.10.
UN General Assembly (1995). Fourth World Conference on Women, Platform for Action, for Equality, Development and Peace. (Beijing). A/CONF.177/20.
UN General Assembly. (1996). Fourth World Conference on Women. (Beijing) A/RES/50/42.
UN General Assembly. (1985). Domestic Violence. Resolution A/RES/40/36.
UN General Assembly. (1990). Domestic Violence. Resolution A/RES/45/114.
UN General Assembly. (1993). Declaration on the Elimination of Violence against Women. Resolution A/RES/48/104.
United Nations Treaty Collection, available at https://treaties.un.org/Pages/ViewDetails.aspx?src=TREATY&mtdsg_no=IV-8&chapter=4&lang=en.
UN Women. Publications available at www.unwomen.org.
Vienna Declaration and Programme of Action. (1993) UN Doc A/CONF.157/23. Available at www.un-documents.net/ac157-23.htm (Accessed 20 December 2016).
Viljoen, F. (2012). *International Human Rights Law in Africa*. Oxford, UK: Oxford University Press.
World Health Organization (WHO). Publications available at www.who.int/violence_injury_prevention (Accessed 20 December 2016).

18

Transnational families

The right to family life in the age of global migration

Edit Frenyo

Introduction

In this era of global capitalism, a family's livelihood is often determined by its mobility and ability to reinvent itself. By reason of improved travel conditions and communication technologies as well as the ever present push and pull factors of economic, social and political forces, more people than ever before are living so called transnational family lives.[1] As a consequence, the "hypermobility"[2] of our times has dramatically increased the number of families caught in the paradox of physical separation and enduring familial cohesion.

The idea of transnational family is not a modern concept. Quite the contrary, families have been separated and divided throughout the centuries due to both forced and voluntary migrations in search of opportunity and security. Nevertheless, the concepts of transnational family and transnational parenting remain under-researched in the legal field. This chapter fills part of this literature gap by illustrating the inadequacy of the normative framework that regulates the lives of transnational families. In doing so, it questions traditional narratives about "family law" and showcases how limited regulatory, social and economic understandings of this phenomenon may interact to facilitate and/or hinder transnational parenting.

The chapter makes four general claims. First, it explains how transnational family has become an essential aspect of family life and needs to be thoroughly understood and addressed by governments, policy makers and academics. The chapter paints a picture of how mobility and distance have become a part of contemporary family life, rather than an exception to one jurisdictional family life.

1 Majella Kilkey and Ewa Palenga-Möllenbeck, *Family Life in an Age of Migration and Mobility: Global Perspectives through the Life Course* (Springer, 2016); Loretta Baldassar and Laura Merla, *Transnational Families, Migration and the Circulation of Care: Understanding Mobility and Absence in Family Life* (Routledge, 2013).

2 Scott A. Cohen, and Stefan Gössling. "A Darker Side of Hypermobility," *Environment and Planning A* 47, no. 8 (August 1, 2015): 1661–1679.

Second, and as a consequence of the new dynamic of contemporary family life, the boundaries of "family law"[3] need to be redrawn to include various legal and policy regimes. It argues, therefore, that the laws of the family – as a lived experience – must be more broadly understood to include laws that regulate the life of members of the transnational household: labor, migration, welfare as well as traditional family law. This argument destabilizes assumptions about the bounded nature of concepts such as "national culture, or political community," or "national civil society."

In a third general claim, the chapter expands the notion of "household." It shows that though the term predates – and in fact was initially used to describe the "family" – it is capable of endless mutations and does not possess a singular legal definition. Locating these families within a transnational social field[4] challenges orthodox definitions of family unity and parentage.

Last, the chapter illustrates how elements under the rights and obligations related to "care" performed in transnational households do not change the core of care obligations, but rather modify the nature of their performance. As such, it maps how the transnational dimension of household does not diminish a central function of the family – the provision of care for children, the sick and the elderly. Quite the contrary, it leads to new opportunities as well as identifies misconceptions regarding the very quality of parenthood.

In support of these assertions, the chapter maps regulatory weaknesses in European Union law through case examples of Central Eastern European transnational families of labor migrants. The examples illustrate how the elements of "parental care" including contact (physical and virtual), support (remittances, gifts, social benefits) and supervision (alternative child care arrangements) need to be adapted to contemporary EU transnational family life.

Transnational households: remodeling family law

Throughout the history of human kinship, family separation due to migration has been a natural coping mechanism and a source of opportunity for individuals and kin groups.[5] In fact, both the phenomenon of migration and the various institutionalized forms of "the family" predate the formation of nation-states and the contemporary landscape of borders. Nonetheless, significant developments have been observed over the last three decades. Improvements in transportation and communication technologies, changes in labor market demands, and increasing dependence of the home countries on remittances are clearly observable.[6] There has also been a surge in the number of policies that encourage circular migration and longer stretches of separation

3 Referring here to family law as limited to its traditional confines: regulations surrounding formation and dissolution of the so called nuclear family: marriage, cohabitation, divorce, custody, support . . . etc. and matters relating to parental status, rights and duties. See more in: Janet Halley and Kerry Rittich, "Critical Directions in Comparative Family Law: Genealogies and Contemporary Studies of Family law Exceptionalism," *Am. J. Comp. L.* 58 (2010): 753, 754.

4 Transnational Social Field theory requires a transnational lens to understand migration and reveals how social life takes place within as well as beyond the nation-state framework. Migration involves migrants and non-migrating members of households, who are part of migrants' social networks through contact, financial and social remittances. See in: Peggy Levitt, and Nina Glick Schiller. "Conceptualizing Simultaneity: A Transnational Social Field Perspective on Society," *International Migration Review* 38, no. 3 (September 1, 2004): 1002–1039.

5 Christopher H. Johnson et al., eds, *Transregional and Transnational Families in Europe and Beyond: Experiences Since the Middle Ages*, 1st edn (New York: Berghahn Books, 2011).

6 "Migration and Development Brief 28 | KNOMAD," accessed October 24, 2017, www.knomad.org/publication/migration-and-development-brief-28.

from the reproductive sphere of the households. In this context, the first goal of this chapter is to understand how transnational activity in the form of transnational parenting has become a normal facet of transnational family life and merits serious attention from researchers, activists and policy makers alike.

In recent decades, anthropological and sociological studies have developed the term transnational family[7] by focusing on familial separation and labor migration. They have characterized this model of family by the geographical dispersion of a family due to the migration of one or more of its members, while maintaining tight relationships across borders. According to the preeminent European experts in the field, Bryceson and Vuorela, transnational families are "families [where family members] live some or most of the time separated from each other, yet hold together and create something that can be seen as a feeling of collective welfare and unity, namely 'familyhood', even across national borders."[8]

Although individual and social contexts may differ widely, much of the tension in the lives of transnational families comes from normatively reinforced assumptions about family life and "good parenting." This is especially relevant to the second goal of this section: tracing the gap between transnational family life as a lived experience and the boundaries and limits of the discipline of "family law." For instance, parent – child relationships in transnational households are commonly viewed through the traditional confines of "family law"[9] that do not represent the multiple forces ordering the daily functioning and labor division in the transnational family. This legal disparity forces transnational families to navigate in the shadow of overlapping structural regimes on the state and supranational levels.

A useful methodological approach to navigating transnational parent – child relationships comes from the "Undoing Family Law Exceptionalism Project" that emerged from a collaboration of scholars from American University, Washington College of Law's Women & International Law Program and the Harvard Law School Program on Law and Social Thought.[10] This movement demonstrates how several fields of public and private law include family targeted provisions that directly shape the functioning, forms and bargaining dynamics among family members within households. In particular, welfare regimes and family care giving policies directly order the status of husbands, wives and children and in some cases, other guardians, who provide primary care. As Hila Shamir puts it "welfare law reshuffles the boundaries between the labor market, the welfare state and the family in providing individual and familial welfare and social

7 The term first created by Rosina Brodber Wiltshire (1986) in relation to migration among Jamaican/North American families. See more in: Helma Lutz. *The New Maids: Transnational Women and the Care Economy*, 1st edn (London: Zed Books, 2012); Majella Kilkey and Laura Merla, "Situating Transnational Families' Care-Giving Arrangements: The Role of Institutional Contexts," *Global Networks* 14, no. 2 (2014): 210.; Baldassar and Merla, *Transnational Families, Migration and the Circulation of Care*, 6.

8 Deborah Fahy Bryceson and Ulla Vuorela, *The Transnational Family: New European Frontiers and Global Networks* (New York: Berg, 2002), 3.

9 Family Law here is understood a contained discipline in its own to legal field. Alternative and more accurate approaches have been adopted to combat this notion. For instance, Janet Halley et al. describe a four prong typology of family law (FL): FL 1 the traditional formal family law governing marriage, divorce, custody etc.; FL 2 explicit family targeted provisions (such as welfare, tax. Labor law); FL 3 legal rules that contribute to the functioning of family life (i.e. gender non-discrimination etc.) but do it silently; and FL 4 non-codified, informal norms and practices. See more in: Janet Halley, "What Is Family Law?: A Genealogy Part I," *Yale Journal of Law & the Humanities* 23, no. 1 (May 8, 2013): 1–109.

10 For more please see: Ann Shalleck. "Introduction Comparative Family Law: What is the Global Family? Family Law in Decolonization, Modernization and Globalization," *American University Journal of Gender Social Policy and Law* 19, no. 2 (2011): 449–458.

security [. . .],"[11] consequently affecting the division of labor within the household. In this context the main driver for migration is welfare maximization for both mobile and immobile members.

As the Family Law Exceptionalism project shows us, family law's traditional boundaries continue to lay claim to the legitimate contours of what the family ought to look like, even though there is no commonly accepted definition of the family and mobility further obscures our understanding of family life. This line of thought suggests a useful shift of focus from the "family" to the "household," with numerous implications for research and policy. By diverting from the often negative public discourse surrounding migration and "family life," it challenges the traditional boundaries of family law and suggests an understanding of the institution of the family through the functions performed within a transnational household as well as through its interaction with the institutions of the labor market and the welfare state.

These insights are also useful insofar as they pave the way to the third goal of this section, which is to map the family law shift from the idea of "family" to the idea of "household."[12] The Family Law Exceptionalism project shows that family and family law are often treated as occupying a unique and autonomous domain – as exceptional – and for a wide variety of reasons based on cultural and political assumptions and loaded with normative consequences: claims that "family law *should* be different because of the unique, special, crucial, affective, altruistic, social-ordering of the relationships that it houses."[13] The focus to guide these social and legal relationships, therefore, shifts from the family to the household.

This distinction becomes necessary to avoid that an artificial segregation of family law from other branches of law would incorrectly map the distributive functions of the household and the economic maintenance and survival of the household. The FLE project, therefore, applies an economic family paradigm to family decision-making by tying the etymology of both "economy" – as household management – and "family" – as members of a same house(hold).

In depth qualitative and ethnographic studies have traced how motherhood, fatherhood and childhood as well as alternative parenting arrangements evolve and change in the face of prolonged separation. Health and personal relationships can become strained and damaged by long and frequent absences especially when parents and children are separated for extended periods. Importantly, these studies explain how family life is redefined in the absence of proximity and its implications for individuals and societies.[14] As such, the dominant social approach to the subject of transnational household highlights both the opportunities and the darker side of living "mobile lives."

11 Hila Shamir "The State of Care: Rethinking the Distributive Effects of Familial Care Policies in Liberal Welfare States," *The American Journal of Comparative Law* 58, no. 4, Critical Directions in Comparative Family Law (Fall 2010), 954.

12 Haidinger helpfully elaborates on the household as a place of reproductive labor, a flexible unit that includes a broader circle of members beyond the nuclear family; and migration can be seen as a household maintenance strategy. See more: Bettina Haidinger, 2008. "Contingencies among Households: Gendered Division of Labour and Transnational Household Organization – The Case of Ukrainians in Austria," in Helma Lutz (ed.) *Migration and Domestic Work: A European Perspective on a Global Theme*, 127–144. Studies in Migration and Diaspora.

13 Janet Halley and Kerry Rittich (2010).

14 Joanna Dreby, "Children and Power in Mexican Transnational Families," *Journal of Marriage and Family* 69, no. 4 (November 1, 2007); Rhacel Salazar Parreñas, "Mothering from a Distance: Emotions, Gender, and Intergenerational Relations in Filipino Transnational Families," *Feminist Studies* 27, no. 2 (n.d.): 361; Pierrette Hondagneu-Sotelo and Ernestine Avila, "'I'M HERE, BUT I'M THERE' The Meanings of Latina Transnational Motherhood," *Gender & Society* 11, no. 5 (October 1, 1997): 548–571; Elisabetta Zontini, *Transnational Families, Migration and Gender: Moroccan and Filipino Women in Bologna and Barcelona*, 1st edn. (New York: Berghahn Books, 2011); Loretta Baldassar, Cora Vellekoop Baldock, and Raelene Wilding, *Families Caring Across Borders: Migration, Ageing and Transnational Caregiving*, 2007 edn. (Basingstoke, UK; New York: Palgrave Macmillan, 2006).

Finally, the study of transnational family therefore calls for a revision of the concept of "care": not as to its normative substance, but as to the manner in which rights and obligations *are* and *can be* performed in the context of transnational families. The idea of "care" has long been acknowledged as the central function of family life, both socially and normatively reinforced. Care is a central function of the family and especially in the context of transnationalism as it reinforces belonging and lends legitimacy to the family unit especially in times of physical separation.[15] Socially, the sense of familyhood is related to the various caregiving activities associated with "doing," or "displaying" family,[16] in both transnational and non-migrant families. From the perspective of law however, it is not that families become transnational, but rather that they transnationalize their households by dividing production and reproduction across borders. This separation is characterized by constant shifts and alterations based on negotiations between members of the household (often entailing non-family members, i.e.: caregivers),[17] their needs and bargaining powers.[18]

An example of this struggle can be seen in EU regulation and jurisprudence attempting to balance often competing interests of the right to free movement and the right to family life; the issue of social rights, especially the transferability of benefits for non-cohabiting children of certain migrant workers; and all of these domestic and supranational frameworks constantly interact with market dynamics. Care obligations and rights also intersect with the welfare and care regimes of the nation-states that transnational family members inhabit.[19] This further problematizes the public – private divide of family law and policy and shows that care is not merely a private concern, but is embedded in the broader political context of migration and transnational labor; consequently, family policy and law must also account for this transnational turn.

Transnational families in the EU – Central and Eastern European[20] migration to West, North and South

European family life is inevitably embedded in transnationalism. The creation of the integrated, transnational market of the EU necessitates the coordination of rights and social entitlements of migrant workers and families. EU citizens naturally migrate to seek better enjoyment of their rights, which can be crucial for founding and maintaining a family. Instead of focusing on the much-debated topic of non-EU citizen's migration to the EU, this chapter focuses on the less

15 Loretta Baldassar, and Laura Merla. *Transnational Families, Migration and the Circulation of Care: Understanding Mobility and Absence in Family Life* (London: Routledge, 2014).

16 David H.G. Morgan, "Locating 'Family Practices,'" *Sociological Research Online* 16, no. 4 (2011): 14; Janet Finch, "Displaying Families," *Sociology* 41, no. 1 (February 1, 2007): 65–81.

17 See for example a similar discussion: Hila Shamir, "What's the Border Got to Do with it? How Immigration Regimes Affect Familial Care Provision – A Comparative Analysis," *American University Journal of Gender, Social Policy, and the Law* 19, no. 2 (2011): 601.

18 Classic example: one, or both parents migrating for work while other parent/relative/alternative caregiver performs care-work (paid or unpaid).

19 See for example in: Hila Shamir (2010); for an overview of comparative family policy see: John Eekelaar and Rob George, eds, *Routledge Handbook of Family Law and Policy*, 1st edn. (London; New York: Routledge, 2014), chap. 6.1.

20 Central and Eastern European Countries (CEECs) is an OECD term for the group of countries comprising Albania, Bulgaria, Croatia, the Czech Republic, Hungary, Poland, Romania, the Slovak Republic, Slovenia, and the three Baltic States: Estonia, Latvia and Lithuania. For purposes of this chapter, I will focus only on EU members of the CEE region. "OECD Glossary of Statistical Terms – Central and Eastern European Countries (CEECs) Definition." 2018. Accessed June 20. https://stats.oecd.org/glossary/detail.asp?ID=303.

For examples of case studies see also: A.V. Tolstokorova. "Where Have All the Mothers Gone? The Gendered Effect of Labour Migration and Transnationalism on the Institution of Parenthood in Ukraine,"

theorized transnational families of EU citizens from member states that are part of the Central and Eastern European region (CEE) making use of free movement and open borders.[21] This specific type of migration is characterized by labor mobility within the European Union, with some members of the family migrating for work while others are left behind for increasingly longer stretches of time.

The CEE region has undergone significant demographic transformations since the fall of the Soviet Union, allowing for greater mobility. The consequent emergence of a transnational family model in Europe was accelerated by the "Eastern enlargement" of the European Union during its 2004 and 2007 accession waves.[22] Both the shocks of the neo-liberal restructuring of the former Eastern Bloc countries – the consequent retreat of the welfare state – as well as the global economic crisis of 2008 and its aftermath have been significant push-factors for migration among CEE households.

In the wake of these overlapping events and trends a mass migrant worker population emerged in the region, both as a continuation of long histories of emigration (Poland and Hungary)[23] as well as a result of sudden changes in the trajectory of migration (such as in the case of Romania, Bulgaria). This not only altered the demographic landscape of the labor market in the destination countries of older, more developed Western and Southern member states of the EU (i.e. Germany, Austria, the UK and Italy); but also resulted in the depletion of the working population in sending countries (i.e., an estimated 50 percent decline in Romania).[24]

Data on the number of children left behind by migrant parent(s) in the European Union is scarce. According to a comprehensive report by the organization *Children Left Behind*, there were an estimated 500,000 children within the EU who had one or both parents working in other EU member states at the beginning of the 2010s.[25] The true extent of this phenomenon is unknown, as parents often do not officially report their move and working arrangements. Most of these children lived within the Central and Eastern European member states of the EU.

Anthropology of East Europe Review 28, no. 1 (Spring 2010): 184–214; UNICEF (2008b) *The Impacts of Migration on Children Left Behind in Moldova.* www.unicef.org/The_Impacts_of_Migration_on_Children_in_Moldova%281%29.pdf.;

URI (2014) *Albanian migration after '90-es and its influence on the economic and social life of children left behind.* www.uri.org.al/wp-content/uploads/2014/02/2.Albanian-migration-after1.pdf.

21 Most of the existing research is financed and conducted by independent, non-governmental organizations such as the Soros Foundation's work on children left behind in Romania; Norwegian and Swiss institutions and some EU initiatives; See for example: www.childrenleftbehind.eu/become-a-member/; COFACE Families Europe www.coface-eu.org/.

22 These accession waves largely involved countries joining the European Union from the CEE region. Specifically in 2004: the Czech Republic, Estonia, Hungary, Latvia, Lithuania, Poland, Slovakia, and Slovenia (also Malta and Cyprus from the Southern regions) and in 2007: Romania and Bulgaria. See in: "EU Enlargement – Consilium." 2018. Accessed June 20. www.consilium.europa.eu/en/policies/enlargement/.

23 The distinction between destination and sending countries is by no means clear-cut. There is in fact migration to Poland from Ukraine and to Hungary from Romania, often that of migrant women entering the domestic care sector, in some cases to augment the care deficit of women from Poland and Hungary migrating abroad, or simply taking up full time paid employment in the home country and needing affordable care-workers.

24 Birgit Glorius, Izabela Grabowska-Lusinska, and Aimee Kuvik, eds. *Mobility in Transition: Migration Patterns after EU Enlargement* (Amsterdam: Amsterdam University Press, 2014); Daniela Andrén, and Monica Roman. "Should I Stay or Should I Go? Romanian Migrants During Transition and Enlargements," in *Labor Migration, EU Enlargement, and the Great Recession* (Springer, Berlin, Heidelberg, 2016) 247–269.

25 N. Belorgey, B. Gerbe-Emden, S. Horstmann, A. Kuhn, D. Vogel, P. Stubbs (2012) Social Impact of Emigration and Rural – Urban Migration in Central and Eastern Europe. (VT/2010/001) Synthesis Report. ec.europa.eu/social/BlobServlet?docId=8804&langId=en.

The majority of children left behind live in Romania and Poland and there is evidence of the phenomenon existing in the Baltic States and Bulgaria as well. Given the increase in overall labor migration in countries such as Hungary and Slovakia more in-depth, quantitative and qualitative studies would be necessary to investigate the impacts of migration on parents and children in those countries.[26] Perhaps no other country in the CEE region generated more studies and attention to the issue of left behind children than the case of Romania. By the summer of 2007 a comprehensive UNICEF Romania study reported an estimated 350,000 children impacted by parental absence due to labor migration, representing 7 percent of the 0–18 year old population, with most of them between 10 and 18 years old.[27] About 126,000 children had both parents working abroad, leaving entire villages with children without parents.[28] Although in most cases the father was away for work, maternal absence was also significant.

Additionally, the migration of CEE mothers for work ties into broader gendered dynamics of mobility and labor in Europe. The EU is experiencing an increasing feminization of migration, particularly in the private domestic and care work sector. The aging of societies in comparatively wealthy EU countries and the decline in state funding and lack of involvement in social care services have resulted in the privatization of care work: housework, personal services, childcare and elderly care.[29] This strongly gendered form of work is predominately relegated to the private sphere of the household. The increase in the labor market participation of local women outside of the household in the Western, Northern and Southern parts of the EU gave rise to the need for foreign women to fill an ensuing care-gap. As a result, many European households are becoming complicated sites where private and public interests and regulatory frameworks are in constant interaction. With the presence of the female migrant care worker in the household, the traditionally private sphere of family life and its regulation is intertwined with the regulation of the labor market, employment and immigration, areas of law that are seemingly far from that of the laws of the family.

Whether it is fathers or mothers leaving children behind for work, the impact on family life and related rights as well as on the general welfare of the family is manifold. Remittances tend to have a positive effect on household consumption, but absence can also result in psychosocial burden for the parent – child relationship.[30] The various ways in which parental care is performed in the transnational family is central to our understanding of what regulations help and hinder family life in the context of migration.

Transnational fatherhood and motherhood: the right and responsibility of "care" in EU family life

The protection of the family and the right to family life are guaranteed in several international human rights instruments. Notably, the Universal Declaration of Human Rights[31] declares the

26 Zs. Blaskó, L. Szabó. "Migrants with left-behind children in Hungary", in Zsuzsa Blaskó, Károly Fazekas (eds) *The Hungarian Labour Market 2016* (Budapest: Institute of Economics, Centre for Economic and regional Studies, Hungarian Academy of Sciences, 2016).

27 Judit Németh-Almasi. "National Analysis of the Phenomenon of Children Left Home by Their Parents Who Migrate Abroad for Employment." (2002 Text. January) https://childhub.org/fr/child-protection-online-library/national-analysis-phenomenon-children-left-home-their-parents-who.

28 Id. 19.

29 Helma Lutz. *Migration and Domestic Work: A European Perspective on a Global Theme* (Aldershot, UK: Ashgate, 2012).

30 Valentina Mazzucato, and Djamila Schans. "Transnational Families and the Well-Being of Children: Conceptual and Methodological Challenges," *Journal of Marriage and the Family* 73, no. 4 (August 2011): 704–712.

31 UN General Assembly, Universal Declaration of Human Rights, 10 December 1948, 217 A (III), www.refworld.org/docid/3ae6b3712c.html (accessed 22 June 2018).

family as the natural and fundamental unit of society. The UN Convention on the Rights of the Child[32] makes it clear that maintaining the family unit is in the best interests of the child. Within the context of fundamental rights in the EU, Article 8 of the European Convention on Human Rights provides the most effective protection for the right to private and family life. It is directly enforceable law applying to all sectors of domestic law, courts and administrators and demands the deference of national constitutions. Its broad understanding of family life is further extended by the jurisprudence of the European Court of Human Rights (ECtHR).[33] According to the Court, the Convention does not merely compel states to abstain from arbitrary interference in private and family life, but also considers positive obligations related to the respect of family life[34] even in the private sphere between individuals themselves.[35]

Much of the jurisprudence on the respect of family life developed in the context of child protection, divorce, custody and family reunification. In these areas, the Court has established cohabitation, or living together, as a central component of the right to family life.[36] However, as this chapter illustrates, living together means something different in transnational families that cohabit in transnational households. These families emphasize their unity as legally intact families, despite their periodic phases of separation. Economic pressures compel them to create living arrangements akin to transnational divorce scenarios. Yet, unlike in the case of transnational divorce and custody, transnational families often do not have specific or adequate welfare or legal-policy frameworks to help navigate their non-divorce based "post-separation" parenting plans.

Instead of fixating on the more narrow family law structures, or jurisprudence of the EU, it is in the interaction of social rights and family life that transnational families are more directly implicated. The ECtHR has helpfully expanded state's obligations to include social and economic rights in relation to family rights, in some cases calling states to protect "certain levels of material conditions" in order to preserve family life.[37] The right to family life as understood to be a right to maintain family relationship may be adversely affected by for example the loss of adequate housing, or minimum levels of subsistence.

The European Charter of Fundamental Rights, specifically its provisions on equality and solidarity related rights,[38] best models the tension between the free market of the EU and the social values of the welfare state as the common structure of member states. The Charter includes social protections and compensation related rights for dependent workers. Article 31 par. 2, on compatibility of work and family life mandates maximum working hours, and rest period as well as

32 UN General Assembly, Convention on the Rights of the Child, 20 November 1989, United Nations, Treaty Series, vol. 1577, 3, www.refworld.org/docid/3ae6b38f0.html (accessed 22 June 2018).

33 In interpreting the ECHR, the European Court of Human Rights has adopted a rather broad and flexible concept of family. See for example: in *Lebbink v The Netherlands* App. No. 45582/99 (ECtHR, 1 June 2004) the Court reiterated its established case-law under Article 8, moving away from understanding family life as a mere matter of biological bond between father and child towards an emphasis on practical personal ties. In this case the Dutch government referred to the Court's judgment in the case of *K. and T. v. Finland* reiterating "that the existence or non-existence of family life within the meaning of Article 8 of the Convention is essentially a question of fact depending on the real existence in practice of close personal ties (no. 25702/94, § 150, ECHR 2001-VII)."

34 In *X and Y against Nederland* from 26/3/1985 (no. 8978/80).

35 As is often the case for domestic care workers.

36 Luis López Guerra, "European Convention on Human Rights and Family Life: Primary Issues," in Maribel González Pascual and Aida Torres Pérez (eds) *The Right to Family Life in the European Union* (London; New York: Routledge, 2017) 12–13.

37 Ibid. 27 specifically citing *Airey v Ireland* 1979 and *Yordanova v Bulgaria* 2012

38 Title III: Equality and Title IV: Solidarity – European Charter of Fundamental Rights (The Charter) 2012/C 326/02.

annual paid leaves. Article 33 par. 1 also states "The family shall enjoy legal, economic and social protection." These are enshrined as fundamental rights not as mere principles under EU law.

The right to family life in European law covers the right to working conditions that respect the need for work – life balance, i.e., for employment and family to be compatible. Among the recent initiatives of the European Commission aimed at modernizing the existing EU legal framework in the area of reconciliation of work and family life, the Proposal for a Directive of the European Parliament and of the Council on work – life balance for parents and carers[39] is a step in the right direction.

There is no direct judgment of the ECtHR about working conditions and family life yet. There are some promising developments as Dorothee Frings points out regarding the Court's more recent judgments about employment which "confirm that member states are obliged to align the whole of employment law, including prevention and monitoring of this law, with protecting the human rights of the weaker side in any asymmetric employment relationship."[40] Such developments may be directly relevant to the parenting abilities of the more vulnerable transnational parents, such as migrant domestic worker mothers.

Additionally, the European Code of Social Security binds member states to guarantee minimum standards in the field of social security on the basis of minimum harmonization of the level of social security. This also provides for the system of transferability of social security benefits and the regulation of benefits eligibility for workers and dependents located in more than one member state. State's leeway in interpreting fundamental rights is significantly narrower in the context of the rights of workers.[41]

Generally speaking, children have a right to be brought up, be cared for (regarding especially health, housing and education) and legally represented by their parents; or in lieu of parental care, to be provided adequate guardianship by other persons determined by competent authorities.[42] For the purposes of this piece in the context of the right of the child to be cared for, this section

39 "A New Start to Support Work – Life Balance for Parents and Carers." https://ec.europa.eu/info/law/better-regulation/initiatives/com-2017-253_en. (accessed October 4, 2017), focusing on the area of family-related leaves and flexible working arrangements: A common critique is that this does little to address the working conditions of those employed in the private domestic care work sector.

40 Dorothee Frings, "Transnational Domestic Work and Right to Family," in Maria Kontos and Glenda Tibe Bonifacio (eds) *Migrant Domestic Workers and Family Life: International Perspectives* (Basingstoke, UK; New York: Palgrave Macmillan, 2015), 45.

41 The European Code of Social Security (ETS No. 48) and its Protocol, as well as the Revised European Code of Social Security (ETS No.139), "set standards in the social security field on the basis of minimum harmonization of the level of social security, providing minimum standards and permitting (or rather encouraging) the contracting parties to exceed these standards." These standard-setting instruments, together with the European Social Charter, set out the underlying principles of what is referred to as the European social security model. See more on EU transnational social security coverage: http://europa.eu/youreurope/citizens/work/unemployment-and-benefits/country-coverage/index_en.htm.

42 In summary of the relevant laws on parental responsibility or parental custody in EU member states, parents have the right and obligation to care for and raise their children; to manage the child's assets; to legally represent their children; and to appoint a guardian, and exclude any particular persons from the guardianship.

Parental custody means that it is the parent's right and obligation to make decisions on, and proceed in, fundamental matters concerning the minor child. Nevertheless the parents must ensure that their child, having reached a certain degree of maturity can express his/her opinion before any decisions are made concerning him/her, and the parents must take the child's opinion into account. See detailed EU and member state legislation: "European Commission – European Judicial Network – Parental Responsibility – Community Law." http://ec.europa.eu/civiljustice/parental_resp/parental_resp_ec_en.htm (accessed June 5, 2017).

introduces three elements of parental care – contact, support and supervision.[43] Through the lenses of gender, labor, social security and family law, case studies will illustrate the difference in the provision of these three elements of care in transnational family life, under the perspective of transnational fathering and mothering.

On the former, the chapter looks at the case of Hungarian construction workers from the small town of Mindszent, in South-Eastern Hungary, working in Harlingen in the Netherlands. For the latter, examples from Viorela Ducu's work on the strategies of transnational motherhood in Romania[44] show migrant mothers in Cluj county circulating between their homes and Italy to meet care needs in two households: that of their children in Romania and the care needs of their employing households in Italy. Their respective testimonies follow:

> "I'm going home every five to six weeks. I'm at home for 10 days. We get vacation hours, at 8 percent of our salary. This is wired to us in May, so that we can go on vacations with the family in the summer. We also get vacation allowances."
>
> "We have perfect working conditions. They don't overwork us. We work 8 hours a day. After that, we have time to relax, and we have all necessary amenities for that. We live in a so-called vacation park. These are otherwise used by Dutch vacationers. They are equipped with everything, there is a gym, sauna, swimming pool, sports court. We all miss the family naturally. We cannot afford to bring them with us however. In order for that we would have to provide for housing (sublet) ourselves which would mean losing a lot of money. I can send more money back home this way. How long can we keep this up? I do not know. For the time being, I would be reluctant to return to the substandard wages back home."
>
> "One of my brothers" [also working for the same company] "was able to save enough in one year that they were able to buy a house with his earnings combined with the social benefits they received from the state after their two children."
>
> *(Peter Bereczki, from Mindszent, Hungarian working in the construction/ carpentry sector in the town of Harlingen, Netherlands)*[45]

Comparatively, the difficulties faced by female workers from the Cluj County in Romania[46] are clearly described below by Ducu:

> Women in Cluj County usually migrate alone, when leaving for short periods of time. They find employment through employment agents or through a network – other women or

43 Framing this three prong focus of the inquiry drew especially from: Jørgen Carling, Cecilia Menjívar, and Leah Schmalzbauer. "Central Themes in the Study of Transnational Parenthood," *Journal of Ethnic and Migration Studies* 38, no. 2 (2012): 191–217.

44 Viorela Ducu, Strategies of Transnational Motherhood: The Case of Romanian Women, PhD thesis summary 2011, http://doctorat.ubbcluj.ro/sustinerea_publica/rezumate/2011/sociologie/FOamte_Ducu_Viorla_En.pdf (accessed August 29, 2017).

Findings were also part of a Study circulated electronically at the International Workshop "The Effects of International Labor Migration on Political Learning", Center for the Study of Democracy, Babes-Bolyai University, Cluj-Napoca, Romania, June 6–7 2008; http://transnationalfamilies.ro/viorela-ducu/.

45 Erika Kovács. "Jó Pénzért Dolgoznak Az Építkezésen, Vakációparkban Laknak a Fiatalok: Kis Mindszent Lett a Hollandiai Harlingen | Hódmezővásárhely Hírek | Szeged – Delmagyar.Hu," www.delmagyar.hu/hodmezovasarhely_hirek/jo_penzert_dolgoznak_az_epitkezesen_vakacioparkban_laknak_a_fiatalok_kis_mindszent_lett_a_hollandiai_harlingen/2530686/ (accessed September 5, 2017).

46 An estimated one million migrant women work in private domestic care and assistance jobs in Italy. The majority come from the CEE region, mainly Romania, and are aged between 30 and 50. "Private Welfare: Challenges to Decent Work for Migrant Care Workers (Italy) | Solidar." www.solidar.org/en/publications/private-welfare-challenges-to-decent-work-for-migrant-care-workers-italy (accessed June 5, 2017).

> relatives. Sometimes they are followed by their husbands. Their migration is rather a cyclic one (3–4 months of work abroad, 2–3 months at home). In many cases they keep their workplace through "shifting" with another migrant woman from their family. Resorting to this type of migration is motivated by their incapability to stay away from their families for a long period of time. This type of migration seems to be associated with one target country, Italy. The women extend their period of migration when another family member starts to accompany them (husbands, sisters, cousins). In the same community, men migrate alone (irrespective of the target country); they spend much more time away from the family. Although the time spent with their family at home is much longer compared to men, the community sees migrant women negatively. Thus, it is preferable in the community that men migrate who also bring back more money, due to their better paid work types and the longer time spent at work. Families that have the female members who migrate are considered families with a high risk of disintegration. The community ignores women as primary breadwinners and their own families do not directly recognize this role. The priority of women's roles as direct caregivers against breadwinning is reinforced by the migrant women themselves: "I need to do this for the money, but being here with them, giving them care is all I really wish for" (Augusta).[47]

Through the explanatory potential of these case examples, this section provides the reader with entryways into the life of male and female migrant workers in the EU so as to better explain the role of law in shaping transnational parenting and family life.[48]

The right to "contact" in family life

Parents and children have the right to family life, that is to say, a right to enjoy a relationship in the form of contact with each other. Whether they are cohabiting in the same physical household, or separated due to divorce or migration across borders, this right is reinforced through various national, international and European legal instruments.[49]

For transnational parents and children, the one element of this relationship is contact that is achieved in two ways: *physically* using the free movement zone for reciprocal parent – child visits; and *virtually* using cellphone calls and messaging and information and communication technologies (ITC).[50] Visitation is made legally easier through the transnational migration law of the EU as expressed in the doctrine of free movement according to European Directive 2004/38. Parents and children as EU citizens have the right to move and reside freely within the territory of the EU. In virtual contact, the EU has abolished roaming charges as of June

47 Ducu, 19.

48 Betty De Hart, Wibo van Rossum, and Iris Sportel. *Law in the Everyday Lives of Transnational Families: An Introduction.* SSRN Scholarly Paper. Rochester, NY, December 11, 2013. https://papers.ssrn.com/abstract=2366404.

49 The following international and regional treaties in particular ensure children's right to protection and care without discrimination, including their rights to health, education, information, and privacy: the International Covenant on Civil and Political Rights; the International Covenant on Economic, Social, and Cultural Rights; the Convention on the Elimination of all forms of Discrimination against Women; and the Convention on the Rights of the Child; European Convention for the Protection of Human Rights and Fundamental Freedoms (ECHR), and the European Social Charter.

50 Mirca Madianou, "Migration and the Accentuated Ambivalence of Motherhood: The Role of ICTs in Filipino Transnational Families," *Global Networks* 12, no. 3 (July 1, 2012): 277–295; Jørgen Carling, Cecilia Menjívar, and Leah Schmalzbauer (2012).

2017,[51] and has extensive regulations on the right to access to the Internet in line with international human rights movement concerning Internet use.[52] This environment significantly reduces the cost of virtual contact that is crucial in providing emotional and practical support for children by parents, often on a daily basis.[53]

Much like in the context of post-divorce family life, parents check in online to catch up on the days' or weeks events. Research shows that transnational families with children rely heavily on communication technologies, in particular ones that allow for video-calls to supervise and assess children's well-being and maintain parent – child bonds, which may be relevant in showing 'good' and 'involved' parenting and the existence of an affective bond in front of authorities in family court proceedings.[54]

Gaps however remain in the area of contact as experienced in reality and they often manifest along gendered lines. Migrant men often enjoy greater access to the right to family life given the labor sectors they are able to enter when compared to those of migrant women. Many transnational fathers, for example, may have the opportunity to migrate for work in labor sectors that are highly formalized with higher salaries and adequate access to housing, time-off for visits with compensation. On the other hand, the economic constraints of their employment, settlement requirements in host countries and the need to send significant amounts of remittances back home all create the environment where for the duration of their employment they must practice transnational parenthood. Peter's story reveals much about contact in transnational parenting as experienced by a father, both by the information revealed and implied.

With fixed working hours – appropriate housing and privacy – these Hungarian construction workers have adequate time, space and privacy to enjoy physical and virtual contact with their families left behind. The visits are subsidized allowing for a reconciliation of work and family life. This seems like a generous gesture; however, it makes perfect sense for the market and the Dutch state that both have a vested interest in keeping productive and reproductive functions of migrant parents firmly separated between home and host countries.[55]

Contact practiced in the transnational household involves the resources of the household in the home country as well as the temporary one in the host country. Visits with adequate time

51 "EU Reaches Agreement to Abolish Roaming Charges by June 2017 – European Consumer Centre (ECC) Ireland." *European Consumer Centre (ECC) Ireland*, June 0, 2015. www.eccireland.ie/eu-reaches-agreement-to-abolish-roaming-charges-by-june-2017/.

52 Regulation (EU) 2015/2120 of the European Parliament and of the Council of 25 November 2015 laying down measures concerning open internet access and amending Directive 2002/22/EC on universal service and users' rights relating to electronic communications networks and services and Regulation (EU) No 531/2012 on roaming on public mobile communications networks within the Union.

53 Although broadband internet coverage is over 80 percent in much of Eastern Europe, all CEE countries have sparsely populated and underserviced rural areas, which present coverage challenges. "Study on Broadband Coverage in Europe (as of 2014)." *Digital Single Market*. https://ec.europa.eu/digital-single-market/en/news/study-broadband-coverage-europe-2014 (accessed December 5, 2017).

54 ICTs change the practice and the intensity of distant parenting. They also have consequences for the way in which parents and the broader family experiences migration and motherhood, or fatherhood. These are also traceable forms of communication and contact, which authorities can rely on when assessing a parent's involvement in the child's upbringing, a topic that may come up in cases of separation, custody or child welfare hearings. Scholarship also highlights that calls, texts and Skype do not substitute proximate, hands-on care, especially in the case of prolonged separation of adolescent children. Virtual contact is often the more draining experience for transnational mothers, who given the gendered nature of child care remain more involved in the day to day organization of family life than their male counterparts.

55 See more on Dutch regulations on foreign workers: "Accommodation for Foreign Workers." https://business.gov.nl/regulation/accommodation-foreign-workers/ (accessed August 5, 2017).

off and resources may be relatively unproblematic. Virtual contact requires appropriate access to technology across the transnational household: within home and host country dwellings, subject to national availability of Internet access. This presumably exists for the men in Harlingen.

The example of the Romanian female workers, on the other hand, suggests that female migrant workers face altogether different challenges. This is particularly true for the majority of women migrants who find jobs in the domestic and care work sector. The very nature of the domestic care sector (often informal) allows for a very different enjoyment of rights. Women and migrant workers are often in a particularly precarious situation and when employed in the domestic care sector they are all but prohibited from most work – life reconciliation benefits. Many are not able to retain worker status that would satisfy Article 7 (3) sense of Directive 2004/38 on freedom of movement, which describes the line at which a worker can continue to retain certain benefits that attach to being a migrant worker under EU law (illness/accident insurance, unemployment assistance, training etc.).[56]

Research shows that migrant mothers remain more actively needed and involved in the day-to-day task of parenting from afar than migrant fathers.[57] This puts significant pressures on Romanian mothers acting as bread-winners and involved parents at the same time. In addition live-in work has been shown to provide less opportunity to leave for necessary visits when needed, or to exercise parenting through calls and internet communications.[58]

The private nature of female transnational work, in family households, means almost twenty-four hour availability with little enforcement of labor protection laws, even if they do apply.[59] Finding time and space in the day to call or Skype is hard for transnational mothers. Children generally cannot visit their mothers in the destination country, as most of them lack adequate means, or housing that would accommodate visitors. Even in the best of circumstances, as the Hungarian example showed, Internet access in Romania, especially in rural areas is often inadequate, further hindering contact between mothers and children.

As such, rules surrounding Internet use and cellphone communication access function as background rules that in their operation have enormous consequences for the family, without referencing directly the family.[60] This background body of policies and law operate as background norms to the right of "family life" and parental contact, directly impacting the ability of parents or parental figures to provide appropriate "care." Likewise, international and European labor rights and their national applications are responsible for creating working-time arrangements for the "family law" of the transnational family, thus impacting how parental contact may be provided.[61] As

56 European Union, *Directive 2004/38/EC of the European Parliament and the Council of 29 April 2004 on the right of citizens of the Union and their family members to move and reside freely within the territory of the Member states amending Regulation (EEC) No 1612/68 and repealing Directives 64/221/EEC, 68/360/EEC, 72/194/EEC, 73/148/EEC, 75/34/EEC, 75/35/EEC, 90/364/EEC, 90/365/EEC and 93/96/EEC*, 29 April 2004, 2004/38/EC, www.refworld.org/docid/4a54bbb00.html (accessed 21 June 2018).

57 "Children Left Behind: The Impact of Labor Migration in Moldova and Ukraine," *Migrationpolicy.Org*, January 23, 2015, www.migrationpolicy.org/article/children-left-behind-impact-labor-migration-moldova-and-ukraine.

58 Flavia Piperno, "The Impact of Female Emigration on Families and the Welfare State in Countries of Origin: The Case of Romania," *International Migration* 50, no. 5 (2012): 189–204.

59 Michael Jandl et al., *Migration and Irregular Work in Austria: A Case Study of the Structure and Dynamics of Irregular Foreign Employment in Europe at the Beginning of the 21st Century*, 01 edn. (Amsterdam: Amsterdam University Press, 2014); Helma Lutz, *Migration and Domestic Work: A European Perspective on a Global Theme* (Aldershot, UK: Ashgate, 2012), chap. 9.

60 In the context of the FLE movement these can be thought of as Family Law 3.

61 In the context of the FLE movement these laws belong to Family Law 2, bodies of law not designed explicitly for the regulation of family life – seemingly for entirely separate purposes – where the family appears only as a category.

Shalleck aptly put it, "These laws, far more than what we normally call family law, directly affect the ongoing functioning of the family . . . Also, seemingly silently, these bodies of law sometimes also structure how families actually form and dissolve."[62]

The provision of support in transnational families

The EU provides combined protection of families and social rights that mandate that states provide certain levels of material conditions in order to facilitate family life. Article 33 paragraph 1 of the European Charter of Fundamental Rights states "the family shall enjoy legal, economic and social protection." EU citizen migrant workers and their families have been afforded important rights and entitlements.[63] The EU has made major efforts to create an environment conducive to worker mobility.[64] Cash transfers and gifts are relatively easily navigated within the EU. In fact, transnational fatherhood has allowed Peter's brother to channel more money into remittances for the daily household maintenance and support of his children with the comparatively lower costs of living in Hungary. This provision of support also enabled the family to buy a new home. Remittances were not only used to this effect, but they were also combined with social benefits available to families with minor children.

In addition to the higher salaries of skilled male workers from the CEE region, migrant workers in the EU may apply for family benefits for children living abroad.[65] This makes migrant child support in the EU uniquely streamlined. The Union, therefore, acknowledges that children are increasingly raised in transnational households and that social policy regulating the family must also reflect this reality. In the case of the Netherlands, Dutch law – in line with EU regulations on social benefits and social protection of families and children – allows for formally full-time employed migrant workers, or private entrepreneurs working in the Netherlands with minor children "in their households" to apply for family benefits. If the child is already receiving family benefits from the Hungarian state, the Dutch state pays the difference between the amount provided by Hungary and that allowed by Dutch law.

Migrant parents' foreign employment may impact the availability of much needed home country (CEE country) social benefits, most often due to lack of proper communication between home and host member states of the EU on which state owes what to the children of the

62 Shalleck, 452. www.researchgate.net/publication/254569222_Introduction_Comparative_Family_Law_What_is_the_Global_Family_Family_Law_in_Decolonization_Modernization_and_Globalization.

63 See: Directive 2004/38/EC, including the right to equal treatment, access to benefits, under various conditions including employment and family status as well as legal residence; Directive 2004/38/EC amended Regulation 1612/68/EEC with regard to family reunification and extended the definition of 'family member'; Directive 2004/38/EC provides for the right to remain in the host country after stopping work as long as one is a bone fide job-seeker.

64 These include: Directive 2011/24/EU on patients' rights in cross-border healthcare; Regulation (EC) No 883/2004 and implementing Regulation (EC) No 987/2009 on the coordination of social security schemes; Directive 2014/50/EU on minimum requirements for enhancing worker mobility between member states by improving the acquisition and preservation of supplementary pension rights; Directive 2014/54/EU on measures facilitating the exercise of rights conferred on workers in the context of freedom of movement for workers, which specifically provides for new means of redress for workers discriminated against.

65 See n 38; between two member states it is the difference between the benefit obtained in the country of employment and the country of the child's habitual residence that is obtainable in the country of employment, on top of the full amount of family benefit from the home country where the child resides.

transnational household.[66] The impact of the particular labor sector – skilled, formalized and full time – cannot be underestimated, given the higher wages and access to benefits.

Female migrants rarely have access to labor markets that provide for the above conditions, significantly impacting upon their ability to provide financial support for their children, compared to men. For instance, though the availability of domestic care work in Italy provides the Romanian transnational mother with the opportunity to send home remittances as a form of child support, the wide spread informality of the care work market means that these mothers miss out on several other employment and social benefits compared to the fathers in the Hungarian case study.[67]

Italy has an increasingly formalized domestic care sector with protective rules[68] on maximum working hours for a live-in family assistant/caregiver (54 hours per week, and for non-live in at 40 hours), overtime pay, time-off (weekly and for vacations) and vocational training opportunities, strict employment contracts; social security benefits including, unemployment benefit, sickness insurance, occupational accident or illness insurance, and maternity and family leave. While all this looks good on paper, the relatively higher cost of formalized employment both for the state and the households, means that migrant women wishing to obtain legal care work employment become far less attractive to employers. Many households still opt for informal care arrangements. Even in the formal care sector, rules around working-time, overtime compensation are notoriously hard to enforce.[69]

In summary, whether they enhance, or hinder transnational parents' ability to provide financial support for their children, the background rules of EU and national labor laws, social security and family-based welfare benefits shape family organization geographically. They also contribute to the construction of a determinate social and familial role for the women and men within this transnational social space.

66 Problems relating to proof of social security contributions are reported in at least four member states (i.e. BG, DK, HU and RO). There are also persistent delays, refusals to pay and other obstacles to family benefits in at least six member states (i.e. AT, CZ, DE, DK, HR and SK). The most frequent issues are the imposition of a residence requirement and bureaucratic problems in accessing necessary documents. For more information see: "Obstacles to the Right of Free Movement and Residence for EU Citizens and Their Families: Comparative Analysis – Think Tank." Accessed August 6, 2017. www.europarl.europa.eu/thinktank/en/document.html?reference=IPOL_STU(2016)571375.

67 Close to a million migrant domestic workers fulfill much of the care needs of the Italian household, transforming it to a migration based family model of care. Despite an amnesty for irregular migrant workers and employers and large scale regularization of the domestic care sector, significant informality remains. Measures to encourage employers to regularize their workers (care vouchers and tax benefits), have proved either too weak or burdensome. See more: *Surveying Romanian Migrants in Italy Before and After the EU Accession: Migration Plans, Labour Market Features and Social Inclusion (Publication)*, https://wiiw.ac.at/p-2629.html. (accessed June 5, 2017); P. Bonizzoni, and A. Cibea. "Family Migration Policies in Italy" (August 2009). https://air.unimi.it/handle/2434/160184#.WiZCfUqnFPY.; F. Van Hooren, "When Families Need Immigrants: The Exceptional Position of Migrant Domestic Workers and Care Assistants in Italian Immigration Policy," *Bulletin of Italian Politics* 2, no. 2 (2010): 21–38.

68 A 2007 collective agreement protects the rights of domestic workers and family assistants/carers.

69 Migrant domestic workers' right to family life is largely invisible in the policy discourse. International frameworks such as the ICRMW or the ILO Convention No 189 on Decent Work for Domestic Workers have not found broad acceptance. The right to family life is often limited to maternity leave, which is not practical, or applicable for domestic care workers, especially live-in caregivers. The EU Working Time Directive (2003/88EC) generally applies to domestic servants, and the European Court of Justice has reaffirmed that standby hours are full working hours. Essentially twenty-four hour work is against EU law. However in migrant domestic work employers and agencies usually don't set fixed working hours and do not count overtime. Women often team up and arrange to take shifts of two weeks a month in the same household to manage their own household responsibilities back home.

Transnational supervision and child care arrangements

As parents are responsible for their children's upbringing, education and property, they also have the right to represent them legally. The corresponding care-rights of children are part of human rights: rights that the EU and member states must respect, protect and fulfill. As highlighted earlier, member states have the duty to facilitate parenting in its various forms, and to abstain from unnecessary interference in private and family life, barring compelling State interest.[70]

Adequate alternative child care arrangements and supervision are part and parcel of transnational parenting. This challenge focuses on the home-country dimension of transnational households. Given the persistent gendered division of labor in European, especially CEE households, women take on the lion's share of child care and household work.[71] In the case of transnational fatherhood, children are most often left in the care of female caregivers: primarily mothers left behind. Research on transnational fatherhood focuses on the father as primary breadwinner, with attenuated hands-on care roles related to the day-to-day activities associated with parenting.[72]

This doesn't mean that transnational fatherhood is unproblematic for the fathers, mothers and children involved. In fact, experts across the board have warned about the promises and perils for childhood and parenting in this adult-focused mobility and the consequent dispersal across the Union. Although the reasons for parents' migration include the best interest and welfare of their children – family separation seemingly contradicts normative assumptions and empirical research about "active parenting" and the importance of hands-on, direct parent – child relationships for child development.[73]

Work – life reconciliation policies that would enhance male caregiver roles are inadequate. This is particularly troubling since throughout its history the EU law and policy on work – life reconciliation had been framed in the context of gender equality and gender mainstreaming.[74] But the economic objectives of increasing overall labor market participation has taken precedence over equality and family life concerns. In addition, given the predominant role of women as care-providers, there is also a deficit in policies facilitating migrant women's reconciliation needs. Bad parenting and care deficit is often assumed in the case of transnational motherhood.[75]

70 For a comprehensive list of all relevant instrument safeguarding children's interest and rights in the EU: "Rights of the Child – European Commission." http://ec.europa.eu/justice/fundamental-rights/rights-child/index_en.htm (accessed April 5, 2017).

71 Giovanni Razzu and Professor of Economics of Public Policy Giovanni Razzu, *Gender Inequality in the Eastern European Labour Market: Twenty-Five Years of Transition Since the Fall of Communism* (London; New York: Routledge, 2016); Charles Walker and Svetlana Stephenson, *Youth and Social Change in Eastern Europe and the Former Soviet Union* (London; New York: Routledge, 2013).

72 Joyce A. Arditti et al., "Fathers in the Fields: Father Involvement Among Latino Migrant Farmworkers," *Journal of Comparative Family Studies* 45, no. 4 (2014): 537–557; Rhacel Salazar Parreñas, "Transnational Fathering: Gendered Conflicts, Distant Disciplining and Emotional Gaps," *Journal of Ethnic and Migration Studies* 34, no. 7 (September 1, 2008): 1057–1072.

73 Karen Clarke, Tony Maltby, and Patricia Kennett, *Social Policy Review 19: Analysis and Debate in Social Policy, 2007* (Bristol, UK: Policy Press, 2007), chap. 15; Helen Stalford, "Parenting, Care and Mobility in the Eu," *Innovation: The European Journal of Social Science Research* 18, no. 3 (September 1, 2005): 361–380.

74 Samantha Currie, "Un-Joined-up Policy Making and Patchy Promotion of Gender Equality: Free Movement and Reconciliation of Work and Family Life in the EU," in Pascual, Maribel González, and Aida Torres Pérez (eds) *The Right to Family Life in the European Union.* 1st edn (London; New York: Routledge, 2017) 232–252.

75 There is already evidence of labor migration being held against third country national mothers seeking to bring their children into an EU member state under family reunification schemes based on the right to family life (Art 8 ECHR) in cases in the European Court of Human Rights. See in: Fulvia Staiano. "Good Mothers, Bad Mothers: Transnational Mothering in the European Court of Human Rights' Case Law," *European Journal of Migration and Law* 15 (2013): 155.

The absence of a mother from the household due to labor migration is almost always considered a greater pathology than that of a father. Women's migration for wage work challenges local gender ideologies of male breadwinners and female caretakers.[76] Social imaginaries of romanticized mother – child relationships are challenged by women's migration, potentially leading to allegations of mothers abandoning or putting their children at risk and subsequent family breakdown.[77]

In her study, Ducu describes the story of Mioara,[78] which serves as a poignant example of the problems transnational mothers can face when arranging substitute caregivers for their children.

> Mioara lived a true nightmare when her son, left in the care of two women, a neighbor and a friend, needed to undergo an urgent surgery. The women took the child to the hospital and stayed with him, but when needed to sign for his complete anesthesia, everybody panicked since both parents were away and there was no legal tutor for the child in the country. Mioara talked to the doctor on the phone and gave him her verbal consent, then sent him an SMS declaring this again.[79]

In most cases, when parents are away, the legal representation of children is not always adequately substituted. As there is no formal break in the parent – child relationship, the state is not automatically involved. In some cases – especially involving emergencies, such as medical care decisions – it may be unclear who is authorized to act and represent the child *in loco parentis*. To address the problem of informal care arrangements, Romania enacted the Child Protection Law (272/2004). The law addresses the issue of parents working abroad in Chapter VI Section 4, under "Child Protection Against Abuse, Neglect, Exploitation and Any Form of Violence." It imposes strict reporting rules when parents migrate for work, including declaring the alternative caregiver's identity to the authorities.[80] Beyond the child-protection objectives, social benefit authorities hope to be able to use parents' self-reporting to adjust household information on parental income and decide to modify benefit levels, or erase certain dependent children from social care lists, given that their parents now have adequate foreign income. In addition, the amended law imposes stringent regulations and penalties, narrowly defining time-frames and who can be named as an alternative guardian (only members of extended family) and requiring court approval of the arrangements. This law seems to be somewhat out of step with the reality of transnational care arrangements. This assessment is reinforced by the findings of Ducu suggesting

76 Hondagneu-Sotelo and Avila (1997); Dreby (2007), Salazar Parreñas (2005).

77 Carola Suârez-Orozco, Irina L. G. Todorova, and Josephine Louie. "Making up for Lost Time: The Experience of Separation and Reunification among Immigrant Families." *Family Process* 41, no. 4 (2002): 625–643.; see also Deborah A. Boehm. "'For My Children': Constructing Family and Navigating the State in the U.S. – Mexico Transnation," *Anthropological Quarterly* 81, no. 4 (December 25, 2008).

78 Ducu, 25.

79 Ibid.

80 Law No. 272/2004 on the protection and promotion of the rights of the child (in Romanian) (Legea nr. 272/2004 privind protecţia şi promovarea drepturilor copilului) www.dreptonline.ro/legislatie/legea_protectiei_copilului.php; See in particular Chapter IV., Section 4 – Child Protection with Parents Left to Work Abroad; Parents, or single parent who are about to go to work abroad have the obligation to report their plans to the local public social assistance and child protection service, at least forty days before leaving the country. Parents must designate a person who will be taking care of the child. This person will be confirmed by the guardianship court. Alternative guardians must be over the age of eighteen and be part of the extended family with necessary material and moral conditions to meet their obligation. Noncompliance carries penalties. There are limited service provisions included mostly aimed at warning against the harms of leaving children behind.

that parents generally perceive this law as "an abusive control of the state" against their private and family lives.[81]

The issue of supervision and care in the case of Romanian transnational motherhood is useful in highlighting the problem of meeting normatively prescribed and culturally reinforced motherhood-roles. Child protection concerns are a legitimate point of entry for the state into family privacy. However, the 2004 law places the matter of transnational parenting clearly within the context of child protection from abuse and neglect. As such it reinforces state authorities' tendency to pathologize families with migrant parents, especially mothers, using punitive measures, whilst the State continues to fall short of providing appropriate support[82] mechanisms for parents to meet their obligations to protect transnational families' right to the full enjoyment of privacy and family life.

Conclusion

The case of transnational parenting – examined through some of its core elements such as contact, support and supervision – allows us to show that "family law" as understood by much of practice and theory is conceptually limited. Through reconsidering inherited assumptions about the family, household and the concept of care, this contribution aims to highlight ways that family law is embedded in other domains of law, along with the law of the market and the law of the state, as well as in informal practices of family networks across the borders of Europe and the world.

This chapter warns of the ways and reasons officials and legal systems often fail to do justice to migrant families and begins to rethink the theoretical underpinnings of legal systems to reconcile policy and theory with "real life." Numerous policy initiatives could be pursued on national and EU levels to enhance the protection of parents and children in transnational families. Everyone interested in family law and policy must be aware of the nature and consequences of living mobile family lives. Since European family life is inevitably embedded in transnationalism, the laws, practices and policies relevant to the European transnational family must be too.

Bibliography

Andrén, Daniela, and Monica Roman. "Should I Stay or Should I Go? Romanian Migrants During Transition and Enlargements," in *Labor Migration, EU Enlargement, and the Great Recession* (Berlin, Heidelberg: Springer, 2016) 247–269.

Arditti, Joyce A., Mathis Kennington, Joseph G. Grzywacz, Anna Jaramillo, Scott Isom, Sara A. Quandt, and Thomas A. Arcury. "Fathers in the Fields: Father Involvement Among Latino Migrant Farmworkers," *Journal of Comparative Family Studies* 45, no. 4 (2014): 537–557.

Baldassar, Loretta. "Transnational Families and Aged Care: The Mobility of Care and the Migrancy of Ageing," *Journal of Ethnic and Migration Studies* 33, no. 2 (March 1, 2007): 275–297.

Baldassar, Loretta, and Laura Merla. *Transnational Families, Migration and the Circulation of Care: Understanding Mobility and Absence in Family Life* (New York; London: Routledge, 2013).

Belorgey, N., Gerbe-Emden, B., Horstmann, S., Kuhn, A., Vogel, D., and Stubbs, P. Social Impact of Emigration and Rural – Urban Migration in Central and Eastern Europe. (VT/2010/001) Synthesis Report (2012). ec.europa.eu/social/BlobServlet?docId=8804&langId=en.

81 Ducu, 26.

82 Most alternative programs supporting transnational parenthood in Romania are funded and organized by NGOs. See for example: "Letter from Abroad: Mother Loves You! | Romania in Contact." www.romaniaincontact.com/en/2013/08/01/silvia-dumitrache-scrisoare-din-strainatate-te-iubeste-mama/ (accessed October 4, 2017).

Blaskó, Zs. and Szabó, L. "Migrants with Left-Behind Children in Hungary," in Zsuzsa Blaskó and Károly Fazekas (eds) *The Hungarian Labour Market 2016* (Budapest: Institute of Economics, Centre for Economic and regional Studies, Hungarian Academy of Sciences, 2016).

Boehm, Deborah A. "'For My Children': Constructing Family and Navigating the State in the U.S. – Mexico Transnation." *Anthropological Quarterly* 81, no. 4 (December 25, 2008): 777–802.

Bonizzoni, P., and A. Cibea. "Family Migration Policies in Italy" (August 2009). https://air.unimi.it/handle/2434/160184#.WiZCfUqnFPY.

Bryceson, Deborah Fahy, and Ulla Vuorela. *The Transnational Family: New European Frontiers and Global Networks* (New York: Berg, 2002).

Carling, Jørgen, Cecilia Menjívar, and Leah Schmalzbauer. "Central Themes in the Study of Transnational Parenthood," *Journal of Ethnic and Migration Studies* 38, no. 2 (February 1, 2012): 191–217.

"Children Left Behind: The Impact of Labor Migration in Moldova and Ukraine," *Migration policy.Org*, January 23, 2015, www.migrationpolicy.org/article/children-left-behind-impact-labor-migration-moldova-and-ukraine.

Clarke, Karen, Tony Maltby, and Patricia Kennett. *Social Policy Review 19: Analysis and Debate in Social Policy, 2007* (Bristol, UK: Policy Press, 2007).

Cohen, Scott A., and Stefan Gössling. "A Darker Side of Hypermobility," *Environment and Planning A* 47, no. 8 (August 1, 2015): 166–1679.

Currie, Samantha. "Un-Joined-up Policy Making and Patchy Promotion of Gender Equality: Free Movement and Reconciliation of Work and Family Life in the EU," in Maribel González Pascual, and Aida Torres Pérez (eds) *The Right to Family Life in the European Union.* 1st edn (London; New York: Routledge, 2017) 232–252.

Ducu, Viorela Strategies of Transnational Motherhood: The Case of Romanian Women, PhD thesis summary 2011, 19. http://doctorat.ubbcluj.ro/sustinerea_publica/rezumate/2011/sociologie/FOamte_Ducu_Viorla_En.pdf (accessed April 29, 2017).

De Hart, Betty, Wibo van Rossum, and Iris Sportel. *Law in the Everyday Lives of Transnational Families: An Introduction.* SSRN Scholarly Paper. Rochester, NY, December 11, 2013. Rochester, NY. https://papers.ssrn.com/abstract=2366404.

Dreby, Joanna. "Children and Power in Mexican Transnational Families," *Journal of Marriage and Family* 69, no. 4 (November 1, 2007): 1050–1064.

Eekelaar, John, and Rob George, eds. *Routledge Handbook of Family Law and Policy.* 1st edn (Abingdon, UK; New York: Routledge, 2014).

"EU Enlargement – Consilium." 2018. www.consilium.europa.eu/en/policies/enlargement/ (accessed June 25, 2018).

"European Convention on Human Rights and Family Life. Primary Issues | The Right to Family Life in the European Union | Taylor & Francis Group." 2018. www.taylorfrancis.com/books/e/9781317287599/chapters/10.4324%2F9781315643960-9 (accessed July 2, 2018).

Finch, Janet. "Displaying Families," *Sociology* 41, no. 1 (February 1, 2007): 65–81.

Frings, Dorothee. "Transnational Domestic Work and Right to Family," in Maria Kontos and Glenda Tibe Bonifacio (eds) *Migrant Domestic Workers and Family Life: International Perspectives* (Basingstoke, UK, New York: Palgrave Macmillan, 2015), 45.

Haidinger, Bettina. "Contingencies among Households: Gendered Division of Labour and Transnational Household Organization – The Case of Ukrainians in Austria," in Helma Lutz (ed.) *Migration and Domestic Work: A European Perspective on a Global Theme*, Studies in Migration and Diaspora (Aldershot, UK: Ashgate, 2008) 127–144.

Halley, Janet. "What Is Family Law?: A Genealogy Part I," *Yale Journal of Law & the Humanities* 23, no. 1 (May 8, 2013). http://digitalcommons.law.yale.edu/yjlh/vol23/iss1/1.

Halley, Janet and Kerry, Rittich. "Critical Directions in Comparative Family Law: Genealogies and Contemporary Studies of Family Law Exceptionalism," *Am. J. Comp. L.* 58 (2010): 753, 754.

Hondagneu-Sotelo, Pierrette, and Ernestine Avila. "'I'm Here, but I'm There': The Meanings of Latina Transnational Motherhood," *Gender and Society* 11, no. 5 (1997): 548–571.

Jandl, Michael, Christina Hollomey, Sandra Gendera, Anna Stepien, and Veronika Bilger. *Migration and Irregular Work in Austria: A Case Study of the Structure and Dynamics of Irregular Foreign Employment in Europe at the Beginning of the 21st Century.* 1st edn (Amsterdam: Amsterdam University Press, 2014).

Johnson, Christopher H., David Warren Sabean, Simon Teuscher, and Francesca Trivellato, eds. *Transregional and Transnational Families in Europe and Beyond: Experiences Since the Middle Ages.* 1st edn (New York: Berghahn Books, 2011).

Kilkey, Majella, and Laura Merla. "Situating Transnational Families' Care-Giving Arrangements: The Role of Institutional Contexts." *Global Networks* 14, no. 2 (2014): 210.

Kilkey, Majella, and Ewa Palenga-Möllenbeck. *Family Life in an Age of Migration and Mobility: Global Perspectives through the Life Course* (New York: Springer, 2016).

Kontos, Maria, and Glenda Tibe Bonifacio, eds. *Migrant Domestic Workers and Family Life: International Perspectives* (Basingstoke, UK, New York: Palgrave Macmillan, 2015).

Kovács, Erika. "Jó Pénzért Dolgoznak Az Építkezésen, Vakációparkban Laknak a Fiatalok: Kis Mindszent Lett a Hollandiai Harlingen | Hódmezővásárhely Hírek | Szeged – Delmagyar.Hu," www.delmagyar.hu/hodmezovasarhely_hirek/jo_penzert_dolgoznak_az_epitkezesen_vakacioparkban_laknak_a_fiatalok_kis_mindszent_lett_a_hollandiai_harlingen/2530686/ (accessed September 5, 2017).

Levitt, Peggy, and Nina Glick Schiller. "Conceptualizing Simultaneity: A Transnational Social Field Perspective on Society," *International Migration Review* 38, no. 3 (September 1, 2004): 1002–1039.

Lutz, Helma. *Migration and Domestic Work: A European Perspective on a Global Theme.* (Aldershot, UK: Ashgate, 2012).

Lutz, Helma. *The New Maids: Transnational Women and the Care Economy.* 1st edn (London: Zed Books, 2012).

López Guerra, Luis. "European Convention on Human Rights and Family Life. Primary Issues," in Maribel González Pascual and Aida Torres Pérez (eds) *The Right to Family Life in the European Union* (London; New York: Routledge, 2017) 12–13.

Madianou, Mirca. "Migration and the Accentuated Ambivalence of Motherhood: The Role of ICTs in Filipino Transnational Families," *Global Networks* 12, no. 3 (July 1, 2012): 277–295.

Mazzucato, Valentina, and Djamila Schans. 2011. "Transnational Families and the Well-Being of Children: Conceptual and Methodological Challenges," *Journal of Marriage and the Family* 73 (4) (August): 704–712.

"Migration and Development Brief 28 | KNOMAD." www.knomad.org/publication/migration-and-development-brief-28 (accessed December 4, 2017).

Mobility in Transition. www.press.uchicago.edu/ucp/books/book/distributed/M/bo18040289.html (accessed December 5, 2017).

Morgan, David H.G. "Locating 'Family Practices,'" *Sociological Research Online* 16, no. 4 (2011): 14.

Németh-Almasi, Judit. "National Analysis of the Phenomenon of Children Left Home by Their Parents Who Migrate Abroad for Employment." Text. January 2008. https://childhub.org/fr/child-protection--online-library/national-analysis-phenomenon-children-left-home-their-parents-who.

"OECD Glossary of Statistical Terms – Central and Eastern European Countries (CEECs) Definition." 2018. https://stats.oecd.org/glossary/detail.asp?ID=303 (accessed June 25, 2018).

Parreñas, Rhacel Salazar. "Transnational Fathering: Gendered Conflicts, Distant Disciplining and Emotional Gaps," *Journal of Ethnic and Migration Studies* 34, no. 7 (September 1, 2008): 1057–1072.

Parreñas, Rhacel Salazar. "Mothering from a Distance: Emotions, Gender, and Intergenerational Relations in Filipino Transnational Families," *Feminist Studies* 27, no. 2 (n.d.): 361.

Pascual, Maribel González, and Aida Torres Pérez, eds. *The Right to Family Life in the European Union.* 1st edn (London; New York: Routledge, 2017).

Piperno, Flavia. "The Impact of Female Emigration on Families and the Welfare State in Countries of Origin: The Case of Romania," *International Migration* 50, no. 5 (2012): 189–204.

Razzu, Giovanni, and Professor of Economics of Public Policy Giovanni Razzu. *Gender Inequality in the Eastern European Labour Market: Twenty-Five Years of Transition Since the Fall of Communism* (London; New York: Routledge, 2016).

Shalleck, Ann. "Introduction Comparative Family Law: What Is the Global Family? Family Law in Decolonization, Modernization and Globalization" (2011). https://works.bepress.com/ann_shalleck/9/.

SHAMIR, HILA. "The State of Care: Rethinking the Distributive Effects of Familial Care Policies in Liberal Welfare States," *The American Journal of Comparative Law* 58, no. 4 (2010): 953–986.

Shamir, Hila. "What's the Border Got to Do with It? How Immigration Regimes Affect Familial Care Provisions – A Comparative Analysis," *American University Journal of Gender, Social Policy & the Law* 19, no. 2 (January 1, 2011). http://digitalcommons.wcl.american.edu/jgspl/vol19/iss2/7.

Staiano, Fulvia. "Good Mothers, Bad Mothers: Transnational Mothering in the European Court of Human Rights' Case Law," *European Journal of Migration and Law* 15 (2013): 155.

Stalford, Helen. "Parenting, Care and Mobility in the EU," *Innovation: The European Journal of Social Science Research* 18, no. 3 (September 1, 2005): 361–380.

Suârez-Orozco, Carola, Irina L. G. Todorova, and Josephine Louie. "Making up for Lost Time: The Experience of Separation and Reunification among Immigrant Families," *Family Process* 41, no. 4 (2002): 625–643.

Tolstokorova, Alissa V. "Where Have All the Mothers Gone? The Gendered Effect of Labour Migration and Transnationalism on the Institution of Parenthood in Ukraine," *Anthropology of East Europe Review* 28, no. 1 (2010): 184–214.

UN General Assembly, *Convention on the Rights of the Child, 20 November 1989*, United Nations, Treaty Series, vol. 1577, p. 3, www.refworld.org/docid/3ae6b38f0.html (accessed June 22, 2018).

UN General Assembly, Universal Declaration of Human Rights, 10 December 1948, 217 A (III), www.refworld.org/docid/3ae6b3712c.html (accessed June 22, 2018).

Van Hooren, F. "When Families Need Immigrants: The Exceptional Position of Migrant Domestic Workers and Care Assistants in Italian Immigration Policy," *Bulletin of Italian Politics* 2, no. 2 (2010): 21–38.

Walker, Charles, and Svetlana Stephenson. *Youth and Social Change in Eastern Europe and the Former Soviet Union* (London: Routledge, 2013).

Zontini, Elisabetta. *Transnational Families, Migration and Gender: Moroccan and Filipino Women in Bologna and Barcelona*. 1st edn (New York: Berghahn Books, 2011).

Index

For Product Safety Concerns and Information please contact our EU
representative GPSR@taylorandfrancis.com
Taylor & Francis Verlag GmbH, Kaufingerstraße 24, 80331 München, Germany

www.ingramcontent.com/pod-product-compliance
Ingram Content Group UK Ltd.
Pitfield, Milton Keynes, MK11 3LW, UK
UKHW050753180926
475701UK00007B/1018

* 9 7 8 1 0 3 2 0 9 3 8 2 6 *